CROSS
ON PRINCIPLES OF
LOCAL
GOVERNMENT
LAW

AUSTRALIA
LBC Information Services
Sydney

CANADA and USA
Carswell
Toronto

NEW ZEALAND
Brooker's
Auckland

SINGAPORE and MALAYSIA
Thomson Information (S.E. Asia)
Singapore

CROSS
ON PRINCIPLES OF
LOCAL
GOVERNMENT
LAW

SECOND EDITION

S. H. Bailey, M.A., LL.B.,
Professor of Public Law, University of Nottingham

London
Sweet & Maxwell
1997

First Edition 1992
Second Edition 1997

Published in 1997 by Sweet & Maxwell Limited of
100 Avenue Road, Swiss Cottage
London NW3 3PF

Phototypeset by
Mendip Communications Limited, Frome, Somerset
Printed and bound in Great Britain by
Butler and Tanner Limited, Frome, Somerset

No natural forests were destroyed to make this product;
only farmed timber was used and replanted

A CIP catalogue record for this book is available from the
British Library

ISBN 0 421 586508

PREFACE
2nd edition

The present work is an offshoot of the 9th edition of *Cross on Local Government Law* which was published in November 1996. The latter is now presented in loose-leaf form and is directed to practitioners rather than students. The former comprises the chapters of *Cross* that relate to the structure, finance and administration of local government, as distinct from the law governing individual services (Chapters 1–16 and Appendices A–F), and reflect the topics that tend to be covered in professional Local Government Law courses. It is hoped that this will be particularly helpful for students.

Since 1992 there has been a steady stream of major legislation and case law affecting the structure and operation of local government, including the establishment of new unitary authorities in Wales and many parts of England.

I am particularly grateful to Colin Crawford of the University of Birmingham, who has prepared the chapters on contracts and competition, finance, audit, grants, non-domestic rates and the council tax.

We have attempted to state the law as in June 1996, in the light of the materials available to us, although some subsequent developments are noted.

In general, the functions of the various Secretaries of State are exercisable, in relation to Wales, by the Secretary of State for Wales.

S.H.B.

14.11.96

CONTENTS

PART I

PART II

TABLE OF CASES

l

TABLE OF STATUTES

TABLE OF STATUTORY INSTRUMENTS

TABLE OF E.C. LEGISLATION

CHAPTER 1

THE LEGAL FRAMEWORK OF LOCAL AUTHORITIES

In this chapter we deal with a number of basic factors that influence the legal **1–01** framework of local government in England and Wales.

A. THE CONSTITUTIONAL POSITION

A fundamental feature is that the United Kingdom is a unitary and not a **1–02** federal state. Subject to overriding provisions of European Community law,[1] an Act of the United Kingdom Parliament is the supreme source of law. The existence and powers of elected local authorities depend on the provisions of Acts of Parliament. There is no compelling legal reason why the United Kingdom could not adopt a written constitution that divides powers between central and local or regional institutions and confers a measure of legal autonomy to the legislature at each level. Under such an arrangement, the existence and powers of elected local government institutions could be entrenched in the constitution, any change being a matter for constitutional amendment and not merely an Act of the central legislature.[2] However, this does not represent the current position and there is little sign that it will change.[3]

B. HISTORICAL BACKGROUND

Throughout the history of the United Kingdom what may be termed **1–03** governmental functions have been performed by both central and local institutions.[4] The nineteenth century saw the establishment at the local level

---

[1] See *R. v. Secretary of State for Transport, ex p. Factortame Ltd* [1990] 2 A.C. 85, *per* Lord Bridge at p. 140; *R. v. Secretary of State for Employment, ex p. Equal Opportunities Commission* [1995] 1 A.C. 1.

[2] See, *e.g.*, Institute for Public Policy Research, *The Constitution of the United Kingdom* (1991), proposing a draft constitution in which legislative power is shared between Parliament and elected assemblies for Scotland, Wales, Northern Ireland and twelve English regions. Each Assembly would establish elected local authorities to perform such functions as the Assembly determines, but also with general competence to undertake measures for the benefit of all those within the authority's areas.

[3] The introduction of national parliaments and regional assemblies, and local government with "an entrenched constitutional status" is policy for the Liberal Democrats (*Here We Stand: Proposals for Modernising Britain's Democracy* Federal White Paper 6, 1993, pp. 32–36). The Labour Party's position is less clear. The Conservative Party has opposed such constitutional reforms.

[4] For a brief survey, see Sir William O. Hart and J. F. Garner, *Hart's Introduction to the Law of Local Government and Administration* (9th edn, 1973), pp. 8–33.

of elected local authorities across England and Wales. These authorities exercised a range of powers, many inherited from the justices of the peace and from a plethora of ad hoc authorities. They were corporate bodies,[5] incorporated either by a charter granted under the royal prerogative or by statute. The law relating to the constitution and general powers of local authorities was simplified by the Local Government Act 1933. A more radical reorganisation was effected by the Local Government Act 1972, as from April 1, 1974. While there have been significant changes since,[6] the 1972 Act (as amended), still sets out the basic framework of local authorities in England and Wales. The pattern of local authorities immediately prior to reorganisation in 1974 was as follows.

(a) Charter Corporations

Boroughs

1–04   The incorporation of boroughs had a long history. From early times local communities petitioned the Crown for charters of incorporation granting rights and privileges and a certain freedom from control by royal officials. Not infrequently a bargain was struck between the community and the Sovereign, the former making substantial contributions to the royal exchequer in exchange for the charter. The Municipal Corporations Act 1835 introduced fundamental reforms in borough government—it established the elective principle, gave powers in relation to police, street lighting, markets and harbours and local by-laws and conferred the right to levy a rate. By this statute the mayor, aldermen and burgesses were incorporated. Formerly, the corporators consisted of a relatively small group prescribed by the charter, and the corporations were conceived to have been created for the sake of the group and for its exclusive benefit. From 1835 the legal *persona* in the case of boroughs became the mayor, aldermen and burgesses of the borough (or the appropriate variant).

County boroughs, cities and counties of cities and boroughs

1–05   In 1888 boroughs with a population of 50,000 or more were created county boroughs, *i.e.* they were given substantially the powers conferred on county councils by the Local Government Act, 1888, in addition to those they already enjoyed as municipal boroughs, and were made independent of the county in the matter of services. The difference between a county borough and non-county borough was therefore one of function, not of legal status. A county borough council provided all local government services within its area and was not dependent on the county council in any way. In the area of a non-county borough the county council provided a number of services, such as police, fire and education, and others, such as public cleansing and street lighting, were the responsibility of the borough council.

Many county and non-county boroughs were also cities—there was again no difference in legal status. A city was a borough which had or had had a

---

[5] On the significance of incorporation, see further § 1–04f.
[6] See §§ 1–13 *et seq.* and Chap. 3.

diocesan bishop, or which by letters patent had been created a city by royal prerogative, or which was so designated in its charter, though some boroughs appeared to have acquired the title by prescription. Several cities (it may be noted in passing) were not boroughs. The city of Ely was an urban district; the city of St David's lay in a rural district and had a parish council.

Some county boroughs were also counties. This again had its origins in history, for certain towns (such as Chester and Canterbury) were designated in their charters as "counties of cities", and when by the Local Government Act 1888 certain boroughs were given the powers of a county council and made independent of the county, these ancient counties of cities successfully claimed to be made county boroughs. And a few non-county boroughs were counties—Haverfordwest was one of them.[7] But again there was no difference in legal status—it was primarily a matter of privilege, the privilege of maintaining a sheriff.

The council as the agent of the corporation

A corporation of a borough could act, and could only act, through the **1–06** council—the council could be regarded as the sole agent of the corporation.[8] All legal transactions were effected in the corporate name by the council acting on behalf of the corporation. It is to be noted, however, that many statutory powers and duties were conferred on the council as such, and it was the council which was the local authority for the purposes of the Local Government Act 1933.[9] A municipal corporation therefore was not a local authority, neither were the mayor, aldermen and burgesses of the borough.

(b) Statutory Corporations

Local authorities other than the boroughs discussed above were all statutory corporations, brought into being by Act of Parliament.

County councils

County councils were created by the Local Government Act 1888. Section **1–07** 1 of this Act provided that a county council should be established in every administrative county as defined by the Act and should be entrusted with the management of the administrative and financial business of the county. Section 3 transferred to county councils many of the administrative functions formerly exercised by the justices of the peace in quarter sessions (for example, their functions in relation to highways), and the Act imposed on county councils other duties such as responsibility for the maintenance of what were then called main roads. Subsequently, many important powers

---

[7] It was declared such by Ordinances in Wales 1542–43 (34 & 35 Hen. 8. c. 26).
[8] Local Government Act 1933, s.17.
[9] s.305.

3

were conferred on county councils or transferred to county councils from other authorities. The areas of the administrative counties covered the whole of England and Wales, excluding the areas of the county boroughs which that Act set up. A few of the counties (with the county boroughs excluded) were divided into several administrative units with the status and functions of counties. Yorkshire and Lincolnshire were divided into three parts (called Ridings and Parts respectively), and Cambridgeshire, Hampshire, Northamptonshire, Suffolk and Sussex were each divided into two.

Urban and rural district councils

1–08   Urban and rural district councils came into existence under those names by the Local Government Act 1894. By the Public Health Acts 1872 and 1875, the country had been divided into urban sanitary districts and rural sanitary districts. The urban sanitary districts were the districts covered by boroughs, improvement commissioners and local boards; the rural sanitary districts covered the areas of the poor law unions, taking out the areas of the urban sanitary districts. The Act of 1894 renamed the urban and rural sanitary authorities, calling them urban and rural district councils, respectively (boroughs of course were unchanged), and dealt with their constitution and membership, matters subsequently set out in Part I of the Local Government Act 1933. These authorities were mainly concerned with public health, housing and roads. Certain boroughs were included in rural districts under section 28 of the Local Government Act 1958.

London borough councils and the Greater London Council

1–09   Metropolitan boroughs were established by Order in Council made under the London Government Act 1899, which provided that the whole of the administrative county of London, excluding the City of London, should be divided into metropolitan boroughs. The Local Government Act 1888 set up the London County Council. The London Government Act 1963 set out the constitution of the London boroughs and the Greater London Council.

Parish councils

1–10   Parish councils were established by the Local Government Act 1894: their constitution and membership were subsequently governed by the Local Government Act 1933.[10] Every rural parish had to have a parish meeting. If it had no parish council the county council was required by order to establish a parish council if the population of the parish was three hundred or more or if, in the case of a parish having a population of two hundred or more but under three hundred, the parish meeting so resolved. Where the population was less than two hundred the county council had a discretion to establish a parish council if the parish meeting so resolved.[11]

---

[10] ss.43(2), 55.
[11] Local Government Act 1933, s.43, as amended.

Councils as bodies corporate

In the case of all the statutory corporations here referred to, the Local **1–11** Government Act 1933, declared the *council* to be the body corporate, having perpetual succession and (except for parish councils) a common seal.[12] An act of a parish council could be signified by an instrument under the hands of two members of the council, or, if the instrument was one which was required to be under seal, under the hands and seals of two members.[13]

Parishes without a parish council

Section 47(3) of the Local Government Act 1933 provided that in a rural **1–12** parish not having a separate parish council the chairman of the parish meeting and the councillor or councillors representing the parish on the rural district council was to be a body corporate by the name of the representative body with the addition of the name of the parish. The representative body had to act as directed by the parish meeting and could signify its acts under the hands of its members (or hands and seals if the instrument must be made under seal).

C. THE FRAMEWORK ESTABLISHED BY THE LOCAL GOVERNMENT ACT 1972

The Local Government Act 1972 gave effect to the proposals contained in **1–13** the White Paper "Local Government in England: Government Proposals for Reorganisation"[14] and in the consultative document "The Reform of Local Government in Wales", published in 1971. It created new structures for local government and allocated functions among the new authorities. It recast the law, modified and in simpler form, with respect to the administrative working of local authorities. It replaced the Local Government Act 1933, and it incorporated, with modification, the provisions of the London Government Act 1963 relating to the constitution of authorities in Greater London. The structure of London government was not materially affected: fundamental reorganisation had taken place in 1965 following the London Government Act 1963 under which the Greater London Council and the London borough councils had been established.

Under the Act of 1972 new areas and new authorities were created in England, outside Greater London, and in Wales.[15] Each country was divided into counties and districts. In England, certain counties were metropolitan counties and the districts within them were metropolitan districts. In England many districts were divided into parishes and in Wales all districts were divided into communities.

Changes were effected in Greater London and in the metropolitan counties by the Local Government Act 1985. That Act abolished, from

---

[12] ss.2, 31, 32 and 48.
[13] s.48.
[14] Cmnd. 4584 (1971).
[15] Local Government Act 1972, s.1.

5

April 1, 1986, the Greater London Council and the metropolitan county councils, giving effect to proposals contained in the White Paper, "Streamlining the Cities."[16] It provided for the transfer of their functions to other authorities—in the main, they were reallocated, respectively, to the London borough councils and the metropolitan district councils. Part III of the Act established the Inner London Education Authority, formerly a special committee of the Greater London Council, as a directly elected authority.[17] Part IV provided for separate "joint authorities" to be established to act as (1) police, (2) fire and civil defence, and (3) passenger transport authorities in the metropolitan counties, and as the fire and civil defence authority for London.[18] Part VII established a "residuary body" in each area to deal with residual matters concerning the abolished authorities.

The Inner London Education Authority was itself abolished, and its powers transferred to London borough councils and the Common Council of the City of London by the Education Reform Act 1988, the change taking effect from April 1, 1990. The residuary bodies have been wound up, and provision made for the transfer of their property, functions, rights and liabilities, usually to designated district or London borough councils. "Pensions authorities" have been established for South Yorkshire and London to take over pensions functions from the respective residuary body for the area.[19]

The Norfolk and Suffolk Broads Act 1988 established a Broads Authority with the function of managing the Broads.

Police authorities were reconstituted as authorities in their own right by the Police and Magistrates' Courts Act 1994, amending the Police Act 1964.

Substantial further changes to the structure of local government in the non-metropolitan counties in England are in the process of being effected by orders made by the Secretary of State under the Local Government Act 1992, following reports by the Local Government Commission for England (see *post*, Chap. 3). Unitary authorities are to be established for a number of the non-metropolitan counties. Two tiers of local government are retained in the others, although in some cases, large cities are to be given unitary status with the county and district councils retaining their responsibilities elsewhere.

In Wales, local government has been completely restructured by the Local Government (Wales) Act 1994, which replaced the eight county councils and 37 district councils by 22 new unitary authorities (11 counties and 11

---

[16] Cmnd. 9063 (1983).

[17] This authority was first established as the Inner London Interim Education Authority with effect from September 1, 1985.

[18] These authorities were established with effect from September 15, 1985: see the Local Government Act 1985 (New Authorities) (Appointed Days) Order 1985 (S.I. 1985 No. 1283).

[19] See further § 3–08.

county boroughs), with effect from April 1, 1996. The new authorities were elected on May 4, 1995, and acted as shadow authorities until April 1, 1996.[20]

The areas of non-metropolitan counties, districts and London boroughs, and in Wales, counties and county boroughs are called principal areas and their councils are called principal councils. Parishes and communities have parish and community meetings and may have parish and community councils. The areas of metropolitan counties continue as local government areas for certain purposes, for example as the areas under the control of joint authorities.

In Wales, the areas of the eight counties in existence before reorganisation **1–14** under the Local Government (Wales) Act 1994 continue as the areas of "preserved counties" for certain purposes.[21] Orders under the Local Government Act 1992 have established new counties for the areas of new unitary authorities.[22]

Many districts bear the style of borough and their councils are called borough councils; certain parishes and communities bear the style of town and their councils are called town councils. Some areas within districts which were formerly cities or boroughs have a body known as the charter trustees of the city or the charter trustees of the town as the case may be.

This, in briefest terms, is the formal structure of local government. The achievement of status and change of status is the subject of detailed statutory provision and this is described in Chapter 3.

The term "local authority" is applied to county, district, London borough **1–15** and parish councils in England and county, county borough and community councils in Wales.[23] Joint authorities and residuary bodies are treated as "local authorities" for specified purposes.[24] All these authorities are corporate bodies and have the characteristics of corporations. In addition, two other bodies have corporate status, namely, the parish trustees of a parish not having a parish council, and the charter trustees of a city or borough.

---

[20] See Sched. 5 of the Local Government Act 1972, as substituted by Sched. 3 of the Local Government (Wales) Act 1994, and the Welsh Principal Councils (Day of Election) Order 1994 (S.I. 1994 No. 2843).

[21] Local Government Act 1972, s.20, as substituted by the 1994 Act, s.1.

[22] See, *e.g.*, the Avon (Structural Change) Order 1995 (S.I. 1995 No. 493), establishing new counties of North West Somerset, Bath and North East Somerset, South Gloucestershire and the City of Bristol; the Humberside (Structural Change) Order 1995 (S.I. 1995 No. 600), establishing new counties of the City of Kingston upon Hull, North Lincolnshire, North East Lincolnshire and the East Riding of Yorkshire; and the Cleveland (Further Provision) Order 1995 (S.I. 1995 No. 1747), establishing new counties for Hartlepool, Middlesbrough, Redcar and Cleveland, and Stockton-on-Tees. The counties of Avon, Humberside and Cleveland were abolished. A new district and county of York was established by the North Yorkshire (District of York) (Structural and Boundary Changes) Order 1995 (S.I. 1995 No. 610), two tiers of local government being retained elsewhere in North Yorkshire.

[23] Local Government Act 1972, s.270(1): definition of "local authority", as amended by the Local Government Act 1985, Sched. 17, and the Local Government (Wales) Act 1994, s.1.

[24] Local Government Act 1985, Scheds. 13, 14; Local Government Residuary Body (England) Order 1995 (S.I. 1995 No. 401); Local Government (Wales) Act 1994, Sched. 13.

D. CORPORATE STATUS

1–16 One feature common to local authorities is their corporate status. A study of the principles of local government law must therefore begin with an examination of the nature of corporate status and the legal consequences which flow from incorporation.

Nature of a corporation

A corporation has been defined by a leading authority in the following terms[25]:

> A collection of many individuals, united into one body, under a special denomination, having perpetual succession under an artificial form, and vested, by the policy of the law, with the capacity of acting, in several respects, as an individual, particularly of taking and granting property, of contracting obligations, of suing and being sued.

The "collection of many individuals" becomes by incorporation one individual, an artificial person, having rights and duties, capable of suing and being sued, of holding property and making contracts. A corporation is a wholly different and separate entity from the individuals who compose it. It is the corporation as such, not its constituent members, which is liable for its obligations and in whom its property vests. It is a legal *persona*. This is perhaps the most significant feature of corporate status: its importance is seen more clearly when an examination is later made of contractual and tortious liability.

1–17 There are other characteristics of an incorporated body. It must have a name, and all legal transactions must be effected in that name. Secondly, it has perpetual succession. Individual members who compose it may die or retire or be replaced by new corporators, but the corporation continues an unbroken existence. Obligations entered into whilst one group of persons makes up the membership bind the corporation even though the whole of the membership has changed. Finally, it has a seal. The acts and decisions of a corporation are authenticated by its seal, which in some respects is like the signature of a natural person. The corporate will is evidenced by the affixing of the seal to the document in which it is expressed. These characteristics are found in the common law rules as to corporations.

Local authority corporations

1–18 In the case of local authorities these rules are, for the most part, expressed in statute. The Local Government Act 1972[26] provides that a principal council shall be a body corporate by the name of the county council or district council (in England) or county or county borough council (in Wales) as the case may be. Similarly worded provisions apply to parish and

---

[25] *Kyd on Corporations* (1793–94) Vol. 1, p. 13.
[26] ss.2 (England) (as amended by the Local Government Act 1985, Sched. 16), 21 (Wales) (as amended by the Local Government (Wales) Act 1994, s.2).

community councils,[27] and to joint authorities and residuary bodies.[28] So far as parish and community councils are concerned it is expressly stated that notwithstanding anything in any rule of law a council need not have a common seal and where it has no seal any of its acts which are required to be signified under seal may be signed and sealed by two members of the council.[29]

Modes of incorporation

Incorporation in modern times has been effected in one of two ways: by the granting of a charter of incorporation by the Sovereign or in pursuance of an Act of Parliament. Under earlier law all boroughs (except London boroughs) were charter corporations, created by the Sovereign in the exercise of the royal prerogative. Prior to 1964, the London metropolitan boroughs were statutory corporations, as were the former county councils, urban and rural district councils, parish councils and parish meetings and the Greater London Council. Under the London Government Act 1963, London boroughs were incorporated under the royal prerogative, but also pursuant to the 1963 Act. In *Hazell v. Hammersmith and Fulham London Borough Council*[30] the House of Lords held that the borough was to be regarded as a statutory corporation.[31] It would have been possible for the Crown to have incorporated a London borough solely under the royal prerogative, in which case the borough corporation would have had the same capacity as a natural person, but that had not been done. A further point is that it is the *council* and not the *corporation* which is the "local authority" for the purposes of the Local Government Act 1972,[32] and

" ... the council cannot ignore their statutory constraints and lawfully exercise in the name of the borough a power which upon the true construction of the statutory powers of the council was not open to the council."[33]

Authorities created under the Act of 1972, whether boroughs or not, are statutory corporations.

E. THE DOCTRINE OF ULTRA VIRES

Perhaps the most important principle to be considered in relation to **1–19** corporate status is the doctrine of *ultra vires*. The term *ultra vires* means

---

[27] ss.14 and 33 (as substituted by the Local Government (Wales) Act 1994, s.13). In the case of a parish not having a separate parish council the chairman of the parish meeting and the proper officer of the district council are incorporated as "the parish trustees": s.13.

[28] Local Government Act 1985, ss.26(1), 27(1), 28(1), 57(1).

[29] Local Government Act 1972, ss.13(5), 14(3), and 33(4) (as substituted by the Local Government (Wales) Act 1994, s.13). As to the occasions where sealing is necessary, see § 7–13.

[30] [1992] 2 A.C. 1. See § 1–27.

[31] *per* Lord Templeman at pp. 39–43.

[32] *Hazell v. Hammersmith and Fulham London Borough Council* [1990] 2 Q.B. 697, 776–779, C.A. Unlike the House of Lords, the Court of Appeal had held that the *corporation* of the borough did have the powers of a natural legal person.

[33] *per* Lord Templeman at [1992] 2 A.C. 1, 43.

"beyond the powers". An act is *ultra vires* an authority if it is beyond its powers; the converse term is "*intra vires*".

1–20 The doctrine as applied to statutory corporations is stated in Lord Watson's speech in *Baroness Wenlock v. River Dee Co.*[34]:

> "Whenever a corporation is created by Act of Parliament, with reference to the purposes of the Act, and solely with a view to carrying these purposes into execution, I am of opinion not only that the objects which the corporation may legitimately pursue must be ascertained from the Act itself, but that the powers which the corporation may lawfully use in furtherance of these objects must either be expressly conferred or derived by reasonable implication from its provisions."

Unlike a natural person who can in general do whatever he pleases so long as what he does is not forbidden by law or contrary to law, a statutory corporation can do only those things which it is authorised to do by statute, directly or by implication. If such a corporation acts otherwise than in this way its acts are *ultra vires*. There must in all cases be statutory authority for what is done, and that authority must either be expressly given or reasonably inferred from the language of an Act of Parliament.

Application of the doctrine generally

1–21 This rule, if rigidly applied to statutory corporations, would greatly handicap their activities and would require empowering legislation to be burdened to an impossible extent by detailed provisions. The courts have therefore held that a corporation may do not only those things for which there is express or implied authority, but also whatever is reasonably *incidental* to the doing of those things. Lord Selborne said in *Att.-Gen. v. Great Eastern Railway Co.*[35]:

> "It appears to me to be important that the doctrine of *ultra vires* ... should be maintained. But I agree ... that this doctrine ought to be reasonably, and not unreasonably, understood and applied, and that whatever may fairly be regarded as incidental to, or consequential upon, those things which the legislature has authorised ought not (unless expressly prohibited) to be held by judicial construction to be *ultra vires*."

1–22 This common law rule is given statutory force in section 111 of the Local Government Act 1972.[36]

The words "incidental to" are not equivalent to the words "in connection with". They have a narrower meaning. This point emerged in *Amalgamated Society of Railway Servants v. Osborne*, where Lord Macnaghten said[37]:

> "The learned counsel for the appellants did not, as I understand their argument, venture to contend that the power which they claimed could be derived by reasonable implication from the language of the legislature. They said it was a power 'incidental', 'ancillary' or 'conducive'. ... If these rather loose expressions are meant to cover something beyond what may be found in the language which the legislature has used, all I can say is that, so far as I know,

---

[34] (1885) 10 App.Cas. 354 at p. 362.
[35] (1880) 5 App.Cas. 473 at p. 478.
[36] See § 1–25, *infra*.
[37] [1910] A.C. 87 at p. 97.

there is no foundation in principle or authority for the proposition involved in their use."

These dicta were relied on in *Att.-Gen. v. Crayford Urban District Council.*[38]

In the application of the doctrine there are then three issues: first, whether **1–23** what is done is specifically authorised by statute; secondly, whether (if there be no specific authority) one can reasonably imply authority from the language of the statute; and, thirdly, whether an act for which no such direct or implied authority is found is reasonably incidental to the carrying into effect of a statutory purpose.

In the many cases which have come before the courts the question has usually centred on implied powers and incidental powers. It must be rare for an authority to perform an act for which there is no statutory authority at all but it has frequently happened that a council has extended and enlarged a service to a point where it is alleged that its statutory powers have been exceeded, and it has then been contended on behalf of the council that authority can reasonably be implied from the language of the statute as a whole. In other cases a council has engaged in some activity for which there is no clear authority in statute, but it has been argued for the council that this activity has been undertaken for the better carrying into effect of a statutory power or duty—the council has relied on the rule as to incidental powers.

Several of the more important cases relating to this topic are now given. **1–24** The first, the *Ashbury Railway Carriage* case, is of particular significance, since it is from this case that the rule in its modern application may be said to stem; *Att.-Gen. v. Fulham Corporation* and *Att.-Gen. v. Manchester Corporation* provide example of activities held to be *ultra vires* and *Att.-Gen. v. Smethwick Corporation* of an *intra vires* activity:

> *Ashbury Railway Carriage Co. v. Riche.*[39] The company was incorporated under the Companies Act 1862 to make, sell or lend on hire all kinds of railway plant. The company entered into a contract for the construction of a railway. *Held*, that the act of the company in entering into the contract was *ultra vires*. The Lord Chancellor said[40]: "Now ... if that is the condition upon which the corporation is established (his Lordship was referring to the procedure of incorporation under the Companies Act) it is a mode of incorporation which contains in it both that which is affirmative and that which is negative. It states affirmatively the ambit and extent of the vitality and power which by law is given to the incorporation, and it states, if it were necessary to state, negatively, that nothing shall be done beyond that ambit, and that no attempt shall be made to use the corporate life for any other purpose than that which is so specified."
> *Att.-Gen. v. Fulham Corporation.*[41] The metropolitan borough of Fulham was a statutory body created under the London Government Act 1899. The corporation, in common with many other authorities, provided facilities for residents to wash their own clothes in separate troughs under powers clearly

[38] [1962] Ch. 575.
[39] (1875) L.R. 7 H.L. 653. The rule in this case was expressly applied to the London County Council, as a statutory corporation, in *Att.-Gen. v. London County Council* [1907] A.C. 131.
[40] At p. 670.
[41] [1921] 1 Ch. 440.

conferred by the Baths and Washhouses Acts 1846 and 1878. In 1920, the corporation introduced a new scheme under which residents brought their washing to the wash-house, leaving it there to be laundered by employees of the council. A collection and delivery service was provided at a small additional charge. An action for a declaration that the scheme was illegal was brought by the Attorney-General at the relation of a ratepayer. It was argued for the corporation that what had been done was incidental to the use of its statutory powers; that it was not material that the washing was undertaken by council servants and not by the customers. *Held*, that the scheme was *ultra vires* the corporation, for there was no authority express or implied to enable the corporation to wash clothes for others as distinct from providing facilities enabling persons to come to the wash-house to wash their clothes.

● *Att.-Gen. v. Manchester Corporation.*[42] The corporation had power conferred under a private Act to use its tramways "for the purpose of conveying and delivering animals goods minerals and parcels". The corporation proposed to establish a general parcels delivery service within and beyond the area covered by the tramways system, not confined to parcels and goods carried on their tramways. An action was brought by the Attorney-General at the relation of a ratepayer to restrain the corporation. The corporation contended that its acts were authorised by statute or if not fully authorised thereby were properly incidental or ancillary to the business for which statutory powers were available. (The corporation also argued that it was a common law corporation and could therefore act without statutory power—it failed on this point for reasons which no longer have relevance.) *Held*, the corporation had statutory power to carry on the business of common carriers upon their tramways and as ancillary to that business to do all things necessary for the collection and delivery of parcels or goods carried on the tramways; but the corporation had no power to carry on a general parcels delivery service apart from their tramways.

Att.-Gen. v. Smethwick Corporation.[43] The corporation passed a resolution providing for the establishment of a printing, bookbinding and stationery works for the purpose of executing work required by them. An action was brought by the Attorney-General at the relation of a ratepayer claiming a declaration that the proposal was *ultra vires*. *Held*, that the formation of a department to do the printing, bookbinding and stationery work of the corporation was incidental to or consequential upon the carrying out of the corporation's statutory duties and was not therefore *ultra vires*. The Master of the Rolls quoted with approval the passage from Lord Selborne's judgment in *Att.-Gen. v. Great Eastern Ry.*[44]

Application of section 111 of the Local Government Act 1972

1–25   Section 111 provides as follows:

"111 Subsidiary powers of local authorities
  (1) Without prejudice to any powers exercisable apart from this section but subject to the provisions of this Act and any other enactment passed before or

---

[42] [1906] 1 Ch. 643.
[43] [1932] 1 Ch. 562.
[44] See § 1–09. For further examples of *ultra vires* actions, see *R. v. Manchester City Council, ex p. King* (1991) 89 L.G.R. 696 (council not entitled to use power to charge reasonable fees for grant or renewal of a street trading licence or consent as a general revenue-raising provision); *R. v. Ealing London Borough Council, ex p. Lewis* (1992) 24 H.L.R. 484 (council not entitled to charge the whole of the cost of its homeless persons unit, its housing advisory service and the salaries of wardens employed in its sheltered housing service to its housing revenue account as these items did not fall entirely within the description of the "management of houses and other property"); *Morgan Grenfell and Co. Ltd v. Sutton London Borough Council, The Times*, March 23, 1995 (guarantee for loan to association that was not a registered housing association expressly prohibited by the Housing Act 1985, s.60(1)).

after this Act, a local authority[45] shall have power to do any thing (whether or not involving the expenditure, borrowing or lending of money or the acquisition or disposal of any property or rights) which is calculated to facilitate, or is conducive or incidental to, the discharge of any of their functions.

(2) For the purposes of this section, transacting the business of a parish or community meeting or any other parish or community business shall be treated as a function of the parish or community council.

(3) A local authority shall not by virtue of this section raise money, whether by means of rates, precepts or borrowing, or lend money except in accordance with the enactments relating to those matters respectively. ... "

It was stated in DoE Circular 121/72[46] that

"The [1972] Act includes a new provision (section 111) which puts beyond doubt that local authorities have power to do anything which is calculated to facilitate, or is conducive or incidental to, the discharge of any of their functions, even if they have no specific statutory power for that action. This proposition has long represented the law (see in particular *A.G. v. Smethwick Corporation* [1932] 1 Ch. 562), but the section has been included for the avoidance of any doubt which might hamper local initiative."

Key points in the interpretation and application of the section are as follows. First, the powers conferred by it must be ancillary to a function of a local authority conferred by some other provision. The term "function" was the subject of comment by Woolf L.J. in *Hazell v. Hammersmith and Fulham London Borough Council*[47] as follows:

"What is a function for the purposes of the subsection is not expressly defined but in our view there can be little doubt that in this context 'functions' refers to the multiplicity of specific statutory activities the council is expressly or impliedly under a duty to perform or has power to perform under the other provisions of the Act of 1972 or other relevant legislation. The subsection does not of itself, independently of any other provision, authorise the performance of any activity. It only confers, as the sidenote to the section indicates, a subsidiary power. A subsidiary power which authorises an activity where some other statutory provision has vested a specific function or functions in the council and the performance of the activity will assist in some way in the discharge of that function or those functions."

This was approved by the Court of Appeal and the House of Lords.[48] The function in question must of course itself be *intra vires*: the test is not whether it is reasonable to have done what in fact was done.[49] It is, however, unclear

---

[45] This term includes the Common Council: s.111(4). The section also applies to joint authorities: Local Government Act 1972, s.146A(1)(a), inserted by the Local Government Act 1985, Sched. 14, para. 16; and to residuary bodies: 1985 Act, Sched. 13, para. 12(a).

[46] para. 16.

[47] [1990] 2 Q.B. 697, 722–723.

[48] [1990] 2 Q.B. 697, 785; [1992] 2 A.C. 1, 29. The suggestion by Parker L.J. in *Allsop v. North Tyneside Metropolitan Borough Council* (1992) 90 L.G.R. 462, 486, that the term "functions" is "plainly referring to the functions set out in Part IX of the Act" is inconsistent with Woolf L.J.'s statement and cannot be supported. Most of the functions of local authorities are conferred by Acts other than the 1972 Act and it is inconceivable that Parliament intended section 111 to have such a narrow application; in any event, Part IX dealt with the transfer of functions to the authorities established by the 1972 Act.

[49] Watkins L.J. in *Allsop v. North Tyneside Metropolitan Borough Council* (1992) 90 L.G.R. 462, 472, D.C., citing Lord Templeman in *Hazell v. Hammersmith London Borough Council* [1992] 2 A.C. 1, 31.

whether the function must be *expressly* conferred by statute or can be *impliedly* conferred. The broader view, that section 111 can extend to support acts which an authority is impliedly authorised to perform, is supported by the passage just cited from Woolf L.J. in *Hazell*'s case, and by Nourse L.J. in *R. v. Eden District Council, ex p. Moffatt*[50] and Watkins L.J. in the Divisional Court in *Allsop v. North Tyneside Metropolitan Borough Council.*[51] However, in *R. v. Richmond Upon Thames London Borough Council, ex p. McCarthy & Stone (Developments) Ltd*[52] the House of Lords held that the giving of pre-planning application advice facilitated and was conducive and incidental to the function of determining planning applications and was not itself a "function" of the council; charging could not be justified by reference to section 111 as that would be something "incidental to the incidental". It was not argued that the giving of pre-application advice was an "implied function" of the local authority, and so the point as to whether there can be such functions must remain open. It is submitted that the broad approach of Nourse L.J. in *ex p. Moffatt* is to be preferred. The enactment of section 111 does not appear to have been intended to narrow the powers of local authorities[53] and acceptance of an argument that powers can only be conferred expressly or by reference to section 111 would have that effect.[54] The decision in *ex p. McCarthy & Stone (Developments) Ltd*[55] can fully be justified by reference to the separate principle that a power for a public authority to charge for its services must be conferred expressly or by necessary implication, the courts being very reluctant to find an *implied* power to charge.[56] It remains the case that where Parliament has made detailed provision as to how certain statutory powers are to be carried out, there is no scope for implying the existence of wholly additional powers outside the statutory code by reference to section 111.[57]

---

[50] *The Times,* November 24, 1988, C.A.
[51] (1992) 90 L.G.R. 462, 480–481. Thus, the Divisional Court held that the functions of the local authority included the maintenance of good staff relationships to avoid industrial strife, the provision of efficient services and making and terminating contracts of employment (although the enhanced voluntary severance scheme that was in issue was *ultra vires* as it was prohibited by other enactments). See further *post,* § 1–28. In the Court of Appeal, Parker L.J. expressed a preference for a narrower approach: see fn. 48, *supra.*
[52] [1992] 2 A.C. 48. See *post,* § 1–28.
[53] See discussion of the relevant parliamentary materials by C. Crawford in C. Crawford and C. Grace (eds.), *"Conducive or Incidental To?" Local Authority Discretionary Powers in the Modern Era* (University of Birmingham, 1992), pp. 5–6.
[54] This view has been expressed in advice by the Audit Commission: see, *e.g.,* Audit Commission Technical Release 28/91, *Further Guidance on Section 111 of the Local Government Act 1972: Charging Powers, Meaning of "Functions".* One ground is that there is no discernible test to identify an implied function. The response is to question whether such a test is necessary: given that there is no "benchmark to determine what is a function anyway" the matter should be left to judicial policy: J. Bennett and S. Cirell, *Municipal Trading* (1992), pp. 154–155.
[55] *supra.*
[56] *Att.-Gen. v. Wilts United Dairies Ltd* (1921) 37 T.L.R. 884, C.A., affirmed (1922) 91 L.J.K.B. 897, H.L.; cited by Lord Lowry in *ex p. McCarthy & Stone (Developments) Ltd* [1992] 2 A.C. 48, 67–68, 74.
[57] *Credit Suisse v. Waltham Forest Borough Council, The Times,* May 20, 1996; *Credit Suisse v. Allerdale Borough Council, The Times,* May 20, 1996: see § 1–30. The point would apply even more strongly to any broader doctrine of implied powers.

14

Secondly, the powers are conferred subject to any restriction or requirement imposed by the 1972 Act or any other enactment.[58]

Thirdly, it is unclear whether the common law doctrine of incidental **1–26** powers as expressed in *Att.-Gen. v. Great Eastern Railway Co.*[59] has been superseded by the enactment of section 111(1). In the Court of Appeal in *ex p. McCarthy & Stone (Developments) Ltd*, Slade L.J. stated[60] that the court was "disposed to think" that it was not open to a local authority to rely on the common law without reference to section 111(1). However, it has been suggested that "the common law rule is arguably wider . . . as it permits activities which are 'consequential upon' other activities and which may not be reflected in 'calculated to facilitate, conducive or incidental to'."[61]

The following cases illustrate the limits of section 111:

> *R. v. Greater London Council and Another, ex p. Westminster City Council.*[62] It was held that the maintenance of good staff relations was a proper function of a local authority and a decision to release staff for that purpose was within s.111, subject to the *Wednesbury* test of reasonableness.[63] But if the object, or a major object, of the decision was to conduct a political campaign in opposition to government policy that was an irrelevant consideration and the decision would be invalid. On that basis a decision by the Inner London Education Authority to release one member of staff to a joint committee or body of trade unions made in the interests of good industrial relations was valid but a decision of the GLC to release seven members of staff with pay to the same body in support of the GLC's campaign against government policy was invalid.

> *Hazell v. Hammersmith and Fulham London Borough Council.*[64] Between **1–27** 1987 and 1989, the council, a London Borough incorporated by royal charter under section 1(2) of the London Government Act 1963, conducted substantial, speculative financial transactions (interest rate "swaps", "swap options", "caps", "floors" and "collars", forward rate agreements and gilt and cash options). An interest rate swap is usually an arrangement by which a borrower at, say, fixed interest contracts with a third party to pay or receive the difference between his interest liability on that basis and what it would have been at variable interest—or vice versa for a borrower at variable interest. The other transactions mentioned are variations on this theme. The transactions were entered into in order to make a profit, but profits were dependent upon interest rates falling: in fact, interest rates increased, and, if the transactions were enforceable, they would result in a loss in excess of £100m.

> Between December 1983 and March 1987 only a few transactions were entered into, but from April 1987 there was a substantial increase. In July 1988, the Audit Commission expressed the view, based on counsel's opinion, that many of the transactions appeared to be *ultra vires*. From August 1988 to

---

[58] This includes delegated legislation: *Allsop v. North Tyneside Metropolitan Borough Council* (1992) 90 L.G.R. 462, *post*, § 1–29.

[59] (1880) 5 App.Cas. 473, *ante*, § 1–21.

[60] [1990] 2 All E.R. 852, 858.

[61] J. Bennett and S. Cirell, *Municipal Trading* (1992), p. 61.

[62] *The Times*, December 27, 1984. Other cases on section 111 include *R. v. Eden District Council, ex p. Moffat*, *The Times*, November 24, 1988 (council entitled to establish a working party of councillors and officials to consider the council's structure and efficiency); *R. v. Wirral Metropolitan Borough Council, ex p. Milstead* (1989) 87 L.G.R. 611 ("factoring" agreement to sell for a current payment the right to receive the proceeds of future sales of land unlawful; disposal of the proceeds of sale could not be said to be incidental to the sale of the property).

[63] As to the *Wednesbury* test, see § 10–25.

[64] [1990] 2 Q.B. 697, D.C.; C.A.; [1992] 2 A.C. 1, H.L.

February 23, 1989, an "interim strategy" was conducted whereby no new transactions were undertaken but existing positions were managed in order to reduce the extent of the council's exposure to loss. On February 22, 1989, the council was advised that the transactions were unlawful, and only seven transactions were conducted thereafter, consequent on other parties exercising options. The transactions were conducted through a capital market fund.

The auditor applied under section 19 of the Local Government Finance Act 1982 for a declaration that the items of account appearing in the capital market fund for 1987–89 were contrary to law, and for an order for rectification of the accounts. The council did not dispute the application, but several of the banks involved in the transactions were joined as respondents. The Divisional Court allowed the application, holding:

(i) The council could not rely on its royal charter as giving it the capacity of a natural person to enter into contracts, as was the case with common law corporations, as this was not the intention of the London Government Act 1963. Accordingly, it could only exercise such powers as were conferred expressly or impliedly by statute.

(ii) There was no express statutory power that authorised the transactions; in particular, they did not fall within Schedule 13 to the Local Government Act 1972.

(iii) The transactions were not authorised by section 111(1) of the 1972 Act (power to do anything calculated to facilitate, or conducive or incidental to, the discharge of any of the council's functions). They did not assist the council to borrow, although they might have been capable of assisting the council to alleviate the consequences of borrowing (i.e. the obligation to pay interest); accordingly, they did not facilitate the management of a function itself, but only the consequence of a function. Moreover, express provision was made in Schedule 13 for the raising and investment of money.

Although not strictly necessary for the judgment, the court expressed views on the other issues argued.

(iv) The undertaking of the transactions was outside the scope of the powers delegated to officers in standing orders or otherwise.

(v) The "capital market fund" was not a fund authorised by Schedule 13, paragraph 16 to the 1972 Act and had never been validly established.

(vi) The conduct of the dealings between April 1987 and August 1989 was unreasonable in the *Wednesbury* sense: no legal advice had been obtained and the officers engaged in the activity were not equipped by training or experience to operate within a highly technical, sophisticated and competitive market.

(vii) The decision to implement, and the actual implementation of, the interim strategy were not *Wednesbury* unreasonable. During the period of the interim strategy the activities were intended to minimise the risks to which the council might be exposed; the fact that the legality of the earlier transactions was in dispute did not negate the fact that it was prudent management to require that risk to be reduced if the transactions were enforceable; if (contrary to the holding in (iii) above) interest risk management was capable of falling within section 111, each transaction would have to be examined on its own facts to decide whether it constituted interest risk management.

(viii) A declaration under section 19 of the 1982 Act concerned only whether an item of expenditure was contrary to law. It was not concerned with the enforceability of rights as between the council and third parties. The court left open the question whether, although a contract was contrary to law as a matter of public law, it might nevertheless not be void under private law, but capable of giving rise to rights enforceable by third parties as long as they did not know and ought not to have known of the facts that made it contrary to law.

The Court of Appeal allowed an appeal (in part): The court *held*:
  (i) that although a borough incorporated by charter had the same capacity as a natural person to enter contracts, it was the council and not the corporation which was the "local authority" for the purposes of the 1972 Act. The general rate fund kept by the council under s.148 of the 1972 Act was applicable only for the purposes of meeting the council's liabilities under the 1972 Act and other legislation. Accordingly, the council's ability to use its funds to defray obligations under the instruments in question depended on the existence of a statutory power, express or implied, authorising it to enter into those transactions;
 (ii) that interest rate risk management was to be regarded as incidental to or consequential upon a local authority's powers of borrowing and investment, and its duty to take reasonable care to manage its borrowings and investments prudently in the best interests of the ratepayers;
 (iii) that the detailed code in Schedule 13 and other statutory provisions regarding borrowing were not inconsistent with local authorities being able, in appropriate circumstances, to enter into swap transactions, with reference to particular debts, as part of interest rate risk management;
 (iv) that, on the other hand, authorities were not empowered to enter into such transactions by way of carrying on a trade or business;
  (v) that all the categories of swap transactions were capable of being lawfully entered into;
 (vi) that all those transactions up to July 1988 were tainted with the improper purposes of trading, but those thereafter were not. After July 1988, the authority was taking defensive steps designed to protect its, and the ratepayers', financial interests;
 (vii) that the authority's resolution of February 1988 to authorise transactions could not ratify what had gone before, and was irrational;
 (viii) that no capital markets fund was validly established by the council;
 (ix) the court also left open the question whether any outstanding contract was enforceable.

The House of Lords restored the decision of the Divisional Court, holding:
  (i) the word "functions" in s.111 embraces all the powers and duties of a local authority;
 (ii) the swap transactions were not incidental to the function of borrowing as they involved speculation in future interest trends with the object of making a profit;
 (iii) Schedule 13 established a comprehensive code which defined and limited the powers of a local authority with regard to borrowing; it was inconsistent with any incidental power to enter swap transactions;
 (iv) if swap transactions were incidental to the function of borrowing, they could only be entered into by the authority, and not a committee or officer, by virtue of s.101(6) of the 1972 Act; this restriction could not be avoided by arguing that the transactions were incidental to debt management as distinct from borrowing, as "debt management" was not itself a function.
  (v) as local authorities had no power to enter into such transactions, the "interim strategy" was as unlawful as the earlier action.[65]

---

[65] There has been considerable litigation on other matters arising from these transactions. See *Statement: Interest Rate Swaps Litigation, The Times*, May 15, 1992; *Statement: Interest Rate*

1-28   *R. v. Richmond Upon Thames London Borough Council, ex p. McCarthy & Stone (Developments) Ltd.*[66] At first instance, Popplewell J.[67] held that s.111(1) gave a local authority power to raise money by charging an individual company for pre-planning application discussions. The words in brackets in subs. (1) were inclusive and not exclusive. The charges were calculated to facilitate, or conducive or incidental to the discharge of the authority's functions. The wording of subs. (3) made it clear that the raising of money by rate, precept or borrowing was within the scope of subs. (1). The restrictions in subs. (3) that raising money had to be in accordance with enactments relating to those matters applied only to the methods of raising money specified, and did not restrict the power to raise money by charges. This was affirmed by the Court of Appeal but reversed by the House of Lords. The House of Lords *held* that section 111(1) could not be interpreted as authorising a local authority to charge for the performance of every function and that, in any event, a power to charge had to be authorised expressly or by necessary implication (*Att.-Gen. v. Wilts United Dairies Ltd*[68]). Furthermore, the giving of pre-application advice was not itself a function of the council, although it was incidental to the discharge of the council's planning functions; that charging for such advice was accordingly "incidental to the incidental"; and that this was too remote to be permitted by section 111(1). The House rejected the council's argument that a distinction was to be drawn between functions which a council has a *duty* to perform (in respect of which it was accepted that no charge could be made) and those which it had a *power* to perform, where a charge could be made. On the other hand, it also rejected the developers' argument that charging under section 111(1) was prohibited by section 111(3), which provides that a local authority "shall not by virtue of this section raise money, whether by means of rates, precepts or borrowing, or lend money except in accordance with the enactments relating to those matters respectively." The argument "would require the addition of the words 'or otherwise' after the word 'borrowing', to get off the ground and, even then, in the context of 'rates, precepts or borrowing,' to equate charging for a service with the raising of money appears to me to demand a very forced interpretation of languages." (*per* Lord Lowry at p. 73).

1-29   *Allsop v. North Tyneside Metropolitan Borough Council.*[69] The council's enhanced voluntary severance scheme provided for payments substantially in excess of those for which the council was liable under the Employment Protection (Consolidation) Act 1978, or specifically empowered to make under the Local Government Superannuation Regulations 1986,[70] the Local Govern-

---

Swap Litigation (No. 2), The Times, July 16, 1992; and *Westdeutsche Landesbank Girozentrale v. Islington London Borough Council* [1994] 1 W.L.R. 938 (council receiving payments under *ultra vires* interest rate swap transactions held them as fiduciary for the payer); *Morgan Grenfell & Co. Ltd. v. Welwyn Hatfield District Council; Islington London Borough Council (Third Party)* [1995] 1 All E.R. 1 (swap deals not wagering contracts); *Kleinwort Benson Ltd v. South Tyneside Metropolitan Borough Council* [1994] 4 All E.R. 972; *South Tyneside Metropolitan Borough Council v. Svenska International plc* [1995] 1 All E.R. 545 (no "change of position" by the bank to prevent the council recovering the full sum paid to the bank under a void agreement); *Kleinwort Benson Ltd v. Birmingham City Council, The Times,* May 20, 1996 (no defence to claim for restitution that bank had or might have hedged the contract so as to suffer no loss).
[66] [1992] 2 A.C. 48.
[67] (1989) 58 P. & C.R. 434.
[68] (1921) 37 T.L.R. 884, C.A.; affirmed (1922) 91 L.J.K.B. 897, H.L.
[69] (1992) 90 L.G.R. 462.
[70] S.I. 1986 No. 24.

ment (Compensation for Premature Retirement) Regulations 1982[71] and the Local Government (Compensation for Redundancy and Premature Retirement) Regulations 1984.[72] The council claimed that the power to make enhanced payments was incidental to the discharge of its functions within section 111(1) and/or section 112 of the Local Government Act 1972, *i.e.* the functions of making and terminating contracts of employment, the delivery of services and the maintenance of good industrial relations. The Divisional Court[73] held that these payments were unlawful, granting the auditor a declaration to that effect. The provisions of section 111(1) were expressly made "subject to the provisions of ... any other enactment," and this limitation included a reference to the delegated legislation; the council's powers were accordingly restricted by reference to the regulations. Moreover, the scheme was no more than a device to promote the council's policy of avoiding compulsory redundancies. The court ordered rectification of the accounts.

An appeal to the Court of Appeal was dismissed. The making of redundancy payments was not expressly authorised by section 112, and power to do so had to be found, if it was to be found at all, in section 111; this was then subject to the restrictions found in other enactments.

Credit Suisse v. Allerdale Borough Council.[74] The bank claimed payment under a guarantee given by the council for sums borrowed by a company established by the council to carry out recreational development (the provision of a leisure pool to be paid for by a time share development) which the council itself was unable to carry out because of government limits on spending and borrowing. The company was now in liquidation. Colman J. *held* that the guarantee was *ultra vires* and void. Local authorities had implied powers to borrow in order to carry out their statutory functions, such as the provision of recreational facilities, but not to guarantee borrowing by distinct legal persons in order to acquire the use of borrowed money without borrowing it themselves. Even if there was such power, the decision to guarantee the loan was unlawful as the reason for it, to evade the spending and borrowing limits, was an irrelevant consideration.

An appeal to the Court of Appeal was dismissed. It was held that the **1–30** development was not authorised by either (1) section 19 of the Local Government (Miscellaneous Provisions) Act 1976 (power to provide recreational facilities, including power to provide buildings, equipment, supplies and assistance of any kind), or (2) by section 111 of the Local Government Act 1972. As to (1), providing time share accommodation was not the provision of a recreational activity, and the provision of "assistance of any kind" covered assistance to users of the facilities and not to those who provided them. As to section 111, as well as identifying the underlying statutory functions (here, s.19(1) of the 1976 Act and s.2(1) of the Local Authorities (Land) Act 1963) it was necessary to examine the context in which supposed implied powers were to be exercised. This included the basic principle that local authority finances were to be conducted on an annual basis; that the scheme involved incurring substantial financial obligations which could not be met out of the council's ordinary income; that powers to spend and borrow were subject to statutory control, Schedule 13 to the 1972 Act containing a comprehensive code defining

[71] S.I. 1982 No. 1009.
[72] S.I. 1984 No. 740.
[73] *The Times*, October 18, 1991.
[74] [1995] 1 Lloyd's L.R. 315, Colman J.; *The Times*, May 20, 1996, C.A.

and limiting borrowing powers. The implied powers in s.111 did not provide an escape route from statutory controls.

> *Credit Suisse v. Waltham Forest London Borough Council.*[75] The local authority gave a guarantee and indemnity for repayments of a loan made for the purpose of establishing a company to acquire properties which were then leased to the authority to provide housing for its homeless in discharge of its statutory duty under section 65 of the Housing Act 1985. The authority subsequently argued that the guarantee and indemnity were *ultra vires*. Gatehouse J., *held* that they were authorised by the Local Government Act 1972, s.111, as calculated to facilitate, and conducive or incidental to the discharge of the authority's functions. An appeal to the Court of Appeal was allowed. Section 102 of the Local Government Act 1972 concerning arrangements for the discharge of functions did not entitle local authorities to discharge any of their functions by means of a partly-owned company. Neither that power nor power to give assistance in the form of a guarantee or indemnity to such a company could be implied by reference to s.111 of the 1972 Act. Where Parliament has made detailed provisions as to how certain statutory functions are to be carried out there is no scope for implying the existence of wholly additional powers which lie outside the statutory code.

Application of doctrine to procedural requirements

1–31 Parliament frequently prescribes the procedure which should be followed in the making of a particular order or decision. This may be done in considerable detail in the relevant statute (or schedule). Alternatively, a Minister may be empowered to lay down procedural rules in a statutory instrument. The traditional position has been that even where there is a duty to observe a procedural step, non-observance will render the ultimate decision *ultra vires* only if it is a *mandatory* or *imperative* requirement. Failure to observe a *directory* requirement does not have that effect. There are many cases illustrating the distinction,[76] but the courts have been unable to formulate clear guidelines as to which steps are mandatory and which directory. Parliament very occasionally indicates the consequences which follow from the non-observance of particular requirements. An example of such an indication, in section 82(1) of the Local Government Act 1972,[77] reads:

> "The acts and proceedings of any person elected to an office under this Act or elected or appointed to an office under Part [...] IV of the Local Government Act 1985 and acting in that office shall, notwithstanding his disqualification or want of qualification, be as valid and effectual as if he had been qualified."

1–32 A court is likely to hold a requirement to be mandatory where, for example, it relates to the exercise of a right or a power rather than the

---

[75] *The Times*, November 8, 1994, Gatehouse J., *The Times*, May 20, 1996, C.A.; *cf. R. v. Greater Manchester Police Authority, ex p. Century Motors (Farnworth) Ltd, The Times*, May 31, 1996 (contract with company organising a vehicle recovery scheme was not an impermissible delegation of statutory powers).

[76] See *Craies on Statute Law* (7th ed.), pp. 260–263; *Maxwell on the Interpretation of Statutes* (12th ed.), pp. 314–322.

[77] As amended by the Local Government Act 1985, Sched. 14, para. 4.

performance of a duty,[78] or it provides an important safeguard to individual interests, such as a requirement to give prior notice of a decision or to hold a hearing,[79] or to give notice of rights of appeal,[80] or rights to make objections,[81] or to give the prescribed period of notice of the implementation of a licensing scheme by council resolution,[82] or to consult appropriate bodies.[83] Similarly a requirement is likely to be mandatory where it reflects the need for justice to be seen to be done[84] or where the procedure leads to the imposition of a financial burden on a member of the public.[85] In *Howard v. Bodington*,[86] Lord Penzance stated[87]:

> "I believe, as far as any rule is concerned, you cannot safely go further than that in each case you must look to the subject-matter; consider the importance of the provision that has been disregarded, and the relation of that provision to the general object intended to be secured by the Act; and upon a review of the case in that aspect decide whether the matter is what is called imperative or only directory."

Bradbury v. Enfield London Borough Council.[88] The reorganisation of **1–33** Enfield's schools on comprehensive lines involved changes which in the case of eight schools did not in the council's view amount to "ceasing to maintain" them. Accordingly, the requirements of s.13(1), (3) and (4) of the Education Act 1944 were not observed. These were that where a local education authority intended to "establish" a county school or "cease to maintain" a county or voluntary school, it was to submit proposals to the Minister, and give public

---

[78] *Montreal Street Railway Co. v. Normandin* [1917] A.C. 170; *Cullimore v. Lyme Regis Corporation* [1962] 1 Q.B. 718. The reasoning here is explained as follows in *Maxwell on the Interpretation of Statutes* (11th edn, 1962), p. 364:

"A strong line of distinction may be drawn between cases where the prescriptions of the Act affect the performance of a duty and where they relate to a privilege or power (*Caldow v. Pixell* (1877) 2 C.P.D. 562, *per* Denman J.). Where powers, rights or immunities are granted with a direction that certain regulations, formalities or conditions shall be complied with, it seems neither unjust nor inconvenient to exact a rigorous observance of them as essential to the acquisition of the right or authority conferred, and it is therefore probable that such was the intention of the legislature. But when a public duty is imposed and the statute requires that it shall be performed in a certain manner, or within a certain time, or under other specified conditions, such prescriptions may well be regarded as intended to be directory only in cases when injustice or inconvenience to others who have no control over those exercising the duty would result if such requirements were essential and imperative." (This paragraph was omitted from the 12th edn.)

[79] *Bradbury v. Enfield London Borough Council* [1967] 1 W.L.R. 1311, *infra*.
[80] *Rayner v. Stepney Corporation* [1911] 2 Ch. 312; *London & Clydeside Estates Limited v. Aberdeen District Council* [1980] 1 W.L.R. 182.
[81] *R. v. Lambeth Borough Council, ex p. Sharp* (1988) 55 P. & C.R. 232.
[82] *R. v. Swansea City Council, ex p. Quietlynn Ltd*, The Times, October 19, 1983; *R. v. Birmingham City Council, ex p. Quietlynn Ltd and other cases* (1985) 83 L.G.R. 461 at pp. 471–479, 512–514.
[83] *Agricultural, Horticultural and Forestry Industry Training Board v. Aylesbury Mushrooms Ltd* [1972] 1 W.L.R. 190; *R. v. Secretary of State for Social Services, ex p. Association of Metropolitan Authorities* [1986] 1 W.L.R. 1; *R. v. Secretary of State for Social Services, ex p. Association of Metropolitan Authorities* (1992) 25 H.L.R. 131.
[84] *Noble v. Inner London Education Authority* (1983) 82 L.G.R. 291.
[85] *Per* Scarman L.J. in *Sheffield City Council v. Graingers Wines Ltd* (1977) 75 L.G.R. 743 at pp. 748–749.
[86] (1877) 2 P.D. 203.
[87] *Ibid.* at p. 211.
[88] [1967] 1 W.L.R. 1311. See also *Lee v. Enfield London Borough Council* (1967) 66 L.G.R. 195; *Lee v. Department of Education and Science* (1967) 66 L.G.R. 211.

notice so that objections could be made to him. The Court of Appeal held that changes in the age group or sex of the pupils did amount here to "ceasing to maintain" the existing schools. The requirements of s.13(1), (3) and (4) were applicable, and were mandatory. In addition, and in relation to all Enfield's secondary schools, the council had failed to comply with s.13(6) and (7) of the 1944 Act, which provided that after the general proposals were approved, the authority had to submit specifications and plans of the school premises to the Minister. The Minister would approve them if they were in conformity with prescribed standards. The court held these requirements to be directory. The only remedy was to complain to the Minister under s.99 of the 1944 Act. The court granted an injunction to restrain the council from implementing the changes only in relation to the group of eight schools.

Howard v. Secretary of State for the Environment.[89] By s.16(2) of the Town and Country Planning Act 1968 (see now s.174 of the 1990 Act), an appeal against an enforcement notice "shall be made by notice in writing to the Minister, which shall indicate the grounds of appeal and state the facts on which it is based." The plaintiff gave notice of appeal within the 42-day period specified in the enforcement notice, but indicated the "grounds" and "facts" concerned after that period had expired. The Court of Appeal held that the section was mandatory as to the giving of notice in writing within the specified time, but directory only as to the contents of the notice of appeal. Accordingly, the Minister had jurisdiction to entertain the plaintiff's appeal.

1–34   There is some authority to the effect that failure to comply with a directory requirement will only be excused where there has been "substantial compliance".

Cullimore v. Lyme Regis Corporation.[90] The borough council prepared a works scheme under the Coast Protection Act 1949, whereby charges were to be levied for certain coast protection works. The scheme required the council within six months of completion of the work to determine the interests in the land benefited by reference to which charges were to be levied, and the amount of such charges. The council determined these matters almost two years after completion. Edmund Davies J. held that the charges were *ultra vires* and void on the grounds that either (1) the six-month time limit was a mandatory requirement, or (2) even if it were a directory requirement, there had been nothing approaching substantial compliance.

1–35   It is not clear, however, whether "substantial compliance" means substantial compliance with the particular procedural requirement that has not been observed or substantial compliance with the procedural code as a whole. In *London & Clydeside Estates Ltd v. Aberdeen District Council,*[91] Lord Hailsham L.C. stated, *obiter*, that "a total failure to comply with a significant part of a requirement cannot in any circumstances be regarded as 'substantial compliance' with the total requirement ... "

A more flexible approach to the effect of failure to comply with procedural requirements was suggested by Lord Hailsham L.C. in the *London & Clydeside* case[92]:

"When Parliament lays down a statutory requirement for the exercise of legal authority it expects its authority to be obeyed down to the minutest detail. But

[89] [1975] Q.B. 235.
[90] [1962] 1 Q.B. 718.
[91] [1980] 1 W.L.R. 182.
[92] *ibid.* at pp. 189–190.

what the courts have to decide in a particular case is the legal consequence of non-compliance on the rights of the subject viewed in the light of a concrete state of facts and a continuing chain of events. It may be that what the courts are faced with is not so much a stark choice of alternatives but a spectrum of possibilities in which one compartment or description fades gradually into another. At one end of this spectrum there may be cases in which a fundamental obligation may have been so outrageously and flagrantly ignored or defied that the subject may safely ignore what has been done and treat it as having no legal consequences upon himself. In such a case if the defaulting authority seeks to rely on its action it may be that the subject is entitled to use the defect in procedure simply as a shield or defence without having taken any positive action of his own. At the other end of the spectrum the defect in procedure may be so nugatory or trivial that the authority can safely proceed without remedial action, confident that, if the subject is so misguided as to rely on the fault, the courts will decline to listen to his complaint. But in a very great number of cases, it may be in a majority of them, it may be necessary for a subject, in order to safeguard himself, to go to the court for declaration of his rights, the grant of which may well be discretionary, and by the like token it may be wise for an authority (as it certainly would have been here) to do everything in its power to remedy the fault in its procedure so as not to deprive the subject of his due or themselves of their power to act. In such cases, though language like 'mandatory', 'directory', 'void', 'voidable', 'nullity' and so forth may be helpful in argument, it may be misleading in effect if relied on to show that the courts, in deciding the consequences of a defect in the exercise of power, are necessarily bound to fit the facts of a particular case and a developing chain of events into rigid legal categories ... "

Lord Hailsham's observations have been applied in a number of cases in the High Court and the Court of Appeal,[93] although references to the distinction between "mandatory" and "directory" requirements are still found.[94] Under the more flexible approach, questions as to the effect of non-compliance with a procedural requirement are to be determined not so much as matters of substantive law but more as matters for the court's discretion, taking account of such considerations as the objective of the procedural requirement, whether the applicant has been prejudiced, timing and the public interest. It remains to be seen whether this will entirely take the place of the traditional approach.

Whether the applicant has been prejudiced may be relevant to the question of the effect of failure to comply with a procedural requirement; however, in appropriate cases an act or decision may be quashed even though the applicant has not been prejudiced.[95]

---

[93] *R. v. Chester City Council, ex p. Quietlynn Ltd, The Times,* October 19, 1983, Woolf J.; *R. v. Secretary of State for the Environment, ex p. Leicester City Council* (1985) 25 R.V.R. 31, Woolf J.; *Main v. Swansea City Council* (1985) 49 P. & C.R. 26, C.A.; *R. v. Lambeth London Borough Council, ex p. Sharp* (1988) 55 P. & C.R. 232; *R. v. Doncaster Metropolitan District Council, ex p. British Railways Board* [1987] J.P.L. 444, Schiemann J.; *Porritt v. Secretary of State for the Environment and Bromley London Borough* [1988] J.P.L. 414, M. T. Pill Q.C.; *cf. R. v. Birmingham City Council, ex p. Quietlynn Ltd* (1985) 83 L.G.R. 461, 471–479, where Forbes J. regarded Lord Hailsham's observations as applicable only to directory requirements.

[94] *Inverclyde District Council v. Lord Advocate* [1982] J.P.L. 313, 314, H.L.

[95] [1980] 1 W.L.R. 182 at p. 183, *per* Lord Hailsham L.C.: compare the position in respect of failure to comply with natural justice: below § 10–46. Failure to comply with a mandatory procedural requirement is fatal even where there is no prejudice: *R. v. Birmingham City Council, ex p. Quietlynn Ltd and other cases* (1985) 83 L.G.R. 461 at pp. 471–479.

In areas where ordinary procedures for judicial review are ousted by a "statutory *ultra vires*" or "time limit" clause (see *infra*, paras. 10–60 and 10–64) the statute generally provides that a person substantially prejudiced by failure to comply with any requirement may apply to the High Court within six weeks for the ultimate order or decision to be quashed.

1–36   Breach of a directory requirement will not render the ultimate decision void, and may not even amount to an *intra vires* error of law which may be challenged on an appeal or on an application for certiorari to quash for error of law on the face of the record.[96] However, if he is in time, a person aggrieved may be able to obtain mandamus to compel observance of the requirement.

> *Brayhead (Ascot) Ltd v. Berkshire County Council.*[97] The Town and Country Planning General Development Order requires that reasons be given by a local planning authority where it refuses planning permission or attaches conditions to a permission. Winn J. held that failure to give reasons did not render a condition void, but that a court would normally grant mandamus to compel the reasons to be divulged.

In some cases, Parliament expressly allows defects to be corrected. For example, section 176(2) of the Town and Country Planning Act 1990 provides that on an appeal against an enforcement notice, the Secretary of State may correct any informality, defect or error in the notice, or give directions for varying its terms, if he is satisfied that the correction or variation can be made without injustice to the appellant or to the local planning authority. Section 176(5) provides that he may disregard the fact that a person entitled to be served with the notice has not been so served if neither he nor the appellant has been substantially prejudiced by the failure. If, however, the notice is a nullity for any reason, the defect cannot be corrected under section 176.[98]

Other aspects of the ultra vires doctrine

1–37   Many of the cases on the application of the *ultra vires* doctrine to local authorities have concerned issues as to whether a particular project could lawfully be undertaken. However, the *ultra vires* doctrine may also be invoked to control the *methods* by which decisions are reached. Accordingly, in *Anisminic Ltd v. Foreign Compensation Commission,*[99] the House of Lords came near to holding that any error of law in the course of decision making will infringe the *ultra vires* doctrine. The courts have also held that powers are exceeded if exercised in bad faith, for improper purposes, where a legally relevant consideration has been ignored, where a legally irrelevant consideration has been taken into account, or where the decision is so unreasonable that no reasonable authority could act in such a manner. A

---

[96] See *Mountview Court Properties Ltd v. Devlin* (1970) 21 P. & C.R. 689.
[97] [1964] 2 Q.B. 303.
[98] See *Miller-Mead v. Minister of Housing and Local Government* [1963] 2 Q.B. 196.
[99] [1969] A.C. 147.

discretion may not be fettered improperly by any contract or undertaking, by the creation of an estoppel, or by any rigid policy rule. Local authorities must not act under the dictation of any other body in the exercise of functions in the absence of express or implied statutory authority. Finally, the courts may hold that there is an obligation to observe natural justice or to act fairly. These are limitations which the courts, in the appropriate context, deem Parliament to have intended to impose, in the absence of express provision to the contrary. These aspects of the *ultra vires* doctrine are considered in Chapter 10.

Legal consequences of a breach of the ultra vires rules
There are two important consequences which may follow from a breach of **1–38** the *ultra vires* rule. First, legal proceedings may be commenced in the High Court. A person aggrieved may apply for "judicial review" of a local authority's decision under Order 53 of the Rules of the Supreme Court. The court may in an appropriate case grant one or more of a number of remedies, some of which are peculiar to public law (the prerogative orders of certiorari, prohibition and mandamus), and the other ordinary remedies also applicable in the private law context (injunction, declaration and damages). The former group may only be sought under Order 53; the latter may also be sought in ordinary High Court proceedings, although the courts will normally require an applicant to proceed under Order 53 if the case is within the scope of that Order. Thus, a remedy may be available to quash an *ultra vires* decision that has been made (certiorari), to prohibit *ultra vires* action which is about to take place (prohibition, injunction), to compel performance of a public duty (mandamus, injunction), or simply to make the legal position clear (declaration). These remedies are considered in Chapter 10.

Where unlawful expenditure is concerned, the traditional procedure was for an action to be commenced in the High Court for a declaration or for a declaration coupled with an injunction. This is what happened in *Att.-Gen. v. Fulham Corporation*,[1] discussed earlier. In a similar way a ratepayer in Birmingham obtained a declaration that the council had acted *ultra vires* in granting free bus travel to old-age pensioners,[2] and in Cardiff tenants of council houses unsuccessfully sought a declaration that a differential rent scheme was *ultra vires*, arguing that a charge based on ability to pay was not within the Housing Act 1936.[3] Such proceedings would now normally be brought by way of an application for judicial review.

An action in the High Court is costly, and in relation to local authorities a more effective check is exercised through statutory audit.[4] Where it appears to the auditor that any item of account is contrary to law he may apply to the court for a declaration to that effect, unless the expenditure has been sanctioned by the Secretary of State. Where the court makes the declaration asked for, it may order repayment by the person concerned and may order

[1] [1921] 1 Ch. 440.
[2] *Prescott v. Birmingham Corporation* [1955] Ch. 210.
[3] *Smith v. Cardiff Corporation* [1955] Ch. 159.
[4] Local Government Finance Act 1982, Part III.

the rectification of accounts, and in some cases disqualification from membership of the local authority follows.

1–39   Any person interested may inspect documents of account and any local government elector may question the auditor about them and may raise an objection to an account.[5]

These matters are considered in more detail in Chapter 7. But the point is noted here that if an authority oversteps its powers or if members (or officers) are responsible for expenditure which is *ultra vires* they are likely to be called to account through the system of statutory audit.

1–40   There is the further practical point that an authority cannot engage in a major scheme or project without involving in some way, and generally at an early stage, one of the central government departments, and departments always must be satisfied, before giving any consent required of them, that adequate statutory authority exists for what is proposed. Some services are grant-earning, and grants are customarily given only in respect of "approved" expenditure, that is to say, approved by a government department. When a local authority needs to acquire land compulsorily it must always rely on a clearly applicable statutory power. In initiating larger schemes, therefore, an authority is in any event unlikely to engage or be able to engage in activities which are *ultra vires*.

Recent trends

1–41   Parliament has given several widely-drawn powers to local authorities, powers which enable them to act for the good of their areas in ways not specified by statute. These general powers do not negative the *ultra vires* rule but they do soften its application. Section 6 of the Local Government (Financial Provisions) Act 1963 enabled a local authority to incur expenditure up to a 0.4p rate for any purpose which in its opinion was in the interests of the area or its inhabitants, provided such activity was not subject to other statutory provision. This provision was important because of its novelty. It was re-enacted in section 137 of the Local Government Act 1972 in somewhat wider terms. An amount up to a prescribed limit[6] may be spent for the benefit of the area or a part of it or for the benefit of all or some of the inhabitants. Section 139 gives a power to local authorities to spend money on

---

[5] *ibid.* s.17.

[6] A prescribed sum (£1.90 for county and non-metropolitan district councils, £3.55 or £3.80 for metropolitan districts, £3.55 for local authorities in Greater London and £3.50 for parish or community councils) multiplied by the population of the area: s.137(4AA), (4AB), inserted by section 36 of the Local Government and Housing Act 1989 and the Local Authorities (Discretionary Expenditure Limits) Order 1993 (S.I. 1993 No. 4). The appropriate sum in relation to a county or district council which has become a unitary authority following a structural change order under the Local Government Act 1992 is £3.80: Local Authorities (Discretionary Expenditure Limits) (England) Order 1995 (S.I. 1995 No. 651). £3.80 is also the figure for county and county borough councils in Wales from April 1, 1996: Local Government (Wales) Act 1994, Sched. 15, para. 30, inserting a new subs. (4C) in section 137 of the 1972 Act. On the calculation of the "relevant population", see the Local Authorities (Discretionary Expenditure) (Relevant Population) Regulations 1993 (S.I. 1993 No. 40). The limit was formerly the product of a 2p rate. See further, §§ 12–15, 12–16.

gifts donated for the benefit of the inhabitants of the area, and a gift may be unrelated to any statutory purpose. Section 137 also gives authorities power to contribute to certain charitable funds and appeals related to the United Kingdom, and section 138 authorises expenditure in dealing with actual or imminent or apprehended disasters and emergencies affecting an area or its inhabitants. Sections 120 and 124 enable local authorities to purchase land for the benefit, improvement or development of their areas; and section 2 of the Local Authorities (Land) Act 1963 empowers local authorities, for the benefit or improvement of their areas, to erect buildings or to construct or carry out works on land. Here again is the concept of benefit to the area generally.

But there has been a converse tendency as well, a tendency to particular- **1–42** ise, and to particularise in such a way that generally implied or incidental powers are curtailed, not only in the field in which the restriction takes place, but at large, since it can be argued that if a particular power is required by statute in one field, it is required in another. There is, in fact, one example of this in the section which extends the scope and activity of local authorities in a generalised way and the two tendencies are seen within one provision. Where an authority develops land for the benefit of the area under section 2 of the Local Authorities (Land) Act 1963, it has power to repair, maintain and insure the buildings or works and generally deal with such buildings or works in the proper course of management. This is not a new kind of provision. It is found in section 235(1)(b) of the Town and Country Planning Act 1990 (a provision originally derived from the 1944 Planning Act). But it can be argued that if an authority has power to put up a building it can, under the doctrine of implied and incidental powers, or under the subsidiary powers conferred by section 111 of the Local Government Act 1972,[7] deal with it in the proper course of management, and indeed one would have thought that there would have been a bounden duty on the authority to do this and to keep the building in repair. There are other statutory provisions enabling authorities to erect buildings and there is no reference in them to insurance. Is it to be assumed in those cases that to effect insurance is *ultra vires*? This particular enabling power is perhaps more restrictive than enabling.

The Royal Commission on Local Government in England[8] took the view **1–43** that all of the main authorities which it proposed should be established should have a general power to spend money for the benefit of their areas and inhabitants, additional to their expenditure on services for which they would have statutory responsibility. The Commission referred to the precedent under section 6 of the Local Government (Financial Provisions) Act 1963. They suggested that the only limit on the use of new power should be the wishes of the electors and such restrictions as have to be placed on local government expenditure in the interests of national economic and financial policy. The White Paper "Reform of Local Government in

[7] See § 1–10.
[8] Vol. I, para. 323.

England"[9] stated that the Government of the day were sympathetic in principle to this proposal.[10] But practical difficulties were noted; for example, unconditional powers, not restricted by any financial limit, might lead to wasteful duplication or to local action which could conflict with national objectives in important fields of policy. In the event, only the "free 2p", and the subsidiary powers referred to above, emerged as law. The Widdicombe Committee on the Conduct of Local Authority Business was not in favour of a general power without a fixed financial ceiling, and this position was endorsed by the Government.[11]

F. LOCAL AUTHORITIES AND EUROPEAN COMMUNITY LAW

1–44 Local authorities are increasingly affected by developments in European Community Law.[12] Areas of substantive law concerning the powers and duties of local authorities may be remodelled by E.C. legislation in pursuit of the process of European integration. Examples include the law applicable to public procurement,[13] waste management, and food safety, where directives have been implemented by subordinate legislation. An unimplemented E.C. directive that is directly effective according to E.C. law principles can be relied on in domestic proceedings against a Member State, and a local authority is regarded as an "emanation of the state" for this purpose.[14] Moreover, under E.C. law a decentralised body such as a local authority is obliged to apply the terms of an unimplemented but directly effective directive in preference to national law.[15]

A Member State may under certain conditions be liable to compensate individuals for damage caused to them by the state's breach of the Community obligations, such as failure to implement a directive within the prescribed period.[16] It has been argued that in appropriate circumstances this principle could render a local authority liable in damages.[17]

The argument that a private person may enforce the terms of an unimplemented directive against another private person has been rejected

---

[9] Cmnd. 4276 (1970).
[10] *ibid.* para. 69.
[11] Cmnd. 9797 (1986) at pp. 180–181; Government Response, Cm. 433 (1988) at pp. 36–40.
[12] See generally B Hessel and K. Mortelmans, 'Decentralised Government and Community Law: conflicting institutional developments?' (1993) 30 C.M.L.Rev. 905.
[13] See §§ 7–25 *et seq.*
[14] Case 152/84, *Marshall v. Southampton and South West Hampshire Area Health Authority* [1986] Q.B. 401 (Article 5(1) of Directive 76/207 EEC, the "Equal Treatment Directive", directly effective against health authority in its capacity as employer); *R. v. London Boroughs Transport Committee, ex p. Freight Transport Association Ltd* [1990] 1 C.M.L.R. 229 (Committee held to be an 'emanation of the state').
[15] Case 103/88, *Fratelli Constanzo SpA v. Comune di Milano* [1989] E.C.R. 1861.
[16] Cases 6 and 9/90, *Francovich & Bonifaci v. Italy* [1991] E.C.R. I–5357; Cases C–46/93 and C–48/93, *Brasserie du Pêcheur SA v. Germany; R. v. Secretary of State for Transport, ex p. Factortame (No. 4)* [1996] 2 W.L.R. 506.
[17] R. Gordon and C. Miskin, *Local Authority Law*, 4/94, p. 8.

by the European Court.[18] Prior to that decision, it was advanced unsuccessfully by the council in *Wychavon District Council v. Secretary of State for the Environment*.[19] Here, the council sought to quash the decision of an inspector allowing an appeal against the council's refusal of planning permission to Velcourt Ltd for the erection of poultry houses and related agricultural dwellings. The council argued that as respondent to the planning appeal and now in bringing an application to quash it was acting, as an 'individual', for the promotion of the interests of the inhabitants of the area under section 222 of the Local Government Act 1972.[20] As such it was entitled to enforce Directive 85/337/EEC (the Environmental Impact Directive) against Velcourt Ltd, the matter arising in advance of implementation of the Directive by the Town and Country Planning (Assessment of Environmental Effect) Regulations.[21] Turner J. rejected these arguments. On the matter of direct effect, his Lordship reasserted the orthodox position as stated in the *Marshall* case.[22] Furthermore, the council could not be regarded as an 'individual' for these purposes.

---

[18] Case C–91/92, *P. Faccini Dori v. Recreb Srl* [1994] I E.C.R. 3325.
[19] *The Times*, January 7, 1994.
[20] See § 12–65.
[21] S.I. 1988 No. 1199.
[22] *supra.*

CHAPTER 2

ACQUISITION OF POWERS

THE powers of local authorities are all derived from statute, from public Acts **2–01** and local Acts. The numerous powers referred to in this book all stem from public Acts, but individual authorities may supplement these general powers and acquire additional powers by means of local legislation. There are, in addition, powers *available* under the general law which cannot be exercised until some formal steps are taken—these powers may be acquired by the adoption of "adoptive" Acts, under provisional order procedure, and under special parliamentary procedure.

Local authorities have an influence in fashioning the powers which Parliament gives them. A note of this appears in the final paragraphs of this chapter.

A. LOCAL LEGISLATION

Procedure in Parliament

The rules governing the promotion of local Bills (and private and personal **2–02** Bills) are found in the standing orders of each House. The first step is the giving of public notice and the presentation of a petition for leave to introduce the Bill to Parliament. Notice of intention is published in the Press and in the *London Gazette*, and if land is to be acquired notice is given to owners, lessees and occupiers. A copy of the Bill is deposited in the Committee and Private Bill Office (of the Commons), with the Clerk of the Parliaments (in the House of Lords), and with the government departments affected. The dates by which these and subsequent steps are to be taken are given in standing orders. Normally, Bills should be deposited by November 27 each session.

Each House has an officer, called an Examiner, to check that all formalities have been observed. The petitioners must prove to one of the Examiners that procedure has been rightly followed, and this may be challenged by any party by presenting a memorial. If the Examiner finds that formalities have not been observed, he reports to each House and a decision is made as to whether to strike out the petition or waive the requirements of standing orders. A decision as to the House in which a private Bill shall proceed is made at a meeting between the Chairman of Committees in the House of Lords or his counsel, and the Chairman of Ways and Means in the House of Commons or counsel to the Speaker.

Where a private Bill proceeds first in the House of Lords, it has a first **2–03** reading, a purely formal process, and a second reading which is normally formal, but which may be opposed. If it passes the second reading, any opposed clauses (*i.e.* clauses against which a Petition or Petitions have been received) are committed to a Select Committee of five Lords. The House may agree to an Instruction to the Committee, usually to the effect that the Committee should have regard or be satisfied on certain matters before passing a provision in the Bill. An Instruction may go beyond the scope of any of the Petitions against a particular provision.

Procedure in this Committee largely follows the pattern of a judicial proceeding. A case is put by the promoters and objectors (or "petitioners"), through counsel practising at the Parliamentary Bar, and witnesses may be called. Government departments may also make representations. If there is opposition to the general principles of the Bill as they appear in the preamble, these arguments are normally taken first. If the Committee refuses to sanction the preamble, a report is made to the House and no further proceedings may be taken in that session unless the Bill is recommitted. If the preamble is approved, then each contested clause is argued and objectors may press for the inclusion of clauses to safeguard their interests.

2–04   Unopposed clauses (the great majority) are usually considered by the Committee on Unopposed Bills. This technically consists of the Lord Chairman of Committees and such Lords as think fit to attend, but usually there is simply an informal meeting conducted by the Lord Chairman with the assistance of his counsel. The promoters are represented by a parliamentary agent rather than counsel. Witnesses do not give evidence on oath. Representatives of government departments may attend. The Committee ensures that the promoters prove the requisite need for the provisions sought. A clause is disallowed (a) if the clause embodies a policy which does not commend itself to the Committee; (b) unless the clause is needed to such an extent as to counterbalance the presumed undesirability of enacting it; or (c) if the clause is wholly or partly covered by a public general Act. Unopposed clauses may instead be referred to a Select Committee. This is thought appropriate, for example, where the House agrees to an Instruction, or where important issues of principle are concerned.

The Bill is then reported to the House, with any amendments made in Committee, and given its third reading; it is then passed to the House of Commons, where all the stages are repeated. Proceedings in the House of Commons are very similar to those in the House of Lords, but there are some differences in detail. The Bill becomes an Act of Parliament on receiving the Royal Assent. The full details of this procedure are given in Erskine May, *Parliamentary Practice*.[1]

Validity of local legislation

2–05   Once a local Act has been passed its validity cannot be impugned on the

---

[1] 21st ed., Part III.

grounds that it had not passed through the proper procedure or that it was improperly obtained.[2]

> *Pickin v. British Railways Board*.[3] Section 18 of the British Railways Act 1968 (a private Act) stipulated that provisions in a large number of pre-1845 Railway Acts, whereby on abandonment or discontinuance of a railway the land was to revert to the owners for the time being of the adjacent land, should not apply to property of the board. P. sought a declaration that he was the owner of part of the land of a disused branch line. Part of his argument was that section 18 was ineffective to deprive him of his rights, on the grounds that standing orders had not been complied with, and that the board had fraudulently concealed certain matters from Parliament and its officers and thereby misled Parliament into passing the section. *Held*, the courts had no power to disregard an Act of Parliament, whether public or private, and could not examine parliamentary proceedings to determine whether there had been any irregularity or fraud.

Enabling powers to promote or oppose legislation

A power to oppose a local or personal Bill is available to all local **2–06** authorities and joint authorities and a power to promote such a Bill is available to all authorities except parish and community councils.[4] A Bill may not be promoted to change a local government area or an area's status or electoral arrangements.[5] A resolution to promote or to oppose a local or personal Bill requires a majority of the whole number of the council members. In the case of the promotion of a Bill 30 days' clear notice of the meeting and of the proposal must be given in the local press, and in the case of a proposal to oppose a Bill the period is 10 days. This is in addition to the ordinary notice.[6] Where the proposal is to promote a Bill, a further meeting must be called as soon as may be after the expiration of 14 days from the deposit of the Bill in Parliament. This second meeting is convened in the same way as the first and unless a majority of the whole members confirms the propriety of promoting the Bill it is withdrawn. A residuary body may oppose a local or personal Bill without complying with these requirements.[7]

A local Bill promoted by the council of a London borough may include provisions requested by another London borough council or by the Common Council; a Bill promoted by the Common Council may include provisions requested by any London borough council; and a Bill promoted by a metropolitan district council may include provisions requested by another metropolitan district council in the same county. The same requirements as to meetings apply to a requesting council as apply to a

---

[2] *Edinburgh and Dalkeith Ry v. Wauchope* (1842) 8 Cl. & F. 710; *Lee v. Bude and Torrington Junction Ry* (1871) L.R. 6 C.P. 576.
[3] [1974] A.C. 765.
[4] Local Government Act 1972, s.239, as amended by the Local Government Act 1985, Sched. 14, para. 32.
[5] *ibid.* s.70, as amended by the Local Government Act 1985, Sched. 14, para. 1.
[6] *ibid.* Sched. 12.
[7] Local Government Act 1985, Sched. 13, para. 12(h).

promoting council. The requesting council may contribute to the expenses of promotion.[8]

Clauses Acts

2–07   In the earlier part of the nineteenth century, a very great number of private Bills were presented to Parliament and an attempt was made to secure a measure of uniformity by the provision of "model Bills" containing clauses usually found in private Acts of a given class, and setting out a convenient order. These models were not incorporated into standing orders and were not in any way formally recognised, but they were printed with the sanction of the Speaker and served as a guide to parliamentary agents.[9] A greater degree of uniformity was made possible by the introduction of the Clauses Consolidation Acts of 1845 and 1847, and the promotion of private legislation in particular fields was simplified and cheapened. The Clauses Acts contained a standard set of provisions which could readily be incorporated into any private Act—and indeed into any public Act. The Waterworks Clauses Act 1847, in the words of its preamble, consolidated " ... in One Act certain Provisions usually contained in Acts authorising the Making of Waterworks for supplying Towns with Water". An undertaker requiring statutory authority to supply water would promote a "special Act" which authorised the construction of works and incorporated some or all of the provisions of the Waterworks Clauses Act. The provisions of the Town Police Clauses Act 1847 and the Towns Improvement Clauses Act 1847 similarly became operative by incorporation with a private Act, but some of the sections were incorporated into the Public Health Act 1875 and extended to all urban districts. The Lands Clauses Consolidation Act 1845 and the Cemeteries Clauses Act 1847 are further examples of statutes providing a set of provisions for incorporation into private legislation.

Construction of private Acts

2–08   In construing private Acts the rule is to interpret them strictly against the promoters, and liberally in favour of the public.[10] In *Altrincham Union Assessment Committee v. Cheshire Lines Committee*[11] Lord Esher M.R. said[12]:

> "Now it is quite true that there is some difference between a private Act of Parliament and a public one, but the only difference which I am aware of is as to the strictness of the construction to be given to it when there is any doubt as to the meaning. In the case of a public Act you construe it keeping in view the fact that it must be taken to have been passed for the public advantage, and you

---

[8] Local Government Act 1985, s.87.
[9] H.C. (1847–48), 556 Qns. 226–228.
[10] *Bristol Guardians v. Bristol Waterworks Company* [1914] A.C. 379, and see *Craies on Statute Law* (7th ed.), Part IV, especially pp. 565–569.
[11] (1885) 15 Q.B.D. 597.
[12] At p. 602.

apply certain fixed canons to its construction. In the case of a private Act, which is obtained by persons for their own benefit, you construe more strictly provisions which they allege to be in their favour, because the persons who obtain a private Act ought to take care that it is so worded that that which they desire to obtain for themselves is plainly stated in it. But when the construction is perfectly clear, there is no difference between the modes of construing a private Act and a public Act, and, however difficult the construction of a private Act may be, when once the court has arrived at the true construction, after having subjected it to the strictest criticism, the consequences are precisely the same as in the case of a public Act. The moment you have arrived at the meaning of the legislature, the effect is the same in the one case as in the other."

Local legislation and local government reorganisation

Section 262 of the Local Government Act 1972 provided that local **2–09** legislation in force on April 1, 1974, remained in force, unless specifically dealt with, in the area to which it applied before that date, but the Secretary of State or any appropriate Minister might, by order, extend it to the whole of the new local government area. In order to encourage the rationalisation of the vast amount of local legislation all local Acts ceased to have effect in metropolitan counties at the end of 1980 (the end of June 1981 for Greater Manchester),[13] and elsewhere in England and Wales outside Greater London at the end of 1986.[14] The Secretary of State or other appropriate Minister had power, however, to exempt a local provision from repeal or postpone the date on which local powers cease to apply.

The Secretary of State stated in DoE Circular 14/74 that there was a great deal of local legislation

> "which should have been repealed many years ago, because it has been overtaken by general law, because it is no longer applicable in modern circumstances, because the powers are spent or because the provisions in question represent the sort of law that Parliament would not now be inclined to pass. ... For the exercise to be worthwhile the process of pruning and redrafting must be drastic. From earlier experience it is thought that most local authorities will not need to re-enact more than a very small percentage of the legislation which they are inheriting. ... "

It was strongly recommended that county councils should co-ordinate the review of local legislation in their area, and that district councils should avoid submitting Bills.

The rationalisation process, and indeed private legislation procedure generally, was considered by the House of Lords Select Committee on Practice and Procedure.[15] The Committee recommended (i) that further Miscellaneous Provisions Bills or Bills on particular topics should be introduced as public legislation; (ii) that consideration should be given to the possibility of making Miscellaneous Provisions Bills subject to a special procedure for non-controversial Bills; (iii) that the arrangements for

---

[13] Metropolitan Counties (Local Statutory Provisions) Order 1979 (S.I. 1979 No. 969); Greater Manchester (Local Statutory Provisions) Order 1980 (S.I. 1980 No. 1845).
[14] Non-Metropolitan and Welsh Counties (Local Statutory Provisions) Order 1983 (S.I. 1983 No. 619).
[15] First Report, 1977–78 H.L. 155.

reaching agreement on common clauses should be continued and extended; and (iv) that the modified procedure for the consideration of clauses common to more than one Bill by a single Select Committee should be used in future cases if the exercise in the 1977–78 session[16] proved successful. Otherwise, there was no need for fundamental change in private legislation procedure although a number of small reforms were desirable.[17] The Committee rejected proposals from counsel to the Lord Chairman of Committees which would in effect, although not in theory, have restricted the right of individual local authorities to petition for private legislation, with requests for additional legislation being channelled through a single local authority agency and a joint committee of the two Houses. These proposals were opposed by the local authority associations.

2–10   In 1973, the Department of the Environment set up a group on an informal basis to consider proposals for public legislation on local authorities' general powers, and the process of rationalising local legislation. This group consists of representatives of government departments, local authority associations and parliamentary agents, counsel to the Lord Chairman, and counsel to Mr Speaker. It participated in the discussions leading to the Local Government (Miscellaneous Provisions) Act 1976. The House of Lords Select Committee on Practice and Procedure recommended that the powers of this group should be continued and expanded. It should be enabled to instruct parliamentary counsel to draft bills on agreed topics, subject to the demands of the Government's main legislative programme. This would assist the introduction of further public Miscellaneous Provisions Acts, a proposal which seems to be generally accepted as more appropriate for the development of local government than reliance on local legislation. A number of provisions of the kind found in local Acts were included in the Local Government (Miscellaneous Provisions) Act 1982.

A full-scale review of the scope of, and procedure for, enacting private legislation was conducted by the Joint Committee on Private Bill Procedure, which reported in 1988.[18] It made recommendations for change falling into three main categories: first, it proposed changes in administrative practice to reduce the volume of private business coming to Parliament. For example, if the primary purpose behind a Bill can be authorised through other means, those means should be pursued first, with the approval of Parliament limited only to the specific components which require its authority. The Department of the Environment and the Welsh Office should keep the case for public local authority legislation under constant review and should introduce Local Government (Miscellaneous Provisions) Bills promptly as the need arises. Secondly, it proposed the establishment of a non-parliamentary authorisation procedure for certain types of proposals for which an Act of Parliament is now required (in particular, new railway and tramway works and a wider range of harbour measures). Thirdly, parliamentary procedures

[16] See Report of the Select Committee, 1977–78 H.L. 137.
[17] 1977–78 H.L. 155, pp. x–xii.
[18] 1987–88 H.L. 97, H.C. 625.

for private Bills and Special Procedure Orders should be streamlined and improved. The Government welcomed many of the proposals, including those in the second category, and was content for Parliament to decide upon many of the others.[19] Part I of the Transport and Works Act 1992 (ss.1–25) introduced new arrangements for authorising transport projects without the need for private legislation. Accordingly, the Secretary of State may make orders in respect of a railway, tramway, trolley vehicle system, mode of guided transport prescribed by order, or inland waterway, normally following an application by the promoter or operator. There is provision for inquiries and hearings in respect of objections. Schemes of national significance must be approved by Parliament at an early stage. In practice, the promotion of private legislation by local authorities is now rare, with the exception of bills promoted by London local authorities.

B. ADOPTIVE ACTS

There are several statutory provisions which are effective within an area **2–11** only after formal adoption by the authority concerned. The tendency in recent years has been to incorporate the provisions of adoptive Acts in legislation having general application. Many of the adoptive provisions of the Public Health Acts Amendment Act 1890 were incorporated in the Public Health Act 1936; and the Local Government Act 1972 extended (with few exceptions) the adoptive provisions of the Public Health Acts 1875 to 1925 to the whole of England and Wales whether adopted or not.[20] The following are examples of adoptive provisions which still remain:

(a) Public Health Act 1925. The provisions with regard to the naming of streets.[21]

(b) Highways Act 1980. The advance payments code.[22] Under the Local Government Act 1972 the code continued to apply where it previously applied: it can now be made to apply elsewhere in parishes and communities by resolution of the county council.[23]

(c) Private Places of Entertainment (Licensing) Act 1967. This provision enables a licensing system to be administered by the adopting authority.

(d) The provisions of the Local Government (Miscellaneous) Provisions Act 1976 which deal with hackney carriages and private hire vehicles.[24]

(e) Local Government (Miscellaneous Provisions) Act 1982. A number of the powers conferred by this Act (*e.g.* in respect of licensing of

---

[19] *Private Bills and New Procedures—A Consultation Document* (The Government Response to the Report of the Joint Committee on Private Bill Procedure), Cm. 1110 (1990).
[20] Sched. 14, para. 23.
[21] ss.17–19; Local Government Act 1972, Sched. 14, paras. 24 and 25.
[22] ss.219–225.
[23] Highways Act 1980, s.204(2)(c).
[24] Part II, ss.45–80.

public entertainments, control of sex establishments and street trading) may be adopted by resolution.[25]

C. PROVISIONAL ORDERS

2–12 Provisional order procedure has been largely superseded by the use of orders subject to special parliamentary procedure, and reference to it is therefore brief. It was introduced in the last century primarily to save local authorities and statutory bodies the expense involved in promoting private Bills, and many statutes made powers available by way of orders made by a Minister and confirmed by Parliament. The procedure to be followed in the making of a provisional order under the Local Government Act 1972, or any enactment passed on or after June 1, 1934, is contained in section 240 of the Local Government Act 1972. Publicity is given by the applicants, objections are considered by the Secretary of State, and a local inquiry is held unless he considers one to be unnecessary. It is open to the Secretary of State to make a provisional order and to submit it for confirmation to Parliament. If, while the confirmation Bill is pending, a petition against the order is presented, the petitioner may appear before the Select Committee to which the Bill is referred and he may oppose the order as if it were a private Bill. An order which extends the area for which any local statutory provision is in force must be provisional only.[26] An example of such an extension is the Royal County of Berkshire (Public Entertainment) Provisional Order Confirmation Act 1976. The procedure which applies to the making of orders under statutes before June 1, 1934, is given in those statutes.

D. ORDERS SUBJECT TO SPECIAL PARLIAMENTARY PROCEDURE

2–13 The Statutory Orders (Special Procedure) Act 1945[27] introduced a simpler way of acquiring powers. An order is first made by the Minister concerned, and when the preliminary proceedings in the enabling Act have been complied with it is laid before Parliament. The procedural requirements include the giving of notice in the *London Gazette*, and, where the order relates to any particular area, in at least one newspaper circulating in that area. The notice must state how objections may be lodged, and if objections are raised and not withdrawn the Minister must consider them, holding a local inquiry unless satisfied that there are special circumstances which render this unnecessary.[28]

When the order is laid before Parliament, petitions against it may be

---

[25] *e.g.* s.1(2) (licensing of public entertainments); s.2 (control of sex establishments); s.3 (street trading).

[26] Local Government Act 1972, ss.254(8) and 262(10).

[27] As amended by the Statutory Orders (Special Procedure) Act 1965 and the Local Government Act 1972, s.240.

[28] See *R. v. Minister of Agriculture, Fisheries and Food, ex p. Wear Valley District Council* (1988) 152 L.G.Rev. 849, D.C., where the Minister wrongly refused to accept a memorial from a local authority objector, holding erroneously that the authority was not "adversely affected".

lodged within 21 days of its submission. Petitions of objection are of two kinds: petitions for amendment, praying for particular and specific amendments, and petitions of general objection, praying against the order generally. All petitions are referred to the Lord Chairman of Committees of the House of Lords and the Chairman of Ways and Means of the House of Commons. In due course they report to each House whether objections have been presented against the order, and, if there have been objections, whether they are proper to be received, and whether they are petitions for amendment or petitions of general objection. If within 21 days of this report either House resolves that the order be annulled it becomes void and no further proceedings may be taken with respect to it. If no such resolution of annulment is passed then one of three things may happen. If there is no petition against the order it comes into operation at the end of the resolution period; if there is a petition for amendment the order stands referred to a joint committee of both Houses; if there is a petition of general objection it stands referred to the joint committee, unless either House resolves to the contrary.

Where an order is referred to the joint committee, the committee may report the order with or without amendment. If it is without amendment the order comes into operation on the day the report is laid before Parliament; if the order contains an amendment it will take effect as amended on a day fixed by the Minister, but if the Minister considers it expedient he may withdraw the order or may cause it to be submitted to Parliament for further consideration by means of a Confirmation Bill.[29]

E. THE INFLUENCE OF LOCAL AUTHORITIES IN THE LEGISLATIVE FIELD

There are two important ways in which this influence has been and is **2–14** exerted. First, over many years individual local authorities have promoted private Bills giving them powers not otherwise available, and other authorities, recognising the general usefulness of some of these provisions, have written them into their private Bills. The inclusion of common form clauses is facilitated by the existence of a code of Model Clauses prepared by a committee appointed by the Chairman of Committees of the House of Lords and the Chairman of Ways and Means of the House of Commons. Many of these clauses have ultimately found their way into general legislation. The Highways Act 1980 contains a number of provisions formerly in a Model.[30] Examples are the provisions in the Act relating to crossings over footways[31] and to the prevention of evasion of private street works charges.[32]

---

[29] See, *e.g.* the Okehampton Bypass (Confirmation of Orders) Act 1985, approving Orders against which the joint committee had reported: H.C.Deb. Vol. 87, cols. 140–224, November 19, 1985; H.L.Deb. Vol. 468, cols. 1412 *et seq.*, December 5, 1985.
[30] Report of the Committee on Consolidation of Highway Law, Cmnd. 630, para. 9.
[31] Highways Act 1980, s.184.
[32] *ibid.* s.235.

Secondly, the local authority associations exert a constant influence in legislative matters, by formal process and informally. This influence is exercised in the following ways:

(a) in bringing to the notice of government departments alleged defects in the law affecting directly or indirectly the status or the work of local authorities;

(b) in examining proposals for new legislation, whether sponsored by the Government, private members or other bodies, and making representations in what is conceived to be the general interest of the member authorities represented;

(c) in expressing views when consulted on drafts of delegated legislation; express requirements to consult representatives of local authorities are commonly found and regarded as mandatory[33];

(d) in furthering what is considered by the associations to be the right kind of relationship between the central government and local authorities, both generally and in particular instances of administrative practice; and

(e) in taking part in that informal process of government—the "sounding" process where senior civil servants informally discuss in the broadest terms ideas for projected legislation and administrative arrangements.

No major change in law or administrative practice which concerns local government is introduced without consultation with the local authority associations, taking the form of an exchange of memoranda or the submission of observations or the holding of conferences. When proposed legislation has reached Bill form it is examined by the associations clause by clause, and new clauses and amendments to existing clauses are submitted and deletions urged. A Bill is rarely the subject of discussion before it is laid on the table, though doubtless the substance of particular clauses may be settled in the light of general consultations. The fact remains, however, that much legislation affecting local government in recent years has been enacted over the objections of local authorities and their representative associations.

---

[33] See § 1–32.

CHAPTER 3

LOCAL AUTHORITY AREAS AND STATUS

THIS chapter deals with the following topics: areas and status; provisions as **3–01** to alteration in area and status; electoral areas; miscellaneous related provisions; financial and other adjustments; changes in name; reorganisation of status and functions under the Local Government Act 1985; reorganisation consequent on the abolition of the Inner London Education Authority; reorganisation under the Local Government Act 1992; and reorganisation under the Local Government (Wales) Act 1994.

A. AREAS AND STATUS

Counties and districts

The Local Government Act 1972 divided England and Wales (excluding **3–02** Greater London) into 53 counties and 369 districts. Six of the counties are metropolitan counties and the districts within them, 36 in number, are metropolitan districts.[1] The areas and names of counties appear in the Act: the areas of metropolitan districts also appear in the Act and their names were given by the Secretary of State by order.[2] The areas of districts in Wales were given in the Act and their names in an order made by the Secretary of State.[3] Non-metropolitan districts were defined and named by order.[4]

The Local Government Act 1985 abolished the metropolitan county councils with effect from April 1, 1986, and redistributed their functions among the metropolitan district councils and a number of joint authorities established to undertake specific functions. The areas of metropolitan counties continue as local government areas for certain purposes, for example as the areas under the control of the new joint authorities.

In many of the non-metropolitan counties new unitary authorities have been or are to be established by orders made by the Secretary of State under the Local Government Act 1992 (see *post*, paras. 3-13—3-16).

In Wales, the Local Government (Wales) Act 1994 replaced the existing counties and districts by 22 new unitary authorities, 11 counties and 11 county boroughs, with effect from April 1, 1996.[5] The new principal areas

---

[1] ss.1 and 20. England does not include what was formerly the administrative county of Monmouthshire or the county borough of Newport: s.1(12). As to London, see Chap. 27.

[2] Sched. 1 and Metropolitan Districts (Names) Order 1973 (S.I. 1973 No. 137).

[3] Sched. 4 and Districts in Wales (Names) Order 1973 (S.I. 1973 No. 34).

[4] English Non-Metropolitan Districts (Definition) Order 1972 (S.I. 1972 No. 2039); English Non-Metropolitan Districts (Names) Order 1973 (S.I. 1973 No. 551).

[5] Local Government Act 1972, s.20, substituted by the Local Government (Wales) Act 1994, s.1.

and their English and Welsh names are set out in Schedule 4 to the 1972 Act.[6] The original counties, in some cases with modified boundaries, do, however, continue in existence for certain purposes.[7] The provisions applicable to the preserved counties are set out in Schedule 2 to the 1994 Act.[8] The counties and county boroughs have equal status and powers. Each county council has the name of the county with the addition of "County Council" or "Council" for the English name and "Cyngor" for the Welsh name.[9] Each county borough has the name of the county borough with the addition of "County Borough Council" or "Council" for the English name and "Cyngor Bwrdeistref Sirol" or "Cyngor" for the Welsh name.[10]

The councils which govern the areas of non-metropolitan counties and all districts are principal councils, a term which includes London borough councils and county and county borough councils in Wales.[11]

Parishes

3–03　　Where rural parishes, whether separate or grouped, were in existence before April 1, 1974, they continued to exist from that date by the name of parishes, and a rural borough, created under section 28 of the Local Government Act 1958, ceased to be a borough but continued in the status of a parish.[12] Provision is made in the Act for a further category. The Local Government Boundary Commission for England (this body is referred to at paragraph 3–13) was required in 1973 to consult existing local authorities with a view to making proposals to the Secretary of State for the constitution of parishes by reference to the areas of existing boroughs and urban districts, areas which were to be merged with other units in local government reorganisation.[13]

3–04　　The Secretary of State's guidelines to the Commission contained the following paragraph:

> "When making proposals in accordance with these provisions the Commission should have regard to the policy of the Government, now reflected in the Act, with regard to statutory authorities at parish level. The Act provides for the retention of existing rural parishes with their parish councils or parish meetings. The Government's further view, as explained in Parliament, is that small towns which are at present boroughs or urban districts should retain elected councils at parish level where such towns are broadly comparable in size and character with other small towns or villages which at present have rural

---

[6] Substituted by the 1994 Act, Sched. 1.
[7] The areas of the "preserved counties" are set out in Part III of Sched. 4 of the 1972 Act, as substituted by the 1994 Act, Sched. 1. The Secretary of State may by order change the name of any preserved county.
[8] The purposes relate to such matters as parliamentary constituency boundaries, Lieutenancies and sheriffs.
[9] "Cyngor Sir" for Abertawe, Caerdydd and Powys: "Sir" is part of the county name in the case of the remaining counties.
[10] 1972 Act, s.21, as substituted by the 1994 Act, s.2.
[11] Local Government Act 1972, s.270 (definition of "principal area") as amended by the Local Government Act 1985, Sched. 15, para. 8(b) and the Local Government (Wales) Act 1994, s.1.
[12] Local Government Act 1972, s.1.
[13] Local Government Act 1972, Sched. 1, Part V.

parish councils. But it is the Government's view that statutory authorities should not be established at parish level (at any rate for the present) for areas which are essentially parts of larger towns or of continuously built-up areas. . . . No absolute maximum figure is prescribed but the limited range of functions available to parish councils and the fact that much of their importance lies in the fact that they act as the focus for local opinion, do not point to the desirability of large units at this level: many towns of the order of 10,000–20,000 (as well as those below this range) might well qualify."

The recommendations of the Commission were accepted by the Government and promulgated by order and the councils of these authorities became successor parish councils.[14] Each order provided that as from the date of its operation members of the existing councils also became parish councillors.[15]

Every parish is required to have a parish meeting.[16] In general terms a **3–05** small parish may have a parish council if it chooses, a large parish is obliged to have a parish council, and parishes whether large or small may be grouped under a common council if they so agree. The detailed rules are as follows. The district council is required to establish a parish council by order if a parish has 200 electors or more, or if the meeting of a parish with more than 150 and less than 200 electors so decides. The district council has a discretion to establish a parish council in a parish with less than 150 electors where the parish meeting so requests. A district council may by order create groups of parishes with a common council at the request and with the consent of the parish meetings concerned.

Where the population of a parish has no more than 150 local government electors the parish meeting may ask the district council to dissolve the parish council and the district council may do so. If the application is rejected two years must elapse before a fresh request may be made.

Communities

Districts in Wales were divided into communities by the 1972 Act. These **3–06** were the areas of what were formerly the boroughs, urban districts and rural parishes in Wales, and certain divided parts of former urban districts. The names of the communities were those of the areas which they succeeded except in the case of the divided urban districts—their names appeared in statute.[17]

A parish council existing on March 31, 1974, automatically became a community council on April 1, 1974. An existing borough or urban district council could apply before 1973 to the Secretary of State for an order creating a community council for the area and where this was done the Secretary of State was obliged to accede to the request. It was open to the Secretary of State to make such an order, after such consultations as he thought proper, if an application was received after 1972 or if the existing council refused to make an application. This provision did not apply to six

---

[14] Local Government (Successor Parishes) Orders 1973 (S.I. 1973 No. 1110, S.I. 1973 No. 1939) and 1974 (S.I. 1974 No. 569).
[15] The enabling power is in the Local Government Act 1972, Sched. 3, para. 13(2).
[16] Local Government Act 1972, ss.9–12.
[17] Local Government Act 1972, s.20(4), Sched. 4, Part III.

large towns—Cardiff, Merthyr Tydfil, Newport, Port Talbot, Rhondda, and Swansea.[18]

A district council was obliged to establish a community council if the community meeting so resolved and it had to dissolve a community council if the meeting so requested.[19]

Fresh provision for communities is made in sections 27 to 29B, 33, 33A of the Local Government Act 1972 (as substituted by the Local Government (Wales) Act 1994, ss.8 to 14). A meeting of the local government electors for a community (a "community meeting") may be convened for the purpose of discussing community affairs and exercising any functions conferred on such meetings by any enactment. The community councils in existence on April 1, 1996, continue in existence after then subject to any provision of the 1994 Act.[20] Each council is a body corporate and may have both an English and a Welsh name. This is the name of the community with the addition, for the English name, of the words "Community Council" and, for the Welsh name, of the words "Cyngor Cymuned."[21] Where the name of a community was given only in its English form or only in its Welsh form, and there is a generally accepted form of the name in the other language, the principal council for the area must before October 1, 1997, take such steps as may be prescribed with a view to securing that there is both an English and a Welsh name for the community.[22]

A community meeting of a community with no separate community council may apply to the principal council for the area for an order establishing such a council. A community meeting where there is such a council may similarly apply to the principal council for an order dissolving the community council. The principal council must make such an order if it is satisfied that the relevant requirements of section 29B of and Schedule 12 to the 1972 Act have been complied with. If the community was previously grouped under a common community council, an order cannot be made unless the community is separated from the group or the group is dissolved.[23] A similar procedure exists for establishing a community council for a group of communities or adding a community to an existing group. Each community must consent and all must lie within the area of the same principal council.[24] The council of a group of communities may apply to the principal council for an order dissolving the group; the community meeting for a community in a group may apply to the principal council for an order separating it from the group.[25]

Section 29B of the 1972 Act[26] provides that an application under section 28, 29 or 29A may be made only if it is supported by a poll of local

---

[18] *ibid.* s.27.
[19] *ibid.* s.28.
[20] 1972 Act, s.27(1), (2) as substituted by the 1994 Act, s.8.
[21] 1972 Act, s.33(1), (2), as substituted by the 1994 Act, s.13.
[22] 1972 Act, s.27(3)(4), as substituted by the 1994 Act, s.8.
[23] 1972 Act. s.28, as substituted by the 1994 Act. s.9.
[24] 1972 Act, s.29, as substituted by the 1994 Act, s.10.
[25] 1972 Act. s.29A, inserted by the 1994 Act, s.11.
[26] Inserted by the 1994 Act, s.12.

government electors for the community (or each community) in question, and that an application for a grouping order must be made jointly by the communities concerned. Any consent expressed by a community meeting must also be supported by a poll of electors. The decision of a community meeting to hold a poll on these matters is only effective if not less than 30 per cent of the electors (or, if that number exceeds 300, 300) are present. Thirty clear days' notice of the meeting must be given, and there is a minimum period of 42 days between the community meeting and the poll.

The Secretary of State may by order designate matters on which principal councils are or may be required to consult community councils in its area.[27]

Joint authorities

Part IV of the Local Government Act 1985 established for each of the six **3–07** metropolitan counties (1) a metropolitan county police authority; (2) a metropolitan county fire and civil defence authority; and (3) a metropolitan county passenger transport authority. They are referred to collectively as "joint authorities." Each is a body corporate. Each is known by the name of the county, with the addition of the relevant description. Part IV also established a London fire and civil defence authority.[28] Police authorities were reorganised as freestanding authorities by the Police and Magistrates' Courts Act 1994.

Residuary bodies and pensions authorities

Part VII of the Local Government Act 1985 established a "residuary **3–08** body" for London and for each of the six metropolitan counties. Each residuary body was a body corporate and consisted of between five and 10 members appointed by the Secretary of State. They had various responsibilities arising out of the abolition of the Greater London Council and the metropolitan county councils, including the making of redundancy and compensation payments, pensions and the custody of property for which provision is not otherwise made.

These residuary bodies could be wound up by order.[29] The six bodies for the metropolitan counties have been wound up, and provision made for the transfer of their property, functions, rights and liabilities, usually to designated district councils.[30] Pensions authorities have been established for South Yorkshire and London to take over pensions functions from the respective residuary body for the area.[31] Each of these authorities is a body

---

[27] 1972 Act, s.33A, inserted by the 1994 Act, s.13.

[28] Local Government Act 1985, ss.23–28.

[29] Local Government Act 1985, s.67.

[30] Tyne and Wear (S.I. 1988 No. 1590, as amended by S.I. 1988 No. 1615); South Yorkshire (S.I. 1989 No. 814); Greater Manchester (S.I. 1989 No. 1359); Merseyside (S.I. 1989 No. 2470, as amended by S.I. 1990 No. 17); West Yorkshire (S.I. 1991 No. 517); West Midlands (S.I. 1991 No. 710). As to the London Residuary Body, see § 30–08.

[31] The South Yorkshire Pensions Authority: the Local Government Reorganisation (Pensions etc.) (South Yorkshire) Order 1987 (S.I. 1987 No. 2110); and the London Pensions Fund Authority: the London Government Reorganisation (Pensions etc.) Order 1989 (S.I. 1989 No. 1815, as amended by S.I. 1990 No. 198).

corporate. The South Yorkshire Pensions Authority comprises 12 members appointed by the district councils in South Yorkshire. The London Pensions Fund Authority comprises between seven and 11 members appointed by the Secretary of State, at least half (excluding the chairman) following consultations with such representatives of local government in London as appear to the Secretary of State to be appropriate. A number of the provisions applicable to joint authorities and residuary bodies are applied to pensions authorities.[32]

Residuary bodies have also been established for the purposes of reorganisation under the Local Government Act 1992 (England) and the Local Government (Wales) Act 1994.[33]

The Broads Authority

The Broads Authority was established by the Norfolk and Suffolk Broads Act 1988 with the general duty of managing the Broads for the purposes of conserving and enhancing their natural beauty, promoting the enjoyment of them by the public, and protecting the interests of navigation. The Authority is a body corporate, and comprises 18 members appointed by the county and district councils for the area, nine appointed by the Secretary of State, six appointed by other bodies, and two appointed by the Authority from members of its Navigation Committee who are not otherwise members of the Authority. A number of provisions of the legislation applicable to local authorities apply to the Authority.

National Park authorities

Under Part III of the Environment Act 1995,[34] the Secretary of State may establish a National Park authority in respect of an existing National Park or in connection with the designation of a new one.[35] The authority is a body corporate and comprises such numbers of local authority members and members appointed by the Secretary of State as are specified in the order; the former must be in the majority. The local authority members must be appointed by the councils for principal areas wholly or partially comprised in the Park, the numbers being specified in the order. They must be members of the appointing council. In England, the members appointed by the Secretary of State must include parish members, who must be a member of the parish council or chairman of the parish meeting for a parish wholly or partially comprised in the park. The members must elect a chairman and deputy

---

[32] See S.I. 1987 No. 2110, Sched. 1 and S.I. 1989 No. 1815, Sched. 1, paras. 5–7. The Public Bodies (Admission to Meetings) Act 1960 is expressly stated not to apply to the London Pensions Fund Authority.

[33] See *post*, §§ 3–34 and 3–35.

[34] ss.61–79 and Scheds. 7–10.

[35] Three National Park authorities have been appointed in Wales: see the National Park Authorities (Wales) Order 1995 (S.I. 1995 No. 2803), as amended by S.I. 1996 No. 534; and seven in England: National Park Authorities (England) Order 1996 (S.I. 1996 No. 1243).

chairman. A number of provisions of the legislation applicable to local authorities apply to these authorities. They are the planning authority for the relevant Park and exercise powers under a series of specified statutes.

The status of borough

A district council may petition Her Majesty for the grant of a charter **3–09** conferring upon the district the status of borough.[36] The resolution authorising the petition requires a two-thirds majority at a specially convened meeting of the council. Where Her Majesty by the advice of the Privy Council grants a charter the district becomes a borough, the district council becomes the borough council and the chairman and vice-chairman of the council are entitled to the style of mayor and deputy mayor respectively. Similar provisions apply enabling the council of a county in Wales to obtain the status of a county borough.[37]

The status of town

The council of a parish, by a simple majority, may resolve to adopt the **3–10** status of town.[38] The council becomes the town council and the chairman and vice-chairman are known as town mayor and deputy town mayor respectively.

Provision for a separate community council in Wales to resolve that the community should have the status of a town is now found in section 245B of the Local Government Act 1972.[39] The council then has the name of the community with the addition, in English, of the words "Town Council" and, in Welsh, of the words "Cyngor Tref". The chairman is entitled to the style of "town mayor" or "maer y dref" and the vice-chairman, "deputy town mayor" or "dirprwy faer y dref". The status of the community as a town is not affected if the council is subsequently dissolved.

Privileges of former cities and boroughs

The 1972 Act makes provision for the retention of some of the privileges **3–11** and dignities of former local authorities.[40] Although it abolished boroughs and cities as units of government and accordingly brought to an end the rights to borough status conferred by royal charter, these charters were neither abrogated nor surrendered. All other rights and privileges belonging to a borough or city were specifically preserved, subject, of course, to any contrary provision appearing in the charter granted to the district of which the borough or city was part, and subject to any contrary provision in the Act itself. An obligation is put on any authority to whom charters and insignia of an abolished borough are transferred to preserve them, so far as practicable, in the area of the former authority.[41]

---

[36] Local Government Act 1972, s.245(1)–(5).
[37] 1972 Act, s.246A, as substituted by the Local Government (Wales) Act 1994, s.5.
[38] *ibid.* s.245(6)–(9), as amended by the Local Government (Wales) Act 1994, Sched. 15, para. 51.
[39] Inserted by the 1994 Act, s.16.
[40] *ibid.* s.246.
[41] *ibid.* s.254(7).

There are several ways in which former rights and privileges survived. First, many former boroughs and cities virtually became the new districts and those new districts were able to incorporate within the new charter many of the inherited rights and privileges. Secondly, many smaller boroughs became successor parishes and their councils adopted the status of town. Thirdly, the Act made provision to enable a former borough, in a district which does not petition for a charter conferring borough status on it, to retain an identity through charter trustees, a body corporate consisting of the district councillors representing the former borough. If the number of councillors is less than three, the district council may make up the difference by appointing local government electors for the area of the former borough. The charter trustees are enabled to elect one of their number as city mayor or town mayor as the case may be.[42]

Where the area of any charter trustees becomes comprised in a borough, upon the grant of a charter under section 245, the charter trustees continue in being without alteration of their powers, and the privileges and rights of the inhabitants of that area are unaffected.[43]

A part of the preserved rights are those concerned with the appointment of local officers of dignity—these would include sheriffs of cities and towns, high stewards, honorary recorders and the like.[44] The status and rights of freemen are undisturbed.[45]

Prerogative titles and armorial bearings

3–12 Many former authorities bore the title of city or royal borough, and their mayors were variously addressed, in some cases by the prefix "the right honourable", or "the right worshipful", and in some cities the mayor held the title of lord mayor. A continuation of these titles lies within the royal prerogative, exercised by the Queen on the advice of the Secretary of State for the Home Department. Such titles are conferred by Letters Patent.

Specific provision is made for the transfer of armorial bearings from the former authorities to the newly created authorities.[46]

B. ALTERATIONS IN AREA AND STATUS

3–13 Part IV of the Local Government Act 1972 established permanent machinery for the review of local government areas. Two Commissions were set up, as bodies corporate, the Local Government Boundary Commission

---

[42] Local Government Act 1972, s.246, as amended by the Charter Trustees Act 1985 and the Local Government (Wales) Act 1994, Sched. 15, para. 52. See also the Charter Trustees Order 1974 (S.I. 1974 No. 176). The Charter Trustees Regulations 1996 (S.I. 1996 No. 263), as amended by S.I. 1996 No. 610, establish charter trustees for a number of areas in consequence of orders for structural change made under the Local Government Act 1992, s.17.

[43] *ibid.* s.246, as amended by the Charter Trustees Act 1985.

[44] *ibid.* s.246.

[45] *ibid.* s.248, as amended by the Local Government (Wales) Act 1994, Sched. 15, para. 54.

[46] *ibid.* s.247, as amended by the Local Government (Wales) Act 1994, Sched. 15, para. 53, and orders made thereunder. This provision extends to transfers from old to new councils in Wales under the 1994 Act.

for England and the Local Government Boundary Commission for Wales.[47] The first consisted of a chairman, deputy chairman and not more than five members. It was replaced by the Local Government Commission for England established by the Local Government Act 1992. The Welsh Commission consists of a chairman, deputy chairman and not more than three members, and one of them must be Welsh speaking. Membership of the Commissions is an office of profit under the Crown—this means that their members cannot sit in the House of Commons. The Commissioners are empowered to delegate to others the work of any particular investigation.

The 1972 Act established the third set of Commissions in the post-war period. There was first the Local Government Boundary Commission of 1945, brought to an end by the Local Boundary Commission (Dissolution) Act 1949, and secondly the Local Government Commission for England and Local Government Commission for Wales set up in 1958 and dissolved by the Local Government (Termination of Reviews) Act 1967. It is noted in passing that the bodies established to deal with parliamentary constituencies, the Boundary Commission for England and Boundary Commission for Wales, established in 1944, are still in operation.

The Commissions are basically advisory bodies. Their recommendations are submitted to the Secretary of State and become effective when contained in an order made by him.

The Local Government Commission for England

Part II of the Local Government Act 1992 (sections 12 to 27) abolished the **3–14** Local Government Boundary Commission for England, established by Part IV of the Local Government Act 1972. In its stead, section 12 established the Local Government Commission for England, a body corporate consisting of between 5 and 15 members appointed by the Secretary of State. One member is appointed as Chairman. The Commission is to appoint a chief executive, subject to the consent of the Secretary of State, and may appoint other staff.[48] It has two main functions. The first is to conduct reviews of areas in accordance with the directions of the Secretary of State and make recommendations for structural, boundary or electoral changes, or that no changes should be made.[49] In particular, the Commission was to consider whether there should be a move to unitary authorities in non-metropolitan counties. Secondly, the Commission has taken over the responsibility for periodic reviews of electoral arrangements from the Local Government Boundary Commission for England. Mandatory reviews must take place between 10 and 15 years from the last review. The changes recommended by the Commission must be such as appear to it desirable having regard to the need (a) to reflect the identities and interests of local communities and (b) to secure effective and convenient local government.[50]

---

[47] *ibid.* ss.46 and 53, and Scheds, 7 and 8.
[48] Local Government Act 1992, Sched. 2, paras. 1, 3.
[49] *ibid.* s.13(2).
[50] *ibid.* s.13(5).

"Structural" changes are those that comprise the establishment of a unitary authority in a non-metropolitan area.[51] "Boundary" changes include the alteration or creation of a local government area; the abolition of a principal area outside Greater London or a metropolitan county; and the creation or abolition of a London borough or parish.[52] Such changes may be designed to facilitate a structural change, but may arise independently (hence the inclusion of references to London and metropolitan counties). Electoral changes include changes in the numbers of councillors and the numbers and boundaries of electoral areas.[53] Such changes may be made in consequence of a structural or boundary change, but may also arise independently.

The Secretary of State may give directions to the Commission as to the performance of its functions in respect of reviews, and these may require it to have regard to any guidance given by the Secretary of State as to matters to be taken into account.[54] *The Policy Guidance to the Local Government Commission for England* was published by the Department of the Environment in July 1992, and replaced by a revised document in November 1993. In *R. v. Secretary of State for the Environment, ex p. Lancashire County Council; R. v. Same, ex p. Derbyshire County Council,*[55] Jowitt J. held that a sentence in the revised guidance was unlawful and should be deleted from the policy guidance. This stated: "But the Government expects that [i.e. a recommendation for continuation of the existing two-tier structure] to be the exception, and that the result will be a substantial increase in the number of unitary authorities in both urban and rural areas." Jowitt J. held that this sentence undermined the statutory criteria laid down in section 13 of the 1992 Act. However, in *R. v. Secretary of State for the Environment, ex p. Lancashire County Council,*[56] Judge J. held that fresh guidance was not unlawful.

The Commission must invite representations, take them into account, prepare and publicise draft recommendations, and subsequently report to the Secretary of State.[57] It may require the Audit Commission to give its opinion on the likely impact of proposed structural changes on economy, efficiency and effectiveness.[58] The Commission's recommendations may be implemented, with or without modification,[59] by an order made by the

---

[51] *ibid.* s.14(1)(a) and (2).
[52] *ibid.* s.14(1)(b) and (3).
[53] *ibid.* s.14(1)(c) and (4).
[54] *ibid.* s.13(6).
[55] [1994] 4 All E.R. 165.
[56] *The Times*, December 9, 1995.
[57] *ibid.* s.15.
[58] *ibid.* s.16.
[59] See *R. v. Secretary of State for the Environment, ex p. Berkshire County Council, The Times,* January 25, 1996, where the Court of Appeal held that the Secretary of State's power of modification was sufficiently broad to enable him to change the Commission's proposal that five new unitary authorities be established in Berkshire, including the combination of two borough councils into one authority, by rejecting this last element and thereby establishing six authorities; *cf. R. v. Secretary of State for the Environment, ex p. Wycombe District Council* [1996] C.O.D. 73.

Secretary of State.[60] The orders made by the Secretary of State fall into the following groups. First, three new counties created by the Local Government Act 1972, Cleveland, Avon and Humberside, have been abolished, the constituent districts (or combinations thereof) becoming unitary authorities.[61] Secondly, in a number of non-metropolitan counties, large urban areas have been constituted as unitary authorities, two tiers of local government remaining elsewhere in the county.[62] Thirdly, a unitary authority has been established for the Isle of Wight.[63] The Secretary of State has announced his intention of making further orders. The Secretary of State has a wide power to make supplementary regulations,[64] and affected bodies may make agreements as to incidental matters.[65] The Secretary of State has made the Local Government Changes for England Regulations 1994[66] which make incidental, consequential, transitional and supplementary provision of general application in respect of orders made by him. Provision is made for continuity of matters, elections of shadow authorities which were to prepare for a change and assume on the relevant reorganisation date the full powers and the status of local authorities, and other specific local matters, including town and country planning and fire and police disciplinary matters.

The Commission has reported generally on its work in Local Government

---

[60] *ibid.* s.17. The Secretary of State's powers are extremely wide: see *R. v. Local Government Commission for England, ex p. Cleveland County Council, The Times,* July 4, 1994, where the council's application for judicial review of the Secretary of State's acceptance of the recommendation that it be abolished was rejected; see also *R. v. Local Government Commission, ex p. Cambridgeshire District Council* [1995] C.O.D. 149.

[61] Cleveland (Structural Change) Order 1995 (S.I. 1995 No. 187) and Cleveland (Further Provision) Order 1995 (S.I. 1995 No. 1747) (new authorities for Hartlepool, Stockton-on-Tees, Middlesbrough, and Redcar and Cleveland); Avon (Structural Change) Order 1995 (S.I. 1995 No. 493) (new authorities for North West Somerset, Bath and North East Somerset, South Gloucestershire and the City of Bristol); and the Humberside (Structural Change) Order 1995 (S.I. 1995 No. 600) (new authorities for the City of Kingston Upon Hull, North Lincolnshire, North East Lincolnshire and the East Riding of Yorkshire). Six unitary authorities are also to be established for Berkshire.

[62] York in North Yorkshire (North Yorkshire (District of York) (Structural and Boundary Changes) Order 1995 (S.I. 1995 No. 610)); Milton Keynes in Buckinghamshire (Buckinghamshire (Borough of Milton Keynes) (Structural Change) Order 1995 (S.I. 1995 No. 1769)); Brighton and Hove (combined) in East Sussex (East Sussex (Boroughs of Brighton and Hove) (Structural Change) Order 1995 (S.I. 1995 No. 1770)); Poole and Bournemouth (separately) in Dorset (Dorset (Boroughs of Poole and Bournemouth) (Structural Change) Order 1995 (S.I. 1995 No. 1771)); Darlington in Durham (Durham (Borough of Darlington) (Structural Change) Order 1995 (S.I. 1995 No. 1772)); the City of Derby in Derbyshire (Derbyshire (City of Derby) (Structural Change) Order 1995 (S.I. 1995 No. 1773); Thamesdown in Wiltshire (Wiltshire (Borough of Thamesdown) (Structural Change) Order 1995 (S.I. 1995 No. 1774)); the Cities of Portsmouth and Southampton (separately) in Hampshire (Hampshire (Cities of Portsmouth and Southampton) (Structural Change) Order 1995 (S.I. 1995 No. 1775)); Luton in Bedfordshire (Bedfordshire (Borough of Luton) (Structural Change) Order 1995 (S.I. 1995 No. 1776)); the City of Stoke-on-Trent in Staffordshire (City of Stoke-on-Trent) (Structural and Boundary Changes) Order 1995 (S.I. 1995 No. 1779)); Leicester and (albeit not a large urban area) Rutland in Leicestershire (Leicestershire (City of Leicester and District of Rutland) (Structural Change) Order 1996 (S.I. 1996 No. 507)).

[63] Isle of Wight (Structural Change) Order 1994 (S.I. 1994 No. 1210).

[64] 1992 Act, s.19.

[65] *ibid.* s.20.

[66] S.I. 1994 No. 867. A large number of further regulations and orders have been made dealing with particular matters.

51

Commission for England, *Renewing Local Government in the English Shires: A Progress Report*,[67] and *A Report on the 1992–1995 Structural Review*.[68]

There is also provision for the establishment of joint authorities, where the Secretary of State considers that joint arrangements should be made for the discharge of any functions.[69]

The Local Government Boundary Commission for Wales

3–15   The first major task of the Welsh Commission was to undertake a review of Wales with a view to the making of changes in the areas, councils and electoral arrangements of communities and with respect to the initial review of electoral arrangements for counties and districts in Wales.[70] Its powers have been amended in a number of respects by the Local Government (Wales) Act 1994. The appointment of a Local Government Commission for Wales on the model of the English Commission was not necessary as the decision to establish a system of unitary authorities in Wales was taken as a policy decision by government.

3–16   It is the continuing duty of the Welsh Commission to keep under review all principal areas in Wales. It is not related to specified periods of time.[71] The Secretary of State may give directions as to the holding of reviews.[72] As is the case in England, the Secretary of State for Wales may give directions to the Welsh Commission for their guidance in conducting reviews.[73] If a direction concerns all reviews, or reviews of any class or a single review of the principal areas in Wales, the Secretary of State must first consult the appropriate local authority associations. A local authority may ask for a review to be carried out.

3–17   If the Commission considers it desirable in the interests of effective and convenient local government, it may make proposals for change to the Secretary of State. The Commission's proposals may consist of any of the following or a combination of one or more of them.

    (a) the alteration of a local government area;

    (b) the constitution of a new local government area by the amalgamation of two or more principal areas or communities or by the aggregation of parts of such areas or by the separation of part of such an area;

    (c) the abolition of a principal area or community and its distribution among other principal areas or communities;

    (d) the constitution of a new community by—

---

[67] H.M.S.O., December 1993.

[68] H.M.S.O., March 1995.

[69] 1992 Act, s.21.

[70] Local Government Act 1972, s.64 and Sched. 10.

[71] *ibid.* ss.54, 55, as amended by the Local Government (Wales) Act 1994, Sched. 15, para. 7, 8.

[72] *ibid.* s.56(1), as substituted by the 1994 Act, Sched. 2, para. 5. The Secretary of State may direct a review of Wales as a whole or any one or more local government areas or parts of such area as or any one or more preserved counties or parts of preserved counties.

[73] *ibid.* s.59, as amended by the 1994 Act, Sched. 15, para. 12(b).

(i) the establishment of any area which is not a community or part of one as a community;

(ii) the aggregation of the whole or any part of any such area with one or more communities or parts of communities;

(e) a change of electoral arrangements for any local government area which is either consequential on any change in local government areas proposed under the foregoing or is a substantive change. Arrangements for substantive change are referred to later at paragraph 3–25.

Whenever a review is undertaken, the Commission must have regard to **3–18** the system of community councils and is required, *inter alia*, to consider whether to make a proposal for the constitution or dissolution of a community council.[74] The Commission may in consequence of a review under Part IV may make proposals for changes in the area of a preserved county.[75] If it proposes the constitution of a new principal area, it must specify whether it should be a county or a county borough.[76]

Where the Welsh Commission has been conducting a review of any area **3–19** and considers that it is in a position to submit a report to the Secretary of State, it must submit a report together with their proposals or a notification that they have no proposals to put forward. The Secretary of State may if he thinks fit by order give effect to any proposals made to him, with or without modifications; if he makes modifications he may direct the Commission to conduct a further review. Any order which alters the area of a principal council or a preserved county or abolishes a principal area is subject to a negative resolution of either House of Parliament.[77]

Reviews of parishes and communities

The duty of each district council in England to keep the whole of its district **3–20** under review for the purpose of considering whether or not to make proposals to the English Commission as to the constitution of new parishes, the abolition of parishes, or the alteration of parishes[78] was abolished by the Local Government Act 1992.[79]

However, a similar duty falls to principal councils in Wales to keep their **3–21** areas under review in order to consider recommendations for the constitution of new communities, the abolition of communities, and the alteration of communities.[80] A principal council is obliged to consider a request made by a community council or community meeting to undertake a review, though the council may refuse the request if in its opinion to do what is asked would impede the proper discharge of its functions in relation to review.

When a council has carried out a review it submits a report to the Welsh Commission and the Commission, in turn, may make proposals to the

[74] Local Government Act 1972, s.55(5), as amended by the 1994 Act, Sched. 15, para. 8(5).
[75] *ibid.* s.54(1A), inserted by the 1994 Act, Sched. 2, para. 4.
[76] *ibid.* s.54(1B), inserted by the 1994 Act, Sched. 15, para. 7.
[77] *ibid.* s.58, as amended by the 1994 Act, Sched. 15, para. 11.
[78] *ibid.* s.48(8), (9).
[79] Sched. 4.
[80] Local Government Act 1972, s.55(2), (3), (5), as amended by the 1994 Act, Sched. 15, para. 8.

Secretary of State, with or without modifications. If the Commission thinks the proposals submitted, even with modification, are not apt for securing effective and convenient local government, or where the principal council has reported that it will not recommend proposals, the Commission may itself undertake a review. The Commission's proposals, whether its own or those of a principal council which it accepts, are submitted to the Secretary of State and he may make an order to give effect to them with or without modifications. If a principal council intends to make proposals for change of a local government area, it must also consider the community council arrangements and the need for any alteration to the boundaries of any preserved county.

Procedure for reviews in Wales

3–22   The procedure originally applied alike to England and Wales and now applies only to Wales.[81] The Commission or a principal council proposing to conduct a review is required to take a number of steps to see that interested parties are aware of what is proposed to be done, and each must take account of representations made. There must first be consultations with all local authorities whose areas are affected and with any other local authorities and public bodies which would appear to be concerned. There must additionally be consultations with bodies representative of staff employed by local authorities who have asked to be consulted and consultations with such other persons as the Commission or principal council thinks fit. Steps must be taken to see that persons who may be interested in the review are informed of draft proposals or recommendations and of the place where the relevant documents may be inspected. The Commission or council must then take account of representations which are made within the period of deposit, and a final decision must take account of them.

Where recommendations are made by a council following a review, the Commission may consult the council of any other local government area affected and such other bodies and persons as it thinks fit.

If a commission or a principal council wishes to hold a local inquiry it may do so, and in that event the provisions with regard to *subpoena*, penalty for failure to attend and the award of costs would apply.[82]

3–23   Particular procedural rules were applied by the 1972 Act to the alteration in boundaries between English and Welsh counties.[83] Joint proposals would be made by the English and Welsh Commissions with the consent of the counties concerned. Powers were not available under earlier legislation to the former Local Government Commissions for England and Wales to propose an alteration to the boundary between the two countries. This procedure was, however, abolished by the Local Government Act 1992.[84]

---

[81] *ibid.* s.60, as amended by the Local Government Act 1992, Sched. 3, para. 13(2) and Sched. 4, and the Local Government (Wales) Act 1994, Sched. 15, para. 13. Regulations may be made prescribing procedure.

[82] *ibid.* s.61, as amended by the Local Government Act 1992, Sched. 3, para. 14 and the Local Government (Wales) Act 1994, Sched. 15, para. 14, and s.250.

[83] *ibid.* s.62, as amended by the Local Government Act 1985, Sched. 16, para. 6.

[84] Sched. 4.

C. Electoral Arrangements

Permanent machinery for the review of electoral arrangements through the **3–24** Local Government Commission for England and the Local Government Boundary Commission for Wales is found, respectively, in the Local Government Act 1992 and Part IV of the Local Government Act 1972.

Arrangements for review[85]

It is the duty of each Commission to carry out periodic reviews for the **3–25** purpose of making proposals for changes in electoral arrangements. The Commissions must do this at intervals of not less than 10 years or more than 15 years, but in Wales an authority or other person may ask the Welsh Commission to carry out a review at any time. When the Commission has finished its review, it submits a report and recommendations to the Secretary of State for the Home Department, and he may make an order giving effect to them as they stand or with modification, in the same way and subject to the same rules which apply to the making of orders as to boundary and other changes.

By section 64 of the Local Government Act 1972[86] (as substituted by the Local Government (Wales) Act 1994, s.6) it was the duty of the Welsh Commission, as soon as practicable after the ordinary elections for principal areas in 1995 to review the electoral arrangements for each area with a view to considering future electoral arrangements and formulate proposals for those arrangements.

It is the duty of a principal council in Wales to review the electoral arrangements of communities within the area and it may make appropriate orders. The council must consider a request for a review made by a community council or by at least 30 electors in the community. A request by a community council or by at least 30 electors may be made to the Welsh Commission and where this is done the Commission may send recommendations to the principal council, who may make an order accordingly, or with such modifications as the Commission may accept. If the principal council does not agree with the Commission or defaults in making a recommended order, the Commission may make its own proposals direct to the Secretary of State for the Home Department.

Similarly expressed provisions used to apply in England as regards the review of electoral arrangements of parishes by district councils.[87] These were repealed by the Local Government Act 1992.[88]

The changes here described are referred to as "electoral changes" in England and "substantive changes" in Wales. An "electoral change" is a change in electoral arrangements for any local government area, whether made in consequence of any structural or boundary change or independently

---

[85] Local Government Act 1992, s.13(2), (3), (4); Local Government Act 1972, s.57, as amended by the 1994 Act, Sched. 15. para. 10.
[86] As substituted by the Local Government (Wales) Act 1994, s.6.
[87] The 1972 Act, s.50.
[88] Sched. 4.

of any such change.[89] A substantive change is defined as a change in electoral arrangements for any local government area which is independent of a change in the boundaries of that area.[90]

Factors relevant to change

3–26 There are a number of rules to be observed in considering electoral arrangements.[91] In the case of counties in England, the number of electors in each electoral division is to be roughly the same, electoral divisions may not be split between districts and parishes may not be split as between electoral divisions. In the case of London boroughs and districts there must be, as nearly as may be, an equal number of electors per councillor in each of the wards, but this principle is overridden by the requirement in section 47(1) of the Act that changes should be "in the interests of effective and convenient local government."[92] As regards counties and county boroughs in Wales, the Welsh Commission is to provide for a single member for each electoral division, unless the Secretary of State directs it to consider the desirability of providing for multi-member electoral divisions for the whole or a specified part of a principal area. Having regard to any change in the number or distribution of the local government electors of the principal area in the next five years,

(a) (subject to (b)), the number of local government electors shall be, as nearly as may be, the same in every electoral division in the principal area;

(b) where there are one or more multi-member divisions, the ratio of the number of electors to the councillors to be elected shall be, as nearly as may be, the same in every electoral division in the principal area (including any that are not multi-member);

(c) every ward of a community having a community council (separate or common) is to lie wholly within a single electoral division; and

(d) every community which is not divided into community wards shall lie wholly within a single electoral division.

In parishes and communities, before deciding whether to introduce wards, regard must be had to the question whether the number and distribution of electors is such as to make a single election of councillors impracticable or

---

[89] Local Government Act 1992, s.14(1)(c). "Electoral arrangements" are defined in s.14(4) for a principal area to cover the number of councillors for the council for the area and for each electoral area within it, the number and boundaries of the electoral areas into which the area is divided, and the name of any electoral area; as regards parish councils, it covers the number of councillors for the council, whether the parish should be divided into wards, the number and boundaries of any such wards, and the number of councillors and name for any such ward.

[90] 1972 Act, s.78(1), referring to s.54(1)(e). "Electoral arrangements" is defined in s.78(1) in similar terms to s.14(4) of the 1992 Act.

[91] *ibid.* Sched. 11, as amended by the Local Government (Wales) Act 1994. This applies to the Local Government Commission for England by virtue of section 27 of the Local Government Act 1992 and to the Welsh Commission and principal councils in Wales by the 1972 Act, s.78(2), as amended by the 1992 Act, Sched. 3, para. 18(2) and the Local Government (Wales) Act 1994, Sched. 15, para. 22.

[92] *Enfield London Borough Council* v. *Local Government Boundary Commission* [1979] 3 All E.R. 747.

inconvenient, and to the desirability of any areas being separately represented on the council.

Whenever changes are being considered, thought must be given to local ties and to the production of easily identifiable boundaries.

D. Miscellaneous Provisions

The Secretary of State has a general power under section 266 of the Local **3–27** Government Act 1972 to revoke by a later order any order made under the Act. But there is a limitation to this power so far as orders made under Part IV of the Act are concerned. The power is limited to the supplementary provisions in the order, and before a change of this kind is made certain procedural steps must be taken.[93]

A restriction is placed on the promotion of private Bills. No local or joint authority has power to promote a Bill for forming or abolishing or altering any local government area or for the alteration of status or for the alteration of electoral arrangements.[94]

The 1972 Act brought certainty into the matter of seaward boundaries. In the case of some authorities, seaward boundaries were fixed by local Act, but generally speaking they were fixed by reference to the limit of medium tides. The matter is now brought within the review of the Commissions.[95]

E. Financial and Other Adjustments[96]

The Secretary of State has power to make regulations of general application **3–28** to deal with consequential and transitional arrangements which are needed following the making of orders under Part IV of the Local Government Act 1972.[97] The regulations may deal with the transfer of property, rights and liabilities, functions and staff. Other matters (the name of a new area and its constitution, for example), may be dealt with in local orders. Agreements may be entered into by the bodies involved to deal with property and finance, and provision is made for arbitration where agreement is not reached.[98]

[93] Local Government Act 1972, s.69, as amended by the Local Government (Wales) Act 1994, Sched. 15, para. 16.
[94] *ibid.* s.70, as amended by the Local Government Act 1985, Sched. 14, para. 1, the Education Reform Act 1988, Scheds. 12, para. 41, and 13.
[95] *ibid.* s.71, as amended by the Local Government (Wales) Act 1994, Sched. 15, para. 17 (Welsh Commission); Local Government Act 1992, s.14(3)(a). As to accretions from the sea, see s.72; as to the alteration of boundaries where the line of a watercourse changes, see s.73.
[96] *ibid.* ss.67 and 68, as amended by the Local Government and Housing Act 1989, s.194 and Sched. 12, and S.I. 1990 No. 431.
[97] See Local Government Area Changes Regulations 1976 (S.I. 1976 No. 246) as amended by S.I. 1978 No. 247, and Local Government (Changes in Electoral Arrangements) Regulations 1985 (S.I. 1985 No. 110).
[98] See *R. v. Secretary of State for the Environment, ex p. Sutton London Borough Council, The Times*, December 14, 1995 (power to appoint arbitrator not restricted by S.I. 1976 No. 246).

F. Changes of Name of Local Authority Areas[1]

3–29 The council of a county, county borough, district or London borough may change its name by a two-thirds majority at a specially convened meeting of the council.[2] The name of a parish in England may be changed by the district council at the request of the parish council, or parish meeting where there is no parish council. The name of a community in Wales may be changed by the principal council for the area at the request of the community council, or community meeting where there is no community council.

Councils in Wales were given power to resolve to adopt the Welsh language form of the council's description.[3] The resolution was to be passed by a two-thirds majority at a specially convened meeting and comes into effect after three months. The same procedure was to be adopted to revert to the English language description. By virtue of the Local Government (Wales) Act 1994, English and Welsh language versions of the name of each principal area were specified by a new Schedule 4 substituted in the Local Government Act 1972.[4] Each principal council similarly has both an English and a Welsh name.[5] Where the name of a community was given only in its English or Welsh form, and there is a generally accepted alternative form, the principal council within whose area the community lies must before October 1, 1997, take prescribed steps for securing that there is both an English and a Welsh name for the community.[6] Each community council has the name of the community with the addition of English and Welsh titles.[7] Similarly, where a community council resolves that the community should have the status of a town, the council is to have the name of the community with the addition of the appropriate English and Welsh titles.[8]

G. Reorganisation of Status and Functions Under the Local Government Act 1985

3–30 As has already been noted, the Local Government Act 1985 abolished the Greater London Council and the six metropolitan county councils. Provision was made under this Act for the transfer of functions, and the new arrangements are set out in this book in the chapters on specific functions.

---

[1] Local Government Act 1972, ss.74–76, as amended by the Local Government (Wales) Act 1994, Sched. 15, paras. 20, 21.
[2] In February 1980, Salop County Council resolved to change the name of the county to Shropshire.
[3] Local Government Act 1972, s.21(4), (5) (county and district councils), 33(2A), (2B) (community councils) and 245A (borough and town councils), inserted by the Local Government and Housing Act 1989, s.160 and Sched. 8.
[4] Local Government Act 1972, s.20 and Sched. 4, substituted by the 1994 Act, s.1 and Sched. 1.
[5] 1972 Act, s.21, substituted by the 1994 Act, s.2.
[6] 1972 Act, s.27(3), (4), substituted by the 1994 Act, s.8.
[7] 1972 Act, s.33, substituted by the 1994 Act, s.13.
[8] 1972 Act, s.245B, inserted by the 1994 Act, s.16.

Provision was also made for the transfer and compensation of staff[9] and the transfer of property. Most functions were transferred to London borough councils and metropolitan district councils respectively. In London and in each metropolitan county, the successor councils were required to establish a joint committee to co-ordinate arrangements for the transfer of functions. Such committees were required, *inter alia*, to consider whether any of those functions could with advantage be discharged jointly by those councils or any of them by virtue of arrangements made under section 101 of the Local Government Act 1972,[10] and to consult and co-operate with the new joint authorities, the Inner London Education Authority, any other body to which functions or property were transferred, and the staff commission.[11] Furthermore, it was the express duty of both the abolished and successor authorities and their officers to co-operate with each other and generally to exercise their functions so as to facilitate the implementation of the 1985 Act and any transfer of functions, property or staff.[12]

The Secretary of State had power to make orders before the abolition date for the transfer on that date of property, rights and liabilities.[13] He may at any time by order make such incidental, consequential, transitional or supplementary provision as appears to him necessary or expedient.[14]

The Secretary of State had special powers of control over joint authorities and the Inner London Education Authority.[15] These powers were to be exercised

> "with a view to securing that the functions of a new authority are discharged economically, efficiently and effectively in the period beginning with its establishment and ending three years after the abolition date. ... "

The Secretary of State had power, by regulations,[16] to provide for the **3–31** submission to him by the authority, or the making by him, of schemes with respect to the discharge of the authority's functions so far as concerned with:

(a) the number of persons employed by the authority, or employed by it for a particular purpose;

(b) the authority's arrangements for obtaining services, supplies or facilities;

(c) the authority's organisation and its arrangements for managing its affairs;

(d) in the case of a police authority, the number of persons constituting the establishment of the police force maintained by it; and

---

[9] See § 4–52, 4–53.
[10] See §§ 4–63, 4–85.
[11] Local Government Act 1985, s.95.
[12] *ibid.* s.97.
[13] *ibid.* s.100.
[14] *ibid.* s.101.
[15] *ibid.* s.85.
[16] See the Police Authorities (Establishment and Support Services Schemes) (Metropolitan Counties and Northumbria Police Area) Regulations 1985 (S.I. 1985 No. 1302); the Fire and Civil Defence Authorities (Establishment, Support Services and Management Schemes) Regulations 1985 (S.I. 1985 No. 1303).

(e) in the case of a fire authority, the number of persons constituting the establishment of any fire brigade maintained by it.

The authority in this initial period was required to discharge its functions in accordance with any scheme approved or made by the Secretary of State.

3–32   The Secretary of State also had special powers of control over the Greater London Council and metropolitan county councils in the period leading up to abolition. These required his consent for:

(a) financial and other assistance to local authorities after July 24, 1984[17];
(b) expenditure after April 1, 1985 under section 137 of the Local Government Act 1972[18];
(c) disposals of land after July 31, 1984[19];
(d) the entering of certain contracts after July 31, 1984[20]; and
(e) arrangements after March 21, 1985, for the assumption of certain liabilities.[21]

Finally, there is provision for the Secretary of State to reorganise the allocation of functions transferred to joint authorities under the 1985 Act.[22] For example, he may by order constitute a metropolitan district council, London borough council or the Common Council as a fire authority. He may allocate passenger transport functions to a metropolitan district or London borough council.

H. Reorganisation Consequent on Abolition of ILEA

3–33 The Education Reform Act 1988 abolished the Inner London Education Authority on April 1, 1990. Part III of the Act provided for the transfer of most of its functions to the councils of inner London boroughs and the Common Council, which became local education authorities.[23] The Secretary of State had power by order to designate the schools for which each authority would assume responsibility, to provide for the transfer of property, rights and liabilities, and to transfer staff.[24] He also had control for five years over the management structure for LEA functions established by each authority,[25] and had control over ILEA's contracts and disposals as from July 22, 1987.[26] A Staff Commission was established.[27] The functions and the life of the London Residuary Body were extended to enable it to

[17] Local Government Act 1985, s.91 and Sched. 15.
[18] Local Government (Interim Provisions) Act 1984, s.7.
[19] *ibid.* s.8.
[20] *ibid.* s.9 and the Local Government Act 1985, s.93.
[21] Local Government Act 1985, s.92.
[22] *ibid.* s.42, as amended by the Transport Act 1985, Sched. 8, and the Police and Magistrates' Courts Act 1994, Sched. 9.
[23] Education Reform Act 1988, s.163.
[24] *ibid.* ss.166, 168, 172.
[25] *ibid.* s.169.
[26] *ibid.* ss.188–191.
[27] *ibid.* s.171.

assist with ILEA's abolition.[28] The London Residuary Body has itself now been wound up.

I. Reorganisation under the Local Government Act 1992

Structural changes in non-metropolitan areas in England are effected by **3–34** orders made by the Secretary of State under section 17 of the Local Government Act 1992.[29] The Secretary of State also has power to make regulations supplementing such orders,[30] and to establish one or more residuary bodies[31] and one or more staff commission.[32]

---

[28] *ibid.* ss.164, 176–187.

[29] See *supra*, § 3–14.

[30] 1992 Act. s.19. Orders under ss.17 and 19 include the Local Government Changes for England Regulations 1994 (S.I. 1994 No. 867), as amended by S.I. 1995 Nos. 590, 1055 and 1748, S.I. 1996 Nos. 330, 611, which, *inter alia*, provide for shadow authorities; the Local Government Changes for England (Finance) Regulations 1994 (S.I. 1994 No. 2825), as amended by S.I. 1995 No. 2862; and S.I. 1996 No. 563; the Local Government Changes for England (Calculation of Council Tax Base) Regulations 1994 (S.I. 1994 No. 2826); the Local Government Changes for England (Collection Fund Surpluses and Deficits) Regulations 1994 (S.I. 1994 No. 3115); the Local Government Changes for England (Finance, Miscellaneous Provisions) Regulations 1994 (S.I. 1994 No. 3223); the Local Government Changes for England (Non-Domestic Rating, Collection and Enforcement and Discretionary Relief) Regulations 1995 (S.I. 1995 No. 212); the Local Government Changes for England (Community Charge and Council Tax, Administration and Enforcement) Regulations 1995 (S.I. 1995 No. 247); the Local Government Changes for England (Property Transfer and Transitional Payments) Regulations 1995 (S.I. 1995 No. 402), as amended by S.I. 1995 Nos. 1748 and 2796, S.I. 1996 No. 312; the Local Government Changes in England (Staff) Regulations 1995 (S.I. 1995 No. 520), as amended by S.I. 1996 No. 455; the Local Government Changes for England (Housing Benefit and Council Tax Benefit) Regulations 1995 (S.I. 1995 No. 531); the Local Government Changes for England (Non-Domestic Rating, Alteration of Lists and Appeals) Regulations 1995 (S.I. 1995 No. 623); the Local Government Changes for England (Community Charge and Council Tax, Valuation and Community Charge Tribunals and Alteration of Lists and Appeals) Regulations 1995 (S.I. 1995 No. 624); the Local Government Changes for England (Capital Finance) Regulations 1995 (S.I. 1995 No. 798); the Local Government Changes for England (School Reorganisations and Admissions) Regulations 1995 (S.I. 1995 No. 2368); the Local Government Changes (Rent Act) Regulations 1995 (S.I. 1995 No. 2451); the Local Government Changes for England (Collection Fund Surpluses and Deficits) Regulations 1995 (S.I. 1995 No. 2889); the Local Government Changes for England (Designation of Authorities) Order 1995 (S.I. 1995 No. 2894); the Local Government Changes for England (Payments to Designated Authorities) (Minimum Revenue Provision) Regulations 1995 (S.I. 1995 No. 2895); the Local Government Changes for England (Local Management of Schools) Regulations 1995 (S.I. 1995 No. 3114); the Local Government Changes for England (Council Tax) (Transitional Reduction) Regulations 1996 (S.I. 1996 No. 176), as amended by S.I. 1996 No. 333; the Local Government Changes for England (Miscellaneous Provision) Regulations 1996 (S.I. 1996 No. 330); the Local Government Changes for England (Miscellaneous Provision) Order 1996 (S.I. 1996 No. 446); the Local Government Changes for England (Magistrates' Courts) Regulations 1996 (S.I. 1996 No. 674); the Local Government Changes for England (Education) (Miscellaneous Provisions) Regulations 1996 (S.I. 1996 No. 710).

There have also been numerous orders concerning staff transfer, the registration service and coroners.

[31] *ibid.* s.22. See the Local Government Residuary Body (England) Order 1995 (S.I. 1995 No. 401).

[32] *ibid.* s.23. See the Local Government Staff Commission (England) Order 1993 (S.I. 1993 No. 1098).

J. Reorganisation under the Local Government (Wales) Act 1994

3–35 Part II of the Local Government (Wales) Act 1994 (ss.17–26) provides for the transfer of functions to the new unitary authorities. Part V (ss.39–45) establishes the Residuary Body for Wales or Corff Gweddilliol Cymru[33] and the Staff Commission for Wales or Comisiwn Staff Cymru and provides for the transfer of staff. Transitional provisions are contained in Part VI (ss.46–59),[34] and include the establishment of a joint "transition" committee of the existing authorities in the area of a new principal council to advise on transitional matters.[35]

Each principal council is to prepare and publish a "service delivery plan" describing how it proposes to perform its functions in the first year from April 1, 1996, and giving particulars of the arrangements for organisation and management which it proposes to adopt. The council must take into account any guidance given by the Secretary of State as to consultation or the contents of the plan and copies must be readily available. A draft must be published by November 1, 1995, and the final plan by February 1, 1996.[36]

Any new principal council (the "contracting council") may enter into an agreement with any other such council (the "supplying council") for the provision by the supplying council of services which the former requires for the purpose of, or in connection with, the discharge of any of its functions.[37] This is subject, *inter alia*, to restrictions imposed by regulations made by the Secretary of State.[38]

---

[33] See the Residuary Body for Wales (Miscellaneous Provisions) Order 1995 (S.I. 1995 No. 102); the Residuary Body for Wales (Appointed Day) Order 1995 (S.I. 1995 No. 103) (establishing the Body on February 1, 1995).

[34] Regulations on aspects of reorganisation in Wales include the Local Government Reorganisation (Wales) (Consequential Amendments) Order 1995 (S.I. 1995 No. 115) and (No. 2) Order 1995 (S.I. 1995 No. 156); the Local Government Reorganisation (Wales) (Limitation of Compensation) Regulations 1995 (S.I. 1995 No. 1039); the Local Government Reorganisation (Wales) (Transitional Provisions No. 2) Order 1995 (S.I. 1995 No. 1042), (Transitional Provisions No. 3) Order 1995 (S.I. 1995 No. 1161), (Transitional Provisions No. 4) Order 1995 (S.I. 1995 No. 2563); the Local Government Reorganisation (Wales) (Finance) (Miscellaneous Amendments and Transitional Provisions) Order 1995 (S.I. 1995 No. 3150); the Local Authorities (Expenditure Powers) Order 1995 (S.I. 1995 No. 3304); the Local Government Reorganisation (Wales) (Council Tax Reduction Scheme) Order 1996 (S.I. 1996 No. 56); the Local Government Reorganisation (Wales) (Finance) Order 1996 (S.I. 1996 No. 88); Local Government Reorganisation (Wales) (Staff) Order 1996 (S.I. 1996 No. 501) and (No. 2) Order 1996 (S.I. 1996 No. 905), and (No. 3) Order 1996 (S.I. 1996 No. 1214); Local Government Reorganisation (Wales) (Consequential Amendments) Order 1996 (S.I. 1996 No. 525) and (No. 2) Order 1996 (S.I. 1996 No. 1008); Local Government Reorganisation (Wales) (Property, etc.) Order 1996 (S.I. 1996 No. 532), as amended by (S.I. 1996 No. 906); Local Government Reorganisation (Wales) (Rent Officers) Order 1996 (S.I. 1996 No. 533).

[35] s.46. As to the payment of allowances to the members of transition committees, see the Local Government Reorganisation (Wales) (Transitional Provisions) Order 1994 (S.I. 1994 No. 3124) and the Local Government Reorganisation (Wales) (Transitional Provisions) Order 1995 (S.I. 1995 No. 570).

[36] Local Government (Wales) Act 1994, s.26.

[37] *ibid.* s.25.

[38] See the Local Government (Wales) (Service Agency Agreements) Regulations 1995 (S.I. 1995 No. 1040), excluding (subject to particular exceptions) work which is subject to competition requirements under Part III of the Local Government, Planning and Land Act 1980 or Part I of the Local Government Act 1988.

CHAPTER 4

THE ADMINISTRATIVE MACHINERY OF LOCAL AUTHORITIES

THE subject-matter of this Chapter is considered under the following **4–01** headings: the constitution of councils, joint authorities and committees; meetings; members; officers; the disposal of local authority business; direct labour services; competition requirements; local authority companies; publication of information and the Commissions for Local Administration for England and Wales. Competition requirements are dealt with in Chapter 7.

A. Constitution of Councils, Joint Authorities and Committees[1]

A principal council consists of the chairman and councillors. The council's **4–02** members are elected at local elections.[2] The chairman is elected annually by the council from among its members and his election is the first business to be transacted at the annual meeting. The council is required to appoint a vice-chairman, and, subject to standing orders, he may undertake whatever is required to be done by the chairman. The council may pay to each a reasonable allowance to cover the expense of office.[3] Similar rules apply to the chairman and vice-chairman of a joint authority.[4] The chairman of a district council has precedence in his district but not so as prejudicially to affect Her Majesty's royal prerogative. Where a district council has been granted a charter the chairman and vice-chairman have the style of mayor and deputy mayor respectively. The chairman of a county borough council in Wales is entitled to the style of mayor or *maer* and the vice-chairman, deputy mayor or *dirprwy faer*.[5]

A parish council consists of the chairman and members of the council. The council's members are elected at local elections. The chairman is elected

---

[1] Local Government Act 1972, ss.2–5, 13–15, 33, 34. As to joint authorities and residuary bodies, see the Local Government Act 1985, Parts IV and VII, the Local Government Act 1992, ss.21, 22, and the Local Government (Wales) Act 1944, ss.34, 39.

[2] See generally Chap. 11.

[3] The power to make an allowance must be exercised in good faith: see *Att.-Gen. v. Blackburn Corporation* (1887) 57 L.T. 385 and *Att.-Gen. v. Cardiff Corporation* [1894] 2 Ch. 337. In the latter case an increase was made in the mayor's salary. The additional amount was not paid to the mayor but carried to a separate account and expended under the direction of a committee to celebrate a royal event. It was held to be a valid payment.

[4] Local Government Act 1985, ss.24–28, 34.

[5] Local Government Act 1972, s.25A, inserted by the Local Government (Wales) Act 1994, Sched. 15, para. 3.

annually by the council from among its members and his election is the first business to be transacted at the annual meeting. A vice-chairman may be appointed by the council from among its members. An allowance may be paid to the chairman, but not to the vice-chairman. Similar rules apply to the constitution of community councils. In certain circumstances the chairman and vice-chairman of a parish or community council may hold the title of town mayor and deputy town mayor respectively.[5a] In Wales, the chairman and vice-chairman may hold the title of *maery dref* and *dirprwy faer y dref*, respectively.[6]

4-03   The members of a joint authority are members of the "constituent councils" appointed by those councils to be members of the authority. The constituent councils are the councils of the metropolitan districts in the county and, in the case of the London Fire and Civil Defence Authority, the London borough councils and the Common Council. The number of members to be appointed by each constituent council is specified in Schedule 10 to the Local Government Act 1985. These numbers may be changed by order of the Secretary of State,[7] who must have regard to the number of local government electors in the areas of the constituent councils and must consult the constituent councils before making such an order.

A constituent council may at any time terminate the appointment of a person appointed by it to a joint authority and appoint another person in his place.[8] The appointment also terminates if the member ceases to be a member of the constituent council.[9] In this event, or if a vacancy arises for some other reason, the constituent council must appoint a replacement, normally within one month.[10] Where a constituent council makes at least three appointments to a joint authority the political balance rules that apply to the appointment of committees and sub-committees must be observed.[11]

4-04   Authorities may appoint committees as they think fit.[12] In certain cases the appointment is obligatory, although the number of such requirements has

---

[5a] Local Government Act 1972, s.245(6); and see § 3–10.

[6] *ibid.* s.245B, inserted by the Local Government (Wales) Act 1994, s.16.

[7] See, *e.g.* the Greater Manchester Passenger Transport Authority (Increase in Number of Members) Order 1995 (S.I. 1995 No. 1522).

[8] Local Government Act 1985, s.31, as amended by the Local Government Act 1986, s.10(2).

[9] *ibid.* s.32(1). A person is not to be treated as ceasing to be a member of a constituent council where he retires by virtue of s.7(3) of (metropolitan district councillors) or Sched. 2, para. 6(3) to (London borough councillors) the Local Government Act 1972 and is re-elected to membership of that council not later than the date of his retirement: *ibid.* s.32(1A), inserted by the Local Government Act 1986, s.10(1).

[10] *ibid.* s.32(2)–(8).

[11] Local Government and Housing Act 1989 (ss.15–17 and Sched. 1), see §§ 4–06, 4–07. These replace a political balance requirement imposed by section 33 of the 1985 Act with effect from August 1, 1990 (S.I. 1990 No. 1552, para. 3).

[12] Local Government Act 1972, ss.101 and 102, as amended. These provisions apply to joint authorities (other than police authorities) by virtue of s.101(13), as amended by the Local Government Act 1985, Sched. 14, para. 15, and to police authorities, with modifications, by virtue of s.107.

steadily declined.[13] Thus, authorities for the purposes of the Local Authority Social Services Act 1970 must appoint a social services committee,[14] and a local fisheries committee must be established for a sea fisheries district.[15] The requirements of the Education Act 1944, s.6(2) and Sched. I, Part II, as to the appointment of an education committee by each local education authority were repealed by the Education Act 1993 with effect from April 1, 1994.[16] This leaves local education authorities with a discretion to appoint an education committee under section 102(1) of the Local Government Act 1972. However, the Secretary of State has power to give directions to any local authority which does appoint any committees wholly or partly to discharge education functions imposed on it in its capacity as local education authority. The directions may require all or some of those committees to include persons appointed to secure the representation of persons who appoint foundation governors for voluntary schools in the area for which the committee acts. Similar powers apply in respect of committees appointed jointly by two or more local education authorities, and in respect of sub-committees.[17] An authority may not arrange for functions subject to the 1972 Act, s.101(9) to be discharged by a committee, sub-committee or other local authority, but may, empower an officer to discharge the relevant function.[18] Separate express provision is made for the appointment of committees to advise the authority on any matter relating to the discharge of its functions.[19]

Two or more authorities may appoint joint committees.[20] Committees and joint committees may appoint sub-committees.[21] These may also be advisory committees.[22]

Membership of committees and sub-committees is fixed by the appointing **4–05** authority, authorities or committee. Except in the case of a committee controlling the finance of the local authority, they may include persons not members of the authority,[23] but, with some exceptions, such co-opted

---

[13] For a list of statutory committees, see Local Government Act 1972, s.101(9), as amended by the Health and Social Services and Social Security Adjudications Act 1983, Sched. 29, the Local Government Act 1985, Sched. 17, the Statute Law Repeals Act 1986, Sched. 1, the Education Act 1993, Sched. 19 and the Police and Magistrates' Courts Act 1994, Sched. 9.

[14] s.2; Local Government Act 1972, s.101(9)(f)); Local Government, Planning and Land Act 1980, s.183. Para (f) does not apply in Wales: 1972 Act s.101(10A) inserted by the Local Government (Wales) Act 1994, Sched. 15, para. 26.

[15] Sea Fisheries Regulation Act 1966, s.1.

[16] s.296; Education Act 1993 (Commencement No. 3 and Transitional Provisions) Order 1994 (S.I. 1994 No. 507).

[17] Education Act 1993, s.297.

[18] Local Government Act 1972, s.101(10).

[19] *ibid*. s.102(4).

[20] *ibid*. s.102(1)(b).

[21] *ibid*. s.102(1)(c). An amendment to s.102(1)(a) by the Local Government and Housing Act 1989, Sched. 11, para. 25(a) enabling the authority to appoint a sub-committee, has not been implemented.

[22] *ibid*. s.102(4). The addition of a new subs. (4A) by the 1989 Act, Sched. 11, para. 25(c) has not been implemented. This would enable the authority to appoint an advisory sub-committee.

[23] *ibid*. s.102(3), as amended.

members are now only non-voting members.[24] The exceptions cover co-opted members of a series of specified committees (and their sub-committees), including sea fisheries, superannuation, and education appeal committees, advisory committees and other committees exercising functions prescribed by regulations.[25] However, other than in the case of advisory committees and other cases prescribed by regulations,[26] to be a voting member of a sub-committee a co-opted member must also be a member of the parent committee. In addition, the Secretary of State may approve arrangements for co-opted members of education committees and sub-committees representing persons who appoint foundation governors of voluntary schools to be voting members.[27]

The composition of a particular committee may be dealt with by statute. At least a majority of members of a social services committee must be members of the authority, and where a sub-committee is established, at least one member must be a member of the local authority.[28]

4-06 Apart from these specific provisions, the Local Government and Housing Act 1989 introduced a requirement that appointments by "relevant authorities" (and committees of relevant authorities) to committees, sub-committees and other bodies achieve a political balance.[29] The "relevant authorities" include county, district and London borough councils, fire authorities, waste disposal authorities, joint authorities and any bodies established as successors to residuary authorities.[30] The appointments covered include appointments:

(a) to an ordinary committee or sub-committee of the authority[31];

---

[24] Local Government and Housing Act 1989, s.13. The Widdicombe Committee had recommended that only elected members should serve on decision-taking committees and sub-committees (Cmnd. 9797, paras. 5.79—5.107), but the government thought it sufficient to withdraw voting rights from co-opted members (*Government Response* (Cm. 433), paras. 2.9–2.14).

[25] See the Parish and Community Councils (Committees) Regulations 1990 (S.I. 1990 No. 2467), reg. 3 and the Local Government (Committees and Political Groups) Regulations 1990 (S.I. 1990 No. 1553), reg. 4, as amended by S.I. 1991 No. 1398 and S.I. 1993 No. 1339. Functions prescribed include land management, the promotion of tourism, the management of a festival (in the case of a county council), functions under *inter alia* the Highways Act 1980 or the Local Authority Social Services Act 1970 discharged by a committee comprising county council and district council members. See also the Local Government (Committees) (Devon and Cornwall) Regulations 1994 (S.I. 1994 No. 961), which extended the ability to vote in respect of certain matters related to the economic development of Devon and Cornwall to those members of the Devon and Cornwall Development Bureau who are not members of the local authorities which established it as a joint committee of theirs.

[26] See the Parish and Community Councils (Committees) Regulations 1990 (S.I. 1990 No. 2476), reg. 4.

[27] S.I. 1990 No. 1553, reg. 5.

[28] Local Authority Social Services Act 1970, s.5.

[29] 1989 Act, ss.15, 16, 17 and Sched. 1; Local Government (Committees and Political Groups) Regulations 1990 (S.I. 1990 No. 1553), as amended by S.I. 1991 No. 1398 and S.I. 1993 No. 1339.

[30] 1989 Act, Sched. 1, para. 4, as amended by the Police and Magistrates' Courts Act 1994, Sched. 4, para. 44.

[31] *i.e.* the authority's education committee or social services committee or any other committee appointed under the 1972 Act, s.102(1)(a), not being a body to which s.15 applies by virtue of Sched. 1, para. 2: *ibid.* as amended by the Education Act 1993, Sched. 21, Pt. II.

(b) to an advisory committee and any sub-committee appointed by an advisory committee; and

(c) to a series of prescribed bodies,[32] where at least three seats have to be filled by the relevant authority or committee.

However, the requirements do not apply to area committees and sub-committees of county, district and London borough councils.[33]

The legislation provides for the *review* of the representation of political groups and the *determination* of the allocation of seats.[34] Where the members of a relevant authority were already divided into political groups, reviews by the authority and by any of its committees with power to make appointments were required as soon as practicable after the coming into force of the 1989 Act. Thereafter, the authority must conduct a review at or as soon as practicable after the annual meeting and at such times as may be prescribed by regulations.[35] Where a relevant authority becomes divided into political groups,[36] a review must take place as soon as practicable thereafter. Where a committee of a relevant authority has power to make appointments, the committee must conduct a review as soon as practicable after any occasion on which the members of the committee are changed in consequence of a determination under the section, except in cases pre-scribed by regulations.[37]

A "political group" comprises two or more members who give written notice of their wish to be treated as a group. It must have a leader and a deputy leader. A member is to be treated as a member of a group if he is party to such a notice, or otherwise gives notice, signed by the leader, deputy leader or a majority of group members, that he wishes to join the group. No person can be a member of more than one group.[38]

A determination of the allocation of seats must take place as soon as **4–07** practicable after a review, and may take place on other occasions, such as when a vacancy arises.

Determinations, so far as reasonably practicable, must give effect to the principles:

(a) that not all the seats on the body to which appointments are made are allocated to the same political group;

---

[32] Prescribed by *ibid*. Sched. 1, para. 2(1), as amended: they include a combined fire authority, a waste disposal authority, a joint authority, any successor to residuary bodies, the Broads Authority, the National Park Planning Boards, a joint planning board in Wales, a National Parks authority, a local fisheries committee, a superannuation committee, a National Parks Committee, a board or committee appointed under a local Act and a joint committee appointed under the 1972 Act, s.102(1)(b). References to the National Park Planning Boards and National Parks Committee are to be repealed by the Environment Act 1995, Sched. 24.
[33] S.I. 1990 No. 1553, reg. 16A, added by S.I. 1991 1398, reg. 6.
[34] Local Government and Housing Act 1989, s.15.
[35] S.I. 1990 No. 1553, reg. 17: *e.g.* on the creation of a new political group and, on request, following changes in a group's membership or the filling of a casual vacancy.
[36] Members of an authority are to be treated as divided into political groups when there is at least one political group in existence constituted in accordance with reg. 8: *ibid*. reg. 7.
[37] *ibid*. reg. 19.
[38] *ibid*. regs. 8–12.

(b) that the majority of seats on the body is allocated to a particular political group if the number of persons belonging to that group is a majority of the authority's membership;

(c) subject to (a) and (b), that the total number of seats on all the ordinary committees of a relevant authority allocated to a particular political group reflects that group's proportion of the membership of the authority;

(d) subject to (a) and (c), that the number of seats on each body allocated to a particular political group reflects that group's proportion of the membership of the authority.

Once a determination has been made, it becomes the duty of the relevant authority or committee to exercise the power to make appointments as soon as practicable thereafter, and to give effect to such wishes about who is to be appointed to the seats allocated to a particular political group as are expressed by that group.[39]

The proceedings of a body are not to be invalidated by any breach of sections 15 and 16,[40] and alternative arrangements not complying with the requirements may be made if no member of the relevant authority or committee votes against.[41]

Under the previous law, it had been held that the majority party on a council could exclude other members from all committees by passing an appropriate resolution complying with standing orders.[42] The requirement of proportionality was introduced on the recommendation of the Widdicombe Committee.[43]

Subject to these requirements, it is open to a council to establish in standing orders its own criteria for appointing members to its committees.[44]

4–08 A member cannot be compelled to serve on a committee against his wish[45] and it is open to a council to dislodge a member from a committee although appointed for the ensuing municipal year. In *Manton v. Brighton Corporation*[46] it was held that as the council had power to revoke the authority of a committee as a whole it also had power to revoke the authority of any single member before the end of his prescribed period of office. However, where a

---

[39] 1989 Act, s.16. Such wishes are to be expressed (a) orally or in writing by the leader or deputy leader, or (b) in writing by a majority of group members; in cases of conflict, wishes expressed as in (b) prevail. If no wishes are expressed within three weeks, the authority or committee may make such appointment as it thinks fit: S.I. 1990 No. 1553, regs. 13–15.

[40] 1989 Act, s.16(3).

[41] *ibid.* s.17; S.I. 1990 No. 1553, reg. 20.

[42] *R. v. Rushmoor Borough Council, ex p. Crawford, The Times*, November 28, 1981; *R. v. Newham London Borough Council, ex p. Haggerty* (1986) 85 L.G.R. 48.

[43] Cmnd. 9797, 1986, pp. 77–81.

[44] *R. v. Newham London Borough Council, ex p. Haggerty* (1986) 85 L.G.R. 48 (members required to disclose a range of personal details); note, however, that any requirement to disclose interests other than those required to be disclosed by section 94 of the Local Government Act 1972 or regulations under section 19 of the 1989 Act is now prohibited by the 1989 Act, s.19(5).

[45] *R. v. Sunderland Corporation* [1911] 2 K.B. 458.

[46] [1951] 2 K.B. 393. See also *R. v. Newham London Borough Council, ex p. Haggerty* (1986) 85 L.G.R. 48; *R. v. Greenwich London Borough Council, ex p. Lovelace* [1991] 1 W.L.R. 506.

person has been appointed, other than for a fixed term, to a body to which section 15 of the 1989 Act applies, in accordance with the wishes of a political group, the relevant authority or committee which made the appointment must act in accordance with the wishes of that group in deciding whether and when to terminate the appointment.[47] Moreover, the power to remove from a committee cannot itself be delegated,[48] and natural justice may have to be observed.[49]

Where an authority appoints a representative to *another* body,[50] that person holds office in accordance with the terms creating the other body.[51] Where this provides for a fixed term of office with no provision for rescinding the appointment, a local authority may not replace the member in order to reflect a change in its political complexion.[52] Provision may, however, be made enabling an appointment to be rescinded.[53] These appointments may be subject to the requirement of proportionality in the representation of political groups and the requirement to act in accordance with the wishes of the member's political group in determining whether an appointment should be terminated.[54]

B. Meetings[54a]

This topic is considered in three parts: the law relating to the calling and **4–09** conduct of meetings; the law of defamation as applied to local authority and committee meetings; the rights of the public and Press.

The calling and conduct of meetings

The rules governing the meetings of local authorities and committees are found, first, in statute—in the main in Schedule 12 to the Local Government Act 1972.[55] Part I of the Schedule regulates meetings and proceedings of all principal councils, Part II those of parish councils, and Part III of parish meetings. Parts IV and V cover community councils and meetings respectively, and Part VI contains general provisions relating to all councils. Part IA applies the provisions of Part I to joint authorities with minor modifications. Secondly, they are found in standing orders. An authority may make standing orders to regulate its proceedings and business, and may vary or revoke them.[56] Standing orders generally contain rules of debate and other

---

[47] Local Government and Housing Act 1989, s.16(2).
[48] *R. v. Brent London Borough Council, ex p. Gladbaum* (1989) 88 L.G.R. 627.
[49] *R. v. Portsmouth City Council, ex p. Gregory* (1990) 89 LG.R. 478 (suspension of councillors following complaints of misconduct).
[50] There is no direct general power enabling this to be done, but such power may be implied from the power to pay allowances to such a representative: see § 4–31, n. 14.
[51] *R. v. Peak Park Joint Planning Board* (1976) 74 L.G.R. 376.
[52] *R. v. Lambeth London Borough Council, ex p. Parker, The Times*, March 1, 1983.
[53] *e.g.* Local Government Act 1985, s.31(1): see § 4–03.
[54] See *supra*.
[54a] See R. S. B. Knowles, *The Law and Practice of Local Authority Meetings* (2nd ed., 1993).
[55] As amended by the Local Government Act 1985, Sched. 14, para. 35, and Sched. 17.
[56] Local Government Act 1972, Sched. 12, para. 42. Regulations made by the Secretary of State may require particular provisions to be incorporated: Local Government and Housing Act 1989, s.20. The Local Authorities (Standing Orders) Regulations 1993 (S.I. 1993 No. 202) require standing orders to be made in relation to the recording of votes and the signing of minutes at extraordinary meetings.

procedural matters in respect of which there is no specific statutory provision. Thirdly, recourse may be had to the common law rules as to meetings. These come into operation only where a point is not covered by statute or standing orders. Thus, if standing orders are silent on such matters as the ejection of unruly members, the adjournment of meetings, the powers and duties of chairmen, then the issue will be decided on common law principles.

Principal councils

4–10   Schedule 12 requires a principal council to hold an annual meeting and such other meetings as the council thinks necessary. The annual meeting in an election year is to be held on the eighth day after the retirement of councillors or on a day within 21 days immediately following the day of retirement. In a year when there is no election the annual meeting may be held in either March, April or May. A joint authority must hold its annual meetings between March 1 and June 30 inclusive of these dates.

The chairman of a council may call a meeting of the council at any time, and he may be required to call a meeting on the requisition of five members (three in the case of a joint authority). If the chairman after a requisition refuses to call a meeting or fails to call it within seven days of receiving the requisition,[57] any five members (or three in the case of a joint authority) may themselves do so as soon as he refuses or on the expiration of the seven days. Notice of the time and place of any meeting of the council is to be published at the council offices three clear days[58] before the meeting, and where the meeting has been called by members the notice is required to be signed by them and it must specify the business.

A summons to attend a meeting, specifying the business and signed by the proper officer of the council, must be sent to each member, and again three clear days' notice is required. No business may be transacted at a meeting unless it is specified in the summons or is urgent business brought before the meeting in accordance with standing orders. If a summons is not served on any member the validity of the meeting is not affected.

The chairman presides at the meeting. In the absence of the chairman the vice-chairman (or deputy mayor where the chairman is a mayor) presides. In London boroughs, the deputy mayor presides in the absence of the mayor if at the time he is still a councillor and the members present choose him. If the chairman and vice-chairman are absent, or, in a London borough council, the deputy mayor although present is not chosen, another member of the council is chosen.

The quorum for a principal council or a joint authority is one quarter of the body—provision is made for exceptional situations where more than a third of the council are disqualified. Here, the quorum is determined by

---

[57] The requirement is that a meeting be *called* within seven days, not that a meeting be called to be *held* within seven days: *Mallon v. Armstrong* [1982] N.1. 112, on similar provisions in the Local Government (Northern Ireland) Act 1972.

[58] The day on which notice is given and the day of the meeting is to be excluded: *R. v. Herefordshire Justices* (1820) 3 B. & Ald. 581; *R. v. Swansea City Council, ex p. Elitestone* (1993) 66 P. & C.R. 422.

reference to the number of members of the authority remaining qualified instead of by reference to the whole number of members.[59]

Parish councils and community councils

The rules are similar to those which apply to principal councils but are **4–11** rather more detailed. It is obligatory to hold an annual meeting and at least three other meetings in a year. They may not be held in licensed premises unless there is no other reasonable alternative. An extraordinary meeting may be called at any time by the chairman or members—the rules follow those which apply to principal councils except that two members only are required to sign the requisition.

The law with respect to community councils is marginally different from the law which applies to parish councils. For example, it is obligatory only to hold an annual meeting: other meetings are held as the council thinks necessary.

The quorum is one-third of the members of the whole council and provision is made to meet exceptional circumstances in which one-third of the council are disqualified (as in the case of principal councils), but the quorum is never less than three.

Parish meetings

A parish meeting is required to assemble annually between March 1 and **4–12** June 1. Other meetings are held as fixed by the parish council, or where there is no council by the chairman of the parish meeting. Where the parish does not have a separate parish council the parish meeting is required to assemble at least twice a year. Proceedings may not begin before 6 p.m. and may not be held on licensed premises unless no reasonable alternative is available. A parish meeting may be convened by the chairman of the parish council, or any two councillors for the parish or any six local government electors for the parish. Where there is no council, a meeting may be convened by the chairman of the parish meeting or any person representing the parish on the district council. Seven days' public notice[60] must be given of the meeting and the notice must specify the time and place of it and the business to be transacted.

Matters discussed at a parish meeting are decided by a majority of those present and voting. The decision of the person presiding as to the result of the voting is final unless a poll is demanded. Such a poll may be demanded before the end of the meeting on any question arising at the meeting.[61] It is open to the person presiding or to the meeting to consent to a poll. If such consent is not given, a poll must be held if demanded by not less than 10, or one-third, of the local government electors present at the meeting, whichever is the less.

---

[59] 1972 Act, Sched. 12, para. 45.
[60] 14 days' notice in the case of business relating to the establishment or dissolution of the parish council or the grouping of the parish with another parish or parishes.
[61] Parish and Community Meetings (Polls) Rules 1987 (S.I. 1987 No. 1), as amended by S.I. 1987 No. 262.

Community meetings

4–13 The rules are somewhat different from those which apply to parish meetings since community meetings are not continuing bodies with executive functions. There is, for example, no requirement as to regular meetings. Thirty clear days' notice (rather than seven) is required when the business relates to the establishment or dissolution of a community council, the grouping of a community with or separation of a community from another community or communities, the dissolution of a common community council or the expression of certain consents.[62] Where a community has a community council the chairman of that council, if present, presides at the community meeting. In any other case the meeting appoints the chairman, but for that meeting only. As in the case of parish meetings, matters are decided by a majority of those present and voting, and a poll may be demanded.[63]

Committee meetings

4–14 Rules for the calling of committees and the procedure to be followed in committee are generally found in standing orders—section 106 of the Local Government Act 1972[64] confers a general power on local authorities to make standing orders respecting the quorum, proceedings and place of meetings of committees and joint committees, and subject to the standing orders these matters are determined by the committee itself. But the general provisions with regard to the conduct of meetings, referred to in the paragraph which follows, apply to meetings of committees as well as to meetings of local authorities.

General provisions

4–15 Except where otherwise provided by statute, decisions are taken by a majority of members present and voting,[65] and the person presiding has a second or casting vote if there is no majority. The principles on which a casting vote can be exercised were considered in the following case:

> *R. v. Bradford Metropolitan City Council, ex p. Corris.*[66] The Lord Mayor of Bradford exercised his second, casting, vote in favour of a series of controversial resolutions at a meeting of the council. A resident at a council home which was the subject of a proposed sale sought judicial review of the exercise of the casting votes on party-political grounds. The Divisional Court (*sub nom. R. v. Bradford Metropolitan City Council, ex p. Wilson* held:
>
> (a) That power to give a second or casting vote in the case of an equality of votes (Local Government Act 1972, Sched. 12, para. 39(2)) was not subject to the implied restriction that it should be exercised without regard to party political considerations. Neither was there any practice to that effect rendering decisions departing from it irrational.

---

[62] 1972 Act, Sched. 12, paras. 30(2)(3)(3A), substituted by the Local Government (Wales) Act 1994, s.12.
[63] See n. 61, *ante.*
[64] This provision applies to joint authorities: s.101(13), as amended by the Local Government Act 1985, Sched. 14, para. 15, and s.107.
[65] Voting can be "on the nod", without a ballot or a show of hands: *R. v. Highbury Corner Magistrates' Court, ex p. Ewing* [1991] 3 All E.R. 192.
[66] [1990] 2 Q.B. 363 (pet. dis. [1990] 2 W.L.R. 255, H.L.).

(b) That the Lord Mayor's actions were not in breach of standing orders. The Lord Mayor did not have a non-pecuniary interest under the National Code of Conduct (see now paras. 4–43, *et seq.*) in a resolution criticising his use of the casting vote. He was entitled to speak and vote against the resolution.

(c) The applicant did not have a legitimate expectation that casting votes would not be cast on party-political lines. Such an expectation did not arise from an inter-party agreement on the rotation of the Lord Mayoralty among three political parties. In any event, the applicant did not assert that she derived any expectation from that agreement. Furthermore, the agreement was not made by or on behalf of the council.

An appeal to the Court of Appeal was dismissed.

The names of those present must be recorded. The minutes of the meeting are entered in a book kept for that purpose, and the book may consist of loose leaves consecutively numbered. They are signed at the same or next suitable meeting of the authority by the person presiding thereat and a minute purporting to be so signed is received in evidence without further proof.

The minutes of a principal council and its committees and sub-committees are available for inspection by members of the public.[67] The minutes of a parish or community council and a parish meeting are available for inspection by electors[68] or by an agent for an elector.[69]

Defamatory statements in council and committee

Statements made in council and committee are subject to the general **4–16** principles of law relating to defamation. A person who issues a defamatory statement (one exposing a person to hatred, ridicule or contempt, or which causes him to be shunned or avoided, or which has a tendency to lower him in the estimation of right thinking members of society generally or injure him in his office, profession or trade) commits a tort, and is liable for the consequences which flow from such an act.

It may be noted in passing that it was previously held that a local authority has a "governing" reputation which it is entitled to protect by a defamation action. In *Bognor Regis Urban District Council v. Campion*[70] the council successfully brought an action against a ratepayer who had published a leaflet defamatory of the council. However, a different view was taken by the

---

[67] Local Government Act 1972, ss.100C, 100E, inserted by the Local Government (Access to Information) Act 1985, s.1. See also §§ 4–21 *et seq.* Formerly, there was no general right of access to the minutes of committees and sub-committees (*Wilson v. Evans* [1962] 2 Q.B. 383), except where the minutes of a committee exercising referred powers were submitted to the council for approval (*Williams v. Manchester Corporation* (1897) 45 W.R. 412) or where this was expressly required by statute (*e.g.* Education Act 1944, Sched. 1, para. 9: education committees). For rights of access to documents concerning local authority accounts, see §§ 13–42 *et seq.* The right to take copies is not a right to be provided with copies: *Russell-Walker v. Gimblett* (1985) 149 J.P. 448.

[68] Local Government Act 1972, s.228, as amended, *inter alia*, by the Local Government (Access to Information) Act 1985, Sched. 2, para. 6.

[69] *R. v. Glamorganshire County Council* [1936] 2 All E.R. 168.

[70] [1972] 2 Q.B. 169.

House of Lords in *Derbyshire County Council v. Times Newspapers Ltd*[71] where it was held that a local authority could not sue for libel in respect of its governing or administrative reputation. Where the law otherwise, legitimate public criticism of its activities would be stifled. Actions would, however, be maintained by individual officers or councillors who were libelled, and members of the Court of Appeal pointed out that the authority itself might in appropriate circumstances secure the institution of a prosecution for criminal libel or (if it suffered economic loss) malicious falsehood. *Bognor Regis Urban District Council v. Campion*[72] was overruled.

Defence of privilege

4–17   It is a general defence in an action for defamation to show that the statement was made on a "privileged occasion", being made in such circumstances as to be exempt from the rule that a man attacks the reputation of another at his own risk. "Privileged occasions" are of two kinds.

As to the first, the privilege is absolute, and the motive prompting the author of a defamatory statement is not material. Absolute privilege attaches to certain proceedings (*e.g.* judicial and parliamentary) and where it is present there is a complete bar against an action. It does not attach to meetings of local authorities, even where functions are exercised which attract an obligation to act judicially and fairly.[73] Communications between a Local Commissioner and a local authority are, however, absolutely privileged.[74]

As to the second, the privilege is qualified, and the "relevant occasion", to use the words of Lord Atkinson in *Adam v. Ward*,[75] is

> "... an occasion where the person who makes a communication has an interest or a duty, legal, social or moral, to make it to the person to whom it is made, and the person to whom it is so made has a corresponding interest or duty to receive it."

An essential feature of qualified privilege is the absence of malice.

4–18   Qualified privilege will accordingly frequently attach to statements made in council and committee. Where it is pleaded in an action for defamation the author of the defamatory statement must prove (a) a duty or interest to make the statement, and (b) a duty or interest on the part of the recipient to receive it. If these things are proved the plaintiff will not succeed unless he proves malice on the defendant's part.

So long as a person believes in the truth of what he says malice cannot normally be inferred.

Horrocks v. Lowe.[76] Councillor Horrocks issued a writ against Alderman

---

[71] [1993] A.C. 534.
[72] *supra.*
[73] *Royal Aquarium etc., Society v. Parkinson* [1892] 1 Q.B. 431; *cf. R. v. London County Council, ex. p. Akkersdyk* [1892] 1 Q.B. 190: meetings held to consider applications for music and dancing licences.
[74] Local Government Act 1974, s.32.
[75] [1917] A.C. 309 at p. 334.
[76] [1975] A.C. 135.

Lowe, each of the Bolton Council, claiming damages for slander. At a meeting of the authority the alderman made a speech defamatory of the councillor. The alderman claimed, *inter alia*, that the words were spoken on a privileged occasion. By his reply the councillor pleaded that the alderman was actuated by express malice. The trial judge held that the occasion was privileged, that the alderman had honestly believed that what he had said was true but that he had shown such gross and unreasoning prejudice as to constitute malice in law sufficient to destroy the privilege. An appeal by the alderman to the Court of Appeal was allowed. The councillor appealed to the House of Lords. The House of Lords *held*, dismissing the appeal, that, the defendant not having misused the privileged occasion by using it for some purpose other than that for which the privilege was accorded to it in the public interest, his positive belief in the truth of what he said entitled him to succeed in his defence of qualified privilege. Lord Diplock stated[77] that, save in the exceptional case where a person may be under a duty to pass on, without endorsing, defamatory reports made by some other person, "what is required on the part of the defamer to entitle him to the protection of the privilege is positive belief in the truth of what he published, or, as it is generally ... termed, 'honest belief' ... Even a positive belief in the truth of what is published on a privileged occasion—which is presumed unless the contrary is proved—may not be sufficient to negative express malice if it can be proved that the defendant misused the occasion for some purpose other than that for which the privilege is accorded by law." Examples of improper purposes or motives include giving vent to "personal spite or ill-will" or obtaining "some private advantage unconnected with the duty or interest which constitutes the reason for the privilege". However, where there is a positive belief in the truth of the statement, it is only where the defendant's "desire to comply with the relevant duty or to protect the relevant interests plays no significant part in his motives for publishing ... that 'express malice' can properly be found".

The second element mentioned above—the duty or interest to receive— **4–19** has the effect of greatly limiting the extent of publication if qualified privilege is to be preserved.

> *De Buse v. McCarthy*.[78] The town clerk of Stepney sent out a notice convening a meeting of the council to consider, *inter alia*, a report of a committee regarding the loss of petrol from one of the council's depots. Included in the notice was a long agenda of business, and a complete copy of the report of the committee. Copies of the notice were sent to the public libraries, in accordance with long-established practice. *Held*, that the extent of the publication of the report destroyed the privilege otherwise attaching to it. There was no common interest between the council and the ratepayers to be informed in what was only a preliminary stage in an investigation.

As will be noted below, under the Public Bodies (Admission to Meetings) Act 1960, s.1, and the Local Government Act 1972, Part VA, the Press and public must on request be allowed access to or, in certain circumstances, be supplied with agenda and certain other documents relating to matters before local authorities and other bodies. Where such matter is made available to the Press or to the public, the agenda and other documents are privileged unless publication is proved to have been made with malice.[79] Qualified privilege therefore attaches to them. However, this statutory privilege

---

[77] At pp. 150–151.
[78] [1942] 1 K.B. 156.
[79] 1960 Act, s.1(5); 1972 Act, ss.100H(5)(6).

covers only the publication to the Press or member of the public. Whether further publication by the Press or members of the public is protected by qualified privilege depends on the common law and section 15 of the Defamation Act 1996.[80]

Other defences

4–20   Certain other defences are available. Justification can be pleaded if the words are true, and justification provides a complete answer. It is also a good defence to show that what was said was a fair comment on a matter of public interest,[81] honestly believed to be true, relevant and not inspired by malicious motive, and that the statements of fact on which the comment was based were materially true.

Defences of apology and fair reporting are open to newspapers. Under section 2 of the Libel Act 1843 it is a good defence to prove that a statement was published without actual malice or gross negligence and that the earliest opportunity was taken to publish an apology. The defendant must, when filing his defence, make payment into court by way of amends. Section 15 of the Defamation Act 1996[81a] provides that fair and accurate reports of meetings of local authorities and their committees are privileged, unless the publication is proved to be made with malice. This qualified privilege does not extend to meetings to which the public and the Press are denied admission. To secure the benefit of this provision the defendant must publish a reasonable letter by way of explanation or contradiction if so requested. A copy or fair and accurate report or summary of any notice or other matter issued for the information of the public by or on behalf of any local authority is similarly protected. The Defamation Act 1996 introduces a new defence of unintentional defamation, a new offer of amends procedure and provision for the summary disposal of claim.

A local authority may in principle be liable in respect of defamatory statements made by an officer within the scope of his authority.[82]

Rights of public and press

4–21   The Public Bodies (Admission to Meetings) Act 1960 provided that meetings of local authorities and certain other bodies which exercise public functions should be open to the public. A list of these bodies was given in the Schedule to the Act, and included as well as local authorities, joint boards, joint committees of local authorities, parish meetings and education committees. Section 100 of the Local Government Act 1972 applied the Public Bodies (Admission to Meetings) Act 1960 to committees, joint committees and advisory committees appointed by local authorities under sections 101 and 102 of the Act, except in so far as the provisions of the 1960 Act already applied. The Local Government (Access to Information) Act 1985 introduced a new regime providing greater public access to local

---

[80] *infra.*
[81] The administration of local affairs by authorities is a matter of "public interest": *Purcell v. Sowler* (1887) 2 C.P.D. 215.
[81a] Replacing section 7 of the Defamation Act 1952 from a day to be appointed.
[82] *Glasgow Corporation v. Lorimer* [1911] A.C. 209. The corporation was held not liable on the facts.

authority meetings, reports and documents. The Public Bodies (Admission to Meetings) Act 1960 continues to apply to parish and community councils, parish meetings, health authorities and certain other bodies. The two sets of provisions are considered separately.

Local Government (Access to Information) Act 1985

Section 1 of this Act inserts a new Part VA (sections 100A—100K) in the **4–22** Local Government Act 1972. It applies to any principal council, which term includes the councils of non-metropolitan counties, districts and London boroughs, and counties and county boroughs in Wales,[83] and, for the purposes of Part VA, a joint authority, the Common Council of the City of London, joint boards and joint committees of two or more principal councils, a police authority, and a combined fire authority.[84] It also applies, with some modifications, to committees and sub-committees of such bodies.[85]

Meetings of the bodies subject to Part VA must normally be open to the public. However, the public *must* be excluded from a meeting during an item of business whenever it is likely that confidential information would otherwise be disclosed to members of the public in breach of an obligation of confidence. For this purpose "confidential information" means (1) information furnished to the council by a government department on terms which forbid the disclosure of the information to the public, and (2) information the disclosure of which to the public is prohibited by or under any enactment or by a court order. Moreover, a council *may* by resolution exclude the public from a meeting during an item of business whenever it is likely that "exempt information" would otherwise be disclosed to members of the public. The resolution must identify the proceedings, or the part of the proceedings, to which it applies, and state the description, in terms of schedule 12A, of the exempt information in question.[86] The descriptions of information which are for the time being exempt information are found in this Schedule, and the descriptions may be varied by order of the Secretary of State. Part I of the Schedule lists 15 descriptions of exempt information. These are subject to qualifications contained in Part II. Part III contains provisions for interpretation of the Schedule. The descriptions in Part I include information relating to particular persons, such as employees, former employees, council tenants and applicants for or recipients of services or financial assistance; information relating to the adoption, care, fostering or education of any particular child; information relating to the

---

[83] Definition of "principal council" and "principal area" in the Local Government Act 1972, s.270(1), the latter as amended by the Local Government Act 1985, Sched. 15, para. 8, and the Local Government (Wales) Act 1994, s.1.
[84] Local Government Act 1972, s.100J, as amended.
[85] *ibid.* s.100E. See *R. v. Warwickshire County Council, ex p. Bailey* [1991] C.O.D. 284.
[86] *ibid.* s.100A(1)–(5). *Cf. R. v. Liverpool City Council, ex p. Liverpool Taxi Fleet Operators' Association* [1975] 1 W.L.R. 701: see § 4–26. In *R. v. Kensington and Chelsea London Borough Council, ex p. Stoop* [1992] 1 P.L.R. 58 Otton J. held that a planning committee meeting at which both the developer and the objectors were present was entitled to go into closed session under section 100A(4) and Schedule 12A, para. 12 of the Local Government Act 1972, to hear the advice of a legal officer on the likelihood of a successful appeal by the developer and costs being awarded against the council if planning permission were refused.

financial or business affairs of any particular person; the amount of proposed expenditure on the acquisition of property or the supply of goods or services; any terms proposed or to be proposed in the course of negotiations for a contract for the acquisition or disposal of property or the supply of goods or services; the identity of the authority or a person as the person tendering for a contract for the supply of goods or services; information concerning legal proceedings; information which would reveal that the authority proposes to serve a notice, or make an order or direction under any enactment; any action taken or to be taken in connection with the prevention, investigation or prosecution of crime; and the identity of a protected informant.[87]

4–23   Public notice of the time and place of a meeting of a body subject to Part VA must be published at the offices of the body three clear days[88] before the meeting, or when the meeting is convened if called at shorter notice. While the meeting is open to the public, the council does not have power to exclude members of the public from the meeting, and duly accredited Press representatives must, so far as practicable, be afforded reasonable facilities for taking a report and (unless the meeting is not held on council premises or the premises are not on the telephone) for telephoning the report at their own expense. However, these provisions are without prejudice to any power of exclusion to suppress or prevent disorderly conduct or other misbehaviour at a meeting.[89]

Copies of the agenda and any reports for a meeting must be open to public inspection at least three clear days before the meeting, or when the meeting is convened, if convened at shorter notice. Part or the whole of a report may be withheld if it relates only to items during which, in the opinion of the proper officer, the meeting is likely not to be open to the public. Late items must be open to inspection from the time they are added to the agenda. Copies of a document are not, however, required to be open to public inspection until copies are available to council members. An item of business may not be considered at a meeting unless either the rules as to publication of the agenda are complied with or, by reason of special circumstances, which must be specified in the minutes, the chairman of the meeting is of the opinion that the item should be considered as a matter of urgency. At a meeting, a reasonable number of copies of the agenda and relevant reports must be available for the use of the public. If the Press so request they must be supplied with a copy of the agenda and relevant reports, such further statements or particulars as are necessary to indicate the nature of the items

---

[87] Schedule 12A, Part II, was amended by the Local Government (Access to Information) (Variation) Order 1992 (S.I. 1992 No. 1497), to provide that information shall not be exempt information by reference to Part I if it relates to proposed development for which the local planning authority can grant itself planning permission pursuant to regulation 3 of the Town and Country Planning General Regulations 1992 (S.I. 1992 No. 1492).

[88] In *R. v. Swansea City Council, ex p. Elitestone* (1993) 66 P. & C.R. 422, the Court of Appeal held that the "three clear days" for which the agenda and report for a meeting of a principal council must be open to public inspection did not include the day that the documents first became available for inspection.

[89] Local Government Act 1972, s.100A(6)–(8). *cf. R. v. Brent Health Authority, ex p. Francis* [1985] Q.B. 869: see § 4–26.

included in the agenda and, if the proper officer thinks fit in the case of any item, copies of any other documents supplied to members of the council in connection with the item.[90]

After a meeting, certain documents must be open to public inspection at **4–24** the council's offices for six years:

(1) the minutes, or a copy of the minutes, of the meeting, excluding so much of the minutes of proceedings during which the meeting was not open to the public as discloses exempt information;

(2) a summary prepared by the proper officer which provides a reasonably fair and coherent record of proceedings without disclosing exempt information, in circumstances where the exclusion of part of the minutes means that the part published does not provide such a record;

(3) a copy of the agenda; and

(4) a copy of so much of any report for the meeting as relates to any item during which the meeting was open to the public.[91]

If and so long as copies of the whole or part of a report for a meeting are required to be open to public inspection, copies of a list of the background papers for the report or the part of the report and at least one copy of each of the documents included in that list must also be open to public inspection. This applies both before and after the meeting, except that the relevant period after the meeting is four years, not six. Nothing in these provisions requires any document which discloses exempt information to be included in the list, and nothing requires or authorises the inclusion in the list of any document which includes confidential information within the meaning of section 100A. "Background papers" are those documents which disclose any facts or matters on which, in the opinion of the proper officer, the reports or an important part of the report is based and which have, in his opinion, been relied on to a material extent in preparing the report. They do not, however, include any published works.[92]

A document directed by any provision of Part VA to be open to inspection **4–25** shall be so open at all reasonable hours. No payment may be required except in the case of access to background papers, in which case a reasonable fee may be required for the facility. A person entitled to inspect a document may make copies of or extracts from it or require a photocopy to be supplied, upon payment of a reasonable fee. This does not, however, require or authorise any infringement of copyright, except that where the owner of the copyright is a principal council, nothing done in exercise of these rights shall constitute an infringement of copyright. Where any accessible document for a meeting is open to public inspection, or is supplied for the benefit of a newspaper, the publication thereby of defamatory matter contained in the document is privileged, unless the publication is proved to be made with malice. The rights conferred by Part VA to inspect, copy and be furnished

[90] *ibid.* s.100B.
[91] Local Government Act 1972, s.100C.
[92] *ibid.* s.100D.

with documents are in addition, and without prejudice, to any such rights conferred by or under any other enactment.[93]

Public Bodies (Admission to Meetings) Act 1960

4–26 This Act now applies only to parish or community councils, the Council of the Isles of Scilly and joint boards or joint committees which discharge functions of any of those bodies (or of any of those bodies and of a principal council, a joint authority or the Common Council of the City of London); parish meetings; the Land Authority for Wales; regional or district health authorities, and, if the order establishing a special health authority so provides, that authority; family practitioner committees as regards the exercise of their executive functions; and other bodies with power to levy a rate, other than bodies subject to Part VA of the Local Government Act 1972 regional and local flood defence committees; and advisory committees established and maintained under the Water Resources Act 1991 and customer service committees maintained under the Water Industry Act 1991.[94] It does not apply to residuary bodies or the London Pensions Fund Authority.[95] The 1960 Act[96] applies to committees of parish and community councils by virtue of section 100 of the 1972 Act.

Power is given to exclude the public from meetings whenever publicity would be prejudicial to the public interest because of the confidential nature of the business or for other special reasons stated in the resolution excluding the public and arising from the nature of the business. One particular ground for exclusion is specifically given, but without prejudice to the generality of the broad rule. A body may treat the need to receive or consider recommendations or advice from sources other than members, committees or sub-committees of the body as a special reason why publicity would be prejudicial to the public interest, without regard to the subject or purport of the recommendations or advice. A body is able under this provision to exclude the public and Press when receiving advice from its officers. The following case relates to these general provisions.

> *R. v. Liverpool City Council, ex p. Liverpool Taxi Fleet Operators' Association.*[97] Forty members of the public wished to attend a committee meeting, but there were only 14 seats available for Press, public and those making representations to the committee. The chairman suggested that the public be excluded because of the limited seating, and because it was desirable that those making representations be heard privately. The committee resolved to exclude members of the public apart from the Press "in view of the limitations of available space and in order that the business of the committee may be carried

---

[93] *ibid.* s.100H.
[94] Public Bodies (Admission to Meetings) Act 1960, Schedule, para. 1, as amended, *inter alia*, by the Local Government (Access to Information) Act 1985, Sched. 2, para. 4, the Water Act 1989, Sched. 25, para. 28, and the Water Consolidation (Consequential Provisions) Act 1991, Sched. 1, para. 10.
[95] Local Government Reorganisation (Miscellaneous Provision) (No. 6) Order 1986 (S.I. 1986 No. 1929); London Government Reorganisation (Pensions etc.) Order 1989 (S.I. 1989 No. 1815), Sched. 1, para. 8.
[96] As amended by the Local Government (Access to Information) Act 1985, Sched. 2, para. 6.
[97] [1975] 1 W.L.R. 701.

out satisfactorily". The applicants sought an order of certiorari to quash the council's decision in the matter considered at the committee meeting on the ground of non-compliance with the Public Bodies (Admission to Meetings) Act 1960. *Held*, (1) the reasons for exclusion amounted to "special reasons" within the Act, (2) the requirement that the reasons be stated in the resolution was directory and not mandatory. Accordingly, the fact that the second reason was expressed too vaguely to meet that requirement did not invalidate the resolution.

Furthermore, these provisions are without prejudice to any power of exclusion to suppress or prevent disorderly conduct or other misbehaviour at a meeting.[98] At common law, there is a power to exclude during a meeting anyone whose behaviour is disruptive or disorderly and, indeed, a power to prevent the entry of the public in circumstances where disruption or disorderly conduct is apprehended. In either case the power may be exercised where exclusion is necessary for the carrying on of the authority's business.[99]

Where a meeting is required to be open to the public, notice of the time and place of the meeting must be published at the offices of the body at least three clear days before the meeting, or when the meeting is convened if called at shorter notice. If the Press so request they must be supplied with a copy of the agenda, together with such further statement or particulars as are necessary to indicate the nature of the items on the agenda. There is no provision for access to background papers.

C. MEMBERS

There is little statute or common law regarding individual members of local **4–27** authorities. This is to be expected, for it is an incident of corporate status that the corporation, rather than the individuals who comprise it, has legal significance. A member in his individual capacity has no executive powers and can exercise no lawful authority. This is the position in law. There are, of course, a number of conventions and commonly accepted practices which govern the rights and powers of members in their individual capacities. Sometimes these matters are covered by standing orders—for example, they frequently give members a qualified right of inspection of land and premises owned by the local authority.

The principal legal rights relate to the inspection of documents and to the payment of allowances. The principal duty consists of an obligation to disclose any pecuniary interest a member may have in a matter before the council. Reference is also made in the following paragraphs to the statutory requirement as to attendance, insurance of members, and the procedure for challenging validity of office.

Inspection of documents

At common law, a member is entitled to see such documents as are **4–28** reasonably necessary to enable him to carry out his duties. He has no right to

---

[98] Public Bodies (Admission to Meetings) Act 1960, s.1(8).
[99] *R. v. Brent Health Authority, ex p. Francis* [1985] Q.B. 869.

a roving commission to examine the books or documents of a corporation—a mere curiosity or wish to see them is not sufficient.[1] Mandamus to compel disclosure will be refused if a member is not actuated solely by his public position but is inspired by an indirect motive, for example, a desire to assist a person in litigation with the council.[2]

R. v. Barnes Borough Council, ex p. Conlan.[3] A councillor strongly opposed his authority's decision to defend an action. He demanded access to the draft case prepared for counsel before it was submitted. *Held*, the common law right arises from a councillor's common law duty to keep himself informed of all matters necessary to enable him properly to discharge his duty as a councillor. The common law right is accordingly limited to access to such documents as might reasonably be necessary to enable him properly to perform his duties. The court refused to compel disclosure in this case.

R. v. Lancashire County Council Police Authority, ex p. Hook.[4] In 1976, a county council police committee received a report on complaints about the conduct of the Chief Constable. In 1977, H. was elected as a county councillor and appointed to the police committee. The committee subsequently dismissed the Chief Constable in the light of the findings of an independent tribunal. However, only an abridged form of the original report was released to the committee as then constituted. H. requested to see the unabridged report. The committee refused the request, acting on the advice of leading counsel to the effect that the suppressed parts of the report contained damaging and potentially defamatory matters of rumour and gossip that were not relevant to the committee's remaining statutory duties and might not now be protected by qualified privilege. The Court of Appeal (Waller and Dunn L.JJ., Lord Denning M.R. dissenting) *held* that though a councillor had an undoubted right in law to see council documents reasonably necessary to enable him to perform his duties, it was for the police committee in the exercise of its discretion to determine whether there was such reasonable necessity. Its decision here was based on proper advice and was not one which no reasonable authority could have made. *R. v. Barnes Borough Council, ex p. Conlan* (*supra*) was approved.

R. v. Birmingham City Council, ex p. O.[5] A councillor, in her capacity as chairman of the housing committee, obtained information which led her to doubt the suitability of a married couple to adopt a child whom they had been fostering. The councillor, who had no direct connection with the social services department, was held by the Court of Appeal to be not entitled, on the grounds of confidentiality, to see the files of the social services department relating to her case. However, this decision was reversed by the House of Lords, which *held* that she was entitled to see the files. A councillor, by virtue of her office, was entitled to have access to all written material in the possession of the local authority as long as she had good reason. In the case of a committee of which she was a member she would normally have good reason for access to all that

---

[1] *R. v. Southwold Corporation, ex p. Wrightson* (1907) 5 L.G.R. 888.
[2] *R. v. Hampstead Borough Council, ex p. Woodward* (1917) 15 L.G.R. 309.
[3] [1938] 3 All E.R. 226.
[4] [1980] Q.B. 603.
[5] [1983] 1 A.C. 578, H.L. See also *R. v. Hackney London Borough Council, ex p. Gamper* [1985] 1 W.L.R. 1229, where Lloyd L.J. held that there was no logical distinction between access to documents and attendance at meetings; *R. v. Sheffield City Council, ex p. Chadwick* (1985) 84 L.G.R. 563 (use of a special sub-committee composed of members of the ruling group for party political purposes could not justify exclusion of an opposition member of the parent committee); *R. v. Eden District Council, ex p. Moffatt, The Times,* November 24, 1988 (principles applicable to meetings of a council working party notwithstanding that it was not formally constituted as a council committee or sub-committee; no "need to know" on the facts).

committee's written material. In the case of other committees a "need to know" had to be demonstrated, and the matter in the last resort was for the council to determine, subject to judicial review under the *Wednesbury* principles. The council had decided to allow access and this decision had not been shown to be *ultra vires*.

The Local Government (Access to Information) Act 1985 creates a **4–29** statutory right of access to documents for members of "principal councils" as defined for the purposes of Part VA of the Local Government Act 1972.[6] Any document which is in the possession or under the control of a principal council and contains material relating to any business to be transacted at a meeting of the council or a committee or sub-committee of the council is to be open to inspection by any council member. However, there is no right of inspection where it appears to the proper officer that a document discloses certain classes of exempt information. Ten of the fifteen descriptions of exempt information specified in Part I of Schedule 12A to the 1972 Act[7] apply here. The Secretary of State may vary this list by order. This right of inspection is expressly stated to be in addition to any other rights that a member may have.[8]

The accounts[9] of a local authority or joint authority and of any proper officer may be inspected by any member and he may make a copy of them or take extracts from them.[10]

Monetary payments

The Local Government Act 1972[11] authorised the payment of allowances **4–30** in respect of attendance, financial loss, special responsibilities, travelling and subsistence to members of local authorities, joint authorities and other bodies. For elected members of the major local authorities, attendance and special responsibility allowances have been replaced, as from April 1, 1991, by arrangements under section 18 of the Local Government and Housing Act 1989. Otherwise, allowances continue to be paid under the provisions of the 1972 Act.

Allowances under the 1989 Act

The details of the new arrangements are found in the Local Authorities **4–31** (Members' Allowances) Regulations 1991.[12] Part II of the Regulations required each county, district and London borough council, and joint authority, and the Council of the Isles of Scilly to make a scheme, before April 1, 1991, for the payment of allowances to members. A scheme can be revoked, but must be replaced by another before the revocation takes effect. The scheme *must* provide for the payment of a "basic allowance" of the same

[6] See § 4–22.
[7] *ibid.*
[8] Local Government Act 1972, s.100F, added by the Local Government (Access to Information) Act 1985, s.1.
[9] See *Buckingham v. Shackleton* (1981) 79 L.G.R. 484.
[10] Local Government Act 1972, s.228, as amended by the Local Government Act 1985, Sched. 14, para. 24. As to the rights of persons interested and electors, see §§ 13–42 *et seq.*
[11] ss.173–178, as amended.
[12] S.I. 1991 No. 351, as amended by S.I. 1995 No. 553 and S.I. 1996 No. 469.

amount to each member. It *may* provide for "special responsibility allowances," which need not be the same, to such councillors as have such special responsibilities as are specified in the scheme, and fall into one or more categories specified in the regulations.[13] It *may* provide for attendance allowances payable in respect of the performance of such duties as are specified in the scheme and fall into one of the categories set out in the regulations.[14] An attendance allowance covers both the carrying out of the duty and the time spent travelling to and from the place where it is performed. The amount of the allowance may vary according to the time of day and the duration of the duty, but must otherwise be the same for all members entitled to the allowance in respect of a duty of any description. A scheme may provide that a member shall not be entitled to payment of more than one attendance allowance in respect of any period of 24 hours. The amount of the various allowances must be set out in the scheme.

Part III of the Regulations originally imposed financial restrictions on the aggregate paid by way of allowances, including an overall ceiling, a provision that no more than £7,500 can be paid to one member by way of special responsibility allowance, and ceilings on the proportions of the total spent on the different kinds of allowance within the scheme. These restrictions were removed by the 1995 amendments to the arrangements.[15]

A scheme may be amended at any time but may only be revoked with effect from the beginning of the financial year on April 1. A councillor may elect to forgo part of his entitlement to an allowance.

Allowances under the 1972 Act[16]

4–32   A member of a parish or community council who is a councillor[17] is entitled to receive an attendance allowance of such reasonable amount, not

---

[13] Acting as leader or deputy leader of a political group; presiding at meetings; representing the authorities at meetings of, or arranged by, any other body; membership of a committee or sub-committee that meets with exceptional frequency or for exceptionally long periods; acting as a spokesman for a political group on a committee or sub-committee; other activities requiring at least the same time and effort as any of the foregoing: *ibid*, reg. 9(1). The regulations originally *required* each scheme to provide for special responsibility allowances; this was replaced by a discretion by S.I. 1995 No. 553.

[14] Attendance at meetings of the authority, or any of its committees or sub-committees, or any other body to which the authority makes appointment or nominations; at other meetings authorised by the authority, one of its committees of sub-committees, or a joint committee (but not private political group meetings); at meetings of local authority associations; duties undertaken on behalf of the authority in pursuance of any standing order requiring a member or members to be present while tender documents are opened; in connection with the discharge of any function of the authority involving the inspection of premises or arrangements for the attendance of pupils at special schools. A member who otherwise receives remuneration cannot claim under the scheme: *ibid*. reg. 10(3), (3A), (4). Reg. 10(3A) was inserted by S.I. 1995 No. 553.

[15] S.I. 1995 No. 553.

[16] ss.173–178 (as amended by the Local Government, Planning and Land Act 1980, ss.24–26; the Miscellaneous Financial Provisions Act 1983, s.7; the Local Government Act 1985, Sched. 14, paras. 18–20, and Sched. 17; and the Local Government and Housing Act 1989, Scheds. 11 and 12).

[17] *i.e.* a member of the council from which payment is claimed: *Hopson v. Devon County Council* [1978] 1 W.L.R. 553 (district councillor appointed to committee of the county council not entitled to claim attendance allowance from the county council).

exceeding the prescribed amount, as the council may determine, for the performance of any approved duty.[18] Such a member may opt instead to receive a financial loss allowance,[19] which is a payment not exceeding the prescribed amount in respect of any loss of earnings necessarily suffered, or any additional expenses (other than for travelling or subsistence) necessarily suffered or incurred in performance of the approved duty.[20] Payment may not be made under these provisions to parish or community councillors in respect of duties performed within the parish or community or grouped parish or grouped community.[21]

A member of a local authority who is not a councillor is also entitled to a financial loss allowance.[22]

A member of a local authority is also entitled to travelling and subsistence **4–33** allowances in respect of expenditure necessarily incurred in the performance of approved duties. Except in the case of parish and community councils travelling expenses are payable in respect of all approved duty, whether within or without the area of the authority, and with no minimum distance, and a subsistence allowance is payable to a member where the expenditure on subsistence is necessarily incurred by him. In the case of parish and community councillors, travelling expenses and subsistence allowances are not payable unless the duty lies outside the parish or community or grouped parish or grouped community.[23] A local authority may pay allowances to any member attending a conference or meeting held inside or outside the United Kingdom for the purposes of discussing matters which in its opinion relate to the interests of the area or its inhabitants; this does not however extend to conferences or meetings convened by a commercial or political organisation.[24] These allowances are payable to members of a number of other prescribed bodies.[25] Maximum rates of

---

[18] 1972 Act, s.173(1)–(3), as amended.

[19] *ibid.* s.173A, as amended.

[20] *ibid.* s.173(4), as amended.

[21] *ibid.* s.173(6).

[22] This is claimed under s.173(4), as amended, by virtue of the saving in the Schedule to the Local Government and Housing Act 1989 (Commencement No. 11 and Savings) Order 1991 (S.I. 1991 No. 344). Members of a number of other prescribed bodies, other than councillors appointed to represent local authorities, may also claim financial loss allowance. These bodies include local valuation panels, joint committees, joint boards and the Cheshire Brine Subsidence Compensation Board: 1972 Act, s.177(1), as saved by the Schedule to S.I. 1991 No. 344, and *ibid.* reg. 19.

[23] 1972 Act, s.174, as amended by the Local Government, Planning and Land Act 1980, s.25(1), (2), Sched. 34.

[24] *ibid.* s.175, as amended by the 1980 Act, s.25(3), and the Local Government and Housing Act 1989, Sched. 11, para. 27.

[25] See *ibid.*, s.177(1), as substituted by the 1989 Act, Sched. 11, para. 28(1)–(3); the Local Authorities (Members' Allowances) Regulations 1991 (S.I. 1991 No. 351), reg. 3, as amended by S.I. 1996 No. 469, reg. 2, specifying the bodies listed in the Local Government and Housing Act 1989, s.21, except the Common Council of the City of London and successors to residuary bodies, and including National Park authorities; and prescribed bodies on which any of the former are represented. The prescribed bodies are a joint committee of two or more authorities, a joint education committee and the Cheshire Brine Subsidence Compensation Board.

payments for certain allowances are specified or prescribed by the Secretary of State.[26]

A local authority has power to defray travelling and other expenses reasonably incurred by or on behalf of any members in making official and courtesy visits, whether inside or outside the United Kingdom, on behalf of the council.[27]

4–34 The term "approved duty" is defined in regulations to cover the duties specified for the purposes of attendance allowance under the 1989 Act,[28] and any other duty approved by the body for the purpose of or in connection with the discharge of the functions of the body or any of its committees or sub-committees.[29]

There are several specific provisions as to conferences—section 83 of the Education Act 1944 enables local education authorities to organise and participate in conferences relating to education.

Disclosure of interest[30]

4–35 The principal duty imposed by statute on members relates to their interest in matters before the authority. A breach of this duty exposes a member to criminal proceedings. If a member has a pecuniary interest, direct or indirect, in any contract or proposed contract or other matter and is present at the meeting when it is discussed, he must disclose the fact and refrain from discussion and voting. An authority may, by standing orders, provide for the exclusion of such members, and this is commonly done, with a proviso that the member may remain if the majority of those present at the meeting so decides. A member has an indirect interest if:

(a) he or any nominee of his is a member of a company or other body with which the contract is made or is proposed to be made or which has a direct pecuniary interest in the matter under consideration; or

(b) he is a partner, or is in the employment, of a person with whom the contract is made or is proposed to be made or who has a direct pecuniary interest in the matter under consideration.

This does not apply to membership of or employment under a public body. In the case of married persons living together the interest of one is deemed to be the interest of the other if known to the other. Where the indirect pecuniary interest of a member arises from his beneficial interest in

---

[26] Local Authorities (Members' Allowances) Regulations 1991 (S.I. 1991 No. 351), reg. 17(2) (allowances under s.175 where there is no attendance allowance scheme), and reg. 18 (allowances under s.173(1) and (4)), as amended by S.I. 1995 No. 553 and S.I. 1996 No. 469. Rates for travelling and subsistence are prescribed by circular: see, *e.g.* DoE Circular 1/86.

[27] Local Government Act 1972, s.176, as amended. The section also authorises expenditure on the reception and entertainment of distinguished persons visiting the area.

[28] See n. 14, *supra*.

[29] The Local Authorities (Members' Allowances) Regulations 1991 (S.I. 1991 No. 351), reg. 16.

[30] Local Government Act 1972, ss.94–98. These provisions apply to local authorities, joint authorities and police authorities: s.98(1A), inserted by the Local Government Act 1985, Sched. 14, para. 13 and amended by the Police and Magistrates' Courts Act 1994, Sched. 4, para. 7; and to the Broads Authority: s.265A, inserted by the Norfolk and Suffolk Broads Act 1988, Sched. 6, para. 10(1). See also the National Code of Local Government Conduct (DoE Circular 8/90). See §§ 4–43, 4–44.

securities which he or his wife holds, then if the total nominal value of these shares does not exceed £5,000[31] (or one-hundredth part of the total nominal value of the issued share capital, whichever is the less), then whilst the member must declare his interest he is not precluded from speaking and voting.

It was a generally held view that the maxim *de minimis non curat lex* could **4–36** not be applied to the interest provisions and that members were under an obligation to declare an insignificant and trifling interest. The matter was cleared up by the Local Government (Pecuniary Interests) Act 1964, which provided that a member should not be treated as having a pecuniary interest by reason only of any interest (a) of that member, or (b) of any company, body or person connected with him, which was so remote or insignificant that it could not reasonably be regarded as likely to influence him in discussion and voting. This rule now appears in section 97(5). The section also excludes an interest which a member has merely as a community charge or council tax-payer, a ratepayer, inhabitant of the area, or water consumer, or as a person entitled to participate in any service offered to the public.[32]

There has been a good deal of case-law on this topic, and indeed this is to **4–37** be expected, for the statutory provisions are expressed in broad terms and without precise definition. The body of case-law helps in two ways. First, because the statutory provisions are in broad terms, the courts have looked at the mischief which the provisions were intended to prevent and have enunciated certain underlying notions. Lord Esher M.R. said in *Nutton v. Wilson*[33]:

> "I adhere to what I have before said with regard to provisions of this kind. They are intended to prevent the members of local boards, which may have occasion to enter into contracts, from being exposed to temptation, or even to the semblance of temptation."

Secondly, in applying the law to particular cases the courts have stated and developed a number of rules—to take one example, pecuniary interest means more than pecuniary advantage, and voting in a matter which is to the financial *detriment* of a member is therefore illegal. The first of the two cases which follow illustrate this rule; in the second the words "or other matter" in section 94 are considered.

Brown v. Director of Public Prosecutions.[34] A motion was submitted to the **4–38** Northampton County Borough Council to abolish a levy charged on council tenants who took in lodgers or sub-let, except in the case where council members were the tenants. An amendment was put to delete the exception, and six members who were tenants voted against the amendment. Three of the six took in lodgers. All six were found guilty of an offence against section 76(1) of the Local Government Act 1933. They appealed to the Divisional Court,

---

[31] Substituted by the Local Government and Housing Act 1989, Sched. 11, para. 23.
[32] 1972 Act, s.97(4), as amended by the Local Government Finance Act 1988 (Miscellaneous Amendments and Repeals) Order 1990 (S.I. 1990 No. 10) and the Local Government Finance Act 1992, Sched. 13, para. 32.
[33] (1889) 22 Q.B.D. 744 at p. 747.
[34] [1956] 2 Q.B. 369.

claiming that they had no pecuniary interest in the matter, but were merely subjecting themselves to a specific pecuniary detriment. Their appeal was dismissed. Lord Goddard C.J. said[35]: "It seems to me that section 76 (this is now section 94 of the Act of 1972) is drawn in such terms that it does not matter whether the result of the vote would be to the pecuniary interest or disinterest of the person voting. Parliament has not said that they may vote against their interest and not for their interest: it has said that they must not vote on any matter in which they have a pecuniary interest."

Rands v. Oldroyd.[36] R., a building contractor and a member of a local authority, decided in 1956 that his company, in which he had a controlling interest, would not in future tender for building contracts for the council. In 1957 a motion came before the council that when public tenders were invited the borough engineer should tender on behalf of his department, and that, where necessary, the direct labour force should be augmented. An amendment to delete that part of the motion dealing with an increase in the labour force succeeded, R. voting for the amendment. It was argued on behalf of R., *inter alia*, that "or other matter" in section 76 was to be construed *ejusdem generis* with "contract or proposed contract", or was at any rate to be construed as meaning a *specified* transaction or matter which, like a contract or proposed contract, gave rise to rights and liabilities. This argument did not prevail. Lord Parker C.J. said[37]: "I find it impossible to give any satisfactory narrower meaning, even if I were so minded, to these words 'any contract or proposed contract or other matter'. . . . the more one does consider the matter the more difficult and impossible it is to cut down those words 'or other matter' to something which was definable and which was a limitation on what appear to be general words. Bearing in mind the mischief aimed at by this Act, I do not think those words are to be read in other than a very general way, and I see no ground for introducing a limitation which, as I said, is one which cannot satisfactorily be defined."

4–39 *Declaration of interest.* A member may disclose his interest in two ways. He may give a general notice of some interest to the proper officer of the authority or he may give particular notice as the occasion arises. A general or particular notice must be recorded, and the book in which the record is kept must be open for inspection by members of the authority.[38]

Under section 19 of the Local Government and Housing Act 1989, the Secretary of State may by regulations require each member to give a general notice to the proper officer of the authority setting out such information about the member's direct and indirect pecuniary interests as may be prescribed by the regulations, or stating that he has no such interests. The regulations may prescribe further notices to be given to keep the information up to date. A failure to comply with the regulations or knowingly or recklessly providing false information is to be a criminal offence punishable on summary conviction by a fine not exceeding level 4 on the standard scale. Section 96 of the 1972 Act does not apply in relation to any notice given under the regulations, but the regulations may provide that such notices be deemed sufficient disclosure for the purposes of section 94 of the Act. The

---

[35] At p. 375.
[36] [1959] 1 Q.B. 204.
[37] At p. 212.
[38] Local Government Act 1972, ss.94(1), 96.

regulations require records of the information contained in the notices to be maintained and to be open to public inspection.[39]

The Secretary of State has made regulations under section 19 of the 1989 Act (the Local Authorities (Members' Interests) Regulations 1992[40]) with effect from May 8, 1992. These require each member to give the proper officer a notice about his direct and indirect pecuniary interests containing the information prescribed by the regulations. However, there is no provision under section 19(4)(a) that the giving of a notice under the regulations shall be deemed to be sufficient disclosure for the purposes of section 94 of the 1972 Act. The prescribed matters include information in respect of the councillor's employment, office, trade, profession or vocation; sponsorship; contracts; land; licences; corporate tenancies and interests in securities.

Local authorities are not able to impose any obligations on their members to disclose any interests other than those required to be disclosed by virtue of section 94 of the 1972 Act or regulations under section 19 of the 1989 Act.[41]

Breach of the rules. A member may commit one or more of three offences: he **4–40** may fail to disclose an interest, he may take part in consideration or discussion, and he may vote. There is no *duty* upon the proper officer to advise members who are in doubt as to their position, or to warn members who may be putting themselves in jeopardy of proceedings, but it is customary for him to put his specialised knowledge at a member's disposal if he is asked for guidance.

Failure to comply with the law renders a person liable on summary conviction to a fine not exceeding level 4 on the standard scale, unless he can prove that he did not know that the matter in which he had an interest was being considered. A prosecution cannot be instituted except by or on behalf of the Director of Public Prosecutions.[42]

There is no precise rule as to where responsibility lies for bringing alleged infringements to the notice of the Director of Public Prosecutions. Anyone may start inquiries simply by reporting the matter to the police, and it would equally be open to a council to resolve that the Director be informed of any incident in which members have apparently contravened the law. But it appears to be a fairly widely accepted view that a responsibility rests with the proper officer or chairman of a council to report a manifest contravention to the chief constable, who in turn will lay the facts before the Director of Public Prosecutions if in his view such course is warranted.[43]

---

[39] s.19 is based on the recommendations of the Widdicombe Committee: Cmnd. 9797, (1986), paras. 6.40–6.56; however, the government rejected the Committee's proposals that the requirements as to registration apply to non-pecuniary as well as pecuniary interests: Government Response (Cm. 433, 1989), paras. 4.5, 4.6.

[40] S.I. 1992 No. 618, as amended by S.I. 1996 No. 1215. The regulations apply to police authorities and National Park authorities.

[41] 1989 Act, s.19(5).

[42] Local Government Act 1972, s.94(3).

[43] See hereon Report of Bognor Regis Inquiry, 1965.

4–41 *Removal of disabilities.* The Secretary of State is empowered by section 97 to remove the disability imposed on members where the number of members disabled at any one time is so great as to impede the transaction of business or where it appears to him that it is in the interests of the inhabitants of the area that the disability be removed. General dispensations have been granted to enable council house tenants to speak and vote on matters of general housing policy (unless there are rent arrears of two months or more),[44] to enable parents of a child in full-time education to speak and vote on questions concerning school refreshments and transport,[45] and to enable members to speak and vote on matters concerning the statutory sick pay scheme under the Social Security and Housing Benefits Act 1982.[46] In the case of parish or community councils it is the district council which may exercise this dispensing power.

The disability of interested members is twofold: they may not take part in the consideration or discussion of the matter and they are precluded from voting. The Secretary of State or district council granting a dispensation may choose to remove only the first disability, enabling a member to give his view but not his vote.

A person may discuss, and vote on, an application for a dispensation even though he is one of the members concerned; and the chairman, vice-chairman or deputy chairman of a principal council is not to be regarded as having a pecuniary interest in the allowance paid him, nor is a member to be so regarded in relation to travelling, subsistence or attendance allowances.[47]

4–42 *Validity of votes cast by interested persons.* A difficult situation arises where a member is clearly under a disability yet persists in speaking and voting. The matter is by no means free from doubt but it is submitted that if the member is manifestly interested the chairman would be justified (and indeed may be under an obligation) to refuse to count his vote, for the "vote" has been cast illegally and therefore can be said not to be a vote at all. An authority for this view is found in *Nell v. Longbottom*.[48] In this case the mayor-elect of Louth voted for himself: it was held that his vote was invalid and could not therefore be regarded as having been cast. It would appear that where a council acts in a quasi-judicial capacity a vote cast by a member having an interest may render the decision void as contrary to natural justice on account of bias.[49]

4–43 *The National Code of Local Government Conduct.* The Redcliffe-Maud Committee on Local Government Rules of Conduct[50] recommended that

---

[44] DoE Circular 25/92. *Cf. Readman v. D.P.P.*, *The Times*, March 4, 1991.
[45] DoE Circular 9/92.
[46] *ibid.*
[47] Local Government Act 1972, s.94(5), as amended.
[48] [1894] 1 Q.B. 767. This case was decided on the somewhat different provisions of the earlier law.
[49] See *R. v. London County Council* [1892] 1 Q.B. 190; *R. v. Hendon Rural District Council, ex p. Chorley* [1933] 2 K.B. 696 and § 12–47.
[50] Cmnd. 5636 (1974).

existing rules, embodied in statutes and standing orders, should be supplemented by a nationally agreed code of conduct. A code was subsequently agreed by central government departments, the local authority associations in England and Wales and the Convention of Scottish Local Authorities.[51] The Widdicombe Committee on the Conduct of Local Authority Business recommended that the Code should be given statutory status and that new councillors in their declaration of acceptance of office should undertake to be guided by it in the performance of their functions.[52] These recommendations were implemented by the Local Government and Housing Act 1989.[53] Section 31 enables the Secretary of State, for the guidance of members of local authorities, to issue a code of recommended practice as regards their conduct. He must consult such representatives of local government as appear to him appropriate, and the Code must be approved by both Houses of Parliament. The Code, a revised version of its non-statutory predecessor, came into operation in 1990.[54]

The code is a guide for all members of councils and their committees and sub-committees, whether elected or co-opted. It emphasises, *inter alia*, that compliance with the law, standing orders and the code is the personal responsibility of each councillor. It is not enough to avoid actual impropriety; each councillor should at all times avoid any occasion for suspicion and any appearance of improper conduct. Although the law requires disclosure of pecuniary interests non-pecuniary interests can be just as important.

> "You should not allow the impression to be created that you are, or may be, using your position to promote a private or personal interest rather than forwarding the general public interest. Private and personal interests include those of your family and friends, as well as those arising through membership of, or association with, clubs, societies and other organisations such as the freemasons, trade unions and voluntary bodies."[55]

A private or personal non-pecuniary interest in a matter arising at a meeting should always be disclosed unless it is insignificant or shared with other members of the public generally as a ratepayer, chargepayer or inhabitant. If the interest is "clear and substantial" then, subject to specified exceptions,[56] the member should take no further part in the proceedings. In deciding whether an interest is clear and substantial,

---

[51] See DoE Circular 94/75.
[52] Cmnd. 9797, paras. 6.7–6.23; Government Response, Cm. 433, paras. 4.7–4.19.
[53] ss.30 and 31. s.30 amended s.83 of the Local Government Act 1972 to enable the form of declaration of office to be prescribed by order of the Secretary of State; see the Local Elections (Principal Areas) (Declaration of Acceptance of Office) Order 1990 (S.I. 1990 No. 932); the Local Elections (Parishes and Communities) (Declaration of Acceptance of Office) Order 1990 (S.I. 1990 No. 2477) and the Local Elections (Declarations of Acceptance of Office) (Welsh Forms) Order 1991 (S.I. 1991 No. 1169).
[54] The Code is set out as an Annex to DoE Circular 8/90.
[55] National Code, para. 9.
[56] See *ibid.* para. 12. Dispensations may be sought where the principles would require at least half the council or committee to withdraw or withdrawals would upset the electoral party balance to such an extent that the decision is likely to be affected: *ibid.* paras. 15–19.

> "you should ask yourself whether members of the public, knowing the facts of the situation, would reasonably think that you *might* be influenced by it. If you think so, you should regard the interest as clear and substantial."[57]

4–44 Interests should also be disclosed in dealings with council officers and at party group meetings. Where a councillor's business or personal interests are closely related to the work of one of the council's committees (or sub-committees), he should not seek or accept membership of that committee (or sub-committee) if that would involve him in disclosing an interest so often that he could be of little value to it or if it would weaken public confidence in the duty to work solely in the general public interest. A councillor should not seek or accept the leadership of the council, or chairmanship of a committee or sub-committee, if he, or an associated body, has a substantial financial interest in, or is closely related to, the business affairs of the council, committee or sub-committee. The Code emphasises that mutual respect between councillors and officers is essential to good local government, and that close personal familiarity between individual councillors and officers can damage this relationship. The Code also notes that it is a betrayal of trust to use confidential information for personal advantage or to the disadvantage of the council and that the receipt or offer of gifts should be reported to the appropriate senior officer.

The National Code may be incorporated into standing orders. Furthermore, a failure to comply with the Code may be regarded by the Commissioner for Local Administration[58] as maladministration by the authority, whether or not the Code has been incorporated in standing orders.[59] The Commission has issued Guidance on Good Practice on Members' Interests.[60]

Restrictions on voting

A member of a local authority,[61] a committee of a local authority or a joint committee of two or more local authorities (or a sub-committee) who has not paid an amount due in respect of community charge or council tax for at least two months after it has become payable, may not vote on matters concerning the level of council tax or the administration of the community charge or council tax. If present at a meeting, he must disclose the fact that this provision applies to him. He may, however, speak. Non-compliance is a criminal offence.[62] It is possible to obtain a dispensation from the Secretary of State or (in the case of a parish council or community council) from the district council or Welsh principal council respectively.[63]

---

[57] *ibid.* para. 11.
[58] *infra.* §§ 4–101—4–110.
[59] See Annual Reports of the English Commission for 1980–81, paras. 27–32; 1981–82, paras. 42–48; 1982–83, paras. 29–40 and Appendix 5.
[60] *Guidance on Good Practice 4*, reproduced in Part 8 of the *Encyclopedia of Local Government Law*. See also § 4–104.
[61] This term has the same meaning as in the Local Government Act 1972, ss.94 and 97.
[62] There are separate offences in respect of (1) failing to disclose and (2) voting: *D.P.P. v. Burton, The Times*, June 8, 1995.
[63] Local Government Finance Act 1992, s.106.

Attendance

A member who for six months fails to attend any meeting of the authority **4–45** or its committees or sub-committees or joint committees or joint boards with which it is linked ceases to be a member unless within that period his absence is approved by the authority. Time begins to run from the date of the member's last attendance. There are exceptions to the general rule in the case of military personnel in time of war or emergency.[64]

Insurance

An authority may insure members against personal accident suffered **4–46** whilst engaged on the authority's business.[65]

Validity of office

A procedure is available under section 92 of the Local Government Act **4–47** 1972, by which an elector can challenge the right of a person to act as a member of a local authority on the grounds that he is disqualified in law. Proceedings may be instituted in either the High Court or a magistrates' court where the person challenged has in fact acted as a member, and in the High Court only where the person challenged merely claims to be entitled to act. If it is proved that a defendant has acted whilst disqualified, a penalty not exceeding £50 (in the High Court) or level 3 on the standard scale (in a magistrates' court) may be imposed for each occasion on which he acted. If the case is heard by the High Court the court may declare the office vacant and grant an injunction restraining the defendant from acting further. Proceedings must be commenced before the expiration of six months from the date on which the defendant acted as a member—the period begins to run from the earliest date on which he acted.[66]

Where the issue is merely a claim to be entitled to act, the High Court may, if it finds that the member is disqualified, make a declaration to that effect and declare that the office is vacant, and it may grant an injunction restraining him from so acting.

Where proceedings are begun in a magistrates' court and the magistrates consider that the matter in question would be more properly dealt with by the High Court, they may order the discontinuance of the proceedings before them; and it is open to a defendant to apply to the High Court for an order that the proceedings in the magistrates' court be discontinued.

---

[64] Local Government Act 1972, s.85. This section applies to local authorities and joint authorities: s.85(4), inserted by the Local Government Act 1985, Sched. 14, para. 7; to the Broads Authority: s.265A, inserted by the Norfolk and Suffolk Broads Act 1988, Sched. 6, para. 10(1); and to National Park authorities: Environment Act 1995, Sched. 7, para. 8.

[65] Local Government Act 1972, s.140, as amended by the Local Government (Miscellaneous Provisions) Act 1982, s.39, Sched. 7. This power is available to residuary bodies and joint authorities: Local Government Act 1985, Sched. 13, para. 12(d) and Sched. 14, para. 16; to the Broads Authority: s.265A, inserted by the Norfolk and Suffolk Broads Act 1988, Sched. 6, para. 10(1); and to National Park authorities: Environment Act 1995, Sched. 8, para. 3(1).

[66] *Bishop v. Deakin* [1936] Ch. 409.

D. OFFICERS

4–48 The following matters are considered in this section: appointment; transfer of staff; tenure and remuneration; responsibilities; advice to the public; pensions; interest, corruption and accountability; political restrictions.

Appointment

Section 112 of the Local Government Act 1972[67] requires an authority to appoint such officers as it thinks necessary for the proper discharge by the authority of its functions and for carrying out commitments on behalf of other authorities. Where an officer is appointed for a particular purpose or to discharge a particular function he is referred to in the Act as the "proper officer". Subsection (3) provides that any provision requiring or empowering local authorities or committees of local authorities to appoint a specified officer was to cease to have effect. This was, however, subject to a number of qualifications. First, it did not extend to committees of local authorities of which some members are required to be appointed by a body or person other than a local authority. This meant that National Park officers had to be appointed under Schedule 17 to the Act of 1972[68] and fishery officers under the Sea Fisheries Regulation Act 1966. Secondly, four statutory requirements as to the appointment of particular officers are preserved in subsection (4).[69] They are as follows:

    (a) Chief education officers appointed under section 88 of the Education Act 1944.

    (b) Chief officers and other members of fire brigades maintained under the Fire Services Act 1947.

    (c) Agricultural analysts and deputy agricultural analysts appointed under section 67(3) of the Agriculture Act 1970.

    (d) Directors of social services appointed under section 6 of the Local Authority Social Services Act 1970.

Thirdly, subsection (3) did not extend to any other person appointed by a local authority to perform a specified function.

4–49 Since the 1972 Act, a number of provisions have required the appointment or designation of specified officers.

First, each food authority must appoint one or more public analysts, and each weights and measures authority must appoint a chief inspector of weights and measures, and such number of inspectors as may be necessary for the efficient discharge of its functions.[70]

Secondly, local authorities must secure that one of their officers has

---

[67] ss.112–119, concerning staff, apply to local authorities and joint authorities (s.146A, inserted by the Local Government Act 1985, Sched. 14, para. 16); to the Broads Authority (Norfolk and Suffolk Broads Act 1988, Sched. 6, para. 10(1)); (except for s.116) to residuary bodies (1985 Act, Sched. 13, para. 12(b)) and to National Park authorities: (Environment Act 1995, Sched. 7, para. 13(6)).

[68] See now the Environment Act 1995, Sched. 7, para. 14.

[69] There were originally seven: see the amendments effected by the Local Government Act 1985, Sched. 17, and the Weights and Measures Act 1985, Sched. 13.

[70] Food Safety Act 1990, s.27; Weights and Measures Act 1985, s.72.

responsibility for the administration of their financial affairs.[71] Those appointed on or after September 29, 1988, must have a recognised accountancy qualification.[72]

Thirdly, local authorities must designate one of their officers as the "head of their paid service," and one (who may be the head of paid service but not the chief finance officer) as "monitoring officer."[73]

A parish council and community council may, under section 112(5) of the **4–50** Local Government Act 1972, appoint one or more persons from among their number to be officers of the council, without remuneration.

A member of an authority cannot be appointed by that authority to any paid office, other than chairman or vice-chairman, and this bar continues for 12 months after membership ceases.[74] The bar applies notwithstanding that the service is given in an honorary capacity.

> *Att.-Gen. v. Ulverston Urban District Council.*[75] A member of the urban district council was appointed clerk of the council on an offer by him immediately to resign his membership and to serve in an honorary capacity for twelve months from the date of his appointment. *Held*, the appointment was to a "paid office."

Every appointment of a person to a paid office or employment under a local authority[76] or parish or community council must be made on merit.[77]

Nothing in the requirement to appoint on merit, or in any enactment, **4–51** standing order or rule of law by virtue of which it is unlawful to take a person's political activities or affiliations into account in making an appointment applies to the appointment of political assistants under section 9 of the Local Government and Housing Act 1989. Each authority may make up to three appointments of persons to act as assistants to a political group. The salary must not exceed £13,500 or a sum specified in regulations[78] and

---

[71] Local Government Act 1972, s.151 (county, county borough, district, London borough, parish and community councils); Local Government Act 1985, s.73 (joint authorities); Local Government Finance Act 1988, s.112 (police authorities and combined fire authorities); Local Government and Housing Act 1989, s.6 (Common Council of the City of London, in its capacity as local authority, police authority or port health authority). It also applies to the Council of the Isles of Scilly and waste disposal authorities. See further, § 12–11.

[72] Local Government Finance Act 1988, s.113; Local Government and Housing Act 1989, s.6.

[73] Local Government and Housing Act 1989, ss.4, 5. See further § 4–57.

[74] Local Government Act 1972, s.116, as amended by the Local Government Act 1985, Sched. 17.

[75] [1944] Ch. 242.

[76] Widely defined by s.21(1) of the Local Government and Housing Act 1989, as amended, to include county, district and London borough councils, the Common Council, the Council of the Isles of Scilly, combined fire authorities, police authorities, waste disposal authorities, joint authorities, successors to residuary bodies, the Broads Authority, joint boards and planning boards.

[77] Local Government and Housing Act 1989, s.7(1). This is subject to particular statutory provisions such as s.113 of the Local Government Act 1988 and s.6 of the 1989 Act (see § 4–47), and s.7 of the Sex Discrimination Act 1975 and s.5 of the Race Relations Act 1976 (discrimination permitted where sex or race is a genuine occupational qualification): see s.7(2).

[78] Currently £25,044; Local Government (Assistants for Political Groups) (Remuneration) Order 1995 (S.I. 1995 No. 2456).

there is a maximum term of office.[79] These appointments are to be filled in accordance with the wishes of the political group to which the post has been allocated under standing orders. Standing orders must prohibit the making of an appointment to any post until posts have been allocated to each qualifying group, the allocation of a post other than to a qualifying group and the allocation of more than one post to the same group. A group qualifies for a post if it has at least one-tenth of the membership and it is one of the three largest groups.[80] If only one group satisfies the one-tenth requirement, two appointments are to be made, one to that group and one to the next largest.[81] Powers may not be delegated under section 101 of the Local Government Act 1972 to a political assistant. No officer or employee of the authority may be required to work under the direction of a political assistant except for the purpose of providing secretarial or clerical services to that person or the relevant political group. The Secretary of State may make regulations as to the division of the authority into political groups, the membership of such groups, requirements as to the review of allocations from time to time and related matters.[82]

The Secretary of State may make regulations imposing a duty to adopt certain standing orders with respect to their staff.[83] He has made the Local Authorities (Standing Orders) Regulations 1993[84] with respect to the appointment of and disciplinary action against chief officers. Standing orders must now require that where the authority proposes to appoint a chief officer[85] and it is not proposed that the appointments be made exclusively from existing officers, a statement specifying the duties and the qualifications and qualities sought must be drawn up; the post must be advertised and copies of the statement sent on request; either all qualified applicants or a short list of such applicants must be interviewed; if there is no qualified applicant, the post must be re-advertised.[86] Every appointment must be made by the authority.[87]

Transfer of staff

4–52 Sections 257 and 258 of the Local Government Act 1972 made provision for the establishment of two staff commissions, one for England and one for

---

[79] *i.e.* where there are whole council elections to the authority, not later than the date of the annual meeting in the period of 12 months beginning with the first such election to be held after the person is appointed; where there are elections by thirds, not later than the date of the annual meeting in the period of 12 months beginning with the third anniversary of that person's appointment.

[80] If the number of other groups of the same size or larger is more than two, the authority must determine which of the groups of the same size should be allocated a post.

[81] If there are two or more groups with the next largest membership, the authority must determine which should be allocated the post.

[82] See Part III of the Local Government (Committees and Political Groups) Regulations 1990 (S.I. 1990 No. 1553), as amended by S.I. 1991 No. 1398, above, §§ 4–06, 4–07.

[83] Local Government and Housing Act 1989, s.8.

[84] S.I. 1993 No. 202.

[85] Non-statutory chief officers (see the 1989 Act, s.2(7)(a) or (b)) and political assistants can be excluded from these requirements by the standing orders.

[86] Standing orders can provide for these steps to be taken by a committee, sub-committee or chief officer of the authority (or, in the case of a joint appointment, the authorities concerned).

[87] Standing orders can provide for the appointment to be made by a committee, sub-committee or joint committee.

Wales. Their objectives were to promote arrangements for the transfer of staff from former authorities to new authorities on an equitable and efficient basis, to encourage the best means of recruitment and appointment of officers, and to safeguard the interests of the staff concerned. The commissions had no mandatory powers but advised the Secretary of State, and he in turn had power to give directions to any authority.

The transfer of staff on reorganisation was governed by regulations made **4–53** under section 255 of the Local Government Act 1972.[88] Section 259 of the Act required the Minister to make regulations for the payment of compensation to persons who suffer loss of employment or loss or diminution of emoluments which is attributable to provisions of the Act or delegated legislation made under it.[89] The loss must be attributable to the legislation and not to changes of policy by the new authorities.[90]

The transfer of staff on the abolition of the Greater London Council and the metropolitan counties is governed by Part VI (ss.50–56) of the Local Government Act 1985. The Secretary of State is advised by the London and Metropolitan Government Staff Commission, first established under the Local Government (Interim Provisions) Act 1984. The Secretary of State may by order designate a person or a class or description of employees for the purposes of their being transferred to the employment of a successor authority. Any person who at any time after July 16, 1985, is in the service of:

(a) the Greater London Council, a metropolitan county or district council, a London borough council or the Common Council of the City of London, or

(b) a new authority or a residuary body,

and who suffers loss of employment or loss or diminution of emoluments which is attributable to any provision made by or under the 1985 Act, is entitled to compensation.[91]

Similar arrangements apply in respect of authorities affected by structural changes under the Local Government Act 1992 and local government reorganisation in Wales. Under the 1992 Act, the Secretary of State may appoint one or more staff commissions by order,[92] and he has appointed the Local Government Staff Commission (England).[93] The Local Government (Wales) Act 1994 established the Staff Commission for Wales or

---

[88] Local Authorities, etc. (Staff Transfer and Protection) Order 1974 (S.I. 1974 No. 483) as amended.

[89] Local Government (Compensation) Regulations 1974 (S.I. 1974 No. 463). See also S.I. 1974 No. 54 (fire services); S.I. 1974 No. 759 (police); S.I. 1975 No. 353 (coroners).

[90] *Mallett v. Restormel Council* [1978] I.C.R. 844; *Harper v. North-West Water Authority* [1978] I.C.R. 884; *Walsh v. Rother District Council* [1978] I.C.R. 1216; *Fleming v. Wandsworth London Borough Council* (1984) 83 L.G.R. 277.

[91] 1985 Act, s.53. See the Local Government Reorganisation (Compensation) Regulations 1986 (S.I. 1986 No. 151), made under the Superannuation Act 1972, s.24. For provisions governing the transfer and compensation of staff following the abolition of the Inner London Education Authority, see the Education Reform Act 1988, ss.170–175.

[92] See 1992 Act, s.23.

[93] Local Government Staff Commission (England) Order 1993 (S.I. 1993 No. 1098). See also the *Policy Guidance to the Local Government Staff Commission (England)* (DoE, 1993) and the Local Government Charges for England (Staff) Regulations 1995 (S.I. 1995 No. 520).

Comisiwn Staff Cymru.[94] Compensation is payable for loss of diminution in remuneration in accordance with regulations made under section 24 of the Superannuation Act 1972.[95]

Tenure and remuneration

4–54   Officers appointed under the Local Government Act 1972 hold office on such reasonable terms and conditions, including terms of remuneration, as the authority appointing them thinks fit.[96] The more specific provisions in the Local Government Act 1933 were not repeated in the Act of 1972: officers are therefore directly subject to the general enactments relating to employment, in particular the Employment Protection (Consolidation) Act 1978, the Equal Pay Act 1970,[97] the Sex Discrimination Act 1975 and the Race Relations Act 1976, and to the terms of the contract of employment into which they have entered.

Special rules apply to particular groups. The remuneration and conditions of service of police officers are regulated by statutory provisions.[98] Similarly, discipline and dismissal and appointments and promotion in the fire services are the subject of statutory provisions.[99] Special provision must be made in standing orders in respect of disciplinary action against chief officers.[1] Such action (other than suspension on full pay for a period not exceeding two months) must be based on a report by a designated independent person appointed by agreement between the authority and the relevant officer, or, in default of agreement, by the Secretary of State.

4–55   The statutory discretion of local authorities to appoint officers on such terms and conditions and remuneration as they think fit is in practice substantially curtailed. The principle of fixing wages and salaries by means of joint negotiating machinery has extended as much to local authorities as to industry. There are over 40 separate negotiating councils or committees. The activities of the employers' side of local government wage-negotiating organisations are co-ordinated by the Local Government Management Board, which also provides a joint secretariat for these bodies, maintains liaison with other employers and obtains and disseminates information on service conditions. This is a non-statutory body, and its members are

---

[94] s.40. See also ss.41–45.
[95] Local Government Reorganisation (Compensation for loss of Remuneration) Regulations 1995 (S.I. 1995 No. 2837), as amended by S.I. 1996 No. 660; Local Government Reorganisation (compensation for Redundancy or Loss of Remuneration) (Education) Regulations 1996 (S.I. 1996 No. 1240).
[96] Local Government Act 1972, s.112(2).
[97] See, *e.g.*, *Ratcliffe v. North Yorkshire County Council* (1995) 93 L.G.R. 571 (school dinner ladies discriminated against in pay; need to compete commercially insufficient to establish that variation was genuinely due to a material factor other than sex).
[98] Police Act 1996, ss.50, 52, 59–64, and the regulations made thereunder. Members of police forces are excluded from the operation of much of the Employment Right Act 1996, such as, for example, the provisions as to unfair dismissal: 1996 Act, s.200.
[99] Fire Services Act 1947, ss.17, 18, 29, as amended by the Fire Services Act 1959, ss.5, 14 and Schedule and the regulations made thereunder.
[1] Local Authorities (Standing Orders) Regulations 1993 (S.I. 1993 No. 202), made by the Secretary of State under section 8 of the Local Government and Housing Act 1989 (see § 4–51).

appointed by the local authorities' associations and the employers' sides of negotiating bodies.[2]

The recommendations of joint negotiating committees are, however, not necessarily to be taken as the measure of "reasonableness" when the authority's discretion is being exercised. In *Carr v. District Auditor for No. 1 Audit District (Alston-with-Garrigill)*[3] Slade J. stated[4]:

> "I think that the sole function of any such recommendations can be, and can only be, to give guidance to the members of the council as to what may be considered to be objectively reasonable. It is only if a remuneration ... is objectively unreasonable that it becomes unlawful."

That payments in excess of national wage settlements are not necessarily *ultra vires* was confirmed in *Pickwell v. Camden London Borough Council*.[5] The payment of gratuities to serving officers is illegal.   **4–56**

> *Re Magrath*.[6] Durham County Council increased the county treasurer's salary by £100 in 1925. In 1931 the council paid him £700 apparently in respect of additional work which had come to him in 1920 and which had not been recognised from 1920 to 1925. The district auditor disallowed the sum of £700 and surcharged the members who voted for the payment. The Court of Appeal held that the district auditor was right in disallowing it as being retrospective and without consideration. Lord Maugham said[6a]: "It is, I think, clear that the local authority cannot out of public moneys give gratuities to their officers or servants over and above their fixed salaries and wages. ... Different considerations might well apply to a case where the officer or servant was asked to perform extra services in respect of a specified job or undertaking, on the understanding that as soon as the work was complete the authority would determine the amount of his special remuneration."

Special provision is made for payments in respect of premature retirement or redundancy.[6b]

Responsibilities

The responsibilities of officers to their councils and to the public at large   **4–57** have been the subject of judicial comment. The first (as to clerks) appear in *Re Hurle-Hobbs, ex p. Riley and Another* (1944),[7] the second (as to

---

[2] These matters were formerly dealt with by the Local Authorities' Conditions of Service Advisory Board (LACSAB) which merged with the Local Government Training Board (LGTB) and the Local Authorities Management Services and Computer Committee (LAMSAC) to form the Local Government Management Board. See the Local Government and Housing Act 1989, s.12, on the steps that must be taken to avoid conflicts of interest in staff negotiation.

[3] (1952) 50 L.G.R. 538.

[4] At p. 545. In the view of Lord Goddard C.J. and Parker J., the question turned on whether certain fees were or were not to be regarded as part of the clerk's salary.

[5] [1983] Q.B. 962. See § 13–24.

[6] [1934] 2 K.B. 415.

[6a] At p. 435.

[6b] Local Government (Compensation for Redundancy) Regulations 1994 (S.I. 1994 No. 3025) as amended by S.I. 1996 Nos. 456 and 1680); Local Government (Discretionary Payments) Regulations 1996 (S.I. 1996 No. 1680).

[7] This case is not reported but a full note of it appears in the appendix to *Hurle-Hobbs on District Audit*. For a critical discussion on this case, see Report of the Bognor Regis Inquiry, paras. 233 *et seq.* Today an officer would have the additional security of the unfair dismissal provisions of the Employment Rights Act 1996.

treasurers) in *Att.-Gen. v. De Winton*[8] to which reference is made at paragraph 12–12.

> *Re Hurle-Hobbs, ex p. Riley and Another.* The auditor surcharged interest amounting to £1,024 paid under an agreement which the auditor held had been entered into by the council as a result of the negligence and misconduct of an alderman of the council and the town clerk, both of whom the auditor found had withheld from the council material information which might have deterred the council from entering into the agreement. Lord Caldecote C.J. said: "Notwithstanding the strenuous contention of counsel on his behalf, the town clerk seems to me wholly to misconceive his duty when he says that although he thought that the matters I have discussed ought to have been disclosed to the council, he was entitled to stand by without taking such steps as were open to him merely because he would otherwise have been liable to dismissal from his office without notice.... The office of town clerk is an important part of the machinery of local government. He may be said to stand between the borough council and the ratepayers. He is there to assist by his advice and action the conduct of public affairs in the borough, and if there is a disposition on the part of the council, still more on the part of any member of the council, to ride roughshod over his opinions, the questions must at once arise as to whether it is not his duty forthwith to resign his office or, at any rate, to do what he thinks right and await the consequences. This is not so dangerous or heroic a course as it may seem. The integrity of the administration of public affairs is such that publicity may be safely relied upon to secure protection for anyone in the position in which the town clerk was said to have been placed."

4–58   The responsibilities of three designated officers, the head of paid service, the monitoring officer and the chief financial officer have been enshrined in statute. The first two are mentioned here and the third in Chapter 12.

The head of paid service is under a duty, where he considers it appropriate, to prepare a report on:

(a) the manner in which the discharge by the authority of its different functions is co-ordinated;

(b) the number and grades of staff required by the authority for the discharge of its functions;

(c) the organisation of the authority's staff; and

(d) the appointment and proper management of the authority's staff.

The report must be sent to each member, and considered by the authority within three months of its despatch to members. The latter duty cannot be delegated.[9]

The monitoring officer is under a duty to prepare a report to the authority, if at any time it appears to him that any proposal, decision or omission by the authority, or one of its committees, sub-committees or officers, or by a joint committee on which the authority is represented, constitutes or may give rise to a contravention of any enactment, rule of law or statutory code of practice, or maladministration under Part III of the Local Government Act 1974. The monitoring officer must consult so far as practicable with the head of paid service and the chief financial officer, and arrange for a copy to be sent to each member. The relevant authority or committee must consider the report within 21 days of its despatch to members, and ensure that no step is

---

[8] [1906] 2 Ch. 106.
[9] Local Government and Housing Act 1989, s.4.

taken for giving effect to any proposal or decision to which the report relates at any time while implementation is suspended. These duties cannot be delegated. Implementation is suspended until the end of the first business day after the day on which consideration of the report is concluded. The monitoring officer's duties must be performed personally, or where he is absent or ill, personally by a nominated deputy.[10] The report is not in itself binding on the authority, but members who decline to follow its recommendations may thereby knowingly act unlawfully within sections 19 and 20 of the Local Government Finance Act 1982.[11]

Each of these officers must be provided with such staff, accommodation and other resources as are, in his opinion, sufficient to allow his duties to be performed.[12]

Advice to the public

It is common practice for officers to give advice to members of the public **4–59** regarding prospective clearance and or road-widening schemes and the like. A responsible officer answering such an inquiry may well owe a duty of care towards the inquirer, so that if he negligently gives wrong information he and the authority may be sued for damages.[13]

Pensions

Employees of local authorities are subject to the provisions of the Superan- **4–60** nuation Act 1972[14] and the detailed regulations made thereunder.[15] Employers of local authorities and a large number of other bodies in the local government field are eligible to join or may be admitted to the Local Government Pension Scheme.[16] Pension funds are maintained by the contributions of employees, at prescribed percentages of remuneration, and equivalent contributions are made by employing authorities. Funds must be actuarially valued every three years and where a fund is deficient a further payment is required from the local authority. Members of the scheme may transfer from one local authority to another and to and from any employment with an approved non-local government scheme without detriment to their pension rights. The regulations provide for retirement pensions, retirement grants, surviving spouses' pensions, children's pensions and death grants. Benefits are based on years of service and on pensionable remuneration.

Interest, corruption and accountability

If it comes to the knowledge of an officer that a contract in which he has a **4–61** direct or indirect pecuniary interest (other than a contract to which he himself is a party) has been or is proposed to be concluded by the authority he must disclose this fact in writing.[17] An officer is forbidden, under colour of

---

[10] *ibid.* s.5.
[11] See §§ 13–22 *et seq.*
[12] Local Government and Housing Act 1989, ss.4(1)(b), 5(1)(b).
[13] See § 8–28.
[14] See especially ss.7–9. The schemes for local authority officers and for teachers are separate: *Secretary of State for the Environment v. Cumbria County Council* [1983] I.C.R. 52.
[15] Local Government Pension Scheme Regulations 1995 (S.I. 1995 No. 1019), as amended.
[16] See *ibid.* Part B and Sched. B.
[17] Local Government Act 1972, s.117(1).

his office or employment, to exact or accept any fee or reward other than his appropriate remuneration.[18] An officer who fails to disclose an interest or accepts a reward is liable on summary conviction to a fine not exceeding level 4 on the standard scale. An officer is under duty to account for money and property committed to his charge.[19]

An authority is under an obligation to take security in relation to officers likely to have control of money and may take security for other officers.[20] Security may also be taken for other persons not employed by the authority but likely to have control of money or property.

Political restrictions

4–62   The Local Government and Housing Act 1989 introduced restrictions on the political activities of officers holding "politically restricted posts". These officers include[21]:

(a) the head of paid service;

(b) the "statutory chief officers" (chief education officer, chief fire officer, director of social services, chief finance officer);

(c) a "non-statutory chief officer" (a person for whom the head of paid service is directly responsible or who, as respects all or most of his duties, reports directly to the head of paid service, the local authority, a committee or sub-committee);

(d) a "deputy chief officer" (a person who, as respects all or most of his duties, reports directly to a chief officer);

(e) the monitoring officer;

(f) political advisers;

(g) other officers included in the authority's list of officers to whom powers are delegated.

A person whose duties are solely secretarial or clerical, or otherwise in the nature of support services, is not to be regarded as a non-statutory or deputy chief officer.

They also include officers in a separate list compiled by the authority, comprising all earning £19,500 (or a higher amount specified by regulations[22]) or more (or the equivalent part-time), and all who regularly give advice to the authority, committee, sub-committee, or joint committee on which the authority is represented, or who regularly speak on behalf of the authority to journalists or broadcasters.

Head teachers, college principals, teachers and lecturers are not to be regarded as holding a politically restricted post or a post required to be included in the list maintained by the authority.

---

[18] *ibid.* s.117(2). See also the Public Bodies Corrupt Practices Act 1889 and the Prevention of Corruption Acts 1906–16.

[19] *ibid.* s.115.

[20] *ibid.* s.114.

[21] Local Government and Housing Act 1989 s.2.

[22] A higher amount has been specified by the Local Government (Politically Restricted Posts) (No. 2) Regulations (S.I. 1990 No. 1447), specifying spinal column point 44 of the scales for local government officers fixed by the National Joint Council for Local Authorities' Administrative, Professional, Technical and Clerical Services (or that point plus London or Fringe Area Allowances).

A person whose post is included in the authority's list may be exempted from the restrictions (1) by regulations made by the Secretary of State, or (2) by the adjudicator appointed by the Secretary of State under section 3.[23] The adjudicator's function in cases referred to him is to determine whether posts fulfil the criteria for inclusion in the authority's list.

The restrictions are (1) that the officer is disqualified from becoming or remaining a member of any local authority[24] or a Member of Parliament,[25] and (2) that his contract of employment is deemed to incorporate such requirements for restricting his political activities as may be prescribed by regulations.[26] These requirements include that the officer cannot announce (or permit the announcement of) an intention to stand as a candidate for Parliament, the European Parliament or local authority without resigning; cannot act as an election agent; cannot be an officer of or participate in the management of a political party, or any branch of such a party; and cannot canvass on behalf of a political party or in an election. An officer other than a political adviser may not speak to the public, or publish any written or artistic work of which he is author or editor, with the apparent intention of affecting public support for a political party. A political adviser may not do these things in circumstances likely to create the impression (respectively) that he is speaking as an authorised party representative, or that publication is authorised by a political party.

E. DISPOSAL OF LOCAL AUTHORITY BUSINESS

Part VI of the Local Government Act 1972[27] (and more particularly section 101) makes provision for the way in which local authorities may arrange for the discharge of their functions. All authorities (including parish and community councils) may discharge their functions through a committee, a sub-committee, through another authority, through joint committees and through officers, including officers loaned by another authority. In certain cases functions may be discharged through a joint board. There is no power to delegate to a member,[28] although powers may be delegated to an officer acting in consultation with a member.[29] **4–63**

---

[23] The first adjudicator to be appointed (in 1989) was William Jackson CBE, formerly Chief Executive of Kent Council. In 1996, he was reappointed to March 31, 1998: DoE Press Notice, March 21, 1996.

[24] Widely defined in s.21(1): see § 4–50, n. 76.

[25] 1989 Act, s.1(1), (2). This, *inter alia*, prevents "twin-tracking" with officers of one local authority being elected members of another.

[26] Local Government Officers (Political Restrictions) Regulations 1990 (S.I. 1990 No. 851), made under the 1989 Act, s.1(5), (6). The validity of these regulations was upheld by the Court of Appeal in *NALGO v. Secretary of State for the Environment, The Times,* December 2, 1992.

[27] Part VI (ss.101–110) applies to local authorities and joint authorities: s.101(13) amended by the Local Government Act 1985, Sched. 14, para. 15; and to the Broads Authority: Norfolk and Suffolk Broads Act 1988, Sched. 6, para. 10(1).

[28] *R. v. Secretary of State for Education and Science, ex p. Birmingham City Council* (1984) 83 L.G.R. 79. The Act cannot be construed as permitting a committee of one: *R. v. Secretary of State for the Environment, ex p. Hillingdon London Borough Council* [1986] 1 W.L.R. 967. *Cf. KLF (UK) Ltd v. Derbyshire County Council, The Times,* August 21, 1985, where it was held that a council could be bound by statements made by a member.

[29] See §§ 4–73 and 4–84.

Committees

4–64   An authority has a general power to arrange for a committee or a sub-committee to discharge any of its functions. The term "to discharge a function" is used in the Act of 1972 in place of the word "delegation" in earlier legislation. There is, in practice, still a division in decision-making into two groups: in the first are those decisions which are subject to confirmation of the council (the power to make such decisions will be spoken of here as "referred powers"), and in the second group are those which are effective as soon as they are made by the committee (the powers to make such decisions are referred to here as "delegated powers"). Technically, the former situation whereby matters are "referred" involves the delegation of a part only of the decision-making process, usually the part that consists of the investigation of the factual background, the consultation of interested parties and the receipt of expert advice. In *some* circumstances, this information must be fully summarised so that it may be considered by the council.

Osgood v. Nelson.[30] Allegations of neglect in the performance of his duties as Registrar of the Sheriff's Court of The City of London were made against O. The Court of Common Council of the City referred the matter to a committee, which heard evidence and submissions and reported that in their opinion irregularities had occurred. The council resolved to dismiss O. They had before them the committee's report and a full transcript of evidence. *Held*, this mode of proceeding was perfectly fair, and did not constitute a violation of the rule against delegation.

Jeffs and others v. New Zealand Dairy Production and Marketing Board.[31] The Board had power to define zones from which particular factories could get cream and milk. The Board set up a committee of three of its members to investigate the question of supply to two factory-owning dairy companies. The committee acting on its own initiative held a public hearing at which farmers and other interested parties gave evidence and made oral and written submissions. The farmers opposed zoning. The committee made a written report, and recommended certain zonings, which were accepted by the Board without alteration. The report did not record, even in a summary form, the evidence given at the hearing, but did state the submissions that had been made. The Board conceded that it was under a duty to act judicially in determining zoning questions affecting the rights of individuals. The Privy Council held that the Board acted in breach of natural justice in failing to hear the interested parties, but that they would have complied with natural justice had the evidence and submissions been fully summarised. The appointment of a person or persons to hear evidence and submissions was appropriate where the credibility of witnesses was not involved.

4–65   R. v. Chester City Council and others, ex p. Quietlynn Ltd.[32] The applicant challenged the decisions of a number of authorities to refuse sex shop licences under the Local Government (Miscellaneous Provisions) Act 1982, on a variety of grounds. One ground raised against Chester City Council was that the committee that decided to refuse the licence had delegated the task of conducting the hearing required by para. 10(19) of Schedule 1 to the 1982 Act to a panel or sub-committee of five members: all that was before the committee

---

[30] (1872) L.R. 5 H.L. 636.
[31] [1967] 1 A.C. 551.
[32] *The Times*, October 19, 1983 and (1984) 83 L.G.R. 308. *Applied in R. v. Birmingham City Council, ex p. Quietlynn Ltd* (1985) 83 L.G.R. 461, 491–492, 501–502.

was the recommendation of the panel that a licence should be refused on the grounds that the grant of a licence would be inappropriate having regard to the character of the locality and that the number of sex establishments appropriate for the locality was nil. Woolf J. held that this procedure would not have been adequate had the statute contemplated a judicial hearing. Similarly it would not have been adequate for the majority of quasi-judicial hearings. Conversely, it would be sufficient in respect of purely administrative matters. The consideration of an application for a licence was not a purely administrative matter and there was a duty to act fairly: in the ordinary way it would be preferable for the committee to be provided with a summary of the applicant's representations as well as the sub-committee's recommendation. However, on the facts of the case there was no actual unfairness to the applicants: the committee's decision was substantially one of policy, based on the characteristics of the locality which could be expected to be known to the committee; there was no suggestion that the applicants had made any representations to the panel which were relevant to the actual grounds for refusal; the members of the panel were members of the committee and present at the committee meeting and could have provided further information had it been sought. This ground of challenge failed. Woolf J.'s decision on this point was reversed by the Court of Appeal. Stephen Brown L.J. held that the appellant's representations should have been considered by the committee and since no report of any kind had been made to it there was a procedural irregularity which could not be cured by the fact that members of the committee could have been expected to know the characteristics of the locality and that they could have asked if they wished for details from the panel members present.

In other circumstances decisions taken under referred powers when **4–66** confirmed become in all respects the decisions of the council and whatever consideration was given to matters in committee is deemed to have been given them by the council.

> *Goddard v. Minister of Housing and Local Government.*[33] The plaintiff sought to challenge the validity of a compulsory purchase order and put forward two contentions, one of which was this: that the council never applied its mind to the issue, for the resolutions of the committees concerned were merely "rubber-stamped," whereas the council were obliged by statute to "satisfy themselves." This point did not succeed. The court held that the council, *acting through their committees*, were satisfied.[34]

Where a council delegates specific matters to committees (where, in the **4–67** terms of the Act, a council discharges any of its functions by a committee) the decision of the committee is effective forthwith.[35] It is specifically provided that an arrangement of this kind does not prevent the authority itself from exercising the relevant function. This right to withdraw delegation must, of course, be subject to any third-party rights which have come into being (by way of contract, for example) in consequence of a committee's decision. Where an authority has delegated a function to a committee then, unless it otherwise directs, the committee may in turn delegate that function to a sub-committee or to an officer.

---

[33] [1958] 1 W.L.R. 1151.

[34] See further, de Smith, Woolf and Jowell, *Judicial Review of Administrative Action* (5th ed.), pp. 359–360, where it is noted (note 27) that the local authority in *Goddard* was not obliged to hold a hearing as to the matters of which it had to be "satisfied".

[35] A council may delegate to a "sub-committee": *Southwark London Borough Council v. Peters* (1971) 70 L.G.R. 41.

There are a number of limitations on an authority's power to delegate which apply in relation to the discharge of functions whether by a committee, a sub-committee, an officer or some other authority. For example, the following powers may only be exercised by the authority: the power to levy or issue a precept for a rate; functions in setting amounts for council tax and issuing a precept under the Local Government Finance Act 1992; the power to approve schemes for local lotteries; the duty to consider a report of the chief finance officer under section 114 of the Local Government Finance Act 1988; the duty to consider a report of the head of paid service under section 4 of the Local Government and Housing Act 1989; the duty to consider a report of the monitoring officer under section 5 of the 1989 Act; the determination of borrowing limits under section 45 of the 1989 Act; the power to designate land as a litter control area; and the duty to consider an auditor's report under section 5 of the Local Government Act 1992.[36]

4–68   The exercise of delegated powers by committees is illustrated in the case which follows:

> *Battelley v. Finsbury Borough Council.*[37] The local authority had appointed a works committee and by its standing orders it was provided that: "The works committee shall be responsible for . . . appointment and management of the staff of the borough engineer's department." The plaintiff, having applied for the post of assistant road superintendent, was interviewed by the works committee which resolved that the plaintiff should be appointed to the post. He was notified by the Town Clerk that he had been selected "subject to confirmation". Subsequently the committee appointed someone else. The plaintiff brought an action for breach of contract. *Held*, on the true construction of the standing orders the local authority had delegated to the works committee the power to appoint the plaintiff to the post, and the committee, having entered into a contract to that end, was in breach.

It will be noted that a standing order was the instrument of delegation and that the words "shall be responsible for" constituted an act of delegation.

Joint committees

4–69   Authorities are enabled to discharge their functions through joint committees,[38] and such committees have a power to co-opt to their membership. Expenses of a joint committee are defrayed by local authorities in such proportions as they may agree. If they cannot agree, it is for the district council to determine the proportions if the joint committee is appointed by the councils of parishes or communities or groups of parishes or communities in the same district. If the appointing authorities are all principal authorities or if the councils of parishes or communities are situated in two or more districts then, if the parties cannot agree, the apportionment is determined by an arbitrator agreed by the authorities or,

[36] Local Government Act 1972, s.101(6), as amended by the Local Government and Housing Act 1989, s.45(5); Local Government Finance Act 1992, s.67; Lotteries and Amusements Act 1976, s.6(3); Local Government Finance Act 1988, s.115(4); Local Government and Housing Act 1989, ss.4(5), 5(5), 45(4); Environmental Protection Act 1990, s.90(5); Local Government Act 1992, s.5(4).
[37] (1958) 56 L.G.R. 165.
[38] Local Government Act 1972, s.102.

in default of agreement, by an arbitrator appointed by the Secretary of State.[39]

The constitution of a joint committee is generally contained in a formal **4-70** agreement entered into by the authorities concerned. The agreement commonly prescribes the number of members of the joint committee, the number of members which each authority may appoint, the terms of office, and other related matters. The joint committee has no corporate status and it cannot therefore hold property. Any property which it uses vests in one of the constituent authorities which holds it in trust for the rest. Alternatively, the constituent authorities may hold the property jointly. A member of a local authority appointed to a joint committee of which the authority forms part ceases to be a member of that committee when he ceases to be a member of the authority. There is a specific power to appoint joint advisory committees.

Statutes may make provision for the appointment of a joint committee for a particular purpose. For example, there is a joint planning committee for Greater London.[40]

Joint boards

A joint board is fundamentally different from a joint committee. There is **4-71** no general power to create joint boards. Specific powers are contained in a number of statutes and in each case the rules as to the constitution are stated in the enabling statute. A power is contained in the Local Government Act 1972, enabling the provisions of the Act to be extended to joint boards, so that the affairs of joint boards may be administered in much the same way as the affairs of local authorities.[41] A joint board is a corporate body, created by order of a Minister, requiring in many cases the approval of Parliament. It has perpetual succession, a common seal, and it can hold land. Unlike a joint committee a joint board cannot be dissolved by agreement. It has independent financial powers, including the power to borrow, and obtains the money it needs from constituent authorities by means of precepts. The term of office of members of a joint board depends on the provisions of the Order by which it is established.[42]

The following are examples of joint boards. The Public Health Act 1936[43] empowers the Secretary of State by order to create a united district under a joint board for any of the purposes of that Act, and certain other public health statutes. A board constituted in this way is declared by the statute to be a corporate body by such name as the order determines, having perpetual succession, a common seal and a power to hold land. Expenses are defrayed out of a common pool to be contributed by the constituent authorities in proportion to their rateable values, and a power is given to issue levies on the

---

[39] *ibid.* s.103.
[40] Town and Country Planning Act 1990, s.3.
[41] Local Government Act 1972, s.241.
[42] *R. v. Peak Park Joint Planning Board* (1976) 74 L.G.R. 376: member appointed to the board by the county council could not be removed by the council before expiry of the term of office specified in the Order.
[43] ss.6 and 309.

constituent authorities for the amounts due. Section 2 of the Town and Country Planning Act 1990[44] empowers the Secretary of State to create a joint planning board to act as the local planning authority over the areas of a number of planning authorities, but unless the councils agree he must hold a public inquiry and the order he makes must be laid before Parliament. If either House within 40 days resolves that the order be annulled, then it ceases to have effect.

Delegation to officers

4–72 The Local Government Act 1972 for the first time gave a general power to local authorities to discharge any of their functions through officers. Several earlier statutes had enabled certain officers to take decisions on behalf of a local authority. Section 17 of the Public Health Act 1961, for example, gave summary powers to medical officers of health and public health inspectors to deal with stopped-up drains, and section 64 of the Town and Country Planning Act 1968 enabled a local planning authority to delegate certain of its decision-making powers to named officers. The implication was, of course, that, in the absence of a direct statutory power, an officer could not act except with the authorisation of his council. This situation made nonsense of the administrative system, but there was a widely accepted practice that whatever action an officer took within the scope of his general authority, or within the terms of a policy settled by the council, would be taken as the act of the council itself. This practice worked sensibly enough on the assumption that the act would be ratified by the council should ratification be necessary.[45] Indeed, as will be seen in Chapter 7, an authority may, in limited circumstances, be bound even against its will by a contract entered into by an officer within his ostensible authority.[46]

4–73 The power to delegate to officers is of particular importance given the absence of any power to delegate to a member (as distinct from a committee or sub-committee).[47] Standing orders commonly provide for a power to be delegated to an officer acting in consultation with a specified member (commonly a committee or sub-committee chairman). Such arrangements are lawful provided that the officer does not simply act under the dictation of the member. This emerges from the following cases.

> *R. v. Port Talbot Borough Council, ex p. Jones.*[48] The council delegated power to grant council tenancies to the chief officer, acting in consultation with the chairman and vice-chairman of the housing tenancy committee. The chief officer granted a tenancy of a three-bedroomed council house to a recently divorced councillor. This decision involved giving her application priority, other than in accordance with the council's housing policy. The chief officer deposed that had it not been for pressure placed upon him by councillors, especially the committee chairman, he would have refused to grant the tenancy.

---

[44] As amended by the Local Government (Wales) Act 1994, s.19, and the Environment Act 1995, Sched. 10, para. 32(2), and Sched. 22, para. 42.

[45] See below, §§ 4–75—4–84.

[46] See §§ 7–15, 10–14—10–18.

[47] See § 4–63.

[48] [1988] 2 All E.R. 207.

Nolan J. granted certiorari to quash the decision to grant the tenancy on the ground, *inter alia*, that the dominant role had plainly been occupied by the committee chairman, who could not lawfully exercise the delegated power.

Fraser v. Secretary of State for the Environment and the Royal Borough of Kensington and Chelsea.[49] A standing order of the Royal Borough of Kensington and Chelsea provided that urgent action arising between meetings or when the council was in recess could be taken by the Town Clerk or the appropriate Director or Head of Service provided that the written approval of the Mayor or the appropriate committee or sub-committee chairman was obtained. The Director of Planning and Transportation, with the written approval of the Chairman of the Town Planning Committee, issued an enforcement notice directed to the appellant. The appellant argued that the standing order was *ultra vires* as it required approval by a councillor, and not merely consultation. Nolan J. *held* that the arrangement was lawful. His Lordship noted that the officer here had formed his opinion before approaching the chairman of the planning committee for his approval. That approval having been obtained, it was the officer alone who gave the instruction. There was nothing in this procedure which exceeded the delegation or transfer of functions contemplated by section 101.

It is now the practice of authorities to specify areas of decision-making **4–74** which fall to specified officers,[50] but the practical question will remain as to the binding effect of an officer's act beyond the scope of formal delegation. These matters are considered at paragraphs 10–14 to 10–18.

Ratification

According to the law of agency, where an agent purports to act on behalf **4–75** of a principal, but in fact lacks power to bind the principal, the principal may nevertheless be bound by that act, with retroactive effect, if he subsequently ratifies it. The basic conditions are:

(a) the principal must be in existence and capable of being ascertained at the time of the act;

(b) the principal must be competent at the time when the act was done by the agent;

(c) it must be shown that the agent was acting on the principal's behalf.[51]

The extent to which these principles are applicable to the acts of an officer or member purportedly taken on behalf of a local authority is uncertain. It is clear that they do not apply where the act is *ultra vires* the authority.

Co-operative Retail Services Ltd v. Taff-Ely Borough Council.[52] The Clerk to **4–76** the Council erroneously took the view that a resolution of the council amounted to a grant of planning permission for a Tesco superstore. In fact the resolution indicated that while the borough council favoured the application, it was a "county matter" and so had to be referred to a joint meeting with the county council.[53] Without consulting the council or the planning committee, he issued the standard notice, backdated, which stated that the council had granted

---

[49] (1987) 56 P. & C.R. 386.
[50] Principal councils are obliged to maintain a list, open to public inspection, of powers delegated to officers: s.100G(2), (4); § 4–96, *infra*.
[51] See *Bowstead on Agency* (15th ed.), pp. 51–84.
[52] (1979) 39 P. & C.R. 223.
[53] See the Local Government Act 1972, Sched. 16, para. 15.

permission. The council subsequently resolved that "the action taken by the clerk in issuing the planning consent be confirmed". The Court of Appeal held that the council had not granted planning permission originally; that the notice issued by the clerk was a nullity; that the "confirmation" had not amounted to a "ratification" but was simply a confirmation of his action in issuing a document giving notice of a non-existent resolution to grant permission; and that, in any event, an act that was *ultra vires* could not be ratified. This decision was subsequently confirmed when the House of Lords unanimously dismissed an appeal by the borough council: *Att.-Gen. ex rel. Co-operative Retail Services v. Taff-Ely Borough Council.*[54]

Furthermore, they do not apply where an authority purports to ratify the decision of a person to whom there is no power to delegate. In *Barnard v. National Dock Labour Board*,[55] dock workers were suspended by a port manager. The Court of Appeal held that this power was only exercisable by the local dock labour board. There was no power of delegation. The court also rejected an argument that the suspensions had been ratified by the board. Denning L.J. stated[56]:

"... if the board have no power to delegate their functions to the port manager, they can have no power to ratify what he has done. The effect of ratification is to make it equal to a prior command; but just as a prior command, in the shape of a delegation, would be useless, so also is a ratification."

4–77 These points were illustrated by the following cases:

Webb v. Ipswich Borough Council.[57] A purported control order under section 379(1) of the Housing Act 1985 was executed by a council officer to whom authority had not been delegated. The council argued that this was subsequently ratified by the appropriate sub-committee with retrospective effect, but the Court of Appeal rejected this argument. Ratification would not be effective if an individual's legal rights had already been affected by the invalid act: a control order came into force the moment it was made. In both the *Miller-Mead* and *B. & Q.* cases,[58] the ratification was made before any effective step in the action had taken place.

R. v. Rochester upon Medway City Council, ex p. Hobday.[59] The council, on November 17, 1987, resolved to issue an enforcement notice in respect of land being used as a market site. In the erroneous belief that the owners were entitled to use the land for that purpose for 14 days, issue of the notice was delayed until the 15th day. On March 30, 1988, the council was advised that the owners were not so entitled, and resolved as a matter of urgency to issue a stop notice. A council officer served an enforcement notice and a stop notice on April 8. The stop notice was subsequently withdrawn, and replaced, successively, by a second and a third stop notice. An application for judicial review to quash the enforcement notice and the third stop notice was dismissed. Rose J. held (1) that the November 17 resolution was *ultra vires* as the council on that date (albeit wrongly) believed that no breach of planning control had yet occurred; (2) that an *ultra vires* act could not be ratified; but (3) that the March 30 resolution could properly be construed as including a fresh decision to issue

---

[54] (1982) 42 P. & C.R. 1.
[55] [1953] 2 Q.B. 18. The decision of Forbes J. in *R. v. Brent Health Authority, ex p. Francis* [1985] Q.B. 869 appears to be inconsistent on this point.
[56] At p. 40.
[57] (1989) 21 H.L.R. 325.
[58] §§ 4–79 and 4–81, *infra.*
[59] (1989) 58 P. & C.R. 424.

an enforcement notice. This seems similar in result to the *B. & Q.* decision, and it is submitted that it is preferable (following the approach of Rose J.) to avoid the use of the term "ratification" in respect of decisions such as that of the policy committee in the *B. & Q.* case and the March 30 resolution in *ex p. Hobday.*

The position with respect to the ratification of an officer's act in **4–78** commencing legal proceedings is unclear. In the following cases it was held that prior authorisation is necessary:

> *St Leonard's Vestry v. Holmes.*[60] A notice was served by a sanitary inspector without authority; and, later, a second notice was served by him after consultation with some members of a sub-committee. But no consideration was given by the vestry before the work was undertaken. After the work was completed, the action of the sub-committee and of the inspector was approved by resolution of the vestry. In proceedings to recover from the owner the cost of executing the work, the vestry failed. Day J. said[61]: "It is important that the vestry should exercise a discretion in each case, and it is not enough that the inspector does what he pleases, and then relies on his acts being afterwards approved by the vestry."
>
> *Bowyer, Philpott & Payne, Ltd. v. Mather.*[62] Proceedings were begun by an inspector. He had not been authorised to institute these particular proceedings and he had received no general authority to prosecute. *Held,* subsequent ratification by the authority was not sufficient.

These cases were, however, distinguished by the majority of the Court of Appeal in the following decision:

> *Warwick Rural District Council v. Miller-Mead.*[63] The authority's solicitors **4–79** issued a writ against the owner of a caravan site under section 100 of the Public Health Act 1936, which enabled proceedings to be taken in the High Court where "the authority are of the opinion that summary proceedings would afford an inadequate remedy". Three days after the issue of the writ the council met and considered a report of its officers on the prevailing conditions. The council authorised proceedings in the High Court "being of opinion that the summary proceedings would afford an inadequate remedy". The preliminary objection was taken that at the date of the issue of the writ there was no resolution of the council. *Held,* the proceedings were correctly instituted for the authority could ratify by its subsequent resolution the earlier act of its servant. The court observed that at the date of the issue of the writ, the authority, had it applied its mind to the question, was capable of issuing the writ.

This decision was affirmed by the Court of Appeal,[64] but on narrower grounds. The court looked at the precise terms of section 100 rather than to the general rules of ratification. The Master of the Rolls said[65]:

> "I do not think that the terms of the section should be so strictly construed as to require in all cases that the formal expression of the local authority's requisite opinion should have preceded in time the issue of the writ, provided, at any rate, that such formal opinion is expressed before any effective stage in the proceedings comes before the court; and, if I were wrong in that view, I think that, on the facts of the present case, including the recorded minutes ... the

---

[60] (1885) 50 J.P. 132.
[61] At p. 134.
[62] [1919] 1 K.B. 419.
[63] [1961] Ch. 590.
[64] [1962] Ch. 441.
[65] At pp. 455–456.

court should properly hold that the opinion formally expressed ... had been held in truth three days before; and that the council so intended to record."

4–80 His Lordship distinguished *St Leonard's Vestry v. Holmes* and *Bowyer, Philpott & Payne Ltd v. Mather*[66] on the following grounds.[67]

> "We are not, as I think, here concerned with the authority of some person or persons to institute proceedings on behalf of the council or in the council's name, but with the much narrower and distinct point not covered by any direct authority, namely: whether the cause of action which the council asserted in the indorsement of the writ was a cause of action which the council could have possessed at any relevant time. Since the writ was issued in the council's name by its duly constituted solicitors, no such question arises as that debated in *Bowyer v. Mather*, and if the only question was as to the solicitors' authority to institute proceedings in the council's name, which the council was itself perfectly competent to bring, then it would in my judgment be clear, upon principle and authority, that subsequent ratification of the solicitors' action by the council would relate back to the date of the issue of the writ. ... [N]o question here arises of the authority of the solicitors acting for the council to issue a writ in the council's name, for no evidence before the court was directed to that point. ... I accept Mr. Francis' submission that the council, being a *persona ficta* established by section 32 of the Local Government Act 1933, is competent in the ordinary course to institute legal proceedings in its own name and the solicitors for the council regularly appointed as such are entitled prima facie to act in that capacity in connection with such proceedings."

Accordingly, the case is essentially an authority on the interpretation of section 100. It is submitted that the suggestion that the doctrine of ratification would apply to the subsequent approval of the solicitors' act in issuing a writ (1) was *obiter*, given that there was no evidence on the point, and (2) is inconsistent with *St Leonard's Vestry v. Holmes* and *Bowyer, Philpott & Payne Ltd v. Mather*[68] unless a distinction is to be drawn between the subsequent approval of an act of an officer and the subsequent approval of an act of a solicitor. It is suggested, however, that a local authority is no more entitled to delegate a decision to institute proceedings to a solicitor than the authorities were entitled to delegate such decisions to inspectors in the two cases cited. The remarks of Danckwerts L.J. were similarly directed to the interpretation of section 100. Willmer L.J. dissented, holding that the only way in which the opinion of a local authority can be expressed is by way of a resolution; and that the opinion that summary proceedings would afford an inadequate remedy must be so expressed before the commencement of proceedings. The case was indistinguishable in principle from *St Leonard's Vestry v. Holmes* and *Bowyer, Philpott & Payne v. Mather*.[69]

4–81 *Warwick Rural District Council v. Miller-Mead*[70] was applied by the Court of Appeal in *Stoke-on-Trent City Council v. B. & Q. Retail Ltd*.[71] The council instituted proceedings for an injunction to restrain the defendants from opening their shops on Sunday contrary to the Shops Act 1950. They relied

---

[66] *supra*, § 4–78.
[67] At pp. 450–451.
[68] (1885) 50 J.P. 132 and [1919] 1 K.B. 419.
[69] *ibid.*
[70] [1961] Ch. 590.
[71] [1984] Ch. 1.

on section 222 of the Local Government Act 1972 as authority for the institution of proceedings without seeking the consent of the Attorney-General for a relator action.[72] The court held that the council was so entitled, provided they considered whether the action proposed was expedient for the promotion or protection of the inhabitants in their area, as required by section 222. On the facts, the sub-committee that had originally caused the proceedings to be instituted in the council's name had given no thought to these limitations. However, the policy committee, which subsequently resolved that the proceedings "be prosecuted and continued" did consider these matters. The Court of Appeal held that this constituted a valid "ratification".[73]

There are two other cases where subsequent ratification has been permitted:

> *Firth v. Staines.*[74] Section 58 of the Metropolis Management Act 1855 **4–82** empowered any metropolitan vestry to appoint a committee "... for any purposes which in the discretion of the ... vestry would be better regulated and managed by means of such committee. ... Provided always that the acts of every such committee shall be submitted to the ... vestry ... for their approval." The committee, in whom public health powers were vested, directed an inspector to serve a notice requiring abatement of a nuisance, and in default to take proceedings. The inspector subsequently started proceedings, and a summons was issued. After the summons was issued but before the proceedings were heard, the vestry approved the committee's action. The defendant argued that prior approval was necessary. *Held*, the vestry's action constituted a valid ratification. *Per* Hawkins J.[75]: "... if at each step in the execution of their powers the committee are first to obtain the sanction of the vestry, the whole object of their appointment is lost. ..."

It will be noted that this case turns entirely on the interpretation of the 1855 Act as authorising delegation, provided that acts are subsequently ratified. It was followed in the next case:

> *R. v. Chapman, ex p. Arlidge.*[76] A by-law of a sanitary authority provided that **4–83** the chairman of a committee might, when the sanitary authority was in vacation, give instructions with respect to urgent matters, provided that such acts should be reported to the sanitary authority. The chairman of the public health committee directed, during the vacation, that a notice be served on A. requiring abatement of a nuisance. His action was subsequently approved at the next meetings of, respectively, the committee and the authority. A complaint was then made against A. for default in complying with the notice, and a magistrate made an order requiring abatement. A. argued that the notice had not been validly served. The Divisional Court *held* (Atkin J. dissenting) that the notice had been validly served. *Firth v. Staines*[77] was applied. *St. Leonard's Vestry v. Holmes*[78] was distinguished on the ground that "in that case there was nothing resembling by-law 130 and giving the inspector authority to act as he acted in

---

[72] See § 10–65.
[73] See Lawton L.J. at pp. 23–24; Ackner L.J. at pp. 29–30. Oliver L.J. agreed with Lawton L.J.: p. 35.
[74] [1897] 2 Q.B. 70.
[75] At p. 74.
[76] [1918] 2 K.B. 298.
[77] *supra*, n. 74.
[78] *supra*, n. 60.

that case." It was noted that by-law 130 "has not been suggested to be *ultra vires* ... ".[79]

Accordingly, it appears that this case was decided on the basis that there was lawful authority for this arrangement, and is on all fours with *Firth v. Staines*.[80]

It is impossible to discern any clear principle from the cases on ratification other than that they "turn on the implications of various statutory provisions: there is no rigid rule. But in general the court is likely to be more strict where the issue is one of substance as opposed to formality."[81]

4–84   Finally, it should be noted that arrangements whereby a committee chairman is authorised to take urgent action between meetings provided that this is subsequently ratified are of doubtful legality. It will be noted that there is no power under section 101 of the Local Government Act to delegate to members,[82] and the decision in *Barnard v. National Dock Labour Board*[83] is against the doctrine of ratification applying in such circumstances. However, delegation to an officer is permissible under section 101, and it would be possible to authorise an officer to take action in consultation with the chairman.[84] Moreover, approval of urgent chairman's action by the council (or a committee acting under delegated powers) would render the action authorised *from that time*, even if not retrospectively.

Other authorities[85]

4–85   An authority may discharge any of its functions by another authority under what is commonly called an agency arrangement. The statutory responsibility for the function remains with the authority to whom the function is statutorily allocated.

There is clear scope for this device in a system where executive functions in any particular area lie with at least two authorities—the county council and the district council. Perhaps the best example is seen in highway administration. The county council is the highway authority, with power to plan, construct, and subject to the district council's strictly limited powers, maintain all highways other than trunk roads, and it exercises all traffic powers. The district council may maintain urban unclassified roads and may construct and maintain footpaths and bridleways. Both authorities may provide off-street car parks, the district council's powers being exercisable with the consent of the county council. The advantage of agency arrangements in this situation is clear.

One authority may place its staff at the disposal of another local authority or health authority,[86] and under the Local Authorities (Goods and Services)

---

[79] [1918] 2 K.B. 298 at p. 308.
[80] *supra*, n. 74.
[81] Sir William Wade C.F. Forsyth, *Administrative Law* (7th ed.), p. 353. See also D. Lanham, "Ratification in Public Law" (1981) 5 Otago Law Review 35.
[82] See § 4–63.
[83] [1953] 2 Q.B. 19.
[84] See §§ 4–72, 4–73.
[85] Local Government Act 1972, s.101.
[86] *ibid.* s.113, as amended by the National Health Service Reorganisation Act 1973, s.57, Sched. 4, and the Health Services Act 1980, s.1, Sched. 1.

Act 1970, local authorities may enter into agreements with other authorities for the supply of goods or materials, the provision of administrative, professional or technical services, the use of plant or the carrying out of works of maintenance, but not construction.[87]

Apart from the general limitation that an authority cannot delegate the power to issue a precept for or levy a rate, there is the specific restriction that an authority cannot discharge its functions under the Diseases of Animals Act 1950 by any other authority.[88]

In Wales, any new county or county borough council, and the Welsh **4–86** Residuary Body ("the contracting council") may enter an agreement with another such council ("the supplying council") for the provision by the latter of services which the former require for the purpose of, or in connection with, the discharge of any of its functions. Such a "service agency agreement" may be on such terms as to payment or otherwise as the parties consider appropriate. This is subject to any other enactment which provides for specific functions to be discharged only by that authority, to any requirements imposed by Part III of the Local Government, Planning and Land Act 1980 and Part I of the Local Government Act 1988 and to regulations made by the Secretary of State. The provisions of the Local Authorities (Goods and Services) Act 1970 do not affect and are not affected by these provisions. For the purposes of any other statutory powers, anything which falls to be done by a supplying council under an agreement is to be treated as one of its statutory functions.[89] These powers are less restrictive than those of the 1970 Act, in that the latter have been regarded by the Audit Commission "as being limited to the supply of services caused by some temporary surplus capacity of resources employed only for the discharge of functions within the authorities' own boundaries".[90]

Contracting Out

Part II of the Deregulation Act 1994 (sections 69–79) makes provision for **4–87** the contracting out of the functions of ministers and office-holders (section 69) and local authorities[91] (section 70). In the case of a local authority this applies to any function[92]

---

[87] These powers are available to joint authorities (s.146A, inserted by the Local Government Act 1985, Sched. 14, para. 16) and to residuary bodies (1985 Act, Sched. 13, para. 12(b)); and to the Broads Authority (Norfolk and Suffolk Broads Act 1988, Sched. 6, paras. 8, 10(1)). See §§ 7–02, 7–32.

[88] Local Government Act 1972, s.101(7). The provisions of the Diseases of Animals Act 1950 have been consolidated in the Animal Health Act 1981. Subs. (7) does not apply to arrangements as between principal councils in Wales: subs. (7A) inserted by the Local Government (Wales) Act 1994, Sched. 15, para. 26.

[89] Local Government (Wales) Act 1994, s.25.

[90] Annotations in *Current Law Statutes Annotated 1994* by P. Griffiths and C. Crawford. A revised view has now been taken of powers under the 1970 Act: see § 7–32.

[91] *i.e.* in England, a county, district or London borough council, the Common Council of the City of London, the sub-treasurer of the Inner Temple, the under treasurer of the Middle Temple, the Council of the Isles of Scilly or a parish council; and in Wales, a county council, county borough council or community council: 1994 Act, s.79(1). References to a local authority include references to a joint board or joint committee: *ibid.* s.79(3)(b).

[92] This includes any power to do any thing which is calculated to facilitate, or is conducive or incidental to, the exercise of a function: *ibid.*, s.79(1).

(a) conferred by or under any enactment; and
(b) which may be exercised by an officer of the authority under section 101 of the Local Government Act 1972; and
(c) which is not excluded by section 71.

A minister[93] may by order provide for a function to which section 70 applies to be exercised by, or by employees of, such person (if any) as may be authorised in that behalf by the local authority whose function it is. The minister must first consult such representatives of local government as he considers appropriate. An order may set limits to the exercise of contracted-out functions. Authorisations are to be for such period, not exceeding 10 years, as is specified, may be revoked at any time[94] and shall not prevent the local authority from exercising the function to which the authorisation relates. Where an order is in force in relation to a function of local authority A, and arrangements are in force under section 101 of the Local Government Act 1972 for the exercise of that function by local authority B, it is to be an implied term of those arrangements that, except with the consent of authority A, authority B shall not give any authorisation by virtue of the order in relation to that function.

Section 71 excludes functions where the exercise would constitute the exercise of jurisdiction of any court or of any tribunal which exercises the judicial power of the state; or its exercise or non-exercise would necessarily interfere with or otherwise affect the liberty of any individual; or it is a power or right of entry, search or seizure into or of any property (other than under specified provisions concerning the enforcement of rates, community charge and council tax); or it is a power or duty to make subordinate legislation.[95]

Where a person is authorised to exercise any function of a local authority, anything done or omitted to be done by or in relation to the authorised person (or an employee of his), in or in connection with the exercise or purported exercise of the function is to be treated for all purposes as done or omitted to be done by or in relation to that authority.[96] However, this does not apply for the purposes of so much of any contract made between the authorised person and the local authority as relates to the exercise of that function, or for the purposes of any criminal proceedings brought in respect of anything done or omitted to be done by the authorised person (or his employee).[97]

Restrictions on the disclosure of information are modified to enable information to be disclosed to contractors and for the contractors to be under the same restrictions as the original recipients.[98]

---

[93] The term "minister" has the same meaning as "minister of the Crown" in the Ministers of the Crown Act 1975: *ibid.*

[94] If an authorisation is revoked while a contract relating to the exercise of the function is subsisting, the authorised person is entitled to treat the contract as repudiated and not frustrated: *ibid.*, s.73.

[95] This expression includes "orders, rules, regulations, schemes, warrants, byelaws and other instruments made or to be made under any Act": Interpretation Act 1978, s.21(1).

[96] s.72(1), (2).

[97] s.72(3).

[98] s.75 and Sched. 15. For exercises of the powers under s.70, see § 7–54.

F. LOCAL AUTHORITY COMPANIES

Local authorities have a number of express powers and duties to form or **4–88**
acquire shares in companies.[98a] It has also been assumed that section 111 of
the Local Government Act 1972 is sufficiently widely drawn to authorise
such moves.[98b] However, recent decisions of the Court of Appeal have held
that the establishment of a company is *ultra vires* where this is done as part of
an arrangement whereby functions will be unlawfully delegated to it, or in
order to evade statutory controls on borrowing.[98c]

Part V of the Local Government and Housing Act 1989 introduced new
controls over companies in which local authorities have interests. The
purpose of this Part is to ensure that:

> "when a company is effectively under the control of a local authority, ... the
> most significant controls that Parliament has laid down for the conduct of local
> authorities should apply to that company."[99]

Local authority companies are divided into three broad categories: (1) local
authority controlled companies; (2) local authority influenced companies;
and (3) companies in which local authorities have a minority interest.
"Companies" include both companies set up under the Companies Act 1985
and societies registered or deemed to be registered under the Industrial and
Provident Societies Act 1965.[1] The term "local authority" is widely defined,[2]
and things done and powers exercisable by delegation to a committee,
sub-committee or officer are treated as done or exercisable by the authority.[3]

A company is to be regarded as for the time being under the *control* of a **4–89**
local authority if:

(a) it is a subsidiary of the authority by virtue of section 736 of the
Companies Act 1985; or

(b) the authority has power to control a majority of votes at a general
meeting; or

(c) the authority has power to appoint or remove a majority of the board
of directors; or

[98a] See Housing Associations Act 1985, s.58; further Education Act 1985, s.2; Transport Act
1985, s.67; Airports Act 1986, s.13; Local Government and Housing Act 1989, s.33;
Environmental Protection Act 1990, s.32.

[98b] DoE Consultation Paper, *Local Authorities' Interests in Companies in England and Wales*
(October 1989), p. 5.

[98c] *Credit Suisse v. Allerdale Borough Council, The Times,* May 20, 1996; *Credit Suisse v.
Waltham Forest London Borough Council, The Times,* May 20, 1996, § 1–30, *supra.*

[99] D. Trippier, Parliamentary Under-Secretary of State for the Environment, Standing
Committee G, col. 751, April 11, 1989, cited by A. Arden, *et al.,* annotations in *Current Law
Statutes Annotated 1989.*

[1] 1989 Act, s.67(1)(2). Thus almost all housing associations will be covered: Arden *et al., op. cit.,
supra.*

[2] *ibid.* s.67(3): it covers county, district, London borough, parish and community councils, the
Common Council of the City of London, the Council of the Isles of Scilly, combined fire
authorities, police and waste disposal authorities, joint authorities, successors to residuary
bodies, the Broads Authority, joint boards and Passenger Transport Executives.

[3] *ibid.* s.73(4). Similarly, things done and powers exerciseable by a joint committee or
sub-committee of two or more local authorities are treated as done or exercisable by each of
the authorities concerned: *ibid.* s.73(5).

(d) the company is under the control of another company which is itself under the control of the authority.

The Secretary of State has power to direct otherwise.[4]

A company which qualifies as "controlled" under these provisions may nevertheless be an "arm's-length company" for a particular financial year of the authority if, before the beginning of that year, the authority has so resolved and, at all times between the resolution and the end of the financial year, a number of conditions are fulfilled:

(a) that each director was appointed for a fixed term of two years;
(b) that no director has been removed by resolution under section 303 of the Companies Act 1985[5];
(c) that not more than one-fifth of the directors have been members or officers of the authority;
(d) that the company has not occupied (as tenant or otherwise) any land in which the authority has an interest otherwise than for the best consideration reasonably obtainable;
(e) that the company has agreed with the authority that the company will use its best endeavours to produce a specified positive return on assets;
(f) that, except to enable the company to acquire fixed assets or to provide it with working capital, the authority has not lent money to the company or guaranteed any sum borrowed by it or subscribed for any securities in the company;
(g) that the authority has not made any grant to the company except under an agreement entered before the financial year of the company in which the grant was made; and
(h) that the authority has not made any grant to the company the amount of which is in any way related to the financial results of the company in any period.[6]

4-90   A company is to be regarded as for the time being subject to the *influence* of a local authority if:

(a) it is not a controlled company;
(b) it is not a banking or insurance company or a member of a banking or insurance group;
(c) there is a "business relationship" between the company and the authority;
(d) the authority has at least a "one-fifth influence."

The Secretary of State may direct otherwise.

A "business relationship" exists if:

[4] *ibid.* s.68(1)–(5).
[5] The Secretary of State may direct that the removal of a director shall be disregarded, if it appears to him that the removal was not done with a view to influencing the management of the company for other than commercial reasons: *ibid.* s.68(7).
[6] *ibid.* s.68(6). It is not clear whether conditions (c), (d), (f) are breached *whenever* the disqualifying event occurred: see Arden *et al., op. cit.,* n. 99, *supra.*

(a) within a period of 12 months up to and including the day on which the question arises, more than half of the company's turnover is made up of payments from the authority, or from a company under the control of the authority; or

(b) more than half of the turnover is derived from the exploitation of assets in which the authority or a company under the authority's control has an interest; or

(c) the aggregate of (i) grants made by the authority (being expenditure for capital purposes) or by a company under the authority's control, and (ii) the nominal value of shares in the company which is owned by the authority or by a company under its control, exceeds one-half of the company's net assets;

(d) the aggregate of (c) above and loans or other advances made or guaranteed by the authority or by a company under its control exceeds one-half of the fixed and current assets of the company;

(e) the company at that time occupies land by virtue of an interest obtained from the authority or a company under its control at less than the best consideration reasonably obtainable;

(f) the company intends at that time to enter into or complete a transaction and when that is done there will be a business relationship under any of (a) to (e).

There is a "one-fifth influence" where:

(a) at least 20 per cent of the total voting rights at a general meeting are held by persons associated with the authority; or

(b) at least 20 per cent of the directors are persons so associated; or

(c) at least 20 per cent of the total voting rights at a meeting of directors are held by persons so associated.

A person is at any time "associated" with an authority if he is at that time a member or officer of the authority, or both an employee and a director, manager, secretary or similar officer of a company under the authority's control, or at any time within the preceding four years has been a member of the authority. The Secretary of State may by order extend the categories of associated persons.[7]

Companies may be regarded as under the control or influence of each of a group of authorities notwithstanding that they are not under the control or influence of any one of them.[8]

The substantive provisions applicable to companies under the control or **4-91** influence of a local authority are to be found in regulations made by the Secretary of State. Each local authority is under a duty to ensure, so far as practicable, that any company under its control complies with these regulations, and if it fails in this duty, any payments made by the authority to the company and any other expenditure incurred by the authority in contravention of the provisions will be deemed to be unlawful expenditure

---

[7] *ibid.* s.69. These provisions may be extended to non-charitable trusts: *ibid.* s.72.
[8] *ibid.* s.73(1)–(3).

for the purposes of Part III of the Local Government Finance Act 1982. Each local authority is also under a duty to comply with any requirements prescribed by the regulations in relation to conditions to be included in leases, licences, contracts, gifts, grants or loans made with or to a company subject to the authority's influence. If the authority fails to comply, any expenditure incurred by it under the lease, licence, etc., is deemed to be unlawful expenditure for the purposes of Part III of the 1982 Act.[9]

4–92 The Secretary of State has made the Local Authorities (Companies) Order 1995,[10] setting out requirements as to controlled and influenced companies, minority interests and capital finance.[10a] Thus, a "regulated company"[11] must mention on all relevant documents that it is controlled or influenced by a local authority, and name the relevant authority or authorities; limits are placed on the allowances payable to directors of such companies; regulated companies are bound by the restrictions on the publication of information imposed by section 2 of the Local Government Act 1986; and directors of regulated companies must be removed if they become disqualified for membership of a local authority other than by being employed by a local authority or a controlled company. Requirements are also imposed as to the provision of information to the local authority's auditor and to members, and of financial information to the authority. A controlled company must obtain the Audit Commission's consent to the appointment of its auditor.

Controlled companies which are not arm's length companies must allow for public inspection of the minutes of any general meeting, subject to certain restrictions.

4–93 Finally, there are controls over *minority interests* in certain companies. In relation to a local authority, they apply to any company other than:

(a) a company which is or, if the action which is subject to the controls is taken, will be under the control of the local authority; and

(b) an "authorised company," *i.e.* a company of a description specified by order of the Secretary of State.[12]

Where the controls apply, except with the approval of the Secretary of State, the authority may not:

---

[9] *ibid.* s.70.

[10] S.I. 1995 No. 849 as amended by S.I. 1996 No. 621.

[10a] The capital finance provisions are considered by R. Hann, *Local Authority Law*, 6/96, pp. 7–8.

[11] *i.e.* (a) a controlled company; or (b) a local authority influenced company (i) which is an unlimited company or society registered under the Industrial and Provident Societies Act 1965 (or the equivalent legislation in Northern Ireland) or (ii) where the relevant local authority would, if it were a registered company, be treated as having the right to exercise (or as having exercised during the previous financial year) a dominant influence over, or be required to prepare group accounts in respect of, the company in question: S.I. 1995 No. 849, para. 1(4). Public transport or airport companies, companies under the control or influence of one or more Passenger Transport Executives, and companies under the control of any such company, are excluded from the scope of the Order: para. 2, Schedule.

[12] *i.e.* Companies, other than regulated companies and companies specified in the Schedule to the 1995 regulations (see n. 90a), in which any person associated with a local authority is a director or has a right to vote at a general meeting: S.I. 1995 No. 849, para. 11.

(a) acquire shares in the company;

(b) become or remain a member of the company if it is limited by guarantee;

(c) exercise any power to nominate any person to become a member of the company;

(d) exercise any power to appoint directors;

(e) permit any officer of the authority, in the course of his employment, to make any nominations or appointment referred to in (c) or (d); or

(f) permit an officer of the authority, in the course of his employment, to become or remain a director of the company.

An approval by the Secretary of State may be general or relate to any specific matter or company.[12a]

A local authority may not take any action, or refrain from exercising any **4–93** right, which would have the result that a person who is disqualified from membership of the authority (otherwise than being employed by a local authority or a controlled company) becomes a member or director of an authorised company, or authorised to act as the authority's representative at a general meeting of an authorised company under section 375 of the Companies Act 1985.[13]

Where a member or officer has become a member or director of an authorised company in specified circumstances, the authority must make arrangements for him to be open to questioning about the company's activities by members of the authority at a meeting of the authority, or a committee or sub-committee. He is not, however, required to disclose confidential information about the company. He must also declare to the authority any remuneration or reimbursement of expenses received from the company as a member or director, in respect of things done on behalf of the company. The requirement as to arrangements for question also applies in respect of any member or officer authorised to act under section 375 of the 1985 Act.[14]

G. PUBLICATION OF INFORMATION

Part II (sections 2 to 4) of the Local Government, Planning and Land Act **4–94** 1980 places on local authorities[15] a duty to publish information about the discharge of their functions and other matters. For this purpose the Secretary of State may issue a code of recommended practice. The code, which may be revised from time to time, may specify that publication be made in periodical reports or in any other specified manner and may also indicate the occasions and form of publication. In particular, the code may provide for the publication of information with or included in rate demands

---

[12a] 1989 Act, s.71(1)–(3).

[13] *ibid.* s.71(4).

[14] *ibid.* s.71(5)–(7).

[15] *i.e.* county, county borough, district and London borough councils, the Common Council, the Council of the Isles of Scilly, combined fire authorities, joint authorities.

or in statements of accounts prepared under section 23 of the Local Government Finance Act 1982 or for its being made available for inspection by members of the public at an authority's offices or elsewhere and, where the information refers to the cost of discharging functions, the way in which the cost is determined. Different codes may be issued covering different classes of information, different kinds of authority or areas or different forms and occasions of publication. Before issuing a code, the Secretary of State must consult such local authority associations as appear to him to be concerned. Codes have been issued concerning the publication of (1) rate demands and supporting information[16]; (2) annual reports and financial statements[17]; (3) staffing information[18]; (4) the handling of planning applications[19]; (5) information about insured and underused land.[20]

If he considers it necessary, the Secretary of State may make regulations by statutory instrument, subject to annulment by either House of Parliament, requiring authorities to publish information in accordance with the code. Regulations have been made to require observance of the codes for the publication of staffing information.[21] A number of authorities either refused to publish information or were not publishing information quarterly in accordance with the original code of practice on this topic. Regulations have also been made to require observance of the code on information about unused and underused land.[22] However, these were revoked in 1996,[23] and the Code was withdrawn.[24] See also para. 13–07 on duties to publish information concerning performance standards.

4–95   Section 100G of the Local Government Act 1972[25] provides that every principal council, as defined for the purposes of Part VA of the 1972 Act,[26] must maintain a register stating the name and address of every member of the council for the time being and the ward or division which he or she

---

[16] 1980: Now obsolete following introduction of the community charge. Information to be supplied with community charge demand notices is now prescribed by regulations under the Local Government Finance Act 1988 (see *e.g.* the Community Charges and Non-Domestic Rating (Demand Notices) (England) Regulations 1991 (S.I. 1991 No. 148), as amended.

[17] 1981: see *Encyclopedia of Local Government Law*, §§ 6–13—6–18.

[18] Local Government (Publication of Staffing Information) (England) Code 1995, published as the Annex to DoE Circular 14/95. This replaced the Local Government (Publication of Manpower Information) (England) Code 1983: see DoE Circular 3/83.

[19] Code of Practice on the Local Publication of Information on Planning Applications: see DoE Circular 28/83, *Encyclopedia of Local Government Law*, §§ 6–97—6–100.

[20] Code of Recommended Practice for the Publication of Information About Unused and Underused Land Owned by Specified Local Authorities in England, published as the Annex to DoE Circular 18/89.

[21] Local Government (Publication of Staffing Information) (England) Regulations 1995 (S.I. 1995 No. 2006. See DoE Circular 14/95. The previous code, on manpower information, was enforced by the Local Government (Manpower Information) (England) Regulations 1983 (S.I. 1983 No. 8), revoked by S.I. 1994 No. 2422. Enforcement regulations (S.I. 1983 No. 615) in respect of the Welsh manpower information code (Welsh Office Circular 7/83) were revoked by S.I. 1994 No. 2677.

[22] Local Government (Publication of Information About Unused and Underused Land) (England) Regulations 1992 (S.I. 1992 No. 73).

[23] S.I. 1996 No. 585.

[24] DoE Circular 3/96.

[25] Inserted by the Local Government (Access to Information) Act 1985, s.1.

[26] See § 4–22.

represents, and, in respect of every committee and sub-committee, the members of the council who are members of the committee or sub-committee or who are entitled to speak at meetings, the name and address of every other person who is a member or entitled to speak (other than as an officer), and the functions in relation to the committee or sub-committee of each of these persons (other than members of the committee or sub-committee).

Each council must also maintain a list specifying the powers which, for the **4–96** time being, are exercisable by officers and stating the title of the officer by whom each power is exercisable. Arrangements for the discharge of a power by an officer for a specified period not exceeding six months are excluded from this requirement. Thirdly, a summary must be kept of the rights to attend meetings and the rights of access to documents conferred by Parts VA and XI of the Local Government Act 1972, and such other enactments as are specified by the Secretary of State. All these documents must be open to inspection at the council's offices.

Apart from these duties to make certain classes of information available **4–97** to the public, there is a general power under section 142 of the Local Government Act 1972[27] for a local authority to make, or assist in the making of, arrangements whereby the public may obtain:

(a) information concerning the services available within the area of the authority provided either by the authority, or by any other local authority, a joint authority, joint board or joint committee, government departments, charities and other voluntary organisations; and
(b) other information relating to the functions of the authority.

An authority may also arrange for the publication of information in these categories within its area, and may arrange for lectures, discussions and exhibitions relating to such matters.

The original version of section 142 was broader and enabled local authorities, *inter alia*, to publish "information on matters relating to local government". Case law on the original version still offers guidance on what constitutes the publication of "information":

> *R. v. Inner London Education Authority, ex p. Westminster City Council.*[28] It was held that a decision of ILEA under section 142 to retain an advertising agency to conduct a campaign with the object of informing the public of the effect of rate-capping and of persuading the public to the view held by the authority was invalid, because in reaching its decision the authority was pursuing an unauthorised purpose, namely that of persuasion, which had materially influenced the making of the decision. Glidewell J. said that the following all came within "information on matters relating to local government": (a) an account of the various facilities provided by and the activities engaged in by an authority; (b) a description of proposed or even hoped for improvements in or increases in those facilities and activities; (c) the cost of the

---

[27] As amended by the Local Government Act 1986, s.3.
[28] [1986] 1 W.L.R. 28. See also *R. v. Greater London Council and another, ex p. Westminster City Council, The Times*, December 27, 1984 (see § 1–12), and *R. v. Greater London Council, ex p. Westminster City Council, The Times*, January 22, 1985.

various facilities and activities present and anticipated for the future; (d) an explanation of the effect of legislation, including the Rates Act 1984; (e) a description of the extent to which ILEA's activities and facilities would probably have to be curtailed if the Secretary of State's maximum expenditure was to be achieved, including estimates or suggestions of particular facilities or activities which would be affected in this way.

But the decision of the authority was intended to serve two purposes, information and persuasion. Where a decision was intended to achieve two purposes for one of which there was no authority, the tests to be applied were as adopted by Megaw J. in *Hanks v. Minister of Housing and Local Government*.[29] namely (i) what was the true purpose for which the power was exercised; and (ii) if any purpose was unauthorised, had it materially influenced the decision? If it had, then the decision was invalid because irrelevant considerations had been taken into account.

4–98   Section 2 of the Local Government Act 1986[30] expressly prohibits the publication by a local authority[31] of "any material which, in whole or in part, appears to be designed to affect public support for a political party". In determining whether material is prohibited, regard is to be had to the content and style of the material, the time and other circumstances of publication and the likely effect on those to whom it is directed, and, in particular, to whether it refers to a political party or persons identified with a political party, or promotes or opposes a point of view on a question of political controversy which is identifiable as the view of one party and not another. Where the material is part of a campaign, regard is to be had to the effect which the campaign appears to be designed to achieve. An authority cannot give financial or other assistance to a person for the publication of material which the authority is itself prohibited from publishing. The Secretary of State may issue one or more codes of recommended practice as regards the content, style, distribution and cost of local authority publicity, and local authorities must have regard to the code in coming to any decision on publicity.[32] Local authorities must also keep a separate account of expenditure on publicity.[33] "Publicity", "publish" and "publication" refer to any communication, in whatever form, addressed to the public at large or to a section of the public.[34]

4–99   A further express restriction is that a local authority must not intentionally promote, or publish material with the intention of promoting homosexuality, or promote the teaching in any maintained school of the acceptability of homosexuality as a pretended family relationship. This is not, however, to be taken to prohibit the doing of anything for the purpose of treating or preventing the spread of disease. In proceeding in connection with this

---

[29] [1963] 1 Q.B. 999.
[30] As amended by the Local Government Act 1988, s.27(1).
[31] County, district, London borough, parish or community councils, joint authorities, a police authority, the Common Council, the Broads Authority and the Council of the Isles of Scilly: 1986 Act, s.6(2). Reference to a county must be taken to include a county borough in Wales: Local Government (Wales) Act 1994, s.74. National Park authorities are treated as local authorities for these purposes: Environment Act 1995, Sched. 8, para. 9.
[32] Local Government Act 1986, s.4, as amended by the Local Government Act 1988, s.27(2).
[33] *ibid.* s.5.
[34] *ibid.* s.6(4).

provision, a court shall draw such inferences as to the intention of the local authority as may reasonably be drawn from the evidence before it.[35]

The council of a non-metropolitan county may conduct, or assist in the **4–100** conducting of, investigations into, and the collection of information relating to, any matters concerning the county or any part of it. It may also make arrangements whereby any such information or the results of any investigation are made available to any other local authority in the county, any government department or the public.[36] These powers may also be exercised by a London borough council, the Common Council and a metropolitan district council. Furthermore, a scheme may be made for these purposes for Greater London or a metropolitan county by the constituent councils. One of the councils is to be designated to carry out the work, although if two-thirds of the constituent councils so decide, any or all of them may be required to carry out specified tasks. Expenses incurred with the approval of two-thirds of the councils may be recovered from all of them in proportion to their population.[37]

Finally, there are various powers whereby a Minister may require local authorities to provide him with information. For example, every local authority, joint authority, joint board, joint committee and residuary body must send the Secretary of State such reports and returns and give him such information with respect to their functions as he may require or as may be required by either House of Parliament.[38]

H. Commissions for Local Administration

Part III of the Local Government Act 1974 introduced the "ombudsman" **4–101** principle into the context of local government.[39] The Act established two Commissions for Local Administration, one for England and one for Wales, with powers similar to those of the Parliamentary Commissioner for Administration in relation to the Civil Service. England is divided into three areas, with one Local Commissioner responsible for each area. From time to time, the areas are adjusted to achieve an even distribution of the workload among the Commissioners. There is one Local Commissioner for Wales. The Parliamentary Commissioner for Administration is a member *ex officio* of each Commission. Each Commission may also include Advisory Commissioners, not exceeding the number appointed to conduct investigations. The functions of each Commission now include the provision of such advice and guidance to local authorities about good administrative practice as appears to the Commission to be appropriate, and the Commission may

---

[35] *ibid.* s.2A, inserted by the Local Government Act 1988, s.28.
[36] Local Government Act 1972, s.141, as amended by the Local Government Act 1985, Sched. 16 and the Local Government (Wales) Act 1994, Sched. 15, para. 32. In Wales, this provision applies to the county and county borough councils in respect of their areas.
[37] Local Government Act 1985, s.88.
[38] Local Government Act 1972, s.230, as amended by the Local Government Act 1985, Sched. 14, para. 26; 1985 Act, Sched. 13, para. 12(g).
[39] The provisions were modified by the Local Government Act 1988, s.29 and Sched. 3 and the Local Government and Housing Act 1989, ss.22–28.

arrange for it to be published. Before providing the advice or guidance the Commission must consult such local authority associations (and authorities not represented by an association) as it thinks appropriate.[40]

The Commissions' expenses are met from the revenue support grant. Each Commission must prepare an estimate of expenses for the forthcoming financial year, for submission to the Secretary of State. Copies must be sent to such representatives of local government as the Secretary of State directs, and their observations must be taken into consideration before the estimate is submitted to him. The Secretary of State is then to take the estimate into account, together with any other available information as to the Commissions' expenses, in determining the amount of grant payable to them.[41]

4–102 A Local Commissioner may investigate written complaints made by or on behalf of a member of the public who claims to have sustained injustice in consequence of maladministration, in connection with action taken or default first arising after April 1, 1974.

The authorities subject to investigation are:

(a) any local authority, defined for the purposes of this Act[42] as county councils, district councils, the Broads Authority, Welsh county and county borough councils, London borough councils, the Common Council of the City of London and the Council of the Isles of Scilly;
(b) the Land Authority for Wales;
(c) any joint board the constituent authorities of which are all local authorities;
(d) the Commission for the New Towns;
(e) any new town development corporation;
(f) the Development Board for Rural Wales;
(g) any urban development corporation;
(h) any housing action trust;
(i) the Urban Regeneration Agency;
(j) any joint authority established by Part IV of the Local Government Act 1985;
(k) any police authority, except the Secretary of State;
(l) the Environment Agency and any regional flood defence committee, in relation to flood defence functions.[43]

Any reference to an authority includes a reference to the members, officers, committees and sub-committees of that authority, to persons or bodies acting on their behalf under section 101 of the Local Government Act

---

[40] s.12A, inserted by the Local Government and Housing Act 1989, s.23(1). It has issued *Guidance on Good Practice* on *Devising a Complaints System, Good Administrative Practice, Council Housing Repairs, Members' Interests* and *Disposal of Land*.
[41] Sched. 4, paras. 6–8, substituted by the 1989 Act, s.24(1). These arrangements replace those involving "representative bodies" under the original version of the 1974 Act. These bodies were dissolved by the 1989 Act, s.25(1).
[42] s.34(1), as amended.
[43] Local Government Act 1974, s.25(1), as amended.

1972, and to any appeal committee constituted under the Education Act 1980, Sched. 2 or the Education Act 1993, Sched. 6.[44]

Complaints may be referred directly or through a member of the authority concerned.[45] Prior to 1988 they had to be referred by a member, and could only be received directly if the member failed to refer it. The change has led to a substantial increase in the number of complaints.[46] In the absence of special circumstances, a complaint must be made to a Commissioner or a member within 12 months of notice to the person aggrieved of the matters alleged in the complaint. Before investigation by the Commissioner, the authority concerned must have notice of the complaint and a reasonable opportunity to investigate and reply to it. The complaint must specify the action alleged to constitute maladministration, although it is sufficient to specify the action taken by the authority in connection with which the complaint of maladministration is made.[47] **4–103**

The expression "maladministration" appears also in the Parliamentary Commissioner Act 1967, s.5(1)(a), but is defined in neither the 1967 Act nor the 1974 Act. In the second reading debate on the Parliamentary Commissioner Bill, Mr. Richard Crossman stated that the characteristics of maladministration include "bias, neglect, inattention, delay, incompetence, ineptitude, perversity, turpitude, arbitrariness and so on".[48] The Commission's booklet, *Complaint about the Council? How to Complain to the Local Government Ombudsman* states that **4–104**

> "If a council does something the wrong way, does something it should not have done, or fails to do something it should have done, that is maladministration. Some examples of maladministration are: neglect and unjustified delay, failure to follow a council's agreed policies, rules or procedures, failure to have proper procedures, malice, bias or unfair discrimination, failure to tell people of their rights, failure to provide advice or information when reasonably requested, providing inaccurate or misleading advice."[49]

Breach of the National Code of Local Government Conduct may constitute maladministration. In *R. v. Commissioner for Local Administration, ex p. Blakey*[50] Popplewell J. rejected an application for judicial review of the Commissioner's decision that a council should have declared a non-pecuniary interest in a matter. His Lordship held that the Commissioner had been correct in concluding that the statement in the National Code of Local Government Conduct that a councillor's "overriding duty" was to the whole local community, did not override the duty to declare a personal interest. The "dispensations" set out in the code would have been

---

[44] *ibid.* s.25(4), (5); (subs. (5) was inserted by the Education Act 1980, s.7(7) and amended by the Education Act 1993, s.269).

[45] *ibid.* s.26(2), as amended by the Local Government Act 1988, Sched. 3, para. 5.

[46] Annual Report of the English Commission for 1988–89, pp. 4, 9–10, Appendix 3(a); and for 1994–95, p. 26.

[47] 1974 Act, s.26(2)(a); *R. v. Local Commissioner, ex p. Bradford Metropolitan City Council* [1979] Q.B. 287, 312–313 (Lord Denning M.R.) and 315–316 (Eveleigh L.J.).

[48] H.C. Deb. Vol. 754, c. 51 (1966).

[49] See also *R. v. Local Commissioner, ex p. Bradford Metropolitan City Council, supra,* at pp. 311–312; *R. v. Local Commissioner, ex p. Eastleigh Borough Council* [1988] Q.B. 855, 863.

[50] [1994] C.O.D. 345.

sufficient to deal with the question but as the councillor took the view that he was not obliged to declare an interest, any question of dispensation was not raised.

4–105   The authority and persons concerned must have an opportunity to comment on any allegations. Investigations are to be in private, but the Commissioner otherwise has a discretion as to the procedure to be adopted. A Local Commissioner has wide powers to require persons to furnish information or disclose documents,[51] although a Minister of the Crown or an authority may give written notice that disclosure of specified information would be contrary to the public interest, in which case there are limitations on the disclosure of that information by the Commissioner to other persons.[52]

4–106   A report of the results of an investigation or of the reasons for a decision not to conduct one must be sent to the member who referred the complaint (if applicable), to the complainant, and to any authority or person alleged to be responsible for the action of which complaint is made. Persons are not normally to be named or identifiable except that a member who is involved in action constituting maladministration and who is in breach of the National Code of Local Government Conduct is to be named and particulars of the breach given, unless the Commissioner is satisfied that that would be unjust. Reports are to be open to public inspection for three weeks, and public notice of this is to be given.

Where the Local Commissioner is of the opinion that injustice has been caused in consequence of maladministration, the authority concerned comes under a duty to consider the Commissioner's report, and, within three months (or a longer period agreed with him), to notify him of the action which has been or will be taken. If no such notification is received, or the Commissioner is not satisfied with the authority's response or he does not within a further three months receive confirmation that the proposed action has been taken, he is to make a further report setting out the facts and making recommendations. The recommendations are such as he thinks fit to make with respect to action which, in his opinion, the authority should take to remedy the injustice and prevent similar injustice being caused in the future. If there is still no satisfactory response, the Commissioner may require the authority to arrange for a statement outlining the position to be published in a local newspaper.[53] Where a Commissioner has made a report, an authority has power to incur expenditure in making a payment or providing a benefit to a person who has suffered injustice.[54] Authorities are

---

[51] See *In re a subpoena issued by the Commissioner for Local Administration, The Times*, April 4, 1996 (subpoena in respect of confidential information from a local authority's adoption files upheld).

[52] 1974 Act, s.32(3), as amended by the Local Government, Planning and Land Act 1980, s.184. See hereon *Re a Complaint against Liverpool City Council* [1977] 1 W.L.R. 995 and *Gaskin v. Liverpool City Council* [1980] 1 W.L.R. 1549.

[53] 1974 Act, s.31(1)–(2H), as amended by the 1989 Act, s.26(1).

[54] 1974 Act, s.31(3), added by the Local Government Act 1978, and amended by the 1989 Act, Sched. 11, para. 39(1). A Local Commissioner's report is a necessary pre-condition to the exercise of this power.

not, however, obliged by law to accept the views of the Local Commissioner. At March 31, 1995, in 5.5 per cent. of the 4,215 cases where injustice had been found, the authority failed to take action satisfactory to the Commissioner.[55] The local authority associations have urged authorities always to respond positively and speedily to Commissioners' findings.[56] The amendments effected by the 1989 Act, which fall short of making Commissioners' reports legally enforceable, appear to have led to a small increase in the rate of compliance.

A Local Commissioner is precluded from investigating any of the **4–107** following particular matters:

(a) any action in respect of which the complainant has or had a right of appeal to a statutory tribunal;

(b) any action in respect of which the complainant has or had a right of appeal to a Minister; or

(c) any action in respect of which the person aggrieved has or had a remedy in law.

But there is a proviso to this. A Commissioner may in fact conduct an investigation into these situations if he is satisfied that in the particular circumstances it was not reasonable to expect the complainant to have taken advantage of the remedies open to him.[57]

> *R. v. Local Commissioner, ex p. Bradford Metropolitan City Council.*[58] A mother made various complaints concerning the actions of the local authority in taking her two children into care in March 1975, and in dealing with them thereafter:
>
>> (1) that the authority had failed in their duty under section 1 of the Children and Young Persons Act 1963 to use their resources to help the complainant look after the children herself;
>>
>> (2) that a senior social worker said that she would strongly oppose the mother having the children back as the girl suffered from fits but later said that she did not so suffer;
>>
>> (3) that the children were separated against the mother's wishes and assigned to different foster parents;
>>
>> (4) that the senior social worker said that she would have the children adopted without the mother's consent and that they were placed with prospective adopters without consulting the mother.
>
> The Court of Appeal *held* that the investigation of these complaints by the Commissioner was not barred by s.26(6). The local authority had applied successfully to the juvenile court for a care order in August 1975, and there were to be adoption proceedings in relation to the children for them to be adopted by their foster parents. Eveleigh L.J. stated[59] that the juvenile court and adoption proceedings did not provide a remedy for the complaints made in this case, as

---

[55] Annual Report of the English Commission for 1994–95, Appendix 3c. The figure was 6 per cent at March 31, 1985 (Annual Report 1984–85, paras. 88–92), and remained at that level at March 31, 1991: Annual Report for 1990–91, para. 4.23.

[56] *ibid.* Appendix 6.

[57] 1974 Act, s.26(6).

[58] [1979] Q.B. 287.

[59] At p. 317.

the issues whether the complainant had suffered injustice and whether there had been maladministration did not arise in those proceedings. Sir David Cairns agreed[60] that none of the remedies mentioned in subs. (6) were applicable to the actions of which complaint was made. Lord Denning M.R. stated[61] that there was no conflict at all in relation to complaints (2) and (4). In relation to complaints (1) and (3) there was no conflict as the Local Commissioner had decided to consider only matters which arose between March and August 1975.

4–108   There are some additional areas of investigation from which a Local Commissioner is excluded. He may not look into cases where the complainant claims to have suffered from a decision affecting the public at large, nor into any of the matters listed in Schedule 5. The list includes legal proceedings, action taken by a police authority in connection with the investigation of crime, certain commercial transactions,[62] and issues relating to appointments, pay, discipline and other personnel matters.

4–109   Local Commissioners are required to submit an annual general report to the Commissions, and each Commission must prepare an annual report and submit it and the Commissioners' reports to the local authority associations (and such authorities as are not represented by an association) for comment. After these associations and authorities have had a reasonable opportunity to comment, the reports must be published.[63] Every three years the Commissions are required to review the operation of these provisions and are empowered to convey to local authorities or to government departments, any recommendations or conclusions reached in the course of their reviews. Copies are to be sent to the local authority associations and to authorities not represented by such associations.[64] Major reviews were conducted in 1978, 1980, 1984, 1990, and 1993.[65] The Secretary of State has generally resisted proposals for the extension of the Commissioners' jurisdiction.

4–110   The local authority associations, in co-operation with the Commission for Local Administration in England, have issued a Code of Practice concerning the complaints procedures of local authorities. It is reproduced in Appendix 9 to the Report of the English Commission for 1977–78. Part 2 of this Code

---

[60] At p. 318.

[61] At pp. 310–311.

[62] Decisions in respect of licences to occupy a pitch or stall in a fair or market, or the provision (other than in connection with a dock or harbour undertaking) of moorings, ceased to be excluded from the Ombudsmen's jurisdiction by virtue of the Local Government Administration (Matters Subject to Investigation) Order 1993 (S.I. 1993 No. 940).

[63] 1974 Act, s.23(11) and s.23A, inserted by the Local Government and Housing Act 1989, s.25(1).

[64] *ibid.* s.23(12), (12B)(a), as amended by the Local Government Act 1988, Sched. 3, para. 2 and the Local Government and Housing Act 1989, Sched. 11, para. 38.

[65] Annual Reports of the English Commission for 1977–78, paras. 62–159, 1980–81, Appendices VII and VIII and 1984–85, Appendices 4 and 5. The Secretary of State's responses may be found, respectively, in the Annual Reports for 1978–79, Appendix 9, 1983–84, paras. 91–98 and Appendix 4, 1985–86, Appendix 4 1991–92, Appendix 5 and 1993–94, Appendix 5. See also the JUSTICE report, *The Local Ombudsman: A review of the first five years* (1982).

covers local action without involving a Local Commissioner. Part 3 concerns complaints to be referred to a Local Commissioner. A supplement was issued in 1982.[66] The Commission has also issued a Guidance Note on *Devising a Complaints System*.[67]

---

[66] See generally P. Birkinshaw, *Grievances, Remedies and the State* (Sweet & Maxwell, 2nd edn., 1995), Chap. 2.
[67] *Guidance on Good Practice 1.*

CHAPTER 5

ACQUISITION, APPROPRIATION, DISPOSAL AND DEVELOPMENT OF LAND

I. ACQUISITION

THIS topic falls under two heads: (A) powers and duties in relation to **5–01** acquisition and (B) procedure for compulsory acquisition.

A. POWERS AND DUTIES

THE Local Government Act 1972 empowers a principal council to acquire by **5–02** agreement any land inside or outside its area (a) for the purposes of its functions under any enactment, or (b) for the benefit, improvement or development of its area, whether it is immediately required for any such purpose or not.[1] The Act also provides that a principal council may be authorised by the Minister concerned to purchase compulsorily any land, inside or outside its area, for any purpose for which it is authorised by any enactment to acquire land, with certain exceptions, namely, (i) the purposes mentioned in (b) above, (ii) purposes of the Local Authorities (Land) Act 1963 (see para. 5–47), or (iii) where the enactment in question specifically limits the power to acquisition by agreement.[2] The fact that land may be acquired by agreement under the Local Government Act 1972, s.121, does not prevent it being acquired compulsorily under section 120.[3] The Act gives similar powers to parish and community councils, save that such councils cannot take compulsory purchase proceedings themselves.[4] These must be taken by the district council in England or the county or county borough council in Wales, where that council thinks it appropriate, on the representation of the parish or community council.[5]

Apart from these general provisions, Acts conferring specific functions on authorities normally confer specific powers of acquisition of land, and, where a specific power is given, it is usual for that power to be used rather than any more general power. Thus the powers in the Education Acts and the Highways Acts would be used for land acquisitions for education and

---

[1] s.120. A joint authority is treated as a principal council for the purposes of s.120 (except subs.(1)(b)) and ss.121–123: s.146A(1)(b), inserted by the Local Government Act 1985, Sched. 14, para. 16.

[2] s.121.

[3] *Brookwood Cemetery Ltd v. Secretary of State for the Environment* [1992] C.O.D. 95.

[4] ss.124 and 125, as amended by the Local Government (Wales) Act 1994, Sched. 15, para. 28.

[5] As from March 31, 1990, a new s.125 was substituted by s.43 of the Housing and Planning Act 1986. Previously, there had been a requirement that the district council hold a public local inquiry.

highways purposes. A list of statutes giving specific powers of compulsory purchase appears in Appendix 3.

5-03 In one case an Act conferring specific functions contains wide powers of acquisition. Sections 226 and 227 of the Town and Country Planning Act 1990 empower certain authorities[6] to acquire compulsorily, or by agreement, any land in their areas which is suitable for, and is required[7] in order to secure the carrying out of, development, redevelopment or improvement, or which is required for a purpose which it is necessary to achieve in the interests of the proper planning of an area in which the land is situated. Moreover, it is immaterial by whom the authority proposes that any activity or purpose mentioned should be undertaken or achieved, and, in particular, it need not propose to undertake the activity or achieve the purpose itself.

The 1990 Act thus gives very wide powers to such an authority to acquire land for development by itself or to acquire and assemble it for disposal to private developers. In considering whether land is suitable for development, redevelopment or improvement, the authority must have regard to the development plan, to whether any planning permission for the development of the land is in force, and to any other considerations which would be material to determining an application for planning permission for development of the land. Accordingly, in exercising these wide powers, the authority is to be guided by planning considerations.

5-04 Where an authority may be authorised to purchase land compulsorily under any Act it may be authorised to acquire, instead of the land itself, new rights, *e.g.* a right of way, over the land.[8]

5-05 Apart from the powers of acquisition mentioned above, a principal council, or a parish or community council, may accept gifts of property for the purpose of any of its functions or for the benefit of the inhabitants of its area.[9]

A local authority may only acquire land for the purposes set out in the relevant enactment or enactments, and not for any ulterior purpose.[10] It may

---

[6] Councils of counties, county boroughs, districts and London boroughs (s.226(8)); the Common Council of the City of London (definition of "London borough" in s.336(1)); Planning Boards (s.244). Where the Secretary of State has power to authorise compulsory purchase by one of these authorities, he may, after the requisite consultation, authorise acquisition by another local authority (as defined in s.336(1) to include, *inter alia*, charging and precepting authorities and levying bodies): s.226(5).

[7] The word "required" means necessary in the circumstances of the case; the council does not have to show that the compulsory purchase is indispensable to the achieving of the proper planning of the area and that there are no other methods available for achieving the same end. *Sharkey v. Secretary of State for the Environment* (1991) 63 P. & C.R. 332. See also *R. v. Bromley London Borough Council, ex p. Frampton* (1992) 32 R.V.R. 173; *Sutton London Borough Council v. Bolton* (1993) 91 L.G.R. 566.

[8] Local Authorities (Miscellaneous Provisions) Act 1976, s.13.

[9] Local Government Act 1972, s.139.

[10] See, *e.g. Gard v. Commissioners of Sewers of the City of London* (1885) 28 Ch.D. 486; *Marquess of Clanricarde v. Congested Districts Board* (1915) 79 J.P. 481; *Municipal Council of Sydney v. Campbell* [1925] A.C. 338; *Hanks v. Minister of Housing and Local Government* [1963] 1 Q.B. 999; *Meravale Builders Ltd v. Secretary of State for the Environment* (1978) 77 L.G.R. 365; *Costello v. Dacorum District Council* (1982) 81 L.G.R. 1; *R. v. Secretary of State for the Environment, ex p. Leicester City Council* (1988) 55 P. & C.R. 364; *Sharkey v. Secretary of State for the Environment* (1991) 63 P. & C.R. 332; *R. v. Essex County Council, ex p. Jackson Projects* [1995] C.O.D. 155. See also § 5–17.

be liable in trespass where work is done beyond the terms of a compulsory purchase order.[11]

Where land is acquired by compulsory purchase the compensation money, or purchase price, is payable on the basis described in paragraphs 5–22 to 5–35. Where, as happens in the majority of cases, the land is acquired by agreement although the authority has power to make a compulsory purchase order if it so desires, the compensation money will normally be negotiated and settled on the same basis. Where an authority acquires land for a purpose for which it has no power of compulsory purchase, and this is unusual, there is nothing to compel the owner to sell, so that the authority will have to pay him the price he wants if it is to have the land. **5–06**

Where land is acquired by agreement in cases where the authority could have made a compulsory purchase order, many of the provisions of the Compulsory Purchase Act 1965 apply as if it was a compulsory purchase, and restrictive covenants on the land acquired may be overridden.[12] **5–07**

Where a body conducting a public function occupies land as a licensee, the landowner cannot terminate the licence without reasonable notice, enabling the body to make practical arrangements to safeguard the public interest.[13]

B. Compulsory Purchase Procedure

Authorisation of the use of statutory powers

An authority cannot exercise a statutory power to acquire land compulsorily in any particular case unless it receives a specific authorisation to do so. The Acquisition of Land Act 1981, replacing the earlier Acquisition of Land (Authorisation Procedure) Act 1946, sets out a uniform procedural code for the authorisation of compulsory purchase which applies to nearly all acquisitions under compulsory powers conferred on local authorities by statutes existing at the time when the 1981 Act was passed and to those under powers conferred by any subsequent statute which incorporates the code by reference. There is one important exception to this rule—the code does not apply to land acquired compulsorily under Part IX of the Housing Act 1985, which deals with clearance areas; a similar code contained in Schedule 22 to the Act of 1985 applies instead. Apart from this and a few other exceptions, including acquisition under the New Towns Act 1981 and the Pipe-lines Act 1962, the code is in general use. **5–08**

Compulsory purchase order

The authority must first make a compulsory purchase order in the prescribed form,[14] describing by reference to a map the land to which it relates and citing the statute on which the authority relies for compulsory powers.[15] The order is submitted to the appropriate Minister for confir- **5–09**

---

[11] *National Provident Institution v. Avon County Council* [1992] E.G.C.S. 56.
[12] Local Government Act 1972, ss.120 and 124 and see, *e.g.* Town and Country Planning Act 1990, s.237.
[13] *In re Hampstead Garden Suburb, The Times*, April 13, 1995.
[14] Compulsory Purchase of Land Regulations 1994 (S.I. 1994 No. 2145).
[15] Part II of the Acquisition of Land Act 1981 sets out the procedure to be followed. And see DoE Circular 6/85.

mation, *i.e.* to the Minister who, under the statute under which the land is acquired, is empowered to authorise the purchase; but before this is done the authority is required to publish in one or more local newspapers in two successive weeks a notice in the prescribed form[16] stating that the order is to be submitted for confirmation, giving details of the contents of the order, and specifying a time (to be not less than 21 days) within which objections may be made. A notice in similar terms is sent to every owner,[17] lessee and occupier (except tenants for a month or a less period). If sent by post, it must be sent by registered letter or by recorded delivery service. A notice for an incorporated company or body is duly served if served on the secretary or clerk thereof. When it is not practicable to find the name and address of an owner, lessee or occupier the notice may be addressed to the "owner", "lessee", or "occupier" and delivered to someone on the land or, if there is no-one on the land to whom it may be delivered, by leaving a copy on or near the land.[18] If no objections are raised, or if objections are withdrawn, the Minister may confirm the order with or without modification. If objections remain (other than those which relate to matters of compensation only), then the Minister must hold a local public inquiry, or alternatively a private hearing, at which the objector and the acquiring authority may state their views.[19] However, where an order is made under section 226 of the Town and Country Planning Act 1990, the Secretary of State may disregard an objection which amounts in substance to an objection to the provisions of the development plan defining the proposed use of the land.[20]

5–10   The Minister then decides whether or not to confirm the order, and is under an obligation to give reasons for his decision.[21] He may not confirm a compulsory purchase order for a purpose different from the original purpose of the acquiring authority.[22]

5–11   A notice to the effect that the order has been confirmed is published in one or more local newspapers and sent, with a copy of the confirmed order, to persons to whom notice was originally given or is addressed as mentioned in paragraph 5–09 and delivered to someone on the premises or affixed to the premises.[23] The order becomes operative, subject to any challenge in the High Court, on the date of the first publication. A person aggrieved by the order may not challenge it except by the proceedings set out in Part IV of

---

[16] *supra*, n. 14.
[17] See hereon *Grimley v. Minister of Housing and Local Government* [1971] 2 Q.B. 96, in which it was held that an easement of support was not "land" so as to entitle the owner of the dominant tenement to notice.
[18] Acquisition of Land Act 1981, s.6, as amended by the Planning and Compensation Act 1991, Sched. 15, para. 8.
[19] Acquisition of Land Act 1981, s.13. As to the procedure to be followed, see the Compulsory Purchase by Non-Ministerial Acquiring Authorities (Inquiries Procedure) Rules 1990 (S.I. 1990 No. 512), and DoE Circular 1/90. A person who does not enter a formal objection to a compulsory purchase order but who is accepted as a late objector cannot be awarded costs as a "statutory objector" under the Rules: *R. v. Secretary of State for the Environment, ex p. Durham County Council* [1993] N.P.C. 92.
[20] Town and Country Planning Act 1990, s.245(1).
[21] Tribunals and Inquiries Act 1992, s.10, and rule 18.
[22] *Procter and Gamble v. Secretary of State for the Environment* (1991) 63 P. & C.R. 317.
[23] Acquisition of Land Act 1981, s.15.

the 1981 Act. The grounds on which the order may be questioned are limited to two: that it is *ultra vires*, which would include failure to observe the principles laid down in the *Wednesbury* case described in paragraph 12–25,[24] or that there has been a failure to comply with some statutory requirement. A person aggrieved on either of these grounds may, within six weeks from the date on which notice of confirmation was first published, apply to the High Court that the order be quashed. The court may quash the order on the second ground only if satisfied that the interests of the applicant have been substantially prejudiced by failure to observe formalities. If the order is not challenged within the six weeks' period it cannot subsequently be questioned, even where fraud is alleged.[25]

Special parliamentary procedure
The Act prescribes a supplementary procedure[26] in the case of land which **5–12** falls within the following groups:

(a) land held inalienably by the National Trust;
(b) land forming part of a common or open space;

A compulsory purchase order in respect of land falling in group (a) is subject to special parliamentary procedure under the Statutory Orders (Special Procedure) Acts 1945 and 1965 if the National Trust have raised objections. A compulsory purchase order relating to land in group (b) is subject to special parliamentary procedure unless the appropriate Minister certifies that equivalent land will be given in exchange or that the land does not exceed 250 square yards, is required for road widening, and the giving of other land in exchange is unnecessary or that the land is being purchased in order to secure its preservation or improve its management.[27] Before issuing a certificate, the Minister must give an opportunity to interested persons to make representations to him.

A ministerial certificate under section 19 of the Acquisition of Land Act 1981 may be challenged on an application to quash under section 23; in assessing whether the exchange land is equally advantageous to users of the land and the public, the appropriate time for comparison of the two pieces of land is the date of exchange.[28]

---

[24] There are no special rules beyond the *Wednesbury* principle applicable to the confirmation order; the test is not whether there is a compelling case for the order with any doubt being resolved in favour of the landowner: *R. v. Secretary of State for Transport, ex p. de Rothschild* [1989] 1 All E.R. 933, C.A.; *Singh v. Secretary of State for the Environment* [1989] 24 E.G. 128, C.A.

[25] *Smith v. East Elloe Rural District Council* [1956] A.C. 736, followed in *R. v. Secretary of State for the Environment, ex p. Ostler* [1977] Q.B. 122. As to the right of challenge, see also *Webb v. Minister of Housing and Local Government* [1965] 1 W.L.R. 755 and *Ashbridge Investments Ltd v. Minister of Housing and Local Government* [1965] 1 W.L.R. 1320 (see § 10–60), a case arising under a similar provision in the Housing Act 1957.

[26] This is found in Part III of the Acquisition of Land Act 1981.

[27] The third of these conditions was added by the Planning and Compensation Act 1991, Sched. 15, para. 12, from September 25, 1991.

[28] *Greenwich London Borough Council v. Secretary of State for the Environment, The Times,* March 2, 1993.

Housing Act 1985, Part IX

5–13 As has been noted, the provisions of the Acquisition of Land Act 1981 do not apply where land is acquired under the clearance provisions of Part IX of the Housing Act 1985. The procedure to be followed is found in the 22nd Schedule to that Act, but it is basically the same as the procedure which the 1981 Act prescribes and it is not therefore separately described.

Procedure following authorisation

5–14 After an order has been confirmed a number of further steps must be taken before the acquiring authority becomes the owner. The rules governing this subsequent procedure are now largely found in the Compulsory Purchase Act 1965, which replaced the Lands Clauses Consolidation Act 1845 so far as acquisitions under the code in the Acquisition of Land (Authorisation Procedure) Act 1946, and now the 1981 Act, are concerned. The 1845 Act, however, has not been wholly repealed and can still operate in a few special cases. The provisions in the 1965 Act deal with such matters as the notice to treat, entry before completion, and completion.

Notice to treat

5–15 When the order has been confirmed, the authority is required by section 5 of the 1965 Act to serve notice on all parties interested in the land, stating that the authority has been authorised to acquire the land and is willing to treat for its purchase. The notice asks the parties concerned for details of their interests and claims. The persons on whom notice is served are those who will be required to convey or join in conveying an estate or interest, and all persons who have an interest in the land by reason of which they could interfere with the authority's possession.[29] The method of service is prescribed in section 6 of the 1981 Act as applied by section 30 of the 1965 Act, now substituted by the 1981 Act: see paragraph 5–009.

Schedule 4 of the Compulsory Purchase Act 1965 prescribes a special procedure for the purchase of common land, including the negotiation of compensation with a committee of five commoners. Where this procedure is followed, it is not necessary to serve notice to treat on each commoner under section 5 of the Act.[30]

5–16 The service of a notice to treat does not create a contract of sale, although establishment of the agreed price pursuant to the notice creates an obligation to convey—the point is discussed in *Birmingham Corporation v. West Midlands Baptist (Trust) Association (Inc.).*[31] Salmon L.J. said[32]:

---

[29] But it need not be served on tenants from year to year or for a year or less period; they are dealt with by notice of entry and s.20 of the Act. The notice to treat must be given to persons interested in the land "so far as known to the acquiring authority after making diligent inquiry." This requires reasonable diligence to be used but not the making of a very great inquiry: *R. v. Secretary of State for Transport, ex p. Blackett* [1992] J.P.L. 1041.

[30] *Mid-Glamorgan County Council v. Ogwr Borough Council* (1993) 68 P. & C.R. 1, affirmed on this point by the House of Lords, *sub nom. Lewis v. Mid-Glamorgan County Council* [1995] 1 W.L.R. 313.

[31] [1970] A.C. 874.

[32] In the Court of Appeal [1968] 2 Q.B. 188 at p. 215.

"It is not until compensation is agreed or assessed that the equitable title in the land passes to the party who has served the notice to treat. Either party can then—but only then—obtain specific performance, the one to have the legal title conveyed to him on payment of the price, the other to have the price paid on conveying the legal title."

Notice to treat may not be withdrawn except by consent unless pursuant to **5–17** some statutory power. An authority is enabled by the Land Compensation Act 1961 to withdraw the notice within six weeks of receiving a claim for compensation, or to withdraw it within six weeks of the determination of the purchase price by the Lands Tribunal if the owner fails to put in a claim.[33] This power is exercisable even if the authority has entered into possession of the land.[34] Further, under section 8 of the Compulsory Purchase Act 1965, where the authority requires part only of any house, building or manufactory, or park or garden belonging to a house, and the owner is willing to sell the whole, he may require the authority to purchase the whole, and the authority in these circumstances may abandon the notice to treat.[35] But although a notice to treat may not be withdrawn except in the circumstances mentioned, the court may infer an abandonment of rights conferred by the notice. The Court of Appeal in *Simpsons Motor Sales (London) Ltd v. Hendon Corporation*[36] reviewed the law on this topic generally and stated the following propositions.

(1) The acquiring authority is under a duty to proceed to acquire the land within a reasonable time and if this is not done the authority may lose its right to enforce the notice to treat.

(2) The authority may evince an intention to abandon the notice to treat in which case the owner may regard it as abandoned, or may refuse to accept abandonment and enforce the notice—but he must make his position clear and proceed within a reasonable time.

(3) If the authority shows a continuing intention to acquire the land but for a purpose not authorised by the compulsory purchase order, the notice may be restrained as *ultra vires*.[37]

(4) Apart from delay or abandonment, a party may so have conducted or misconducted himself in relation to the other party as to lose, against him, the right to enforce the notice to treat.

The decision of the Court of Appeal was upheld by the House of Lords, where the particular point was made that the court may interfere in its equitable jurisdiction to prevent an acquiring authority from enforcing its legal rights under a notice to treat, but only if to do so would be against good conscience because of bad faith or abuse of power by the authority, or an

---

[33] s.31.

[34] *R. v. Northumbrian Water Ltd, ex p. Able UK Ltd* (1995) 72 P. & C.R. 95 (the landowner was also required to return an advance payment of compensation under the Land Compensation Act 1973, s.52).

[35] *King v. The Wycombe Railway Company* (1860) 29 L.J. Ch. 462.

[36] [1963] Ch. 57, C.A.; [1964] A.C. 1088, H.L. See also *R. v. Carmarthen District Council, ex p. Blewin Trust Ltd* (1989) 59 P. & C.R. 379.

[37] See hereon *Grice v. Dudley Corporation* [1958] Ch. 329.

alteration in his position by the owner making it unfair in the particular circumstances.

Section 5(2A)–(2E) of the Compulsory Purchase Act 1965[38] now provides that a notice to treat ceases to have effect at the end of the three years, unless the compensation has been agreed or awarded, or paid or paid into court; a general vesting declaration has been executed; the acquiring authority has taken possession of the land; or the question of compensation has been referred to the Lands Tribunal. However, the period may be extended by agreement between the owner and the acquiring authority. When the notice to treat ceases to have effect, the acquiring authority must notify the owner and is liable to compensate him for any consequential loss or expenses.

5–18   If notice to treat is not served within three years of the coming into operation of the compulsory purchase order, the order lapses.[39]

Notice of entry and interest

5–19   In the ordinary course of events a purchaser enters the land on completion, but under the Compulsory Purchase Act 1965 the acquiring authority may at any time after notice to treat has been served give notice of entry, to take effect not less than 14 days after service. Interest is payable at the prescribed rate[40] on the purchase price as finally assessed from the date of entry to the date of payment.[41] When possession has been taken the claimant has a right upon request to an advance payment of 90 per cent of the agreed or estimated compensation.[42]

Conveyance

5–20   When notice to treat has been served and the amount of compensation has been settled the land is conveyed in accordance with normal conveyancing practice. The Compulsory Purchase Act 1965 provides for the vesting of the land in the acquiring authority where the parties refuse to take compensation or to convey, or do not show title, or cannot be found: the purchase-money is lodged in court and a deed poll is executed by which the land vests in the authority.[43] The costs of all conveyances, including all incidental expenses, are to be borne by the acquiring authority.[44] The Act of

---

[38] Inserted by the Planning and Compensation Act 1991, s.67, September 25, 1991.

[39] Compulsory Purchase Act 1965, s.4. Service by the acquiring authority on persons affected by an order of the particulars prescribed by section 3(3) of the Compulsory Purchase (Vesting Declarations) Act 1981 is insufficient: *Co-Operative Insurance Society v. Hastings Borough Council* (1993) 91 L.G.R. 608 (*Westminster City Council v. Quereshi* (1990) 88 L.G.R. 826 not followed).

[40] Acquisition of Land (Rate of Interest after Entry) Regulations 1995 (S.I. 1995 No. 2262).

[41] s.11; Land Compensation Act 1961, s.32. The date of entry for the purposes of assessing compensation and interest is that of the first entry onto any part of the land described in the notice: *Chilton v. Telford Development Corporation* [1987] 1 W.L.R. 872 (under analogous provisions of the New Towns Act 1965). For special powers of entry when a general vesting declaration has been made, see ss.8 and 9 of the Compulsory Purchase (Vesting Declarations) Act 1981: see § 5–21.

[42] Land Compensation Act 1973, s.52, as amended by the Planning and Compensation Act 1991, s.63(1). There is also a right to an advance payment of accrued interest: s.52A, inserted by the 1991 Act, s.63(2).

[43] ss.5(3), 9 and Sched. 2.

[44] Compulsory Purchase Act 1965, s.23.

1965 also contains provisions relating to conveyance by persons under disability, but these provisions are now rarely invoked, for under modern law the power of sale has been greatly extended.[45]

General vesting declarations

The Compulsory Purchase (Vesting Declarations) Act 1981, replacing **5–21** powers which earlier appeared in the Town and Country Planning Act 1968, makes possible a speedier vesting process by means of general vesting declarations. Where this procedure is followed, legal title to the land which is the subject of a confirmed compulsory purchase order passes to the acquiring authority on the date on which the declaration takes effect, and thereafter the authority is able to deal with the land as it chooses, and may resell the land, without having to await the investigation of title and without having to wait for completion in the conveyancing sense. Compensation in respect of the acquisition can be claimed by the former owner as if notice to treat had been served, and he would then be required to establish his title to the land acquired.[46]

This procedure is available to all authorities possessing compulsory powers under whatever legislation those powers are conferred.

Principles of compensation

The acquiring authority will have served notice to treat on interested **5–22** parties, requiring them, *inter alia*, to submit particulars of their claims. Their claims may, of course, be settled by agreement, and in practice generally are, but if the parties fail to agree (or if no claim is made) the matter will be determined by the Lands Tribunal in accordance with the principles laid down in the Land Compensation Acts 1961 and 1973.[47] In the case of tenants from year to year or for a year, or lesser period, who are not entitled to notice to treat, provision for compensation is made by section 20 of the Compulsory Purchase Act 1965.

Compensation on compulsory purchase is made up of three principal **5–23** elements—(a) the value of the land taken; (b) if only part of the owner's land is taken, compensation for severance and/or injurious affection in respect of the land retained; and (c) compensation for disturbance or any other matter not directly based on the value of the land.

The fundamental principle underlying this basis of compensation was stated in the often repeated words of Lord Justice Scott in *Horn v. Sunderland Corporation*,[47a] when he said that the owner:

> "has the right to be put, so far as money can do it, in the same position as if his land had not been taken from him. In other words, he gains the right to receive a money payment not less than the loss imposed on him in the public interest, but, on the other hand, no greater."

[45] ss.2, 3 and Sched. 1.
[46] See hereon the Compulsory Purchase of Land (Vesting Declarations) Regulations 1990 (S.I. 1990 No. 497).
[47] Compulsory Purchase Act 1965, s.6.
[47a] [1941] 2 K.B. 26 at p. 42.

141

The totality of the compensation should recompense the owner accordingly.[48]

5-24 The Land Compensation Act 1961 lays down (a) certain general rules for assessing compensation; (b) certain special rules concerning the appreciation or depreciation in the value of land resulting from the compulsory purchase scheme; and (c) what assumptions may be made in valuing the land as to the grant of planning permission for its future development.

The general rules

5-25 The Lands Tribunal in fixing the *total* amount of compensation must have regard to the rules in section 5 of the Land Compensation Act 1961. These are as follows:

(a) No allowance shall be made on account of the acquisition being compulsory.

(b) The value of land shall be taken to be the amount which the land if sold in the open market by a willing seller might be expected to realise.[49]

(c) The special suitability or adaptability of the land for any purpose shall not be taken into account if that purpose is a purpose to which it could be applied only in pursuance of statutory powers, or for which there is no market apart from the requirements of any authority possessing compulsory purchase powers.[50]

(d) Where the value of the land is increased by reason of the use thereof or of any premises thereon in a manner which could be restrained by any court, or is contrary to law, or is detrimental to the health of the occupants of the premises or to the public health, the amount of that increase shall not be taken into account.[51]

(e) Where land is, and but for the compulsory acquisition would continue to be, devoted to a purpose of such a nature that there is no general demand or market for land for that purpose, the compensation may, if

---

[48] In *Wimpey & Co. Ltd v. Middlesex County Council* [1938] 3 All E.R. 781 a claim for prospective profits of a building developer was disallowed.

[49] The words "expected to realise" refer to the expectations of properly qualified persons who have taken pains to inform themselves of all the particulars ascertainable about the property, its capabilities, the demand for it and likely buyers: *Church Cottage Investments v. Hillingdon London Borough* [1990] 15 E.G. 51.

[50] See *Lambe v. Secretary of State for War* [1955] 2 Q.B. 612; *Batchelor v. Kent County Council* (1989) 59 P. & C.R. 357 (emphasising that the words are "specially suitable" not merely "most suitable") and *Hertfordshire County Council v. Ozanne* [1991] 1 W.L.R. 105 (the statutory powers must relate to the use of the land acquired, and not, *e.g.*, the stopping-up of a highway on other land). The words "the special needs of a particular purchaser or" after "from" were repealed by the Planning and Compensation Act 1991, Sched. 15, Pt. I, para. 1.

[51] See *Hughes v. Doncaster Metropolitan Borough Council* [1991] 1 A.C. 382, where the House of Lords held (1) that this bars a claim for disturbance where a use has been contrary to law; but (2) that unauthorised development is not "contrary to law" if it is immune from enforcement action.

the Lands Tribunal is satisfied that reinstatement in some other place is bona fide intended, be assessed on the basis of the reasonable cost of equivalent reinstatement.

(f) The provisions of rule 2 shall not affect the assessment of compensation for disturbance or any other matter not directly based on the value of land.

The special rules

In applying the rules contained in section 5 the Tribunal must leave certain **5-26** matters out of account and must take certain matters into account. They are contained in sections 6–9 of the 1961 Act and may be summarised as follows:

(a) No account shall be taken of any increase or decrease in the value of the land which is attributable to development, or the prospect of development, under the kinds of scheme of development specified in Schedule 1 to the Act for which the land is being acquired.

(b) Where the owner of the land acquired retains ownership of contiguous or adjacent land and the value of the land he retains is enhanced by the general scheme, the amount by which the value is increased is to be deducted.

(c) No account shall be taken of any depreciation in the value of the land attributable to the fact that an indication has been given that the land was to be acquired by a public authority.

It was decided in *Pointe Gourde Quarrying and Transport Co. Ltd v. Sub-intendent of Crown Lands*[52] that compensation should not be increased by reason of the acquiring authority's scheme[53] and this common law principle still applies in addition to the statutory provisions.[54] However, neither the *Pointe Gourde* rule nor section 9 of the Land Compensation Act 1961 applies to require a covenant reserving a plot of land for a school to be disregarded in assessing compensation when the land is compulsorily acquired for that purpose; the *Pointe Gourde* principle bears on the value of the interest once the interest has been determined, not on the determination of the interest itself.[55]

The planning assumptions

The grant of planning permission can substantially increase the value of **5-27** the land taken, and the Lands Tribunal must take into account any planning

---

[52] [1947] A.C. 565.

[53] As to the meaning of "scheme", see *Wilson v. Liverpool City Council* [1971] 1 W.L.R. 302. "Scheme" in this context is not confined to the kinds of scheme in the 1961 Act as at (a) above.

[54] See also *Melwood Units Pty. Ltd v. Commissioner of Main Roads* [1979] A.C. 426; *Batchelor v. Kent County Council* (1989) 59 P. & C.R. 357. The principle also requires a decrease in value entirely due to the scheme underlying the development to be disregarded: *Jelson Ltd v. Blaby District Council* [1977] 1 W.L.R. 1020; *cf. Birmingham District Council v. Morris and Jacombs* (1976) 33 P. & C.R. 27. See also *Ward Construction (Medway) Ltd v. Barclays Bank plc* (1994) 68 P. & C.R. 391, where the Court of Appeal emphasised that once the Lands Tribunal had correctly directed itself as to the test to be applied, whether land would have a substantial premium value in the no-scheme world is a question of fact to be determined by the tribunal.

[55] *Abbey Homesteads (Developments) Ltd v. Northamptonshire County Council* (1992) 64 P. & C.R. 377.

permission in force at the date of the notice to treat. But section 14 of the Land Compensation Act 1961[56] provides that various assumptions as to the grant of other planning permissions may be made in addition. These are divided into two kinds:

(a) assumptions not derived from development plans and
(b) assumptions derived from development plans.

Assumptions not derived from development plans[57]

5–28   (1) That planning permission would be given for the development envisaged in the proposals of the acquiring authority in relation to the land.[58]

(2) That planning permission would be given for development of any class specified in the Town and Country Planning Act 1990, Schedule 3, paragraph 1, (rebuilding)[58a] and 2 (the use as to two or more dwelling houses of any building which at a material date was used as a single dwelling house). However, if compensation has become payable in respect of an order under section 102 of the 1990 Act, requiring the removal of a building or the discontinuance of a use, it will not be assumed that permission would be granted for rebuilding or for the resumption of the use.

(3) That planning permission would be given for development in respect of which a certificate of appropriate alternative development has been issued by the local planning authority under Part III of the Land Compensation Act 1961.

Under this procedure either the owner of the interest to be acquired or the acquiring authority may apply to the local planning authority, under section 17 of the Land Compensation Act 1961,[59] for a certificate, known as a certificate of appropriate alternative development, stating the classes of development, if any, for which planning permission would have been granted if the land were not to be acquired by a public authority. It is for the applicant to specify the class or classes of development which he thinks appropriate. The local planning authority may issue a certificate for all or any of the specified classes or some other class or classes, and the certificate must in any event state that permission would have been granted for any development for which the land is to be acquired. Regard may properly be paid to the possibility of development on a site comprising both the applicant's site and other land not under his ownership or control and to the possibility of a particular development of an exceptional nature.[60] The

---

[56] As amended, from September 25, 1991, by the Planning and Compensation Act 1991, s.64 and Sched. 15, para. 15.
[57] Land Compensation Act 1961, s.15 as amended by the 1991 Act, s.31(4) and Sched. 6, para. 1.
[58] See *Myers v. Milton Keynes Development Corporation* [1974] 1 W.L.R. 696.
[58a] Subject to the condition laid down in the 1990 Art, Shed. 10.
[59] s.17; as amended by the Local Government, Planning and Land Act 1980, s.121 (from September 25, 1991) the Planning and Compensation Act 1991, s.65 and Sched. 15, Part II, para. 16; and Land Compensation Development Order 1974 (S.I. 1974 No. 539), as amended by S.I. 1986 No. 435. See also *Grampian Regional Council v. Secretary of State for Scotland* [1983] 1 W.L.R. 1340.
[60] *Sutton v. Secretary of State for the Environment* (1984) 50 P. & C.R. 147.

content of a certificate of appropriate alternative development must be determined by reference to factors in existence at the date of the authority's offer to purchase the land and not, for example, at the date of the decision.[61] Moreover, not only is the authority's proposal to acquire the land compulsorily to be ignored in assessing what the land might otherwise have been used for, but the planning policies underlying the proposal are also to be ignored.[62] The competing need for public open space in the area may amount to a valid planning objection to the hypothetical development.[63] Where the relevant land is to be acquired for use for, or in connection with, the construction of a highway, or such a use is being considered by a highway authority, it must be assumed that if the relevant land were not so used, no highway would be constructed to meet the same or substantially the same need.[64] An appeal lies to the Secretary of State by the owner or the acquiring authority.

Assumptions derived from development plans[65]

(1) Where land is included in a development plan and is shown in the plan **5–29** as intended for *specified development*, then it will be assumed that planning permission would be given for that development.

(2) Where the land is shown in the development plan as an area allocated primarily for a specified use (for example, residential) or a range of two or more primary uses (for example, commercial and industrial) it will be assumed that permission would be granted for any development, falling within the specified primary use or range of uses, for which permission might reasonably have been expected if none of the land in question had been proposed to be acquired.

(3) Where land is to be comprehensively developed, and this is to be construed as an action area for which a local plan is in force, it will be assumed that planning permission would be given for any development falling within the range of uses allowed for the area. This is subject to it being development for which planning permission might reasonably have been granted on the assumptions:

(a) that the area had not been defined as an area of comprehensive development and no particulars or proposals relating to any land in the area had been comprised in the current plan, and

(b) that no development or redevelopment already carried out in accordance with the plan had taken place, and

---

[61] *Fox v. Secretary of State for the Environment* (1991) 31 R.V.R. 171.
[62] *ibid.*
[63] *Maidstone Borough Council v. Secretary of State for the Environment* (1994) 69 P. & C.R. 1.
[64] Land Compensation Act 1961, s.14(5)–(8), inserted by the Planning and Compensation Act 1991, s.64, with effect from September 25, 1991. References to construction of a highway include its alteration or improvement: *ibid.* s.14(8).
[65] Land Compensation Act 1961, s.16; Town and Country Planning Act 1990, s.54(5), Sched. 2, Pt. III, para. 5. And see *Re Croydon Development Plans 1954 and 1959; Harrison v. London Borough of Croydon* [1968] Ch. 479; *Margate Corporation v. Devotwill Investments Ltd* [1970] 3 All E.R. 864; and *Provincial Properties (London) Ltd v. Caterham and Warlingham Urban District Council* [1972] 1 Q.B. 453.

(c) that no part of the land was proposed to be acquired by a public authority.

In determining whether planning permission might reasonably have been expected, in a case where the relevant land is to be acquired for use for or in connection with the construction of a highway, or such a use is being considered by a highway authority, it must be assumed that if the relevant land were not so used, no highway would be constructed to meet the same or substantially the same need.[66]

All the assumptions derived from the development plan are on the basis that they are subject to any conditions which might reasonably have been imposed and any indication in the current development plan that the development might only be allowed to take place at some future date.

Where in any area structure and local plans are in force, these together will provide the planning assumptions: where, in the transitional period, the structure plan but not a local plan is in force either the structure plan or the former development plan will be taken to be the development plan, whichever gives rise to those assumptions as to the grant of planning permission which are more favourable to the owner.

Where a unitary development plan is in force this plan will provide the planning assumptions.

5–30 Having set out these various rules and assumptions for the assessment of compensation, consideration is now given to the three elements of compensation mentioned in paragraph 5–23.

Value of the land taken

5–31 Compensation for the value of the land taken will be assessed at either (a) the open market value provided for by rule 2 of section 5 of the 1961 Act or (b) the equivalent reinstatement basis in rule 5. It is only in rare cases that the rule 5 basis is applicable.

Compensation for a church or mission would generally fall to be assessed on the basis of the cost of equivalent reinstatement under rule 5,[67] but where this rule is applied there must be a bona fide intention on the part of the claimant to rebuild in some other place.

> *Edgehill Light Ry v. Secretary of State for War.*[68] The company, whose land had been acquired compulsorily, claimed that in calculating the amount of compensation the principle of equivalent reinstatement applied, since the land acquired was devoted to a purpose for which no general demand or market existed. But the company failed to establish its claim for compensation based on rule 5 on the ground that it had no intention to rebuild the railway in some other place.

In the expression "no general demand or market for land for that purpose"

---

[66] See n. 64.
[67] *Zoar Independent Church Trustees v. Rochester Corporation* [1975] Q.B. 246. See also *Nonentities Society v. Kidderminster Borough Council* (1971) 22 P. & C.R. 224 and *Manchester Homeopathic Clinic v. Manchester Corporation, ibid.* at p. 243 (theatre and clinic respectively within rule 5).
[68] (1956) 6 P. & C.R. 211.

in rule 5, the term "general" qualifies only "demand" and not "market" as well.

> *Harrison & Hetherington Ltd v. Cumbria County Council.*[69] The House of Lords *held* on the facts that rule 5 applied in respect of the compulsory purchase of land used for a livestock auction market. "General demand" did not include a special demand which might only arise in particular circumstances, such as when an existing market was offered for sale. The evidence was that in the north of England a state of equilibrium had been reached and that there had been no sale of virgin land for such a market which was not a replacement of an existing market.

Furthermore, the application of rule 5 is in any case in the discretion of the Lands Tribunal so that, *e.g.* if the cost of reinstatement would be out of all proportion to the benefits resulting from reinstatement the Tribunal could reject the basis.[70]

The Land Compensation Act 1973 specifically provides for the application of rule 5 to the acquisition of any dwelling substantially modified for a disabled person.[71]

5–32 The date for valuation will in a rule 2 case be the date on which the authority takes possession or on which the compensation is settled, whichever is the earlier, and in a rule 5 case the earliest date at which reinstatement could reasonably have been carried out.[72]

There may, of course, be more than one interest in the land to be valued, *e.g.* a freehold interest and a leasehold interest, and there may also be a lesser interest to be compensated under section 20 of the 1965 Act.

Compensation for severance and injurious affection

5–33 Compensation under this head stems from section 7 of the Compulsory Purchase Act 1965. It applies where the owner holds other land with the land taken and that other land, called the retained land, is depreciated in value, *e.g.* where the value of the retained land plus the compensation for the value of the land taken is worth less than the value of the whole before the compulsory acquisition; indeed, the depreciation would usually be valued by taking a before and after valuation of the rule 2 open market value.[73] Thus, if most of the front garden of a house is acquired for a road widening scheme, the value of the land taken may be small and the retained house may be depreciated much more because it now has practically no front garden, and the noise, dust and lights of traffic are brought nearer to it. The retained land need not be contiguous to the acquired land for compensation to be claimed

---

[69] (1985) 50 P. & C.R. 396.

[70] See *Festiniog Ry v. Central Electricity Generating Board* (1962) 13 P. & C.R. 248—here the cost of reinstatement was found to be disproportionately high; *cf. Sparks v. Leeds City Council* (1977) 34 P. & C.R. 248.

[71] s.45.

[72] *Birmingham Corporation v. West Midlands Baptist (Trust) Association (Inc.)* [1970] A.C. 874. This rule 2 principle will also apply where the purchase is by agreement leaving the price to be fixed as if a notice to treat had been served: *Washington Development Corporation v. Bamblings (Washington) Ltd* (1984) 83 L.G.R. 561.

[73] *Exors. of J. R. Bullock, deceased v. Ministry of Transport* (1969) 211 E.G. 235. See, generally, *Duke of Buccleuch v. Metropolitan Board of Works* (1872) L.R. 5 H.L. 418; (injurious affection); *Holt v. Gas Light and Coke Co.* (1872) L.R. 7 Q.B. 728 (severance).

under this head, provided that the owner's possession and control of each of the relevant pieces of land gives an enhanced value to all of them.[74]

Under section 44 of the Land Compensation Act 1973, where damage is caused by works constructed partly on land taken and partly on other land, a claim for injurious affection may include the effect of the works as a whole. If injury or depreciation arises from a wrongful use of statutory powers, the appropriate remedy would be by way of an action for damages or for an injunction or both.

Compensation for disturbance or any other matter not directly based on the value of the land taken

5–34   This compensation derives from case law and is expressly preserved by rule 6 of section 5 of the Land Compensation Act 1961. Broadly, it covers all the expenditure or loss which an owner may incur in having to uproot himself from the land taken and re-establish himself elsewhere. The Court of Appeal considered the principles in the following case:

> *Harvey v. Crawley Development Corporation.*[75] This was an appeal on case stated by the Lands Tribunal. Mrs Harvey agreed with the Crawley Development Corporation to sell her house at an agreed price. She claimed in addition as "compensation for disturbance" (1) the expenses of moving her furniture and having curtains and carpets adjusted to fit a new house, and (2) surveyor's fees, legal costs and travelling expenses incurred by her, first, in an abortive proposed purchase of a new home, and secondly, in the purchase of a new home. The corporation admitted that the items at (1) were so claimable, but disputed those at (2). *Held*, Mrs Harvey was entitled to the costs claimed, for any loss sustained by a dispossessed owner-occupier of a house which flowed from the compulsory acquisition could properly be the subject of compensation for disturbance, provided (a) that it was not too remote, and (b) that it was the natural, direct and reasonable consequence of dispossession.

Compensation for disturbance may cover many items, especially in commercial cases, such as the cost of transferring plant and equipment to new premises,[76] loss of goodwill attached to the premises taken, loss of profits while re-establishing a business, and, in a case where it is not reasonably possible to re-establish the business, loss from the extinction of the business. By section 46 of the 1973 Act where a person occupying business premises is over 60 and does not wish to relocate the business, it may be assumed that it is not reasonably practicable to re-establish the business provided that he has not disposed of the goodwill and undertakes that he will not do so and will not re-engage in a similar business elsewhere within an area and for a time laid down by the acquiring authority.[77] Compensation under this head

---

[74] *Cowper Essex v. Acton Local Board* (1889) 14 App.Cas. 153; *Sisters of Charity of Rockingham v. R.* [1922] 2 A.C. 315.

[75] [1957] 1 Q.B. 485. See also *Horn v. Sunderland Corporation* [1941] 2 K.B. 26; *Woolfson v. Strathclyde Regional Council* (1978) 38 P. & C.R. 521.

[76] The amount of any regional development grant received by the claimant is not to be deducted from disturbance compensation: *Palatine Graphic Arts Co. v. Liverpool City Council* [1986] Q.B. 335.

[77] A person may be entitled to compensation under section 46 where he ceases trading before he is required to give up the land provided that it is established that the cessation of the business was the consequence of the acquisition: *Sheffield Development Corporation v. Glossop Sectional Buildings Ltd* (1994) 70 P. & C.R. 1.

may also be payable where only part of the land is taken, *e.g.* where part of a farm is taken and the farmer suffers a loss by having to make a forced sale of part of his stock. It is usual to leave the quantification of a disturbance claim until the loss or expenditure concerned has materialised.[78] But, if this is not done, the Lands Tribunal will have to make the best estimate they can on the available evidence. Costs incurred prior to acquisition but in reasonable anticipation of it may be recoverable.[79]

The costs of preparing and negotiating the claim may be claimed as a matter not directly based on the value of the land under rule 6,[80] but this rule does not include either the costs of opposing a compulsory purchase order or the costs incurred in obtaining, on appeal to the Secretary of State, a certificate of appropriate alternative development to enable the value of the land to be assessed on a higher basis.[81] The costs of any reference to the Lands Tribunal are not a subject of claim but will be awarded by the Tribunal according to the outcome of the case.[82] The costs of the conveyance to the authority will be payable by it under section 23 of the 1965 Act.

As mentioned in paragraph 5–22, a tenant from year to year or for a year **5–35** or less period is separately provided for by section 20 of the Compulsory Purchase Act 1965. This provides that such a person shall be entitled to compensation for the value of his unexpired term or interest in the land, for damage from severance and injurious affection if only part of his land is taken, for any just allowance which ought to be made to him by an incoming tenant, and for any loss or injury he may sustain. In short, it puts him in very much the same position as any other claimant. Where he is a business tenant his right to apply for a new tenancy will be taken into account,[83] and where he is a tenant farmer his security of tenure under the Agricultural Holdings Act 1986 may be taken into account.[84]

Compensation where permission for additional development is granted after acquisition

Part IV (sections 23–29) of and Schedule 3 to the Land Compensation Act **5–36** 1961, inserted by the Planning and Compensation Act 1991, Schedule 14, provides that where an interest in land is compulsorily acquired, or acquired by an authority possessing compulsory powers, and, within 10 years of the date of completion, permission is granted for additional development, a claim to further compensation may arise.[85] Thus, if the original compen-

---

[78] *Birmingham Corporation v. West Midlands Baptist (Trust) Association (Inc.)* [1970] A.C. 874 at p. 896.

[79] *Prasad v. Wolverhampton Borough Council* [1983] Ch. 333 (a case concerning a disturbance payment claimed under the Land Compensation Act 1973, s.37 (see § 5–40), approved by the Privy Council in *Director of Buildings and Lands v. Shun Fung Ironworks Ltd* [1995] 2 A.C. 111).

[80] *London County Council v. Tobin* [1959] 1 W.L.R. 354; *Radnor Trust Ltd v. Central Electricity Generating Board* (1960) 12 P. & C.R. 111.

[81] *Hull and Humber Investment Co. Ltd v. Hull Corporation* [1965] 2 Q.B. 145.

[82] Land Compensation Act 1961, s.4.

[83] Land Compensation Act 1973, s.47.

[84] *ibid.* s.48, as amended by the Agricultural Holdings Act 1986, Sched. 14, para. 53.

[85] The forms of notice have been prescribed by the Land Compensation (Additional Development) (Forms) Regulations 1992 (S.I. 1992 No. 271).

sation or purchase price would have been larger had the new permission been granted then, a claim can be made for the additional amount. This does not, however, apply where the land is acquired under the Local Government, Planning and Land Act 1980, ss.142 or 143 (acquisitions by urban development corporations or by highway authorities in connection with urban development areas), under the New Towns Act 1981, or where the compulsory purchase order included a direction under section 50 of the Planning (Listed Buildings and Conservation Areas) Act 1990 (minimum compensation where a building is deliberately allowed to fall into disrepair).

Special statutory payments and benefits

5–37   Apart from the settlement of the compensation under the foregoing provisions the Land Compensation Act 1973 contains a number of special provisions in relation to persons displaced from land by compulsory purchase, or, in some cases, by other means also.

The provisions of the 1973 Act apply to those displaced from land whether or not, in cases (a), (c) and (d) below, they have sufficient interest in the land to entitle them to compensation under the rules appearing in the preceding paragraphs. These provisions relate to home loss payments, farm loss payments, disturbance payments, and the right to rehousing. In some cases a claimant is entitled as of right; in others a discretion lies with the authority.

5–38   (a) *Home loss payments.*[86] This payment is due to a person displaced from his home in consequence of a compulsory acquisition of the premises, or on account of redevelopment by the authority, or because of the making of certain orders under the Housing Acts, the more common being a closing order or a demolition order. He must have occupied the dwelling as his main residence throughout the previous year. A displaced caravan dweller may also be qualified unless he is given an alternative site on which to place his caravan. This payment is mandatory. Payment to the vendor is discretionary where the authority acquires by agreement though having compulsory powers, but any person other than the vendor who is displaced in such a case is entitled to a payment. A discretionary payment can also be made to a residential occupier who, on the date of displacement, has been in occupation for less than a year.

Where the date of displacement is on or after November 16, 1990, the amount of the home loss payment is £1,500, except in the case of a displaced owner, who is entitled to a payment of 10 per cent of the market value, subject to a maximum of £15,000 and a minimum of £1,500.[87]

5–39   (b) *Farm loss payment.*[88] This is due to a farmer displaced from the whole of his land because of the compulsory acquisition of his interest in it, provided that he is the owner of the farm or is a tenant for a year or from year to year (or with a greater interest) and provided that he begins to farm

---

[86] 1973 Act, ss.29–33, as amended by the Planning and Compensation Act 1991, ss.68, 69 and Sched. 15, para. 22, as from September 25, 1991.
[87] *ibid.* s.30, inserted by the 1991 Act, s.68(3).
[88] Land Compensation Act 1973, ss.34–36, as amended by the 1991 Act, Sched. 15, para. 6.

elsewhere within three years of displacement. In general terms the amount due is a sum equal to the average annual profit from the land acquired for a three-year period after deducting a notional rent. It is not payable where the compensation paid for the interest of the farmer includes development value and exceeds the existing use value plus the farm loss payment.

An authority has a discretionary power to make a farm loss payment where the acquisition is by agreement under the shadow of compulsory powers.

(c) *Disturbance payment.*[89] A person who is displaced from land for any of the reasons mentioned in (a) above and who has no compensatable interest (he may, for example, be a lodger who occupies under a licence[90]) is entitled to a disturbance payment. Where there is no legal entitlement under this provision an authority is empowered to make a discretionary payment. The disturbance payment consists of removal expenses,[91] and, in appropriate cases, the loss sustained by reason of the disturbance of trade or business consequent upon the claimant having to quit his land. Particular provision is made for the disabled. The Lands Tribunal has jurisdiction to determine a dispute in respect of the amount of the payment, whether made as a matter of entitlement or of discretion.[92] **5-40**

(d) *Rehousing.*[93] A housing authority is under a duty to secure the provision of suitable alternative accommodation, where this is not otherwise available on reasonable terms, for any person displaced from residential accommodation for any of the reasons mentioned under (a) above, unless the displacement results from his serving a blight notice. The provision also applies to a caravan dweller displaced from a site with no suitable alternative site. Power is given to offer an owner-occupier or lessee with more than three years of his lease to run a mortgage advance repayable on maturity. In the case of a short-term tenant the displacing authority may pay any reasonable expenses he incurs, other than the purchase price, in connection with the acquisition of an alternative dwelling. **5-41**

Compensation to adjoining owners

So far in this chapter we have been considering compensation to persons whose land is taken for some public project. But often the property of **5-42**

---

[89] *ibid.* ss.37 and 38. In *R. v. Islington London Borough Council, ex p. Knight* [1984] 1 W.L.R. 205, a council tenant rehoused by agreement was held not to be entitled to claim a disturbance payment, as the relinquishment of the tenancy did not amount to the acquisition of land by the council.

[90] To qualify for a disturbance payment under the 1973 Act, s.37, the claimant must be in "lawful possession"; "possession" means physical occupation with the intention to exclude unauthorised intruders. Accordingly, a licensee may be eligible for a disturbance payment: *Wrexham Maelor Borough Council v. MacDougall* (1993) 69 P. & C.R. 109.

[91] See *Nolan v. Sheffield Metropolitan District Council* (1979) 38 P. & C.R. 741, L.T.

[92] *Gozra v. Hackney London Borough Council* (1988) 57 P. & C.R. 211, C.A.

[93] Land Compensation Act 1973, ss.39–43. See *R. v. Bristol Corporation, ex p. Hendy* [1974] 1 W.L.R. 498.

neighbouring owners, none of whose land is taken, may be depreciated by the construction of the works or the use of them. Such owners may be entitled to claim under section 10 of the Compulsory Purchase Act 1965, which confers a right to compensation on an adjoining owner whose lands are injuriously affected by the *works* which the acquiring authority carries out in lawfully exercising statutory powers: compensation, it is to be observed, is payable only when lands have been injuriously affected by the execution of works and not, under this section, by the subsequent user of those works.[94] An action in tort might, of course, lie if there were a negligent or otherwise wrongful use of a statutory power. Not every injurious act entitles an adjoining owner to compensation—the act complained of must be one which, if it had been committed by someone other than an authority acting under statutory powers, would have been actionable at common law. The compensation will be the amount by which the claimant's land is depreciated by the construction of the works.

If there are easements, *e.g.* a right of way over, or restrictive covenants affecting the land compulsorily acquired in favour of an adjoining owner's land, he cannot maintain an action against the acquiring authority for obstruction of the easement or breach of the covenants[95]; his remedy is compensation under section 10 of the Act of 1965.[96] Section 14 of the Local Government (Miscellaneous Provisions) Act 1976 extends section 10 to cases where the land on which the works are constructed was acquired by agreement.

5–43   A right to compensation for depreciation caused by the *use* of public works is given by the provisions in Part I of the Land Compensation Act 1973.[97] A right to compensation is given where the value of an interest in land is depreciated by certain physical factors caused by the *use* of highways, aerodromes and other works on land provided or used in the exercise of a statutory power. The physical factors are noise, vibration, smell, fumes, smoke and artificial lighting, and the discharge on to the land of any solid or liquid substance. The right to claim is available only in cases where the persons concerned are debarred by statute from bringing an action for nuisance at common law. Generally speaking the property owner has no redress at common law since the use is immune, expressly or by implication, from an action in nuisance.

This right to compensation is available to resident owner-occupiers of residential property, owner-occupiers of agricultural units, and owner-occupiers of other premises where the rateable value does not exceed £2,250. The owner must have a freehold interest or a tenancy with not less than three years to run.

[94] *Metropolitan Board of Works v. McCarthy* (1874) L.R. 7 H.L. 243.
[95] *Kirby v. Harrogate School Board* [1896] 1 Ch. 437; Town and Country Planning Act 1990, s.237; Local Government Act 1972, s.120(3); and Local Government (Miscellaneous Provisions) Act 1976, s.14.
[96] *Long Eaton Recreation Grounds Co. v. Midland Railway* [1902] 2 K.B. 574; *Re Simeon and Isle of Wight Rural District Council* [1937] Ch. 525.
[97] ss.1–19, as amended by the Local Government, Planning and Land Act 1980, s.112. See also the Noise Insulation Regulations 1975 (S.I. 1975 No. 1763), as amended by S.I. 1988 No. 2000.

II. APPROPRIATION, DISPOSAL AND DEVELOPMENT

Appropriation

A local authority may appropriate land held for one statutory purpose, **5–44** and which is no longer required for that purpose, to some other statutory purpose.[98] Common land may not be appropriated under this provision if it exceeds an area of 250 square yards; if it does an appropriation may be undertaken under section 229 of the Town and Country Planning Act 1990. This involves special parliamentary procedure unless equally advantageous land is provided in exchange, or the land is required for the widening or drainage of a highway and the Secretary of State is satisfied that exchange land is not necessary. Common land having an area of 250 square yards or less, or land forming part of an open space, may not be appropriated until after public notice has been given and any objection considered by the authority.

Under section 232 of the Town and Country Planning Act 1990 land held for planning purposes may be appropriated to other purposes.

Disposal

Section 123 of the Local Government Act 1972[99] enables a principal **5–45** council, and section 127[1] enables a parish or community council to dispose of any of its land as it chooses.[2] But an authority may not dispose of open space land under either section until after public notice has been given and any objections considered.[3]

Except in the case of a short tenancy, the consent of the appropriate Minister[4] is required if it is intended to dispose of the land at less than the best consideration that can reasonably be obtained.[5] "Consideration" here

---

[98] Local Government Act 1972, ss.122 and 126, as amended by the Local Government, Planning and Land Act 1980, Sched. 23. The question whether land is no longer required for its existing purpose is for the local authority to decide and not the court: *Att. Gen. v. Manchester Corporation* [1931] 1 Ch. 254; *Dowty Boulton Paul Ltd. v. Wolverhampton Corporation (No. 2)* [1976] Ch. 13. Joint authorities are treated as principal councils for the purposes of s.122: s.146A(1)(b), inserted by the Local Government Act 1985, Sched. 14, para. 16.

[99] As amended by the Local Government, Planning and Land Act 1980, Sched. 23 and the Local Government and Housing Act 1989, Sched. 12.

[1] As so amended.

[2] This enables a local authority to grant an option to renew a lease: *West Middlesex Golf Club Ltd v. Ealing London Borough Council, Local Authority Law* 8/93, p. 5.

[3] "Open space" includes "land ... used for the purposes of public recreation" (definition in s.290(1) of the Town and Country Planning Act 1971 (now s.336(1) of the 1990 Act), applied by s.270(1) of the 1972 Act; for this purpose, use by the public does not have to be of right provided it is lawful: *R. v. Doncaster Metropolitan Borough Council, ex p. Braim* (1986) 85 L.G.R. 233 (lease of part of a common to a golf club to be advertised under s.123(2A)).

[4] A direction by the Secretary of State under s.98 of the Local Government, Planning and Land Act 1980 requiring land to be sold at auction without reserve may carry an implied consent under this provision: *R. v. Secretary of State for the Environment, ex p. Manchester City Council* (1988) 87 L.G.R. 207.

[5] In *R. v. Darlington Borough Council, ex p. Indescon* [1990] 1 E.G.L.R. 278, Kennedy J. held that in principle a court was only likely to find a breach of section 123(2) of the Local Government Act 1972 if a council has (a) failed to take proper advice, or (b) failed to follow proper advice for reasons which cannot be justified, or (c) followed advice which was so plainly erroneous that in accepting it the council must have known that it was acting unreasonably. See also *Disposal of Land for less than the Best Consideration that can reasonably be obtained—Guidance for Authorities* (DoE Circular 6/93, W.O. Circular 19/93).

means the price payable for the land, which may comprise both a sum of money and other elements such as an easement or a right to repurchase reserved by a selling authority, provided those elements have a commercial or monetary value; the fact that a particular development is considered by the authority to be especially desirable cannot form part of the consideration.[6] In deciding what is the best consideration "reasonably obtainable", the authority is entitled to have regard to ethical as well as commercial considerations. However, where there are opposing bidders, the authority must take reasonable steps to see how far each will go to commit himself to the highest offer he is prepared to make.[7] If the obligation to obtain the best consideration can only be fulfilled by putting the land up for sale by tender, this will take precedence over Department of Environment "Crichel Down" guidelines to the effect that land compulsorily acquired should first be offered back to the original owner.[8]

Section 233 of the Town and Country Planning Act 1990 contains a wide power for the disposal of land held for planning purposes. In *R. v. Thurrock Borough Council, ex p. Blue Circle Industries plc*,[9] the Court of Appeal held that an agreement to vary terms of covenants in proposed leases so as to permit the deposit of certain types of waste material on a piece of land did not amount to a "disposal" within section 233 of the Town and Country Planning Act 1990; a disposal was a transaction by which there was an out and out parting with an asset or proprietary interest in an asset.

The Secretary of State may by order apply Part X of the Local Government, Planning and Land Act 1980 to the area of any district or London borough council, and he has so applied it to all areas in England and Wales. He may then for any area to which the Part is so applied maintain a public register of land owned by certain public bodies in the area, including local authorities other than parish or community councils, which in his opinion is not being used, or sufficiently used, for the functions of the body concerned. He may, subject to certain conditions, direct the disposal of any land on the register.

Section 176 of the Leasehold Reform, Housing and Urban Development Act 1993 amended section 98 of the Local Government, Planning and Land Act 1980 to enable the Secretary of State to require the disposal of land

---

[6] *R. v. Middlesbrough Borough Council, ex p. Frostree Ltd* (unreported, December 16, 1988) (council's decision to accept a lower tender for premises from a person who wished to establish a health and fitness club quashed; the Minister's consent should have been obtained). See also *R. v. Essex County Council, ex p. Clearbrook Contractors Ltd* (unreported, April 3, 1981).

[7] *R. v. Essex County Council, ex p. Clearbrook Contractors Ltd* (unreported, April 3, 1981); *R. v. Lancashire County Council, ex p. Telegraph Service Stations, The Times*, June 25, 1988.

[8] *R. v. Commission for the New Towns, ex p. Tomkins and Leach* (1988) 87 L.G.R. 207. The "Crichel Down" rules have been revised: see *Disposal of Surplus Government Land: Obligation to offer land back to former owners or their successors—the "Crichel Down Rules"* (October 30, 1992), issued jointly by the Department of the Environment and the Welsh Office. This is reproduced in the *Encyclopedia of Compulsory Purchase and Compensation*, para. 4–430. See *R. v. Trent Regional Health Authority, ex p. Westerman Ltd* [1995] E.G.C.S. 175.

[9] (1994) 69 P. & C.R. 79.

whether or not it is on a public register under Part X, provided that the conditions for registration are fulfilled. Part X was previously amended by the Local Government 1988,[10] which, *inter alia*, conferred on the Secretary of State power to authorise entry on land to discover if it is suitable for a direction. This power is now exercisable whether or not the land is registered.

Capital money received by a local authority on a disposal of land is subject **5–46** to provisions relating to the capital receipts of local authorities contained in Part IV of the Local Government and Housing Act 1989, referred to at paragraphs 12–19 to 12–35.

Development

Section 235 of the Town and Country Planning Act 1990 enables an **5–47** authority to construct any building or carry out any work on land acquired or appropriated for planning purposes—this power may not, however, be relied on for carrying out work or building for which express statutory power already exists under some other enactment.

The Local Authorities (Land) Act 1963[11] gives certain development powers to local authorities. For the benefit or improvement of its area, an authority may erect buildings and construct and carry out works on land. For such benefit or improvement it may lend money to any person to enable him to acquire land or to erect buildings on land. Money may be loaned in pursuance of building agreements. Garages may be erected and buildings converted into garages.

---

[10] s.31 and Sched. 5.
[11] ss.2 to 5, as amended, in particular in the case of s.3, by the Local Government (Miscellaneous Provisions) Act 1982, s.43.

CHAPTER 6

BY-LAWS

A LOCAL authority by-law may be defined in simple terms as a law which **6–01** operates over the area of the authority, having been made by the authority under a power conferred by statute and confirmed by the Secretary of State for the Home Department or other appropriate Minister. Lord Russell C.J. said in *Kruse v. Johnson*[1]:

> "A by-law, of the class we are here considering, I take to be an ordinance affecting the public, or some portion of the public, imposed by some authority clothed with statutory powers ordering something to be done or not to be done, and accompanied by some sanction or penalty for its non-observance. It necessarily involves restriction of liberty of action by persons who come under its operation as to acts which, but for the by-law, they would be free to do or not do as they please. Further, it involves this consequence—that, if validly made, it has the force of law within the sphere of its legitimate operation."

The law on this topic is considered under the following headings: the source of by-law making powers; the procedure to be followed in the making of by-laws; judicial tests as to the validity of by-laws; penalties and enforcement; waiver, relaxation and repeal.

A. BY-LAW MAKING POWERS

All local authority by-laws derive from statute. There is a doctrine that **6–02** corporate bodies have an inherent power—that is to say, apart from statute—to make by-laws regulating any matter connected with the purposes for which they are established, but it is doubtful if this doctrine has had any significance in modern times so far as local authorities are concerned. It is in any case certain that local authorities do not rely on a common law right.

There are a number of statutes which authorise the making of by-laws, and these are listed in Appendix 5. One general power is mentioned here, namely that conferred by section 235 of the Local Government Act 1972, enabling the councils of districts and London boroughs to make by-laws for good rule and government and for the suppression of nuisances. This provision makes possible a wide range of by-laws—indeed the section is so widely drawn that there would appear to be no limit to the number of offences which could be created. There are, however, two restrictive factors. First, a by-law is not effective unless confirmed by the Secretary of State for the Home Department or other Minister, and, secondly, the courts apply

[1] [1898] 2 Q.B. 91 at p. 96.

certain stringent tests when the validity of a by-law is challenged; so that in practice the form and substance of by-laws made under this section follow a fairly constant pattern. These matters are referred to in succeeding paragraphs.

6–03   By-laws for good rule and government and for the suppression of nuisances do in practice cover a wide variety of topics, as may be seen from the model code which the Secretary of State for the Home Department has issued, notwithstanding the limiting factors referred to above. The model contains clauses on the following topics: music near houses, churches, hospitals; noisy hawking; touting; wireless loudspeakers, gramophones and organs; shooting galleries; indecent language; violent behaviour on school premises; fighting; indecent bathing; indecent shows; nuisances contrary to public decency; wilful jostling; loitering at church doors; advertising vehicles; flags; defacing pavements; advertising bills; broken glass; carrying soot; carrying carcasses; dangerous games near streets; spitting; bulls; cycling on footpaths; the fouling of footpaths by dogs; and noisy animals.

A by-law taken from the model code may nevertheless be open to judicial challenge: see *R. v. Bristol City Council, ex p. McDonough*,[2] where a by-law directed, *inter alia*, against gypsies was quashed; the by-law had appeared in the Home Office list of model by-laws until 1969.

B. Procedure for the Making of By-Laws

6–04   A common procedure is contained in section 236 of the Local Government Act 1972.[3] It applies to all by-laws made by a local authority under the 1972 Act or made by a local authority, or a metropolitan county passenger transport authority under any other enactment, unless specific statutory provision is otherwise made or unless the procedure is specifically excluded. This common code requires a by-law to be made under the seal of the council, or under the hands and seals of two members in the case of a parish or community council not having a seal. The next step is a submission to the confirming authority named in the statute under which the by-law is made. The confirming authority in the case of by-laws for good rule and government and for the suppression of nuisances is the Secretary of State for the Home Department. The council is required to publish in one or more local newspapers notice of its intention, after the expiration of one month, to submit the by-law for confirmation, and during this period it is open to anyone to inspect the by-law and to purchase copies. The confirming authority as a matter of practice examines the by-law to see, first, whether it is *intra vires* in the narrow sense, secondly, whether it is likely to satisfy the

---

[2] [1993] C.L.Y. 3891.
[3] As amended by the Local Government Act 1985, Sched. 14, para. 31(1), and the Local Government (Wales) Act 1994, Sched. 15, para. 50. National Park authorities are treated as local authorities for the purposes of ss.236–238: Environment Act 1995, Sched. 7, para. 17.

other judicial tests as to validity if it is challenged in the courts, and, thirdly, whether in any case the by-law is necessary.

It is common practice for the confirming authority to issue model by-laws, **6–05** and it is often difficult to secure the confirmation of a by-law which is outside the model or which departs from it in some important respect. In many cases the models have been built up out of practical experience over the years, which means that a by-law in the form of the model is unlikely to be upset in the courts. Moreover, the use of the model makes for some measure of uniformity, a generally desirable feature.

The confirming authority may confirm or reject the by-laws, and if they are confirmed may fix a time when they are to take effect. A copy of the by-laws when confirmed is to be made available for public inspection at the offices of the council, and must be available for sale at a cost not exceeding 20p. Copies are sent to other related authorities.

C. Judicial Tests as to Validity

It has been said that by-laws have the force and effect of law. There is, **6–06** however, an important respect in which by-laws differ from statute law—in the case of statutes the courts have no alternative but to enforce them as they stand, whatever the consequences and howsoever they are framed. By-laws, on the other hand, are subject to scrutiny by the courts and certain rules as to validity have emerged from a long line of cases. The jurisdiction of the courts in such matters dates from earliest times. Lord Hobhouse said in *Slattery v. Naylor*[4]:

> "The jurisdiction of testing by-laws by their reasonableness was originally applied in such cases as those of manorial bodies, towns, or corporations having inherent powers or general powers conferred by charter of making such laws. As new corporations or local administrative bodies have arisen, the same jurisdiction has been exercised over them."

The rules which the courts have applied when the validity of a by-law has been challenged may be stated as follows: the by-law must be reasonable, certain in its terms, consistent with the general law, and *intra vires* the authority which made it. It should be noted that all these rules may be regarded as aspects of the *ultra vires* doctrine.[5]

Reasonableness

The principle of reasonableness is dealt with fully in the first of the **6–07** following two cases:

> *Kruse v. Johnson.*[6] The Kent County Council made a by-law prohibiting any

---

[4] (1888) 13 App.Cas. 446 at p. 452.
[5] *Per* Diplock L.J. in *Mixnam's Properties Ltd v. Chertsey Urban District Council* [1964] 1 Q.B. 214 at pp. 237–238.
[6] [1898] 2 Q.B. 91. See also *Cinnamond v. British Airports Authority* [1980] 1 W.L.R. 582; *Staden v. Tarjanyi* (1980) 78 L.G.R. 614; *R. v. Bristol City Council, ex p. McDonough* [1993] C.L.Y. 3891; *Anderson v. Alnwick District Council* [1993] 1 W.L.R. 1156 (see § 6–11; challenge based on unreasonableness rejected).

person from playing music or singing in any place within fifty yards of any dwelling-house after being requested to desist. A person convicted under this by-law appealed to the Divisional Court, contending that the by-law was bad because it was unreasonable. *Held* (one member of the court dissenting) that the by-law was valid. Lord Russell C.J. expressed the view that by-laws made by local authorities, being bodies of a public representative character entrusted by Parliament with delegated authority, should be supported if possible. On the other hand this did not mean that the courts ought to be slow to condemn as invalid any by-law on the grounds of supposed unreasonableness. He said: "But unreasonable in what sense? If, for instance, they were found to be partial and unequal in their operation as between classes; if they were manifestly unjust; if they disclosed bad faith; if they involved such oppressive or gratuitous interference with the rights of those subject to them as could find no justification in the minds of reasonable men, the court might well say, 'Parliament never intended to give authority to make such rules; they are unreasonable and *ultra vires*.' But it is in this sense, and in this sense only, as I conceive, that the question of unreasonableness can properly be regarded. A by-law is not unreasonable merely because particular judges may think that it goes further than is prudent or necessary or convenient, or because it is not accompanied by a qualification or an exception which some judges may think ought to be there."

Arlidge v. Islington Corporation.[7] A by-law under the Public Health (London) Act 1891 required the landlord of a lodging-house to cause every part of the premises to be cleansed in April, May or June every year. The by-law applied even to landlords who had no right of entry, and who would commit a trespass or be in breach of contract if they complied with it. *Held*, the by-law was unreasonable and bad.

Certainty of terms

6–08   In *Kruse v. Johnson*[8] Mathew J. said:

> "From the many decisions on the subject it would seem clear that a by-law to be valid must, among other conditions, have two properties—it must be certain, that is, it must contain adequate information as to the duties of those who are to obey, and it must be reasonable."

Certainty includes positiveness and an absence of ambiguity.

> *Scott v. Pilliner.*[9] A by-law made by the Staffordshire County Council imposed a penalty on any person frequenting and using any street or public place "for the purpose of selling or distributing any paper or written or printed matter devoted wholly or mainly to giving information as to the probable result of races, steeplechases, or other competitions." *Held* (by a majority of the court), that the by-law was bad. Kennedy J. based his decision on the grounds of unreasonableness. Lord Alverstone C.J. relied on the principle of certainty. He said[10]: "I think that this court ought not to interfere with a by-law made by a local authority if it can be supported on reasonable grounds: but I also think that it is desirable for the good government of a locality that by-laws should be clear and definite and free from ambiguity, and also that such by-laws should not

---

[7] [1909] 2 K.B. 127.
[8] [1898] 2 Q.B. 91 at p. 108. But *cf. Percy v. Hall, The Times*, May 31, 1996, where the Court of Appeal preferred, *obiter*, the test for uncertainty set out in *Fawcett Properties Ltd v. Buckingham County Council* [1996] A.C. 636, 676, 677 whether the words were "absolutely senseless" or could be "given no meaning or no sensible or ascertainable meaning.
[9] [1904] 2 K.B. 855.
[10] At p. 858.

make unlawful things which are otherwise innocent. ... It seems to me that the main objection to this by-law is that it is too wide, and that it would include cases where the sale of the paper was not in aid of street betting or of any betting at all. ... There may be perfectly innocent sales of such papers, and their publication and distribution might not conduce to any betting offence at all, and yet they would fall within this by-law. ... Therefore, both on the ground of uncertainty, and mainly on the ground that it may strike at perfectly innocent sales of papers, I think that this by-law is bad and cannot be supported."

United Bill Posting Co. Ltd v. Somerset County Council.[11] The Divisional Court upheld a by-law (under the Advertisements Regulation Act 1907, s.2(2)), which provided that "No advertisements shall be exhibited on any hoarding, stand or other similar erection so as to be visible from any public highway, ... public waterway ... or ... any railway, and to disfigure the natural beauty of the landscape." Lord Hewart C.J. said[12]: "The degree of certainty required must obviously be related to the subject matter, and in my opinion this by-law dealing with a necessarily somewhat ambiguous matter cannot be said to be invalid on the ground of uncertainty." Shearman J. said[13]: " 'Natural beauty' is a thing which cannot be defined by specific instances, and the only complaint of the appellants really is that the county council have not attempted to define the indefinable."

Nash v. Finlay.[14] A by-law in terms that "no person shall wilfully annoy passengers in the street" was held to be void on account of uncertainty.

Staden v. Tarjanyi.[15] Adur District Council made a by-law under section 164 of the Public Health Act 1875, in respect of a pleasure ground, which provided: "A person shall not in the pleasure ground ... (ii) take off, fly or land any glider, manned or unmanned, weighing in total more than four kilogrammes. ... " The respondent flew a hang glider over the pleasure ground and was prosecuted under the by-law. It was conceded that "in" meant "in or over". The Divisional Court held that the by-law was invalid for uncertainty. *Per* Lord Lane C.J.[16]: " ... [To] be valid, a by-law ... must be certain and clear in the sense that anyone engaged upon the otherwise lawful pursuit of hang gliding must know with reasonable certainty when he is breaking the law and when he is not breaking the law ... [T]o be valid the by-law must set some lower level below which the glider must not fly."

Woolf J. agreed, although he stated that this was an "exceptional case", which in relation to uncertainty should not be regarded as having a wide application.

Consistency with the general law

A by-law is invalid if it is inconsistent with or repugnant to the general law **6–09** or if it deals with a matter already precisely covered by statute law. It cannot permit what a statute expressly forbids (this point is added merely for completeness, for by-laws would rarely attempt this); nor can it forbid what is expressly or impliedly permitted by statute. It is not often that a statute expressly permits an act—the law is generally negative in form. But there are occasions where a group of acts are forbidden, with certain exceptions, or are forbidden unless certain conditions are fulfilled. In such cases it can be said that the law expressly or by necessary implication permits the excepted acts

[11] (1926) 42 T.L.R. 537.
[12] At p. 538.
[13] *ibid.*
[14] (1901) 85 L.T. 682. See also *Leyton Urban District Council v. Chew* [1907] 2 K.B. 283.
[15] (1980) 78 L.G.R. 614.
[16] At p. 623.

BY-LAWS

and permits the other acts if the specified conditions are fulfilled. A by-law making unlawful one of these acts expressly or impliedly approved by the law would be invalid as being in conflict with the general law.

> *Powell v. May.*[17] A by-law made by the Glamorgan County Council prohibited betting in a public place, although both the Street Betting Act 1906, and the Betting and Lotteries Act 1934, allowed betting in a public place provided that certain requirements were complied with. *Held*, the by-law was bad, for it prohibited the doing of an act which the law expressly or impliedly allowed.

Similarly, a by-law may be invalidated by the courts if repugnant to some basic principle of the common law.

> *London Passenger Transport Board v. Sumner.*[18] A by-law of the Board provided that "each passenger shall, immediately upon demand, or, in case no demand shall have been made, before leaving the carriage, pay to the conductor the fare legally demandable for his journey and accept a ticket therefor". An information was preferred against a passenger who paid her fare to a certain point but went beyond it without tendering or being asked for the extra fare. She offered to pay when challenged by an inspector, but payment was refused. The Chief Magistrate at Bow Street who heard the case dismissed it on the ground that the by-law was bad, being repugnant to the laws of England for "no act or omission can be a crime unless *mens rea* is present, or there is express statutory provision that the act or omission is a crime without any criminal intent, or it can be clearly inferred from the terms of the statute that the mere act or omission is in itself an offence". The Divisional Court upheld the decision on appeal, adopting the reasoning of the Chief Magistrate.
> *Staden v. Tarjanyi.*[19] The by-law in this case[20] was held not be repugnant to the Civil Aviation Rules of the Air and Air Traffic Control Regulations 1976, which exempted "any glider while it is hill-soaring", from the rules prohibiting low flying. The circumstances envisaged by the regulations and those envisaged by the by-law were "entirely different".[21]

A by-law may, of course, add to the law, making an offence where none existed—indeed, this is the effect of most by-laws. Such an addition, if rightly made, is in the nature of an extension to the law, a supplement to the law in keeping with it.

> *Morrissey v. Galer.*[22] Justices convicted a man for an offence against a local authority by-law prohibiting the keeping on any premises of "any noisy animal which shall be or cause a serious nuisance to residents in the neighbourhood". It was argued that this by-law was *ultra vires* as it dealt with the same subject-matter as section 92 of the Public Health Act 1936, under which "any animal kept in such a place or manner as to be prejudicial to health or a nuisance" was a statutory nuisance: *Held*, the by-law was valid. Section 92 did not cover noisy animals, but only nuisance arising from the conditions under which animals were kept. Lord Goddard C.J. stated[23]: "No one doubts, that if

---

[17] [1946] K.B. 330.
[18] (1935) 99 J.P. 387. See also *Nicholls v. Tavistock Urban District Council* [1923] 2 Ch. 18.
[19] (1980) 78 L.G.R. 614.
[20] See § 6–08.
[21] *per* Lord Lane C.J. at p. 619.
[22] [1955] 1 W.L.R. 110.
[23] At p. 112.

162

the statute deals with precisely the same matter, the by-law would be *ultra vires* because if it deals with precisely the same matter as the statute there is no necessity for it, and if it tries to go beyond the statute it is bad."

It is submitted, however, that not every by-law which "tries to go beyond the statute" is bad. In *Thomas v. Sutters*[24] Sir F. H. Jeune said[25]:

"An Act of Parliament for the whole country renders certain things illegal. It does not at all follow that a by-law speaking for a particular locality may not make some more stringent regulations with the same object. . . . When an Act of Parliament has forbidden certain things to be done in certain places, it seems to me perfectly consistent with that that a municipality, with regard to their particular locality, should go somewhat beyond the Act, not contravening its spirit, but carrying it out, and making regulations somewhat wider than those to be found in the Act."

In *Owen v. D.P.P.*,[26] the Divisional Court upheld a by-law which created an offence of indecency in a public place. The range of conduct covered by the by-law and its purpose were sufficiently different from other enactments which dealt with indecency. See also *D.P.P. v. Gawecki and Bazar*.[27]

In relation to the power of councils to make by-laws for good rule and government and suppression of nuisances, section 235(3) of the Local Government Act 1972 now expressly provides that: "By-laws shall not be made under this section for any purpose as respects any area if provision for that purpose as respects that area is made by, or is or may be made under, any other enactment."

Intra vires

Reference was made in the opening paragraphs of this Chapter to the fact **6–10** that the by-laws of local authorities must stem from statute law. They must have their source there, and in addition, must be wholly within the scope of the statutory provision, going no further than the precise wording of the statute allows.

> *R. v. Wood*.[28] The Public Health Act 1848 enabled a local board of health to make by-laws with respect to the removal by the occupier of dust, ashes, rubbish, filth, manure, dung and soil. A board made a by-law under this provision directing all occupiers to remove all snow from the footpath opposite to their premises. *Held*, the by-law was *ultra vires*, for it went beyond the enabling powers.[29]

A power to "regulate" an activity by a by-law would not authorise the complete prohibition of that activity: "a power to regulate and govern seems to imply the continued existence of that which is to be regulated or

---

[24] [1900] 1 Ch. 10.
[25] At p. 16.
[26] [1994] Crim.L.R. 192; [1994] C.O.D. 85.
[27] [1994] Crim.L.R. 202.
[28] (1855) 5 E. & B. 49.
[29] Powers to make by-laws in regard to the clearance of snow are now available under s.81 of the Public Health Act 1936.

governed."[30] However, a power to make by-laws for regulating the use and operation of an aerodrome was held sufficient to authorise the prohibition of the use of the aerodrome by certain persons for certain specified purposes, *viz.* taxi drivers plying for hire without permission.[31]

D. Penalties and Enforcement

6–11 By-laws made under the procedure contained in the Local Government Act 1972 may provide for the imposition of fines, recoverable on summary conviction, not exceeding such sum as may be fixed by the enabling statute, or if no sum is fixed, level 2 on the standard scale.[32] The new figure is applicable to existing as well as to future by-laws. Where the offence is a continuing one, a by-law may provide for a further fine for each day during which the offence continues. The maximum continuing penalty is that fixed by the enabling statute, or £5 if no sum is prescribed.[33] Where by-laws have been made under some other code then the rules contained in that code as to penalties apply. For example, by-laws as to pleasure fairs, roller skating rinks and seaside pleasure boats, under sections 75 and 76 of the Public Health Act 1961, may provide for a maximum fine not exceeding level 3 on the standard scale or not exceeding a lesser amount.[34]

Questions of construction of a by-law may arise in the course of a prosecution for breach. In *Anderson v. Alnwick District Council*[35] the Divisional Court allowed A's appeal against conviction for contravention of a by-law prohibiting digging on a beach for lugworms without lawful right or authority. The restricted area was to be understood by reference to a map approved, with the by-law, by the Secretary of State, and A had dug bait outside the area as shown on the map. Moreover, a public right to take worms from the foreshore was recognised by common law as ancillary to the right to fish.

It is open to any person to institute proceedings for a breach of a by-law unless the statute under which the by-law is made restricts the right to prosecute.

> *R. v. Stewart.*[36] The Secretary of the Royal Society for the Prevention of Cruelty to Animals preferred an information against the master of a steamship for offences against an order under the Diseases of Animals Act 1894. The stipendiary magistrate upheld an objection that under the Act only the borough council could institute proceedings. *Held*, the objection was ill-founded. Kay L.J. said[37]: "Prima facie there is no doubt that anybody may take proceedings to recover a penalty. That is an old rule and is well established. The Act now under

---

[30] *per* Lord Davey in *City of Toronto Municipal Corporation v. Virgo* [1896] A.C. 88 at p. 93.
[31] *R. v. British Airports Authority, ex p. Wheatley* [1983] R.T.R. 147, 466. *cf. Anderson v. Alnwick District Council* [1993] 1 W.L.R. 1156.
[32] Local Government Act 1972, s.237, as amended by the Criminal Justice Act 1982, s.46.
[33] Local Government Act 1972, s.237.
[34] Criminal Law Act 1977, s.31(4)(a) and (b); Criminal Justice Act 1982, s.46(1)(2).
[35] [1993] 1 W.L.R. 1156.
[36] [1896] 1 Q.B. 300.
[37] At p. 303.

consideration in terms provides that penalties shall be imposed for certain acts, and that those penalties shall be regarded as though they were penalties incurred under the Summary Jurisdiction Acts. In order to prevent the application of the general rule, it must be shown that the Act in plain terms prevents anyone, except certain specified persons, from prosecuting for offences under the Act."

An example of a statutory restriction on the right to institute proceedings **6–12** appears in section 298 of the Public Health Act 1936. Only an aggrieved party or the council or other body whose function is to enforce the by-law in question may prosecute without the written consent of the Attorney General. Notwithstanding this or any similar provision, a constable may take proceedings in respect of an offence against a by-law, made by a local authority under any enactment, without the consent of the Attorney General.[38] It has been held in an Irish case[39] that the general right to prosecute might apply only where the by-laws concern the public interest.

A breach of a by-law may be insufficient to sustain an action in damages. **6–13** This depends on the application of the principles relevant to determine whether breach of a statute gives rise to civil liability.[40]

> *Newman v. Francis.*[41] A London County Council by-law forbade a person to allow his dog to annoy or injure anyone in any open space. The plaintiff was knocked down by the defendant's dog. He claimed damages alleging, first, negligence and, secondly, a breach of the by-law. *Held*, the by-law was intended for enforcement by the council; it was not intended to give a cause of action to members of the public, either one against the other, or, for breach of them, against the county council.

There are dicta in this case in support of the view that only the London County Council could have proceeded under the by-law.

In *Anns v. Merton London Borough Council*,[42] the House of Lords held that the council owed the plaintiff a duty to take reasonable care to ensure that builders complied with building by-laws. In addition, Lord Wilberforce stated[43] that "since it is the duty of the builder ... to comply with the byelaws, I would be of opinion that an action could be brought against him, in effect, for breach of statutory duty by any person for whose benefit or protection the byelaw was made." It was subsequently doubted, *obiter*, whether building by-laws or regulations were to be regarded as imposing an absolute duty on the builder, as distinct from a duty of care.[44] Moreover, the House of Lords has held, overruling *Anns*, that local authorities and builders do not owe a duty of care in negligence in respect of economic loss caused to purchasers as the result of the construction of defective houses.[45]

---

[38] Local Government (Miscellaneous Provisions) Act 1982, s.12.
[39] *Kenealey v. O'Keefe* [1901] 2 I.R. 39.
[40] See §§ 8–15 *et seq.*
[41] (1953) 51 L.G.R. 168.
[42] [1978] A.C. 728.
[43] At p. 759.
[44] Woolf J. in *Worlock v. S.A.W.S.* (1981) 260 E.G. 920, 926; Waller L.J. in *Taylor Woodrow Construction (Midlands) Ltd v. Charcon Structure* (1982) 266 E.G. 40, 44; Judge Newey Q.C. in *Perry v. Tendring District Council* (1984) 30 Build.L.R. 118.
[45] *Murphy v. Brentwood District Council* [1990] 3 W.L.R. 414. See §§ 8–20 *et seq.*

The threatened breach of a by-law may be restrained by an injunction.

Burnley Borough Council v. England and others.[46] The defendants objected to a new by-law which made it an offence for a person to cause a dog belonging to him or in his charge to enter or remain in any of a number of pleasure grounds, other than a guide-dog in the charge of a blind person. They organised a protest walk in the grounds by a large number of people with their dogs. This also involved breaches of a by-law which prohibited meetings or processions in the grounds without the council's prior consent. The walk took place, but no-one was prosecuted. However, when another protest was organised the council sought an interlocutory injunction to restrain the breaches of the two by-laws. *Held,* the injunction should be granted. The council had made out a prima facie case that the by-laws were valid, and if the defendants were not restrained by injunction until trial, serious damage to the public interest was likely. The defendants would continue to encourage members of the public to flout the by-laws, and this would place the park rangers and police in a most difficult and invidious position in any attempt to enforce the law. Had the defendants acted individually in breach of the by-laws, and not in concert, the judge would probably have left the council to their remedy under the criminal law.[47] The by-law relating to dogs was subsequently held to be reasonable,[48] and injunctions were granted against two of the defendants in respect of that by-law. The other defendants undertook not to break that by-law.

The defendant in a criminal prosecution before the magistrates for breach of a by-law may argue in his defence that the by-law is invalid. This long-established practice was endorsed by the Divisional Court in *R. v. Reading Crown Court, ex p. Hutchinson.*[49] However, where the by-law is *ultra vires,* in that it is drawn more widely than the powers of the enabling Act, but the defendant's conduct would have contravened the by-law if it had been properly drawn, the defendant may in some circumstances be lawfully convicted. This appears from the following joined cases.

D.P.P. v. Hutchinson; D.P.P. v. Smith.[50] The facts in *D.P.P. v. Hutchinson* were that the defendant was convicted of entering a prohibited area without authority, contrary to the R.A.F. Greenham Common By-Laws, made under the Military Lands Act 1892, s.17(2). As made, the by-laws were *ultra vires* in that, on their face, they prejudicially affected rights of common, which was specifically prohibited by the enabling Act. The Divisional Court[51] held that the defendant, who did not assert any right of common, was rightly convicted. It was clear that the by-law maker, if he had appreciated the limitation of his powers, would have made the by-laws in such a way as to apply to all the world except commoners: and that would have covered the case here. However, the House of Lords allowed an appeal. The House accepted the principle that, in an appropriate case, an *ultra vires* part of a legislative instrument might properly be regarded as severable from the good part, and disregarded, leaving the good part valid and effectual. Moreover, the principle of severance was not confined to cases of textual severability where a particular clause, sentence, phrase or word can be disregarded, with what remains still grammatical and coherent. However, the proper test to be applied where textual severance is impossible is

---

[46] (1977) 76 L.G.R. 393.
[47] Slade J. at p. 400.
[48] *Burnley Borough Council v. England* (1978) 77 L.G.R. 227.
[49] [1988] Q.B. 384.
[50] [1990] 2 A.C. 783.
[51] [1989] Q.B. 583.

to abjure speculation as to what the law-maker might have done if he had applied his mind to the relevant limitation on his powers and to ask whether the instrument with the invalid portion omitted would be substantially a different law as to the subject-matter dealt with. Applying that test, the by-law in question was *ultra vires* in its entirety: a by-law drawn in such a way as to permit free access to all parts of Greenham Common air-base to persons exercising rights of common would be a by-law of a totally different character.

In *Bugg v. Director of Public Prosecutions*[52] it was held that collateral challenge is only available where a by-law is invalid on its face.

E. WAIVER, RELAXATION AND REPEAL

An authority has no power to waive its by-laws or to relax them in any **6–14** respect unless the by-laws themselves contain provisions enabling this to be done (it is highly improbable that by-laws containing a dispensing power would be confirmed) or else there is specific statutory provision for waiver or relaxation.

> *Yabbicom v. King.*[53] An urban district council "approved" a plan though in fact it was contrary to the by-laws. Before the building was erected the area was transferred to the City of Bristol, the council of which instituted proceedings against the respondent for unlawfully erecting the house. *Held*, an "approved" plan is one which is lawfully approved by a local authority and not one which is merely approved in fact. The urban district council had no power to sanction plans for a building which would contravene the by-laws. Day J. said[54]: "The district council could not control the law, and by-laws properly made have the effect of laws; a public body cannot any more than private persons dispense with laws that have to be administered; they have no dispensing power whatever."

The Highways Act 1980 contains provisions for the relaxation of new **6–15** streets by-laws. Section 190 enables an authority, with the consent of the Secretary of State for the Environment, to relax the requirements of a by-law as to new streets or to dispense with its compliance if it considers its operation to be unreasonable in any particular case. The authority must give notice of its intention to apply for the Secretary of State's consent, and, in reaching his decision, he must have regard to any objection which may have been raised.

It is open to an authority to repeal its by-laws with the consent of the appropriate confirming authority. Section 4 of the Interpretation Act 1978 reads:

> "Where an Act ... confers power to make ... by-laws, the power shall, unless the contrary intention appears, be construed as including a power, exercisable in the like manner and subject to the like consent and conditions, if any, to rescind, revoke, amend, or vary ... by-laws."

In practice a by-law made in substitution of another would itself contain a clause repealing the one it replaces. In certain cases, by-laws cease to be valid

[52] [1993] Q.B. 473.
[53] [1899] 1 Q.B. 444.
[54] At p. 448.

after the expiration of a prescribed period unless a Secretary of State by order extends their life. By-laws made under the Water Act 1945 fell in this category—they were effective for a period of 10 years from the date on which they were made, unless the Secretary of State for the Environment extended them.[55] In a few instances, by-laws have been wholly repealed by statute or statutory instrument.[56]

By-laws made under a statute which is then repealed cease to have effect unless either the repealing Act contains some provision preserving the validity of the by-law,[57] or the by-law making power is itself re-enacted, with or without modification.[58] In the latter case, unless the contrary intention appears, the by-law has effect as if made under the new provision.

---

[55] Water Act 1945, s.19(6)(*a*).

[56] All by-laws made under section 235(1) of the Local Government Act 1972 dealing with the burning of crop residues on agricultural land were repealed by the Burning of Crop Residue (Repeal of Byelaws) Order 1992, (S.I. 1992 No. 693).

[57] *Watson v. Winch* [1916] 1 K.B. 689, *per* Lord Reading C.J. at p. 690. In *D.P.P. v. Jackson* (1990) 88 L.G.R. 876, the Divisional Court, with some difficulty, construed s.272(2) of the Local Government Act 1972 as preserving good rule and government by-laws made under the Local Government Act 1933, s.249.

[58] Interpretation Act 1978, s.17(2)(b). This provision was not in force at the time of the passage of the Local Government Act 1972: see *D.P.P. v. Jackson, supra.*

CHAPTER 7

CONTRACTS AND COMPETITION

LOCAL authorities have always had power to enter into contracts in relation **7–01** to their functions. This is necessary for any organisation employing staff, purchasing materials, services and other resources. However, the private law context of contract must also take account of the public law context of local government. The contracts of local authorities are therefore governed by the general principles of the law of contract but subject to special considerations which fall into three parts—the powers of local authorities to enter into contracts and to be bound by them; the particular rules which apply when these powers are exercised; and the exclusion of liability.

Although the dominant model of the local authority had until recently been one of the authority undertaking its functions and providing services through its own staff, the trend in recent years has been making the local authority an "enabler" and subjecting its activities to the "discipline" of the market. This has resulted not only in increased interest in the use of contracts as a technique of service delivery but also in a growing body of law designed to ensure that competition with the private sector is introduced as far as possible into local authority activities and which extends the particular rules which apply when contract powers are exercised. This has become so extensive as to be given separate treatment within this chapter.

Control over the contracting process to ensure competition has come not only from domestic policies but also from the law of the European Union, designed to ensure that there is no discrimination against nationals of other member states, or products from those states, in the award of public contracts. These provisions are also given separate treatment.

I. GENERAL PRINCIPLES

A. POWERS TO CONTRACT

A local authority is enabled, by section 111 of the Local Government Act **7–02** 1972,[1] to do anything which is calculated to facilitate, or is conducive or incidental to, the discharge of any of its functions. It has therefore a general

---

[1] This power applies also to joint authorities (s.146A, inserted by the Local Government Act 1985, Sched. 14, para. 16) and to residuary bodies (1985 Act, Sched. 13, para. 12(a)).

power to enter into contracts for the discharge of any of its functions.[2] In a number of statutes a *specific* power to contract is conferred. Thus, for example, an authority is enabled to enter into an agreement as to payment for kitchen waste[3]; an authority has specific power to enter into agreements for the supply of heat, and electricity produced in association with heat[4]; and an authority has power for the use by others of spare capacity on a local authority computer.[5] The Local Authorities (Goods and Services) Act 1970 enables a local authority[6] to make an agreement on appropriate terms with another local authority and, subject to the Secretary of State for the Environment making appropriate regulations,[7] with other public bodies, for that authority or body to supply to the other goods, materials, services, transport and equipment and to carry out maintenance works.[8] But a specific power is not simply a duplication of general power; a statute enabling authorities to enter into agreements in respect of specified matters in effect confers a power to do whatever is involved—in the first example given, to pay for kitchen waste.

In a few instances there is an express statutory prohibition against entering into certain agreements—a fire authority, for example, is precluded by section 3(4) of the Fire Services Act 1947 from making a charge for services except as provided for in the Act.

7–03   A special power, which has been of great significance in recent years, is the power to enter obligations or agreements, with persons with an interest in the land, regulating or restricting the development or the use of land; requiring specified operations or activities to be carried out; requiring land to be used in a specified way; or requiring sums to be paid to the authority.[9] Such agreements are enforceable against successors in title.[10] While the power to enforce such obligations is now given by statute,[11] an analogous agreement under a local Act was enforced as a matter of contract in *Beaconsfield District Council v. Gams*[12] and an injunction was obtained by a local authority to enforce a section 106 agreement in *Avon County Council*

---

[2] But in regard to the inability to apply s.111 to matters which are themselves incidental to the functions of the authority see *R. v. Richmond-upon-Thames London Borough Council, ex p. McCarthy & Stone (Developments) Ltd.* [1990] 2 All E.R. 852; and *Credit Suisse v. Allerdale Borough Council, The Times*, May 20, 1996. See also §§ 1–25, *et seq.*

[3] Section 9 of the Agriculture (Miscellaneous Provisions) Act 1954.

[4] Local Government (Miscellaneous Provisions) Act 1976, ss.11 (as amended by the Electricity Act 1989, Sched. 16, para. 20) and 12.

[5] *ibid.*, s.38. This power applies also to joint authorities (s.44(1), as amended by the local Government Act 1985, Sched. 14, para. 53(b)) and to residuary bodies (1985 Act, Sched. 13, para. 13(g)).

[6] The Act applies also to joint authorities and residuary bodies; § 4–85.

[7] See the Local Authorities (Goods and Services) (Public Bodies) Orders 1972, 1975, 1981, 1990, 1992, 1993, 1994, 1995 (S.I. 1972 No. 853; S.I. 1975 No. 193; S.I. 1981 No. 1049; S.I. 1990 No. 433; 1992 No. 2380; 1993 No. 2097; 1994 Nos. 37 and 1389; 1995 No. 2626; 1996 Nos. 342 and 1814).

[8] See § 7–29 and § 7–32.

[9] Town and Country Planning Act 1990, s.106 as substituted by the Planning and Compensation Act 1991, s.12. An earlier version of this power was s.52 of the Town and Country Planning Act 1972, and Local Government (Miscellaneous Provisions) Act 1982, s.33.

[10] *ibid.*, s.106(3).

[11] *ibid.*, s.106(5).

[12] (1974) 234 E.G. 749.

v. Millard.[13] A council may not, however, by entering a section 106 agreement fetter its exercise of other statutory powers.[14] Since the power was amended in the Planning and Compensation Act 1991, all such obligations must be entered into by deed.[15] Many planning agreements had been made in this way already, but the new provision was to deal with the legal uncertainty which existed over whether such agreements were contracts which had adequate consideration, in that it was doubted that whether a local planning authority could provide as consideration the exercise of a statutory power, namely the grant of planning permission.[16]

The power to contract (whether given generally or specifically) is a limited **7–04** power: it may be exercised only in the discharge of an authority's functions. If an authority enters into a contract in regard to some matter which is *ultra vires* the authority then, in strict legal theory, the contract is null and void and neither party can sue on it: it is as if no contract has been made. Moreover, it is no avail to the party who thinks he has entered into a contract to establish that he was not aware of the limits to the authority's statutory powers.

> *Ashbury Railway Carriage and Iron Co. v. Riche.*[17] The company entered into a contract the purpose of which was beyond the objects expressed or implied in the memorandum of association. The contract was therefore *ultra vires* the company. The company repudiated the contract as being *ultra vires* and the respondent brought an action to recover damages for its non-fulfilment. *Held*, the contract, being *ultra vires* the company, was wholly void (though not necessarily illegal). It could not, therefore, be enforced against the company.[18]

An authority cannot by its own acts enlarge the powers given by statute.

> *Rhyl Urban District Council v. Rhyl Amusements Ltd.*[19] The council had granted a lease relying on certain private Act powers. These powers did not in fact cover the particular transaction, so that, if the lease were to be *intra vires*, the council would have to rely on the general law. Section 177 of the Public Health Act 1875 (the relevant provision in the general law) required the consent of the Local Government Board (the predecessor of the Ministry of Health) to the lease of land, but such consent was not obtained. *Held*, that the lease was null and void, for the council in granting it had acted *ultra vires*. It was further held that the council, having acted *ultra vires* in granting the lease, could not be estopped for denying its validity. On this point Harman J. said[20]: "If the plaintiffs were private people this would be a strong plea, but in my judgment a plea of estoppel cannot prevail as an answer to a claim that something done by a statutory body is *ultra vires*."

The application of this rule presents no difficulty where there is a complete absence of a statutory power or an expressed prohibition. But problems of

---

[13] (1985) 274 E.G. 1025.
[14] *Windsor and Maidenhead Royal Borough v. Brandrose Investments Ltd* [1983] 1 W.L.R. 509.
[15] Town and Country Planning Act 1990, s.106(9).
[16] See also § 7–12.
[17] (1875) L.R. 7 H.L. 653.
[18] It may be noted that the *ultra vires* rule was modified in respect of companies registered under the Companies Acts by s.9(1) of the European Communities Act 1972, now section 35(1) of the Companies Act 1985.
[19] [1959] 1 W.L.R. 465.
[20] *ibid.*, at p. 474.

construction and interpretation arise where a prohibition is to be implied from the terms of the statute[21] and where an otherwise lawful act becomes *ultra vires* because a power has been unreasonably exercised.[22]

7–05   However, in recent years, this strict position has been challenged in two ways. First, within general contract law, since the *Riche* decision there have been "judicial attempts, on the whole successful, to attenuate the doctrine so that a person ... will not be prejudiced by the ... lack of capacity except in exceptional circumstances".[23] Secondly, as a result of developments in administrative law the terms void and voidable have been criticised as being too rigid and the view has been taken by some that more flexibility is needed.[24] In *Hazell v. Hammersmith and Fulham London Borough Council*,[25] the House of Lords, having found the contracts effecting "swaps" transactions to be *ultra vires*, left open the question of the enforceability of the contracts in private law. Subsequent cases in regard to the position in private law have proceeded largely on the basis of restitutionary and equitable remedies.[26] However, on the issue of whether *ultra vires* contracts are void, the Court of Appeal has confirmed the traditional approach.

> In *Credit Suisse v. Allerdale Borough Council*,[27] it was held that the authority had no power to give a guarantee in relation to sums borrowed by a company established to build recreational facilities which the Council could not borrow because of capital finance controls. The argument by the bank that administrative law principles should be applied to allow contractual remedies was rejected, Hobhouse L.J. being of the opinion that:

> > "Private law issues must be decided in accordance with the rules of private law. The broader and less rigorous rules of administrative law should not without adjustment be applied to the resolution of private law disputes in civil proceedings."

7–06   There is one further limitation on the power to contract—an authority may not enter into a contract incompatible with the due exercise of its powers or the discharge of its duties or which divests the authority of its statutory powers or which obliges the authority not to exercise its powers.[28]

---

[21] *Melliss v. Shirley Local Board* (1885) 16 Q.B.D. 446.

[22] *Municipal Mutual Insurance Ltd v. Pontefract Corporation* (1917) 116 L.T. 671.

[23] *Chitty on Contracts*, 27th ed., 1994, at § 9–016.

[24] See, *e.g.*, *London and Clydeside Estates v. Aberdeen District Council* [1980] 1 W.L.R. 182, *per* Lord Hailsham at p. 189.

[25] [1991] 2 W.L.R. 372. See also § 1–27.

[26] See the opinion of the House of Lords in *Westdeutsche Landesbank Girozentrale v. Islington London Borough Council*, *The Times*, May 30, 1996. See also *Kleinwort Benson Ltd v. South Tyneside Metropolitan Borough Council* [1994] 4 All E.R. 972; *Morgan Grenfell & Co. Ltd v. Welwyn Hatfield District Council* [1995] 1 All E.R. 1; and *South Tyneside Metropolitan Borough Council v. Svensksa International plc* [1995] 1 All E.R. 545.

[27] *The Times*, May 20, 1996. Leave to appeal to the House of Lords was granted.

[28] *York Corporation v. Henry Leetham & Sons Ltd* [1924] 1 Ch. 557; *Birkdale District Electric Supply Co. v. Southport Corporation* [1926] A.C. 355, *per* Lord Birkenhead at p. 364; *Wm. Cory & Son Ltd v. London Corporation* [1951] 2 K.B. 476; *Stringer v. Minister of Housing and Local Government* [1970] 1 W.L.R. 1281, *per* Cooke J. at p. 1289; *Re Staines Urban District Council's Agreement, Triggs v. Staines Urban District Council* [1969] 1 Ch. 10, *per* Cross J. at p. 18; *cf. Dowty Boulton Paul Ltd v. Wolverhampton Corporation* [1971] 1 W.L.R. 204. See §§ 10–11 to 10–13.

B. The Exercise of Contractual Powers

Compliance with standing orders

7–07 The Local Government Act 1972, section 135,[29] provides that a local authority

(i) may make standing orders with respect to the making of contracts; and

(ii) must make such orders with respect to contracts for the supply of goods or materials or for the execution of works.

In relation to the latter, the standing orders must include provisions for securing competition and for regulating the manner in which tenders are invited. But they may exempt contracts for a price below that specified in the standing orders and may authorise the authority to exempt any contract from the relevant standing order when the authority is satisfied that the exemption is justified by special circumstances. A person contracting with a local authority is not bound to inquire whether standing orders have been complied with, and non-compliance with such orders does not invalidate any contract entered into by or on behalf of the authority. This provision will not, however validate a contract which is otherwise invalid, for example, by being *ultra vires*.[30]

Model standing orders for local authority contracts have been issued by the Department of the Environment after consultation with the local authority associations, government departments and other bodies.[31]

7–08 It would appear that there is no immediate sanction against an authority which acts in breach of these rules, though mandamus might issue to compel compliance.

> *R. v. Hereford Corporation, ex p. Harrower.*[32] The council invited the local gas and electricity boards and the National Coal Board to submit schemes and prices for the installation of central heating apparatus in council houses, and one submission was accepted. Several electrical contractors on the council's approved list applied to the Court for an order of mandamus directing the authority to comply with standing orders relating to public advertisement and public tender. The standing orders provided that there should be no exceptions to the rules contained in them otherwise than by a direction of the council. It was held that an order of mandamus would issue, for there was a clear statutory duty on the authority to comply with standing orders. But since the council had a right to suspend standing orders, the order would not issue immediately so that the council might have an opportunity to suspend them. It was further held that the applicants, as ratepayers, but not as electrical contractors, had a sufficient legal right to apply for the order.

---

[29] This section applies also to joint authorities: s.146A, inserted by the Local Government Act 1985, Sched. 14, para. 16.

[30] *North West Leicestershire District Council v. East Midlands Housing Association Ltd* [1981] 1 W.L.R. 1396.

[31] *Model Standing Orders: Contracts* (3rd ed., 1983): see DoE Circular 15/83.

[32] [1970] 1 W.L.R. 1424. See also *McKee v. Belfast Corporation* [1954] N.I. 122.

In practice, an auditor might well comment on any breach in his statutory report.[33]

7–09   There must be compliance with the E.U. Treaties and any relevant Directives, in addition to compliance with standing orders. The Notes to the Model Standing Orders draw attention to Article 30 of the Treaty, which prohibits quantitative restrictions on imports between member states and measures having equivalent effect to such restrictions. The directives also lay down common advertising procedures and award criteria for public contracts with an estimated value above the prevailing threshold. Contracts must be advertised in the Official Journal of the European Communities. For further details, see paragraphs 7–25 to 7–28 below.

In addition to the requirements of standing orders and the competition requirements imposed by European law, there are competition requirement imposed by domestic law. Special rules apply where work is to be undertaken by direct labour departments. Furthermore, Part I of the Local Government Act 1988 requires local authorities to expose certain activities to competitive tendering. Part II of the 1988 Act requires authorities to disregard non-commercial considerations in relation to public supply or works contracts. For further details, see paragraphs 7–29 to 7–53 below.

Consideration of Tenders

7–10   An invitation to tender may give rise to an implied contractual obligation to consider the invitee's tender in conjunction with all other conforming tenders, or at least that the tender will be considered if others are.[34] However, in *Fairclough Buildings Ltd v. Borough Council of Port Talbot*[35] the Court of Appeal held that there had been no breach of that obligation where the council removed a company originally invited to tender for a project from the tender list on the ground that the council's principal architect was married to a director of the company; the council had acted reasonably in the circumstances.

In *General Building and Maintenance plc v. Greenwich London Borough Council*[36] it was held that health and safety are among the matters that a local authority is entitled to take into account when deciding whether to invite a contractor to tender for a contract; these matters fall within the issue of "technical capacity" which is one of the grounds for excluding a contractor specified in regulation 12 of the Public Works Contracts Regulations 1991.[37]

Disclosure of interest

7–11   When matters relating to contracts are discussed in council or committee, there is a duty on members and officers having an interest to declare it.[38]

---

[33] See § 13–14.
[34] *Blackpool and Fylde Aero Club Ltd v. Blackpool Borough Council* [1990] 1 W.L.R. 1195.
[35] (1992) 62 B.L.R. 82.
[36] (1993) 92 L.G.R. 21.
[37] S.I. 1991 No. 2680, and see § 7–26.
[38] Local Government Act 1972, ss.94 to 98, and see §§ 4–35 to 4–42.

Sealing of contracts

The Corporate Bodies' Contracts Act 1960 brought order and certainty to **7–12** the law with respect to the sealing of local authority contracts and greatly simplified administrative practice. It was formerly a rule of the common law that a corporation (other than a trading corporation) could not bind itself in contract except by seal,[39] a rule sensible enough where large sums were involved but administratively impossible in trifling matters. The effect of the Act of 1960 is as follows. If a contract is one which, if made between private persons would be required by law to be in writing, then it may be made by a local authority in writing, signed by a person acting under its authority, express or implied: if a contract made between private persons would by law be valid although made verbally, then such a contract can be made verbally on behalf of a local authority by any person acting under its authority express or implied. A local authority is, therefore, in substantially the same position in respect to the *formalities* attaching to contracts as is a private person. But an authority may continue to seal contracts which now need not be sealed, if only to preserve the safeguards which the formalities of sealing might be considered to give. Local authorities generally systematise the position through standing orders, frequently authorising the appropriate officers to sign all contracts below a certain amount and requiring all others to be sealed. Or the authority may authorise several officers to sign contracts of particular kinds and below specified sums.

Formalities

The formalities to be observed in the making of contracts (applicable as **7–13** well to local authorities as to private persons) are to be found in common law and statute. It is a general rule of the common law that a contract is binding upon the parties to it if it is made verbally: there is no need in common law to have a contract reduced to writing for oral evidence can be given of its terms. But statute has provided exceptions to this broad rule. Certain contracts are void unless they are reduced to writing. These include, for example, assignments of copyright,[40] agreements to submit differences to arbitration[41] and contracts for the sale or other disposition of an interest in land.[42] There are certain contracts which still require to be under seal—generally speaking all conveyances of land or interests therein,[43] and contracts made without consideration.[44]

It will be seen, therefore, that most local authority contracts can be made **7–14** under hand and indeed orally. They may be signed by a person acting under the authority of the corporation, and that authority may be express or implied. The rules as to implied authority are found in the common law and

---

[39] *Austin v. Bethnal Green Guardians* (1874) L.R. 9 C.P. 91, *per* Lord Coleridge C.J. at p. 94.
[40] Copyright, Designs and Patents Act 1988, s.90.
[41] Arbitration Act 1950, s.32.
[42] Law of Property (Miscellaneous Provisions) Act 1989, s.2.
[43] Law of Property Act 1925, s.52.
[44] See § 7–03.

in their application to local authorities two of them are of particular importance. In the first place, if a contracting party has good reason to suppose, in all the circumstances, that an officer or servant has power to bind his corporation, then the corporation may be bound in contract by the act of that officer or servant.[45] Secondly, where an officer or servant has express authority, then that authority extends by implication to all acts which are incidental to the main purpose.[46]

7–15   A contracting party is not bound to satisfy himself as to the authority which the officer holds. Authority in such circumstances would generally be express, but if this were not so it could well be implied. Where a corporation is committed by the acts of its officers to whom express or implied authority is given it will be no defence to the corporation to say that a particular act was unauthorised. Conversely, a clause in a contract agreed to by a council officer will not bind the council if the officer has no authority, whether actual, implied or usual, to assent to that clause.[47]

C. Exclusion of Liability and Unfair Terms

7–16   The Unfair Contract Terms Act 1977 limits the extent to which civil liability for breach of contract or negligence can be avoided by contract terms or other notices. The main limitations are applied only to "business liability", but "business" is defined so as to include the activities of any local or public authority.[48]

An authority is unable to exclude or restrict by reference to any contract term, or to a notice given to persons generally or to particular persons, liability for death or personal injury resulting from negligence.[49] Similar exclusions or limitations relating to other loss or damage resulting from negligence are subject to the test of reasonableness.[50] Clauses of various kinds (including exemption clauses) affecting contractual liability are also subject on the test of reasonableness, where one party "deals as consumer or on the other's written standard terms of business".[51] A party "deals as consumer" if "(a) he neither makes the contract in the course of a business nor holds himself out as doing so; and (b) the other party does make the contract in the course of a business; and (c) in the case of a contact governed by the law of sale of goods or hire purchase, or by section 7 of this Act, the goods passing under or in pursuance of the contract are of a type ordinarily supplied for private use and consumption".[52] A contract with a member of the public acting in an individual capacity (e.g. one arising out of enquiries made of local authorities in the course of conveyancing) will be subject to

[45] *Brady v. Todd* (1861) 9 C.B. (N.S.) 592. But see §§ 10–14 to 10–18.
[46] *Bayley v. Wilkins* (1849) 7 C.B. 886.
[47] *North West Leicestershire District Council v. East Midlands Housing Association Ltd* [1981] 1 W.L.R. 1396.
[48] Unfair Contract Terms Act 1977, s.1(1) and (3) and s.14.
[49] *ibid.*, s.2(1).
[50] *ibid.*, ss.2(2) and (11).
[51] *ibid.*, ss.3, 11 and 13.
[52] *ibid.*, s.12(1).

section 3 where the other party "deals as consumer". Contract terms authorised or required by an enactment are unaffected; and terms approved by a competent authority "acting in pursuance of a statutory jurisdiction or function" are taken to be "reasonable".[53] Any contract is unaffected by section 2 to 4 in so far as it relates to the creation or transfer of an interest in land.[54]

While the Unfair Contract Terms Act 1977 deals mainly with exclusion **7–17** clauses, a wider, but overlapping, system was introduced to apply to all contractual terms by Directive 93/13/EEC on Unfair Terms in Consumer Contracts, implemented by the Unfair Terms in Consumer Contracts Regulations 1994.[55] These Regulations apply to a contract concluded between a seller or supplier and a consumer where the term has not been individually negotiated.[56] A term is regarded as not having been individually negotiated where it has been drafted in advance and the consumer has not been able to influence the substance of the term and, even where a specific term or aspects of it have been individually negotiated, the regulations will apply to the rest of the contract if an overall assessment indicates that it is a pre-formulated standard contract.[57] "Seller" and "supplier" are defined as a person who sells goods and supplies goods and services respectively and who, in making the contract, is acting for purposes relating to his business.[58] "Business" includes not only trades and professions but also the activities of any government department and any local or public authority.[59] Unlike the 1977 Act, a consumer is restricted to natural persons for whom the contract is outside his business, so business contracts are excluded from the provisions of the regulations.[60] In addition, contracts relating to employment, succession rights, rights under family law, and to the incorporation and organisation of companies and partnerships are excluded from the scope of the regulations, as are any terms which comply with or reflect statutory domestic provisions or international conventions to which the member States or the Community are party.[61]

An unfair term is defined as one which, contrary to the requirement of good faith, causes a significant imbalance in the parties' rights and obligations under the contract to the detriment of the consumer.[62] Excluded from this, however, is any challenge to the main subject matter of the contract or whether a bad bargain has been struck.[63] An indicative list of

[53] ibid., s.29.
[54] ibid., Sched. 1, para. 1(b).
[55] S.I. 1994 No. 3159.
[56] ibid., reg. 3.
[57] ibid.
[58] ibid., reg. 2.
[59] ibid.
[60] ibid.
[61] ibid., Sched. 1.
[62] ibid., reg. 4. "Good faith" is not defined as such, but Sched. 2 provides that in making an assessment of good faith, regard is to be had in particular to the strength of the bargaining positions of the parties; whether the consumer had an inducement to accept the term; whether the goods or services were sold or supplied to the special order of the consumer; and the extent to which the seller or supplier has dealt fairly and equitably with the consumer.
[63] ibid., reg. 3(2).

unfair terms is given in Schedule 3 to the regulations. Where a term is unfair, it shall not be binding on the consumer, and the remainder of the contract will continue in existence if it is capable of doing so without the term.[64] In addition to direct remedies, the consumer may also invoke the assistance of the Director General of Fair Trading, who may apply for an injunction against any person using or recommending unfair terms.[65]

II. THE REQUIREMENTS OF COMPETITION[65a]

D. OVERVIEW

7–18   Local authorities are subject to two sets of controls over the contracting process to ensure competition. The first comes from the law of the European Union and the second from domestic policies. The relationship between the two is that they are separate but overlapping systems with different purposes, principles and remedies. Thus each is given separate treatment in this chapter.

Procurement controls

7–19   The public procurement controls of the E.U. are designed to ensure that there is no discrimination against nationals of other member states, or products from those states, in the award of public contracts for works, supplies and services. The strategy is based on three stages—initial information, technical specification, and selection of tenders. Thus, there must be advertising across the Community for contracts above a specified monetary threshold; there must not be the use of discriminatory technical standards; and there must be objective and open criteria for evaluation and selection of tenders.

Domestic controls

7–20   To understand the current position in regard to the domestic provisions, it is necessary to understand how the legislative and administrative framework has changed since 1980. Two powers had provided the basis for the dominant approach in local government which was to provide services directly through employees. First, the power to employ persons to carry out the functions of the local authority,[66] including those in "direct works departments" relating to construction and maintenance. Secondly, the power to enter into contracts. While the dominant approach in local government was to provide services directly through employees, it was thus always possible for authorities to engage the private sector to carry out work for the authority, and this was done either on specific small tasks, such as legal work, or more major works such as construction. Competitive tendering was voluntary. However, requirements for compulsory competitive tendering have been introduced through four key legislative stages and through the delegated

---

[64] *ibid.*, reg. 6.
[65] *ibid.*, reg. 8.
[65a] See S. Arrowsmith, *The Law of Public and Utilities Procurement* (1996); S. Cirell and J. Bennett, *Compulsory Competition Tendering: Law and Practice.*
[66] Local Government Act 1972, s.101.

legislation and informal "advice" issued by the government. The main purpose of this legislation has been to turn local authorities from the direct providers of services to "enablers" of service provision and to have services subjected to market "discipline". The changes in the law have also been accompanied by increased financial and management controls through audit.[67] The strategy of increasing private sector involvement in the activities of local authorities also involves financial controls and the Private Finance Initiative.[68]

The 1980 Act

The first stage was the Local Government, Planning and Land Act 1980, **7–21** which introduced controls in relation to direct labour organisations (D.L.O.). It imposed a regime of regulation of all functional and works contracts relating to construction and maintenance to ensure that they were entered into and undertaken only under conditions which required a measure of competition with other non-public contractors. This Act was limited not only in its coverage, but also in regard to the rigour of the competition requirements.

The 1988 Act

It was therefore followed by the Local Government Act 1988 which **7–22** introduced three important changes: it expanded the scope of the functions covered by the tendering rules; tightened the rules to ensure a higher degree of compulsory competition and privatisation of service provision; and outlawed the use of "non-commercial matters" in functions of the authority.

First, compulsory competitive tendering (C.C.T.) was extended to collection of household and trade waste; cleaning of buildings; other cleaning such as streets, litter etc; catering for schools and welfare establishments such as old-peoples' homes; other catering; management of sports and leisure facilities; maintenance of grounds, parks etc; and repair and maintenance of vehicles. This list can be amended or expanded by means of an order of the Secretary of State.

Secondly, more detailed tendering procedures were introduced for both external and internal contracts. For an "external" works contract, not only must it be opened up to tender from the private sector, but the other contracting party has also not to act "in a manner having the effect or intended or likely to have the effect of restricting, distorting, or preventing competition". For internal functional work, a number of conditions were introduced and the bid from the council's own direct labour or service organisation (DLO or DSO) is required to have been prepared on the same basis as that for the private sector. In determining the terms of the contract or in choosing the tenders or successful bid, the council must not act in a manner restricting competition and must not vary the terms of the specification if it awards the work to its own labour force. In regard to the

---

[67] See Chap. 13.
[68] See Chap. 12.

conditions the Secretary of State has power to modify and otherwise regulate their terms. For both external and internal contracts, there are also more detailed and stringent regimes for accounting, annual reporting and access to information. Policing of these requirements is given, not to the authority itself or an independent auditor or other person, but to the Secretary of State. He may issue notices requiring further information to be supplied to him if it appears that there has been a breach of these conditions. If, in the light of that information, he decides that there has been a breach, he may issue a direction either requiring compliance with his decision or removing the power of the authority to carry out the work. There is no appeal against the decision of the Secretary of State and actions by councils under judicial review have met with little success because of the widely expressed powers in the legislation.

The third aspect expanded by the 1988 Act is the concept of anti-competitive behaviour or "non-commercial" matters. The duty for authorities not to take account in contracts extends beyond the matters covered by CCT and a long list of non-commercial matters is listed in the Act but can be supplemented by regulations made by the Secretary of State. These rules are designed to prohibit the use of "contract compliance" as a device for enforcing other policies of the authority. Aggrieved contractors may sue for damages on the basis that these restrictions have not been followed.

The 1992 Act

7–23   All aspects covered by the 1988 Act were then further tightened in the third stage by the Local Government Act 1992. CCT has been extended to other areas including other manual services, theatre, library and arts management, and also includes professional services, such as legal, architectural, financial, and engineering. The latter in particular raise more complicated issues abut how to reconcile cost and quality, a matter which has not been adequately resolved. While the authority are not under a duty to accept the lowest tender, cost can be seen as the most important consideration since many other matters are excluded as being "non-commercial". Indeed, the 1992 Act created a new power for the Secretary of State to make further regulations specifying and enforcing what is deemed to be "anti-competitive", which goes beyond the provisions relating to "non-commercial" matters in the 1988 Act.

The 1994 Act

7–24   The fourth stage is provided by Part II of the Deregulation and Contracting Out Act 1994 which makes provision for the contracting out of the functions of ministers and office-holders and, by section 70, local authorities.[69] This is aimed at removing the remaining statutory obstacles to

---

[69] In England, a county, district or London borough council, the Common Council of the City of London, the sub-treasurer of the Inner Temple, the under treasurer of the Middle Temple, the Council of the Isles of Scilly or a parish council; and in Wales, a county council, county borough council or community council: Deregulation and Contracting Out Act 1994, s.79(1). References to a local authority include references to a joint board or joint committee: *ibid.*, s.79(3)(b).

the use of private contractors, and to overcome the general presumption against delegation in as much as it has not been overcome by s.101 of the Local Government Act 1972.

E. EUROPEAN PUBLIC PROCUREMENT CONTROLS

There must be compliance with the E.U. Treaties and any relevant **7-25** Directives. Article 30 of the Treaty prohibits quantitative restrictions on imports between member states and measures having equivalent effect to such restrictions. The relevant directives require the abolition of any restrictive or discriminatory practices which might prevent contractors from other member states from participating in public contracts on equal terms with national contractors. Not all public contracts are so included, only those as defined and above the appropriate monetary threshold. For these purposes, not only the local authority itself, but also bodies financed or controlled by the authority, will be subject to these controls and where there is government subsidy of more than 50 per cent for certain construction projects the rules also apply. Once triggered, the controls are based on three stages. First, there must be advertising across the Community through a prior information notice to the Official Journal of the European Communities (OJEC) for contracts above a specified threshold. Secondly, the authority must use non-discriminatory technical standards and specifications. Thirdly, there must be objective and open criteria for evaluation and selection of tenders, following the appropriate procedure.

There are three sets of regulations which have implemented the relevant **7-26** Directives relating to public works, public supplies, and public services.

In regard to works contracts, Directive 71/305, as amended by Directive 89/440 and part of Directive 89/665, was enacted in the Public Works Contracts Regulations 1991.[70] "Works", is defined as any activities falling with Schedule 1 to the regulations, and covers a number of building and civil engineering operations. These regulations were amended by the Utilities Supplies and Works Contracts Regulations 1992,[71] to ensure that not more than one set of regulations applies to any contract to overcome the ambiguity of such issues as whether maintenance was "works" or "services". The threshold for the application of these regulations is 500,000 ECU.

For supply contracts, EEC Directive 77/62, as amended by Directives 80/767 and 88/295, and part of Directive 89/665 were enacted in the Public Supply Contracts Regulations 1991,[72] which were subsequently revoked and replaced by the Public Supply Contracts Regulations 1995[73] which implemented the consolidated Directive 93/36. "Public supply contract" is defined as a contract in writing for consideration of whatever nature for the purchase or hire of goods, whether by instalments or not. The threshold for the application of these regulations is 200,000 ECU.

---

[70] S.I. 1991 No. 2680.
[71] S.I. 1992 No. 3279.
[72] S.I. 1991 No. 2679.
[73] S.I. 1995 No. 201.

In regard to services, Directive 92/50 was implemented by the Public Services Contracts Regulations 1993.[74] "Public service contract" is defined, somewhat negatively, as a contract in writing for consideration of whatever nature under which the contracting authority engages a person to provide services, but excluding a contract of employment and contracts which fall within the works and supplies regimes. However, not all services fall under the full control of these regulations. Services are divided, by Schedule 1, into Part A and Part B services. Only in regard to the former do all the provisions of the regulation apply. In regard to Part B services, a more restricted regime operates. In deciding whether a service falls within Part A or Part B, it is the activity, not the person or agency, which is crucial. Thus, for example, legal services would remain as Part B even if related to auditing which is defined as a Part A service. The threshold for the application of these regulations is 200,000 ECU.

7–27 When the regulations do apply, the requirements of each set are very similar. In outline, the contracting authority is required to publicise its intention to seek offers in the OJEC.[75] The contracting authority, in seeking offers for relevant contracts, must use one of three procedures.[76] First, the open procedure whereby any person may submit a tender. Secondly, the restricted procedure whereby only those selected by the contracting authority may submit tenders. Thirdly, the negotiated procedure whereby the contracting authority negotiates the terms of the contract with one or more persons selected by it. The last of these is available in very restricted circumstances. Detailed provision is made in the regulations in regard to which procedure may be adopted and the requirements of that procedure, including the time limits within which a decision must be made. While the contracting authority may reject certain contractors or tenders, the regulations lay down detailed provisions relating to business and professional status, economic and financial standing, ability and technical capacity, and the information on which such assessments may be made.[77] The contract must be awarded on the basis of the lowest cost or the most economically advantageous, but in regard to the latter, the criteria to be adopted must be disclosed in advance.[78] Detailed provision is made for technical specifications to comply with European standards.[79] Following the award of the contract, the contracting authority must send a contract award notice to the OJEC which must be published except in specified circumstances.[80] The

---

[74] S.I. 1993 No. 3228.
[75] Public Works Contracts Regulations 1991 (S.I. 1991 No. 2680), reg. 9; Public Supply Contracts Regulations 1995 (S.I. 1995 No. 201), reg. 9; Public Services Contracts Regulations 1993 (S.I. 1993 No. 3228), reg. 9.
[76] *ibid.*, reg. 10 of each set of regulations.
[77] *ibid.*, Part IV of each set of regulations.
[78] Public Works Contracts Regulations 1991 (S.I. 1991 No. 2680), reg. 20; Public Supply Contracts Regulations 1995 (S.I. 1995 No. 201), reg. 21; Public Services Contracts Regulations 1993 (S.I. 1993 No. 3228), reg. 21.
[79] *ibid.*, reg. 8 of each set of regulations.
[80] Public Works Contracts Regulations 1991 (S.I. 1991 No. 2680), reg. 21; Public Supply Contracts Regulations 1995 (S.I. 1995 No. 201), reg. 22; Public Services Contracts Regulations 1993 (S.I. 1993 No. 3228), reg. 22.

contracting authority must keep specified records of the award and inform any unsuccessful contractor of the reasons for being unsuccessful should this be requested.[81]

Where there has been a breach of the rules on procurement the **7–28** Commission may commence proceedings against the member state in the European Court of Justice.[82] Otherwise, the remedies are those provided domestically. The regulations provide that breach of the regulations is not a criminal offence, but that interim relief suspending the procedure, or the award of damages, or both, may be given on application by the contractor where the contract has not already been entered into, but where the contract has already been entered into the only remedy is the award of damages.[83]

F. Direct Labour Organisations—Maintenance and Construction Functions

Local authorities commonly operated direct labour departments to carry **7–29** out works of maintenance and construction for their own functions under powers contained in section 111 of the Local Government Act 1972.[84] Such direct labour organisations, as they are called, may also carry out work for other authorities and bodies in accordance with agency arrangements under section 101 of the Local Government Act 1972, sections 5 and 18 of the London Government Act 1963, or under local legislation. Works of maintenance, but not construction, may also be carried out for other authorities under the Local Authorities (Goods and Services) Act 1970.[85]

Part III of the Local Government, Planning and Land Act 1980[86] introduced a system of control by the Secretary of State over the power of local authorities to enter into agreements to carry out construction and

---

[81] Public Works Contracts Regulations 1991 (S.I. 1991 No. 2680), reg. 22; Public Supply Contracts Regulations 1995 (S.I. 1995 No. 201), reg. 23; Public Services Contracts Regulations 1993 (S.I. 1993 No. 3228), reg. 23.

[82] Article 169 of the EEC Treaty.

[83] Public Works Contracts Regulations 1991 (S.I. 1991 No. 2680), reg. 31; Public Supply Contracts Regulations 1995 (S.I. 1995 No. 201), reg. 29; Public Services Contracts Regulations 1993 (S.I. 1993 No. 3228), reg. 32.

[84] See §§ 1–25, et seq.

[85] See § 7–02 and § 7–32.

[86] As amended by the Local Government Act 1985, Sched. 17, and the Local Government Act 1988, s.32 and Sched. 6, and the Local Government Act 1992, ss.9, 10 and Sched. 1, paras. 1–9. The amendments effected by the 1988 Act bring Part III of the 1980 Act into line with the competition requirements introduced by Part II of the 1988 Act: below §§ 7–42 to 7–45. See also the Local Government (Direct Labour Organisations) (Competition) Regulations 1989 (S.I. 1989 No. 1588); the Local Government (Direct Labour Organisations) (Competition) (Exemption) (England) Regulations 1992 (S.I. 1992 No. 582); the Local Government (Direct Service Organisations) (Competition) Regulations 1993 (S.I. 1993 No. 848, as amended); the Local Government (Direct Labour Organisations) (Competition) (Exemption) (England) Regulations 1994 (S.I. 1994 No. 567); and the Local Government (Direct Labour Organisations) (Competition) (Amendment) (England) Regulations 1994 (S.I. 1994 No. 1439); and the Local Government (Direct Labour Organisations) (Competition) (Amendment) (Crown Courts) Regulations 1995 (S.I. 1995 No. 1377).

maintenance work for other bodies, referred to in the Act as "works contracts", and over "functional work" carried out by direct labour organisations for their parent authorities.

The philosophy of the 1980 Act, as amended in 1988 and 1992, is to achieve two main objectives. First, that much of the authority's construction and maintenance work over a certain value should be subject to tendering on a detailed specification, and that the direct labour or service organisation should win work only in fair competition with the private sector. Secondly, that separate accounts must be kept by each authority for its own construction and maintenance force, on a trading basis so that a true financial picture can be given, and calculated on the assumption that the direct labour or service organisation achieves such financial objectives as are specified by the Secretary of State, and earns a real rate of return on the opportunity cost of its capital, equivalent to the average private sector rate.

In recognition of the additional administrative work entailed by local government reorganisation in Wales, the Local Government (Direct labour organisations) (Competition) Regulations 1989[87] ceased to apply to local authorities in Wales on April 1, 1994. Revised arrangements are contained in the Local Government, Planning and Land Act 1980 (Competition) (Wales) Regulations 1994.[88] The application of Part III of the 1980 Act to local authorities affected by structural change under the Local Government Act 1992 is dealt with in the Local Government Changes for England (Direct Labour and Service Organisations) Regulations 1994.[89]

Works contracts

7–30   A works contract comprises[90]:

(a) an agreement under
  (i) section 5(3)(c) of the London Government Act 1963[91] (agreements between London authorities for the carrying out of works of maintenance by one party in connection with land or buildings for the maintenance of which another party is responsible), or
  (ii) section 1 of the Local Authorities (Goods and Services) Act 1970 which provides for the carrying out by a local authority of certain works of maintenance; or
(b) an agreement made by virtue of any other enactment (including a provision of a local Act) which provides for the carrying out by a local authority of any construction or maintenance work.[92]

---

[87] S.I. 1989 No. 1588.
[88] S.I. 1994 No. 338.
[89] S.I. 1994 No. 3167, as amended by S.I. 1995 No. 1326 and S.I. 1996 Nos. 330 and 1882.
[90] Local Government, Planning and Land Act 1980, s.5.
[91] As amended by the Local Government Act 1985, Sched. 17.
[92] This term is defined in the Local Government, Planning and Land Act 1980, s.20, as amended. By ss.20 and 21, it excludes work in parks; routine maintenance carried out by employees such as caretakers; dock and harbour undertakings; training schemes; small D.L.O.s with 15 or less employees, excluding those not providing the construction and maintenance work; and urgent work where the DLO temporarily increases its workforce. It includes painting: *Wilkinson v. Doncaster Metropolitan Borough Council* (1985) 84 L.G.R. 257.

A local authority may not enter into a works contract, except for those **7–31** exempted by regulation,[93] whose value exceeds an amount prescribed by the Secretary of State[94] except as a result of acceptance of a tender where the invitation to tender was extended to at least three other persons, who are not, or include at least three other persons who are not, local authorities or development bodies.[95] However, this does not mean that contracts under this limit are not required to be subjected to the same process or other restrictions. For contracts at or below the prescribed amount, there must be compliance with conditions prescribed in regulations made by the Secretary of State.[96] Such regulations may prescribe the manner in which the value of a contract is to be determined, exclude certain descriptions of contract and vary the number of persons tendering, but at present the regulations in effect draw no distinction between contracts over and under the prescribed amounts.[97]

In addition, the authority may not enter a works contract in which it will undertake the work if the other party acted in a manner having the effect or intended or likely to have the effect of restricting, distorting or preventing competition.[98] However, there is no failure to fulfil tendering conditions unless the local authority has become aware of the failure of the other authority before entering into the contract (rather than at the time the contract is proposed to be entered into).[99]

There has been confusion over the ability of one local authority to tender **7–32** for the work of another authority. For many years the conventional wisdom was that this was implicitly recognised by the Local Authorities (Good and

[93] The Local Government (Direct Labour Organisations) (Competition) Regulations 1989 (S.I. 1989 No. 1588, as amended), reg. 7, excludes certain categories of emergency work, and some contracts extending for works of new construction, highway and sewer works. Other exemptions in the original regulations relating to snow clearance and competition free allowances have since been omitted. The term "works of new construction" as they appeared in s.17 of the 1980 Act (since repealed) was considered in *R. v. Hackney London Borough Council, ex p. Secretary of State for the Environment* (1989) 88 L.G.R. 96, where it was held that major renewals and improvements to two blocks of flats including conversion of a flat roof to a pitched roof and window replacement were works of maintenance and not new construction.

[94] *ibid.*, reg. 3, prescribes the amounts. These are £50,000 for the construction or maintenance of a sewer, and works of new construction; £25,000 for general highway works and £10,000 for works of maintenance, with provisions for aggregating contracts of a lower value in reg. 4. However, while still in force, these are now in effect redundant, see fn. 97.

[95] Local Government, Planning and Land Act 1980, s.7.

[96] *ibid.*, s.7(1).

[97] Initial tendering requirements were imposed by condition for certain of these contracts by the Local Government (Direct Labour Organisations) (Competition) Regulations 1989 (S.I. 1989 No. 1588), regs. 5 and 6, the latter of which deals with highway works. Since exemptions in earlier regulations had been repealed there was a period when only reg. 6 provided an exception, and no provision was made for the other areas so no exemption exists for construction work falling below £50,000 or maintenance work falling below £10,000. Now, however, the exception relating to highway works has itself been omitted by the Local Government (Direct Labour Organisations) (Competition) (Amendment) (England) Regulations 1994 (S.I. 1994 No. 1439), reg. 3.

[98] Local Government, Planning and Land Act 1980, s.7(1A), as inserted by the Local Government Act 1988, s.32 and Sched. 6, para. 2.

[99] *ibid.*, s.7(1B), inserted by the Local Government Act 1992, Sched. 1, para. 1.

Services) Act 1970.[1] However, following the Local Government Act 1988 which opened up many other areas to competitive tendering, there was political concern over the use of "cross boundary tendering". Both the Government and the Audit Commission stated that such tendering was possible only using the spare capacity of staff already employed for the functions of the authority wishing to tender.[2] However, this interpretation was subject to much debate and now, without any binding legal authority, the Government has, on the basis of another counsel's opinion, accepted that the previous advice was too restrictive.[3] While there remains doubt over how far the authority may engage in trading for profit, it is clear that it is possible for it to undertake maintenance and other work in accordance with the express provisions of s.1 of the Local Authorities (Good and Services) Act 1970.

Functional work

7–33 Functional work means construction or maintenance work[4] undertaken by a local authority otherwise than under a works contract for the performance of, or in connection with:

(a) their functions[5]; or
(b) their obligations under any arrangements, agreement or requirement made under any enactment and providing for the discharge by them of any functions of:
  (i) a Minister of the Crown; or
  (ii) a sewerage authority; or
  (iii) a local authority under Part VI of the Local Government Act 1972 (discharge of functions, *e.g.* by delegation under section 101).[6]

7–34 It does not include work done by placing a contract with another person, either directly or through a sub-contractor, unless the work done under such a contract is dependent upon, or incidental or preparatory to, other work undertaken or to be undertaken by persons in the employment of the local authority.[7]

When a local authority is about to undertake functional work it must first, in accordance with regulations made by the Secretary of State, prepare a written statement of the amount which will be credited to the direct labour

---

[1] See § 7–02.
[2] DoE press release June 7, 1990, and Audit Commission Technical Release 23/90, on the basis of counsel's opinion.
[3] DoE letter to local authorities, December 7, 1995. See also *Local Authority Law* 1/96, pp. 1 and 4–6.
[4] See n. 92.
[5] On the meaning of "functions" see *Hazell v. Hammersmith London Borough Council* [1991] 2 W.L.R. 372, where Lord Templeman accepted that "functions embraces all the duties and powers of a local authority; the sum total of the activities Parliament has entrusted to it". See also §§ 1–25, *et seq.*
[6] Local Government, Planning and Land Act 1980, s.8(1).
[7] *ibid.*, s.8(2) and (3).

organisation revenue account (to which reference is made below) or of a method by which it intends that the amount to be so credited shall be calculated.[8] In the case of functional work of a type prescribed by the Secretary of State[9] the authority may not proceed to undertake the work until it has invited at least three other persons to tender for it who are not, or include at least three persons who are not, local authorities or development bodies and who are included in a list of persons willing to undertake such work maintained by the authority.[10] The authority must include in the invitation the matters prescribed by regulation, comply with prescribed requirements as to responses to the invitation and must not act in a manner having the effect or intended or likely to have the effect of restricting, distorting or preventing competition.[11]

In *R. v. Walsall Metropolitan Borough Council, ex p. Yapp*[12] the Court of Appeal held that a council which decided to seek fresh tenders for building works which had already been awarded to its own workforce for a four-year period was not in breach of its public law duty to act fairly. The standard contract with outside contractors was couched in flexible terms and the award of the work to its own workforce was as nearly as possible on the same terms; the workforce was not entitled to assume that the council was committed, as if by contract, to give all the specified types of work to the workforce throughout the four-year period.

If an authority is asked by any person to furnish him with a written statement showing the tender figures and who is to undertake the work and its estimated costs, the authority must comply with the request.[13]

In regard to issues relating to the Transfer of Undertakings (Protection of Employment) Regulations 1981 (S.I. 1981 No. 1794), see paragraph 7–48.

Accounting and financial provisions

There are rules laid down as to accounting practice. Each authority **7–35** undertaking construction or maintenance work under works contracts or by way of functional work must keep a revenue account and such other

---

[8] *ibid.*, s.9(2), as amended.

[9] The Local Government (Direct Labour Organisations) (Competition) Regulations 1989 (S.I. 1989 No. 1588, as amended), reg. 8, prescribes the following categories: a job consisting or consisting principally of general highway works; construction or maintenance of a sewer with an estimated cost exceeding £50,000; and works of new construction or works of maintenance. By reg. 9, as amended, the following are exempt: certain categories of emergency work; some contracts extending for works of new construction, highway and sewer works; and work undertaken for the purposes of Crown Court. The term "works of new construction" as they appeared in s.17 of the 1980 Act (since repealed) was considered in *R. v. Hackney London Borough Council, ex p. Secretary of State for the Environment* (1989) 88 L.G.R. 96, where it was held that major renewals and improvements to two blocks of flats including conversion of a flat roof to a pitched roof and window replacement were works of maintenance and not new construction.

[10] Local Government, Planning and Land Act 1980, s.9(3)–(6). See also the Local Government (Direct Service Organisations) (Competition) Regulations (S.I. 1993 No. 848, as amended), and DoE Circular 5/96, WO Circular 11/96.

[11] *ibid.*, s.9(4).

[12] (1993) 92 L.G.R. 110.

[13] Local Government, Planning and Land Act 1980, s.9(8) and (9).

accounts as the Secretary of State may direct in respect of specified descriptions of work.[14] However, the specific rules, other than the need to keep general accounts, do not apply to small direct labour organisations of less than 15 persons.[15]

An authority may not credit any revenue account in respect of the cost of carrying out functional works with a sum in excess of the appropriate amount, that is to say, the amount appearing in the written statement referred to above or calculated in accordance with the method in that statement.[16]

Authorities are required to meet such financial objectives as the Secretary of State may specify, defined by him by reference to such factors as he thinks fit.[17]

7–36 Authorities are under a duty to prepare, not later than September 30 in respect of the preceding financial year, a revenue account and a statement of whether the authority have complied with the financial objectives set by the Secretary of State.[18] In addition, each authority which has undertaken construction or maintenance work under works contracts or by way of functional work or both is obliged to prepare an annual report not later than September 30 in the financial year following that to which it relates, and to send it to the Secretary of State and the auditor not later than October 31.[19]

Sanctions

7–37 Where it appears to the Secretary of State that a local authority or development body has carried out or undertaken construction or maintenance work in breach of the various requirements imposed in Part III of the 1980 Act, or will do so, he may serve a written notice on the authority or body requiring a written response.[20] The response must either show that the allegation is unjustified, or admit that it is correct and show why the Secretary of State should not give a direction.[21] If he receives no written response, or is not satisfied with it, he may issue directions that the authority shall cease to have power to carry out the work identified in the direction, or shall only have such power if specified conditions are fulfilled such as re-tendering, or vary a previous direction.[22]

G. OTHER COMPETITIVE TENDERING REQUIREMENTS

7–38 While the Local Government Planning and Land Act 1980 applied to construction and maintenance, Part I of the Local Government Act 1988

[14] *ibid.*, s.10, as amended by the Local Government (Direct Labour Organisations) (Accounts) Regulations 1981 (S.I. 1981 No. 339).
[15] *ibid.*, ss.11 and 21.
[16] *ibid.*, s.12.
[17] *ibid.*, s.16, as amended by the Local Government Act 1988, Scheds. 6, 7, and the Local Government Act 1992, Sched. 1, para. 4, and Sched. 4, Pt. I.
[18] *ibid.*, s.13, as amended by the 1988 Act, Sched. 6 and the 1992 Act, Sched. 1, para. 3, and Sched 4, Pt. I.
[19] *ibid.*, s.18.
[20] *ibid.*, s.19A(1), as amended by the Local Government Act 1992, Sched. 4, Pt. I.
[21] *ibid.*, s.19A(3).
[22] *ibid.*, s.19B, as amended by the Local Government Act 1992, Sched. 1, para. 7.

enacted a series of provisions designed to ensure that local and other public authorities[23] undertake certain other activities only if they can do so competitively.[24] In a number of respects they are modelled on the provisions applicable to Direct Labour Organisations under Part III of the 1980 Act.[25]

The restrictions apply to "defined activities", which are listed in the Act. **7–39** The list in section 2(1), and defined in detail in Schedule 1, of the 1988 Act, as amended, comprises:

(a) collection of refuse (*i.e.* household and commercial waste other than sewage);

(b) cleaning of buildings (cleaning of interior and window-cleaning of buildings other than dwellings, residential establishments or police establishments);

(c) other cleaning (litter removal, street cleaning, the emptying of gullies, the cleaning of traffic signs and street name plates);

(d) catering for the purposes of schools and welfare (*i.e.* catering for schools, residential establishments or day centres, unless excepted; meals-on-wheels);

(e) other catering;

(ee) managing sports and leisure facilities (except where provided on premises not predominantly used for sport or physical recreation or on premises occupied by educational institutions)[26];

(f) maintenance of grounds (*i.e.* cutting and tending grass, planting and tending trees, hedges, shrubs, flowers and other plants (excluding landscaping) and controlling weeds, but not if its primary purpose is research or securing the survival of any plant);

(ff) supervision of parking (parking and fixed charge notices, immobilisation devices, and removal of vehicles)[27];

(g) repair and maintenance of vehicles (other than police vehicles and the repair of accident damage)[28];

(gg) management of vehicles[29];

[23] The Local Government Act 1988, s.1, defines these as an English county, district, London borough, parish or community council, a Welsh county, county borough or community council, the Common Council, the Council of the Isles of Scilly, an urban or new town development corporation, the Commission for the New Towns, a police authority, fire authority, metropolitan county fire and civil defence or passenger transport authority, the London Fire and Civil Defence Authority, a waste disposal authority, and a joint education committee.

[24] The application of Part I of the 1988 Act to local authorities affected by structural change under the Local Government Act 1992 is dealt with in the Local Government Changes for England (Direct Labour and Service Organisations) Regulations 1994 (S.I. 1994 No. 3167, as amended).

[25] See §§ 7–29 to 7–37.

[26] Local Government Act 1988 (Competition in Sports and Leisure Facilities) Order 1989 (S.I. 1989 No. 2488).

[27] Local Government Act 1988 (Competition) (Defined Activities) Order 1994 (S.I. 1994 No. 2884).

[28] *ibid.*

[29] *ibid.*

    (h) housing management (extensive activities relating to letting, rent collection, inspection, evictions, security systems, compensation, and other matters[30];

    (i) security work (for land in which the authority has an interest)[31];

    (j) legal services (advice to members and other persons, work in connection with proceedings, contracts, conveyancing etc.)[32];

    (k) construction and property services (white collar services such as architecture, engineering, surveying, valuation etc.)[33];

    (l) financial services[34];

    (m) information technology services[35]; and

    (n) personnel services.[36]

7–40   The Secretary of State also has power to prescribe exemptions for matters which are otherwise included in the competitive regime.[37] This power has been exercised in respect of:

    (a) an activity whose gross cost in the immediately preceding financial year does not exceed £100,000;

    (b) work carried out through an employee who is required as a condition of employment to live in particular accommodation for the better performance of his duties and the work forms part of his duties;

    (c) the repair or maintenance of fire service vehicles;

    (d) work carried out pursuant to an agreement with the Training Commission.[38]

Apart from this general *de minimis* exception, there are numerous other more specific exemption orders which are used for different purposes. Some are used to phase in new activities generally, specify contract lengths or impose higher *de minimis* limits for a specific function, while others are used to exempt specific projects in single authorities.[39]

7–41   Where work falls within more than one defined activity (*e.g.* the removal of litter from flower beds), it is to be treated as falling within one of them as specified by the authority. Work carried out through an employee is not to fall within a defined activity if it is incidental to the greater part of work he is employed to do, and the greater part does not itself constitute a defined

---

[30] Local Government Act 1988 (Competition) (Defined Activities) (Housing Management) Order 1994 (S.I. 1994 No. 1671).

[31] Local Government Act 1988 (Competition) (Defined Activities) Order 1994 (S.I. 1994 No. 2884).

[32] *ibid.*

[33] Local Government Act 1988 (Competition) (Defined Activities) (Construction and Property Services) Order 1994 (S.I. 1994 No. 2888).

[34] Local Government Act 1988 (Competition) (Defined Activities) 1995 (S.I. 1995 No. 1915).

[35] *ibid.*

[36] *ibid.*

[37] Local Government Act 1988, s.1(9).

[38] Local Government Act 1988 (Defined Activities) (Exemptions) (England) Order 1988 (S.I. 1988 No. 1372), as amended by S.I. 1990 No. 1565.

[39] See *e.g.* the Local Government Act 1988 (Defined Activities) (Exemptions) (England) Order 1988 (S.I. 1988 No. 1372, as amended) and the Local Government Act 1988 (Defined Activities) (Exemptions) (Wales) Order 1988 (S.I. 1988 No. 1469, as amended). On the last group, see *e.g.* the Stockport Borough Council Order (S.I. 1992 No. 3009).

activity (*e.g.* cleaning by a school caretaker). Work is not to fall within a defined activity if it is calculated to avert, alleviate or eradicate the effects of an emergency or disaster. Conversely, work which cannot be carried out efficiently separately from a particular defined activity is to be treated as falling within it.[40]

Works contracts and functional work

Separate requirements apply to works contracts and functional work, **7–42** which are defined in slightly different terms to the same expressions in the Local Government, Planning and Land Act 1980. Thus, a "works contract" is a contract constituting or including an agreement which provides for the carrying out of work by a defined authority (other than for a Minister, another defined authority or a sewerage undertaker). "Functional work" is work carried out by a defined authority, other than work carried out under a works contract, and work carried out other than by a defined authority but which is dependent upon or incidental to such work.[41] Work carried out by a direct labour or service organisation for its own authority is "functional work".

By the Local Government Act 1992, section 8, the Secretary of State is enabled to introduce by order modified tendering procedures in relation to certain professional and other services, the intention being initially to cover architectural, engineering and property management services.[42] What was contemplated was that tenderers would have to cross an initial quality threshold, with the choice between tenders that cross the threshold being on the basis of price. The proposal to introduce such a "double envelope" procedure has since been dropped by the government, and accordingly, section 8 has not been implemented.

Works contracts

The competition requirements applicable in respect of works contracts **7–43** are that a defined authority (the "bidding authority") may not enter into such a contract unless two conditions are fulfilled. The first condition is fulfilled if either four or more persons (three of whom must not be defined authorities) willing to carry out work of the kind concerned are invited to offer to do the work; or public notice inviting the submission of offers is given in a local newspaper and an appropriate trade publication. The second condition is that the other party to the contract did not act in a manner having the effect or intended or likely to have the effect of restricting, distorting or preventing competition. Anything amounting to a failure to fulfil a condition only has that effect if the bidding authority is aware of the failure.[43]

[40] Local Government Act 1988, s.2(5)–(8).
[41] *ibid.*, s.3.
[42] *Competing for Quality: Competition in the Provision of Local Services: A Consultation Paper* (November 1991).
[43] Local Government Act 1988, s.4. This applies to works contracts entered into after April 1, 1989; where works contracts entered into before that date would have infringed s.4 if entered subsequently, the parties cease to have power to carry it out: *ibid.*, s.5.

Functional work

7-44   The competition requirements applicable in respect of functional work are that a defined authority may not carry out functional work, or a specified proportion of it,[44] falling within a defined activity unless each of six conditions in section 7 is fulfilled, and conditions (b) to (e) may be further amplified by regulations.[45]

   (a) The authority must publish a notice in a local newspaper and an appropriate trade publication, giving a brief description of the work, stating (*inter alia*) that the authority intends to make a tender invitation and that a detailed specification will be available for inspection for a specified period; and requiring notification to the authority within a specified period by any person wishing to carry out the work.

   (b) The arrangements under condition (1) must be reasonable; the detailed specification must be made available and must include a statement of the period during which the work is to be carried out.[46]

   (c) If any person notifies the authority that they wish to carry out the work, an invitation must be made between three and six months after publication of the notice in condition (1), to at least three persons who are not defined authorities (or to every person interested if there were less than four such persons) and (if the authority thinks fit) to any interested defined authority.[47]

   (d) Before carrying out the work, the authority, through its direct labour or similar organisation, must prepare a written bid indicating its wish to carry out the work.

   (e) The authority in reaching the decision that it should carry out the work must not act in a manner having the effect or intended or likely to have the effect of restricting, distorting or preventing competition.

   (f) In carrying out the work, the authority must comply with the detailed specification.

7-45   The fifth condition is one which goes further than the concept of non-commercial consideration introduced by the 1988 Act.[48] However,

---

[44] This qualification was introduced by the Local Government Act 1992 to allow for some services to be gradually subjected to competition. This has been applied to specified proportions of legal services and construction and property services. See the Local Government Act 1988 (Competition) (Legal Services) (England) Regulations 1994 (S.I. 1994 No. 3164, as amended); Local Government Act 1988 (Defined Activities) (Competition) (Construction and Property Services) (England) Regulations 1994 (S.I. 1994 No. 3166, as amended).

[45] Local Government Act 1988, s.8.

[46] Local Government Act 1988 (Defined Activities) (Specified Periods) (England) Regulations 1988 (S.I. 1989 No. 1373) and similar regulations for Wales (S.I. 1988 Nos. 1470 and 1520), specifying the minimum and maximum periods for which offers may be sought as part of condition (2).

[47] This has been amended in regard to the specific functions of legal services, see the Local Government Act 1988 (Competition) (Defined Activities) Order 1994 (S.I. 1994 No. 2884); and construction and property services, see the Local Government Act 1988 (Competition) (Defined Activities) (Constructions and Property Services) Order 1994 (S.I. 1994 No. 2888).

[48] See § 7-51.

initially there was no regulation making power associated with this condition so the Secretary of State relied on circular advice to disseminate his opinion of what has the effect of restricting, distorting or preventing competition, but the Local Government Act 1992 provided for such regulation making power to define conduct as "competitive" or "anti-competitive" and to structure the tendering process.[49] Accordingly, the Secretary of State has made the Local Government (Direct Service Organisation) (Competition) Regulations 1993,[50] which make provision for a number of matters. These are the time limits with respect to the tendering procedure for work outside the Public Works Contracts Regulations 1991[51] or Public Services Contracts Regulations[52]; the period that must elapse before the commencement of certain work; the preparation of bids; the evaluation of bids and tenders; matters which the authority must take into account in evaluating tenders and its own bid of the work, such as costs of disabled persons, trainees, and redundancy[53]; and the issue of guidance as to how to conduct restricting, distorting or preventing competition is to be avoided. Thus the statement of what has the effect of restricting, distorting or preventing competition, remains only in circular form but with legislative backing.[54]

The circular advice states that the purpose of C.C.T. is to stimulate greater **7–46** efficiency and secure better value for money by requiring full and fair competition between local authorities' own in-house teams and private contractors.[55] In order to satisfy the Secretary of State that competition has not been prevented, the authority will be required to demonstrate that proper regard has been given to the way in which markets for individual services operate in practice and, while it is accepted that this will need to be balanced against the authority's service requirements, it is the view of the Secretary of State that a competitive response will secure that such requirements are met at an acceptable cost.[56] Detailed advice is given on good tendering practice which is classified under five principles:

(i) ensuring that the competition process is conducted, and is seen to be conducted, in a fair and transparent manner;

(ii) identifying the way in which the market operates for the service in question, and ensuring that tendering practices are consistent with securing a good competitive response;

(iii) generally specifying the output to be achieved rather than the way in which the service is to be performed in detail, so that the evaluation of bids and the monitoring of performance can concentrate on the ability

---

[49] Local Government Act 1992, s.9.
[50] S.I. 1993 No. 848, as amended.
[51] S.I. 1991 No. 2680.
[52] S.I. 1993 No. 3228.
[53] Such matters are crucial for the issue of whether private and public authorities compete on equal terms.
[54] See DoE Circular 5/96, WO 11/96. This repeals DoE Circular 10/93, WO Circular 40/93.
[55] *ibid.*, para. 7.
[56] *ibid.*, para. 8.

of contractors to achieve the full requirements of the specification including real service quality;

(iv) adopting clear procedures for evaluating tenders to ensure that the required quality can be achieved; and

(v) acting fairly between potential contractors to ensure that the conduct of tendering does not put any one of them at a disadvantage.

7–47   While there is no decision of the courts directly on the point, guidance on the approach which the local authority should take has been given *obiter*. In *R. v. Secretary of State for the Environment, ex p. Knowsley Borough Council*[57] Popplewell J. accepted the view put forward in 1991 in the Scottish case of *Colas Roads Ltd. v. Lothian Regional Council*[58] where he said, in regard to the authority having taken redundancy costs into account when applying the Local Government, Planning and Land Act 1980

> "if the placing of a contract with an outside contractor would indeed lead to the local authority incurring major liabilities, I cannot regard taking notice of that fact, and giving it weight in the decision making process, as within the category of actings covered by [s.9(4)] ... A responsible regard for the truth does not seem to me to be something which can be said to restrict, distort or prevent competition, unless one has decided that competition is more important than both truth and the interests of the citizens for whom the local authority are responsible. I see nothing in the language of the statute which indicate such a pre-eminence for competition over all else, nor I am prepared to accept that Parliament intended local authorities to enter into contracts regardless of perhaps disastrous, if indirect consequences."

However, this must be read in the light of the powers of the Secretary of State to issue directions reflecting his view of the reasonableness of the balance struck by the authority: see § 7–48.

Transfer of Undertakings

7–48   One matter which had caused uncertainty is whether the Transfer of Undertakings (Protection of Employment) Regulations 1981[59] (T.U.P.E.), would apply to the transfer of an activity from a council to a private company or other body in the context of competitive tendering.[60] Where these regulations apply, the new employer takes over responsibility for the employees who transfer on the same terms and conditions, with consequences for the ability of the new employer to reduce labour costs. In 1993 the regulations were amended to remove the exclusion relating to non-commercial ventures and, without binding authority, it has been generally

---

[57] *The Times*, 28 May 1991, CO/1720/90; *The Independent*, September 25, 1991, C.A.
[58] 1994 SLT 396.
[59] S.I. 1981 No. 1794, implementing the Acquired Rights Directive of 1977.
[60] See *Kenny v. South Manchester Colleges* [1993] I.C.R. 934 where T.U.P.E. regulations were held to apply to the transfer of prison education service from local education authority to a college; and *Wren v. Eastbourne Borough Council* [1993] I.C.R. 955 (E.A.T.) where the transfer of street cleaning and refuse collecting from council to private company was held to be capable of being a relevant transfer for the purposes of T.U.P.E. regulations. See also *Dines v. Initial Healthcare Services Ltd* [1995] I.C.R. 11, (C.A.); *Council of the Isles of Scilly v. Brintel Helicopters Ltd* [1995] I.C.R. 249 (E.A.T.); *Kelman v. Care Contract Services Ltd* [1995] I.C.R. 260 (E.A.T.).

accepted that T.U.P.E. will apply in most circumstances. Government advice on this matter was given in a communication sent to local authorities, which amended the advice given in the then current circular.[61] Such advice is now given by circular.[62] The advice lays down, *inter alia*, that an authority may state whether, in its opinion, T.U.P.E. will or will not apply, and there must be full disclosure to prospective tenderers of all matters relating to the current workforce to allow them to make an appropriate bid.

Accounting and financial provisions

An authority which carries out work falling within a defined activity must **7–49** keep separate accounts for each such activity, meet financial objectives specified by the Secretary of State, prepare a report for each financial year, and make publicly available information about bids to carry out functional work made in competition with an authority's direct labour organisation, and about the annual financial report.[63]

Sanctions

If it appears to the Secretary of State that an authority has failed to comply **7–50** with any requirement, he has similar powers to serve a written notice on the authority and give directions as are available in regard to direct labour or service organisations under Part III of the Local Government, Planning and Land Act 1980. He may serve a written notice on the authority or body requiring a written response.[64] The response must either show that the allegation is unjustified, or admit that it is correct and show why the Secretary of State should not give a direction.[65] If he receives no written response, or is not satisfied with it, he may issue directions that the authority shall cease to have power to carry out the work identified in the direction, or shall only have such power if specified conditions are fulfilled such as re-tendering, or vary a previous direction.[66]

Challenges have been made to the exercise by the Secretary of State of these powers. However, given the width of the powers of the Secretary of State these have been largely unsuccessful. The general approach was laid down by the Court of Appeal in *R. v. Secretary of State for the Environment, ex p. Knowsley Borough Council*[67] where an attempt to argue that the powers could be used only where the local authority acted unreasonably was rejected.[68] In addition the decision of the High Court in that case[69] that a power to give a direction under section 14(2) of the Local Government Act 1988 may not be used to impose a requirement that, having fulfilled

---

[61] Issues Paper on T.U.P.E., dated January 21, 1994, and DoE Circular 10/93.
[62] DoE Circular 5/96, WO 11/96.
[63] Local Government Act 1988, ss.9–12.
[64] *ibid.*, s.13(1) and (2), as amended by the Local Government Act 1992.
[65] *ibid.*, s.13(3).
[66] *ibid.*, s.14, as amended by the Local Government Act 1992.
[67] *The Independent*, September 25, 1991, C.A.
[68] The principle laid down in *Secretary of State for Education and Science v. Tameside Metropolitan Borough Council* [1977] A.C. 1014 was distinguished on the wording of the respective provisions.
[69] *The Times*, May 28, 1991, CO/1720/90.

requirements under section 7, the council should seek the Secretary of State's consent before continuing to carry out the work, was reversed by the Court of Appeal. The Court of Appeal in *R. v. Secretary of State for the Environment, ex p. Haringey London Borough Council*[70] followed this general approach to the discretion of the Secretary of State and also held that the Secretary of State was entitled to direct that the council should cease to have power to collect refuse on the ground that he considered it had acted in breach of the fifth condition set out in section 7(7) of the Local Government Act 1988. Having regard to the primary purpose of the Act a baring order may be used as a deterrent to conduct which restricts, distorts or prevents competition.

H. Exclusion of Non-Commercial Considerations

7-51 Part II of the Local Government Act 1988 makes detailed provision for the exclusion of non-commercial considerations in the exercise by specified authorities[71] of functions in relation to public supply or works contracts (*i.e.* contracts for the supply of goods or materials, for the supply of services, or for the execution of works).[72]

The relevant functions include the preparation of lists of approved contractors or persons who may be invited to tender, the invitation of tenders, the acceptance of the submission of tenders, the selection of contractors, the approval of subcontractors, and the termination of existing contracts.[73]

A series of matters are specified as "non-commercial"[74]:

(a) the terms and conditions of employment by contractors of their workers[75];

(b) whether sub-contractors provide their services as self-employed persons;

(c) any involvement of contractors' activities with irrelevant fields of government policy;

(d) the conduct of contractors or workers in industrial disputes;

(e) the country of origin of supplies to or the location of contractors' business activities;

(f) any political, industrial or sectarian affiliations or interests of contractors, or their directors, partners or employees;

(g) financial support or lack of financial support by contractors for any institution to or from which the authority gives or withholds support;

---

[70] (1994) 92 L.G.R. 538.

[71] Local Government Act 1988, Sched. 2. They comprise the defined authorities for the purposes of Part I (see § 7–38) plus the Broads Authority, the planning boards, passenger transport executives, probation and after-care committees and residuary bodies.

[72] *ibid.*, s.17(1) and (3).

[73] *ibid.*, s.17(4).

[74] *ibid.*, s.17(5).

[75] *e.g.* contract clauses providing that a contractor should at all times comply with ss.6(1)(a), (c), and (2)(b) of the Sex Discrimination Act 1975: *R. v. Islington London Borough Council, ex p. Building Employer's Confederation* (1989) 153 L.G.Rev. 948, (D.C.).

(h) the use or non-use by contractors of technical or professional services provided by the authority under the Building Act 1984.

Corresponding matters referable to, *inter alia*, suppliers, customers, sub-contractors and associated bodies are to be regarded as non-commercial matters for the contractor.[76]

Section 71 of the Race Relations Act 1976 provides that local authorities **7–52** must have regard to the need to eliminate unlawful racial discrimination and promote equality of opportunity, and good relations between persons of different racial groups. It does not require or authorise a local authority to exercise any function regulated by section 17 by reference to a non-commercial matter. However, section 17 does not preclude a local authority asking an "approved question" or making an "approved request for evidence" or including terms or conditions in a draft contract or tender, if that is reasonably necessary to secure compliance with section 71.[77]

The duty imposed by section 17 does not create a criminal offence. **7–53** However, potential contractors (and any body representing contractors) have a sufficient interest for proceedings for judicial review and a failure to comply with the duty is actionable by any person who, in consequence, suffers loss or damage. In any such action brought by a tenderer, the damages, are, however, limited to damages in respect of expenditure reasonably incurred for the purpose of submitting the tender.[78]

Reasons must be given on request from the person concerned about the following decisions made in the exercise of functions regulated by section 17:

(a) in relation to an approved list, a decision to exclude a person from the list;

(b) in relation to a proposed public supply or works contract, a decision not to invite a person to tender, not to accept the submission by him of a tender, or not to enter the contract with him, or a decision to withhold approval for, or to select or nominate sub-contractors;

(c) in relation to a subsisting public supply or works contract, a decision to withhold approval for, or to select or nominate sub-contractors, or a decision to terminate the contract.[79]

A public authority which maintains a list of approved contractors may not charge a contractor a fee in order to be included or retained in the list.[80]

J. FURTHER CONTRACTING OUT

Part II of the Deregulation and Contracting Out Act 1994 makes provision **7–54** for the contracting out of the functions of ministers and office-holders and

---

[76] Local Government Act 1988, s.17(7). The Secretary of State may add other matters by Order: *ibid.*, s.19(1)–(4).

[77] *ibid.*, s.18.

[78] *ibid.*, s.19.

[79] *ibid.*, s.20. See *R. v. Enfield London Borough Council, ex p. T. F. Unwin (Roydon) Ltd* (1989) 46 Build.L.R. 1, D.C., where a decision to remove a company from the list of approved contractors was quashed, *inter alia*, on the ground of a breach of this section.

[80] *ibid.*, s.22.

local authorities.[81] This is aimed at removing the remaining statutory obstacles to the use of private contractors, and to overcome the general presumption against delegation in as much as it has not been overcome by s.101 of the Local Government Act 1972. This could cover functions such as revenue collection and investment management.

In the case of a local authority this applies to any function[82]

(a) conferred by or under any enactment; and
(b) which may be exercised by an officer of the authority under section 101 of the Local Government Act 1972; and
(c) which is not excluded by section 71 of the 1994 Act.

A minister[83] may by order provide for a function to which section 70 applies to be exercised by, or by employees of, such person (if any) as may be authorised in that behalf by the local authority whose function it is. The minister must first consult such representatives of local government as he considers appropriate. An order may set limits to the exercise of contracted-out functions. Authorisations are to be for such period, not exceeding 10 years, as is specified, may be revoked at any time[84] and shall not prevent the local authority from exercising the function to which the authorisation relates. Where an order is in force in relation to a function of local authority A, and arrangements are in force under section 101 of the Local Government Act 1972 for the exercise of that function by local authority B, it is to be an implied term of those arrangements that, except with the consent of authority A, authority B shall not give any authorisation by virtue of the order in relation to that function.

Section 71 excludes functions where the exercise would constitute the exercise of jurisdiction of any court or of any tribunal which exercises the judicial power of the state; or its exercise or non-exercise would necessarily interfere with or otherwise affect the liberty of any individual; or it is a power or right of entry, search or seizure into or of any property (other than under specified provisions concerning the enforcement of rates, community charge and council tax); or it is a power or duty to make subordinate legislation.[85]

Where a person is authorised to exercise any function of a local authority,

---

[81] Deregulation and Contracting Out Act 1994, s.70, *i.e.* in England, a county, district or London borough council, the Common Council of the City of London, the sub-treasurer of the Inner Temple, the under treasurer of the Middle Temple, the Council of the Isles of Scilly or a parish council; and in Wales, a county council, county borough council or community council: 1994 Act, s.79(1). References to a local authority include references to a joint board or joint committee: *ibid.*, s.79(3)(b).

[82] *ibid.*, s.79(1). This includes any power to do any thing which is calculated to facilitate, or is conducive or incidental to, the exercise of a function.

[83] *ibid.* The term "minister" has the same meaning as "minister of the Crown" in the Ministers of the Crown Act 1975.

[84] *ibid.* If an authorisation is revoked while a contract relating to the exercise of the function is subsisting, the authorised person is entitled to treat the contract as repudiated and not frustrated.

[85] This expression includes "orders, rules, regulations, schemes, warrants, byelaws and other instruments made or to be made under any Act": Interpretation Act 1978, s.21(1).

anything done or omitted to be done by or in relation to the authorised person (or an employee of his), in or in connection with the exercise or purported exercise of the function is to be treated for all purposes as done or omitted to be done by or in relation to that authority.[86] However, this does not apply for the purposes of so much of any contract made between the authorised person and the local authority as relates to the exercise of that function, or for the purposes of any criminal proceedings brought in respect of anything done or omitted to be done by the authorised person (or his employee).[87]

Restrictions on the disclosure of information are modified to enable information to be disclosed to contractors and for the contractors to be under the same restrictions as the original recipients.[88]

The first orders made under section 70 concern the contracting out of tax billing, collection and enforcement functions and investment functions.[89]

---

[86] Deregulation and Contracting Out Act 1994, s.72(1), (2).
[87] *ibid.*, s.72(3).
[88] *ibid.*, s.75 and Sched. 15.
[89] Local Authorities (Contracting Out of Tax Billing, Collection and Enforcement Functions) Order 1996 (S.I. 1996 No. 1880); Local Authorities (Contracting Out of Investment Functions) Order 1996 (S.I. 1996 No. 1883).

CHAPTER 8

TORT AND CRIMINAL LIABILITY

I. TORT

A TORT is a civil wrong (which is not exclusively a breach of contract or a **8–01** breach of trust), the remedy for which is a common law action for damages and, where necessary, a decree of the court such as an injunction. The law of tort is therefore concerned with such matters as trespass to persons, lands and goods, nuisance, negligence, defamation, deceit. A tort is to be distinguished from a crime, which is an offence for which punishment is meted out by the State as a result of criminal proceedings. The same facts may, of course, form a basis for a criminal charge and for an action in tort, *e.g.* manslaughter and negligence arising from an act of careless driving.

A local authority, as a corporate body, may itself sue in tort. Section 222 of the Local Government Act 1972 gives a general power to prosecute and defend legal proceedings.[1] Examples of such proceedings are *Ilford Urban District Council v. Beal*[2] (nuisance), *Esso Petroleum Co. Ltd v. Southport Corporation*[3] (trespass, nuisance and negligence), and *Shoreham-by-Sea Urban District Council v. Dolphin Canadian Proteins Ltd*[4] (public nuisance). Naturally, an authority may sue to recover possession of its land.[5]

In *Derbyshire County Council v. Times Newspapers Ltd*,[6] the House of Lords held that a local authority could not sue for libel in respect of its governing or administrative reputation. Were the law otherwise, legitimate public criticism of its activities would be stifled. In the Court of Appeal,[7] it was suggested that actions could, however, be maintained by individual officers or councillors who were libelled, and the authority itself might in appropriate circumstances secure the institution of a prosecution for criminal libel or (if it suffered economic loss) an action for malicious falsehood.

The general rules of tortious liability apply both to corporate bodies and natural persons: they are not therefore examined here except in so far as they are of particular importance in local administration.[8] The following

---

[1] See also §§ 10–65 *et seq.*
[2] [1925] 1 K.B. 671.
[3] [1956] A.C. 218.
[4] (1972) 71 L.G.R. 261.
[5] *Manchester Corporation v. Connolly* [1970] 1 Ch. 420; *Bristol Corporation v. Persons Unknown* [1974] 1 W.L.R. 365; *Greater London Council v. Jenkins* [1975] 1 W.L.R. 155; R.S.C., Ord. 45, r. 13 and Ord. 113.
[6] [1993] A.C. 534, overruling *Bognor Regis Urban District Council v. Campion* [1972] 2 Q.B.
[7] *ibid.*
[8] See *Clerk and Lindsell on Torts* (17th ed.) for general principles.

matters are considered to fall in this category: the general liability of corporate bodies for tortious acts; the construction of statutory powers, *i.e.* whether a defence can be raised that an act is committed in order to comply with a statutory requirement; failure to perform duties; negligence in the performance of statutory functions; the liability of local authorities as occupiers of premises; the application of the rule in *Rylands v. Fletcher* to local authorities; misfeasance in a public office; and the personal liability of individual members of local authorities and their officers. The payment of compensation following a finding of maladministration by a Local Commissioner is also considered.

In *Rookes v. Barnard*,[9] the House of Lords held that the award of "exemplary" or "punitive" damages should be confined to three situations. The first of these, of relevance here, is where there is "oppressive, arbitrary or unconstitutional action by the servants of the government".[10] These limitations were endorsed by the House in *Broome v. Cassell & Co.*[11] Here it was stated *obiter* that Lord Devlin's first category was not confined to Crown servants, but extended to all those exercising governmental functions, including local authorities.[12]

In *A.B. v. South West Water Services Ltd*,[13] the Court of Appeal held that there was a further limitation to the award of exemplary damages that the tort must be one in respect of which an award of damages was made prior to 1964, when *Rookes v. Barnard*[14] was decided. Accordingly, such damages could not be awarded in public nuisance. This point had not been raised in cases where it had been suggested that exemplary damages might be available in race and sex discrimination cases and private nuisance cases.

It is not contrary to public policy for local authorities and chief constables to insure against their vicarious liability to pay damages, including exemplary damages, for the criminal acts of employees or police officers.[15]

A claim for damages may now be made on an application for judicial review, in combination with a claim for mandamus, certiorari, prohibition, an injunction or a declaration.[16] Prior to 1978 an application for one of the prerogative orders could not be coupled with a claim for damages. This development is purely procedural; it confers no new right to damages, and leaves unaffected the power of a plaintiff to choose to commence an action in the ordinary way.

---

[9] [1964] A.C. 1129.
[10] *Per* Lord Devlin at p. 1226.
[11] [1972] A.C. 1027.
[12] See Lord Reid at pp. 1087–1088, and Lord Diplock at p. 1130; *cf.* Lord Hailsham at pp. 1077–1078, and Lord Kilbrandon at p. 1134. Applied in *Bradford City Metropolitan Council v. Arora* [1991] 2 Q.B. 507.
[13] [1993] 2 W.L.R. 507.
[14] [1964] A.C. 1129.
[15] *Lancashire County Council v. Municipal Mutual Insurance Ltd, The Times*, April 8, 1996.
[16] R.S.C. Ord. 53, r. 7, substituted by S.I. 1977 No. 1955.

A. GENERAL PRINCIPLES OF TORTIOUS LIABILITY

It was at one time doubted whether a statutory corporation could commit a **8–02** tort, since it can do only those things for which it has specific authority in law, and clearly it has no authority to commit a wrong. The position was clarified in *Mersey Docks and Harbour Board Trustees v. Gibbs*[17] which laid down the general rule that a corporate body may be liable in tort in the same way as a natural person. This is obviously so when the function in which the act occurs is *intra vires*, and it appears that an authority cannot escape liability by pleading that the function in which the wrongful act occurs is *ultra vires*, notwithstanding the doubts which have been expressed on this point.[18]

> *Campbell v. Paddington Corporation.*[19] In this case the act complained of was specifically authorised by the council. A resolution was passed instructing the council's servants to erect a stand in the highway from which councillors and their friends could watch the funeral procession of Edward VII. The act was held to constitute a nuisance for which the council was made liable. The council put as one defence that, being a corporation, it could not be sued in tort because it had no authority in law to authorise the erection of the stand. On this Avory J. said[20]: "To say that because the borough council had no legal right to erect it [the stand], therefore the corporation cannot be sued, is to say that no corporation can ever be sued for any tort or wrong. ... That would be absurd."

The liability of a local authority for tortious acts is normally a vicarious liability: it acts through its employees, agents or contractors. Since somewhat different principles apply to each of these categories it is important, in any particular case, to establish the relationship of the local authority to the tortfeasors, whether it be that of employer and employee, principal and independent contractor, or principal and agent.

Servants

Generally speaking, a local authority is vicariously liable for a tort **8–03** committed by its employee whilst engaged on the work of the authority and during the course of his employment. The term "during the course of employment" has been the subject of much litigation and the courts have tended to give it an extended meaning.

> *Smith v. Martin and Hull Corporation.*[21] A school teacher directed a child to attend to the fire in the teachers' common room in preparation for the teachers' lunch, and the child was injured in so doing. *Held*, that the relation of master and servant existed between the local education authority and the teachers employed by them, and that the act of the teacher was within the scope of her employment, which was not strictly confined to teaching alone. The corporation was accordingly held liable for the act of the teacher.

An employee of a local authority may not in fact be carrying out the work

---

[17] (1866) L.R. 1 H.L. 93.
[18] *e.g.* by P. S. Atiyah, *Vicarious Liability in the Law of Torts*, pp. 383–387; *cf. Salmond on the Law of Torts* (19th ed.), pp. 480–481.
[19] [1911] 1 K.B. 869.
[20] At p. 875.
[21] [1911] 2 K.B. 775.

of the authority but duties imposed by law on government departments. The employing authority may not be liable for the torts of such employees.

> *Stanbury v. Exeter Corporation.*[22] An inspector appointed by the council under the Diseases of Animals Act 1894 negligently carried out a duty imposed upon him by an Order of the Board of Agriculture. *Held,* the corporation could not be made liable, for the inspector was not acting in performance of a duty imposed by statute on the local authority.[23]

8–04   An employee is commonly defined for the purposes of liability in tort as a person subject to the control and direction of his employer as to the manner in which he shall do his work.[24] The question has been raised as to whether professional persons in the employment of an authority come under this definition so far as tortious liability is concerned. The issue was of particular importance prior to the National Health Service Act 1946, when many local authorities maintained public hospitals. There was then some doubt as to whether medical practitioners and other skilled employees were "servants" (*i.e.* employees) of a hospital authority so as to make the authority liable for negligence, but this was resolved in the two cases which follow. In view of these decisions it is doubtful whether professional staff of a local authority are ever excluded from the term "employee" so as to excuse the local authority from liability for tortious acts committed during the course of their employment and in the work of the authority.

> *Gold v. Essex County Council.*[25] A visiting doctor ordered ray treatment for a child patient suffering from warts, and a qualified radiographer employed by the county council administered the treatment negligently so that the child was permanently disfigured. *Held,* one who employs a servant is liable to another person if the servant does an act within the scope of his employment so negligently as to injure that other. That principle applies even though the work which the servant is employed to do is of a skilful or technical character as to the method of performing which the employer is himself ignorant.
>
> *Cassidy v. Ministry of Health.*[26] The plaintiff entered hospital for an operation on his hand which necessitated post-operational treatment. Whilst undertaking that treatment he was under the care of the surgeon who performed the operation, the house surgeon and members of the nursing staff, all of whom were employed under contracts of service. At the end of his treatment the plaintiff's hand became useless. *Held,* a hospital authority is liable for the negligence of doctors and surgeons employed by the authority under a contract of service arising in the course of the performance of their professional duties. It was no answer for them to say that their staff were professional men and women who do not tolerate any interference by their lay masters in the way they do their work. The reason why employers are liable in such cases is not that they can control the way in which the work is done but that they employ the staff and have chosen them for the task and have in their hands the ultimate sanction for good conduct, the power of dismissal.

---

[22] [1905] 2 K.B. 838.
[23] *cf. Ministry of Housing and Local Government v. Sharp* [1970] 2 Q.B. 223; local authority not vicariously liable for the clerk to the council when acting in the capacity of Registrar of Local Land Charges.
[24] *Yewens v. Noakes* [1880] 6 Q.B.D. 530, *per* Bramwell L.J. at p. 532.
[25] [1942] 2 K.B. 293.
[26] [1951] 2 K.B. 343.

It will be observed that the medical and nursing staff in the *Cassidy case* **8–05** were under contracts of service, that it is say, they were employees in the sense in which this term is commonly understood, giving all their time to the hospital authority. Denning L.J. would have taken the matter further and would have imputed liability to the hospital authority even though the medical staff were under *contracts for services*, being employed, for example, on a sessional basis of work of a highly specialised nature. The point is mentioned here to illustrate a tendency of the courts to widen the scope of vicarious liability of public authorities arising from acts of all who are employed by them, whether employees whose work they can "control" or specialists about whose techniques they are wholly ignorant. There is a tendency, too, to take all the factors in the relationship into account—the terms of the contract, the degree of control, the economic risk.[27]

There are particular rules with respect to liability for tortious acts committed by police constables.[28]

Independent contractors

There is a distinction between an employee as considered above and an **8–06** independent contractor—a person engaged to give some service or to undertake a particular piece of work in the carrying out of which the council exercises no detailed control. A firm engaged in the building of houses or the construction of a road under a contract with the authority is an independent contractor. The firm will work to a specification provided by the authority and the authority will satisfy itself that the work done conforms to the requirements of the contract. But there will be no supervision of workmen, and orders will not be given to employees, as would be the case in a direct works scheme, *i.e.* where the work itself is entrusted to one of the council's departments.

A local authority is not liable for the torts of an independent contractor **8–07** except in the following circumstances: (a) where the independent contractor is carrying out a duty imposed by law upon the local authority,[29] (b) where the authority interferes to prescribe how the work shall be undertaken,[30] (c) where the authority specifically authorises the tortious act (*qui facit per alium facit per se*), or (d) where the work required to be undertaken is particularly hazardous.[31] In the case of (a), the authority is liable if a legal duty has not been discharged but not for the collateral negligence of a contractor. Lord Blackburn stated the law in *Dalton v. Angus*.[32] He said:

---

[27] See *Market Investigations Ltd v. Minister of Social Security* [1969] 2 Q.B. 173. For a further discussion on this issue, see *Stevenson, Jordan and Harrison Ltd v. Macdonald and Evans* [1952] 1 T.L.R. 101, *Ready Mixed Concrete (South East) Ltd v. Minister of Pensions and National Insurance* [1968] 2 Q.B. 497 and *Lane v. Shire Roofing Co. (Oxford) Ltd*, *The Times*, February 22, 1995.

[28] See Police Act 1996, s.88 and Chap. 24.

[29] See *Penny v. Wimbledon Urban District Council* [1899] 2 Q.B. 72; *Hardaker v. Idle District Council* [1896] 1 Q.B. 335; Highways Act 1980, s.41.

[30] *McLaughlin v. Pryor* (1842) 4 M. & G. 48.

[31] *Honeywill and Stein Ltd v. Larkin Bros. Ltd* [1934] 1 K.B. 191.

[32] (1881) 6 App.Cas. 740 at p. 829.

"Ever since *Quarman v. Burnett* (1840) 6 M. & W. 499 it has been considered settled law that one employing another is not liable for his collateral negligence unless the relation of master and servant existed between them. So that a person employing a contractor to do work is not liable for the negligence of that contractor or his servants. On the other hand, a person causing something to be done, the doing of which casts on him a duty, cannot escape from the responsibility attaching on him of seeing that duty performed by delegating it to a contractor. He may bargain with the contractor that he shall perform the duty and stipulate for an indemnity from him if it is not performed, but he cannot thereby relieve himself from liability to those injured by the failure to perform it."

Lord Blackburn here contrasts a contractor's negligence, which he calls "collateral", with failure on the part of a contractor to perform the duty falling by law to his employer. For the first the employer is not liable; for the second he is, whether the failure is attributable to negligence or not.

> *Hardaker v. Idle District Council.*[33] A district council, being about to construct a sewer under their statutory powers, employed a contractor to construct it for them. In consequence of his negligence in carrying out the work a gas-main was broken, and the gas escaped from it into a house in which the plaintiffs (a husband and wife) resided, and an explosion took place, by which the wife was injured, and the husband's furniture was damaged. In an action by the plaintiffs against the district council and the contractor: *Held*, that the district council owed a duty to the public (including the plaintiffs) so to construct the sewer as not to injure the gas-main; that they had been guilty of a breach of this duty; notwithstanding that they had delegated the performance of the duty to the contractor, they were responsible to the plaintiffs for the breach.

In the course of his judgment Lindley L.J. said[34]:

> "I pass now to consider the duty of the district council in the present case. Their duty in sewering the street was not performed by constructing a proper sewer. Their duty was, not only to do that, but also to take care not to break any gas-pipes which they cut under: this involved properly supporting them. This duty was not performed. They employed a contractor to perform their duty for them, but he failed to perform it. It is impossible, I think, to regard this as a case of collateral negligence. The case is not one in which the contractor performed the district council's duty for them, but did so carelessly; the case is one in which the duty of the district council, so far as the gas-pipes were concerned, was not performed at all."

These general principles were reaffirmed in *Cassidy v. Ministry of Health.*[35] Denning L.J. said[36]:

> "The truth is that, in cases of negligence, the distinction between a contract of service and a contract for services only becomes of importance when it is sought to make the employer liable, not for a breach of his own duty of care, but for some collateral act of negligence of those whom he employs. He cannot escape the consequences of a breach of his own duty but he can escape responsibility for collateral or casual acts of negligence if he can show that the negligent person was employed, not under a contract of service but only under a contract for services. ... Take now an instance where an employer is under a duty

[33] [1896] 1 Q.B. 335.
[34] At p. 342.
[35] [1951] 2 K.B. 343.
[36] At p. 364.

himself. Suppose an employer has a lamp which overhangs his shop door; he is himself under a duty to his customers to use reasonable care to see that it is safe and he cannot escape that duty by employing an independent contractor to do it. He is liable, therefore, if the independent contractor fails to discover a patent defect which any careful man should have discovered, and in consequence the lamp falls on a customer; but he is not liable if the independent contractor drops a hammer on the head of a customer, because that is not negligence in the employer's department of duty. It is collateral or casual negligence by one employed under a contract for services."

Agents

A local authority is in general answerable for the acts of its agents where it **8–08** has expressly authorised them or subsequently ratifies them. The agent also may be liable, for a person cannot excuse himself by saying that he was acting as the agent of another. In applying this principle to particular cases regard must be had to the extent to which the authority controls the conduct of the agent in the discharge of the work entrusted to him. The agent may in this regard be nearer either to a servant or to an independent contractor, and the appropriate rules apply whichever might be the case.

In *S. v. Walsall Metropolitan Borough Council*,[37] the Court of Appeal held that where a child in the care of a local authority is boarded out with approved foster parents, the foster parents are not agents of the authority. Accordingly, the local authority is not vicariously liable for the foster parents' negligence in causing injury to the child.

B. CONSTRUCTION OF STATUTORY POWERS

Whether an authority is liable for a wrongful act depends, amongst other **8–09** things, on the construction of the authorising statute. The statute itself may specifically require or authorise the doing of things which would otherwise be tortious. It may require or authorise something to be done which is necessarily an infringement of a legal right. In such a case the authority is absolved from liability, provided there is no negligence on the part of the authority in what it does.

In deciding whether a defence of statutory authority can be raised, a number of factors may be relevant.

The precision of the statutory authorisation

The more precisely defined are the acts authorised by the statute, so it is **8–10** more easily established that the legislature intended to authorise the performance of acts otherwise tortious.

> *Metropolitan Asylum District v. Hill*.[38] Section 5 of the Metropolitan Poor Act 1867 enacted that "asylums . . . may be provided under this Act for reception or relief of the sick, insane, or infirm, or other class or classes of the poor. . . . " The managers of the Metropolitan Asylum District, in accordance with the Board's

---

[37] [1985] 1 W.L.R. 1150.
[38] (1881) 6 App.Cas. 193. See also *Jordeson v. Sutton, Southcoates and Drypool Gas Co.* [1898] 2 Ch. 614 and *Dormer v. Newcastle upon Tyne Corporation* [1940] 2 K.B. 204.

directions, built a smallpox hospital in a residential area of Hampstead. It was alleged by the residents to be a nuisance. *Held*, that the statutory authority by which the managers acted was no defence. Lord Selborne L.C. said[39]: "The result is: (1) that this Act does not necessarily require anything to be done under it which might not be done without causing a nuisance; (2) that as to those things which may or may not be done under it, there is no evidence on the face of the Act that the legislature supposed it to be impossible for any of them to be done (if they were done at all) somewhere and under some circumstances, without creating a nuisance; and (3) that the legislature has manifested no intention that any of these optional powers, as to asylums, should be exercised at the expense of ... private rights ... [N]o place, or limit of space, is defined within which the establishment of such an asylum is made lawful." Lord Watson said[40]: "The respondents did not dispute that if the appellants ... had been ... expressly empowered to build the identical hospital which they have erected at Hampstead, upon the very site which it now occupies, and that with a view to its being used for the treatment of patients suffering from smallpox, the respondents would not be entitled to the judgment which they have obtained."

Allen v. Gulf Oil Refining Ltd.[41] Gulf were authorised by a private Act of Parliament to construct an oil refinery on certain land. The House of Lords held that this was sufficient to confer on Gulf immunity from proceedings for any nuisance which might be the inevitable result of constructing a refinery on the land, however carefully sited, constructed and operated. Unlike the situation in *Metropolitan Asylum District v. Hill, supra*, the statute in question here specified the land on which the works were to be constructed.[42]

Whether functions are "imperative" or "permissive"

8–11   In *Metropolitan Asylum District v. Hill, supra*, Lord Watson stated[43]:

"If the order of the legislature can be implemented without nuisance, they cannot, in my opinion, plead the protection of the statute; and, on the other hand, it is insufficient for their protection that what is contemplated by the statute cannot be done without nuisance, unless they are also able to show that the legislature has directed it to be done. Where the terms of the statute are not imperative, but permissive, when it is left to the discretion of the persons empowered to determine whether the general powers committed to them shall be put into execution or not, I think the fair inference is that the legislature intended that discretion to be exercised in strict conformity with private rights. ... "

This statement has been influential, but is not a strict rule. Certainly, the presence of a discretion as to the execution of powers makes it more difficult to establish a defence of statutory authority, but it does not make it impossible.[44]

The presence of a "compensation clause"

8–12   Many statutes contain express provision for the payment of compensation to persons who are affected by authorised works. The presence of a

---

[39] At p. 201.
[40] At p. 212.
[41] [1981] A.C. 1001. See also *Tate & Lyle Food and Distribution Ltd v. Greater London Council* [1983] 2 A.C. 509.
[42] See Lord Diplock at p. 1014.
[43] At p. 213.
[44] See, *e.g. Dormer v. Newcastle upon Tyne Corporation* [1940] 2 K.B. 204 and *Marriage v. East Norfolk Rivers Catchment Board, infra.*

"compensation clause" will normally indicate that the legislature did authorise the performance of acts which would otherwise be tortious, but that the only remedy in respect of such acts is that provided by the clause. Hence, an injunction would not be available; compensation would not be obtainable in an action for damages at common law, but only under the statutory procedure. The absence of a compensation clause makes it more difficult to establish a defence of statutory authority, given that the plaintiff in such a case would be without a remedy of any description.

Marriage v. East Norfolk Rivers Catchment Board.[45] The Board had dredged the River Waveney in the exercise of a statutory power and had deposited the spoil on the south bank, raising the level of the bank. This prevented the water at a time of flood from escaping over the south bank as had happened before, and as a consequence a by-pass channel on the north side received an abnormal spate, which swept away the plaintiff's bridge. The plaintiff claimed an injunction and damages for nuisance, alternatively for negligence. *Held*, the injury was of the kind contemplated by the Act, and the plaintiff's sole remedy was therefore a claim for compensation under section 34(3) of the Land Drainage Act 1930. Singleton L.J. said[46]: "Wide powers are given to the board, and it is clear that they have a discretion as to what work they shall undertake, and when; and, speaking generally, the way or manner in which they shall perform the work is left to them. It is equally clear from the nature of the work that the doing of it may cause nuisance and damage to a number of people. One cannot interfere with the course of a river ... without causing upset: the operation of dredging or cleansing a river or a ditch results in soil which has to be put somewhere, and that may create a nuisance. This was recognised by Parliament and s.34 subsection 3 provides [the remedy]."

Jenkins L.J.[47] drew a distinction "between (a) statutory powers to execute some particular work or carry on some particular undertaking (for example, the construction and operation of the reservoir, in *Geddis v. Proprietors of Bann Reservoir*,[48] the provision of hospitals, in *Metropolitan Asylum District Managers v. Hill*,[49] and the construction and operation of the generating station in *Manchester Corporation v. Farnworth*[50]) and (b) statutory powers to execute a variety of works of specified descriptions in a given area (the works in question being of such a kind as necessarily to involve some degree of interference with the rights of others) and as when the body invested with the powers deem it necessary or expedient to do so in furtherance of a general duty imposed on it by the Act (for example, the powers conferred on the board in the present case ...) ... In cases of the former class, the powers are, in the absence of clear provision to the contrary in the Act, limited to the doing of the particular things authorised without infringement of the rights of others, except in so far as any such infringement may be a demonstrably necessary consequence of doing what is authorised to be done. ... In cases of the latter class, such as the present, it is obvious that, if the powers are subjected to an implied limitation to the effect that they are not to be exercised so as to cause any avoidable infringement of the rights of others, the powers will in great measure be nullified and the manifest

[45] [1950] 1 K.B. 284.
[46] At p. 297.
[47] At pp. 307–309.
[48] (1878) 3 App.Cas. 430.
[49] (1881) 6 App.Cas. 193.
[50] [1930] A.C. 171.

object of the Act will be largely frustrated. ... The Act including, as it does, a provision for compensation ... the considerations stated seem to me to lead irresistibly to the conclusion that the intention of the Act was to make the board, acting in good faith and within their powers, the sole judge of what was necessary or proper to be done in the way of drainage operations. ... "

Jenkins L.J. left open the question whether this distinction should be applied where there is no "compensation clause".

The absence of a compensation clause is not, however, conclusive.[51]

The presence of a "nuisance clause"

8–13   Several statutes contain express provisions retaining liability for nuisance. These will negative any defence of statutory authority, but have also been interpreted as requiring a plaintiff to prove fault, thus excluding any liability under the rule in *Rylands v. Fletcher*[52] or any strict liability in nuisance, although in either case perhaps only where the liability relates to the performance of a statutory duty as distinct from the exercise of a statutory power.[53] Two cases where, as a matter of interpretation, "nuisance clauses" have been held not to relate to the acts in question are *Manchester Corporation v. Farnworth*,[54] and *Dormer v. Newcastle upon Tyne Corporation*.[55]

The onus of proof

8–14   It is clear that the onus of establishing a defence of statutory authority lies on the public body concerned.

> *Manchester Corporation v. Farnworth.*[56] A private Act empowered the corporation to establish an electricity generating station on a certain site. The plaintiff, a farmer, sought an injunction and damages in respect of the damage to his property from sulphur fumes emitted by the station. *Held*, damages were to be awarded, and an injunction granted (after a one year suspension). The injunction would be dissolved, and damages would cease to be payable when the corporation established that they had exhausted all reasonable modes of preventing mischief to the plaintiff, and undertook to adopt "the most effective of these modes until they have replaced them by other reasonable but more effective modes of prevention which may thereafter be discovered. ... "
> Viscount Dunedin said[57]: "When Parliament has authorised a certain thing to be made or done at a certain place, there can be no action for nuisance caused by the making or doing of that thing if the nuisance is the inevitable result of the making or doing so authorised. The onus of proving that the result is inevitable is on those who wish to escape liability for nuisance, but the criterion for inevitability is not what is theoretically possible but what is possible according to the state of scientific knowledge at the time, having also in view a certain

---

[51] *Edgington v. Swindon Corporation* [1939] 1 K.B. 86; *Allen v. Gulf Oil Refining Ltd* [1981] A.C. 1001 at p. 1016.

[52] (1869) L.R. 3 H.L. 330. See, *e.g. Smeaton v. Ilford Corporation* [1954] Ch. 450 at p. 477 (see also § 16–11) and *Dunne v. North Western Gas Board* [1964] 2 Q.B. 806.

[53] *Per* Webster J. in *Department of Transport v. North West Water Authority* [1984] A.C. 336 at p. 344, approved by the House of Lords: [1984] A.C. 336 at pp. 359–360. See also § 8–14.

[54] [1930] A.C. 171.

[55] [1940] 2 K.B. 204.

[56] [1930] A.C. 171.

[57] At p. 183.

commonsense appreciation, which cannot be rigidly defined, of practical feasibility in view of the situation and of expense. It is true that in this case we can hold so far that by their callous indifference in planning the construction of the station to all but its own efficiency, the defendants have not discharged the onus incumbent on them." Viscount Sumner concluded: "that the defendants have not shown that a generating station ... could not have been erected then and cannot be used now without causing a nuisance, but that they have failed to show that they have used all reasonable diligence and taken all reasonable steps and precautions to prevent their operations from being a nuisance. ... "

The overall position was summarised as follows by Webster J. in *Department of Transport v. North West Water Authority*[58]:

"1. In the absence of negligence, a body is not liable for a nuisance which is attributable to the exercise by it of a duty imposed upon it by statute.[59] 2. It is not liable in those circumstances even if by statute it is expressly made liable, or not exempted from liability, for nuisance.[60] 3. In the absence of negligence, a body is not liable for a nuisance which is attributable to the exercise by it of a power conferred by statute if, by statute, it is not expressly either made liable, or not exempted from liability, for nuisance.[61] 4. A body is liable for a nuisance attributable by it to the exercise of a power conferred by statute, even without negligence, if by statute it is expressly either made liable, or not exempted from liability, for nuisance.[62]

In these rules, references to absence of negligence are references to: 'the qualification, or condition, that the statutory powers are exercised without "negligence"—that word here being used in a special sense so as to require the undertaker, as a condition of obtaining immunity from action, to carry out the work and conduct the operation with all reasonable regard and care for the interest of other persons ... ': see *Allen v. Gulf Oil Refining Ltd.*[63]

References to nuisance are to be taken as references either to liability in nuisance simpliciter, or to liability under the rule in *Rylands v. Fletcher.*"[64]

These propositions were expressly approved by the House of Lords.[65] It should be noted, however, that as the House held the nuisance in question to be attributable to the performance of a statutory duty, the principles stated to be applicable in cases of statutory powers are *obiter*.

C. FAILURE TO PERFORM STATUTORY DUTIES

It is not possible to state concisely the principle on which an action for **8–15** damages can be sustained against a local authority for a breach of a statutory duty, or a failure to exercise a statutory power. The cases on this subject indicate clearly the circumstances in which an action will *not* lie—indeed the grounds for excluding such an action are so comprehensive that it is

---

[58] [1984] A.C. 336 at p. 344.
[59] *Hammond v. Vestry of St Pancras* (1874) L.R. 9 C.P. 316.
[60] *Stretton's Derby Brewery Co. v. Mayor of Derby* [1894] 1 Ch. 431; *Smeaton v. Ilford Corporation* [1954] Ch. 450.
[61] *Midwood & Co. Ltd v. Manchester Corporation* [1905] 2 K.B. 597; *Longhurst v. Metropolitan Water Board* [1948] 2 All E.R. 834; *Dunne v. North Western Gas Board* [1964] 2 Q.B. 806.
[62] *Charing Cross Electricity Supply Co. v. Hydraulic Power Co.* [1914] 3 K.B. 772.
[63] [1981] A.C. 1001, *per* Lord Wilberforce, at p. 1011.
[64] (1868) L.R. 3 H.L. 330.
[65] [1984] A.C. 336 at pp. 359–360.

frequently said that an action for damages will not lie against an authority for nonfeasance, *i.e.* for failure to do an act which ought to have been done. This, it is submitted, goes too far. Vaughan Williams L.J. said in *Groves v. Wimborne*[66] (an action to recover damages for an alleged breach of a statutory duty to fence machinery):

> " ... it cannot be doubted that, where a statute provides for the performance by certain persons of a particular duty, and someone belonging to a class of persons for whose benefit and protection the statute imposes the duty is injured by failure to perform it, prima facie, and if there be nothing to the contrary, an action by the person so injured will lie against the person who has so failed to perform the duty."

It is clear from the cases, however, that certain stringent tests must be applied.[67] It must first be ascertained whether the relevant statute confers a power or imposes a duty—whether the function is one which the council may undertake or not, as it chooses, or one which the authority has an absolute duty in law to carry out.

Secondly, the relevant statute as a whole must be examined to see whether a remedy for the injury complained of is prescribed. It may be taken as a general rule that the provision of a specific remedy excludes a common law action in tort. Two cases are cited: in the first it was held that the prescribed remedy excluded all others; in the second that, *taking the statute as a whole*, the common law remedy (*i.e.* an action for damages) was available.

> *Hesketh v. Birmingham Corporation.*[68] The corporation owned a sewer which ran alongside a natural stream. A number of storm water outlets were made in the sewer to relieve pressure on it in times of heavy rain by discharging the surplus water into the stream. At the time the outlets were made the stream was of sufficient capacity to carry off all the water that was discharged into it, but in course of time, owing to the neighbouring land having been almost entirely built over, it had become insufficient. After a heavy storm so much surplus water was discharged from the sewer into the stream that adjoining land was flooded and certain houses of the plaintiff were damaged. *Held*, the defendant's neglect to enlarge the capacity of the stream or otherwise improve their drainage system to meet the requirements of the increased population was not negligence for which an action would lie; it was nonfeasance, the remedy, if any, for which was by an application to the Local Government Board under section 299 of the Public Health Act 1874, and assessment of compensation by arbitration under section 308.
>
> *Read v. Croydon Corporation.*[69] The corporation was under a statutory duty to maintain a supply of pure and wholesome water, but it failed in this and the water supply became contaminated with typhoid bacilli. A ratepayer's daugh-

---

[66] [1898] 2 Q.B. 402 at p. 415.

[67] See generally *Cutler v. Wandsworth Stadium Ltd* [1949] A.C. 398; *Lonrho Ltd v. Shell Petroleum Co. Ltd* [1982] A.C. 173; *Hague v. Deputy Governor of Parkhurst Prison* [1992] 1 A.C. 58; and *X v. Bedfordshire County Council* [1995] 3 W.L.R. 152.

[68] [1924] 1 K.B. 260. For other examples of cases where the existence of a statutory remedy has been held to exclude a private right of action, see *Pasmore v. Oswaldtwistle Urban District Council* [1898] A.C. 387; *Watt v. Kesteven County Council* [1955] 1 Q.B. 408; *Bradbury v. Enfield London Borough Council* [1967] 1 W.L.R. 1311 at p. 1324; *Wyatt v. Hillingdon London Borough Council* (1978) 76 L.G.R. 727; *Strable v. Borough Council of Dartford* [1984] J.P.L. 329.

[69] [1938] 4 All E.R. 631.

ter, who lived in his house, contracted typhoid fever. The ratepayer claimed damages for expenses to which he had been put by his daughter's illness, and his daughter claimed damages for pain and suffering. *Held*, that on a proper construction of the Act, an action lay for damages, founded on a breach of statutory duty, *at the suit of the ratepayer*. Stable J. said[70]: "While there is no doubt that, for breaches of some of the statutory duties imposed by the Waterworks Clauses Act, the penalty (provided in the Act) is exclusive, it is difficult to believe that the legislature intended that it should be exclusive in the case of each breach of every duty under the Act. I find it impossible to hold, unless compelled by authority so to do, that the legislature intended that there should be one remedy, and one remedy only, equally applicable to so trivial a breach as the failure to maintain a certain pressure of water behind a fire plug and to a deliberate dereliction of duty resulting in the destruction of a large community by the supply of poisonous water."

It will be noted that the court in the *Croydon* case held that the action **8–16** would lie *on the proper construction of the Act*. The court will look at the general scope of the Act, the nature of the statutory duty, the nature of the injuries likely to arise from a breach of that duty, and the amount of the penalty imposed.[71]

In some cases it has been suggested that the existence of a statutory remedy excludes any private right of action for breach of the statutory duty in question *only* where there is *nonfeasance*, and not where there is *misfeasance*. It is submitted that this is clearly correct where the allegations of misfeasance amounts to an allegation that the defendant authority has tortiously infringed the legal rights of the plaintiff apart from any consideration of the statutory provisions,[72] or where the alleged misfeasance comprises a positive act *ultra vires* the authority (and *a fortiori* a positive act expressly prohibited by the statute).[73] However, where there is merely an incompetent attempt to perform the statutory duty, the case is on proper analysis one of nonfeasance: the essence of the plaintiff's complaint is still that he has not received the benefit of performance of the duty in question.

The alternative remedies discussed in these cases were expressly given in the relevant statute. The possibility of seeking judicial review will not exclude an action for damages.[74]

Thirdly, if the duty is an imperative one and no special remedy is provided then a further test must be applied. It must be ascertained whether a duty to give the service is owed to the community at large or to persons of whom the plaintiff is one. If an action is to lie the duty must be to individuals of whom the plaintiff is one. This principle is illustrated in *Read v. Croydon Corporation*. It will be observed from the words in italics in the note of the

---

[70] At p. 652.
[71] *Per* Lord Cairns in *Atkinson v. Newcastle Co.* (1877) 2 Ex.D. 441. See also *Cutler v. Wandsworth Stadium Ltd* [1949] A.C. 398, *per* Lord Normand at p. 413.
[72] The *Pride of Derby* case (§ 8–18) may be an example of this.
[73] *Gateshead Union v. Durham County Council* [1918] 1 Ch. 146; *Wood v. Ealing London Borough Council* [1967] Ch. 364, 386; *Bradbury v. Enfield London Borough Council* [1967] 1 W.L.R. 1311 at p. 1326; *Meade v. Haringey Council* [1979] 1 W.L.R. 637; *R. v. Secretary of State for the Environment, ex p. Ward* [1984] 1 W.L.R. 834, *cf. R. v. Secretary of State for the Environment, ex p. Lee* (1985) 54 P. & C.R. 311.
[74] *Thornton v. Kirklees Metropolitan Borough Council* [1979] Q.B. 626.

case above that, in so far as the action was founded on a breach of statutory duty, only the ratepayer could sue, for on the construction of the Act the statutory duty was owed to a class of persons of whom the ratepayer was one, but the daughter was not.

8-17 If these tests are satisfied—if injury is sustained through a failure of a local authority to exercise a *duty*, an imperative duty that is, and if that duty is owed to the aggrieved person, as opposed to the community at large, and if the statute itself provides no adequate remedy for such default, then an action for damages may lie at the suit of the injured party.

> *Reffell v. Surrey County Council.*[75] A girl hurrying along a corridor in a controlled school put out her hand to stop a swing door that was swinging towards her, and she was injured. The plaintiff succeeded in a claim for damages for breach of statutory duty under section 10 of the Education Act 1944, and regulation 51 of the Standards for School Premises Regulations 1959. Veale J. asked,[76] three questions (drawn from *Charlesworth on Negligence*, 4th ed., at p. 454) in relation to the facts of the case. First, was the action brought in respect of the kind of harm which the statute was intended to prevent? Secondly, was the person bringing the action one of the class which the statute desired to protect? Thirdly, was the special remedy by the statute adequate for the protection of the person injured? He found that the first two questions were answered in the affirmative, and the third in the negative. The provisions imposed an absolute duty, the test of breach was an objective test, *viz.*, that there would be a breach of duty if safety were not reasonably assured, and, on the facts, safety had not been reasonably assured. The authority was also liable in negligence at common law, since it knew that the door was a real danger and was a reasonably foreseeable risk.

By contrast, civil actions for breach of statutory duty do not lie against local authorities in respect of breaches of the statutory codes concerning the special educational needs of children[77] or the protection of children from abuse.[78] Indeed it has been stated that regulatory or welfare legislation is not to be treated as being passed for the benefit of individuals affected by the regulated activity but for the benefit of society in general and that the cases where a private right of action for breach of statutory duty has been held to arise are all cases where the duty has been very limited and specific, as opposed to general administrative functions imposed on public bodies involving the exercise of administrative discretions.[79]

8-18 In each of the cases so far considered, the plaintiff either based his action on negligence, alleging that a failure on the part of an authority to perform

---

[75] [1964] 1 W.L.R. 358. It was held in *Thornton v. Kirklees Metropolitan Borough Council* [1979] Q.B. 626 that since the Housing (Homeless Persons) Act 1977 imposed a duty on a housing authority for the benefit of a specified category of persons and provided no special remedy, an action in damages would lie against an authority which failed to provide accommodation in an appropriate case. However, no private right arises until the local authority's public law decision-making function has been concluded in the applicant's favour: *R. v. Northavon District Council, ex p. Palmer, The Times,* August 1, 1995.

[76] At pp. 362, 363.

[77] *X v. Bedfordshire County Council and other cases* [1995] 2 A.C. 633 (*E (A Minor) v. Dorset County Council, Keating v. Bromley London Borough Council*).

[78] *ibid.* (*X v. Bedfordshire County Council, M (A Minor) v. Newham London Borough Council*).

[79] *ibid.,* per Lord Browne-Wilkinson at pp. 731–732.

its statutory duty amounted in itself to negligence; or claimed damages for breach of statutory duty as a cause of action distinct from negligence. But different considerations may well arise if an action is based on nuisance, for a plaintiff may have a right of action notwithstanding the presence of a remedy in the relevant statute if he suffers injury through nuisance, even though it is brought about through an authority's inactivity. This proposition emerges from *Pride of Derby and Derbyshire Angling Association v. British Celanese*,[80] a case dealing with sewers and sewerage systems at a time when there were a local authority responsibility. The rule clearly applied where a system had been constructed by an authority or "adopted" by an authority within the principles laid down in *Sedleigh-Denfield v. O'Callaghan*[81]; its application was doubtful where an authority had "inherited" drains and sewers, and those drains and sewers constituted a nuisance by reason only that they had ceased to deal adequately with the sewage of the authority's area, the local authority not having itself been at fault except that it had not used its statutory powers to enlarge the sewerage system.

> *Pride of Derby and Derbyshire Angling Association v. British Celanese.*[82] One of the defendants, the Derby Corporation, had polluted the River Derwent by discharging insufficiently treated sewage into the river. It was argued on behalf of the corporation that the sewerage system, which had been constructed in accordance with the statutory powers, did not cause pollution at the time it was completed. The present pollution had resulted from the increase in the population of Derby which had caused the system to become inadequate. The council, it was contended, could not be made liable since the injury was the result of nonfeasance. *Held*, as regards sewers and drains it was necessary to keep in mind the possibility of two distinct causes of action, namely, nuisance and negligence. As regards negligence, it may be that nonfeasance, in the sense of failing to perform some positive statutory duty, did not give rise to a cause of action for negligence against the local authority in respect of its sewerage system. In regard to nuisance, however, the question of nonfeasance as distinct from misfeasance had no real relevance. Evershed M.R. said[83]: "Now it is clear that if a public authority so exercises any of its functions as to cause a private nuisance to any person, the authority is liable ... to be sued in these courts, ... unless it can rely upon some statute as providing, by express language or necessary or proper inference, a defence to such an action. So much appears, for example, from *Metropolitan Asylum District v. Hill*."[84]

It appears, however, that there was an element of *misfeasance* in this case, an active dealing with the sewage which came into the council's works. Denning L.J.[85] based his decision on the fact that

> "When the increased sewage came into their sewage disposal works ... they took it under their charge, treated it in their works, and poured the effluent into

---

[80] [1953] Ch. 149, see also *Page Motors Limited v. Epsom and Ewell Borough Council, supra.*
[81] [1940] A.C. 880.
[82] *supra*, n. 80.
[83] At p. 163.
[84] (1881) 6 App.Cas. 193.
[85] At p. 191.

the River Derwent. ... Their act in pouring a polluting effluent into the river makes them guilty of nuisance."

A plaintiff claiming damages from a local authority for *failure to carry out a statutory duty*, if he relies solely on the *Derby* case, may well be faced with the substantial point that, on the facts, this case was not wholly one of nonfeasance. The law on this topic is by no means settled.

A statutory duty may be held not to be absolute, but to be a duty to exercise care.[86]

8–19   Until the coming into force of section 1 of the Highways (Miscellaneous Provisions) Act 1961, the failure of a highway authority to perform the duties of repair and maintenance imposed by the common law or by statute was held not to give rise to a liability to pay damages to persons injured as a result. This much-criticised immunity was not extended to other authorities,[87] and was subsequently abrogated by section 1(1) of the 1961 Act. Section 1(2) provided that in an action against a public authority for damage resulting from their failure to maintain a highway it shall be a defence to prove that the authority has taken such care as is reasonable in the circumstances to secure that the part of the highway to which the action relates was not dangerous for traffic. The test of whether a highway is "dangerous" for these purposes is whether the condition of the road is foreseeably dangerous "to traffic being driven in the way normally expected on that highway."[88]

Parliament is frequently exhorted to indicate expressly whether failure to perform a statutory duty may lead to liability in damages. Occasionally this is done. Section 1(5) of the Refuse Disposal (Amenity) Act 1978 read:

"No action shall lie against a local authority in respect of damage resulting from their failure to carry out their duty under this section [to provide places where the public may dispose of refuse]; but if the Secretary of State is satisfied, after holding a local inquiry, that a local authority have failed to carry out that duty he may by order require the authority to take such steps for carrying it out as are specified in the order."

No such provision is, however, found in the Environmental Protection Act 1990, which repeals section 1 of the 1978 Act and makes fresh provision for the duties of waste disposal authorities.

---

[86] See *Sephton v. Lancashire River Board* [1962] 1 W.L.R. 623; *Rippingale Farms v. Black Sluice Internal Drainage Board* [1963] 1 W.L.R. 1347; *Ministry of Housing and Local Government v. Sharp* [1970] 2 Q.B. 223.
[87] See, *e.g. Att.-Gen. v. St Ives Rural District Council* [1960] 1 Q.B. 312.
[88] *Per* Sachs L.J. in *Rider v. Rider* [1973] 1 All E.R. 294 at p. 300. See also *Griffiths v. Liverpool Corporation* [1967] 1 Q.B. 374; *Meggs v. Liverpool Corporation* [1968] 1 W.L.R. 689; *Littler v. Liverpool Corporation* [1968] 2 All E.R. 343; *Burnside v. Emerson* [1968] 1 W.L.R. 1490; *Haydon v. Kent County Council* [1978] Q.B. 343; *Bird v. Pearce and Another, Somerset County Council* [1979] R.T.R. 369; and *Tarrant v. Rowland* [1979] R.T.R. 144.

D. Negligence in the Performance of Statutory Functions

Negligence principles

Local authorities may be held liable in negligence in respect of acts and **8–20** omissions occurring in the performance of their statutory functions. The act or omission may be that of the authority itself or of a person for whom the authority is vicariously liable. The plaintiff must establish that he was owed a duty of care, that there was a breach of that duty, that the breach caused harm to him and that the harm was not too remote a consequence.

In situations where a private citizen or corporation would be liable in negligence, the mere fact that the defendant is a local authority of itself makes no difference to liability. The defence of statutory authority will rarely if ever be available.

> *Geddis v. Proprietors of the Bann Reservoir.*[89] The defendants, acting under statutory authority, constructed a reservoir. They neglected to cleanse a channel leading from the reservoir, although they had statutory power to do so, with the result that the plaintiff's land was flooded. *Held*, the defendants were liable. Lord Blackburn stated[90]: "It is now thoroughly well established that no action will lie for doing that which the legislature has authorised, if it be done without negligence, although it does occasion damage to anyone; but an action does lie for doing that which the legislature has authorised if it be done negligently. And I think that if by a reasonable exercise of the powers, either given by statute to the promoters, or which they have at common law, the damage could be prevented, it is, within this rule, 'negligence' not to make such reasonable exercise of their powers."

Many well-known cases in the law of negligence in fact involve local authorities as defendants. In *Fisher v. Ruislip-Northwood Urban District Council*,[91] the council was held liable where it built an air raid shelter in the road but left it unlit at night so that a motorist collided with it. In *Carmarthenshire County Council v. Lewis*,[92] the council was held liable where precautions were not taken to prevent a four-year-old child straying from school into the highway, with the result that a lorry driver was killed when he swerved to avoid him. In *Rimmer v. Liverpool City Council*[93] the council was held liable for constructing a flat with an interior glass panel of insufficient thickness. Other examples include cases on occupiers' liability[94] and negligent misstatement.[95]

The position is more complex where a public authority is performing functions not generally undertaken by private citizens. Here it may be difficult to establish that the authority owes a duty of care. The case law on

---

[89] (1878) 3 H.L. 430.
[90] At pp. 455, 456.
[91] [1945] K.B. 584.
[92] [1955] A.C. 549.
[93] [1985] Q.B. 1. *Cf. Targett v. Torfaen District Council* (1991) 24 H.L.R. 164 (council liable for personal injuries caused by a design defect in a council house designed and constructed by the council itself).
[94] §§ 8–29 *et seq.*
[95] §§ 8–28 *et seq.*

the duty of care in negligence is now very substantial, the attitude and generally approach of the courts having changed over time.[96] Where it is reasonably foreseeable that a positive act of the defendant may cause physical damage to the plaintiff, it is commonly, although not invariably,[97] recognised by the courts that a duty of care is owed.[98] However, the courts are more cautious where, for example, loss is caused by an *omission*[99] rather than an act, or by a *statement*,[1] or where the harm caused was not physical damage but *psychiatric injury*[2] or *economic loss*.[3] The fact that negligence has occurred in the course of the exercise of statutory *discretionary powers* has also been thought to give rise to special difficulties.[4] In these areas, the courts have been prepared either to limit the scope of the duty of care or hold that no duty arises. However, the courts have not been consistent in their approach.

In the 1970s and early 1980s, the courts were relatively willing to recognise duties of care in novel situations, expanding the scope of the tort of negligence. Particularly influential was the decision of the House of Lords in *Anns v. Merton London Borough Council*[5] where it was held that a local authority owed a duty to take reasonable care to ensure that a builder complied with building by-laws, the duty being owed to the purchaser of a house that turned out to be defective because of non-compliance with those by-laws.[6] The recognition of a duty here was significant in that in essence the local authority could be held liable in respect of an omission (*i.e.* the failure to control the builder) that gave rise to economic loss (*i.e.* the purchase of a house that turned out to be worth less than the purchase price, but which did not itself cause damage to other property).[7] Furthermore, the House indicated that consideration of whether a duty of care should be owed should proceed in two stages. First, where "as between the alleged wrongdoer and the person who has suffered damage there is a sufficient relationship of proximity or neighbourhood such that, in the reasonable contemplation of the former, carelessness may be likely to cause damage to the latter" a *prima facie* duty of care arose. It was then necessary to determine whether there were "considerations which ought to negative, or limit the scope of the duty."[8]

This "two-stage approach" was subsequently employed to expand liability

---

[96] See W.V.H. Rogers, *Winfield and Jolowicz on Tort* (14th ed., 1994), Chap. 5.
[97] *Marc Rich & Co. AG v. Bishop Rock Marine Co.* [1996] 1 A.C. 211, H.L.
[98] *Donoghue v. Stevenson* [1932] A.C. 562, H.L.
[99] See § 8–25.
[1] See § 8–28.
[2] See *Alcock v. Chief Constable of South Yorkshire* [1992] 1 A.C. 310, H.L.
[3] *Candlewood Navigation Corp. v. Mitsui O.S.K. Lines Ltd* [1986] A.C. 1, P.C.; *Murphy v. Brentwood District Council* [1991] 1 A.C. 398, H.L.
[4] § 8–25.
[5] [1978] A.C. 728. See § 8–21. The leading speech was given by Lord Wilberforce.
[6] In *Anns* it was claimed that maisonettes had been built on inadequate foundations and did not conform to the plans approved under the by-laws.
[7] These points were inadequately recognised in the speeches in the *Anns* case itself.
[8] [1978] A.C. 728, 751.

in negligence for economic loss[9] and psychiatric injury.[10] At the same time, a large body of case law was generated by the uncertainties as to the limits of the duty of care owed by a local authority in respect of the exercise or non-exercise of its building control powers.[11]

From the mid-1980s, the courts have reverted to a more cautious **8–21** approach. The "two-stage test" has been disapproved. The typical approach now involves consideration of (1) whether damage was reasonably foreseeable, (2) whether there was a sufficient relationship of proximity[12] between the parties for a duty of care to be imposed, and (3) whether it was "fair, just and reasonable" in the light of the relevant policy considerations for a duty of care to be owed. Furthermore, any developments in the law of negligence should preferably be incremental, by analogy with the existing case law.[13] The courts have restated the limits of liability in respect of economic loss, psychiatric injury and negligent misstatement more narrowly.[14] Of particular importance to local authorities, the House of Lords in the following case overruled its previous decision in the *Anns* case:

> *Murphy v. Brentwood District Council.*[15] Plans for the building of a house were submitted to the council. The council referred them to consulting engineers acting as independent contractors, and, relying on their advice, passed the plans. The house was built on a concrete raft foundation. The design of the raft was defective. While the plaintiff was in occupation, the raft cracked, leading to extensive damage to the walls and pipes. The trial judge and the Court of Appeal held that the engineers had been negligent, and that the council's duty to take reasonable care had not been discharged by acting on the advice of independent contractors. The council was accordingly liable under the *Anns* case for the diminution in value of the plaintiff's house.
>
> The House of Lords allowed an appeal by the council, holding—
>
> > (a) A builder who constructs a building owes a duty of care (under *Donoghue v. Stevenson*) in respect of injury to persons or damage to other property, arising from a latent defect; but does not normally owe a duty of care in tort to persons who acquire the building and who suffer economic loss because the building is defective in quality.
> >
> > (b) Where a dangerous defect is discovered before it causes personal injury or property damage it is now to be regarded as a defect in quality. The building is either capable of repair at economic cost or must be abandoned, and the cost of repairs and/or the diminution in value of

---

[9] *Junior Books Ltd v. Veitchi Co. Ltd* [1983] 1 A.C. 520, H.L., holding that a duty of care could arise in respect of purely economic loss where there was a sufficient relationship of proximity between the parties.

[10] *McLaughlin v. O'Brian* [1983] 1 A.C. 410, H.L.

[11] See *Lyons v. Booth (F.W.) (Contractors) and Maidstone Borough Council* (1982) 262 E.G. 981; *Worlock v. S.A.W.S.* (1983) 265 E.G. 774; *Dennis v. Charnwood Borough Council* [1983] Q.B. 409; *Peabody Donation Fund Governors v. Parkinson (Sir Lindsay) & Co.* [1985] A.C. 210; *Investors in Industry Commercial Properties Ltd v. South Bedfordshire District Council* [1986] Q.B. 1034 *Richardson v. West Lindsey District Council* [1990] 1 W.L.R. 522.

[12] A different, and narrower concept than that of foreseeability: *Yuen Kun Yeu v. Attorney-General of Hong Kong* [1988] A.C. 175, P.C.

[13] See *e.g. Caparo Industries plc v. Dickman* [1990] 2 A.C. 605, H.L.

[14] *Alcock v. Chief Constable of South Yorkshire* [1992] 1 A.C. 310, H.L. (psychiatric injury); *Caparo Industries plc v. Dickman, supra* (statements).

[15] [1991] 1 A.C. 398.

the building is properly analysed as economic loss. Such losses can be recovered in contract but not, in the absence of a special relationship of proximity, as in *Hedley Byrne & Co. Ltd v. Heller & Partners Ltd*,[16] in tort.

(c) A building the whole of which has been erected and equipped by the same contractor is to be regarded as one unit; it is not correct to regard damage to walls and pipes caused by a defective foundation to be damage to "other property" and so actionable under *Donoghue v. Stevenson*. (The position might be different where a building is destroyed or damaged as a result of defective wiring installed by a sub-contractor or the explosion of a negligently manufactured central heating boiler.)

(d) A local authority does not owe a duty of care to protect building owners from such economic losses; the duty of care owed by the authority can be no wider than that of the builder. The decision in *Anns* was contrary to principle and difficult to apply and should be overruled. It should be left to Parliament to determine how far as a matter of policy builders and local authorities should be liable for such losses (*cf.*, in relation to builders, the Defective Premises Act 1972).

The House left open the question whether a local authority owes a duty of care to prevent builders constructing a building with a latent defect that does cause personal injury or damage to other property, and the question whether the council was liable for the negligence of the independent contractors.

8–22 There has been a similar reluctance to recognise a duty of care in other areas where the essence of the plaintiff's complaint is that the local authority has failed to protect him from harm caused by a third party.[16a] Furthermore, the courts have become increasingly receptive[17] to arguments that a duty of care should not be imposed on a public authority for reasons of public policy, noting that recognition of a duty may unduly inhibit the proper performance of statutory functions or constitute a disproportionate drain on the limited resources of the authority through both the costs of litigation and the payment of damages.

The leading case is *X (a minor) v. Bedfordshire County Council*.[18] Here the House of Lords heard five appeals on questions whether particular causes of action should be struck out. Two cases (*X (a minor) v. Bedfordshire County Council* and *M (a minor) v. Newham London Borough Council*) concerned alleged negligence in the exercise or non-exercise of powers under the Child Care Act 1980 and then the Children Act 1989 to protect children from abuse. In the *Bedfordshire* case, the child plaintiffs claimed damages for personal injuries, alleging that the council had negligently failed to act on reports that they were being abused. In the *Newham* case, it was alleged that a consultant psychiatrist employed by the area health authority and a social worker employed by the council, negligently identified the

---

[16] [1964] A.C. 465. See § 8–28. For the rejection of a claim that a statement that premises had been inspected under the building regulations was sufficient to found liability under *Hedley Byrne*, see *King v. North Cornwall District Council* [1995] N.P.C. 21.

[16a] See further §§ 8–25, *et seq.*

[17] This argument received short shrift in *Home Office v. Dorset Yacht Co.* [1970] A.C. 1004, 1033, *per* Lord Reid.

[18] [1995] 2 A.C. 633, H.L.

cohabitee of M's mother as M's abuser, leading to M's placement in foster care. Here M and her mother claimed damages for psychiatric injury. Three cases (*E (a minor) v. Dorset County Council, Christmas v. Hampshire County Council* and *Keating v. Bromley London Borough Councils*) arose out of alleged failures to diagnose special leaning disorders in children or deal appropriately with the children's special educational needs once they had been identified. In the *Dorset* and *Bromley* cases it was also alleged that the parents had been wrongly advised by psychologists and other staff employed by the council. The House of Lords struck out all the causes of action in negligence save those based on allegations of the giving of negligent advice by officers. Causes of action based on breach of statutory duty were also struck out. The leading speech was given by Lord Browne-Wilkinson, with whom all the other members of the House agreed.[19] The points made included the following. First, the careless performance of statutory powers or duties does not give rise to a cause of action unless the circumstances are such as to raise a duty of care at common law.[20] Secondly, a distinction has to be drawn between (a) cases in which it is alleged that the authority owes a duty of care in the manner in which it exercises a statutory discretion, and (b) cases in which a duty of care is alleged to arise from the manner in which the statutory duty has been implemented in practice.

As to (a) to establish common law liability for negligence it is necessary first to show that the decision was outside the ambit of the discretion: a local authority cannot be liable for doing that which Parliament has authorised and so decisions within the ambit of such statutory discretion cannot be actionable. Conversely a decision that is so unreasonable that it falls outside the ambit of the discretion conferred on the authority is not immune from liability. In deciding whether this requirement is satisfied, the court has to assess the relevant factors taken into account by the authority. However, the court cannot enter upon the assessment of such policy matters as "social policy, the allocation of finite financial resources ... or the balance between pursuing desirable social aims as against the risk to the public inherent in so doing".[21] These matters are not justiciable. Accordingly,

> "if the factors relevant to the exercise of the discretion include matters of policy, the court cannot reach the conclusion that the decision was outside the ambit of the statutory discretion. Therefore, a common law duty of care in relation to the taking of decisions involving policy matters cannot exist."[22]

Subject to this, the test appears to be whether the decision is so unreasonable that no reasonable authority could have reached them.[23]

As to (b), the question whether a duty of care is owed depends upon the

---

[19] Apart from Lord Nolan on one point: pp. 771–772.

[20] pp. 732–735. The decision in *Geddis v. Proprietors of Bann Reservoir* (1878) 3 App.Cas. 430, H.L.; (§ 8–20) merely established that the defence of statutory authority is not available if powers or duties are exercised or performed carelessly.

[21] pp. 736–737.

[22] p. 738. See further §§ 8–25, *et seq.* on the policy-operational dichotomy.

[23] This is *Wednesbury* unreasonableness (see § 10–25). At the same time Lord Browne-Wilkinson stated that other aspects of the *ultra vires* doctrine had no part to play in the determination of this question: p. 736.

application of the usual principles of the law of negligence. However, a duty of care cannot be imposed

"if the observance of such common law duty of care would be inconsistent with, or have a tendency to discourage, the due performance by the local authority of its statutory duties."[24]

8–23   Applying these principles to the facts of the cases, Lord Browne-Wilkinson concluded that the claims against the council directly in the *Bedfordshire* case should not be struck out on the ground of non-justiciability as at least some of the allegations did not necessarily involve any question of the allocation of resources or the determination of general policy; moreover, it was possible that the plaintiffs might be able to demonstrate at trial that the local authority's decisions were so unreasonable that no reasonable local authority could have reached them and therefore fell outside the ambit of the statutory discretion. Furthermore, the local authority accepted that it could foresee damage and that there was a sufficient relationship of proximity. However, the claim should be struck out on the ground that it was not fair, just and reasonable for a duty of care to be owed.[25] First, to recognise such a duty "would cut across the whole statutory system set up for the protection of children at risk". This system was inter-disciplinary, involving the police, educational bodies, doctors and others, taking joint decisions. To impose liability of all "would lead to almost impossible problems of disentangling ... the liability, both primary and by way of contribution, of each for reaching a decision found to be negligent". Secondly, the task of those dealing with children at risk was "extraordinarily delicate". Thirdly, the imposition of liability on local authorities might lead to the adoption of "a more cautious and defensive approach to their duties". Fourthly, this area was a "fertile ground in which to breed ill-feeling and litigation, often hopeless, the cost of which both in terms of money and human resources will be diverted from the performance of the social service for which they were provided." Fifthly, they were alternative remedies for maladministration in the statutory complaints procedure and the Local Government Ombudsman. Finally, in the nearest analogous cases it had been held that the police did not owe a duty of care to protect vulnerable members of society from wrongs done to them by others[26] and that statutory regulators of financial dealings did not owe a duty of care to investors to protect them from wrongdoing.[27]

"In my judgment the courts should proceed with great care before holding liable in negligence those who have been charged by Parliament with the task of protecting society from the wrongdoings of others."[28]

Claims in the *Bedfordshire* and *Newham* cases based on vicarious liability for the negligence of such officers as a psychiatrist or a social worker were

[24] p. 739.
[25] pp. 748–751.
[26] *Hill v. Chief Constable of West Yorkshire* [1989] A.C. 53.
[27] *Yuen Kun Yeu v. Attorney-General of Hong Kong* [1988] A.C. 175.
[28] *per* Lord Browne-Wilkinson at p. 751.

struck out on the ground that these officers were retained to advise the local authority as to whether the child care legislation should be invoked and not to advise or treat the plaintiff and so their duty was owed to the authority and not to the plaintiff. In addition, it was not just and reasonable for a duty of care to be owed for the same reasons that ruled out a direct duty of care owed by the authority.[29] Similar reasons were applied in striking out the majority of the negligence claims in the education cases (*Dorset, Hampshire,* and *Bromley*),[30] including the existence of a right to appeal to the Secretary of State under tne Education Act 1981; the great expenditure of time and money that would be involved in the defence of many hopeless (and possibly vexatious) cases; the courts

> "should hesitate long before imposing a common law duty of care in the exercise of discretionary powers and duties conferred by Parliament for social welfare purposes."

However, claims based squarely on the *Hedley Byrne* principle[31] were not struck out.[32]

Other recent cases decided both before and since *X (a minor) v.* **8–24** *Bedfordshire County Council* are consistent with the approach adopted in those cases. Thus, in *Ephraim v. Newham London Borough Council*[33] the council was held not liable in respect of injuries suffered by the plaintiff in a fire at a bed and breakfast establishment. The plaintiff was homeless and was advised to go to the establishment by the council as local housing authority. However, the essence of the complaint was a failure to inspect the premises and it was not fair, just and reasonable for a duty of care to be owed. In *Martine v. South East Kent Health Authority*[34] it was held that the authority owed no duty of care in respect of an investigation into a registered nursing home. The police have been held not to owe a duty of care to protect members of the public from physical danger or crime.[35] Fire authorities have been held not normally to owe a duty of care to the owner of premises on

---

[29] pp. 751–754.

[30] pp. 760–763 (*Dorset*); p. 770 (*Bromley*).

[31] See § 8–28.

[32] See *e.g.* pp. 762–763 (*Dorset*): claims in respect of allegedly negligent advice given by Dorset's psychology advice service and by particular educational psychologists; pp. 765–767 (*Hampshire*): claims in respect of allegedly negligent advice as to educational needs given by a head teacher and the county advisory service; pp. 770–771 (*Bromley*).

[33] (1992) 25 H.L.R. 207.

[34] *The Times*, March 8, 1993.

[35] *Hill v. Chief Constable of West Yorkshire* [1989] A.C. 530 (no duty owed to the last victim of Peter Sutcliffe); *Clough v. Bussan* [1990] 1 All E.R. 431 (claim in respect of alleged police failure to respond quickly where traffic lights became defective struck out); *Ancell v. McDermott* [1993] 4 All E.R. 355 (claim in respect of alleged police failure to deal adequately with traffic hazard resulting from spillage of oil leading to fatal accident struck out); *Alexandrou v. Oxford* [1993] 4 All E.R. 328 (claim in respect of allegedly negligent response to burglar alarm dismissed); *Osman v. Ferguson* [1993] 4 All E.R. 344 (claim in respect of alleged police failure to prevent a person known to have threatened P from injuring him struck out).

fire.[36] On the other hand, cases falling within the *Hedley Byrne* principle have succeeded.[37]

Failure to exercise powers; the policy-operational dichotomy

8–25   A further argument against liability in negligence may arise where the plaintiff's complaint is that there has been a failure to exercise powers for his benefit.

Where the legislature has given a local authority a power to act for the benefit of individual citizens, or for the community at large, but has not imposed a duty so to act,[38] it follows logically that the authority should not normally be liable in damages where it chooses not to exercise that power in a particular case. The fact that it has a discretion whether to exercise the power means that it is legally entitled not to do so if it so wishes.

> *Sheppard v. Glossop Corporation.*[39] The council resolved that street lamps be extinguished at about 9 p.m. each night in the interests of economy. Because a lamp was unlit the plaintiff strayed onto private land and then fell onto the highway from the private land over a retaining wall at a point where the level of the street was lower than the private land. The plaintiff sued the council for damages. *Held*, that section 161 of the Public Health Act 1875 conferred on urban authorities a discretion, but imposed on them no obligation, to light the streets in their districts; consequently that the defendants, who had begun, were not bound to continue to light the street; and that having done nothing to make the street dangerous they were under no obligation, whether by lighting or otherwise, to give warning of danger. The defendants were not, therefore, liable.

Similarly, there should normally be no liability where there is a delay before the power is exercised.

There is a House of Lords authority to the effect that where a power to confer a benefit is incompetently exercised, an authority will be liable for "fresh damage" which would not have occurred had the power not been exercised at all, but not merely for failure to confer the benefit in question. The authority's intervention must in some respect make the situation worse, and damages will only be payable in respect of the "worsening".

> *East Suffolk Rivers Catchment Board v. Kent.*[40] An exceptionally high spring tide caused the River Deben to overflow its banks and many pastures were

---

[36] *John Munroe (Acrylics) Ltd v. London Fire and Civil Defence Authority, The Times*, May 22, 1996 (no sufficient proximity between fire brigade and owner of premises which might be ablaze to give rise to a duty to respond to a call for assistance; also contrary to public policy for such a duty to be recognised; once the fire brigade did respond, it would only be liable if it undertook a personal responsibility to some individual during the course of its activity); *Church of Jesus Christ of Latter-Day Saints (Great Britain) v. Yorkshire Fire and Civil Defence Authority, The Times*, May 9, 1996 (contrary to public policy for duty of care to be recognised arising out of failure to take reasonable steps to ensure an adequate supply of water at the scene of a crime); *cf. Capital and Counties plc. v. Hampshire County Council, The Times*, April 26, 1996 (fire brigade liable where officer negligently ordered sprinkler system in a burning building to be turned off; no public policy immunity). In *Stovin v. Wise* [1996] 3 W.L.R. 388, 416, Lord Hoffman doubted whether a duty should be owed; see further, § 8–27.

[37] See § 8–28; see *e.g. T. v. Surrey County Council* [1994] 4 All E.R. 577 (council held liable for failing to warn a parent of suspicions concerning a registered childminder.

[38] In which case an action for breach of statutory duty might lie: see §§ 8–15, *et seq.*

[39] [1921] 3 K.B. 132.

[40] [1941] A.C. 74.

flooded. The trial judge found that the Board's staff had so inefficiently carried out repair works that it took them 178 days, whereas with reasonable skill the gap should have been closed in 14 days. The Board had no statutory *duty* to repair the breach but had a statutory power to do this. *Held*, the Board could not be made liable in damages. Lord Romer said[41]: "Where a statutory authority is entrusted with a mere power it cannot be made liable for any damage sustained by a member of the public by reason of a failure to exercise that power. If in the exercise of their discretion they embark upon an execution of that power, the only duty they owe to any member of the public is not thereby to add to the damages that he would have suffered had they done nothing. So long as they exercise their discretion honestly, it is for them to determine the method by which and the time within which and the time during which the power shall be exercised; and they cannot be made liable, except to the extent that I have just mentioned, for any damage that would have been avoided had they exercised their discretion in a more reasonable way." Given that the duty was limited to the avoidance of extra damage there was no causal link between any breach of that duty and the damage of which the plaintiff complained, namely the continuance of the inundation for 164 extra days.

The principles applied in the *East Suffolk* case are illustrations of the general reluctance of the courts to impose duties of affirmative action within the framework of the law of negligence. There are, however, certain situations where such duties are well established, and a local authority will be liable here just as other defendants would be. For example, the law requires persons who exercise control over others to exercise care (1) to protect them from harm, and (2) to prevent them from causing harm to third parties. Thus, a local authority will owe a duty to take reasonable affirmative steps to protect children in its care or attending its schools,[42] and to prevent such children causing harm to others.[43] The law also requires the occupiers of premises to take reasonable affirmative action to prevent visitors suffering harm from defects in the premises (see also below, paras 8–29, *et seq.*). Even where there is no special relationship of this sort, someone in the position of the plaintiff in the *East Suffolk* case might be able to recover damages if he had acted to his detriment, reasonably expecting that the authority would perform its task competently. In the *East Suffolk* case itself, Slesser L.J. in the Court of Appeal found for the plaintiff on this basis.[44] However, it was held in the House of Lords that detrimental reliance had not been established on the facts as pleaded.[45]

The *East Suffolk* case was criticised and distinguished by the House of **8–26** Lords in *Anns v. Merton London Borough Council*[46] on the ground that

---

[41] At p. 102.

[42] *e.g. Carmarthenshire County Council v. Lewis* [1955] A.C. 549; *Shepherd v. Essex County Council* (1913) 29 T.L.R. 303; *Fryer v. Salford Corporation* [1937] 1 All E.R. 617; *Fowler v. Bedfordshire County Council, The Times*, May 22, 1995 (council liable where plaintiff at youth centre was injured during unsupervised gymnastics). *Cf. P. v. Harrow London Borough Council, The Times*, April 22, 1992 (local education authority not liable in negligence where boys with emotional difficulties sent by it to an independent school approved by the Secretary of State were sexually abused by the Headmaster).

[43] *e.g. Ricketts v. Erith Borough Council* [1943] 2 All E.R. 629.

[44] See [1940] 1 K.B. at pp. 327–328 and *cf.* MacKinnon L.J. at p. 333.

[45] [1941] A.C. 74, *per* Lord Porter at p. 107; *cf.* Lord Romer at p. 97.

[46] [1978] A.C. 728.

"the conception of a duty of care, not limited to particular accepted situations but extending generally over all relations of sufficient proximity, and even pervading the sphere of statutory functions of public bodies, had not at that time become fully recognised."[47]

As we have seen,[48] the House of Lords in *Anns* in effect extended the liability of local authorities in respect of failure to protect the purchasers of houses from the consequences of defective building work. At the same time, a qualification was recognised, to take account of the fact that the local authority was exercising (or failing to exercise) discretionary statutory powers.[49] In *Anns*, Lord Wilberforce said:[50]

"Most, indeed probably all, statutes relating to public authorities or public bodies, contain in them a large area of policy. The courts call this 'discretion' meaning that the decision is one for the authority or body to make, and not for the courts. Many statutes also prescribe or at least presuppose the practical execution of policy decisions: a convenient description of this is to say that in addition to the area of policy or discretion, there is an operational area. Although this distinction between the policy area and the operational area is convenient, and illuminating, it is probably a distinction of degree; many 'operational' powers or duties have in them some element of 'discretion'. It can safely be said that the more 'operational' a power or duty may be, the easier it is to superimpose upon it a common law duty of care.

I do not think that it is right to limit this to a duty to avoid causing extra or additional damage beyond what must be expected to arise from the exercise of the power or duty. That may be correct when the act done under the statute *inherently* must adversely *affect* the interest of individuals. But many other acts can be done without causing any harm to anyone—indeed may be directed to preventing harm from occurring. In these cases the duty is the normal one of taking care to avoid harm to those likely to be affected."

Accordingly, where the impugned decision to exercise or not to exercise the powers, or decision as to the method of exercise, fell within the "policy" or "discretionary" area, the plaintiff had to show not merely that there was a failure to take reasonable care but also that the decision was *ultra vires*.[51] The underlying principles were explained as follows by Robert Goff L.J. in *Fellowes v. Rother District Council*[52]:

"The underlying basis appears to be that citizens are entitled to expect that powers conferred on public authorities will be exercised, and entitled therefore to expect that such powers will be exercised with due care, subject to being unable to found a cause of action on an act done within the limit of a discretion bona fide exercised and to the ordinary criteria of an action in negligence being fulfilled. Such powers cannot be regarded as mere liberties, or as mere authority to invade the proprietary interests of another, as under private Acts of Parliament. So, although a mere omission by a public authority to exercise a statutory power will not ordinarily be actionable by a private citizen as such

---

[47] *per* Lord Wilberforce at p. 757.
[48] § 8–20, *supra.*
[49] The local authority had a discretion to make building by-laws, and, once made, a discretion to inspect foundations etc. to ensure compliance with the by-laws.
[50] At p. 754.
[51] The principles under which an exercise or non-exercise of discretion will be held to be *ultra vires* are set out at §§ 10–06—10–35.
[52] [1983] 1 All E.R. 513 at p. 522.

(being within the area of discretion), nevertheless the local authority may be responsible for the consequences of a negligent act done in a purported exercise of the power (but not in fact within the limits of a discretion bona fide exercised) even though no fresh or additional damage is caused."

Furthermore, the courts appeared to regard this qualification as relevant not only in cases of the *East Suffolk* or *Anns* type, where the complaint was of an authority's omission to confer a benefit upon or protect the plaintiff, but in all cases where the plaintiff alleged that there had been a negligent exercise or non-exercise of a statutory discretion.[53]

The distinction between the "policy" and "operational" areas is difficult to **8–27** draw.[54] The Privy Council has expressed the view that the distinction is not helpful[55] and most recent negligence cases against public authorities have been decided without reference to it.[56] The *Anns* case has itself been overruled in *Murphy v. Brentwood District Council*.[57] However the House of Lords in that case did not deal expressly with Lord Wilberforce's general observations concerning the distinction between the "policy" and "operational" areas. The House of Lords in *X (a minor) v. Bedfordshire County Council*[58] regarded it as retaining significance, in particular in confirming that non-justiciable policy decisions are immune from challenge.

However, in *Stovin v. Wise (Norfolk County Council, Third Party)*[59] a differently constituted House of Lords unanimously doubted whether the distinction was of any utility.[60] Here, the highway authority was aware of a visibility problem at a junction, caused by a bank of earth. It agreed it would pay for the necessary work, and that it would pursue the matter with the owner of the land, but then did not follow the matter up. The House of Lords held by a majority that the authority owed no duty of care to road users to act with reasonable expedition in these circumstances, and was liable to the plaintiff in respect of personal injuries suffered in an accident at the junction. The statements of principle by majority and minority were broadly similar; the difference lay in their application to the facts. Thus, the whole House emphasised that this was the case of an omission and that there had to be a

---

[53] See, *e.g. Department of Health and Social Security v. Kinnear* (1984) 134 New L.J. 886 where actions in negligence against the Department in respect of the policy of promoting immunisation against whooping cough were struck out as the policy could not be shown to be *ultra vires*.

[54] See Lord Wilberforce in *Anns v. Merton London Borough Council* [1978] A.C. 728, 755, 757; *Bird v. Pearce and Somerset County Council (Third Party)* [1978] R.T.R. 290 and (1979) 77 L.G.R. 753, C.A.; *Haydon v. Kent County Council* [1978] Q.B. 343, 361, 363–364; *Vicar of Writtle v. Essex County Council* (1979) 77 L.G.R. 656; *Hallett v. Nicholson* 1979 S.C. 1, Ct. of Session; *Fellowes v. Rother District Council* [1983] 1 All E.R. 513; *West v. Buckinghamshire County Council* (1984) 83 L.G.R. 449.

[55] *Rowling v. Takaro Properties Ltd* [1988] A.C. 473, 500–503. See also *Lonrho plc v. Tebbitt* [1992] 4 All E.R. 280.

[56] See, *e.g., Jones v. Department of Employment* [1989] Q.B. 1; *Hill v. Chief Constable of West Yorkshire* [1989] A.C. 53; *Calveley v. Chief Constable of Merseyside* [1989] A.C. 1228.

[57] [1991] 1 A.C. 398, § 8–21.

[58] [1995] 2 A.C. 633, H.L. See § 8–22.

[59] [1996] 3 W.L.R. 388.

[60] See Lord Hoffman (for the majority) at p. 413 and Lord Nicholls of Birkenhead (for the minority) at p. 401. Only Lord Jauncey of Tullichettle (who agreed here with Lord Hoffman) sat on both *X v. Bedfordshire* and *Stovin v. Wise*.

special reason for imposing a duty of care in such a case.[61] A duty to act might arise where the defendant has "undertaken to do so or induced a person to rely upon one doing so" or out of the occupation of land,[62] but none of these factors was present here. The majority held that where it was sought to base a duty of care simply on the existence of a statutory power, the "minimum preconditions" for doing so

> "if it can be done at all, are, first that it would in the circumstances have been irrational not to exercise the power, so that there was in effect a public law duty to act, and secondly, that there are exceptional grounds for holding that the policy of the statute requires compensation to be paid to persons who suffer loss because the power was not exercised."[62a]

However, the fact that Parliament had chosen to confer a power rather than impose a duty was a strong pointer against such an inference, especially as to breach a statutory *duty* by no means necessarily gives rise to a civil action.[62b] On the facts, the majority found that it was not established on the evidence that it would have been irrational for the council not to have done the work, and that there was no discernible legislative intents that there should be a duty of care in respect of the use of the power under section 29 of the Highways Act 1980 to deal with hazards. It was primarily the duty of the drivers to take care and there was compulsory insurance if they did not; there was no reason of policy or justice that required the highway authority to be an additional defendant.[62c]

One remaining issue is the extent to which the *East Suffolk* case[62d] remains good law. Lord Hoffman accepted that

> "if a public authority was under no duty to act, either by virtue of its statutory powers or on any other basis, it cannot be liable because it has acted but negligently failed to confer a benefit on the plaintiff or to protect him from loss."[62e]

He rejected the particular criticisms of *East Suffolk* made by Lord Wilberforce in *Anns*, and stated that a common law duty of care could not be founded merely on the public law duty to give proper consideration to the question of whether a power should be exercised. However, he was not prepared to say that a statutory power could never give rise to a common law duty and preferred to leave open the question whether the *Anns* case had been wrong to create any exception to Lord Romer's statement of principle in *East Suffolk*.[66f] Given, however, the rarity with which exceptions are likely to be recognised, the decision can be seen largely to have been rehabilitated.

---

[61] Lord Hoffman at pp. 405–407; *cf.* Lord Nicholls at pp. 393–394.

[62] Lord Hoffman at pp. 406, 415; *cf.* Lord Nicholls at pp. 393–394, 400.

[62a] Lord Hoffman at p. 415; *cf.* Lord Nicholls at pp. 398–399.

[62b] Lord Hoffman at p. 414 and Lord Nicholls at p. 399. One possible justification was where there was general reliance by the public on the routine provision of a particular service, but this factor was not present here: pp. 415–416.

[62c] Lord Hoffman at pp. 417–419. The minority's reasons for holding that it was just and reasonable to impose a duty to act were set out by Lord Nicholls at pp. 402–404.

[62d] *supra.*

[62e] p. 411.

[66f] pp. 411–414. *Cf.* Lord Nicholls's more favourable view of *East Suffolk*: p. 394.

Negligence in the performance of professional services

In *Hedley Byrne & Co. Ltd v. Heller and Partners Ltd*,[63] the House of Lords **8–28**
held that there may in some circumstances be liability in negligence where a
careless misstatement causes financial loss. The exact scope of this liability is
not clear. The principle was stated as follows by Lord Morris of Borth-y-
Gest in the *Hedley Byrne* case.[64]

> "If someone possessed of a special skill undertakes, quite irrespective of
> contract, to apply that skill for the assistance of another person who relies upon
> such skill, a duty of care will arise. The fact that the service is to be given by
> means of or by the instrumentality of words can make no difference.
> Furthermore, if in a sphere in which a person is so placed that others could
> reasonably rely upon his judgment or his skill or upon his ability to make careful
> inquiry, a person takes it upon himself to give information or advice to, or allows
> his information or advice to be passed on to, another person who, as he knows or
> should know, will place reliance upon it, then a duty of care will arise."

Lord Hodson agreed with this formulation.[65] Lord Reid stated[66] that a
duty would arise from:

> "all those relationships where it is plain that the party seeking the information
> or advice was trusting the other to exercise such a degree of care as the
> circumstances required, where it was reasonable for him to do that, and where
> the other gave the information or advice when he knew or ought to have known
> that the inquirer was relying on him."

Lord Pearce stated[67]:

> "If persons holding themselves out in a calling or situation or profession take
> on a task within that calling or situation or profession, they have a duty of skill
> and care. ... To import [a duty of care,] the representation must normally, I
> think, concern a business or professional transaction whose nature makes clear
> the gravity of the inquiry and the importance and influence attached to the
> answer."

Lord Devlin was prepared to accept any of their Lordships' statements as
showing the general rule,[68] although he did suggest that liability would attach
to a "voluntary assumption of responsibility", and that "wherever there is a
relationship equivalent to contract (*i.e.* there would be a contract but for the
absence of formal consideration), there is a duty of care".

It was also established that there would be no liability in respect of words
spoken on a social or informal occasion[69] or where there was an express
disclaimer of liability (as in the *Hedley Byrne* case itself), although express
disclaimers are subject to the test of reasonableness under the Unfair
Contract Terms Act 1977.[70] The House of Lords has emphasised the need for
"proximity" between the plaintiff and defendant, in that

---

[63] [1964] A.C. 465.
[64] At pp. 502–503.
[65] At p. 514.
[66] At p. 486.
[67] At pp. 538 and 539.
[68] At p. 530.
[69] See Lord Pearce in *Hedley Byrne* at p. 539; Lords Reid and Morris in *Mutual Life and
Citizens' Assurance Co. v. Evatt* [1971] A.C. 793, 810–811, P.C.
[70] *Smith v. Eric S. Burton*; *Harris v. Wyre Forest District Council* [1990] 1 A.C. 831, H.L.

"the defendant knew that his statement would be communicated to the plaintiff, either as an individual or as a member of an identifiable class, specifically in connection with a particular transaction or transactions of a particular kind ... and that the plaintiff would be very likely to rely on it for the purpose of deciding whether or not to enter on that transaction or on a transaction of that kind."[71]

Finally, the House of Lords has stated that the *Hedley Byrne* principle extends beyond the provision of information and advice to cover assumptions of responsibility for the performance of services for the plaintiff.[72] Here a plaintiff may rely on the defendant to exercise due care and skill without himself taking any action in reliance on any statement by the defendant.[73]

A duty to take care may accordingly be imposed on a local authority which gives information or advice to members of the public. An action for damages might lie where a plaintiff is unable to establish that an authority is bound by a statement given by an officer (see paras. 10–14—10–18). Such a statement may be given in the course of the officer's employment, so as to render the authority vicariously liable in tort if it was negligently made.

A local authority was held liable under the *Hedley Byrne* principle in the following case:

> *Coats Patons (Retails) Ltd v. Birmingham Corporation.*[74] The plaintiff, in the course of searches before purchasing a shop, asked the council whether any proposals had been approved for the construction of a subway opposite the shop. A clerk entered the answer "No" on the search form without making the appropriate enquiries. In fact, the council had approved such a proposal two years previously, and the plaintiffs claimed that they had suffered financial loss when the subway was constructed. The search form included the following clause: "The replies below are furnished after appropriate enquiries, and in the belief that they are in accordance with the information at present available to the officers of the council, but on the distinct understanding that neither the council nor any officer of the council is legally responsible therefor." *Held*, that (1) as a result of the sending in of the enquiries form with the appropriate fees, and the giving of the answers, a contract was created; (2) the exclusion clause only operated to negative contractual liability, there being no clear words to exclude tortious liability; (3) the council was liable in tort under the *Hedley Byrne* principle; (4) alternatively, it was liable in contract as the making of appropriate enquiries by the council was a fundamental term of the contract, breach of such a term preventing reliance on the exemption clause.

As a consequence of the *Coats Patons* case, the exemption clause in the standard enquiries form (CON 29) was altered by the addition of the words "except for negligence". This does not seem to alter the authorities' liability in tort in respect of incorrect answers.[75]

---

[71] *per* Lord Bridge in *Caparo Products plc v. Dickman* [1990] 1 All E.R. 568, 576; *cf.* Lord Olivier at p. 589. Here, the House of Lords held that a company's auditors owed a duty of care to the company but not to persons (whether or not an existing shareholder) who bought shares in the company in reliance on the company's accounts.

[72] *Henderson v. Merrett Syndicates* [1994] 3 W.L.R. 761, H.L.

[73] *per* Lord Goff at p. 776.

[74] (1971) 69 L.G.R. 356. See also *Co-operative Retail Services Ltd v. Taff-Ely Borough Council* (1983) 133 New L.J. 577; *L. Shaddock & Associates Pty. Ltd v. Parramatta City Council* (1981) 55 A.L.J.R. 713.

[75] See J. F. Garner, *Local Land Charges* (9th ed.), pp. 94–95.

On the other hand, in *Tidman v. Reading Borough Council*,[76] Buxton J. held that a response by council officers to an informal planning enquiry by a member of the public did not give rise to a duty of care. It would be inconsistent with the council's public duties to recognise an overriding obligation to give advice in the interests of particular individuals engaged in the planning process. Moreover, the approach here had been informal, over the telephone, and on the basis of very slight information. His Lordship thought it possible, although unlikely, that a formal approach to a council, which was known by the council to have very serious implications, and to which the council did choose to respond, might generate a duty of care.

Local authorities have also been held vicariously liable for the negligence of their surveyor in inspecting and valuing a house.[77]

The following case illustrates the point that these may be liability under the *Hedley Byrne* principle outside situations where the plaintiff relies on information or advice from the local authority. While at the time the case was decided, it was difficult to fit it within the *Hedley Byrne* principle as then understood, these difficulties disappear once the principle is restated in the broader sense recognised by the House of Lords in *Henderson v. Merrett Syndicates*.[77a]

> *Ministry of Housing and Local Government v. Sharp*.[78] A landowner was refused permission to develop his land and obtained compensation from the Ministry under Part II of the Town and Country Planning Act 1954. Notice of compensation was registered in the local authority's register of local land charges as required by section 28(5) of the Act of 1954. Two years later, permission was granted, on a fresh application by the landowner. Prospective purchasers of the land, who as developers would be liable to repay the compensation, caused a search to be made in the register. The search was negligently carried out by a clerk of the second defendant (Hemel Hempstead Rural District Council), and a certificate signed by S., the registrar of local land charges, omitted any reference to the notice. The Court of Appeal *held* that (1) the omission entitled the developers to refuse to repay the compensation; (2) (*per* Salmon and Cross L.JJ., Lord Denning M.R. dissenting), the registrar was not liable, as section 17(2) of the Land Charges Act 1925 did not impose an absolute obligation on him to make an effective search and issue a complete certificate, and negligence was not alleged against him; (3) (Cross L.J. *reservante*), the clerk who made the search was under a duty of care to anyone whom he knew or ought to have known might be injured if he made a mistake, and the local authority was vicariously liable for his negligence. Lord Denning stated[79] that his decision on the clerk's liability was based squarely on the *Hedley Byrne* principle, although he gave that principle a wide interpretation:

---

[76] *The Times*, November 10, 1994. *Cf. King v. North Cornwall District Council* [1995] N.P.C. 21 (no *Hedley Byrne* liability where purchaser was told on inquiry that final inspection had taken place under the building regulations, and subsequently found departures from the regulations; no specific relationship of proximity or assumption of responsibility).

[77] *Westlake v. Bracknell District Council* (1987) 19 H.L.R. 375; *Harris v. Wyre Forest District Council, supra*, n. 70.

[77a] n. 72, *supra*.

[78] [1970] 2 Q.B. 223.

[79] At pp. 268–269. This broad approach cannot now stand with the decision of the House of Lords in *Caparo Products plc v. Dickman*, n. 71, *supra*.

"the duty to use due care in a statement arises, not from any voluntary assumption of responsibility, but from the fact that the person making it knows, or ought to know, that others, being his neighbours in this regard, would act on the faith of the statement being accurate." This duty was owed "to any person whom he knows, or ought to know, will be injuriously affected by a mistake...." Salmon L.J. held that this case did not fit into any category of negligence yet considered by the courts: "The plaintiff has not been misled by any careless statement made to him by the defendant or made by the defendant to someone else who the defendant knew would be likely to pass it on to a third party, such as the plaintiff, in circumstances in which the third party might reasonably be expected to rely upon it ... I am not, however, troubled by the fact that the case is, in many respects, unique."[80] His Lordship was much influenced by the fact that in some situations under the regulations, a clear certificate did not protect the purchaser, who would pay full value on the faith of the certificate and then discover that the land was encumbered. Such a purchaser would clearly be able to sue under the *Hedley Byrne* principle: "Our law would be grievously defective if the council did owe a duty of care to the purchaser in the one case but no duty to the incumbrancers in the other. The damage in each case is equally foreseeable."[81]

E. LIABILITY OF LOCAL AUTHORITIES AS OCCUPIERS OF PREMISES IN RELATION TO VISITORS AND TRESPASSERS

8–29 The rules which regulate the duty which an occupier of premises owes to his visitors in respect of dangers due to the state of the premises are contained in the Occupiers' Liability Act 1957. These rules replace the common law rules as to the nature and extent of this duty, but the common law rules as to who is the occupier and who are the visitors remain. Stated shortly, the duty prescribed in the Act is owed to those known to the common law as invitees and licensees and the duty is the same whether a visitor falls in the first or the second of these classes. An invitee is a person who is "invited into the premises by the owner or occupier for some purpose of business or of material interest"[82]; a licensee is "a person whom the proprietor has not in any way invited—he has no interest in his being there—but he has either expressly permitted him to use his lands or, knowledge of his presence ... having been brought home to him, he has then either accorded permission or shown no practical anxiety to stop his further frequenting the lands."[83]

8–30 Section 2 describes the occupier's duty:

"(1) An occupier of premises owes the same duty, the 'common duty of care', to all his visitors, except in so far as he is free to and does extend, restrict, modify or exclude his duty to any visitor or visitors by agreement or otherwise.

---

[80] At p. 278.
[81] At p. 280. See now Local Land Charges Act 1975, s.10.
[82] *Latham v. Johnson* [1913] 1 K.B. 398, *per* Hamilton L.J. at p. 410.
[83] *Addie & Sons v. Dumbreck* [1929] A.C. 358, *per* Lord Dunedin at p. 371.

(2) The common duty of care is a duty to take such care as in all the circumstances of the case is reasonable to see that the visitor will be reasonably safe in using the premises for the purposes for which he is invited or permitted by the occupier to be there.

(3) The circumstances relevant for the present purpose include the degree of care, and want of care, which would ordinarily be looked for in such a visitor, so that (for example) in proper cases—

    (a) an occupier must be prepared for children to be less careful than adults; and

    (b) an occupier may expect that a person, in the exercise of his calling, will appreciate and guard against any special risks ordinarily incident to it, so far as the occupier leaves him free to do so.

(4) In determining whether the occupier of premises has discharged the common duty of care to a visitor, regard is to be had to all the circumstances, so that (for example)—

    (a) where damage is caused to a visitor by a danger of which he had been warned by the occupier, the warning is not to be treated without more as absolving the occupier from liability, unless in all the circumstances it was enough to enable the visitor to be reasonably safe; and

    (b) where damage is caused to a visitor by a danger due to the faulty execution of any work of construction, maintenance or repair by an independent contractor employed by the occupier, the occupier is not to be treated without more as answerable for the danger if in all the circumstances he had acted reasonably in entrusting the work to an independent contractor and had taken such steps (if any) as he reasonably ought in order to satisfy himself that the contractor was competent and that the work had been properly done.

(5) The common duty of care does not impose on an occupier any obligation to a visitor in respect of risks willingly accepted as his by the visitor (the question whether a risk was so accepted to be decided on the same principles as in other cases in which one person owes a duty of care to another).

(6) For the purposes of this section, persons who enter premises for any purpose in the exercise of a right conferred by law are to be treated as permitted by the occupier to be there for that purpose, whether they in fact have his permission or not."

These rules apply to local authorities as they apply to other occupiers of property: they would apply, for example, in the case of persons who enter public offices to transact business. Most of the cases against local authorities in this context have concerned visitors to public parks[84]; children and visitors on school premises[85]; and persons injured in council houses and flats.[86] Cases

---

[84] e.g. *Glasgow Corporation v. Taylor* [1922] 1 A.C. 44; *Ellis v. Fulham Corporation* [1938] 1 K.B. 212; *Dyer v. Ilfracombe Urban District Council* [1956] 1 W.L.R. 218; *Simkiss v. Rhondda Borough Council* (1983) 81 L.G.R. 460. See also *Cotton v. Derbyshire Dales District Council*, *The Times*, June 20, 1994 (no breach of duty in absence of a notice warning of dangerous cliffs on a high path where the danger was obvious to visitors); *Staples v. West Dorset District Council* (1995) 93 L.G.R. 536 (no breach of duty where danger of slipping on the Cobb at Lyme Regis was obvious to visitors).

[85] e.g. *Fryer v. Salford Corporation* [1937] 1 All E.R. 617; *Lyes v. Middlesex County Council* (1962) 61 L.G.R. 443; *Reffell v. Surrey County Council* [1964] 1 W.L.R. 358; *Murphy v. Bradford Metropolitan Council* [1992] P.I.Q.R. p. 68.

[86] *Hawkins v. Coulsdon and Purley Urban District Council* [1954] 1 Q.B. 319; *Greene v. Chelsea Borough Council* [1954] 2 Q.B. 127; *Moloney v. Lambeth London Borough Council* (1966) 64 L.G.R. 440.

decided under the common law in relation to invitees may be of some relevance as illustrations of the standard of care appropriate in particular situations. However, an occupier of land does not owe a duty of care under the Occupier's Liability Act 1957 or at common law in respect of negligent non-feasance to a person using a public right of way over his land.[87]

8–31   Officers of a local authority who enter premises under a statutory power (for the purpose of inspection or to carry out works) and police officers acting on a search warrant are "visitors" and the occupier owes them the "common duty of care" as regards his premises.[88] They are to be treated as permitted by the occupier to be there for that purpose, whether they in fact have his permission or not.[89]

The attempted exclusion or restriction of liability for negligence by the use of a notice, operating either as a contractual exclusion clause[90] or as a condition attached to a licence to enter the property[91]; is now subject to the Unfair Contract Terms Act 1977 (see para. 10–14). An appropriately worded notice may, however, enable the authority to discharge the common duty of care under section 2(4)(a) of the Occupiers' Liability Act 1957, *supra*. This kind of notice is unaffected by the 1977 Act. Moreover, a notice drawing a visitor's attention to dangers may be relevant to the establishment of the defence of *volenti non fit injuria*, which is expressly preserved by section 2(5) of the 1957 Act.[92] This is to be distinguished from a notice which merely purports to "exclude or restrict liability for negligence". A person's agreement to or awareness of such a notice "is not of itself to be taken as indicating his voluntary acceptance of any risk".[93]

8–32   An occupier of property does not owe the "common duty of care" towards a trespasser—one who comes to the land without right or permission—but it has long been established that he must not set a trap deliberately to injure a trespasser, and if he does he may be liable to the trespasser in tort.[94]

The common law liability of an occupier towards a trespasser was extended by the House of Lords in *British Railways Board v. Herrington*,[95] where the House of Lords unanimously held the Board liable to a child who was injured when he strayed on to an electrified line through a broken fence: the stationmaster knew that children had been seen on the line and that the fence had not been repaired. Their Lordships used varying terms in formulating both (1) the circumstances in which a duty to a trespasser, commonly termed a duty of common humanity, would arise, and (2) the content of that duty. As a result it was difficult to ascertain the precise *ratio*

---

[87] *McGeown v. Northern Ireland Housing Executive* [1995] 1 A.C. 233.
[88] *Salmond on the Law of Torts* (19th ed.), pp. 315–317.
[89] Occupiers' Liability Act 1957, s.2(6).
[90] See *White v. Blackmore* [1972] 2 Q.B. 651.
[91] *Ashdown v. Samuel Williams Ltd.* [1957] 1 Q.B. 409; *White v. Blackmore, supra*.
[92] *Supra*.
[93] Unfair Contract Terms Act 1977, s.2(3).
[94] *Bird v. Holbrook* (1828) 4 Bing. 628; 6 L.J.(o.s.) C.P. 146.
[95] [1972] A.C. 877. See also *Pannett v. McGuiness & Co.* [1972] 2 Q.B. 599; *Melvin v. Franklins Builders and another* (1972) 71 L.G.R. 142; *Penny v. Northampton Borough Council* (1974) 72 L.G.R. 733; *Harris v. Birkenhead Corporation* [1976] 1 W.L.R. 279.

of the case.[96] In respect of events occurring on or after May 13, 1984, the liability of an occupier to a trespasser is regulated by section 1 of the Occupiers' Liability Act 1984, and not by the law as stated in *Herrington's* case. This section provides that an occupier of premises owes a duty to another (not being his visitor) in respect of any risk of that person suffering injury on the premises by reason of any danger due to the state of the premises or to things done or omitted to be done on them if

"(a) he is aware of the danger or has reasonable grounds to believe that it exists;
(b) he knows or has reasonable grounds to believe that the other is in the vicinity of the danger concerned or that he may come into the vicinity of the danger (in either case, whether the other has lawful authority for being in that vicinity or not); and
(c) the risk is one against which, in all the circumstances of the case, he may reasonably be expected to offer the other some protection."

If a duty is owed,

"the duty is to take such care as is reasonable in all the circumstances of the case to see that he does not suffer injury on the premises by reason of the danger concerned."

The duty may in an appropriate case be discharged by taking reasonable steps to warn of the danger or to discourage persons from incurring the risk. No duty is owed by virtue of these provisions to any person in respect of risks willingly accepted and a person does not by reason of any breach of the duty incur any liability in respect of any loss of or damage to property. Furthermore, no duty is owed by virtue of this section to persons using the highway and the section does not affect any duty owed to such persons. The terms "occupier" and "visitor" in this section carry the same meanings as in the Occupiers' Liability Act 1957.

Under the *Herrington* principle, it was held that it was proper to take into account the defendant's skill and resources in deciding what it was reasonable to expect of *him*,[97] unless perhaps he had created the danger himself.[98] It is not clear whether resources can be taken into account under the Occupiers' Liability Act 1984.

The Occupier's Liability Act 1984 was considered in *White v. St Albans City and District Council.*[99] The plaintiff claimed damages for personal injuries sustained when he fell into a 12 foot trench while walking across fenced-off council property, taking a short cut to a car park. The Court of Appeal dismissed his appeal against the rejection of his claim by Judge

---

[96] See Law Commission Report No. 75, Cmnd. 6428, paras. 5–7.
[97] *British Railways Board v. Herrington* [1972] A.C. 877 at pp. 899, 920, 942. A similar principle applies in respect of liability in nuisance for natural hazards occurring on land: *Goldman v. Hargrave* [1967] 1 A.C. 645; *Leakey v. National Trust* [1980] Q.B. 485; *Page Motors Ltd v. Epsom & Ewell Borough Council* (1981) 80 L.G.R. 337. In the *Page Motors* case, the Court of Appeal held that the court was not limited to considering the council's physical and financial resources only, but was entitled to take into account matters arising from its public responsibilities, such as the need to engage in a democratic process of dialogue with interested parties.
[98] *Southern Portland Cement v. Cooper* [1974] A.C. 623 at p. 644.
[99] *The Times*, March 12, 1990.

Lovegrove, sitting as a judge of the Queen's Bench Division, who held the council had no reason to believe that the plaintiff would be in the vicinity of the trench. The Court of Appeal rejected the plaintiff's argument that once it was established that precautions had been taken to stop people getting to the land on which there was a danger, it followed that the person taking the precautions had reason to believe someone was likely to come into the vicinity of the danger for the purpose of section 1(3)(b).

Section 4 of the Defective Premises Act 1972[1] provides that:

"(1) Where premises are let under a tenancy which puts on the landlord an obligation to the tenant for the maintenance or repair of the premises, the landlord owes to all persons who might reasonably be expected to be affected by defects in the state of the premises a duty to take such care as is reasonable in all the circumstances to see that they are reasonably safe from personal injury or from damage to their property caused by a relevant defect.

(2) The said duty is owed if the landlord knows (whether as the result of being notified by the tenant or otherwise) or if he ought in all the circumstances to have known of the relevant defect.

(3) In this section 'relevant defect' means a defect in the state of the premises existing at or after the material time and arising from, or continuing because of, an act or omission by the landlord which constitutes or would if he had had notice of the defect, have constituted a failure by him to carry out his obligation to the tenant for the maintenance or repair of the premises; and for the purposes of the foregoing provision 'the material time' means—

(a) where the tenancy commenced before this Act, the commencement of this Act; and

(b) in all other cases, the earliest of the following times, that is to say—

(i) the time when the tenancy commences;

(ii) the time when the tenancy agreement is entered into;

(iii) the time when possession is taken of the premises in contemplation of the letting.

(4) Where premises are let under a tenancy which expressly or impliedly gives the landlord the right to enter the premises to carry out any description of maintenance or repair of the premises, then, as from the time when he first is, or by notice or otherwise can put himself, in a position to exercise the right and so long as he is or can put himself in that position, he shall be treated for the purposes of subsections (1) to (3) above (but for no other purpose) as if he were under an obligation to the tenant for that description of maintenance or repair of the premises; but the landlord shall not owe the tenant any duty by virtue of this subsection in respect of any defect in the state of the premises arising from, or continuing because of, a failure to carry out an obligation expressly imposed on the tenant by the tenancy.

(5) For the purposes of this section obligations imposed or rights given by any enactment in virtue of a tenancy shall be treated as imposed or given by the tenancy.

(6) This section applies to a right of occupation given by contract or any enactment and not amounting to a tenancy as if the right were a tenancy, and 'tenancy' and cognate expressions shall be construed accordingly."

---

[1] Replacing the Occupiers's Liability Act 1957, s.4.

A local authority may be liable under this provision.[1a] Liability under it may extend to persons who are not visitors to the premises.

F. TRESPASS, NUISANCE AND THE RULE IN RYLANDS V. FLETCHER

The defence of statutory authority has most commonly been raised in **8–33** respect of actions in nuisance. This matter has already been considered.[2] Local authorities have been held liable in nuisance in respect of such matters as noise from a children's playground,[3] flooding caused by the bad state of repair of drains,[4] encroachment by tree roots from council land,[5] and the nuisance caused by a gypsy encampment on land leased from the council by the plaintiffs.[6]

An analogous principle to the defence of statutory authority can apply where planning consent is given for a development: the question of nuisance thereafter falls to be decided by reference to the neighbourhood with that development or use and not as it was previously.[7] However, the grant of planning permission cannot itself be taken as authorising any nuisance that inevitably flows from it.[8]

Wherever local authority officials take or retain possession of premises in reliance on an order which is *ultra vires*, an action for damages will lie in trespass.[9]

It is uncertain whether the doctrine of *Rylands v. Fletcher*[10] is applicable to **8–34** the exercise of functions by public authorities. The rule was stated by Blackburn J., in the Court of Exchequer Chamber, as "that the person who for his own purposes brings on his lands and collects and keeps there anything likely to do mischief if it escapes, must keep it in at his peril, and if

---

[1a] *Smith v. Bradford Metropolitan City Council* (1982) 80 L.G.R. 713 (s.4(4)); *cf. McAuley v. Bristol City Council* [1992] Q.B. 134, where liability under s.4 was based on an implied right to enter the premises to carry out repairs to remedy any defects which might expose lawful visitors (or the tenant) to the risk of injury.

[2] See §§ 8–09—8–14.

[3] *Dunton v. Dover District Council* (1977) 76 L.G.R. 87 (damages awarded and use of the playground restricted by injunction; *Tetley v. Chitty* [1986] 1 All E.R. (council liable in respect of go-karting activities permitted on its land) *cf. Hall v. Beckenham Corporation* [1949] 1 K.B. 716 (use of recreation ground by members of the public for flying noisy model aircraft: corporation held not liable as it did not "occupy" the ground in the strict sense of the word, being merely custodian on behalf of the public).

[4] *Att.-Gen. v. St Ives Rural District Council* [1961] 1 Q.B. 366.

[5] *Davey v. Harrow Corporation* [1958] 1 Q.B. 60; *Masters v. Brent London Borough Council* [1978] Q.B. 841; *Bridges v. Harrow London Borough Council* (1981) 260 E.G. 284; *Russell v. Barnet London Borough Council* (1984) 83 L.G.R. 152; *Paterson v. Humberside County Council, The Times*, April 19, 1995.

[6] *Page Motors Ltd v. Epsom and Ewell Borough Council* (1981) 80 L.G.R. 337.

[7] *Gillingham Borough Council v. Medway (Chatham) Dock Company Ltd* [1993] Q.B. 343.

[8] *Wheeler v. J. J. Saunders Ltd* [1995] 2 All E.R. 697.

[9] *Smith v. East Elloe Rural District Council* (1952) 160 E.G. 148 (a requisition of land continued although the lawful purposes for requisition had ceased); *Cooper v. Wandsworth Board of Works* (1863) 14 C.B.(N.S.) 180 (a decision to demolish a house which was erected without notice to the Board was held to be *ultra vires* on the ground that there was a breach of natural justice).

[10] (1868) L.R. 3 H.L. 330.

he does not do so is *prima facie* answerable for all the damage which is the natural consequence of its escape".[11] In *Cambridge Water Co. v. Eastern Counties Leather plc*,[12] the House of Lords held that foreseeability by the defendant of the relevant type of damage is a prerequisite of liability in damages under *Rylands v. Fletcher*. It has been held that there will be no liability unless the user of the land is "non-natural".[13] In *Rickards v. Lothian*, Lord Moulton[14] described "non-natural" user as "some special use bringing with it increased danger to others, and ... not merely ... the ordinary use of the land or such a use as is proper for the general benefit of the community." It has been argued that the collection by a public authority of such things as sewage, water and gas for public purposes is accordingly not within the rule, as it is "for the general benefit of the community"[15] and not for the authority's "own purposes".[16] However, other judges have taken a different view. Evershed M.R. in the *Pride of Derby* case stated that he was "not satisfied" that local authorities have a special immunity from the rule in *Rylands v. Fletcher*.[17] In *Smeaton v. Ilford Corporation*,[18] Upjohn J. held that the collection of sewage in sewers vested in the Corporation did amount to a "non-natural" user of land, and he rejected the arguments outlined above. Nevertheless, his Lordship held that the rule did not apply in this case in view of section 31 of the Public Health Act 1936, which provided: "A local authority shall so discharge their functions under the foregoing provisions of this Part of this Act as not to create a nuisance." "That section necessarily implies, in my judgment, that, provided the defendant corporation does not create a nuisance in carrying out its duties, it is to be absolved from liability." Accordingly, his Lordship did not have to express a "concluded view" on the difference of opinion between Denning L.J. and Evershed M.R. in the *Pride of Derby* case.[19]

G. MISFEASANCE IN A PUBLIC OFFICE

8–35 The law does not provide a general right of damages for maladministration.[20] However, public authorities or officers may be held liable in damages if they are responsible for an act which is *ultra vires*, which causes loss, and where

---

[11] At p. 279.
[12] [1994] 2 A.C. 264.
[13] See Lord Cairns in *Rylands v. Fletcher* (1868) L.R. 3 H.L. 330 at p. 340; *Rickards v. Lothian* [1913] A.C. 263; *Read v. Lyons* [1947] A.C. 156.
[14] At p. 280. See n. 13.
[15] Denning L.J. in *Pride of Derby Angling Association v. British Celanese* [1953] Ch. 149 at p. 189.
[16] *Dunne v. North Western Gas Board* [1964] 2 Q.B. 806, 831.
[17] [1953] Ch. 149 at p. 176.
[18] [1954] Ch. 450.
[19] At p. 478.
[20] *per* Schiemann J. in *R. v. Knowsley Metropolitan Borough Council, ex p. Maguire* (1992) 80 L.G.R. 653.

there is either malice[21] or (possibly) knowledge of the absence of *vires*.[22] Most of the authorities are from Commonwealth jurisdictions, but in *Dunlop v. Woollahra Municipal Council*[23] the Privy Council described the tort as "well-established". In *Smith v. East Elloe*[24] the House of Lords held that an action for damages could proceed against the council's clerk on the allegation that he had procured the compulsory purchase of the plaintiff's property wrongfully and in bad faith, even though the compulsory purchase order was rendered immune from challenge by the Acquisition of Land (Authorisation Procedure) Act 1946.[25] The action subsequently failed on the merits.[26] In *Dunlop v. Woollahra Municipal Council*,[27] the Council passed two resolutions which were subsequently held to be void. The Privy Council held that, in the absence of malice, the passing of a void resolution without knowledge of its invalidity was not conduct capable of amounting to "misfeasance"; for the purpose of the tort. Furthermore, in *Bourgoin S.A. v. Ministry of Agriculture, Fisheries and Food*,[28] Mann J. held that in order to establish the tort it was not necessary to prove that an officer had been actuated by malice towards the plaintiff if it could be shown that the officer had known that his conduct was *ultra vires*, and would, or was foreseeably likely to, injure the plaintiff and that the plaintiff had been injured by it. The requirements of the two separate limbs of this tort were further considered by Clarke J. in *Three Rivers District Council v. Governor and Company of the Bank of England*,[29] on a preliminary issue in litigation where the council and others who were depositors in the failed Bank of Credit and Commerce International SA were suing the Bank of England. His Lordship confirmed that malice in the sense of (1) an intention to injure the plaintiff or a person in the class of which the plaintiff was a member and (2) knowledge by the officer both that he had no power to do the act complained of and that the act would probably (not inevitably) injure the plaintiff were alternative ingredients. To establish the requirement under (2) that the officer knew he had no power to do the act complained of, it was sufficient to show that the officer had actual knowledge that the act was unlawful, or, in circumstances in which he believed or suspected that the act was beyond his powers, that he did not ascertain whether or not that was so or failed to take such steps to do so as would be taken by an honest and reasonable man. The same approach applied to proof of knowledge that the act would probably injure the plaintiff or a person in the class of which the plaintiff was a member. Thus the

---

[21] The proof of malice requires proof of an intent to injure and not merely recklessness: *Bennett v. Metropolitan Police Commissioner* [1995] 1 W.L.R. 488.

[22] *Halsbury's Laws of England* (4th ed.), Vol. 1 (1) (Reissue), para. 203; Sir William Wade and C. F. Forsyth, *Administrative Law* (7th ed.), pp. 789–796.

[23] [1982] A.C. 158 at p. 172.

[24] [1956] A.C. 736.

[25] Sched. 1, Pt. IV, para. 16.

[26] *Smith v. Pywell* (1959) 178 E.G. 1009.

[27] *supra*, n. 17.

[28] [1985] Q.B. 716. Mann J.'s decision on this point was approved by the Court of Appeal: *ibid.*

[29] *The Times*, April 22, 1996. See also *Northern Territory v. Mengel* (1995) 64 A.L.J.R. 527.

second limb extended to recklessness as well as actual knowledge and to omissions as well as acts.

8–36 The application of the tort to collective decisions of local authorities was considered by the House of Lords in the following case.

> *Jones v. Swansea City Council.*[30] The council voted by 28 to 15 to rescind a consent previously given by the council as landlord to the change of use of a site from that of a shop or office to a club. The plaintiff, who held the land under an agreement for a lease, sued the council, claiming *inter alia*, that by maliciously refusing consent to the change of use, with the object of injuring her and her husband, the council had been guilty of the tort of misfeasance in a public office. The plaintiff's husband had been a councillor, and a political opponent of the ruling Labour group. All 28 votes for the motion had been from Labour councillors.
>
> The House of Lords *held* that, generally speaking, if a plaintiff alleges and proves that a majority of the councillors present, having voted for a resolution, did so with the object of damaging the plaintiff, he thereby proves against the council misfeasance in a public office.[31] However, the plaintiff's case, as pleaded, alleged that all 28 Labour councillors were infected by their leader's malice. On the evidence, this was not proved, and so the plaintiff's case was bound to fail, even if malice were proved against the group leader. The House left open the question whether or not the tort was applicable in respect of any abuse of powers exercisable by a public authority or officer, whether private powers or powers with a statutory or public origin; the Court of Appeal had held that it was.[32]

If an officer commits the tort of misfeasance, the employing authority may be vicariously liable unless the unauthorised acts are so unconnected with the officer's authorised duties as to be quite independent of and outside those duties.[33]

H. Personal Liability of Members and Servants

8–37 It is one of the incidents of incorporation that the corporate body is distinct from the members who compose it. Individual members of local authorities are not, therefore, personally liable for corporate acts. If, however, a corporation authorises a wrongful act and damages are awarded against the authority, the members who were parties to the authorisation may find themselves the subject of proceedings following audit.[34] The view is sometimes expressed that if a council expressly authorises an act which is *ultra vires* the authority and which proves to be tortious, the members who authorised it may themselves be sued, but the law on this point is not clearly settled. Members might well be liable if a wrongful act were wilful and malicious.[35] The position is somewhat different in the case of servants. The injured party may sue either the corporation or the servant (except where

---

[30] [1990] 1 W.L.R. 1453.
[31] See Lord Lowry at pp. 1458–1459.
[32] [1990] 1 W.L.R. 54: the Court of Appeal left open the question of whether or not the power here could in any event properly be regarded as a purely "private" power.
[33] *Racz v. Home Office* [1994] 2 A.C. 45.
[34] See the Local Government Finance Act 1982, Part III.
[35] *R. v. Watson* (1788) 2 T.R. 199.

statutory protection is given to the servant as indicated below), but where the servant has acted outside the scope of his authority or not in the course of his employment, so that the council cannot be made liable, an action may lie only against the servant.

These common law rules as to immunity of individual members of **8–38** corporations and as to actions against servants as well as employing authorities are affected by certain statutory provisions. Section 265 of the Public Health Act 1875 provides:

> "No matter or thing done, and no contract entered into by any local authority ... and no matter or thing done by any member ... or by any officer of such authority or other person whomsoever acting under the direction of such authority shall if the matter or thing were done or the contract were entered into *bona fide* for the purposes of executing this Act, subject them or any of them personally to any action liability claim or demand whatsoever; and any expense incurred by any such authority member officer or other person acting as last aforesaid shall be borne and repaid out of the fund or rate applicable by such authority to the general purposes of this Act."

This immunity does not extend to protect members from action by the auditor.[36] Section 265 was extended to cover other public health functions[37] and highways functions.[38] Officers enjoy specific protection under the Rag Flock and Other Filling Materials Act 1951[39] and the Food Safety Act 1990.[40] The Local Government (Miscellaneous Provisions) Act 1976 extends section 265 to cover all local authorities including joint authorities and parish and community councils and other specified bodies[41] and the execution of any public general or local Act.[42] Other statutes extended section 265 to water authorities[43] and the various health authorities.[44]

A claim to the special defence under section 265 raises a question of fact, which in a libel action is the same as the issue of malice and a question for the jury.[45]

I. COMPENSATION FOR MALADMINISTRATION

A Local Commissioner[46] has no power to order the award of compensation **8–39** where he finds that maladministration has caused injustice. However, the payment of compensation has followed an adverse report by a Local

---

[36] Proviso to s.265, as amended by the Local Government Finance Act 1982, Sched. 5, para. 1.
[37] Public Health Acts 1936, s.305, and 1961, s.1; Building Act 1984, s.115; Public Health (Control of Disease) Act 1984, s.69.
[38] Highways Act 1959, s.261 and Highways (Miscellaneous Provisions) Act 1961, s.16(3).
[39] s.28.
[40] s.44.
[41] See s.44(1), definition of "local authority" as substituted by the Local Government Act 1985, Sched. 14, para. 53(b), and amended by the Local Government Reorganisation (Miscellaneous Provisions) Order 1990 (S.I. 1990 No. 1765), art. 4(5), and the Environment Act 1995, Sched. 22, para. 33.
[42] s.39.
[43] Control of Pollution Act 1974, s.86.
[44] National Health Service Act 1977, s.125.
[45] *Kirby-Harris v. Baxter, The Times*, June 15, 1995.
[46] See §§ 4–101, *et seq.*

Commissioner in a number of cases. It is not the practice for a Commissioner to propose remedies in his first report, although this may be done in a second report issued under section 31(2) of the Local Government Act 1974 where the Commissioner is not satisfied with the local authority's response to the finding of maladministration.[47] The Local Government Act 1978 added a new subsection (3) to section 31 of the 1974 Act, empowering a local authority to incur such expenditure as appears to them appropriate in making a payment to, or providing a benefit for, a person found by a Local Commissioner to have suffered injustice in consequence of maladministration. This met difficulties which arose where the Secretary of State refused to sanction such expenditure under section 161 of the Local Government Act 1972 (which removed the possibility of proceedings by the District Auditor, without rendering the expenditure lawful), and where there have been delays before sanction has been forthcoming.[48]

II. CRIMINAL LIABILITY

8–40 A body corporate may be convicted of criminal offences except those for which the only punishment is imprisonment or death and those which cannot be vicariously committed, *e.g.* bigamy. Similarly, a local authority may be convicted of offences under public health and similar statutes, *e.g.* for a statutory nuisance.[49] The common law offence of misconduct in a public office applies to officers of local authorities and not only to officers and agents of the Crown: *R. v. Bowden.*[50]

---

[47] Report of the Commission for Local Administration in England for 1975–76, paras. 61 and 74–79.
[48] See now the Local Government Finance Act 1982, s.19(1).
[49] See *R. v. Epping Justices, ex p. Burlinson* [1948] K.B. 79. For a full discussion of criminal liability of incorporated bodies see *Tesco Supermarkets v. Nattrass* [1972] A.C. 153.
[50] (1995) 159 J.P. 502.

CHAPTER 9

CENTRAL CONTROL OF LOCAL AUTHORITIES

A. GENERAL POWERS OF CONTROL

IN one sense local authorities are wholly subject to central control, for **9–01** Parliament is omnipotent. Parliament may allocate functions to local bodies or take them away. It may prescribe how those functions shall be carried out and may change the structure of local government as it chooses. The control here considered is, however, the control exercised by Ministers of the Crown and by the departments for which they are responsible, and in this connection the point must first be made that neither ministers nor departments have an overall control of the work of local authorities. All formal control must be specifically authorised by statute. Certain statutes, it is true, appear to vest supervisory powers in Ministers of the Crown. It is the duty of the Secretary of State for Education and Science, under section 1 of the Education Act 1944,

> "to promote the education of the people of England and Wales and the progressive development of institutions devoted to that purpose, and to *secure the effective execution by local authorities, under his control and direction*, of the national policy for providing a varied and comprehensive educational service in every area."

It is commonly held that the powers of control and direction referred to here **9–02** are those specifically given in a number of sections in the Act, such as the power to issue directions under section 68 to prevent the unreasonable exercise of functions, and that these general words do not in themselves give any direct supervisory authority. Section 7 of the Local Authority Social Services Act 1970, confers a vaguer power on the Secretary of State. It reads:

> "Local authorities shall, in the exercise of their social services functions, including the exercise of any discretion conferred by any relevant enactment, act under *the general guidance* of the Secretary of State."

A similar provision appears in section 12 of the Housing (Homeless Persons) Act 1977 (now section 71 of the Housing Act 1985):

> "(1) In relation to homeless persons and persons threatened with homelessness, a relevant authority shall have regard in the exercise of their functions to such guidance as may from time to time be given by the Secretary of State.
> (2) The Secretary of State may give guidance either generally or to specified descriptions of authorities."

A Code of Guidance was issued by the Department of the Environment, the Department of Health and the Welsh Office under this section.[1]

The legal significance of these provisions is not clear. Presumably an authority which fails to have regard to "guidance" from the Secretary of State in the exercise of the powers concerned may be said to have ignored a "relevant consideration" and thereby abused its discretion. On the other hand, a minister may not rely on a power to give "guidance" in order to give mandatory directions.[2]

9–03   Apart from these provisions, it is safe to say that central government departments have no legal control over the work of local authorities other than that directly conferred by statute. There is no doubt, however, that control is in fact exercised informally in the process of consultation between local authorities and officers of the various ministries and in the issue by the departments of circulars and memoranda. By these means the policy of a department works its way into the practice of local authorities, perhaps imperceptibly. It is referred to sometimes as "government by circular". An example of this was found in the building licensing work undertaken by the local authorities work from 1945 to 1954 on behalf of the Ministry of Works. There was no statutory authority which enabled the Ministry to delegate its function to local authorities[3] and there was no statutory authority empowering local authorities to undertake this work and to spend money on it. The precise form that the licensing should take and its limits and extent were prescribed in ministry circulars and followed by authorities.

9–04   No examination of the relationship between central and local government can therefore be satisfactory unless due regard is had to the conventions of control—the "pressures" of advice, consultations, practice codes, memoranda and circulars which explain or amplify a minister's policy. This acceptance of non-statutory control may rest on several factors. In spite of the criticisms by local authorities of the nature and extent of central control, there has to be a working partnership with a common purpose. A working partnership invariably involves some flexibility in the matter of rights and duties. There is, too, the very extensive practice of prior consultation between local authority associations and the central government departments under which the formulae of control are often jointly considered before they are imposed. This aspect of central control is considered further in the concluding paragraphs of this Chapter. The statutory forms of control are now examined.

B. STATUTORY FORMS OF CONTROL

Control of borrowing, capital expenditure and revenue expenditure

9–05   Part IV of the Local Government and Housing Act 1989 established a new, detailed, regime for the capital finance of local authorities.[4] This is the

---

[1] See *Homelessness: Code of Guidance for Local Authorities* (HMSO, Revised 3rd edn., 1994).
[2] *Laker Airways Ltd v. Department of Trade* [1977] Q.B. 643.
[3] *Jackson, Stansfield & Sons v. Butterworth* [1948] 2 All E.R. 558.
[4] See §§ 12–19—12–37.

latest in a series of different mechanisms for control. Formerly, apart from certain exemptions, local authorities could not borrow money except with the approval of the Secretary of State.[5] It was the practice of ministers, in the exercise of the power to give approval, to examine the merits of every capital scheme, ensuring that it was technically sound, adequate for its purpose, and within the resources of the authority seeking the sanction. From April 1, 1971, a general sanction to borrow in relation to specified kinds of schemes was given by Department of the Environment Circular. Part VIII of the Local Government, Planning and Land Act 1980 changed the emphasis from control of *borrowing* to control over the level of each authority's capital *expenditure*. The minister could prevent an authority from incurring "prescribed expenditure" above a limit set by a combination of an amount specified by the minister and, *inter alia*, the amount of the authority's net capital receipts.

Under Part IV of the 1989 Act, there is an "aggregate credit limit" for each local authority. This is calculated in accordance with section 62 of the Act, but may be increased for a specified period by the Secretary of State. There is a general power to borrow,[6] but that power may not be exercised so that the total principal outstanding plus the aggregate cost of certain other "credit arrangements"[7] exceeds the aggregate credit limit applicable to the authority for the time being.[8] Similarly, a local authority may not enter into a credit arrangement if that would cause the authority to exceed its aggregate credit limit.[9] Furthermore, each year the Secretary of State is to issue a "basic credit approval" for a specified amount to each local authority. Supplementary credit approval may be issued by any minister. These approvals give authority for incurring liability under credit arrangements or for spending on capital purposes.[10]   **9–06**

The objectives of Part IV include those of ensuring that the total amount of local authority net capital expenditure in any financial year does not exceed the government's expenditure plans, and to allow the government to target spending and borrowing allocations having regard to local authorities' own resources.

The Secretary of State was empowered by the Rates Act 1984 to prescribe a maximum for the rate made or precept issued by an individual local authority or local authorities generally. This was replaced by a power to "cap" community charges and precepts under Part VII of the Local Government Finance Act 1988, and now a power to cap council tax or precepts under Part I, Chapter V of the Local Government Finance Act 1992.[11]

---

[5] Local Government Act 1972, Sched. 13, para. 1(b).
[6] s.43.
[7] s.48.
[8] s.44.
[9] s.50.
[10] ss.53, 54, 56.
[11] See § 16–17.

These powers of control are considered in greater detail in Chapters 12 and 16.

Control through the system of grants

9–07   Exchequer grants fall broadly under two headings, specific grants in aid of particular services and general grants. Fairly detailed control has been a feature of specific grants. It has commonly been the rule that a grant is not payable unless the appropriate minister is broadly satisfied with the service in respect of which the grant is claimed, and in most cases grant-earning expenditure must be "approved" expenditure; that is, approved, in one way or another, by the appropriate minister. The withholding of a grant is a rarity—in practice it is the power to withhold that enables the department to exercise an influence in the conduct of the service to which the grants relate.

9–08   The police grant payable under section 31 of the Police Act 1964, prior to its replacement by provisions of the Police and Magistrates' Courts Act 1994, was an example of a specific grant (it was a percentage grant, roughly one-half of the police authority's expenditure) and it illustrated the measure of control which could accompany the payment of such grants. Section 31 of the Police Act 1964 provided that the grants shall be:

> "of such amounts, be payable at such times, in such manner, and subject to such conditions, and be carried to such funds, as the Secretary of State may with the approval of the Treasury by order determine."

Payment was conditional upon the Secretary of State being satisfied that:

> "the police area in question is efficiently policed, that adequate co-operation is afforded by the police force to other police forces, that the police service is efficiently and properly maintained, equipped and administered, and that the rates of pay and allowances of the force are as prescribed or approved by him; and if he is not satisfied on any of these matters he may withhold the grant in whole or in part permanently or for such time as he may determine."[12]

9–09   In practice, however, refusal of a certificate of efficiency, as in the case of the Derbyshire constabulary, did not lead to the withholding of grant. These provisions do not appear in the arrangements for the payment of grant to the newly-constituted police authorities.

A housing subsidy is payable to housing authorities under sections 79–84 of the Local Government and Housing Act 1989. Under section 86 of that Act, the Secretary of State may recoup the whole or a part of the subsidy, in accordance with rules published by him.

9–10   These are two examples of a minister's power of control through his ability to withhold or withdraw financial aid if schemes or activity are not of the kind or to the standards which he approves. It is, however, the case that the balance between special and general grants has, since the 1960s, shifted decisively towards the latter. The distribution of the general revenue support grant is not tied to the enforcement of specific standards, and

[12] Police (Grant) Order 1966 (S.I. 1966 No. 223), para. 2.

indeed, unlike rate support grant, will not vary according to the expenditure of the authority.[13]

Control through regulation

It is common for statutes conferring powers or duties on local authorities **9–11** to authorise a minister to make regulations prescribing how the work shall be carried out or the standards to which the service shall conform or conditions subject to which a grant is payable. The statute lays down the broad principles on which a power or duty shall be undertaken and the detailed working rules are often left to a minister to prescribe.

The Town and Country Planning Act 1990 contains a number of examples **9–12** which show how this form of control works out in practice. In many sections authority is given to the Secretary of State to make regulations setting out the way in which the Act is to be administered. He may under section 53 make regulations with respect to the form and content of structure and local plans and with respect to the procedure to be followed in their preparations, submission, approval and amendment. The regulations made under this section[14] minutely prescribe the procedure which planning authorities must follow. The Secretary of State is empowered by section 59 to make general development orders which have the effect of granting permission to such classes of development as he specifies subject to such conditions or limitations as he may lay down. The Town and Country Planning (General Permitted Development) Order 1995[15] made under this provision specifies those classes of development which are permitted by the Order and which may be undertaken without the consent of the local planning authority. Section 55(2)(f) enables the Secretary of State by Order to specify "use classes" within which there can be made a change from one use to another without having to obtain the permission of the local planning authority.[16] By his powers under these two sections he can limit or extend the discretionary powers of local planning authorities in the granting or withholding of planning permission.

There are a number of similar provisions in planning legislation but the examples given indicate the significance of control by regulation. It is true that the rules must be laid before Parliament and that in most cases they may be annulled by a resolution of either House. But Parliament does not often use its right of challenge. The power to make regulations, illustrated by reference to planning legislation, is found in many statutes relating to local authority services.

Control through inspection

This form of control operates in a limited field: it is used principally in the **9–13** education, police and fire services. In section 77(2) of the Education Act 1944, a duty is put on the Secretary of State for Education and Science to

---

[13] See further, Chapter 14.
[14] Town and Country Planning (Development Plan) Regulations 1991 (S.I. 1991 No. 2794).
[15] S.I. 1995 No. 418, as amended.
[16] S.I. 1987 No. 764, as amended.

cause an inspection to be made of every educational establishment at such intervals as he considers appropriate and to arrange a special inspection of any establishment whenever he thinks it desirable. The inspectorate exercises a considerable influence by way of advice, the interchange of ideas, the pooling of experience and the provision of a personal link between the administration in Whitehall and those who teach.

9–14   Inspectors of Constabulary are appointed under section 54 of the Police Act 1996. They have a duty to inspect and to report to the Secretary of State for the Home Department on the efficiency and effectiveness of police forces, and to carry out other duties for furthering police efficiency and effectiveness as he may direct. The Report of the Royal Commission on the Police[17] said of the inspectorate:

> "Thus the inspectors of constabulary will have four duties. They will continue, as now, to inspect each separate police force and report to the Secretary of State whether or not it is efficient, and in particular they will indicate any misgivings they may have about the competence of its chief constable, including the manner in which he deals with complaints against the police. Secondly, arising from their inspection of the force, they will form an opinion about the adequacy of the provision made by a police authority, and report any shortcomings in this respect to the Secretary of State. Thirdly, they will ensure that the results of central research are made available to the forces they inspect, and that new knowledge and up-to-date techniques are being applied. Fourthly, they will be responsible for advising upon arrangements for promoting collaboration between forces and the development of ancillary services. Although their duty will continue to be to the Secretaries of State, the inspectors should, in addition, keep in close touch with police authorities."

9–15   Section 24 of the Fire Service Act 1947 enables the Crown and the Secretary of State for the Home Department to appoint inspectors and assistant inspectors respectively, and precisely specifies what the inspectors are to do. They are to obtain information, first as to the manner in which fire authorities are carrying out their functions, and secondly as to technical matters relating to the fire service. In practice their second function is the one in which their influence is perhaps the more felt. In some ways like the school inspectorate the fire service inspectors can, by advice, encourage the acceptance of improved systems and techniques. They have a statutory duty to keep in touch with technical developments affecting the service and it is reasonable to suppose that the guidance they offer, based on their specialised knowledge, is carefully noted by fire authorities.

Powers in relation to authorities in default

9–16   In a number of cases, Parliament has given to Ministers of the Crown specific powers of control should authorities fail to carry out certain of their statutory functions. In several cases the minister concerned may issue directions or may transfer particular functions of a defaulting authority to

---

[17] Cmnd. 1728 (1962).

himself or to another authority. These are legal powers which are very rarely used, but as they are available to the central government departments they must be noted. Two examples are given. Where the Secretary of State for the Environment is satisfied, after a local inquiry or hearing, that a planning authority has failed to carry out its functions in connection with the preparation and submission of a structure or local plan he may, under section 51 of the Town and Country Planning Act 1990, take over those functions himself or may transfer them to another planning authority with an interest in the proper planning of the area. The cost of carrying out the work involved falls to the defaulting authority.

The Secretary of State for Education and Science is given directive powers **9–17** under section 99 of the Education Act 1944, where he is satisfied, on complaint or otherwise, that a local education authority, or the governors of any county or voluntary school, have failed to carry out any of their statutory duties. The Secretary of State may declare the authority or governors to be in default and may issue appropriate directions, enforceable by mandamus. He is not obliged to hold a local inquiry before exercising such powers. These default powers are available where there has been a failure to carry out statutory duties. But the powers of the Secretary of State under section 68 of the Act are wider still. The section provides that if he is satisfied on complaint or otherwise that a local education authority or the governors of a county or voluntary school have acted or are proposing to act unreasonably in exercising their functions, he may give such directions to them as he thinks expedient. The default here dealt with is not the failure to carry out a legal duty, but the failure to carry out statutory duties in a reasonable manner. However, the Secretary of State may only intervene where an authority is acting, or proposing to act, so unreasonably that no reasonable authority could act in that manner. He may not intervene merely because he disagrees with the authority's action.[18]

Control over officers

It is generally true to say that a local authority has control over the **9–18** appointment and dismissal of its officers and may stipulate what qualifications those officers shall hold. There are, however, exceptions to this general rule.[19] The extent of this control is relatively slight: its purpose, presumably, is to ensure minimum standards.

Section 18 of the Fire Services Act 1947, for example, enables the **9–19** Secretary of State for the Home Department, after consultation with the Central Fire Brigades Advisory Council, to make regulations prescribing the method of appointment of chief fire officers and the qualifications for appointment and promotion in all ranks.[20] It is illustrative of the preciseness of the regulations to note, for example, that minimum and maximum height

---

[18] *Secretary of State for Education and Science v. Tameside Metropolitan Borough Council* [1977] A.C. 1014; *cf. R. v. Kent County Council, ex p. Bruce, The Times*, February 8, 1986.
[19] See, *e.g.*, Local Government Act 1972, s.112(4) and §§ 4–48 *et seq.*
[20] Fire Services (Appointment and Promotion) Regulations 1978 (S.I. 1978 No. 438), as amended.

limits are specified, together with tests for lung function, aerobic capacity, eyesight and the strength of the handgrip and lifting strength. A previous requirement as to chest size and expansion has been removed.

Central control over officers was reduced by section 112 of the Local Government Act 1972. However, the discretion of local authorities has also been restricted by the conferment of independent responsibilities on particular designated officers[21]; by the new express duty to appoint staff "on merit"[22]; and by regulations made by the Secretary of State prescribing standing orders with respect to the appointment and dismissal of officers.[23]

The confirmation of by-laws

9–20   As has been observed in Chapter 6, no local by-laws are effective until confirmed by the appropriate minister. Central control is here absolute, as one might expect, for by-laws in the main create penal offences. The department concerned examines proposed by-laws first on the score of validity in law. As will have been noted, a local by-law is open to challenge in the courts on one or more of the following grounds: that it is repugnant to or inconsistent with statute or common law, that it is unreasonable, that it is uncertain in its terms, that it is *ultra vires* the authority, and, in the case of good rule and government by-laws, that a summary remedy already exists for the prevention or suppression of the nuisance at which the by-law is aimed. The minister will not confirm a by-law which, in his opinion, will not satisfy the judicial tests as to validity. Additionally, the department is to be assured that the need exists in the particular locality for the by-law proposed, for it is clearly undesirable to have by-laws for their own sake. Some attempt is made, through the use of model codes, to secure a measure of uniformity in wording and substance.

The issue of directions

9–21   The directions here considered are of a particular character, addressed to an individual authority. If the power to issue directions of this kind were greatly extended then local autonomy would be severely jeopardised. The number of instances in which this power is conferred on Ministers is fairly substantial but except in the first example given the power is not widely used. Section 77 of the Town and Country Planning Act 1990, enables the Secretary of State for the Environment to give directions to any local planning authority (or to local planning authorities generally) requiring that any application for permission to develop land, or all applications of a specified class, shall be referred to him instead of being dealt with by the local planning authority. Reference has earlier been made to the powers of direction which vest in the Secretary of State for Education and Science under section 99 of the Education Act 1944, when he is satisfied that an

---

[21] *e.g.* the chief finance officer: Local Government Finance Act 1988, ss.114–116; the head of paid service: Local Government and Housing Act 1989, s.4; and the monitoring officer: *ibid.* s.7.

[22] 1989 Act, s.7.

[23] *ibid.*, s.8.

authority is in default, and under section 68 of that Act where, in his opinion, an authority or the governors of any county or voluntary school have acted or are proposing to act unreasonably in carrying out their functions.

Section 19 of the Clean Air Act 1993 enables the Secretary of State for the Environment to require an authority to create a smoke control area and to carry out a smoke control programme. The Secretary of State may be concerned with a particular footpath—he has power under section 26 of the Highways Act 1980 to make a public path creation order. Powers of direction contained in the Local Government, Planning and Land Act 1980 included the powers of the Secretary of State to require a public body to dispose of land which in his opinion is not being used, or not being sufficiently used, for the authority's purposes,[24] and to restrict capital expenditure.[25] The first of these remains in force.

Perhaps more significant than any of the powers already mentioned are the powers of the Secretary of State to "cap" the expenditure of individual charging and precepting authorities under Part I, Chapter V of the Local Government Finance Act 1992.[26]

Appellate jurisdiction

In a number of statutes a right of appeal against a decision of a local **9–22** authority lies to a minister. An applicant for planning permission who is aggrieved by the decision of the local planning authority may appeal to the Secretary of State for the Environment under section 78 of the Town and Country Planning Act 1990. Section 233 of the Highways Act 1980 gives a right of appeal to the Secretary of State against certain decisions of local authorities when acting under the street works code.

Ministers have appellate jurisdiction in certain cases of dispute between authorities and between authorities and employees. It is the Secretary of State for Health who settles a question between authorities as to a person's "ordinary residence" for the purposes of Part III of the National Assistance Act 1948.[27] The Superannuation Act 1972 and the regulations made thereunder provide that any question of rights or liabilities of an employee shall be decided in the first instance by the employing authority, and if the employee is dissatisfied with the decision reached he may appeal to the Secretary of State for the Environment, whose determination is final.[28]

Consent to individual acts

There are a number of cases in which a local authority may act only with **9–23** the consent of a Minister. For example, an authority may only use money accruing from a local lottery for a purpose other than that originally specified as the object of the lottery with the consent of the Secretary of State.[29]

---

[24] s.98.
[25] s.78.
[26] See § 16–17.
[27] s.32(3).
[28] See Local Government Pension Scheme Regulations 1995, Part J (S.I. 1995 No. 1019), as amended.
[29] Lotteries and Amusements Act 1976, s.7(4).

The power to require information

9–24   There are many examples of the power to hold inquiries and to require information from local authorities. There is an example of the former in section 46 of the Coast Protection Act 1949. The Secretary of State may cause a local inquiry to be held in any case where it appears to him to be advisable to do so in connection with any matter arising under that Act. As to the latter, section 168 of the Local Government Act 1972 requires the submission of financial returns to the Secretary of State in the form directed. The Department of Trade and Industry, under section 26 of the Trade Descriptions Act 1968, can require at any time a report from a weights and measures authority on the exercise of its functions under section 9 of the Hallmarking Act 1973 and the report must contain such particulars as the Department directs. Under section 97 of the Local Government, Planning and Land Act 1980, the Secretary of State may direct a public body to give him such information as he may specify about land being held by it. These are a few examples.

Audit

9–25   District Audit was historically one of the more important ways in which Parliament secured the subordination of local authority to its will as expressed in statute. It had its origin in the Poor Law Act 1834, which provided that payments made contrary to the terms of the Act or the Orders of the Poor Law Commissioners should be illegal. The auditors appointed under the provisions of the Act had power to disallow illegal payment and to surcharge those responsible for making them.

Sections 154 to 167 of the Local Government Act 1972 (applicable up to 1982/83) required authorities to submit their accounts to audit by the district auditor appointed by, or an auditor approved by, the Secretary of State. The system was designed to ensure that local authorities in matters of expenditure and financial practice kept within the law: the auditor was to see, amongst other things, that expenditure was authorised by law, that it was within the powers of the authority, that statutory limits on expenditure had not been exceeded and that statutory salary scales had been observed. In a sense, the system was a mechanism of central control, in that it would be central government that set the legal limits in question, either by securing the passage of legislation or by exercising delegated legislative powers, and one at least of the functions of statutory audit to ensure that those limits were observed. This point is well illustrated by the litigation arising out of the conduct of Clay Cross Urban District Council in the early 1970s and Liverpool City Council in the 1980s.[30] On the other hand it was also true that auditors were independent in the actual performance of their responsibilities. Approved auditors were approved by the Secretary of State on the test of professional skills, and district auditors, though appointed by him, were

---

[30] *Asher v. Lacey* [1973] 1 W.L.R. 1412; *Asher v. Secretary of State for the Environment* [1974] Ch. 208; *Lloyd v. McMahon* [1987] A.C. 625. See § 13–33.

independent of him in decision-making and were not answerable to him. He could not be questioned in Parliament as to their findings.

With the changes to the audit system made by the Local Government Finance Act 1982 for 1983/84 onwards,[31] it may be considered that the independence of audit from central government is increased, since auditors are no longer employed or approved by the Secretary of State. The Audit Commission, which appoints the auditors, is itself appointed by the Secretary of State, however, and he is empowered to issue directions which the Commission must observe. But this does not detract from the independence of the auditors in carrying out their statutory functions (now extended to include that of checking that the authority has made proper arrangements for securing economy, efficiency and effectiveness in its use of resources). Their duties continue to be laid upon them directly by statute and therefore neither the Commission nor the Secretary of State has power to direct or influence them in the performance of those duties. It also, however, remains the case that one aspect of the auditor's functions is to secure compliance with the law, and, indeed, the Local Government Act 1988 gave auditors additional powers to that end.

C. Trends in Central Control

An attempt was made in 1949 to simplify administrative procedures involved **9–26** in central control of local authority work. A committee, called the Local Government Manpower Committee, was set up to examine the problem generally. It consisted of representatives of government departments and local authority associations, and its terms of reference included a duty "to examine in particular the distribution of functions between central and local government and the possibility of relaxing departmental supervision of local authority activities and delegating more responsibility to local authorities". The Committee was concerned primarily with matters of procedure rather than with the forms of control prescribed by statute, though it did in fact make certain recommendations for an amendment of the law. It approached the problem with the view that "local authorities are responsible bodies competent to discharge their own functions and that ... they exercise their responsibilities in their own right", and accordingly "the objective should be to leave as much as possible of the detailed management of a scheme or service to the local authority and to concentrate the department's control at key points where it can most effectively discharge its responsibilities for government policy and financial administration".

The Committee made a number of recommendations for the loosening of **9–27** central control by simplifying and shortening administrative procedures. The recommendations were accepted by the Government and were subsequently embodied in departmental circulars addressed to local authorities. It is doubtful whether a substantial or even measurable reduction of control stemmed from the acceptance of the recommendations of the

[31] See Chap. 13.

Committee, but at least the problem was reviewed with some realism. This examination of the procedures involved and the reforms proposed indicated in an authoritative way how the statutory forms of control were exercised in practice.

9–28　　The objectives of the Local Government Manpower Committee were noted with approval by the Committee on the Management of Local Government[32] which recommended that the Government, in consultation with the local authority associations, should examine existing legislation to see what provisions might be repealed with a view to leaving local authorities the maximum freedom in organising their affairs and carrying out their work.

These consultations did in fact take place and a great many items of control were removed by the Local Government Act 1972. Here are some examples. Though a chief education officer must be appointed, there is no longer a requirement to submit a short list to the Secretary of State for approval or veto.[33] The control exercised by the Secretary of State over charges in connection with ferry undertakings run by a local authority or passenger transport executive was removed.[34] The Act of 1972 cleared away many such minor and relatively unimportant forms of control.

Still more were removed or modified by the Local Government Act 1974. Schedule 8 contained a long list of repeals and amendments which had the effect of dispensing with the consent of ministers to particular acts, and the Secretary of State was empowered by regulation to make further amendments to statute to achieve this end.[35]

The process was taken a step further by the Local Government, Planning and Land Act 1980,[36] which removed many minor controls, particularly over functions relating to clean air and pollution, amenity, weights and measures, and allotments, and controls over charges and rates of interest. However, as has been noted above, the Act also contained significant extensions of central control over levels of expenditure, a process taken further by the Rates Act 1984, Part IV of the Local Government and Housing Act 1989 and Part I, Chapter V of the Local Government Finance Act 1992 (see Chapters 12 and 16). Indeed, the practical effect of the removal of many detailed controls has been more than outweighed by the severe financial constraints set by central government under recent legislation.

D. Consultations

9–29　An examination of these issues would be incomplete without some reference to the processes, statutory and otherwise, involved in reaching decisions as to the controls to be imposed, and more particularly as to how they shall be

---

[32] Vol. I, para. 251.
[33] Local Government Act 1972, s.112 and Sched. 30.
[34] *ibid.*, s.186(6).
[35] s.35.
[36] s.1 and Scheds. 1–6, which give effect to proposals in the White Paper "Central Government Controls over Local Authorities" (Cmnd. 7634).

exercised. In many cases a minister is required by statute first to consult some advisory body, generally one set up by statute and representative of all interested parties, before he makes regulations. An example of this is found in the Central Fire Brigades Advisory Council which the Secretary of State for the Home Department is required to establish under section 29 of the Fire Services Act 1947. This Council is composed of persons representing the interests of fire authorities, fire brigade members and such other persons as the Secretary of State chooses, being persons having special qualifications in this field. The Secretary of State is required to consult the Council before making certain regulations, those with respect to qualifications, for example, and the Council may offer advice on its own initiative. Section 78 of the Local Government Finance Act 1988, to take another example of statutory consultations, requires the Secretary of State for the Environment to consult with local authority associations before making a determination in relation to revenue support grant payable under Part V of the Act.

Perhaps of greater significance than the formal statutory consultations (made in the main with bodies appointed by the minister who consults them) are the non-statutory discussions which invariably take place between government departments and the associations of local authorities on any major administrative change and on any new or amending legislation affecting local government.

The main local authority associations, as constituted following the reorganisation of local government under the Local Government Act 1972, have been the Association of County Councils, the Association of Metropolitan Authorities, the Association of District Councils, the National Association of Local Councils (for parish and community councils), the London Boroughs Association and the Association of London Authorities. A single Local Government Association was established in 1996. There are also more specialised bodies, such as the Council of Local Education Authorities and the British Fire Service Association; and there are various associations of officers (*e.g.* the Society of Local Authority Chief Executives and the Society of Education Officers), and associations of members. These are not statutory bodies, but a local authority may pay reasonable subscriptions to

(a) any association of local authorities formed (inside or outside the United Kingdom) for the purpose of consultation as to the common interests of those authorities and discussion of matters relating to local government; or

(b) any association of officers or members formed for those purposes.[37]

The limits of these powers were considered in the following cases.

R. v. Greater London Council, ex p. Bromley London Borough Council.[38] In 1982, the London Boroughs Association, then with a Conservative majority,

---

[37] Local Government Act 1972, s.143. This power is also available to the Common Council (s.143(2)) and to joint authorities (s.146A(1), inserted by the Local Government Act 1985, Sched. 14, para. 16).

[38] *The Times*, March 27, 1984.

resolved to support the government policy of abolition of the G.L.C. In consequence, the Association of London Authorities was established, whose objects included retention of the G.L.C., the local accountability of the police in London and the establishment in London of a nuclear free zone. Although membership was open to all London borough councils, the G.L.C. and I.L.E.A., the objects were designed to attract only Labour controlled authorities. It was conceded that a local authority was not permitted to pay subscriptions under section 143 of the Local Government Act 1972 to bodies whose objects were to express party political views. *Held*, the A.L.A. was such a body and the subscriptions paid by the G.L.C. were *ultra vires* section 143. After this decision, all the defects of the original constitution of the A.L.A. which had caused Forbes J. to grant the declaration were removed by amendment, and in *R. v. Bromley London Borough Council, ex p. Lambeth London Borough Council*,[39] Hodgson J. held that a subscription to the association would now be *intra vires*.

9–30   A particular forum for consultation on financial matters is the Consultative Council on Local Government Finance (CCLGF), a non-statutory body first established in 1975. It is chaired by the Secretary of State for the Environment, and comprises ministers and civil servants from all departments concerned with local government and members selected by the local authority associations. Detailed, preliminary consideration is given to the Council's business by an Official Steering Group, comprising civil servants, the secretary of each local authority association, specialist professional staff of the associations and officer advisers. Among the consequences of the establishment of the Council have been closer contacts among the main local authority associations, and the displacement of direct contacts on policy between individual local authorities and government departments.

Expectations that the council would be a forum for negotiation have not been fulfilled. Indeed, some have doubted its efficacy as a consultative body, viewing it rather as a forum for the announcement of decisions by central government.[40] It has certainly been in matters concerning the levels of expenditure that local authority influence has been weakest. There is a separate Council for Wales.

---

[39] *The Times*, June 16, 1984.
[40] See A. Alexander, *Local Government in Britain since Reorganisation* (1982), pp. 158–164.

CHAPTER 10

JUDICIAL CONTROL OF LOCAL AUTHORITIES AND LEGAL PROCEEDINGS BY AND AGAINST LOCAL AUTHORITIES

I. JUDICIAL CONTROL OF LOCAL AUTHORITIES[1]

LOCAL authorities are subject to the control of the courts in much the same **10–01** way as any other kind of corporate body or any natural person, in the sense that if they infringe a private right or are in breach of contract, they may be sued in tort or contract, and if they commit a criminal offence, proceedings may be taken against them. The liability of local authorities in these matters is considered in Chapter 10. But the term "judicial control of local authorities" is commonly used in another sense. The courts have a limited kind of supervisory jurisdiction over certain acts of any executive agency, including local authorities, and in the exercise of this jurisdiction may grant the orders of mandamus, prohibition and certiorari where such orders run, may issue declarations and injunctions in relation to acts or proposed acts which are *ultra vires*, and may hear appeals against acts or decisions where a right of appeal is conferred by statute. The courts will not take the initiative in any of these matters; they will act only at the suit of a litigant with sufficient "standing", a matter discussed at paragraphs 10–51—10–53 and 10–59.

The courts are rarely concerned with the *merits* of a particular decision. They can only correct an *error of fact* where (1) Parliament has enacted that an appeal shall lie on the merits, or (2) the error has caused the authority to act *ultra vires*. These situations are exceptional. The normal situations where a court may intervene are those where an authority has made an *error of law*. Any error of law may be corrected (1) if there is a statutory right of appeal, or (2) if an error of law appears on the face of the record of proceedings, or (3) if it causes the authority to act *ultra vires*. In practice, the error of law on the face of the record doctrine is obsolete.

The most straightforward examples of the application of the *ultra vires* doctrine are discussed in Chapter 1. Here we consider the applications of that doctrine in the context of "jurisdictional control". We also consider the

---

[1] The leading work on judicial review is de Smith, Woolf and Jowell, *Judicial Review of Administrative Action* (5th ed.). Other works which deal with the principles at length include Sir William Wade and C. F. Forsyth, *Administrative Law* (7th ed.); J. F. Garner and B. L. Jones, *Garner's Administrative Law* (7th ed.); P. P. Craig, *Administrative Law* (3rd ed.).

issues that arise in connection with limits on the exercise of statutory powers implied by the courts. The most significant of these limits relate to the use of discretionary powers, and the application of the rules of natural justice. Other matters considered are: statutory appeals; other remedies; the exclusion of judicial review.

10–02   In *Council of Civil Service Unions v. Minister for Civil Service*,[2] Lord Diplock suggested[3] the following three-fold classification of the grounds of judicial review:

> "Judicial review has I think developed to a stage today when without reiterating any analysis of the steps by which the development has come about, one can conveniently classify under three heads the grounds upon which administrative action is subject to control by judicial review. The first ground I would call 'illegality', the second 'irrationality' and the third 'procedural impropriety'. That is not to say that further development on a case by case basis may not in course of time add further grounds. I have in mind particularly the possible adoption in the future of the principle of 'proportionality' which is recognised in the administrative law of several of our fellow members of the European Economic Community; but to dispose of the instant case the three already well-established heads that I have mentioned will suffice.
>
> By 'illegality' as a ground for judicial review I mean that the decision-maker understands correctly the law that regulates his decision-making power and must give effect to it. Whether he has or not is par excellence a justiciable question to be decided, in the event of dispute, by those persons, the judges, by whom the judicial power of the state is exercisable.
>
> By 'irrationality' I mean what can by now be succinctly referred to as '*Wednesbury* unreasonableness' (*Associated Provincial Picture Houses Ltd v. Wednesbury Corporation*).[4] It applies to a decision which is so outrageous in its defiance of logic or of accepted moral standards that no sensible person who had applied his mind to the question to be decided could have arrived at it. Whether a decision falls within this category is a question that judges by their training and experience should be well equipped to answer, or else there would be something badly wrong with our judicial system. ...
>
> I have described the third head as 'procedural impropriety' rather than failure to observe basic rules of natural justice or failure to act with procedural fairness towards the person who will be affected by the decision. This is because susceptibility to judicial review under this head covers also failure by an administrative tribunal to observe procedural rules that are expressly laid down in the legislative instrument by which its jurisdiction is conferred, even where such failure does not involve any denial of natural justice."

This classification has been cited on many occasions since, and has been described by Lord Scarman as a "valuable, and already 'classical', but certainly not exhaustive analysis".[5] It is suggested that while these are convenient broad labels, an examination of the case law discussed in the following paragraphs will reveal that the grounds of challenge are rather more complex and extensive than the labels would suggest.

---

[2] [1985] A.C. 374.
[3] At pp. 410–414.
[4] [1948] 1 K.B. 223. See § 10–25.
[5] *R. v. Secretary of State for the Environment, ex p. Nottinghamshire County Council* [1986] A.C. 240, 249.

A. JURISDICTIONAL CONTROL

One of the most complex areas of administrative law is that concerning the **10–03** distinction between those errors which cause a public authority to act outside its jurisdiction (variously termed "jurisdictional" errors; errors on "preliminary" or "collateral" questions) and those which do not ("errors relating to the merits" or "errors with jurisdiction"). Many of the relevant cases concern decisions by justices and tribunals rather than by local authorities.[6]

The following points may be noted:

(a) "Preliminary" or "jurisdictional" questions may be questions of law or fact: "a court with jurisdiction confined to the City of London cannot extend such jurisdiction by finding as a fact that Piccadilly Circus is in the ward of Chepe."[7] However, where the determination of a question of fact depends on the conflicting testimony of witnesses, a superior court will normally decline to interfere with the decision of the tribunal which saw the witnesses.[8]

(b) The distinction between jurisdictional and non-jurisdictional questions has been of less practical significance in the light of the revival of the use of certiorari to quash for any error of law on the face of the record (para. 10–48), and the broad interpretation given to the powers of the court to quash compulsory purchase and other orders on applications under statute (para. 10–60).

The following case illustrates the application of the principles of **10–04** jurisdictional control to local authorities:

> *Re Ripon (Highfield) Housing 1938, White and Collins v. Minister of Health.*[9] Under the Housing Act 1936, a local authority had power to acquire land compulsorily, provided that it did not form "part of any park, garden or pleasure ground or is otherwise required for the amenity or convenience of any house" (s.75). The Minister confirmed Ripon Borough Council's order for the purchase of 23 acres of land let for grazing which were part of the grounds of a house. The owners applied to the High Court for the order to be quashed. Affidavit evidence was given to the effect that the land was part of a park, which evidence was not before the Minister. Charles J. held that the Minister's decision that the land was not part of a park was a finding of fact with which he could not interfere. On appeal, the Court of Appeal *held* that the order should be quashed. Jurisdiction to make the order was dependent on this finding of fact, and the Minister's decision could be reviewed. There was no evidence to

---

[6] See *e.g. R. v. City of London etc., Rent Tribunal, ex p. Honig* [1951] 1 K.B. 641.
[7] *Per* Farwell L.J. in *R. v. Shoreditch Assessment Committee, ex p. Morgan* [1910] 2 K.B. 859 at p. 880.
[8] Devlin L.J. in *R. v. Fulham, etc., Rent Tribunal, ex p. Zerek* [1951] 2 K.B. 1, 11; Lord Goddard C.J. in *ex p. Honig* [1951] 1 K.B. 641 at p. 646, *supra* n. 6.
[9] [1939] 2 K.B. 838.

support the Minister's decision. Indeed, the court was satisfied on the evidence that the land was part of a park.[10]

In *Anisminic Ltd v. Foreign Compensation Commission*,[11] a leading modern case on jurisdictional control, Lord Pearce said[12]:

> "Lack of jurisdiction may arise in various ways. There may be an absence of those formalities or things which are conditions precedent to the tribunal having any jurisdiction to embark on an inquiry. Or the tribunal may at the end make an order that it has no jurisdiction to make. Or in the intervening stage, while engaged on a proper inquiry, the tribunal may depart from the rules of natural justice; or it may ask itself the wrong questions; or it may take into account matters which it was not directed to take into account. Thereby it would step outside its jurisdiction. It would turn its inquiry into something not directed by Parliament and fail to make the inquiry which Parliament did direct. Any of these things would cause its purported decision to be a nullity."

10–05   The *Anisminic* decision broadened significantly the range of errors that were to be regarded as causing a body to exceed its jurisdiction, but did not indicate the limits of that range with precision. *Pearlman v. Keepers and Governors of Harrow School*[13] raised the question whether an error by a county court judge on a rating matter was such as to cause him to exceed his jurisdiction. The members of the Court of Appeal were agreed that the judge had made an error of law. Lord Denning M.R. expressed the view that any error of *law* would cause a statutory body to exceed its jurisdiction.[14] Eveleigh L.J. was not prepared to go so far, but, applying *Anisminic*, agreed that the judge had exceeded his jurisdiction. Geoffrey Lane L.J. held that the error of law was not such as to cause an excess of jurisdiction.

As regards administrative tribunals and authorities, as distinct from courts of law, the wide approach in *Anisminic* has been endorsed *obiter* by Lord Diplock and Lord Keith in *In re Racal Communications Ltd.*[15] Per Lord Diplock[16]:

> "In *Anisminic* this House was concerned only with decisions of administrative tribunals. Nothing I say is intended to detract from the breadth of the scope of application to administrative tribunals of the principles laid down in that case. It is a legal landmark; it has made possible the rapid development in England of a rational and comprehensive system of administrative law on the foundation of the concept of *ultra vires*. It proceeds on the presumption that

---

[10] See also *Dowty Boulton Paul Ltd v. Wolverhampton Corporation* [1971] 1 W.L.R. 204 *per* Russell L.J. at pp. 26, 27: see § 5–44, n. 98; *Cocks v. Thanet District Council* [1983] 2 A.C. 286, 296 (for the local authority to determine whether a person is homeless or threatened with homelessness, is in priority need and not intentionally homeless, so as to give rise to duties under the Housing (Homeless Persons) Act 1977 (now Part III of the Housing Act 1985); *R. v. Westminster City Council, ex p. Tansey* (1988) 20 H.L.R. 520 (for the authority to determine whether accommodation is "suitable"); *R. v. Tower Hamlets London Borough Council, ex p. Ferdous Begum* [1993] A.C. 509 (question whether a person was an "applicant" for housing under the Housing Act 1985 was for the authority to determine). See also *R. v. Monopolies and Mergers Commission, ex p. South Yorkshire Transport Ltd* [1993] 1 W.L.R. 23.
[11] [1969] 2 A.C. 147.
[12] At p. 195.
[13] [1979] Q.B. 56.
[14] At pp. 69–70.
[15] [1981] A.C. 374.
[16] At pp. 382–383.

where Parliament confers on an administrative tribunal or authority, as distinct from a court of law, power to decide particular questions defined by the Act conferring the power, Parliament intends to confine that power to answering the question as it has been so defined, and if there has been any doubt as to what the question is this is a matter for courts of law to resolve in fulfilment of their constitutional role as interpreters of the written law and expounders of the common law and rules of equity. So, if the administrative tribunal or authority have asked themselves the wrong question and answered that, they have done something that the Act does not empower them to do and their decision is a nullity. Parliament can, of course, if it so desires, confer on administrative tribunals or authorities power to decide questions of law as well as questions of fact or of administrative policy; but this requires clear words, for the presumption is that where a decision-making power is conferred on a tribunal or authority that is not a court of law, Parliament did not intend to do so. The breakthrough made by *Anisminic* was that, as respects administrative tribunals and authorities, the old distinction between errors of law that went to jurisdiction and errors of law that did not was for practical purposes abolished. Any error of law that could be shown to have been made by them in the course of reaching their decision on matters of fact or of administrative policy would result in their having asked themselves the wrong question with the result that the decision they reached would be a nullity."

This view was not mentioned by the other members of the House of Lords. It has nevertheless been accepted (*obiter*) as representing the law by Lord Denning M.R. in the Court of Appeal and by the Divisional Court.[17] As regards courts of law, the dissenting judgment of Geoffrey Lane L.J. in *Pearlman v. Keepers and Governers of Harrow School*[18] was endorsed in *Racal* by Lords Diplock, Keith and Edmund-Davies[19] and by the Privy Council in *South East Asia Fire Bricks Sdn. Bhd. v. Non-Metallic Mineral Products Manufacturing Employees Union*.[20] Nevertheless, the Divisional Court has held that the *Anisminic* principle is applicable to a court of law (here, a coroner's inquest).[21]

Most recently, in *R. v. Hull University Visitor, ex p. Page*[22] the House of Lords held that in general any error of law made by an administrative tribunal or inferior court in reaching its decision can lead to the quashing of the decision on the ground that it is *ultra vires*.

B. Failure to Exercise Discretion

A local authority entrusted by Parliament with a statutory discretion will, by **10–06** definition, have some element of choice as to whether or how it will act. However, a power may be coupled with a duty to consider whether the power should be exercised in any particular case. An authority may not delegate the exercise of discretion without statutory authorisation, and must

---

[17] *R. v. Chief Immigration Officer, Gatwick Airport, ex p. Kharrazi* [1980] 1 W.L.R. 1396 at p. 1403; *R. v. Surrey Coroner, ex p. Campbell* [1982] Q.B. 661.
[18] [1979] Q.B. 56.
[19] [1981] A.C. 374 at pp. 639, 645, 644.
[20] [1981] A.C. 363.
[21] *R. v. Greater Manchester Coroner, ex p. Tal* [1985] Q.B. 67; *R. v. Surrey Coroner, ex p. Campbell, supra*, not followed.
[22] [1993] A.C. 682.

not act under the dictation of any other authority, unless that authority has statutory power to give directions. It may not improperly fetter its discretion by entering a contract or other undertaking, and it may not be estopped by its conduct from exercising its powers. It may be required to consider the exercise of discretion in each individual case and not by reference to an inflexible policy rule.

Unlawful delegation

10–07   A public authority may not delegate its decision-making functions without express or implied statutory authority. A power to delegate is not readily implied, particularly where the decision in question is judicial.[23] A local authority has wide powers under section 101 of the Local Government Act 1972 to arrange for the discharge of any of its functions by a committee, a sub-committee or officer of itself or any other local authority.[24] A local authority may lawfully place considerable reliance on the views of other persons or bodies, provided that the power of decision is in the last resort retained by the authority. This emerges from cases concerning the licensing of cinemas. In *Ellis v. Dubowski*,[25] the Divisional Court struck down a condition which provided that no film be shown which had not been certified for public exhibition by the British Board of Film Censors, a non-statutory body established by the film industry. However, a condition which provided that no film which had not been passed by the Board for universal exhibition should be shown to unaccompanied children under 16 "*without the express consent of the Council*" was upheld by the Divisional Court in *Mills v. London County Council*.[26] The licensing of cinemas can be regarded as an administrative function. Where judicial functions are concerned any other body involved in the decision-making process may normally only be used for gathering information—and this information must be fully summarised for the benefit of the authority which is to make the final decision.[27]

A lawful decision to delegate a function does not mean that the delegating authority may not continue to exercise that function concurrently with the delegate.[28] However, where the delegate makes a decision in the proper performance of the function delegated, that decision will be as binding as if it had been made by the delegating authority.[29]

10–08   The express powers of a local authority to delegate its functions under section 101 are so wide that it is difficult to see that there is room for the

[23] See *Vine v. National Dock Labour Board* [1957] A.C. 488; *R. v. Gateshead JJ., ex p. Tesco Stores Ltd* [1981] Q.B. 470.

[24] See §§ 4–63—4–85.

[25] [1921] 3 K.B. 621.

[26] [1925] 1 K.B. 213 (approved by the Court of Appeal in *R. v. Greater London Council, ex p. Blackburn* [1976] 1 W.L.R. 550).

[27] Compare *Osgood v. Nelson* (1872) L.R. 5 H.L. 636 with *Jeffs v. New Zealand Dairy Production and Marketing Board* [1967] 1 A.C. 551 and *R. v. Chester City Council and others, ex p. Quietlynn Ltd* (1984) 83 L.G.R. 308, and see *Selvarajan v. Race Relations Board* [1976] 1 All E.R. 12, per Lord Denning M.R. at p. 20; *R. v. Chief Constable of Avon and Somerset, ex p. Clarke, The Independent*, November 28, 1986; *R. v. Derbyshire Police Authority, ex p. Wilson, The Times*, August 8, 1989, D.C. See also § 4–64.

[28] See *Huth v. Clarke* (1890) 25 Q.B.D. 391, and s.101(4) of the Local Government Act 1972.

[29] *Battelley v. Finsbury Borough Council* (1958) 56 L.G.R. 165. See § 4–68.

implication of any further powers to delegate. However, the following case suggests that this may be possible.

> *Provident Mutual Life Assurance Association v. Derby City Council.*[30] Schedule 1, para. 8, of the General Rate Act 1967 provides that where "a rating authority are of opinion" that a new building has been completed or can reasonably be expected to be completed within three months, a "completion notice" may be served on the owner. Rates thereafter become payable. Section 151 of the Local Government Act 1972 provides that "without prejudice to section 111 above, every local authority shall make arrangements for the proper administration of their financial affairs and shall secure that one of their officers has responsibility for the administration of those affairs."
>
> The council appointed their treasurer as the "proper officer" for rating purposes. The treasurer signed a typed form of completion notice. Copies were made, and were filled in where necessary by the principal rating assistant. The assistant decided when a notice should be served. Such decisions were not referred to the treasurer. There was no formal delegation of powers by the local authority to the assistant. The House of Lords *held* by four to one that this arrangement was *intra vires*. Per Lord Roskill[31]: "Parliament plainly contemplated that the actual machinery of enforcement and collection would not be operated personally by some senior local government official but would be so operated by the relevant senior official's staff." These were "administrative" matters, and what was done was "done as part of the proper administration of the respondents' financial affairs". Moreover, "the question is not whether the respondents' treasurer delegated power to Mr Wells [the assistant]. The question is whether what Mr Wells did was authorised by the respondents' treasurer so as to be the relevant opinion of the respondents. For the reasons I have given I think that it was ..."

It is suggested that local authorities would be best advised to make formal arrangements for the delegation of functions rather than to rely upon the implication of powers to delegate, or to make "authorisations" of the kind contemplated by Lord Roskill (which seems, with respect, to amount to delegation by another name). The *Provident Mutual* case has, however, subsequently been applied by the High Court[32] and the Court of Appeal,[33] and, although not mentioned, its principle appears to lie behind the decision in *R. v. Southwark London Borough Council, ex p. Bannerman.*[34]

Acting under dictation

The converse of the situation described in the previous section is that a **10–09** local authority may not formally exercise its powers under the real or imagined dictation of another authority.

---

[30] (1981) 79 L.G.R. 297.

[31] At pp. 306, 307.

[32] *Cheshire County Council v. Secretary of State for the Environment* [1988] J.P.L. 30 (power to issue enforcement notice delegated to County Secretary and Solicitor; effective decision taken by a member of his staff; notice held valid).

[33] *Fitzpatrick v. Secretary of State for the Environment* (1990) 154 L.G.Rev. 72, C.A. (council instructed district secretary to issue enforcement notices; notices prepared by a member of his staff and endorsed with his facsimile signature; notices held valid). (Note, however, that as the notices were prepared on the council's instructions, reliance on the *Provident Mutual* case seems unnecessary.)

[34] (1989) 22 H.L.R. 459 (possession proceedings instituted on the recommendation of a member of the Borough Valuer's staff, acting in the name of the Borough Valuer; proceedings held to be validly instituted).

R. v. Stepney Corporation.[35] A vestry clerk was entitled to compensation for the loss of his office which resulted from the transfer of the vestry's functions to a new local authority. The corporation had a discretion as to the amount, but mistakenly thought they were bound by the practice of the Treasury in relation to civil servants to deduct a quarter of the amount where an office was held part-time. *Held*, mandamus should be granted to compel the corporation to exercise its discretion in the light of the particular circumstances of the case.[36]

10–10   The extent to which councillors may take account of party group decisions was considered in the following case:

R. v. Waltham Forest London Borough Council, ex p. Baxters[37] Members of the majority group on the council held a private, party meeting where they discussed what the policy of the group would be as to the setting of the rate at the forthcoming council meeting. After discussion, the group agreed to support a rate increase of 62 per cent for the domestic rate and 56.6 per cent for the non-domestic rate. The group's standing orders provided that members were required to refrain from voting in opposition to group decisions, the sanction being withdrawal of the party whip. A number of members who voted against this level of increase at the group meeting voted in favour at the council meeting, at which a resolution to increase the rate by the previously agreed amounts was passed by 31 votes to 26. A number of ratepayers sought judicial review, *inter alia*, on the ground that six or seven councillors had voted contrary to their personal views.

The Court of Appeal *held* that had the councillors in question voted for the resolution not because they were in favour of it but because their discretion had been fettered by the vote at the group meeting, then the councillors would have been in breach of their duty to make up their own minds as to what rate was appropriate. However, that was not established on the facts. The councillors were entitled to take account of party loyalty and party policy as relevant considerations provided that they did not dominate so as to exclude other considerations. The court noted that the sanction was only withdrawal of the party whip: there was nothing to prevent a councillor who voted against the party line continuing as an independent member. Furthermore, these procedures were widely adopted by political groups throughout the country and this had not been regarded by the Widdicombe Committee on the Conduct of Local Authority Business[38] as a matter for concern.

An officer to whom power has been delegated under section 101 of the Local Government Act 1972 must not act under the dictation of a member.[39]

Parliament may, of course, expressly authorise a Minister to issue directions with which a local authority must comply.[40]

A power to give "guidance" may be distinguished from a power to give "directions".[41] On the other hand, Parliament may enable sanctions to be imposed for non-compliance with "guidance".[42]

---

[35] [1902] 1 K.B. 317.
[36] *cf. Lavender v. Minister of Housing and Local Government* [1970] 1 W.L.R. 1231; *R. v. Manchester City Council, ex p. Fulford* (1982) 81 L.G.R. 292; *R. v. Inner London Education Authority, ex p. Brunyate* [1989] 1 W.L.R. 542; *R. v. Warwickshire County Council, ex p. dill-Russell* (1990) 89 L.G.R. 640; *R. v. Cornwall County Council, ex p. Cornwall and Isles of Scilly Guardians ad litem and Reporting Officers Panel* [1992] 1 W.L.R. 427.
[37] [1988] Q.B. 419.
[38] Cmnd. 9797, (1986).
[39] *R. v. Port Talbot Borough Council, ex p. Jones* [1988] 2 All E.R. 207: see § 4–73.
[40] See § 9–21.
[41] *Laker Airways Ltd v. Department of Trade* [1977] Q.B. 643 at pp. 699–700, 714–717, 724–725.
[42] See, *e.g.* s.59(6)(cc) of the Local Government, Planning and Land Act 1980 (since repealed).

Fettering discretion by contract or undertaking

A public authority may not enter into a contract or other agreement which **10–11** is incompatible with the due exercise of its powers or the discharge of its duties or which divests the authority of its statutory powers or which obliges the authority not to exercise its powers. This principle has been invoked in a number of different situations. It has been relied on by local authorities to resist enforcement of an *express* contract,[43] covenant,[44] or non-contractual undertaking.[45] Terms can only be *implied* into existing agreements where they are compatible with the performance of statutory functions.[46] A plaintiff may challenge an exercise or non-exercise of discretion by a local authority on the ground that that discretion has been fettered by an agreement between the authority and a third party.[47]

It is of course clear that any contract by definition binds an authority to a **10–12** course of action and this in turn limits its discretion in a particular field of activity. This is illustrated in *Dowty Boulton Paul Ltd v. Wolverhampton Corporation*.[48] Here the corporation had sold land to the plaintiff company and had granted to it certain rights over an adjoining municipal airfield. During the currency of the lease the corporation decided to develop the airfield as a housing estate. Counsel for the corporation argued, *inter alia*, that under the general law regarding the exercise of statutory powers, the corporation was at any time entitled to override the licence it had granted to the company containing the rights referred to if the corporation required to use the airfield for any of its statutory purposes. Counsel based his contention on the principle that a body entrusted with statutory powers cannot by contract fetter the exercise of those powers. Pennycuick V.-C. said[49]:

> "I have said that the principle laid down . . . is established beyond doubt. That seems to me, however, a principle wholly inapplicable to the present case. What has happened here is that the corporation has made what is admittedly a valid disposition in respect of its land for a term of years. What is, in effect, contended . . . is that such a disposition—and, indeed, any other possible disposition of property by a corporation for a term of years, for example, an ordinary lease—must be read as subject to an implied condition enabling the corporation to determine it should it see fit to put the property to some other use in the exercise of any of its statutory powers. Nothing in the cases cited supports this startling proposition. The cases are concerned with attempts to fetter in advance the future exercise of statutory powers otherwise than by the valid exercise of a statutory power. The cases are not concerned with the position which arises after a statutory power has been validly exercised. Obviously, where a power is exercised in such a manner as to create a right extending over a

---

[43] *Birkdale District Electric Supply Co. v. Southport Corporation* [1926] A.C. 355, at p. 364, *per* the Earl of Birkenhead.

[44] *Stourcliffe Estates Company v. Bournemouth Corporation* [1910] 2 Ch. 12.

[45] *R. v. Liverpool Corporation, ex p. Liverpool Taxi Fleet Operators' Association* [1972] 2 Q.B. 299: § 12–40.

[46] *William Cory & Son Ltd v. London Corporation* [1951] 2 K.B. 476; *British Transport Commission v. Westmorland County Council* [1958] A.C. 126.

[47] *Stringer v. Minister of Housing and Local Government* [1970] 1 W.L.R. 1281.

[48] [1971] 1 W.L.R. 204. See also *Kirklees Metropolitan Borough Council v. Yorkshire Woollen Transport Company Limited* (1978) 77 L.G.R. 448.

[49] At p. 210.

term of years, the existence of that right *pro tanto* excludes the exercise of other statutory powers in respect of the same subject matter, but there is no authority and I can see no principle upon which that sort of exercise could be held to be invalid as a fetter upon the future exercise of powers."

The court refused the remedy prayed for—a mandatory injunction—on the technical ground that the court would not order what amounted, in this case, to specific performance of an obligation. The only remedy of the company lay in damages.[50]

10–13   An agreement will be invalid where it purports to divest the authority of a statutory power of primary importance, such as a power to make by-laws,[51] a power to purchase land,[52] or a discretion under the Town and Country Planning Acts to grant, refuse or revoke a planning permission.[53] In *Stringer v. Minister of Housing and Local Government*,[54] a county council and a rural district council entered into a formal agreement with Manchester University whereby they undertook to discourage development in the vicinity of Jodrell Bank radio telescope. Cooke J. held that the latter council's decision to refuse permission in a particular case, in accordance with this agreement, was void.

Failure to comply with a non-contractual undertaking may amount to a breach of the duty to act fairly.[55]

Estoppel

10–14   The powers of a local authority cannot be extended by the creation of an estoppel.[56] Similarly, an authority cannot sanction the unlawful act of another,[57] and cannot be prevented by an estoppel from performing a statutory duty.

> *Maritime Electric Co. Ltd v. General Dairies Ltd.*[58] The plaintiff electricity company was under a statutory duty to make certain charges. Through its own error, it undercharged the defendants over 28 months. The defendants relied on the accuracy of the sums charged to them in making their pricing decisions. *Held*, the plaintiff company was not estopped from recovering the full amount that should have been charged.

An example of a duty which cannot be hindered by the creation of an estoppel is the duty of an authority not to fetter or divest itself of its statutory discretions.

> *Southend-on-Sea Corporation v. Hodgson (Wickford) Ltd.*[59] The borough engineer wrote to a builder to the effect that certain land had an existing use and that planning consent was not necessary for a builder's yard. Relying on this

---

[50] *cf. Blake v. Hendon Corporation* [1962] 1 Q.B. 283.
[51] *William Cory & Son Ltd v. City of London Corporation* [1951] 2 K.B. 476.
[52] *Triggs v. Staines Urban District Council* [1969] 1 Ch. 10.
[53] *Ransom & Luck Ltd v. Surbiton Borough Council* [1949] Ch. 180.
[54] [1970] 1 W.L.R. 1281.
[55] See §§ 10–37 *et seq.*
[56] *Rhyl Urban District Council v. Rhyl Amusements Ltd* [1959] 1 W.L.R. 465.
[57] *Yabbicom v. King* [1899] 1 Q.B. 444; *Redbridge London Borough Council v. Jacques* [1970] 1 W.L.R. 1604; *Cambridgeshire County Council v. Rust* [1972] 2 Q.B. 426.
[58] [1937] A.C. 610.
[59] [1962] 1 Q.B. 416.

statement the builder purchased the land and used it as a builder's yard. The authority later took the opposite view and served an enforcement notice on the builder. He contended that the authority was estopped from saying that the premises had not been used throughout the period necessary to confer the right of an existing use. *Held*, estoppel cannot be raised to hinder the exercise of a statutory discretion conferred on a public authority.

Princes Investment Ltd v. Frimley and Camberley Urban District Council.[60] The company was granted planning permission for housing development on condition that it would connect the houses to the public sewer to the satisfaction of the planning authority. The sewer was more than 100 feet from the nearest house. The company applied to the engineer for approval for the layout of the company's sewers and the engineer did in fact approve them. The company then claimed against the council for the cost of the excess of the sewers over 100 feet. The Divisional Court held that the authority had not "required" the connection of the public sewer and undertaken to bear a proportion of the cost under the Public Health Act since it could only act by resolution (and there had in fact been none) and the "requirements" could not be notified informally by the engineer.

The court in this case rejected the view that this matter fell within those recurring routine matters of day-to-day administration where no resolution was necessary and in doing so at least recognised the practice of informal delegation in routine matters.

The authority of the *Southend* case was somewhat diminished by *Lever* **10–15** *(Finance) Ltd v. Westminster (City) London Borough Council.*[61] A planning officer had informed a developer that a particular alteration to a plan was not a material alteration so as to require a fresh planning consent. The authority later called for a planning application and refused it. It was held that the planning officer's decision was a representation within the officer's ostensible authority, and having been acted on by the developers, it was binding on the planning authority. Lord Denning M.R. said[62]:

> "If the planning officer tells the developer that a proposed variation is not material, and the developer acts on it, the planning authority cannot go back on it. I know that there are authorities which say that a public authority cannot be estopped by any representations made by its officers. It cannot be estopped from doing its public duty. See, for instance, the recent decision of the Divisional Court in *Southend-on-Sea Corporation v. Hodgson (Wickford) Ltd.* But these statements must now be taken with considerable reserve. ... If an officer, acting within the scope of his ostensible authority, makes a representation on which another acts, then a public authority must be bound by it, just as a private concern would be."

The following decisions of the Court of Appeal restored the earlier **10–16** principle.

Western Fish Products Ltd v. Penwith District Council.[63] The company claimed that there was an established user right to use a factory for a particular purpose. The matter was discussed between company representatives and the council's chief planning officer, the company supplying information as to the

---

[60] [1962] 1 Q.B. 681.
[61] [1971] 1 Q.B. 222.
[62] At p. 230.
[63] [1981] 2 All E.R. 204. See also *Co-operative Retail Services Ltd v. Taff-Ely Borough Council* (1979) 39 P. & C.R. 223; appeal dismissed (1982) 42 P. & C.R. 1.

previous use. Subsequently, the officer wrote that the information had been checked and that "it is confirmed that the limits of the various component parts of the commercial undertaking as now existing appear to be established." The company's later applications for planning permission and for an established use certificate were refused. They sought a declaration, *inter alia*, that the representations made by the council estopped it from asserting that planning permission was necessary, from refusing planning permission and from taking enforcement action. The Court of Appeal *held* (1) that the representation in the letter related to the existing position and did not amount to confirmation of an existing user right in relation to the proposed project; (2) that the plaintiffs had not in fact changed their position in reliance on the representation as they would have gone ahead with their project anyway; (3) that even if the decision on the first two points had been otherwise, their claim would still have failed for the following reasons: (i) since "proprietary estoppel" was concerned only with the creation by estoppel of rights and interests in or over land; and (ii) since the council could not be estopped from performing its statutory duties under the Town and Country Planning Act 1971, or from exercising its statutory discretions. On the second point, an officer, even when acting within the apparent scope of his authority, could not do what the Act required the council to do. Although there was a power to delegate under section 101(1) of the 1972 Act, there had to be a formal act of delegation. By Standing Orders, designated officers had been authorised to perform specified functions including those arising under sections 53 (determinations as to whether planning permission was required) and 94 (applications for established use certificates). Those officers had no authority to make any other kinds of determination. The only exceptions to the principle that authorities cannot be estopped from performing statutory duties were (a) where a decision was made by a person acting within delegated powers, and (b) where an authority waived a procedural requirement (*Wells v. Minister of Housing and Local Government*[64]). Exception (a) could be established either where there was a decision made by a person acting under powers formally delegated, or where there was "some evidence justifying the person dealing with the planning officer for thinking that what the officer said would bind the planning authority. Holding an office, however senior, cannot ... be enough by itself" (*per* Megaw L.J.). The court disagreed with Lord Denning's view that a person is entitled to assume that all necessary resolutions have been passed.

On the facts of *Western Fish*, (i) there was no formal delegation except in relation to section 53 and section 94 matters; (ii) there was no evidence justifying the belief that representations on other matters would bind the authority; (iii) the plaintiffs had not made the necessary formal application for a section 53 determination (the *Wells* decision being confined to situations where an application for planning permission was to be regarded as impliedly containing an invitation to make a section 53 determination); (iv) there was no formal application under section 94; and (v) in any event, a certificate under section 94 would have to be a document complying with the prescribed formalities.

10–17   *Rootkin v. Kent County Council*.[65] The plaintiff's daughter was allocated a place at a school measured by the authority to be over three miles from her

---

[64] [1967] 1 W.L.R. 1000.

[65] [1981] 2 All E.R. 227. See also *R. v. Birmingham City Council, ex p. Sheptonhurst Ltd* [1990] 1 All E.R. 1026 (council entitled to refuse renewal of a sex establishment licence, even where there was no change in the character of the locality, provided that rational reasons were given, and the council had regard to the fact that a licence had been granted in previous years); *Costain Homes Ltd v. Secretary of State for the Environment* (1988) 57 P. & C.R. 461 P.L.R. 101; *R. v. Secretary of State for the Environment, ex p. Barratt (Guildford) Ltd, The Times*, April 3, 1989.

home. On that basis, the authority was under a duty either to provide transport or to reimburse travelling expenses, under section 39(2) of the Education Act 1944. It chose the latter course, and issued a bus pass, in the exercise of the discretionary power under section 55(2) of the 1944 Act. Shortly after, the authority made a more precise measurement and found the distance to be less than three miles. It then withdrew the bus pass. The plaintiff argued (1) that the authority was not entitled to rescind its determination that a bus pass should be issued, and (2) that the authority was estopped from revoking its decision. The Court of Appeal *held* that the authority was entitled to withdraw the pass. On the first point it was stated that "if a citizen is entitled to payment in certain circumstances and a local authority is given the duty of deciding whether the circumstances exist and, if they do exist, of making the payment, then there is a determination which the local authority cannot rescind. That was established in *Livingston v. Westminster Corpn.*[66] But that line of authority does not apply … to a case where the citizen has no right to a determination on certain facts being established, but only to the benefit of the exercise of a discretion by the local authority.[67] On the second point, it was held that an estoppel could not arise where that would prevent the exercise of a statutory discretion (*Southend-on-Sea Corporation v. Hodgson (Wickford) Ltd, supra*), that there was here no exceptional situation of a kind contemplated in the *Western Fish* case, and that in any event the plaintiff had not altered her position so as to entitle her to rely on the doctrine of estoppel.

The decision of the Court of Appeal in *Lever (Finance) Ltd v. Westminster (City) London Borough Council*[68] remains good law on its own facts, having been distinguished but not overruled by the Court of Appeal in *Western Fish Products Ltd v. Penwith District Council.*[69] This point was affirmed by Malcolm Spence Q.C., sitting as a deputy High Court Judge, in the following case.

> *London Borough of Camden v. Secretary of State for the Environment.*[70] An architect acting for the owners of a residential property wrote to the council seeking officer's approval for a minor variation to approved plans for a roof extension. The council replied by letter, stating that the variation was minor and did not constitute development requiring planning permission. The letter was signed by an officer acting for the Head of Planning, Transport and Employment Services. The occupiers began to construct the roof extension. The council served an enforcement notice. The occupiers' appeal against the notice was upheld by an Inspector, who found that the signatory of the letter had ostensible authority to make the decision and that the delegation of such decisions to officers was normal practice in the authority. Malcolm Spence Q.C. *held*, refusing leave to appeal, that the council was estopped by the letter from asserting that the extension constituted development requiring planning permission. The signatory had actual, or at least ostensible authority to take such a decision. (It should, however, be noted that evidence that the signatory of the letter did not have delegated power or ostensible authority was not put before the Inspector; the High Court had to take the Inspector's conclusions of fact as they were.)

It is clear from *Western Fish Products Ltd v. Penwith District Council* **10–18** (*supra*) and cases decided since then that it is only in exceptional

---

[66] [1904] 2 K.B. 109.
[67] *Per* Lawton L.J. at p. 233; *cf.* Eveleigh L.J. at pp. 234–235 and Sir Stanley Rees at p. 237.
[68] [1971] 1 Q.B. 222.
[69] [1981] 2 All E.R. 204.
[70] (1993) 67 P. & C.R. 59.

circumstances that a public authority will be bound by an estoppel arising out of informal undertakings or representations made by itself or on its behalf, so as to preclude it altogether from making a decision inconsistent with that undertaking or representation. Instead, the courts have developed alternative mechanisms for reconciling the interests of public authorities with the legitimate interests and expectations of others arising from such informal undertakings or representations. Accordingly, an authority's subsequent failure to take account of such an undertaking or representation may constitute failure to take account of a relevant consideration, and thus an abuse of discretion.[71] A decision to act inconsistently with a previous undertaking or representation may be held to be irrational or unreasonable in the *Wednesbury* sense.[72] The undertaking or representation may give rise to a legitimate expectation entitling the person affected to an opportunity to make representations before the authority can lawfully decide to act inconsistently.[73]

Fettering discretion by self-created rules of policy

10–19   A local authority may wish to ensure consistency in its decision making by establishing policy rules or guidelines. These must not (1) be based on considerations which are legally irrelevant,[74] nor (2) be applied so rigidly that an exercise of discretion in each individual case is precluded.

The latter principle was stated as follows by Bankes L.J. in *R. v. Port of London Authority, ex p. Kynoch Ltd*[75]:

> "There are on the one hand cases where a tribunal in the honest exercise of its discretion has adopted a policy, and, without refusing to hear an applicant, intimates to him what its policy is, and that after hearing him it will in accordance with its policy decide against him, unless there is something exceptional in his case. I think counsel for the applicants would admit that, if the policy has been adopted for reasons which the tribunal may legitimately entertain, no objection could be taken to such a course. On the other hand there are cases where a tribunal has passed a rule, or come to a determination not to hear any application of a particular character by whomsoever made. There is a wide distinction to be drawn between these two classes."

> *R. v. London County Council, ex p. Corrie.*[76] The county council made by-laws prohibiting the selling of an article in the parks under its control except with the consent of the council. The council later resolved that no new permission should be granted and that the existing permissions should be withdrawn. *Held*, the by-law conferred a discretion on the council. In passing the general resolution to grant no permissions it had failed to exercise its

---

[71] See §§ 10–25, 10–26.
[72] See *ibid*.
[73] See §§ 10–37, 10–40, 10–45.
[74] See §§ 10–25, 10–35.
[75] [1919] 1 K.B. 176, at p. 184.
[76] [1918] 1 K.B. 68.

discretion at all. Mandamus accordingly lay to make the council hear an application and decide on its merits.[77]

In most cases which have arisen the issue has not been as clear-cut. There **10–20** are several areas of uncertainty. First, does an authority comply with the *Kynoch* principle if it *considers* all applications made to it, even though the operation of the policy will mean that each application will fail? In *British Oxygen Co. Ltd v. Minister of Technology*,[78] Lord Reid cited the passage from the judgment of Bankes L.J. in *R. v. Port of London Authority, ex p. Kynoch Ltd, supra*, and continued[79]:

> "I see nothing wrong with that. But the circumstances in which discretions are exercised vary enormously and that passage cannot be applied literally in every case. The general rule is that anyone who has to exercise a statutory discretion must not 'shut his ears to an application' (to adapt from Bankes L.J. on p. 183). I do not think there is any great difference between a policy and a rule. There may be cases where an officer or authority ought to listen to a substantial argument reasonably presented urging a change of policy. What the authority must not do is to refuse to listen at all. But a Ministry or large authority may have had to deal already with a multitude of similar applications and then they will almost certainly have evolved a policy so precise that it could well be called a rule. There can be no objection to that, provided the authority is always willing to listen to anyone with something new to say—of course I do not mean to say that there need be an oral hearing."

However, it may not be sufficient for an authority to listen to all that an **10–21** applicant has to say, if in fact it is not prepared to make any exception to its general policy.

> *Sagnata Investments Ltd v. Norwich Corporation.*[80] The corporation by a majority of 41 to 1 took a policy decision not to grant permits for amusements with prizes for any amusement arcade in Norwich. The plaintiffs applied for a permit. The committee to which the power to determine applications had been delegated afforded the plaintiffs a full hearing, but rejected the application. On appeal to quarter sessions, the recorder held that the committee had so fettered its discretion following the council's policy decision that no application could succeed, and that the committee had failed to exercise its discretion at all. The case ultimately came to the Court of Appeal, where Lord Denning M.R. (dissenting) held that the recorder had erred in law on these points, given that the committee had considered the application. However, the recorder's view was endorsed by Phillimore L.J.[81]: "[According to the recorder], the council had *not* exercised any form of discretion, they had simply dismissed this application after going through the necessary motions without regard to its individual merits or demerits. I take this to be a finding of fact with which this court is in no position to interfere. Incidentally, I cannot see that the recorder could avoid this

---

[77] See also *R. v. County Council of West Riding of Yorkshire* [1896] 2 Q.B. 386; *R. v. Flintshire County Council Licensing Stage Plays Committee, ex p. Barrett* [1957] 1 Q.B. 350; *Docherty v. South Tyneside Borough, The Times*, July 3, 1982; *R. v. Secretary of State for the Environment, ex p. Brent London Borough Council* [1982] Q.B. 593; *R. v. Hampshire Education Authority, ex p. J.* (1985) 84 L.G.R. 547; *R. v. Canterbury City Council, ex p. Gillespié* (1986) 19 H.L.R. 7; *R. v. Inner London Education Authority, ex p. F, The Times*, June 16, 1988; *R. v. Harrow London Borough Council, ex p. Carter* (1992) 91 L.G.R. 46.
[78] [1971] A.C. 610.
[79] At p. 625.
[80] [1971] 2 Q.B. 614.
[81] At p. 630.

decision. ... " Edmund Davies L.J. agreed with the recorder's view that it was "entirely proper" for the authority to adopt a general policy of refusing such application "provided that no inflexible, invarying attitude was adopted and that the local authority was prepared to depart from it where the justice of a particular case so required."[82]

10–22 Secondly, the legality of reliance on a policy *may* depend on the number of applications to be processed. A court may be sympathetic to the adoption of fairly rigid guidelines where large numbers of applications are involved: see Lord Reid in the *British Oxygen* case (*supra*). Indeed, Viscount Dilhorne in the same case felt "some doubt whether the words used by Bankes L.J. ... are really applicable to a case of this kind. It seems somewhat pointless and a waste of time that the Board should have to consider applications which are bound as a result of its policy decision to fail. Representations could of course be made that the policy should be changed."[83] This case concerned the discretion of the Board of Trade (subsequently the Ministry of Technology) to award investment grants in respect of new plant. They had a rule of practice not to make grants in respect of items which cost individually less than £25. This was held to be a lawful ground for rejecting an application, and as they had not declined to consider the application the plaintiffs had no cause for complaint. Where the case load is of more manageable proportions, the exercise of discretion on a more individualised basis may be called for.

10–23 Thirdly, there is some authority for the proposition that reliance on a predetermined policy must not preclude the consideration of "all the issues which are relevant to each individual case as it comes up for decision".[84]

It is to be noted in this connection that Parliament may expressly authorise the adoption of inflexible policies of the kind not permitted by the common law. For example, the Lotteries and Amusements Act 1976 enables a local authority to pass a resolution that it will not grant, or will neither grant nor renew, any permits for the commercial provision of amusements with prizes in respect of premises of a class specified in the resolution.[85]

Error of law in construing the scope of a discretion

10–24 A public authority may be held to have fettered its discretion by making an error of law in construing the statute that confers the power in question.

> *R. v. St Pancras Vestry.*[86] The vestry had a discretionary power to grant pensions to its officers at amounts up to two-thirds of the final salary. It erroneously thought it had no discretion over the amount and so refused a pension to an officer thought not to deserve the full amount. The officer obtained mandamus requiring the vestry to reconsider his claim.
>
> *R. v. Secretary of State for the Environment, ex p. Dudley Metropolitan*

[82] p. 632.
[83] [1971] A.C. 610 at p. 631.
[84] *Per* Cooke J. in *Stringer v. Minister of Housing and Local Government* [1970] 1 W.L.R. 1281 at p. 1298, and see *Lavender & Son Ltd v. Minister of Housing and Local Government* [1970] 1 W.L.R. 1231; *Att.-Gen., ex rel. Tilley v. Wandsworth Borough Council* (1980) 78 L.G.R. 677; affirmed [1981] 1 W.L.R. 854.
[85] Sched. 3, para. 2: see *R. v. Herrod, ex p. Leeds City Council* [1978] A.C. 403.
[86] (1890) 24 Q.B.D. 371.

Borough Council.[87] Section 11(1) of the Radioactive Substances Act 1960 provides that where the minister (*inter alia*) attaches any conditions to an authorisation for the disposal of radioactive waste, he "shall afford to the person directly concerned, and may afford to such local authorities ... as he may consider appropriate an opportunity to appear before, and be heard by, a person appointed for the purpose . . . ." The minister construed this provision as requiring him to consider whether to afford a hearing to a local authority only where the person directly concerned (the applicant for authorisation) requested a hearing. The Divisional Court *held* that this was a misconstruction: the minister had a discretion to afford the local authority a hearing even where the applicant did not request one. He might well have a policy that he would not exercise this discretion save in exceptional or defined circumstances, but on the facts here, he had fettered his discretion.

C. ABUSE OF DISCRETION

Discretionary powers must not be abused in such a way that *express* or **10–25** *implied* limits in the relevant statute are exceeded. The leading statement of the relevant principles was made by Lord Greene M.R. in the following case:

Associated Provincial Picture Houses Ltd v. Wednesbury Corporation.[88] The corporation granted the plaintiffs a licence to give cinema performances on a Sunday on condition that no children under the age of 15 should be admitted. The plaintiffs sought a declaration that the condition was *ultra vires. Held,* the condition was valid. *Per* Lord Greene M.R.[89]: "It is not to be assumed prima facie that responsible bodies like the local authority in this case will exceed their powers; but the court, whenever it is alleged that the local authority have contravened the law, must not substitute itself for that authority. ... When an executive discretion is entrusted by Parliament to a body such as the local authority in this case, what appears to be an exercise of that discretion can only be challenged in the courts in a strictly limited class of case. ... It must always be remembered that the court is not a court of appeal. When discretion of this kind is granted the law recognises certain principles upon which that discretion must be exercised, but within the four corners of those principles the discretion, in my opinion, is an absolute one and cannot be questioned in any court of law. What then are those principles? ... The exercise of such a discretion must be a real exercise of the discretion. If, in the statute conferring the discretion, there is to be found expressly or by implication matters which the authority exercising the discretion ought to have regard to, then in exercising the discretion it must have regard to those matters. Conversely, if the nature of the subject-matter and the general interpretation of the Act make it clear that certain matters would not be germane to the matter in question, the authority must disregard those irrelevant collateral matters. ...

It is true the discretion must be exercised reasonably. Now what does that mean? Lawyers familiar with the phraseology commonly used in relation to exercise of statutory discretions often use the word 'unreasonable' in a rather comprehensive sense. It has frequently been used and is frequently used as a general description of the things that must not be done. For instance, a person entrusted with a discretion must, so to speak, direct himself properly in law. He must call his own attention to the matters which he is bound to consider. He must exclude from his consideration matters which are irrelevant to what he has to consider. If he does not obey those rules, he may truly be said, and often is

---

[87] *The Times*, June 14, 1989, [1989] C.O.D. 540.
[88] [1948] 1 K.B. 223.
[89] At pp. 228, 229, 230.

said, to be acting 'unreasonably'. Similarly, there may be something so absurd that no sensible person could ever dream that it lay within the powers of the authority. Warrington L.J. in *Short v. Poole Corporation*[90] gave the example of the red-haired teacher, dismissed because she had red hair. That is unreasonable in one sense. In another sense it is taking into consideration extraneous matters. It is so unreasonable that it might almost be described as being done in bad faith; and in fact, all these things run into one another. . . . It is clear that the local authority are entrusted by Parliament with the decision on a matter which the knowledge and experience of that authority can best be trusted to deal with. The subject-matter with which the condition deals is one relevant for its consideration. They have considered it and come to a decision upon it. It is true to say that, if a decision on a competent matter is so unreasonable that no reasonable authority could ever have come to it, then the courts can interfere. That, I think, is quite right; but to prove a case of that kind would require something overwhelming, and, in this case, the facts do not come anywhere near anything of that kind."

10–26   The following points may be noted: First, the concept of abuse of discretion, as explained by Lord Greene M.R. in the *Wednesbury* case, covers situations where powers have been used for an improper purpose or "contrary to the object of the statute";[91] where irrelevant considerations have been taken into account or relevant considerations ignored; or where decisions are so unreasonable that no reasonable authority could have so decided. More recently, the courts have begun to consider the circumstances in which decisions that are unfair, or disproportionate to the object to be achieved may be held to be an abuse of discretion.[92] These are not wholly discrete categories. The focus for argument in a given case depends very much on the state of the evidence available. For example, if it is not clear what is the decision-maker's purpose, or what considerations have been taken into account, attention has to centre on the quality of the decision itself; here, the task of establishing that there has been an abuse of discretion is particularly onerous.

Secondly, the courts frequently affirm that they can only intervene where decisions are clearly unlawful. The views of the elected representatives of the people are entitled to considerable respect, both where it is alleged that an act of a local authority is *ultra vires*,[93] and where an appeal lies on the merits against a local authority's decision.[94]

Thirdly, the courts are no longer deterred by the enactment of powers in subjective form from exercising the usual measure of control in relation to discretionary powers. For example, powers to take action if *it appears* or if *the authority is satisfied* that it is *necessary* or *expedient* were interpreted literally in cases decided in wartime, or shortly thereafter.[95] The courts

[90] [1926] Ch. 66 at pp. 90, 91.
[91] *Padfield v. Minister of Agriculture, Fisheries and Food* [1968] A.C. 997.
[92] See § 10–27.
[93] Lord Russell of Killowen C.J. in *Kruse v. Johnson* [1898] 2 Q.B. 91 at p. 99.
[94] *Sagnata Investments Ltd v. Norwich Corporation* [1971] 2 Q.B 614 at pp. 636–637 (Edmund Davies L.J.) and p. 640 (Phillimore L.J.); *cf. R. v. Hillingdon London Borough Council, ex p. Puhlhofer* [1986] A.C. 484, 518 (Lord Brightman).
[95] See, *e.g. Point of Ayr Collieries Ltd v. Lloyd George* [1943] 2 All E.R. 546; *Carltona Ltd v. Commissioners of Works* [1943] 2 All E.R. 560; *Robinson v. Minister of Town and Country Planning* [1947] K.B. 702.

would defer to an authority's assertion that it was so "satisfied" or that it so "appeared", provided that they had acted in good faith. However, the courts have been unwilling to be as deferential in relation to the exercise of other statutory powers in peacetime.[96]

Fourthly, all the discretionary decision-making of local authorities is potentially reviewable in accordance with the *Wednesbury* principles, including decisions closely analogous to those taken by private citizens. Examples include the decision of a local authority as landlord to serve notice to quit on a council tenant,[97] as proprietor of a private as distinct from a statutory market,[98] or as owner of land.[99]

Fifthly, it has been suggested that where items of account of expenditure of local authorities are challenged, a failure to take into account relevant matters or the taking into account of irrelevant matters does not amount to illegality in itself; it is merely evidence that the authority may have acted *ultra vires* or contrary to law. Attention must be directed to the quality of the decision, and to establish illegality it must be shown that the decision was not really made in exercise of the authority's powers but for some ulterior purpose, or that no reasonable authority could have reached such a decision.[1]

Sixthly, where a challenge is based on "unreasonableness" in the *Wednesbury* sense (now commonly termed "irrationality": see para. 10–02) it has been emphasised in recent cases that it is necessary to show that there has been "perversity", "absurdity" or that the decision-maker "must have taken leave of his senses".[2] However, in *R. v. Devon County Council, ex p. G.*[3] Lord Donaldson M.R.[4] expressed a preference for the term "*Wednesbury* unreasonable":

> "I eschew the synonym of 'irrational', because, although it is attractive as being shorter than 'Wednesbury unreasonable' and has the imprimatur of Lord Diplock in *Council of Civil Service Unions v. Minister for the Civil Service*,[5] it is widely misunderstood by politicians, both local and national, and even more by their constituents, as casting doubt on the mental capacity of the decision-maker, a matter which in practice is seldom, if ever, in issue and certainly is not in this case."

[96] See *Commissioners of Customs and Excise v. Cure and Deeley Ltd* [1962] 1 Q.B. 340; *Secretary of State for Education and Science v. Tameside Metropolitan Borough Council* [1977] A.C. 1014 at pp. 1024–1025 (Lord Denning M.R.), 1030–1031 (Scarman L.J.), 1047 (Lord Wilberforce).

[97] *Cannock Chase District Council v. Kelly* [1978] 1 W.L.R. 1 (where the tenant's challenge failed on the merits).

[98] *R. v. Basildon District Council, ex p. Brown* (1981) 79 L.G.R. 655.

[99] cf. *R. v. Wear Valley District Council, ex p. Binks* [1985] 2 All E.R. 699; cf. *West Glamorgan County Council v. Rafferty* [1987] 1 W.L.R. 457, distinguished in *R. v. Barnet London Borough Council, ex p. Grumbridge* (1992) 24 H.L.R. 433; *R. v. Somerset County Council, ex p. Fewings* [1995] 1 W.L.R. 1037 (§ 10–34).

[1] *Per* Ormrod L.J. in *Pickwell v. Camden London Borough Council* [1983] Q.B. 962: see § 13–24.

[2] See *R. v. Secretary of State for the Environment, ex p. Nottinghamshire County Council* [1986] A.C. 240, 247, *per* Lord Scarman; *R. v. Hillingdon London Borough Council, ex p. Puhlhofer* [1986] A.C. 484, 518, *per* Lord Brightman.

[3] [1989] A.C. 573.

[4] At p. 577.

[5] [1985] A.C. 374.

Seventhly, in recent cases, the courts have recognised that there may be an abuse of discretion where an authority fails to take any or sufficient account of undertakings it has previously given, or criteria it has announced indicating how a discretionary power is to be exercised.[6] The abuse of discretion may take the form of failure to take account of a relevant consideration or *Wednesbury* unreasonableness. (A previous undertaking may also give rise to a legitimate expectation of being given a hearing.)[7]

10–27   In each of the following cases it was alleged that there had been a wrongful use of a discretionary power. They illustrate challenges based on purposes,[8] relevant and irrelevant considerations[9] and unreasonableness,[10] and also the relationship between abuse of discretion issues and issues of illegality.[11] A recurrent theme is that the use of powers to express disapproval of the political views of others is likely to be unlawful.[12] Of particular significance in the more recent judicial review case law have been attempts by the courts to identify with greater precision the principles by reference to which decisions may be held to be unreasonable.[13] These principles are in the course of development and have not as yet had much impact on the case law in the field of local government; they are, nevertheless, worthy of note. Thus, it has been suggested that decisions may be struck down on the ground of uncertainty,[14]

---

[6] See § 10–18.

[7] See §§ 10–37, 10–40, 10–45.

[8] See *Westminster Corporation v. London and North Western Railway Co.* [1905] A.C. 426 (*infra*); *Westminster Bank v. Beverley Borough Council* [1971] A.C. 508 (*infra*); *R. v. Liverpool City Council, ex p. Secretary of State for Employment* [1989] C.O.D. 404 (§ 10–31); *R. v. London Borough of Lewisham, ex p. Shell UK Ltd* [1988] 1 All E.R. 938 (§ 10–32). The *Shell* case offers guidance on the approach to be adopted when purposes are mixed.

[9] See cases on the "fiduciary duty" of local authorities: *Roberts v. Hopwood* [1925] A.C. 578, §§ 13–22, *et seq.*; *Bromley London Borough Council v. Greater London Council* [1983] 1 A.C. 768 (§ 10–28); and, on the extent to which councillors may take account of moral or ethical considerations, *R. v. Somerset County Council, ex p. Fewings* [1995] 1 W.L.R. 1037 (§ 10–34). See also § 10–26 (the fifth and seventh points) and § 10–35.

[10] *R. v. Barnet London Borough Council, ex p. Johnson* (1990) 89 L.G.R. 581 (§ 10–33); Lord Brandon in *Bromley London Borough Council v. Greater London Council* [1983] 1 A.C. 768, 853 (§ 10–28). For other examples, see *R. v. London Borough of Tower Hamlets, ex p. Ali* [1993] C.O.D. 314; *R. v. Hammersmith and Fulham London Borough Council, The Independent*, September 7, 1993 (uncertain licence condition); *R. v. Newham London Borough Council, ex p. Laronde, The Times*, March 11, 1994. See also § 10–26 (the sixth point).

[11] See the "fares" cases: *Bromley London Borough Council v. Greater London Council* [1983] 1 A.C. 768 (§ 10–28); *R. v. Merseyside County Council, ex p. Great Universal Stores Ltd* (1982) 80 L.G.R. 639 (§ 10–29); *R. v. London Transport Executive, ex p. Greater London Council* [1983] Q.B. 484 (§ 10–30).

[12] See the *Liverpool, Shell* and *Wheeler* cases (§§ 10–31, 10–32).

[13] See generally, de Smith, Woolf and Jowell, *Judicial Review of Administrative Action* (5th edn., 1995), Chap. 13.

[14] See *R. v. Barnet London Borough Council, ex p. Johnson* (1990) 89 L.G.R. 58 (§ 10–33); *cf.* challenges to by-laws on this ground: § 6–08.

or of unfair interference with a substantive legitimate expectation,[15] or where "manifestly excessive or manifestly inadequate weight has been accorded to a relevant consideration.[16] It has also been stated that

> "The court may not interfere with the exercise of an administrative discretion on substantive grounds save where the court is satisfied that the decision is unreasonable in the sense that it is beyond the range of responses open to a reasonable decision-maker. But in judging whether the decision-maker has exceeded this margin of appreciation the human rights context is important. The more substantial the interference with human rights, the more the court will require by way of justification before it is satisfied that the decision is reasonable in the sense outlined above."[17]

Conversely,

> "the greater the policy content of a decision, and the more remote the subject matter of a decision from ordinary judicial experience, the more hesitant the court must necessarily be in holding a decision to be irrational. That is good law and, like most good law, common sense. Where decisions of a policy-laden, esoteric or security-based nature are in issue even greater caution than normal must be shown in applying the test...."[18]

In either case the *test* applied is the same, being "sufficiently flexible to cover all situations",[19] but the manner of its application varies.[20] Notwithstanding this, it remains the case that the fact that a decision-maker has failed to take account of obligations under the European Convention on Human Rights is not of itself a ground for impugning the decision.[21] Challenge for lack of proportionality, while available in respect of decisions subject to directly effective Community law, is not recognised as an independent ground of challenge elsewhere in English law,[22] although its possible application to decisions below the governmental level has not been ruled out.[23]

---

[15] *R. v. Secretary of State for the Home Department, ex p. Khan* [1984] 1 W.L.R. 1337; Sedley J. in *R. v. Ministry of Agriculture, Fisheries and Food, ex p. Hambles Fisheries (Offshore) Ltd* [1995] 2 All E.R. 714; *cf.* Simon Brown L.J. in *R. v. Devon County Council, ex p. Baker* [1995] 1 All E.R. 73, 88–89; however, it has also been argued that a legitimate expectation can only properly give rise to a right to a hearing: Laws J. in *R. v. Secretary of State for Transport, ex p. Richmond-upon-Thames London Borough Council* [1994] 1 W.L.R. 74. *Cf.* below, § 10–38 and see de Smith, Woolf and Jowell, *op. cit.* pp. 563–576.

[16] de Smith, Woolf and Jowell, pp. 557–559, citing, *inter alia, West Glamorgan County Council v. Rafferty* [1987] 1 W.L.R. 457.

[17] Submission of David Pannick Q.C. approved by the Court of Appeal in *R. v. Ministry of Defence, ex p. Smith* [1996] 2 W.L.R. 305, 336, 342, 346, based on the decisions of the House of Lords in *R. v. Secretary of State for the Home Department, ex p. Bugdaycay* [1987] A.C. 514 and *R. v. Secretary of State for the Home Department, ex p. Brind* [1991] 1 A.C. 696. In *ex p. Smith,* the Court of Appeal rejected arguments that the Ministry's policy of discharging homosexuals from the armed forces was irrational.

[18] Sir Thomas Bingham M.R. in *ex p. Smith, supra,* at pp. 337–338. See de Smith, Woolf and Jowell, *op. cit.* pp. 586–593.

[19] *ibid.*

[20] In the Divisional Court, in *ex p. Smith,* Simon Brown L.J. explained this by saying that where fundamental human rights was at stake, there would be a "more intensive review process and a greater readiness to intervene than would ordinarily characterise a judicial review challenge" [1996] 2 W.L.R. 305, 324.

[21] *Per* Sir Thomas Bingham M.R. in *ex p. Smith* [1996] 2 W.L.R. 305, 340; *ex p. Brind, supra; R. v. Secretary of State for the Environment, ex p. NALGO* (1992) 5 Admin.L.R. 785, 797–798.

[22] *ex p. Brind, supra; ex p. NALGO, supra;* de Smith, Woolf and Jowell, *op. cit.,* pp. 593–606.

[23] Neill L.J. in *ex p. NALGO, supra.*

The leading cases include the following:

Westminster Corporation v. London and North-Western Railway Co.[24] The corporation had power to construct public lavatories underground but no power to construct a subway as such. It constructed lavatories under Parliament Street leading off an underground passage with entrances on each side of the street. There had been some reference in correspondence to the need for a subway at this point. The chairman of the works committee testified that "the primary object of the committee was to provide these conveniences." *Held*, the works were *intra vires. Per* Lord Macnaghten[25]: "In order to make out a case of bad faith it must be shewn that the corporation constructed this subway as a means of crossing the street under colour and pretence of providing public conveniences which were not really wanted at that particular place." On the evidence, the "primary object" was the construction of the conveniences.

Westminster Bank v. Beverley Borough Council.[26] The council refused planning permission for the extension of bank premises on the ground that "it might prejudice the future widening" of the street. Compensation was not payable. The council might have achieved the same result by prescribing an improvement line under the Highways Act 1959, but compensation would then have been payable. *Held*, the council was entitled to choose which of the powers to exercise. *Per* Lord Reid[27]:

"Parliament has chosen to set up two different ways of preventing development which would interfere with schemes for street widening. It must have been aware that one involved in paying compensation but the other did not. Nevertheless it expressed no preference, and imposed no limit on the use of either. No doubt there might be special circumstances which make it unreasonable or an abuse of power to use one of these methods but here there were none. Even if the appellants' view of the facts is right, the authority had to choose whether to leave the appellants without compensation or to impose a burden on its ratepayers. One may think that it would be most equitable that the burden should be shared. But the Minister of Transport had made it clear in a circular sent to local authorities in 1954 that there would be no grant if a local authority proceeded in such a way that compensation would be payable, and there is nothing to indicate any disapproval of this policy by Parliament and nothing in any of the legislation to indicate that Parliament disapproved by depriving the subject of compensation. I cannot in these circumstances find any abuse of power in the local authority deciding that the appellants and not its ratepayers should bear the burden."

10–28   *Bromley London Borough Council v. Greater London Council.*[28] Section 1 of the Transport (London) Act 1969 imposed on the GLC the duty to develop policies and encourage measures which promote "the provision of integrated, efficient and economic transport facilities and services for Greater London". Those policies were to be implemented by the London Transport Executive. Section 5(1) required the LTE to have due regard to "efficiency, economy and safety of operation". Section 7(3)(b) provided that if at the end of an accounting period there was a deficit in the LTE's revenue account, the LTE was required as far as practicable, to make up that deficit in the next accounting period. Under section 7(6) the GLC could take action to enable the LTE to comply with

---

[24] [1905] A.C. 426.
[25] At p. 132.
[26] [1971] A.C. 508. See also *Hoveringham Gravels Ltd v. Secretary of State for the Environment* [1975] Q.B. 754; *R. v. London Borough of Lewisham, ex p. Shell U.K. Ltd* [1988] 1 All E.R. 938; *R. v. Exeter City Council, ex p. J. L. Thomas & Co. Ltd* (1989) 58 P. & C.R. 397.
[27] At p. 530.
[28] [1983] 1 A.C. 768.

its duty under section 7(3)(b). In July 1981, the GLC resolved to implement one of the election manifesto commitments of the controlling Labour group to cut fares on London Transport buses and tubes by an average of 25 per cent. A supplementary precept was issued to cover the deficit that the LTE would incur as a result. The money would be paid by the GLC to the LTE in the exercise of the former's power to make grants to the LTE "for any purpose" (1969 Act, s.3(1)). The GLC was aware that its fare reduction policy would result in the loss of approximately £50m of the rate support grant from the government. Bromley Council, one of the authorities to which the precept had been directed, sought certiorari to quash the supplementary rate on the grounds it was (1) *ultra vires* and (2) an invalid exercise of discretion. Lord Diplock and Lord Scarman regarded the separate arguments based on *ultra vires* and abuse of discretion as two ways of making the same point.[29] Lord Wilberforce and Lord Keith dealt with the case from the *ultra vires* standpoint. Lord Brandon dealt with both arguments.

The House of Lords held that certiorari should be granted, on a variety of grounds.

(a) The LTE was required to run its transport undertaking on "ordinary business principles". This requirement was derived from the common law (*Prescott v. Birmingham Corporation*[30]) and (*per* Lords Wilberforce, Keith and Scarman), from the requirement that the LTE have regard to "economy" (s.5(1)). This did not require the LTE to try to make a profit, but to ensure, so far as practicable, that outgoings were met by revenue.[31]

(b) Section 7(3) was to be interpreted as requiring the LTE to operate, so far as possible, on a break-even basis. Grants could be made by the GLC on the revenue account to make good unavoidable losses, actual or prospective, but not to achieve some object of social policy in total disregard of the LTE's obligations in (a) above and in section 7(3).[32]

(c) There was a breach of the fiduciary duty owed to the ratepayers. The GLC had failed to balance its duty to the ratepayers against the duty to transport users.[33] Lord Diplock said[34] that the fiduciary duty owed to the ratepayers from whom it obtains moneys "includes a duty not to expend those moneys thriftlessly but to deploy the full financial resources available to it to the best advantage".

(d) The decision to implement this policy in the knowledge that the original contemplated cost to the ratepayers would be nearly doubled by the loss of rate support grant was not a decision which the council, directing itself properly in law, could reasonably have made.[35]

(e) The majority group on the GLC had misdirected itself by regarding the GLC as irrevocably committed by the election manifesto to carry out the policy.[36]

---

[29] See pp. 820–821 and 836–837.
[30] [1955] Ch. 210.
[31] See Lord Wilberforce at pp. 815, 819; Lord Keith, *passim*; Lord Scarman at pp. 838–839, 841–842, 843; Lord Brandon at pp. 851, 852.
[32] See Lord Wilberforce at pp. 815–819; Lord Keith at pp. 833–834; Lord Scarman at pp. 844–846; Lord Diplock took a broader view of s.7(3): see pp. 825–828.
[33] See Lord Wilberforce at pp. 815, 819–820; Lord Diplock at pp. 829–830; Lord Scarman at pp. 838–839, 842.
[34] At p. 829.
[35] See Lord Brandon at p. 853; *cf.* Lord Wilberforce at p. 820 and Lord Diplock at p. 830, who regarded this factor as an element in establishing a breach of the fiduciary duty.
[36] See Lord Diplock at pp. 830–831 and Lord Brandon at p. 853; *cf.* Lord Wilberforce at p. 815. See also the analysis of the *ratio decidendi* of the *Bromley* case, derived from the speeches of Lords Wilberforce, Keith of Kinkel and Scarman, set out by Glidewell J. in *R. v. London Transport Executive, ex p. Greater London Council* [1983] Q.B. 484 at pp. 509–510.

10–29   *R. v. Merseyside County Council, ex p. Great Universal Stores Ltd.*[37] In this case, Woolf J. rejected a challenge to the validity of the council's policy of subsidising bus fares from the rates. The *Bromley* case, *supra*, was distinguished on a variety of grounds.

(a) The Council's powers were derived from the Transport Act 1968 and this was different in material respects from the Transport (London) Act 1969. Section 9(3) of the 1968 Act required the council to perform its functions "so ... as to secure or promote the provision of a properly integrated and efficient system of public passenger transport to meet the needs of that area with due regard to the town planning and traffic and parking policies of the councils of constituent areas and to economy and safety of operation." The equivalent provision in the 1969 Act required the GLC to promote the provision of "integrated, efficient *and economic* transport facilities". Moreover, under the 1968 Act the general duty of the executive was not made expressly subject to its financial duty. Woolf J. held that the council could require the executive to run a service which the executive considered would not be justified on ordinary business principles if the authority was prepared to undertake to meet the extra cost of running the service, although it was under a duty to balance the interests of the ratepayers against the advantage to the area of the proposed transport service.

(b) In the present case there was no question of the reduction in fares producing an automatic loss of rate support grant.

(c) The policies adopted by the council were in accord with the Merseyside Structure Plan.

(d) The members of the council here had not regarded themselves as committed to the implementation of their manifesto promise of a cheap fares policy. The proposal had been considered afresh on its merits after the elections.

(e) It could not be said that the new policy was manifestly inconsistent with the duty owed to the ratepayers.

In any event, relief would have been refused on the ground of delay, as the application for judicial review had been delayed pending the outcome of proceedings in the *Bromley* case. At the least the applicants should have warned the council of their intention to make the present application.

10–30   *R. v. London Transport Executive, ex p. Greater London Council.*[38] Following the decision in the *Bromley* case, fares were approximately doubled. Subsequently, the Divisional Court upheld the validity of a revised plan for London Transport fares, involving a reduction of about 25 per cent in the new fares and an increase in the deficit on the LTE's revenue account of about 17 per cent, to be made good by a grant from the GLC The GLC was entitled to make grants to the LTE to meet continuing losses, provided there was no breach of the principles laid down in the *Wednesbury* and *Prescott* cases. Kerr L.J. expressed broad agreement with the submission on behalf of the GLC that the references in *Bromley* and *Prescott* to the requirement to conduct a transport system on business principles were primarily intended to exclude philanthropic considerations and to emphasise the need for proper and cost-effective use of resources; they did not mean that fare revenue had to be maximised on ordinary business principles of profit and loss.[39] The court granted declarations to the effect that the revised plan was within the powers of the GLC and the LTE on the true construction of the Transport Act 1969. It did not decide whether there was any breach of the *Wednesbury* and *Prescott* principles: both parties were agreed that

[37] (1982) 80 L.G.R. 639.
[38] [1983] Q.B. 484.
[39] See pp. 497, 499.

there was no such breach and Kerr L.J. stated that "nothing has emerged in the evidence and argument presented to us which has led us to think the contrary",[40] but the court expressly left the point open.[41]

R. v. Liverpool City Council, ex p. Secretary of State for Employment.[42] The **10–31** Divisional Court granted certiorari to quash a resolution of the council rejecting all use and support for the government's Employment Training Scheme. The council had threatened to withdraw grant aid from any organisation participating in the scheme. This was held to constitute an abuse of power with the purpose of punishment or coercion of organisations that did not toe the line.

R. v. London Borough of Lewisham, ex p. Shell U.K. Ltd.[43] The council **10–32** passed a resolution to boycott Shell products. The Divisional Court found that it had two purposes: (1) a lawful purpose to promote good race relations in the borough in accordance with its duty under s.71 of the Race Relations Act 1976; and (2) an unlawful purpose to put pressure on Shell to withdraw from South Africa. The court held that where two reasons or purposes could not be disentangled, and one was bad, or, where they could be disentangled the bad reason demonstrably exerted the substantial influence, the court could interfere to quash the decision. Here, the two purposes were inextricably mixed up and the unlawful purpose had the effect of vitiating the decision as a whole.

R. v. Barnet London Borough Council, ex p. Johnson.[44] The committee of the **10–33** East Finchley Community Festival, which had been established for some years, applied to the council for permission to hold the festival in the council's pleasure ground, and for a grant. The council gave consent, and awarded a grant, subject to conditions, *inter alia*, that political groups were not to be allocated exhibition space; that the committee were not to allow the land to be used for or in connection with any political activity whatsoever; that no political party or group affiliated to a political party participate in the festival; that no political party nor organisation which sought to promote or oppose any political party be permitted to attend. The Court of Appeal *held* that these conditions were *ultra vires*. They had such a variety of possible meanings as to be in effect meaningless and to be unreasonable in the *Wednesbury* sense. Alternatively, if they had any real meaning they were clearly discriminatory and thus outside the statutory purpose.

R. v. Derbyshire County Council, ex p. The Times Supplements Ltd and **10–34** *others.*[45] Shortly after the *Sunday Times* published articles concerning the activities of the council, in respect of which the council leader, Councillor Bookbinder, instituted libel proceedings, the council resolved to remove all its advertising from newspapers owned by Mr Rupert Murdoch. This decision involved switching advertisements for teaching posts from *The Times Educational Supplement* to *The Guardian*, notwithstanding that the cost was greater and the likely readership among teachers much smaller. The Divisional Court granted certiorari to quash the decision. The court was satisfied, on the evidence, that there was no educational ground for the decision, and that the Labour group on the Council had been activated by bad faith or vindictiveness.

R. v. Somerset County Council, ex p. Fewings.[46] The council, by a majority, resolved to ban deer hunting with hounds on council-owned land at Over

---

[40] At p. 497.
[41] See the form of the declarations set out at p. 502.
[42] *The Times*, November 12, 1988, [1989] C.O.D. 404.
[43] [1988] 1 All E.R. 938. *Cf. Wheeler v. Leicester City Council* [1985] A.C. 1054, where the House of Lords held that the council could not lawfully bar a rugby club from using a public recreation ground in order to punish the club for failing to endorse in full the council's views in opposition to a tour by the Rugby Football Union to South Africa.
[44] (1990) 89 L.G.R. 581.
[45] (1991) 155 L.G.Rev. 123.
[46] [1995] 1 W.L.R. 1037.

Stowey Customs Common. The land had been acquired under section 120(1)(b) of the Local Government Act 1972, which provided that land could be acquired by a local authority for "the benefit, improvement or development" of its area. Laws J. quashed the ban.[47] The words of para. (b) were not wide enough to permit the council to take a decision about activities carried on on its land which was based on free-standing moral perceptions as opposed to an objective judgment about what would conduce to be better management of the estate. Here, it was plain that the decision was based solely on the view of the councillors in the majority that hunting was morally repulsive. An alternative ground on which the decision was open to challenge was that the council had not considered the effect of a ban on the future management of the deer herd. On appeal, the decision of Laws J. was upheld, but on narrower grounds. Sir Thomas Bingham M.R. stressed the point that the council's attention had not been drawn to the governing statutory provision, a paper circulated to councillors concluded that the council had to come to a decision "largely on the grounds of ethics, animal welfare and social considerations", which would be read as an invitation to councillors to give free rein to their personal views and reference to the council "as landowners" appeared to equiperate the positions of private and local authority landowners and reflected a failure to appreciate the overriding statutory constraint. Swinton Thomas L.J. agreed with the Master of the Rolls on this point; Simon Brown L.J. dissented, holding that the cruelty argument was relevant in determining what would benefit the area. On this last point, Swinton Thomas L.J. agreed with Laws J., but the Master of the Rolls refused to hold that it was necessarily irrelevant. All the members of the Court of Appeal rejected Laws J.'s alternative ground. Leave was given to appeal to the House of Lords.

10–35 The specific considerations that are relevant to an exercise of discretion may be set out in the statute. For example, section 604(1) of the Housing Act 1985 lists matters to which regard shall be had in determining whether a house is unfit for human habitation. Section 71 of the Race Relations Act 1976 requires local authorities to carry out their various functions with due regard to the need to eliminate unlawful racial discrimination and to promote equality of opportunity, and good relations, between persons of different racial groups.[48] Alternatively, the relevant considerations may be identified by the courts. There is, for example, much case law on the question of what are material planning considerations under the Planning Acts. The Court of Appeal in *Bristol District Council v. Clark*[49] identified a number of factors which were relevant to decisions to evict council tenants.

Where the exercise of a power is expressly limited to occasions where there are "reasonable grounds" for its exercise, the courts normally require the authority to show that objectively reasonable grounds do exist.[50]

---

[47] [1995] 1 All E.R. 513.

[48] See *Wheeler v. Leicester City Council* [1985] A.C. 1054 (*supra*) where it was held that s.71 did not justify the actions there held to be unlawful. *Cf. R. v. London Borough of Lewisham, ex p. Shell U.K. Ltd* [1988] 1 All E.R. 938; *R. v. Birmingham City Council, ex p. Equal Opportunities Commission* [1989] A.C. 1155 (on s.25 of the Sex Discrimination Act 1975); *R. v. Secretary of State for Education and Science, ex p. Malik* [1992] C.O.D. 31; *R. v. Birmingham City Council, ex p. Equal Opportunities Commission (No. 2)* (1992) 91 L.G.R. 14.

[49] [1975] 1 W.L.R. 1443. See also *Cannock Chase District Council v. Kelly* [1978] 1 W.L.R. 1 and *Sevenoaks District Council v. Emmott* (1979) 78 L.G.R. 346.

[50] See *Nakkuda Ali v. Jayaratne* [1951] A.C. 66, distinguishing *Liversidge v. Anderson* [1942] A.C. 206.

However, in the context of the power of a local authority to charge "reasonable" rents under housing legislation, the court will only interfere where a rent is unreasonable in the narrower sense expounded by Lord Greene in the *Wednesbury* case.[51] Thus an increase of rent from £7 to £18,000 (a device to evade certain aspects of the Housing Finance Act 1972) was held to be unreasonable and *ultra vires* in *Backhouse v. Lambeth London Borough Council.*[52]

D. NATURAL JUSTICE

Local authorities may be required to observe natural justice in the course of **10–36** their decision-making. Traditionally, the rules of "natural justice" have been regarded as comprising the rules *audi alteram partem* and *nemo judex in causa sua.* Respectively, these apply to require the maker of a decision to give prior notice to persons affected by it and an opportunity for those persons to make representations, and to disqualify him from acting if he has a direct pecuniary or proprietary interest, or might otherwise be biased. These rules originated in relation to courts of law, but have been applied to judicial and quasi-judicial decision-making by administrative authorities, albeit with the emphasis that administrators were not expected to adopt the procedures of courts of law.[53] In *Ridge v. Baldwin,*[54] the House of Lords held that a duty to act judicially may arise wherever a decision "affects the rights of subjects", and not solely in situations where a decision is made as between two contending parties. More recently, it has been suggested that a duty to observe natural justice, or at least an attenuated "duty to act fairly", may attach to all decision-making whether judicial or administrative.[55] Alternatively, it has been suggested that a duty to observe natural justice attaches to judicial or quasi-judicial decision-making, and a duty to act fairly to administrative decision-making.[56] This distinction is, however, difficult to draw satisfactorily, and it is submitted that the better view is that the courts should determine the appropriate content of the duty to observe natural justice or act fairly (however it is described) in the light of the particular circumstances of the case. In the case of decisions which are "purely" administrative, the content of the duty to act fairly may simply amount to an obligation to refrain from an *ultra vires* abuse of discretion.[57]

---

[51] See *Luby v. Newcastle-under-Lyme Corporation* [1964] 2 Q.B. 64; [1965] 1 Q.B. 214.

[52] (1972) 116 S.J. 802.

[53] *Local Government Board v. Arlidge* [1915] A.C. 120 (§ 10–38).

[54] [1964] A.C. 40 (§ 10–39).

[55] See *Re H.K., an Infant* [1967] 2 Q.B. 617; *R. v. Birmingham City Justice, ex p. Chris Foreign Foods (Wholesalers)* [1970] 1 W.L.R. 1428; *Breen v. Amalgamated Engineering Union* [1971] 2 Q.B. 175; *R. v. Liverpool Corporation, ex p. Liverpool Taxi Fleet Operators' Association* [1972] 2 Q.B. 299 (§ 10–40); *R. v. Commission for Racial Equality, ex p. Cottrell & Rothon* [1980] 1 W.L.R. 1580 at pp. 1586–1587; *Bushell v. Secretary of State for the Environment* [1981] A.C. 75; *R. v. Commission for Racial Equality, ex p. Hillingdon London Borough Council* [1982] A.C. 779 at p. 787.

[56] See Lord Pearson in *Pearlberg v. Varty* [1972] 1 W.L.R. 534 at p. 547.

[57] See *Breen v. Amalgamated Engineering Union* [1971] 2 Q.B. 175 at pp. 195, 200.

Audi alteram partem

10–37   The following are examples of situations where *procedural* standards have been imposed:

(a) Where there is a *lis inter partes*, as when objections to a compulsory purchase order made by a local authority are submitted to the minister,[58] or where a local authority has to determine whether a landlord or a tenant should receive compensation for a "well maintained" house[59];

(b) Where a decision affects a person's reputation[60] or livelihood[61]; including situations where a licence necessary for pursuit of a person's livelihood has been revoked or not renewed, or (possibly) not granted on an initial application[62];

(c) Where a decision is taken to dismiss the holder from an office or employment terminable only for cause[63];

(d) Where a decision infringes property rights.[64]

10–38   Even where a person's right or interests are not themselves sufficient to attract procedural protection, the conduct of the decision-maker may give rise to a "legitimate expectation" on the part of the person affected entitling him to an opportunity to make representations.[65] There may be, for

---

[58] *Errington v. Minister of Health* [1935] 1 K.B. 249.

[59] *Hoggard v. Worsborough Urban District Council* [1962] 2 Q.B. 93.

[60] *R. v. Wandsworth London Borough Council, ex p.* (1988) 87 L.G.R. 370; *R. v. Norfolk County Council Social Services Department, ex p. M.* [1989] Q.B. 619 (§ 10–43).

[61] *R. v. Liverpool Corporation, ex p. Liverpool Taxi Owners Association* [1972] 2 Q.B. 299 (*per* Lord Denning M.R. at pp. 307, 308) (§ 10–40); *R. v. Enfield London Borough Council, ex p. T. F. Unwin (Roydon)* (1989) 46 B.L.R. 1 (§ 10–44).

[62] See *McInnes v. Onslow-Fane* [1978] 1 W.L.R. 1520; *R. v. Barnsley Metropolitan Borough Council, ex p. Hook* [1976] 1 W.L.R. 1052 (revocation of market trader's licence for alleged misconduct); *R. v. Huntingdon District Council, ex p. Cowan* [1984] 1 W.L.R. 501 (refusal of entertainment licence) (§ 10–41).

[63] *Osgood v. Nelson* (1872) L.R. 5 H.L. 636 (clerk); *Cooper v. Wilson* [1937] 2 K.B. 309 (police officer); *Fullbrook v. Berkshire Magistrates' Courts Committee* (1971) 69 L.G.R. 75 (justices' clerk); *R. v. Kent Police Authority, ex p. Godden* [1971] 2 Q.B. 662 and *Ridge v. Baldwin* [1964] A.C. 40 (police officers); *Stevenson v. United Road Transport Union* [1977] I.C.R. 893 (union official); *R. v. British Broadcasting Corporation, ex p. Lavelle* [1983] 1 W.L.R. 23 (B.B.C. employee); *Chief Constable of the North Wales Police v. Evans* [1982] 1 W.L.R. 1155 (police officer). *Cf. R. v. Brent London Borough Council, ex p. Assegai* (1987) 151 L.G.Rev. 891, D.C. (school governor); *R. v. Portsmouth City Council, ex p. Gregory* (1990) 89 L.G.R. 478 (suspension of councillors from committees).

[64] *Cooper v. Wandsworth Board of Works* (1863) 14 C.B.(N.S.) 180 (board held liable in trespass where a house was demolished by the board's employees without prior notice to the owner).

[65] See *Schmidt v. Secretary of State for Home Affairs* [1969] 2 Ch. 149 (*per* Lord Denning M.R. obiter at p. 170); *Breen v. Amalgamated Engineering Union* [1971] 2 Q.B. 175 (*per* Lord Denning M.R. at p. 191); *O'Reilly v. Mackman* [1983] 2 A.C. 237 (*per* Lord Diplock at p. 275); *Att.-Gen. v. NgYuen Shiu* [1983] 2 A.C. 629. See de Smith, Woolf and Jowell, *Judicial Review of Administrative Action* (5th edn. 1995), pp. 417–430, noting that the principles underlying (a) the identification of interests worthy of procedural protection and (b) legitimate expectations based on the decision-maker's conduct are distinct, although both may arise on the same set of facts.

example, a statement, promise or established practice that some benefit will be conferred,[66] or that there will be a hearing.[67]

The leading cases include the following:

Local Government Board v. Arlidge.[68] A local authority had made a closing order in respect of an unfit house. The Housing, Town Planning, etc., Act 1909 (since repealed), under which the order was made, gave the owner a right of appeal to the Local Government Board. The owner's appeal to the Board was dismissed. He then applied to the court for a writ of certiorari for the purpose of quashing the order on the ground that the appeal had not been determined in the manner provided by law, for he had been refused permission to be heard orally by the officer who decided the case and had been refused permission to see the report made by the Board's inspector upon the public local inquiry. He did not succeed. Lord Shaw said[69]: "The words 'natural justice' occur in arguments and sometimes in judicial pronouncements in such cases. My Lords, when a central administrative board deals with an appeal from a local authority it must do its best to act justly, and to reach just ends by just means. If a statute prescribes the means it must employ them. If it is left without express guidance it must still act honestly and by honest means. In regard to these, certain ways and methods of judicial procedure may very likely be imitated: and lawyer-like methods may find especial favour from lawyers. But that the judiciary should presume to impose its own methods on administrative or executive officers is a usurpation."

Lord Parmoor said[70]: "The power of obtaining a writ of certiorari is not limited to judicial acts or orders in a strict sense, that is to say, acts or orders of a court of law sitting in a judicial capacity. It extends to the acts and orders of a competent authority which has power to impose a liability or to give a decision which determines the rights or property of the affected parties. Where, however, the question of the propriety of procedure is raised in a hearing before some tribunal other than a court of law there is no obligation to adopt the regular forms of legal procedure. It is sufficient that the case has been heard in a judicial spirit and in accordance with the principles of substantial justice."

---

[66] *e.g.* permission to stay in the country, or the grant of a licence: see *Schmidt v. Secretary of State for Home Affairs* [1969] 2 Ch. 149; *McInnes v. Onslow-Fane* [1978] 1 W.L.R. 1520; *R. v. Secretary of State for the Home Department, ex p. Khan (Asif Mahmood)* [1984] 1 W.L.R. 1337 (statement of conditions applicable to entry to UK of children adopted abroad); *Costain Homes Ltd v. Secretary of State for the Environment* (1988) 57 P. & C.R. 416 (indication of likely decision on a planning appeal); *R. v. Brent London Borough Council, ex p. MacDonagh* (1989) 21 H.L.R. 494 (promise that gypsies would not be evicted until alternative sites found) (§ 10–45); *R. v. Rochdale Metropolitan Borough Council, ex p. Schemet* (1992) 91 L.G.R. 425 (parents of children already receiving travel passes had legitimate expectation that that benefit would not be withdrawn without an opportunity to comment); *R. v. Devon County Council, ex p. Baker; R. v. Durham County Council, ex p. Curtis* [1995] 1 All E.R. 73 (resident of home for the elderly entitled to be consulted about closure of the home, although duty could be discharged by meetings with residents generally).

[67] *e.g. R. v. Liverpool Corporation, ex p. Liverpool Taxi Owners Association* (§ 10–40) (promise of consultation); *Att.-Gen. of Hong Kong v. Ng Yuen Shiu* [1983] 2 A.C. 629 (promise of hearing); *Council of Civil Service Unions v. Minister for the Civil Service* [1985] A.C. 374, 401, 408–409 (practice of consultation); *R. v. Brent London Borough Council, ex p. Gunning* (1985) 84 L.G.R. 168 (§ 10–42) (practice of consultation); *R. v. London Borough of Bexley, ex p. Barnehurst* [1992] C.O.D. 382 (intention to consult expressed in document not communicated to applicant, but subsequently discovered by applicant in a public document); *R. v. Birmingham City Council, ex p. Dredger* (1993) 91 L.G.R. 532 (practice of consulting market traders as to the level of rents).

[68] [1915] A.C. 120.

[69] At p. 138.

[70] At p. 140.

Lord Moulton said[71]: "It is said, truthfully, that on such an appeal the Local Government Board must act judicially, but this, in my opinion, only means that it must preserve a judicial temper and perform its duties conscientiously, with a proper feeling of responsibility, in view of the fact that its acts affect the property and rights of individuals."

10–39   *Ridge v. Baldwin.*[72] A Watch Committee had power under section 191(4) of the Municipal Corporations Act 1882 to dismiss any constable whom they thought negligent in or unfit for the discharge of his duty. R., the chief constable of Brighton, was acquitted on criminal charges of conspiracy, but his conduct was adversely criticised by the trial judge. R. was summarily dismissed by the committee without prior notice or an opportunity to make representations, and without compliance with regulations under the Police Act 1919, s.4(1), establishing disciplinary procedures. The committee subsequently heard representations from R.'s solicitor, but gave no particulars of the case against him. R. appealed to the Home Secretary under the Police (Appeals) Act 1927, without prejudice to any right to contend that the purported dismissal was bad in law. He subsequently sought a declaration that the dismissal was *ultra vires*, and damages. The Court of Appeal held that natural justice did not have to be observed as the committee's action was "administrative" or "executive". R.'s appeal to the House of Lords was allowed. *Held*, the dismissal was void for breach of natural justice, and for non-compliance with the regulations. A duty to act judicially was to be inferred from the nature of the power, and this duty had not been observed. The defect was cured neither by the second meeting of the committee, as it did not amount to a full rehearing with disclosure of the case against R., nor by the appeal to the Secretary of State, as the committee's decision was a nullity and R. so maintained during the appeal.

10–40   *R. v. Liverpool Corporation, ex p. Liverpool Taxi Owners' Association.*[73] The City Council had power under section 37 of the Town Police Clauses Act 1847 to license such number of hackney carriages as it thought fit. From 1948 onwards it limited the number to 300. In 1970 and 1971 the taxi cab operators' associations were assured by the town clerk that they would be consulted if any change in the numbers was contemplated. In 1971 a special sub-committee recommended increases for 1972 and 1973 and no restriction in numbers thereafter, and heard the applicants' case against the proposal. The chairman gave a public undertaking that the numbers would not be increased until proposed legislation in the form of a private Bill had come into force. This undertaking was confirmed orally both by the chairman and by letter from the town clerk. In November the sub-committee resolved on an increase for 1972. The committee, and later the council, confirmed the resolution. The applicants applied *ex parte* to the Divisional Court for leave to apply for orders of prohibition, mandamus and certiorari. Leave was refused without reasons being given. The Court of Appeal allowed the appeal and held that though the determination as to the number of taxi cab licences was a policy decision and the court could not interfere with such a policy decision, the court could and should intervene to ensure that the council acted fairly in deciding that policy after due regard to conflicting interests. In view of the past history, and in particular the undertaking publicly given, the applicants were justifiably aggrieved by the council's subsequent unfair conduct. Accordingly the court should order prohibition to go to prohibit action upon the resolutions or the granting of further licences without first hearing representations. Lord Denning M.R. said[74]: "... when the corporation consider applications for licences under the

[71] At p. 150.
[72] [1964] A.C. 40.
[73] [1972] 2 Q.B. 299. *Cf. R. v. Gravesham Borough Council, ex p. Gravesham Association of Licensed Hackney Carriage Owners, The Independent,* January 14, 1987.
[74] At pp. 307, 308.

Town Police Clauses Act 1847, they are under a duty to act fairly. This means that they should be ready to hear not only the particular applicant but also any other persons or bodies whose interests are affected. . . . It is perhaps putting it a little high to say they are exercising judicial functions. They may be said to be exercising an administrative function. But even so, in our modern approach, they must act fairly: and the court will see that they do so."

R. v. Huntingdon District Council, ex p. Cowan.[75] When dealing with an **10–41** application for an entertainment licence under Part I of the Local Government (Miscellaneous Provisions) Act 1982 a local authority must (1) inform the applicant of the substance of any objection or representation in the nature of an objection (not necessarily the whole of it, nor necessarily to say who has made it); and (2) give the applicant an opportunity to make representations in reply.

R. v. Brent London Borough Council, ex p. Gunning.[76] Hodgson J. *held* that **10–42** while there was no statutory duty placed upon local education authorities to consult parents of pupils before making proposals for the closure or amalgamation of schools, parents nevertheless had a legitimate expectation that they would be consulted. The interest of parents in the educational arrangements in the area in which they lived was self-evident, and was explicitly recognised in the legislation (*e.g.* section 6 of the Education Act 1980). The legislation placed clear duties on parents, backed by draconian criminal sanctions. Local authorities (including Brent) habitually consulted on these matters, and were exhorted to do so by the Secretary of State. On the facts here, the consultative document was wholly inadequate and misleading as to the cost of the proposals and the period allowed for consultation was unreasonably short. Furthermore, as the proposals ultimately adopted were materially different from those on which consultation had taken place, the parents of school children in the area should have been given a further opportunity to be consulted. The authority's decision to make the proposals was quashed.

Hodgson J. stated[77] that their legitimate expectation gave them the same right as if it had been specifically given by statute. In *R. v. Gwent County Council, ex p. Bryant*[78] his Lordship stated that he had gone too far in equating a legitimate expectation with a statutory right. In the former case, a defect in consultation could be rectified by the Secretary of State, in the latter, it could not.[79]

R. v. Wandsworth London Borough Council, ex p. P.[80] The Council removed **10–43** the applicant from its list of approved foster mothers following allegations of sex abuse made by a child in her care, and confirmed that decision two and a half years later. The decision was quashed on the ground that there had been a breach of natural justice, in that she had not been given sufficient information about the allegations in order to meet them. She was entitled to more than the bare allegations, although not to see the case notes or other documents held by the council. *Cf. R. v. Norfolk County Council Social Services Department, ex p. M,*[81] where Waite J. quashed (1) a decision of a case conference purporting to name the applicant as a child abuser; (2) entries on the council's child abuse register identifying him as a known or suspected child abuser, *inter alia* on the

[75] [1984] 1 W.L.R. 501. For other illustrations of the application of the duty to act fairly in licensing cases, see *R. v. Preston Borough Council and others, ex p. Quietlynn Ltd* (1984) 83 L.G.R. 308; *R. v. Bristol City Council, ex p. Pearce* (1984) 83 L.G.R. 711; *R. v. Wear Valley District Council, ex p. Binks* [1985] 2 All E.R. 699; *R. v. Durham City, ex p. Robinson, The Times,* January 31, 1992; *R. v. Torbay Borough Council, ex p. Cleasby* [1991] C.O.D. 142.
[76] (1985) 84 L.G.R. 168.
[77] At p. 187.
[78] *The Independent,* April 19, 1988.
[79] *R. v. Northampton County Council, ex p. Tebbutt* (Unreported, June 26, 1986) applied. See also *R. v. Haberdashers' Aske's Hatcham School Governors, ex p. Inner London Education Authority, The Times,* March 7, 1989.
[80] (1988) 87 L.G.R. 370.
[81] [1989] Q.B. 619.

ground of the council's unfairness in acting without prior notification or consultation, and without a hearing.

10–44   *R. v. Enfield London Borough Council, ex p. T. F. Unwin (Roydon) Ltd.*[82] The Divisional Court *held* that the council had acted unfairly in removing the company from its lists of approved building contractors without informing it of the nature of accusations that had been made against it, and giving it a chance to answer. (There was also a clear breach of section 20 of the Local Government Act 1988: see para. 10–08.) This was so notwithstanding that a police investigation was being made into the allegations against the company and the police had advised against disclosure of the details on the ground that that would be likely to prejudice the investigations. There was no evidence that the authority's interests would have suffered if the company had been allowed to continue working for it until the investigation was complete. No attempt had been made to interview any officer or employee of the company.

10–45   *R. v. Brent London Borough Council, ex p. MacDonagh.*[83] Gypsies occupying an unauthorised site were given a letter informing them that they would not be evicted until alternative sites had been found, but were subsequently evicted. Roch J. *held* that (1) the council's decision to evict them was *ultra vires* as it had failed to take the letter, and the consequences for the gypsies and the neighbouring authorities, into account; (2) that the letter gave rise to a legitimate and reasonable expectation that the council would not go back on its undertaking without giving reasons and a chance to make representations.

10–46   These cases may be compared with a number of cases where procedural standards have not been imposed on the ground that the decision in question has been "administrative." Local authorities are not obliged to give anybody a hearing before passing a resolution declaring an area to be a clearance area.[84] The Minister is not obliged at common law to act judicially in relation to the process of compulsory purchase before objections to an order are made.[85] In *Essex County Council v. Minister of Housing and Local Government,*[86] Plowman J. held that the Minister was not obliged to observe the *audi alteram partem* rule when exercising his discretion under section 14 of the Town and Country Planning Act 1962 (now sections 58–61 of the 1990 Act) to grant planning permission by means of a special development order. Accordingly, he was not obliged to consider representations by the county council against the proposed development of the third London airport at Stansted.

The principles of natural justice do not apply to legislative functions such as the making of a statutory instrument[87] or, presumably, a by-law. Similarly, a local authority need not give an opportunity for persons to be heard before making a decision which is universal in its application such as the fixing by the authority of the rates for the year or the scale upon which fees are to be charged.[88]

---

[82] (1989) 46 Build.L.R. 1.
[83] (1989) 21 H.L.R. 494.
[84] *Fredman v. Minister of Health* (1935) 154 L.T. 240; Housing Act 1985, s.289.
[85] *Frost v. Minister of Health* [1935] 1 K.B. 286; *Miller v. Minister of Health* [1946] K.B. 626; *Price v. Minister of Health* [1947] 1 All E.R. 47; *Summers v. Minister of Health* [1947] 1 All E.R. 184; *Johnson & Co. v. Minister of Health* [1947] 2 All E.R. 395. See also *Bushell v. Secretary of State for the Environment* [1981] A.C. 75.
[86] (1967) 66 L.G.R. 23.
[87] *Bates v. Lord Hailsham of St Marylebone* [1972] 1 W.L.R. 1373.
[88] *R. v. Greater London Council, ex p. The Rank Organisation, The Times,* February 19, 1982.

The content of the *audi alteram partem* principle varies according to the context.[89] The basic features are that the person affected by a decision should be given prior notice of what is proposed and an opportunity to make representations. For example, the basic requirements of a fair consultation process were described as follows by Hodgson J. in *R. v. Brent London Borough Council, ex p. Gunning*[90]:

> "First, that consultation must be at a time when proposals are still at a formative stage. Second, that the proposer must give sufficient reasons for any proposal to permit of intelligent consideration and response. Third, ... that adequate time must be given for consideration and response and, finally, fourth, that the product of consultation must be conscientiously taken into account in finalising any statutory proposals."

Those conducting preliminary investigations are under a duty to act fairly, and a person adversely affected should be told the case against him and be afforded a fair opportunity of answering it. However, the "investigating body is ... master of its own procedure. It need not hold a hearing. It can do everything in writing. It need not allow lawyers. It need not put every detail of the case against a man. Suffice it if the broad grounds are given. It need not name its informants. It can give the substance only".[91] In some situations, it will be sufficient for an authority to afford an opportunity to make written representations.[92] Where there is a hearing, cross-examination of witnesses need not be permitted,[93] and, if initially permitted, may be withdrawn.[94] An applicant cannot, however, complain of a breach of natural justice where this arises out of the default of his own advisers.[95]

In appropriate circumstances, fairness may require reasons to be given for a decision.[96] In *R. v. Higher Education Funding Council, ex p. Institute of*

---

[89] *Russell v. Duke of Norfolk* [1949] 1 All E.R. 109, *per* Tucker L.J. at p. 118.
[90] (1985) 84 L.G.R. 168, 189, adopting the submission of Stephen Sedley Q.C.; approved by Webster J. in *R. v. Sutton London Borough Council, ex p. Hamlet* (Unreported, March 26, 1986) and Woolf L.J. in *R. v. Northamptonshire County Council, ex p. Tebbutt* (Unreported, June 26, 1986); and the Court of Appeal in *R. v. Devon County Council, ex p. Baker* [1995] 1 All E.R. 73.
[91] *per* Lord Denning M.R. in *R. v. Race Relations Board, ex p. Selvarajan* [1975] 1 W.L.R. 1686, 1694; *cf. In re Pergamon Press Ltd* [1971] Ch. 388; *R. v. Monopolies and Mergers Commission, ex p. Elders IXL Ltd* [1987] 1 W.L.R. 1221; *R. v. Monopolies and Mergers Commission, ex p. Matthew Brown plc* [1987] 1 W.L.R. 1235; *R. v. Avon County Council, ex p. Crabtree, The Independent*, November 29, 1995.
[92] *Lloyd v. McMahon* [1987] A.C. 625, (see § 7–28); *R. v. Harrow London Borough Council, ex p. D.* [1990] Fam. 133; *R. v. North Yorkshire County Council, ex p. M. (No. 2)* [1989] 2 F.L.R. 79; *R. v. Harrow London Borough Council, ex p. Hobbs, The Times*, October 13, 1992.
[93] *R. v. Commission for Racial Equality, ex p. Cottrell & Rothon* [1980] 1 W.L.R. 1580; *cf. Bushell v. Secretary of State for the Environment* [1981] A.C. 75; *R. v. London Regional Passenger Committee, ex p. Brent London Borough Council, The Times*, May 23, 1995.
[94] *R. v. Haringey London Borough Leader's Investigative Panel, ex p. Edwards, The Times*, March 22, 1983.
[95] *R. v. Secretary of State for the Home Department, ex p. Al-Mehdawi* [1990] 1 A.C. 876, H.L.
[96] *R. v. Secretary of State for the Home Department, ex p. Doody* [1994] 1 A.C. 531, where the House of Lords held that it was unfair for a mandatory life sentence prisoner not to be given reasons, *inter alia*, for any departure by the Secretary of State from the judge's recommendation as to the penal element of the sentence.

Dental Surgery,[97] Sedley J. stated that in determining the requirements of fairness it was necessary to balance a series of factors for and against the giving of reasons; there was no single test. In *R. v. London Borough of Lambeth, ex p. Walters*,[98–99] Sir Louis Blom-Cooper Q.C., sitting as a deputy High Court judge, took a broader approach, holding that there is a general duty to give reasons whenever the statutorily-impregnated administrative process is infused with the concept of fair treatment to those potentially affected by administrative action. Accordingly, reasons had to be given for decisions under Part III of the Housing Act 1985 apart from those where an express duty to give reasons was prescribed. It remains to be seen which approach will prevail; it should be noted, however, that in *R. v. Secretary of State for the Home Department, ex p. Doody*,[1] Lord Mustill stated[2] that "the law does not at present recognise a general duty to give reasons for an administrative decision", and this point was reaffirmed by the Court of Appeal in *R. v. Kensington and Chelsea Royal London Borough Council, ex p. Grillo*[3] in holding (contrary to the view expressed by Sir Louis Blom-Cooper at first instance) that the housing authority did not have to give reasons for its finding that accommodation offered was suitable.

The courts are disinclined to intervene unless there is at least a risk that someone has been prejudiced. They may decline, in the exercise of their discretion, to grant a remedy[4] or simply hold that there has been no "breach of natural justice".[5]

A breach of natural justice may in some circumstances be cured by an appellate hearing at which natural justice has been observed, provided that, overall, there has been a fair result reached by fair methods.[6–7]

Nemo judex in causa sua

10–47   It is not clear whether this rule applies in all situations to which the *audi alteram partem* principle or the duty to act fairly now extends (see *supra*), or whether it is still relevant only to judicial or quasi-judicial decisions. In *Franklin v. Minister of Town and Country Planning*[8] the House of Lords held

---

[97] [1994] 1 W.L.R. 242. Here, fairness did not require the giving of reasons for a decision as to the rating of an institution's research as the matter was essentially one of academic judgment; moreover, the decision was not so aberrant as to call for an explanation.

[98–99] (1993) 26 H.L.R. 170.

[1] *supra.*

[2] p. 172.

[3] *The Times*, May 13, 1995.

[4] *Glynn v. Keele University* [1971] 1 W.L.R. 487; *Malloch v. Aberdeen Corporation* [1971] 1 W.L.R. 1578 at p. 1595 (Lord Wilberforce).

[5] *Lake District Planning Board v. Secretary of State for the Environment* [1975] J.P.L. 20; *George v. Secretary of State for the Environment* (1979) 38 P. & C.R. 609; *Cinnamond v. British Airport Authority* [1980] 1 W.L.R. 582, *per* Brandon L.J. at p. 593; *Swinbank v. Secretary of State for the Environment, ex p. Leicester City Council* (1987) 55 P. & C.R. 371, D.C. (but *cf. Annumunthodo v. Oilfield Workers' Trade Union* [1961] A.C. 945 at p. 956; *Kanda v. Government of Malaya* [1962] A.C. 322 at p. 337).

[6–7] *Calvin v. Carr* [1980] A.C. 574; *R. v. Oxfordshire Local Valuation Panel, ex p. Oxford City Council* (1981) 79 L.G.R. 432 at p. 446; *Lloyd v. McMahon* [1987] A.C. 625, C.A. and H.L.; *R. v. Governors of St Gregory's RC Aided High School, ex p. Roberts, The Times*, January 27, 1995.

[8] [1948] A.C. 87.

that the decision of the Minister to make an order designating Stevenage a new town under the New Towns Act 1946 was "purely administrative". The complaint that he had been biased was accordingly irrelevant. The only possible ground of challenge was that the Minister had not complied with his statutory duty to consider objections to the order, and the report of the local public inquiry. However, the *nemo judex* rule has been applied in a number of situations which are not strictly analogous to the decisions of a court of law.

> *R. v. London County Council, ex p. Akkersdyk.*[9] A committee decided by a majority to recommend to the Council that a music and dancing licence should not be renewed. Three members of the committee, who had voted with the majority, instructed counsel to oppose the renewal at the meeting of the Council. They attended the meeting, but did not vote. One of the three took an active part in the discussions. The Council refused renewal. The Divisional Court granted mandamus to compel the Council to hear and determine the application according to law, on the ground that the councillors had "acted both as accusers and judges at the same time" contrary to natural justice.

This decision may be compared with *Royal Aquarium and Summer and Winter Garden Society v. Parkinson,*[10] where the Court of Appeal held that a similar meeting of the Council was not "judicial" for the purpose of being protected by absolute privilege in the law of defamation.

> *R. v. Hendon Rural District Council, ex p. Chorley.*[11] The council approved an application under the Town Planning Act 1925 by the potential purchaser of a certain site, for permission to build on that site. This permission safeguarded the applicants' right to compensation under section 10 of the Act, in the event of their property being injuriously affected by the making of a proposed town planning scheme. One of the councillors who voted for the grant of permission was an estate agent acting for the site owner. *Held,* (1) the councillor "was biased, or had such an interest in the matter as to disqualify him from taking part or voting"[12]; and (2) since the decision of the council to grant permission conferred a legal right to compensation and affected the rights of subjects, it was sufficiently near to a judicial decision to be the subject of certiorari. The decision was accordingly quashed.

High Court judges have differed on the question whether the *nemo judex* principle applies in any form to the decision of a local authority to grant or refuse planning permission under the Town and Country Planning Act 1990.[13] In *R. v. Holderness Borough Council, ex p. James Robert Developments Ltd,*[14] the Court of Appeal seemed prepared to contemplate the application of the *nemo judex* principle to planning decisions, the majority (Simon Brown and Butler-Sloss L.JJ., Dillon L.J. dissenting) holding,

---

[9] [1892] 1 Q.B. 190.
[10] [1892] 1 Q.B. 431.
[11] [1933] 2 K.B. 696.
[12] *per* Lord Hewart C.J. at p. 702 and Avory J. at p. 703.
[13] In favour: Webster J. in *Steeples v. Derbyshire County Council* [1985] 1 W.L.R. 256. Against: Glidewell J. in *R. v. Sevenoaks District Council, ex p. W. J. Terry* [1985] 3 All E.R. 234 and Stocker J. in *R. v. St Edmundsbury Borough Council, ex p. Investors in Industry Commercial Properties Ltd* [1985] 1 W.L.R. 1168. *Cf. R. v. Hereford and Worcester County Council, ex p. Wellington Parish Council, The Times,* April 7, 1995.
[14] (1992) 66 P. & C.R. 46.

however, that it was not necessarily improper for a builder to sit on a local authority planning committee considering applications for detailed planning permission submitted by a rival builder. On the other hand, it has been held that a panel appointed by a council to consider and determine applications for sex establishment licences was not a judicial body so as to be subject to the rule against bias.[15] Following a full review of the authorities, Sedley J. in *R. v. Secretary of State for the Environment, ex p. Kirkstall Valley Campaign Ltd*[15a] held that the *nemo judex* principle is not limited to judicial or quasi-judicial bodies. His Lordship took account of the broad application of the *audi alteram partem* principle and the restatement of the test for bias in a narrow form by the House of Lords in *R. v. Gough.*[15b]

At common law, an adjudicator is disqualified if he has a direct personal or pecuniary interest in the subject-matter of the adjudication.[16] He must not act both as "prosecutor" and "judge".[17] Moreover, be will be disqualified if there is a "real danger" of bias.[18]

E. Error of Law on the Face of the Record

10–48 If a local authority, acting within its jurisdiction, reaches a decision which discloses *on the face of the record* an error in law, then certiorari will lie to bring the decision into the High Court to be quashed.

> *R. v. Northumberland Compensation Appeal Tribunal, ex p. Shaw.*[19] A decision of the tribunal was expressed in a "speaking order", *i.e.* one which contained the reasons which led the tribunal to its decision. These reasons disclosed that the tribunal had taken an erroneous view of the law. The tribunal admitted that its decision was wrong but argued that the court had no power to make an order of certiorari since the tribunal had not acted without jurisdiction. It was held that certiorari lay. Denning L.J. said[20]: "The answer to this argument, however (*i.e.* the contention of the tribunal), is that the Court of King's Bench has an inherent jurisdiction to control all inferior tribunals, not in an appellate capacity, but in a supervisory capacity. This control extends not only to seeing that the inferior tribunals keep within their jurisdiction, but also to seeing that they observe the law. The control is exercised by means of a power to quash any determination by the tribunal which, on the face of it, offends

---

[15] *R. v. Reading Borough Council, ex p. Quietlynn Ltd* (1987) 85 L.G.R. 387. Kennedy J. held that the panel's composition could only be impugned for bias where it was clear that when the panel came to consider applications that it could not exercise a proper discretion. It was not sufficient that a councillor who held, and had expressed, strong views as to whether in general such licences should be granted, or who was a member of a political group which had resolved that it was not in favour of sex establishments, was appointed to the panel.

[15a] [1996] 3 All E.R. 304.

[15b] n. 18, *infra*.

[16] *Dimes v. Grand Junction Canal Proprietors* (1852) 3 H.L.Cas. 759.

[17] *R. v. London County Council, ex p. Akkersdyk, supra*; *R. v. Barnsley Metropolitan Borough Council, ex p. Hook* [1976] 1 W.L.R. 1052.

[18] In *R. v. Gough* [1993] A.C. 646, the House of Lords held that in all cases of apparent bias, whether concerning justices, members of inferior tribunals, jurors or arbitrators, the applicable test was whether there was a "real danger" of bias; the House settled the uncertainty as to whether the proper test was "real likelihood" or "reasonable suspicion" by, in essence, preferring the former.

[19] [1952] 1 K.B. 338.

[20] At p. 346.

against the law. The King's Bench does not substitute its own views for those of the tribunal, as a Court of Appeal would do. It leaves it to the tribunal to hear the case again, and in a proper case may command it to do so. . . . Of recent years the scope of certiorari seems to have been somewhat forgotten. It has been supposed to be confined to the correction of excess of jurisdiction, and not to extend to the correction of errors of law; and several learned judges have said as much. But the Lord Chief Justice has, in the present case, restored certiorari to its rightful position and shown that it can be used to correct errors of law which appear on the face of the record, even though they do not go to jurisdiction."

Courts have jurisdiction under this ground of challenge only where a tribunal is seen from the record to have acted in error of law. Decisions published without reasons would be difficult to challenge in this way, but section 10 of the Tribunals and Inquiries Act 1992 provides that tribunals listed in Schedule 1 to the Act and any Minister notifying a decision taken after a statutory inquiry must furnish a statement of reasons if requested by a person primarily concerned and may only refuse on grounds of national security. Any such statement is deemed to form part of the record.

In *R. v. Hull University Visitor, ex p. Page*,[21] the House of Lords referred to the concept of error of law on the face of the record as obsolete in the light of the general principle that all errors of law go to jurisdiction (see para. 10–05).

F. Remedies

The legality of a decision of a local authority may be raised, directly or **10–49** collaterally, in a number of ways: (1) on an "application for judicial review", where the court may award one or more of a number of remedies, namely, certiorari, mandamus, prohibition, an injunction, a declaration and damages; (2) in an action for an injunction, a declaration or damages; (3) on an appeal; (4) by way of defence to enforcement proceedings; (5) in proceedings before the district auditor[22]; and (6) by a request to a Minister to exercise a default power.

Application for judicial review

Order 53 of the Rules of the Supreme Court provides a common procedure for seeking remedies in administrative law, termed an "application for judicial review". The main features of Order 53 were enacted in section 31 of the Supreme Court Act 1981. An application for judicial review must be brought in the Queen's Bench Division.

An application for an order of mandamus, prohibition or certiorari, or for an injunction under section 30 of the Supreme Court Act 1981 restraining a person from acting in any office in which he is not entitled to act, *must* be made under Order 53.[23]

An application for a declaration or an injunction *may* be made by way of application for judicial review under Order 53. The court may grant the

---

[21] [1993] A.C. 682.
[22] See §§ 7–14–7–36.
[23] R.S.C., Ord. 53, r. 1(1); Supreme Court Act 1981, s.31(1).

declaration or injunction claimed if it considers that it would be just and convenient so to do under Order 53, having regard to the nature of the matters in respect of which, and the persons and bodies against whom mandamus, prohibition or certiorari may be granted, and all the circumstances of the case.[24] Alternatively, a declaration or injunction may be obtained in an ordinary action. In *O'Reilly v. Mackman*[25] the House of Lords held that as a general rule it would be contrary to public policy and an abuse of the process of the court for a plaintiff complaining of a public authority's infringement of his public law rights to seek redress by ordinary action. However, this was a general rule to which there might be exceptions:

> "particularly where the invalidity of the decision arises as a collateral issue in a claim for infringement of a right of the plaintiff arising under private law, or where none of the parties objects to the adoption of the procedure by writ or originating summons. Whether there should be other exceptions should ... be left to be decided on a case by case basis."[26]

10–50 Accordingly, in *Cocks v. Thanet District Council*,[27] the House of Lords held that challenges to determinations by a housing authority, under the Housing (Homeless Persons) Act 1977, whether a person (1) was homeless or threatened with homelessness; (2) had a priority need; and (3) was homeless intentionally, should be brought on an application for judicial review. This was so notwithstanding that determinations in favour of that person would give rise to rights in the field of private law. Similarly, in *Davy v. Spelthorne Borough Council*[28] the Court of Appeal struck out proceedings in the Chancery Division seeking an injunction restraining the council from implementing an enforcement notice and an order that the notice be set aside. On the other hand, the court refused to strike out an alternative claim for damages for negligent advice alleged to have been given by the council resulting in a failure to appeal against the notice, and this was affirmed by the House of Lords.[29] Furthermore, it has been held that the principle of *O'Reilly v. Mackman*[30] does not prevent the defendant in a criminal case (here, a prosecution under the Town and Country Planning Act 1971 for breach of a stop notice) from relying on the *ultra vires* doctrine in his defence,[31] and that in a civil case a person may raise a matter of *vires* in

---

[24] *ibid.* r. 1(2); *ibid.* s.31(2).

[25] [1983] 2 A.C. 237.

[26] *Per* Lord Diplock at p. 285.

[27] [1983] 2 A.C. 286. See also *Luxclose Ltd v. London Borough of Hammersmith and Fulham* [1983] J.P.L. 662.

[28] (1983) 81 L.G.R. 580.

[29] [1984] A.C. 262. See also *Roy v. Kensington and Chelsea Family Practitioner Committee* [1992] 1 A.C. 624, where the House of Lords held that it was not an abuse of process to seek to enforce a private right to remuneration by an ordinary action.

[30] *supra* n. 25.

[31] *R. v. Jenner* [1983] 1 W.L.R. 873. See also *Canterbury City Council v. Bern* (1981) 44 P. & C.R. 178 and *Scarborough Borough Council v. Adams* (1983) 47 P. & C.R. 133; *R. v. Oxford Crown Court, ex p. Smith* [1990] C.O.D. 211. However, the decision to issue an enforcement notice is not challengeable on *Wednesbury* grounds by way of a defence to an indictment: *R. v. Wicks, The Times*, April 19, 1995. The defendant to a criminal prosecution before magistrates for breach of a by-law is entitled to challenge the validity of the by-law by way of defence: *R. v. Reading Crown Court, ex p. Hutchinson* [1988] Q.B. 384 (pet. dis. [1988] 1 W.L.R. 308).

defence of his private law rights, where those rights are not dependent on a public law decision.[32]

An applicant for judicial review must first obtain leave from a High Court **10–51** judge. Leave may not be granted unless the court "considers that the applicant has a sufficient interest in the matter to which the application relates". This is the only reference in the Rules to the problem of *locus standi*. The intention appears to be that there should be a uniform test for *locus standi* irrespective of the nature of the relief sought. Previously, the requirements for *locus standi* varied according to the remedy applied for.

The case law on the subject was complex and contradictory, the courts usually being less strict in applications for the prerogative orders than in actions for a private law remedy. Lord Denning M.R. formulated a general test in *R. v. Greater London Council, ex p. Blackburn*,[33] where Mr Blackburn was held to have *locus standi* to be granted an order of prohibition restraining the council from exercising their powers of film censorship according to the wrong legal test:

> "I would ask: Who then can bring proceedings when a public authority is guilty of a misuse of power? Mr Blackburn is a citizen of London. His wife is a ratepayer. He has children who may be harmed by the exhibition of pornographic films. If he has no sufficient interest, no other citizen has. I think he comes within the principle which I stated in *McWhirter's* case[34] which I would recast today so as to read: I regard it as a matter of high constitutional principle that if there is good ground for supposing that a government department or a public authority is transgressing the law, or is about to transgress it, in a way which offends or injures thousands of Her Majesty's subjects, then any one of those offended or injured can draw it to the attention of the courts of law and seek to have the law enforced, and the courts in their discretion can grant whatever remedy is appropriate."

However, this broad approach was not adopted by the other judges. In **10–52** *Gouriet v. Union of Post Office Workers*,[35] the House of Lords held that only the Attorney-General could sue on behalf of the public for the purpose of preventing public wrongs, such as breaches of the criminal law, and that a private individual could only take proceedings where he would sustain injury as the result of the public wrong. The private law remedies of declaration and injunction were only available to persons whose legal rights were affected by unlawful action. *Per* Lord Wilberforce[36]:

> "There is no support in authority for the proposition that declaratory relief can be granted unless the plaintiff, in proper proceedings, in which there is a

[32] *Wandsworth London Borough Council v. Winder* [1985] A.C. 461 (council tenant entitled to raise in defence to an action for arrears of rent that the authority's decision to increase the rent was an *ultra vires* abuse of discretion under the *Wednesbury* principles; the tenant's contentions subsequently failed on the merits: *Wandsworth London Borough Council v. Winder (No. 2)* (1988) 20 H.L.R. 400).
[33] [1976] 1 W.L.R. 550 at p. 558.
[34] *Att.-Gen., ex rel. McWhirter v. Independent Broadcasting Authority* [1973] Q.B. 629 at p. 649.
[35] [1978] A.C. 435.
[36] At p. 483.

dispute between the plaintiff and the defendant concerning their legal respective rights or liabilities, either asserts a legal right which is denied or threatened, or claims immunity from some claim of the defendant against him, or claims that the defendant is infringing or threatens to infringe some public right so as to inflict special damage on the plaintiff. The present proceedings do not possess the required characteristics."

10–53   The question of *locus standi* under Order 53 was considered by the House of Lords in *R. v. Inland Revenue Commissioners, ex p. National Federation of Self Employed and Small Businesses Ltd.*[37] Here, the applicants sought a declaration that an "amnesty" in respect of tax evasion granted by the Inland Revenue to Fleet Street casual workers was unlawful and also sought mandamus requiring the Revenue to assess and collect income tax from those workers. The House of Lords held unanimously that the arrangement had been made by the Commissioners for reasons of good management and was not *ultra vires* or unlawful. The majority (Lords Wilberforce, Fraser and Roskill) held, further that the Federation did not have a sufficient interest in the matter, and that it would only be in a rare case that a taxpayer would have the standing to seek judicial review of decisions concerning other taxpayers.[38] Lords Diplock and Scarman held that the Federation would have had *locus standi* had the arrangement been shown to be *ultra vires*.[39] A number of points of general significance emerged:

(a) The question of *locus standi* cannot be considered in isolation from the legal and factual context of the application. A decision that an applicant has sufficient interest to be granted leave under Order 53, r. 3, does not preclude the issue of *locus standi* being raised at the full hearing, where the context of the application can be properly examined. Accordingly, it is inappropriate for the issue to be taken as a preliminary issue of law.[40]

(b) The question of *locus standi* is one of mixed law and fact which the court must decide on legal principles. It is not simply a matter for the court's discretion.[41]

(c) The courts should not take an unduly restrictive approach to questions of *locus standi*. The decision in *R. v. Lewisham Guardians*,[42] which had laid down a requirement for an applicant for mandamus to show a specific legal right in the matter, was expressly disapproved.[43] Lord Fraser stated[44] that the new Order 53 had the effect of removing

---

[37] [1982] A.C. 617.
[38] See Lord Wilberforce at pp. 633, 635–636; Lord Fraser at pp. 644–645, 647; Lord Roskill at pp. 662–663, 664.
[39] See Lord Diplock at p. 644 and Lord Scarman at p. 654.
[40] See Lord Wilberforce at pp. 629–630; Lord Diplock at p. 636; Lord Fraser at p. 645; Lord Scarman at pp. 649, 653–654; and Lord Roskill at p. 656.
[41] See Lord Wilberforce at p. 631. Lords Fraser and Roskill expressly agreed with Lord Wilberforce's reasoning: pp. 644–645, 664.
[42] [1897] 1 Q.B. 488.
[43] See Lord Diplock at p. 639, Lord Fraser at p. 646, Lord Scarman at p. 653. Lord Roskill expressly agreed with Lord Fraser's reasoning: p. 664.
[44] At pp. 645–646.

technical and procedural differences between the prerogative orders, although all the older law had not been overthrown. Lord Scarman cited[45] with approval a statement by Lord Wilberforce in respect of the prerogative orders to the effect that the courts have allowed individuals "liberal access under a generous conception of *locus standi*".[46] Lord Roskill regarded old decisions on the prerogative orders to be of little assistance, the former and stricter rules determining when they might issue having been greatly relaxed.[47] Lord Diplock went further,[48] approving Lord Denning M.R.'s statement in *R. v. Greater London Council, ex p. Blackburn*.[49] A "mere busybody", however, will not have *locus standi*.[50]

(d) A ratepayer has *locus standi* to challenge rating decisions concerning other ratepayers in the same area.[51]

(e) The decision in *Gouriet v. Union of Post Office Workers*[52] was distinguished on the ground that it was not concerned with government bodies or judicial review.[53]

Since this decision, *locus standi* under Order 53 has been accorded to persons and bodies such as amenity societies who oppose grants of planning permission,[54] but denied to a local authority which sought to challenge a decision by the Department of Health and Social Security on a matter concerning social security payments,[55] and denied to a trust company formed

---

[45] At p. 653.

[46] *Gouriet v. Union of Post Office Workers* [1978] A.C. 435 at p. 482.

[47] [1982] A.C. 617 at pp. 656, 658.

[48] At p. 641.

[49] [1976] 1 W.L.R. 550, 559, *supra*. This view was, however, expressly disapproved by Lord Roskill (with whom Lord Fraser agreed) at [1982] A.C. 617 at pp. 660–661.

[50] See Lord Fraser at p. 646.

[51] See Lord Wilberforce at pp. 632–633; Lord Diplock at pp. 641–642; Lord Fraser at p. 646. These remarks are of course *obiter*. See also *Arsenal Football Club Ltd v. Ende* [1979] A.C. 1.

[52] *supra*, n. 35.

[53] See Lord Diplock at pp. 638–639; Lord Scarman at p. 649; Lord Roskill (with whom Lord Fraser expressly agreed) at pp. 657–658. See also Lord Wilberforce in the *Gouriet* case [1978] A.C. 435 at pp. 482–483.

[54] *Covent Garden Community Association Ltd v. Greater London Council* [1981] J.P.L. 183 (certiorari refused on the merits); *R. v. Hammersmith and Fulham Borough Council, ex p. People Before Profit Ltd* (1981) 80 L.G.R. 322 (*locus standi* for certiorari accepted, but leave refused in absence of a reasonable case to put forward); *R. v. Stroud District Council, ex p. Goodenough* (1982) 43 P. & C.R. 59 (mandamus); *R. v. Poole Borough Council, ex p. Beebee* [1991] C.O.D. 264. In *R. v. H.M. Inspectorate of Pollution, ex p. Greenpeace Ltd (No. 2)* [1994] 4 All E.R. 329 Otton J. held that Greenpeace had *locus standi* to challenge variations of authorisations to permit testing of BNFL's new thermal oxide processing plant Thorp at Sellafield, although the application was dismissed on the merits. This seems to reflect the approach in earlier cases concerning amenity societies rather than the narrower approach adopted in *R. v. Secretary of State for the Environment, ex p. Rose Theatre Trust Co.* (n. 56, *infra*). See also *R. v. Sheffield City Council, ex p. Power*, *The Times*, July 7, 1994 (action group had sufficient interest to challenge established use certificate); *R. v. Canterbury City Council, ex p. Springimage* (1994) 68 P. & C.R. 171 (rival developer has *locus standi* to challenge grant of planning permission).

[55] *R. v. Secretary of State for Social Services, ex p. Greater London Council*, *The Times*, August 16, 1984: appeal by the G.L.C. dismissed on another ground: *The Times*, August 8, 1985. *Cf. R. v. Secretary of State for Social Services, ex p. Child Poverty Action Group* [1990] 2 Q.B. 540.

by persons of distinction in archaeology, the theatre, literature and other fields, and local residents, with the object of preserving the remains of the Rose Theatre, in respect of the Secretary of State's refusal to schedule the remains as an ancient monument.[56]

It is not clear whether an unincorporated association has the capacity (as distinct from the standing) to apply for judicial review.[57]

10–54 Leave to apply for judicial review will be granted unless the applicant has no "reasonable" or "arguable" case to put forward.[58]

Once leave is granted, the application is made to a judge sitting in open court, unless the court directs that it should be made to a judge in chambers or to a Divisional Court of the Queen's Bench Division. In a criminal case, the application must be made to a Divisional Court.[59] The court may entertain interlocutory applications for orders such as those for discovery, interrogatories and cross-examination on affidavits.[60]

An application for leave must be made promptly, and in any event within three months from the date when grounds for the application first arose, unless the Court considers there is good reason for extending the period.[61] In addition, section 31(6) of the Supreme Court Act 1981 provides that where the High Court considers that there has been undue delay in making an application for judicial review, the court may refuse to grant (a) leave for the making of the application; or (b) any relief sought on the application, if it considers that the granting of the relief sought would be likely to cause substantial hardship to, or substantially prejudice the rights of, any person or would be detrimental to good administration. This is stated to be without prejudice to any enactment or rule of court which has the effect of limiting the time within which an application or judicial review may be made.[62] The three-month period specified in rule 4(1) is not an entitlement: leave may be refused or the substantive application dismissed on the ground that the application for leave, although made within three months, was nevertheless not made promptly.[63] A finding on an *inter partes* hearing of an application for leave that the application, brought within three months, has been made promptly, does not prevent the court at the substantive hearing finding that there has been undue delay, and exercising its discretion under section 31(6)

[56] *R. v. Secretary of State for the Environment, ex p. Rose Theatre Trust Co.* [1990] 1 Q.B. 504.
[57] In *R. v. Darlington Borough Council, ex p. Association of Darlington Taxi Owners, The Times,* January 21, 1994, it was held that it does not; costs were, however, awarded against the members of the applicant associations: *R. v. Darlington Borough Council, ex p. Association of Darlington Taxi Owners (No. 2), The Times,* April 14, 1994. A different view was taken by Sedley J. in *R. v. London Borough of Tower Hamlets, ex p. Tower Hamlets Combined Traders Association* [1994] C.O.D. 325 and by Turner J. in *R. v. Traffic Commissioners for the North Western Traffic Area, ex p. "Brake"* [1996] C.O.D. 248.
[58] *R. v. Hammersmith and Fulham Borough Council, ex p. People Before Profit Ltd supra; per* Lord Diplock in *Inland Revenue Commissioners v. National Federation of Self-Employed and Small Businesses Ltd* [1982] A.C. 617 at p. 644.
[59] R.S.C., Ord. 53, r. 5(1), (2).
[60] *ibid.* r. 8(1).
[61] *ibid.* r. 4(1).
[62] Supreme Court Act 1981, s.31(7).
[63] *R. v. Greenwich Borough Council, ex p. Cedar Transport Group Ltd* [1983] R.A. 173, D.C.; *Re Friends of the Earth* [1988] J.P.L. 93, C.A.

to refuse relief.[64] An extension of time may be granted if good cause is shown.[65] However, wherever there is a failure to act promptly or within three months, there is "undue delay" for the purpose of section 31(6), and relief may be refused, even though there has been "good reason" for an extension of time under rule 4(1).[66]

The Court will not entertain an application for judicial review where there **10–55** is some equally convenient and beneficial remedy, such as an appeal to a specialised tribunal, or to the High Court by case stated or to a more appropriate Division of the High Court. In *Ex parte Waldron*[67] Glidewell L.J. said[68]:

> "Whether the alternative statutory remedy will resolve the question at issue fully and directly, whether the statutory procedure would be quicker or slower, than procedure by way of judicial review, whether the matter depends on some particular or technical knowledge which is more readily available to the alternative appellate body, these are amongst the matters which a court should take into account when deciding whether to grant relief by way of judicial review when an alternative remedy is available."

Indeed, it has emphasised that where there is a statutory remedy, the mere fact that an application for judicial review might be more convenient and effective may not be sufficient for the court to intervene by way of judicial review: judicial review in such circumstances will only be granted in exceptional cases.[69]

Even where an applicant for judicial review establishes one of the grounds for review, the court retains a discretion whether to grant a remedy. Relevant factors that have already been mentioned include the nature of the applicant's standing, any delay and the existence of alternative remedies. In *R. v. Monopolies and Mergers Commission, ex p. Argyll Group plc*,[70] Sir John Donaldson M.R. stated[71] that in exercising this discretion the court should approach its duties with a proper awareness of the needs of public

---

[64] *R. v. Swale Borough Council, ex p. Royal Society for the Protection of Birds* [1991] J.P.L. 39.
[65] *R. v. Stratford-upon-Avon District Council, ex p. Jackson* [1985] 1 W.L.R. 1319 (time taken in an attempt to persuade the Secretary of State to call in a planning application, and to obtain legal aid); *R. v. Port Talbot Borough Council, ex p. Jones* [1988] 2 All E.R. 207 (time taken by an internal inquiry by the council); *R. v. Commissioner for Local Administration, ex p. Croydon London Borough Council* [1989] 1 All E.R. 1033 (challenge to Commissioner's jurisdiction postponed until receipt of report).
[66] *R. v. Stratford-upon-Avon Council, ex p. Jackson* [1985] 1 W.L.R. 1319; *R. v. Dairy Produce Quota Tribunal for England and Wales, ex p. Caswell* [1990] 2 A.C. 738.
[67] [1986] Q.B. 824.
[68] At p. 852.
[69] *R. v. Chief Constable of the Merseyside Police, ex p. Calveley* [1986] Q.B. 424; *R. v. Secretary of State for the Home Department, ex p. Swati* [1986] 1 W.L.R. 4772; *R. v. Westminster City Council, ex p. Hilditch, The Independent*, June 26, 1990 (leave refused where a complaint was already under investigation by the auditor). *Cf.* cases where leave has been granted notwithstanding the existence of an appeal or a default power: *R. v. Hillingdon London Borough Council, ex p. Royco Homes Ltd* [1974] 1 Q.B. 720; the *Calveley* case, *supra*; *R. v. Ealing London Borough Council, ex p. Times Newspapers* (1987) 85 L.G.R. 316; *R. v. Birmingham City Council, ex p. Equal Opportunities Commission* [1989] A.C. 1155.
[70] [1986] 1 W.L.R. 763.
[71] At p. 774.

administration. Among the factors relevant there were that good public administration is concerned with substance rather than form, and with the speed of decision, particularly in the financial field; it requires a proper consideration of the public interest and of the legitimate interest of individual citizens, and requires decisiveness and finality unless there are compelling reasons to the contrary. The court declined to quash a decision of the chairman of the commission to lay aside a reference of a take-over bid to the commission, which decision should have been made by a group of members and not by the chairman alone.[72]

The prerogative orders

Mandamus

10–56   The order of mandamus issues from the High Court to some person or body to compel the performance of a public duty imposed by law where no other effective means of redress is available. It may therefore be used to compel a local authority to carry out some duty cast upon it by statute or common law.[73] But there are several limitations on the power to issue an order.

In the first place the duty must be an absolute one, and not one which may be exercised if the authority chooses. A council may not be compelled by this means to undertake some activity which is merely permissive (*e.g.* the making of by-laws), or which is discretionary. But mandamus lies to compel the exercise of a discretion in a way that extraneous considerations are excluded and that issues are dealt with on merit.[74] Secondly, the traditional principle is that the applicant for the order must show that he himself has a substantial, personal interest in the performance of the duty—it is not sufficient for him to show that a public duty has been neglected. How "substantial" that interest must be is not clear from the cases.[75] Thirdly, an order will not be made if there is some other remedy equally convenient, beneficial and effective.

The following are examples of the use of mandamus:

> *R. v. Poplar Borough Council.*[76] The borough council refused to pay sums under precepts issued by the London County Council and the Metropolitan District Asylums Board. *Held*, mandamus lay to compel the council to levy a rate to meet the precepts, for this was the only effective means of securing the performance of a public duty. The London Government Act 1899 (under which the London County precept was issued), did not provide a remedy for breach of

---

[72] See also Dillon L.J. at pp. 778–779 and Neill L.J. at pp. 782–783. For further examples of the exercise of this discretion see §§ 10–57, 10–58.

[73] *e.g.* the duty to entertain an application for registration as the keeper of a common lodging-house: *R. v. Hounslow London Borough Council, ex p. Pizzey* [1977] 1 All E.R. 305.

[74] See *R. v. Flintshire County Council Licensing County (Stage Plays) Committee, ex p. Barrett* [1957] 1 Q.B. 350; *R. v. Stepney Corporation* [1902] 1 K.B. 317; *R. v. London County Council, ex p. Corrie* [1918] 1 K.B. 68; *Padfield v. Minister of Agriculture* [1968] A.C. 997.

[75] See *R. v. Paddington Valuation Officer, ex p. Peachey Property Corporation (No. 2)* [1966] 1 Q.B. 380; *R. v. Commissioner of Police of the Metropolis, ex p. Blackburn* [1968] 2 Q.B. 118; *R. v. Hereford Corporation, ex p. Harrower* [1970] 1 W.L.R. 1424, 1427.

[76] [1922] 1 K.B. 95.

duty: in the case of the precept of the Asylums Board, the remedy of distress (if in fact it were available) was wholly inadequate.

R. v. Braintree District Council, ex p. Willingham.[77] Section 71 of the Shops Act 1950 provides that it is the duty of every local authority to enforce the Act. The council decided not to prosecute the operators of a Sunday market for offences under the Act. The Divisional Court found that they had taken into account the expense of prosecuting and the fact that the market was popular in the locality. *Held*, these were irrelevant considerations, and mandamus should go, requiring the council to perform their duty under section 71. The council had no general discretion not to enforce the Act; the only scope for discretion was whether any particular proceedings were necessary to secure observance, and, as an aspect of that, the council could take account of the likelihood of failure.

The remedy is discretionary, and may be refused if, for example, the **10–57** applicant's motives are unacceptable,[78] or the authority's failure to meet a statutory obligation arises out of circumstances over which it has no control.[79]

The order so far referred to is derived from the prerogative writ of mandamus which issued from the King's courts upon principles of law settled by decided cases. There are, however, several instances where mandamus is available by virtue of a specific statutory provision. The Secretary of State for Education and Science has, under section 99 of the Education Act 1944, a power to issue directions to a local education authority, which, in his opinion, has failed to discharge its duties. These directions are enforceable, on the application of the Secretary of State, by mandamus. The court is bound to grant the application if the correct legal procedure is followed.

If a local authority disobeys an order of mandamus, whether derived from the prerogative writ or statute, the members of the authority responsible for the failure are liable to attachment, *i.e.* to arrest and to imprisonment until the order is obeyed.[80]

Prohibition and certiorari

The orders of prohibition and certiorari issue from the High Court to **10–58** prevent inferior courts from exceeding the limits of their legitimate powers or from otherwise acting unlawfully. Prohibition restrains an inferior court from acting unlawfully in the future or from completing an act already begun; certiorari enables a decision already made to be reviewed and if necessary quashed. These orders lie not only against inferior courts. It was held in *R. v. Electricity Commissioners*[81] that they lie:

"whenever any body of persons having legal authority to determine questions affecting the rights of subjects, and having the duty to act judicially, act in excess of their legal authority."

However, recent developments have made it clear that these remedies are

---

[77] (1982) 81 L.G.R. 70.
[78] *e.g.* business rivalry: *R. v. Customs and Excise Commissioners, ex p. Cook* [1970] 1 W.L.R. 450.
[79] *per* Scarman L.J. in *R. v. Bristol Corporation, ex p. Hendy* [1974] 1 W.L.R. 498 at p. 503.
[80] *R. v. Worcester Corporation* (1905) 69 J.P. 296; *R. v. Poplar Borough Council (No. 2)* [1922] 1 K.B. 95.
[81] [1924] 1 K.B. 171, *per* Atkin L.J. at p. 205.

no longer limited to cases where there is a duty to act judicially.[82] For example, certiorari has been granted to quash a grant of planning permission to which *ultra vires* conditions had been attached.[83] An order of prohibition has been granted to restrain a local authority from increasing the number of taxicab licences in their area without hearing objections from existing cab owners.[84]

The orders may lie if an authority acts or proposes to act without jurisdiction (*e.g.* in breach of natural justice). In addition, certiorari may be awarded where an error of law is apparent on the face of the record (see para. 10–48) or where an order is procured by fraud,[85] or where there is unfairness arising from conduct that can fairly be categorised as analogous to fraud.[86]

The courts traditionally have not applied a strict test for *locus standi*.[87] The remedies are discretionary, and may be refused, for example, where the plaintiff has delayed unreasonably,[88] or has been guilty of unreasonable conduct.[89] Moreover, they may be refused where another equally beneficial remedy is available,[90] where there would be no more than a theoretical prospect that the decision would be changed if the matter were remitted[91] or where the point of law is technical and without merit and the applicants have suffered no injustice.[92] In *R. v. Secretary of State for Social Services, ex p. Association of Metropolitan Authorities*,[93] Webster J. granted a declaration that the Secretary of State had failed to comply with a mandatory duty to consult local authority associations before making housing benefit regulations, but declined to quash the regulations in the exercise of his discretion. His Lordship gave several reasons, including that only one of six associations had applied for judicial review, that the applicant's main complaint

---

[82] See *Ridge v. Baldwin* [1964] A.C. 40; *R. v. Hillingdon London Borough Council, ex p. Royco Homes Ltd* [1974] Q.B. 720; *O'Reilly v. Mackman* [1983] 2 A.C. 237, 239 (Lord Diplock); *cf. R. v. Barnet London Borough Council, ex p. Nilish Shah* [1983] 2 A.C. 309 (certiorari granted to quash a decision refusing a mandatory award to a student); *R. v. Manchester City Council, ex p. Fulford* (1982) 81 L.G.R. 292 (certiorari granted to quash a decision to abolish corporal punishment in schools).

[83] *R. v. Hillingdon London Borough Council, ex p. Royco Homes Ltd* [1974] Q.B. 720.

[84] *R. v. Liverpool Corporation, ex p. Liverpool Taxi Fleet Operators' Association* [1972] 2 Q.B. 299.

[85] *R. v. Wolverhampton Crown Court, ex p. Croft* [1983] 1 W.L.R. 204.

[86] *R. v. Secretary of State for the Home Department, ex p. Al-Mehdawi* [1990] 1 A.C. 876; *R. v. Bolton JJ., ex p. Scally* [1991] 1 Q.B. 537; *R. v. Burton upon Trent Magistrates Court, ex p. Woolley, The Times*, November 17, 1994.

[87] See Lord Denning M.R. in *R. v. Paddington Valuation Officer, ex p. Peachey Property Ltd (No. 2)* [1966] 1 Q.B. 380 at pp. 400–401, and *R. v. Liverpool Corporation, ex p. Liverpool Taxi Fleet Operators' Association* [1972] 2 Q.B. 299 at pp. 308–309.

[88] See *R. v. Stafford Justices* [1940] 2 K.B. 33; *R. v. Herrod, ex p. Leeds City Council* [1978] A.C. 403.

[89] *Ex p. Fry* [1954] 1 W.L.R. 730.

[90] *cf. R. v. Hillingdon London Borough Council, ex p. Royco Homes* [1974] Q.B. 720 (statutory right of appeal to the Secretary of State not as beneficial as certiorari where planning conditions are to be challenged on a point of law alone).

[91] *R. v. Secretary of State for the Environment, ex p. Stewart* (1979) 39 P. & C.R. 534; *cf. R. v. Greater Manchester Valuation Panel, ex p. Shell Chemicals U.K. Ltd* [1982] Q.B. 255 at pp. 264–265.

[92] *R. v. Knightsbridge Crown Court, ex p. Marcrest Properties Ltd* [1983] 1 W.L.R. 300.

[93] [1986] 1 W.L.R. 1.

concerned the lack of consultation rather than the substance of the regulations, that the regulations had already been in force for some six months and that claimants would only benefit for a limited period as the regulations had now been consolidated.

Declarations and injunctions

A declaratory judgment is, as the name implies, the finding of a court on a question of law or rights. An injunction is an order by which a party to the proceedings is required to do, or to refrain from doing, a particular thing. **10–59**

Before the introduction of the application for judicial review, it had become increasingly common for persons wishing to challenge or test the legality of an act or decision of a public authority to proceed by commencing an action in the High Court for a declaration or injunction, in preference to seeking one of the prerogative orders. However, a litigant was faced with the difficulty that proceedings in respect of *public rights* were theoretically at the instigation of the Attorney-General, as the protector of public rights. It was necessary to ask the Attorney-General to consent to the institution of "relator proceedings".[94] Here, the proceedings were brought in the name of the Attorney-General "at the relation of" the aggrieved party, but at the latter's expense. The Attorney-General had an absolute discretion as to whether he would lend his name.[95]

There were two exceptions to the rule that the Attorney-General was to be a party to proceedings in respect of public rights. A private party might sue in his own name (i) where the interference with the public right was such that some private right of his was at the same time interfered with, or (ii) where the plaintiff suffered special damage peculiar to himself from an interference with a public right.

> *Boyce v. Paddington Corporation.*[96] The plaintiff, shortly before the action, erected buildings on land abutting on an open space under the control of the borough council. The council resolved to erect a hoarding which would obstruct the access of light to the plaintiff's windows. The plaintiff brought an action to restrain the council from doing this. *Held*, that as the plaintiff was suing in respect of an alleged private right to the access of light, or in respect of an alleged interference with a public right from which he personally sustained special damage, he could sue without joining the Attorney-General as a plaintiff. The action failed on grounds unconnected with the right to sue.

There were a number of cases where a declaration or injunction was awarded to a person without these requirements being fulfilled, but where the point as to *locus standi* was not raised.[97] However, the House of Lords strongly reasserted the traditional position in *Gouriet v. Union of Post Office Workers.*[98]

---

[94] See *Ware v. Regent's Canal Co.* (1858) 3 De G. & J. 212 at p. 228, *per* Lord Chelmsford; *Att.-Gen., ex. rel. McWhirter v. Independent Broadcasting Authority* [1973] 1 Q.B. 629.
[95] *Gouriet v. Union of Post Office Workers* [1978] A.C. 435.
[96] [1903] 1 Ch. 109.
[97] *e.g. Prescott v. Birmingham Corporation* [1955] 1 Ch. 210; *Lee v. Department of Education and Science* (1967) 66 L.G.R. 211.
[98] [1978] A.C. 435. See also *Gregory v. Camden London Borough Council* [1966] 1 W.L.R. 899.

As has been noted above,[99] a declaration or injunction may now be sought either on an application for judicial review under R.S.C. Ord. 53, or in ordinary proceedings in the High Court. However, under the principle of *O'Reilly v. Mackman*,[1] ordinary proceedings against a public authority will be struck out as an abuse of process, save in exceptional circumstances.

On an application for judicial review, the liberal "sufficient interest" test for *locus standi* is applicable.[2] Accordingly, a person may now seek a declaration or injunction in his own name under this procedure even though he has suffered no special damage or interference with his private rights in accordance with the tests applied in *Boyce v. Paddington Corporation*.[3] On the other hand, these tests remain applicable as the tests for *locus standi* where a declaration or injunction is sought in ordinary proceedings against a public authority.[4] Indeed these are among the exceptional circumstances in which the courts will permit such proceedings to be brought.[5]

Statutory appeals

10–60 Many statutes give a right of appeal to a person aggrieved by a decision of a local authority. A litigant relying on a statutory right must be able to bring his case within the statute—there is no discretionary power in any court to extend its jurisdiction beyond that specifically conferred. The following are examples of appeal provisions.

To a magistrates' court

Private street works code.[6] A frontager may object to the proposals of a local authority on the ground, for example, that the works are insufficient or unreasonable, or that the street is not a private street. The authority must ask the court to determine the objection if it is not itself prepared to meet it. The court may quash the proposals in whole or in part or may amend them, or may adjourn the hearing or direct that further notices be given.

Building Act 1984, s.79: A local authority may, in the interests of amenity, require the owner of a ruinous building to repair or to demolish it. An appeal against a requirement lies to the magistrates' court.

Statutes conferring jurisdiction on the justices usually provide a right of appeal on the part of a "person aggrieved" to the Crown Court. This is by the way of a rehearing of the case. Either party in a proceeding before the justices may require them to state a case to the High Court on a point of law or as to a want or excess of jurisdiction.[7]

---

[99] § 10–49, 10–50.

[1] [1983] 2 A.C. 237: see §§ 10–49, 10–50.

[2] *Inland Revenue Commissioners v. National Federation of Self-Employed and Small Businesses Ltd* [1982] A.C. 617: see § 10–53.

[3] *supra*, n. 96.

[4] *Barrs v. Bethell* [1982] Ch. 194. In this case, Warner J. disagreed with the view expressed by Webster J. in *Steeples v. Derbyshire County Council* [1985] 1 W.L.R. 256 that a person with "sufficient interest" under Order 53 would have *locus standi* in ordinary proceedings.

[5] See §§ 10–49, 10–50.

[6] Highways Act 1980, s.209.

[7] See the Magistrates' Courts Act 1980, ss.108, 111.

REMEDIES

To a county court

Housing Act 1985, ss.191, 269 and Sched. 10, para. 6: A person aggrieved by a notice requiring him to carry out works of repair, or by a demand for the recovery of expenses where the authority has acted in default, or by a demolition or closing order, may appeal to the county court. The court may quash or vary the notice, demand or order as it thinks fit.

To the Crown Court

Highways Act 1980, s.56: This section deals with the enforcement of a liability to maintain a highway and enables the complainant who claims that a highway maintainable at the public expense is out of repair first to require the authority to admit that the highway is in fact so maintainable. If this is disputed the complainant may ask the Crown Court for an order requiring the authority, if the court finds that the way is publicly maintainable and is out of repair, to put it in a state of proper repair.

The Lotteries and Amusements Act 1976, Sched. 3: The grant of a permit for amusements with prizes is "at the discretion of the local authority". Paragraph 8 gives a right of appeal against refusal of a permit to the Crown Court.

To the High Court

Acquisition of Land Act 1981, ss.23, 24: An appeal lies to the High Court on the grounds that the purpose for which a compulsory purchase order is made is not one which is authorised by statute or that some statutory requirement has not been complied with to the substantial prejudice of the applicant.

There are a number of such appeal provisions on the statute book, mostly in the context of town and country planning and compulsory purchase. The grounds of challenge which may be raised under these procedures were stated as follows by Lord Denning M.R. in *Ashbridge Investments Ltd v. Minister of Housing and Local Government*,[8] in relation to the Housing Act 1957, Sched. 4, para. 2 (now the Housing Act 1985, Sched. 22, para. 7):

> "The Court can only interfere on the ground that the Minister has gone outside the powers of the Act or that any requirement of the Act has not been complied with. Under this section it seems to me that the court can interfere with the Minister's decision if he has acted on no evidence; or if he has come to a conclusion to which on the evidence he could not reasonably come; or if he has given a wrong interpretation to the words of the statute; or if he has taken into consideration matters which he ought not to have taken into account, or vice versa; or has otherwise gone wrong in law. It is identical with the position when the court has power to interfere with the decision of a lower tribunal which has erred in point of law."

To a minister

Town and Country Planning Act 1990, s.78: An applicant for planning permission may appeal to the Secretary of State for the Environment against a refusal or a conditional grant of planning permission by a local authority.

[8] [1965] 1 W.L.R. 1320 at p. 1326.

Town and Country Planning Act 1990, s.174: A person having an interest in the land to which an enforcement notice relates, or a relevant occupier may appeal to the Secretary of State on any of eight specified grounds.

Locus standi and statutory appeals

10–61 Many appeals established by statute may only be brought by a "person aggrieved". This term has been considered by the courts on many occasions. The view most commonly relied on as to its meaning is that expressed by James L.J. in *ex p. Sidebotham*[9]:

> "... The words 'person aggrieved' do not really mean a man who is disappointed of a benefit which he might have received if some other order had been made. A 'person aggrieved' must be a man who has suffered a legal grievance, a man against whom a decision has been pronounced which has wrongfully deprived him of something, or wrongfully refused him something, or wrongfully affected his title to something."

The attitude of the court has, however, varied according to the context.

10–62 In many areas of local government law, a local authority is empowered to serve a notice requiring a private person to have works done on his property, and a person aggrieved by the notice may appeal to a court. That private person is a "person aggrieved" by the notice, and by a decision of a court upholding a notice. Is the local authority a "person aggrieved" by a decision of the justices against them? A series of decisions of the Divisional Court established that it was not, unless a legal burden was placed upon it as a result of the decision, such as a financial burden beyond the costs of the proceedings.[10] However, the cases conflicted on whether the obligation to pay costs alone was sufficient to render the authority a "person aggrieved".[11] Similarly, a person refused a licence by a local authority was a "person aggrieved" for the purposes of an appeal,[12] but it was held that the local authority might not be a "person aggrieved" by the reversal of its decision.[13]

The whole question was reconsidered by the Court of Appeal in the following case:

> *Cook v. Southend Borough Council.*[14] C.'s hackney carriage vehicle and driver's licences were revoked by the council under ss.60 and 61 of the Local Government (Miscellaneous Provisions) Act 1976. C. successfully appealed to the magistrates' court, which made an order for costs against the council. The council appealed to the Crown Court, claiming to be a "person aggrieved" and therefore entitled to appeal by virtue of s.77(1) of the 1976 Act and s.301 of the Public Health Act 1936. The Crown Court allowed the appeal. C. appealed by

---

[9] (1880) 14 Ch.D. 458 at p. 465. See also *Buxton v. Minister of Housing and Local Government* [1961] 1 Q.B. 278.

[10] *e.g., Phillips v. Berkshire County Council* [1967] 2 Q.B. 991, where justices decided that a street was not a private street, and thus made maintainable at the public expense.

[11] Compare *R. v. Surrey Quarter Sessions, ex p. Lilley* [1951] 2 K.B. 749 with *R. v. Dorset Quarter Sessions Appeals Committee, ex p. Weymouth Corporation* [1960] 2 Q.B. 230.

[12] *Stepney Borough Council v. Joffe* [1949] 1 K.B. 599.

[13] *R. v. London Quarter Sessions, ex p. Westminster Corporation* [1951] 2 K.B. 508; *R. v. Southwark London Borough Council, ex p. Watts* (1989) 88 L.G.R. 86; *cf. R. v. Penwith District Council, ex p. McCartan-Mooney*, The Times, October 20, 1984.

[14] [1990] 2 Q.B. 1 (pet. dis. [1990] 1 W.L.R. 480, H.L.).

case stated to the High Court, and the judge dismissed the appeal, holding that he was constrained by authority to hold that the council was a "person aggrieved" on the ground that an order for costs had been made against it by the magistrates. The Court of Appeal dismissed C.'s appeal, but was free to reconsider the basis of the council's standing. Woolf L.J. held that the term "person aggrieved" is to be given its ordinary natural meaning rather than the narrow interpretation adopted in previous cases. It is not necessary for a legal burden to be placed on a party to proceedings; it is enough that an adverse decision has been given against the party appealing, unless the decision amounts to an acquittal of a purely criminal offence (in which case the statutory context is all important). The fact that the decision against which the person wishes to appeal reverses a decision which was originally taken by that person, does not prevent that person being a "person aggrieved". A body corporate, including a local authority, is just as capable of being a "person aggrieved" as an individual.

In recent cases concerning third parties affected by planning decisions, the courts have shown a less rigid attitude to the question of *locus standi*, while still emphasising that a person's interests must be prejudicially affected.[15]

Collateral challenges

An allegation that the act of a local authority is unlawful may be made by **10–63** way of defence to enforcement proceedings. For example, on a prosecution for breach of a by-law, it may be argued that the by-law is *ultra vires*,[16] and on a prosecution for the offence of demolishing a building subject to a building preservation notice it may be argued that the notice was not validly served.[17] In *Allingham v. Minister of Agriculture*,[18] a notice requiring farmers to grow sugar beet on certain fields was held to be invalid because the task of specifying the fields had been delegated unlawfully by a county agricultural committee to an officer. A prosecution for non-compliance with the notice accordingly failed.[19]

G. EXCLUSION OF JUDICIAL REVIEW

Where Parliament wishes to reduce the scope for judicial intervention in **10–64** administrative decision-making, the technique most commonly adopted is to draft powers in a wide discretionary form. Alternatively, Parliament may seek expressly to exclude judicial review. By section 12(1) of the Tribunals and Inquiries Act 1992, any provision in an Act passed before August 1, 1958 that any order or determination shall not be called into question in any court, or any provision in such an Act which by similar words excludes any of the powers of the High Court, shall not have effect so as to restrict applications

---

[15] See *Turner v. Secretary of State for the Environment* (1973) 72 L.G.R. 380.
[16] *R. v. Reading Crown Court, ex p. Hutchinson* [1988] Q.B. 384: see § 6–13. In *Bugg v. Director of Public Prosecutions* [1993] Q.B. 473 it was held that collateral challenge to a by-law was only available where the by-laws was invalid on its face.
[17] See *Maltglade v. St Albans R.D.C.* [1972] 1 W.L.R. 1230.
[18] [1948] 1 All E.R. 780.
[19] See also *Stroud v. Bradbury* [1952] 2 All E.R. 76; *Canterbury City Council v. Bern* (1981) 44 P. & C.R. 178; *R. v. Jenner* [1983] 1 W.L.R. 873; *Wandsworth London Borough Council v. Winder* [1985] A.C. 461.

for certiorari or mandamus. Section 12(3), however, preserves exclusion clauses "where an Act makes special provision for application to the High Court . . . within a time limited by the Act". The special applications to quash orders discussed at para. 10–60 above must be brought within six weeks. No other administrative law remedies may be sought even within that period, and applications made after expiry of the six week period may not be entertained. Another "exclusion clause" expressly preserved by the forerunner of section 12(3)[20] was in issue in *Anisminic Ltd v. Foreign Compensation Commission*.[21] Here, the House of Lords held that section 4(4) of the Foreign Compensation Act 1950, which provided that "the determination by the Commission of any application made to them under this Act shall not be called in question in any court of law," did not protect from judicial review a purported determination which was in truth a nullity as made in excess of jurisdiction. However, the House of Lords in *Smith v. East Elloe Rural District Council*[22] and the Court of Appeal in *R. v. Secretary of State for the Environment, ex p. Ostler*[23] have held that "time limit" clauses are effective to exclude judicial review on any ground. As a matter of strict logic, these two decisions are difficult to reconcile with *Anisminic*. It is significant that in *Anisminic* there was no provision for a statutory appeal even of a limited nature as in the other two cases.

II. LEGAL PROCEEDINGS BY AND AGAINST LOCAL AUTHORITIES

10–65 Section 222 of the Local Government Act 1972 provides that where a local authority consider it expedient for the promotion or protection of the interests of the inhabitants of their area they may:

(a) prosecute or defend or appear in any legal proceedings and, in the case of civil proceedings, may institute them in their own name; and

(b) in their own name, make representations in the interests of the inhabitants at any public inquiry.

These powers are available to local authorities including the Common Council of the City of London, and the Broads Authority.[24]

This section authorises the authority, for example, to commence or defend criminal prosecutions and proceedings in contract or tort.[25] A local authority may apply for judicial review of a decision of the Secretary of State or of

---

[20] Tribunals and Inquiries Act 1958, s.11(3).
[21] [1969] 2 A.C. 147. Applied in *Pearlman v. Keepers of Harrow School* [1979] Q.B. 56.
[22] [1956] A.C. 736.
[23] [1977] Q.B. 122. Applied in *R. v. Secretary of State for the Environment, ex p. Kent* [1990] J.P.L. 124; by the Court of Appeal in *R. v. Cornwall County Council, ex p. Huntingdon; R. Devon County Council, ex p. Isaac* [1994] 1 All E.R. 694 and by the Divisional Court in *R. v. London Borough of Camden, ex p. Woolf* [1992] C.O.D. 456.
[24] 1972 Act, ss.222(2), 265A, inserted by the Norfolk and Suffolk Broads Act 1988, Sched. 6, para. 10(1). The power is not available to an urban development corporation: *London Docklands Development Corporation v. Rank Hovis McDougall Ltd* (1985) 84 L.G.R. 101.
[25] See Chaps. 7 and 8.

another local authority.[26] Furthermore, the provision that civil proceedings may be instituted "in their own name" enables local authorities to seek an injunction or a declaration to protect the public without obtaining the consent of the Attorney-General. The authority must consider whether the institution of civil proceedings is in the interests of the inhabitants of their area, although there is a rebuttable presumption that this is so.[27] This last point has arisen in a number of cases where a local authority has sought an injunction to restrain a breach of the criminal law, such as contravention of a stop notice or enforcement notice or infringement of the laws on Sunday trading.

The special considerations that arise where it is sought to use the civil law **10–66** to restrain breaches of the criminal law were set out by Lord Templeman in *Stoke-on-Trent City Council v. B. & Q. (Retail) Ltd*[28] (a Sunday trading case):

> "The right to invoke the assistance of the civil court in aid of the criminal law is a comparatively modern development. Where Parliament imposes a penalty for an offence, Parliament must consider the penalty is adequate and Parliament can increase the penalty if it proves to be inadequate. It follows that a local authority should be reluctant to seek and the court should be reluctant to grant an injunction which if disobeyed may involve the infringer in sanctions far more onerous than the penalty imposed for the offence. In *Gouriet v. Union of Post Office Workers*,[29] Lord Wilberforce said[30] that the right to invoke the assistance of civil courts in aid of the criminal law is 'an exceptional power confined, in practice, to cases where an offence is frequently repeated in disregard of a, usually, inadequate penalty ... or to cases of emergency. ...'
> It was said that the council should not have taken civil proceedings until criminal proceedings had failed to persuade the appellants to obey the law. As a general rule a local authority should try the effect of criminal proceedings before seeking the assistance of the civil courts. But the council were entitled to take the view that the appellants would not be deterred by a maximum fine which was substantially less than the profits which could be made from illegal Sunday trading. Delay while this was proved would have encouraged widespread breaches of the law by other traders, resentful of the continued activities of the appellants."

In this case, the company had traded in breach of the requirements of the Shops Act 1950 and an injunction was granted to restrain future breaches.

In *Runnymede Borough Council v. Ball*,[31] the Court of Appeal granted an **10–67** interlocutory injunction to restrain the defendants from establishing a gypsy

---

[26] As well as satisfying the requirements of s.222, the authority must also have a sufficient interest under R.S.C., Ord. 53: see *R. v. Secretary of State for Social Services, ex p. Greater London Council, The Times*, August 16, 1984 see § 10–54.

[27] *Stoke-on-Trent City Council v. B. & Q. (Retail) Ltd* [1984] A.C. 754.

[28] [1984] A.C. 754 at p. 776.

[29] [1978] A.C. 435.

[30] At p. 481.

[31] [1986] 1 W.L.R. 353. See also *Wychavon District Council v. Midland Enterprises (Special Events) Ltd* (1987) 86 L.G.R. 83; *City of London Corp. v. Bovis Construction Ltd* (1988) 86 L.G.R. 660.

caravan site in contravention of enforcement and stop notices. No prosecutions had been brought. The penalties were not insubstantial, but the court accepted that prosecutions would have been too slow. The site would have been well established before the proceedings, including appeals, would be completed. The council were also justified in doubting the effectiveness of a financial penalty against gypsies. The control of the user of Green Belt land was a matter of public importance. The court's jurisdiction was not confined to cases where the defendant was "deliberately and flagrantly flouting the law". This expression appeared in Lord Fraser's speech in *Stoke-on-Trent City Council v. B. & Q. (Retail Ltd)*[32] but did not form part of the *ratio* of Lord Templeman's leading opinion.

In *Staffordshire Moorlands District Council v. Cartwright*,[33] the Court of Appeal held that the court had jurisdiction to grant declarations concerning the planning status of particular property in civil proceedings brought by a local authority under section 222, although this jurisdiction should only be exercised in exceptional circumstances, the authority normally being expected to take enforcement action under the planning legislation.

The jurisdiction extends to the restraint of breaches of the civil law.[34]

A local authority seeking to enforce the law is not be required to give a cross-undertaking in damages.[35]

10–68   Local authorities may also take proceedings in their own name to protect the public where expressly permitted to do so by specific statutory provisions.[36]

10–69   Under section 223 of the Local Government Act 1972,[37] any member or officer[38] of a local authority[39] who is authorised by that authority to prosecute or defend on its behalf, or to appear on its behalf in proceedings before a magistrates' court, is entitled to do so, and, notwithstanding anything in the Solicitors Act 1974, to conduct the proceedings although he is not a solicitor holding a current practising certificate.

The authorisation should be given by the authority before the commencement of court proceedings[40] and must be properly made.[41] If the authoris-

---

[32] [1984] A.C. 754 at p. 767, quoting Bridge L.J. in *Stafford Borough Council v. Elkenford Ltd* [1977] 1 W.L.R. 324 at p. 330.

[33] (1991) 63 P. & C.R. 285.

[34] *City of London Corp. v. Bovis Construction Ltd* (1988) 86 L.G.R. 660 (deliberate breaches of a notice under s.60 of the Control of Pollution Act 1974 controlling noise on a building site).

[35] *Kirklees Borough Council v. Wickes Building Supplies Ltd* [1993] A.C. 227; *Rochdale Borough Council v. Anders* [1988] 3 All E.R. 490; *Coventry City Council v. Finnie, The Times,* May 2, 1996.

[36] See, *e.g.* the Public Health Act 1936, s.100 (statutory nuisances; see § 16–40, *et seq.*); the Control of Pollution Act 1974, s.58(8) (noise nuisances: see § 16–89).

[37] As amended by the Water Act 1973, Sched. 8, para. 98 and the Local Government Act 1985, Sched. 14, para. 21.

[38] Not a police officer: *Fisher v. Oldham Corporation* [1930] 2 K.B. 364.

[39] This power is also available to the Common Council and joint authorities, by virtue of the Local Government Act 1985, Sched. 13, para. 12(f) to residuary bodies, and by virtue of the 1972 Act, s.265A, inserted by the Norfolk and Suffolk Broads Act 1988, Sched. 6, para. 10(1) to the Broads Authority.

[40] *Bowyer, Philpott and Payne Ltd v. Mather* [1919] 1 K.B. 419. See § 4–78.

[41] *Bob Keats Ltd v. Farrant* (1951) 49 L.G.R. 631.

ation is challenged, the proper method of proof is by production of the minute of proceedings that records the council's resolution authorising proceedings, or a certified copy thereof.[42]

If, and to the extent that, an order under section 70 of the Deregulation and Contracting Out Act 1994 so provides (see *ante*, para. 4–85/1) section 223 of the Local Government Act 1972 is to have effect as if any person authorised by virtue of the order to exercise a function of a local authority, and any employee of his, were an officer of the authority.[43]

---

[42] *Dee and Clwyd River Authority v. Parry* (1967) 65 L.G.R. 488. However, the court may not interfere if the magistrates' court expresses itself satisfied on less than strict proof that proceedings are authorised: *cf. R. v. Turner* [1910] 1 K.B. 346; *Westminster Coaching Services Ltd v. Piddlesden* (1933) 31 L.G.R. 245.
[43] Deregulation and Contracting Out Act 1994, Sched. 16, para. 3.

CHAPTER 11

LOCAL ELECTIONS[1]

THE following topics are considered in this Chapter: electoral areas; the **11–01** franchise; the registration of electors; qualifications for candidature and disqualifications; the conduct of elections; the questioning of elections; election offences; and the filling of casual vacancies. The law relating to the franchise, the registration of electors, the conduct of elections, the questioning of elections and election offences was consolidated in the Representation of the People Act 1983, and the regulations made thereunder.[2] Certain changes were made by the Representation of the People Acts 1985, 1989 and 1990. The law as to electoral areas, candidature and the filling of casual vacancies is principally found in the Local Government Act 1972.

A. ELECTORAL AREAS[3]

The following table lists the various kinds of electoral units and the number **11–02** of councillors elected for each:

Local government area	Electoral area	Representation
Non-metropolitan Counties	Electoral division	One councillor for each electoral division
Metropolitan districts	Ward	A number of councillors divisible by three
Non-metropolitan districts	Ward	Such number of councillors as may be provided by order under Part II of the Local Government Act 1992
Principal areas in Wales	Electoral division	Such number of councillors as may be provided by order made under the Local Government Act 1972[4]
Parishes	The parish as a whole or wards of the parish	The number of councillors for each parish or ward of a parish is fixed by the district council

---

[1] See R. Clayton, *Parker's Law and Conduct of Elections* (1996); A.J. Little, *Schofield's Election Law* (1984).

[2] See the Representation of the People Regulations 1986 (S.I. 1986 No. 1081), as amended by S.I. 1990 No. 520, S.I. 1991 No. 1198, S.I. 1992 No. 722 and S.I. 1995 No. 1948. The 1983 Act has been amended by the Representation of the People Acts 1985 and 1989, and the 1989 Act by the Representation of the People Act 1990.

[3] Local Government Act 1972, ss.6, 16, 25 and 35 and Sched. 2, para. 7 as amended.

[4] Sched. 5, para. 2, substituted by the Local Government (Wales) Act 1994, Sched. 3, para. 2.

Local government area	Electoral area	Representation
Communities	The community as a whole or wards of the community	Such number of councillors for each community or ward of a community as is fixed by order made under Part IV of the Local Government Act 1972[5]
London borough councils	Ward	Such number of councillors as is specified by order made under Part II of the Local Government Act 1992[6]

Electoral areas in counties, county boroughs, districts and London boroughs may be, and usually are, further divided into polling districts.[7]

B. THE FRANCHISE[8]

11–03 A person is entitled to vote at a local government election who:

(a) at the qualifying date has a qualification based on residence or *alternatively* has a service qualification or a qualification as a merchant seaman or a qualification as a voluntary mental patient, and

(b) on the qualifying date and the date of the poll is a Commonwealth citizen, a citizen of the Republic of Ireland or a relevant citizen of the European Union[9] and not suffering from a legal incapacity to vote, and

(c) on the date of the poll is of voting age, *i.e.* is 18 years or over[10]

provided that he is registered as an elector. The qualifying date is defined as October 10 for elections falling within the period of 12 months beginning on February 16 in the following year.[11]

A person is qualified under (a) if on the qualifying date he is *resident* in the electoral area. The term "residence" was considered in *Fox v. Stirk*,[12] a case concerned with student residence. It was held that the word "residence" has

---

[5] A special community review of the whole of Wales was conduct by the Local Government Boundary Commission for Wales under the 1972 Act, Sched. 10 (repealed by the Local Government (Wales) Act 1994, Sched. 15, para. 60).

[6] Until an order is made the number is that specified in the borough's charter.

[7] Representation of the People Act 1983, s.31, as amended by the Local Government Act 1985, Sched. 17, and the Local Government (Wales) Act 1994, Sched. 16, para. 68(6).

[8] 1983 Act, ss.2–7, 14–17.

[9] *i.e.* a citizen of any Member State of the European Union who is not either a Commonwealth Citizen or a Citizen of the Republic of Ireland: 1983 Act, s.202(1), as amended by the Local Government Elections (Changes to the Franchise and Qualification of Members) Regulations 1995 (S.I. 1995 No. 1948), referring to the definition of a "citizen of the Union" in Article 8(1)/EC as amended by Title II of the Treaty on European Union, and implementing Article 8b(1)/EC.

[10] *ibid.* ss.2, 4–7, 14, 17.

[11] *ibid.* s.4

[12] *Fox v. Stirk and Another; Ricketts v. Cambridge Electoral Registration Officer* [1970] 2 Q.B. 463.

314

no technical or special meaning but in the ordinary sense implies a degree of permanence. Lord Denning M.R. observed that the general principles in accordance with which the Representation of the People Act 1949 (now 1983) directs questions of residence as to the qualifying date are (1) that a person may have two residences, (2) that temporary presence at an address does not make a person resident there, and (3) that temporary absence does not deprive a person of his residence. A person may be resident in more than one place and where each such residence has the necessary degree of permanence he may be registered as an elector in more than one place.[13]

In *Hipperson v. Electoral Registration Officer for the District of Newbury*[14] it was held that a number of women who were living at the Greenham Common peace camp were "resident" there. The fact that camping on the land involved the commission of offences contrary to by-laws and the Highways Act 1980, s.137 (obstruction of the highway) was irrelevant: it was not necessary for the residence to be "lawful residence". Had any of the women been present on the land in breach of an injunction they could not have relied upon their residence there, but this was not the case on the facts.

The service qualification may be claimed by anyone who is a member of the forces or is employed in the service of the Crown or British Council in a post outside the United Kingdom or is the spouse of a person having a service qualification and (except in the case of spouses of members of the armed forces) who is resident outside the United Kingdom to be with his or her spouse.[15] A merchant seaman may be qualified as an elector in respect of an address at which he would be residing but for his occupation, or a hostel or club for merchant seamen where he normally stays in the course of his occupation.[16]

A mental patient, whether voluntary[17] or detained, who by the application of ordinary principles is regarded as resident at an address other than the mental hospital in which he is a patient or place where he is detained, is entitled to be registered at that other address. However, if by the application of those principles a voluntary mental patient would be regarded as resident only at the hospital, he may make a "patient's declaration" under section 7 of the Representation of the People Act 1983, provided that he is able to do so without assistance (other than assistance necessitated by blindness or other physical incapacity). The declaration must state, *inter alia*, the address where the declarant would be resident in the United Kingdom if he were not a voluntary mental patient or, if he cannot give any such address, an address (other than a mental hospital) at which he has resided in the United Kingdom. The declaration entitles the patient to be registered as an elector

---

[13] Though a person may have two residences it is an offence to vote in more than one electoral area at an ordinary election for councillors for a local government area which is not a single electoral area, or to vote more than once in the same electoral area: Representation of the People Act 1983, s.61.

[14] [1985] Q.B. 1060.

[15] Representation of the People Act 1983, s.14.

[16] *ibid.* s.6.

[17] *i.e.* "a person who is a patient in a mental hospital but is not liable to be detained there by virtue of any enactment": Representation of the People Act 1983, s.7(2).

at that address. A detained mental patient may not be treated as resident at the place of detention.[18]

11–04   Legal incapacity is of two kinds, derived from common law and defined in statute. At common law an idiot is debarred from voting[19] and also a person of unsound mind except during lucid periods.[20] The Forfeiture Act 1870[21] incapacitates a person convicted of treason until he has suffered his punishment or been pardoned. A convicted person during the time that he is detained in a penal institution (prison, remand centre, youth offender institution or secure training centre in the United Kingdom) in pursuance of his sentence is legally incapable of voting.[22] Persons guilty of corrupt practices and illegal practices are debarred from being registered as an elector or voting for five years—in the case of illegal practices the incapacity is effective only in the local government area in which the illegal practices took place.[23] Under the Public Bodies Corrupt Practices Act 1889[24] a person who is convicted for the second time of bribery or corruption of public officials is liable at the court's discretion to be disqualified for five years from being registered or from voting.

C. The Registration of Electors

11–05   A register of electors must be prepared each year. It is to be published not later than February 15 and is effective for elections occurring in the 12 months commencing February 16. Its preparation is dealt with in the Representation of the People Act 1983,[25] and the rules made thereunder.[26] The register serves both parliamentary and local government elections: the names of those who are entitled to vote only at local elections, *i.e.* peers of the realm, are appropriately marked. If a person reaches voting age during the currency of a register, the date of his eighteenth birthday is entered on the register, though he may not vote until an election which falls on or after that date.[27]

The compilation of the register falls to the registration officer, an officer appointed by each district and London borough council and the Common Council in England and each county and county borough council in Wales.[28] Where constituency boundaries and local government boundaries are not coterminous the appointment is dealt with by regulation.[29] The compilation of the register is based on a house-to-house or other sufficient inquiry and

---

[18] *ibid.* s.7(1).
[19] *Bedford (County) Case, Burgess'* Case (1785) 2 Lud.E.C. 381, 567.
[20] *Okehampton Case, Robin's* Case (1791) 1 Fras. 69, 162.
[21] s.2, as amended.
[22] Representation of the People Act 1983, s.3.
[23] *ibid.* s.160.
[24] s.2, as amended.
[25] ss.9–13.
[26] Representation of the People Regulations 1986 (S.I. 1986 No. 1081), as amended by S.I. 1990 No. 520, S.I. 1991 No. 1198, S.I. 1992 No. 722 and S.I. 1995 No. 1948.
[27] Representation of the People Act 1983, s.12(5).
[28] *ibid.* s.8, as amended by the Local Government (Wales) Act 1994, Sched. 16, para. 68(1).
[29] *ibid.* Sched. 2, para. 1(1). See S.I. 1986 No. 1081, reg. 5.

the registration officer has authority to require the giving of information.[30] The lists on which the register is based are made available for public inspection on or before November 28 each year and persons aggrieved by an omission or entry in the lists may lodge a claim or objection in the prescribed form, and provision is made in the regulations for the claim or objection to be formally heard by the registration officer. An appeal lies to the county court against a decision of the registration officer in specific matters (generally speaking all matters connected with registration and non-registration) provided that the aggrieved person has first exercised his right to submit a claim or objection to the registration officer within the prescribed time.[31] There is a right of appeal from the county court to the Court of Appeal.

When the register as published "does not carry out the registration officer's intention" by omitting certain particulars from the register as published (*e.g.* because of printer's errors) the registration officer is authorised to make the necessary correction: any such correction is not effective at a particular election if it is made on or after the date of giving notice of election.[32]

The compilation of certain other lists falls to the registration officer—a list of persons who have been convicted or reported guilty of corrupt or illegal practices (this list is based on information supplied to the registration officer by the local authority), the absent voters list and proxy list.

D. CANDIDATURE[33]

A person is qualified to be elected to a local authority if he is a British **11–06** subject,[34] a citizen of the Republic of Ireland or a "relevant citizen of the Union"[35] and on the "relevant day" he is 21 years of age and

(a) on that day he is and thereafter continues to be a local government elector for the area of the authority; or

(b) he has during the whole of the 12 months preceding that day occupied as owner or tenant any land or other premises in that area; or

---

[30] *ibid.* See S.I. 1986 No. 1081, reg. 29.

[31] *ibid.* s.56, as amended by the Representation of the People Act 1985, Sched. 2, para. 1 and Sched. 4, para. 16.

[32] Representation of the People Act 1983, s.11.

[33] Local Government Act 1972, ss.79–81, as amended by the Local Government Act 1985, Sched. 14, paras. 2, 3 and Sched. 17, the Education Reform Act 1988, Sched. 13, the Local Government and Housing Act 1989, Sched. 11, para. 21, and Sched. 12 and the Environment Act 1995, Sched. 10, para. 10(1). The election of persons who are not qualified can be challenged on an election petition: see §13–14, and n. 71.

[34] *i.e.* now a Commonwealth citizen or British subject under the British Nationality Act 1981: see s.5(1) and (3) of that Act.

[35] *i.e.* every person holding the nationality of a Member State of the European Union, except a commonwealth citizen or a citizen of the Republic of Ireland: 1972 Act, s.79(1), as amended and (2A) inserted by the Local Government Elections (Changes to the Franchise and Qualification of Members) Regulations 1995 (S.I. 1995 No. 1948), reg. 3(1), with effect from January 1, 1996.

(c) his principal or only place of work[36] during that 12 months has been in that area; or

(d) he has during the whole of those 12 months resided in that area; or

(e) in the case of a member of a parish or community council he has during the whole of those 12 months resided either in the parish or community or within three miles of it.

The "relevant day" is the day of nomination and the day of the poll if there is one. Where an election is not preceded by nomination (where, for example, a parish councillor is co-opted) it is the day of election.

11–07 The foregoing are positive requirements; a person is disqualified from being elected or being a member of a local authority if he:

(a) holds any paid office or employment (other than the office of chairman, vice-chairman or deputy chairman) appointments to which are made or confirmed by the local authority or a committee or sub-committee of the authority, or by a joint committee or National Park authority on which the authority is represented, or by any person holding any such office or employment[37]; or

(b) holds any employment in a company which, in accordance with Part V of the Local Government and Housing Act 1989 (other than section 73) is under the control of the local authority[38]; or

(c) is a person who has been adjudged bankrupt, or made a composition or arrangement with his creditors; or

(d) has within five years before the day of election or since his election been convicted of any offence and has had passed on him a sentence of imprisonment (whether suspended or not) for a period of not less than three months without the option of a fine; or

(e) is disqualified from being elected or being a member of that authority under Part III of the Representation of the People Act 1983 (which relates to corrupt or illegal practices); or

(f) is disqualified from membership for a specified period by order of the court because of his involvement in expenditure contrary to law[39]; or

(g) is disqualified from membership for five years following an auditor's certificate that a loss or deficiency has been caused by his wilful misconduct while a member of a local authority[40]; or

(h) holds a politically restricted post[41] under that local authority or any other local authority in Great Britain.[42]

---

[36] A qualification relying on a person's "principal place of work" may be based upon that person's work as a councillor: *Parker v. Yeo* (1992) 90 L.G.R. 645.

[37] A person is not disqualified from membership of a council by reason of an appointment to a paid position in a substantially independent company, notwithstanding that the appointments panel included a person paid by the council and seconded to the company: *R. v. Tower Hamlets London Borough Council, ex p. Jalal, The Times*, May 17, 1994.

[38] See § 4–89; s.80(1)(aa), inserted by the Local Government and Housing Act 1989, Sched. 11, para. 21: in force from a day to be appointed.

[39] Local Government Finance Act 1982, s.19: see § 13–29.

[40] *ibid.* s.20: see § 13–32.

[41] See above, § 4–62.

[42] Local Government and Housing Act 1989, s.1.

This last provision eliminates "twin-tracking," whereby members of one local authority were employees of another, and was enacted on the recommendation of the Widdicombe Committee on the Conduct of Local Authority Business.[43] The term "local authority" has a wide meaning in this context.[44]

The disqualification attaching to a person by reason of his having been **11–08** adjudged bankrupt ceases:

(a) unless the bankruptcy order made against that person is previously annulled, on his discharge from bankruptcy; and

(b) if the bankruptcy order is so annulled, on the date of the annulment.[45]

The disqualification attaching to a person by reason of his having made a composition or arrangement with his creditors ceases:

(a) if he pays his debts in full, on the date on which payment is completed; or

(b) in any other case, on the expiration of five years from the date on which the terms of the deed of composition or arrangement are fulfilled.

There are a number of particular rules on the matter of disqualification and paid office.[46] A teacher or person otherwise employed in a school or other educational establishment maintained or assisted by a county council is not precluded from becoming a member of a district council on the grounds that the district council nominates members to the county education committee[47] and in any case may become a member of the education committee or a committee which discharges duties under the Public Libraries and Museums Act 1964.[48]

An employee of a local authority who works under the direction of a committee or sub-committee of his employing authority on which there are representatives of other authorities is disqualified from membership of those other authorities. Similarly, employees who work under the direction of a joint committee, joint authority, joint board or National Parks authority may not serve on the constituent authorities.[49]

A teacher in a school maintained but not established by the authority (*i.e.*

---

[43] Cmnd. 9797, para. 6.29; Government Response (Cm. 433, 1988), paras. 5.16–5.32.

[44] 1989 Act, s.21(1), specifying county, district and London borough councils, the Common Council of the City of London, the Council of the Isles of Scilly, combined fire authorities, police authorities, waste disposal authorities, joint authorities, successors to residuary bodies, the Broads Authority, joint boards, joint or special planning boards.

[45] Local Government Act 1972, s.81(1), substituted by the Insolvency Act 1985, Sched. 8, para. 22, with effect from December 29, 1986.

[46] As to disqualification for appointment to a joint authority, see the Local Government Act 1985, s.35.

[47] Local Government Act 1972, s.81(4), as amended by the Local Government Act 1985, Sched. 17, and the Education Reform Act 1988, Sched. 13, Part II. See hereon *Lamb v. Jeffries* [1956] 1 Q.B. 431 and *Boyd v. Easington Rural District Council* [1963] 1 W.L.R. 1281.

[48] Local Government Act 1972, s.104(2), as amended by the Education Reform Act 1988, Sched. 13 and the Education Act 1993, Sched. 19, para. 50.

[49] *ibid.* s.80(2), as amended by the Local Government Act 1985, Sched. 14, para. 3, and the Environment Act 1995, Sched. 10, para. 10.

a voluntary school), is in the same position as a teacher employed directly by the authority—he is disqualified from membership.[50]

E. The Conduct of Elections

Election day and frequency of elections

11–09 Ordinary local government elections are held on the first Thursday in May, unless the Secretary of State fixes another day by order made before February 1 in the previous year or, in the case of an order affecting more than one year, the first year.[51] Where the date of a general election is the same as the ordinary day for local government elections, any poll for the election of parish or community councillors is postponed for three weeks.[52]

County council elections take place every four years and all the councillors retire together. Those first elected in 1973 retired in 1977.[53] An election for metropolitan district councillors takes place in each year other than 1977 and every fourth year thereafter, and members retire by thirds.[54] Non-metropolitan district councils may, by the passing of a "requisite resolution" ask the Secretary of State to make an order (a) providing for whole council elections, all the councillors retiring simultaneously, or (b) for a system of retirement by thirds.[55] Where the Secretary of State receives a request under (a), he may order simultaneous elections. Where he receives a request under (b) he may direct the Local Government Commission for England to conduct a review and make recommendations as to the number, boundaries and names of wards into which the district is to be divided and the number of councillors to be elected for each ward and the order of retirement of councillors elected for wards not returning a number of councillors which is divisible by three. The "requisite resolution" is passed at a specially convened meeting of the council with notice of the object and a two-thirds majority is required. An option may not be exercised again for 10 years. Whole council elections took place in 1976, 1979, 1983, 1987, 1991 and 1995, and will take place every four years thereafter, in the year midway between county council elections. Elections which by order of the Secretary of State are to be by thirds are to take place in the year the order comes into force and in each year in which there is no county council election.

Ordinary elections in Wales for the new principal councils established by the Local Government (Wales) Act 1994 took place in 1995 and will take place in every fourth year after 1995.[56] The term of office of each councillor is

---

[50] *ibid.* s.80(3).
[51] Representation of the People Act 1983, s.37, as amended by the Representation of the People Act 1985, s.18. In 1986, the date was May 8: *ibid.*
[52] Representation of the People Act 1985, s.16.
[53] Local Government Act 1972, ss.7(1) and 26(1). Elections have accordingly been held in 1977, 1981, 1985, 1989 and 1993.
[54] *ibid.* s.7(2), as amended by the Local Government Act 1985, Sched. 16, para. 3.
[55] Local Government Act 1972, ss.7(4)–(7), as amended by the Local Government Act 1992, Sched. 3, para. 7.
[56] Local Government Act 1972, s.26, as substituted by the Local Government (Wales) Act 1994, s.4(2). The first elections were on May 4, 1995: Welsh Principal Councils (Day of Election) Order 1994 (S.I. 1994 No. 2843).

four years and all councillors retire together; it is no longer possible to opt to have election by thirds.

Parish councillors elected in 1973 held office for three years, retiring in 1976. Those elected in 1976 retired in 1979, and thereafter parish councillors have been elected for a four-year term.[57] There were ordinary elections of community councillors in 1995 and elections will take place every four years thereafter.[58]

An election for London borough councillors took place in 1974 and 1978 and has taken place every fourth year thereafter.[59]

Procedure at elections

The principal steps to be taken in the conduct of an election are prescribed **11–10** in detail in the Local Elections (Principal Areas) Rules 1986.[60] The latest time at which the various steps are taken is set out in the following table.

Proceeding	*Latest time*
Publication of notice of election	Twenty-fifth day before the day of election
Delivery of nomination papers	Noon on the nineteenth day before the day of election
Publication of statement as to persons nominated	Noon on the seventeenth day before the day of election
Delivery of notices of withdrawals of candidature	Noon on the sixteenth day before the day of election
Applications and notices *re* postal and proxy voting	Thirteenth day before the day of election[61]
Notice of poll	Sixth day before the day of election
Notice of appointment of polling or counting agents	Fifth day before the day of election[62]
Polling	On the day of election

A Saturday, Sunday, Christmas Eve, Christmas Day, Maundy Thursday, Good Friday or a bank holiday or a day appointed for public thanksgiving or mourning are disregarded.[63]

The conduct of elections is largely in the hands of the returning officer. At **11–11** district, county borough or county council elections, he is an officer appointed by the council. At parish or community elections he is an officer appointed by the district council in which the parish lies (in England) or the

---

[57] Local Government Act 1972, s.16.

[58] *ibid.* s.35, as amended by the Local Government (Wales) Act 1994, s.15.

[59] *ibid.* Sched. 2, para. 6(3), as amended by the London Councillors Orders 1976 (S.I. 1976 No. 213), altering previous arrangements.

[60] S.I. 1986 No. 2214, as amended by S.I.s 1987 No. 26, 1990 No. 158 and 1995 No. 1945. There are parallel provisions (with some differences) in the Local Elections (Parishes and Communities) Rules 1986 (S.I. 1986 No. 2215), as amended by S.I.s 1987 No. 260, 1990 No. 157 and 1995 No. 1945. See also the Elections (Welsh Forms) Order 1995 (S.I. 1995 No. 836), modifying the forms.

[61] See the Representation of the People Regulations 1986 (S.I. 1986 No. 1081), reg. 69, as amended by S.I. 1990 No. 520, reg. 22. For exceptions where later applications may be permitted see reg. 69(3).

[62] 1986 Rules, r. 24.

[63] 1986 Rules, r. 2.

county or county borough council in which the community lies (in Wales).[64] At elections for the London boroughs the returning officer is the proper officer of the borough.[65] A returning officer may appoint one or more persons to discharge all or any of his functions.

The first step in an election is the publication by the returning officer of the notice of election in the prescribed form.[66] It indicates, *inter alia*, where nominations are to be lodged, the latest time for lodging, and the latest date by which applications to be treated as absent voters, and other applications and notices about postal or proxy voting, must reach the registration officer.

11–12 A candidate is required to complete a nomination paper which follows the prescribed form, signed by a proposer and seconder and by eight other electors of the electoral area as assenting to the nomination.[67] The signatures on the nomination form must be the usual signatures.[68]

Formerly, if the candidate's description were omitted the nomination was bad. It is now not essential to include any description at all. If a description is included (and it customarily is) it may contain a reference to a candidate's political activities or associations, but it may not in any event exceed six words in length. It is not the function of the returning officer to determine whether the description included is that which a candidate can properly claim to use.

It is the duty of the returning officer to decide, as soon as practicable after delivery, on the validity of the nomination paper.[69] A paper may be rejected as invalid on one or other of two grounds only, that the *particulars* of the candidate or person subscribing the paper are not as required by law or that the *paper* is not subscribed as required by law. The decision of the returning officer that a nomination paper is valid in form is final and may not be questioned in any proceeding whatsoever. The returning officer may not investigate the authenticity of particulars given which on their face are unobjectionable.[70] Objections on grounds other than form may be raised on an election petition.[71] If the returning officer decides the nomination paper to be bad his decision may also be reviewed by way of election petition.

The purpose of the rule that a returning officer's decision on the validity of a nomination paper is final is to err on the side of inclusiveness and to allow

---

[64] Representation of the People Act 1983, s.35, (1), (1A) as amended by the Local Government Act 1985, Sched. 16, paras. 11 and 17, and the Local Government (Wales) Act 1994, Sched. 16, para. 68(7).

[65] *ibid.*, s.35(3).

[66] Local Elections (Principal Areas) Rules 1986 (S.I. 1986 No. 1081), r. 3.

[67] rr. 4, 5. In the case of parish and community councils only a proposer and seconder are required: Local Elections (Parishes and Communities) Rules 1986 (S.I. 1986 No. 2215), rr. 4, 5.

[68] *Re Melton Mowbray (Egerton Ward) U.D.C. Election* [1969] 1 Q.B. 192.

[69] r. 7.

[70] *Greenway-Stanley v. Paterson* [1977] 2 All E.R. 663.

[71] r. 7(7); *R. v. Election Court, ex p. Sheppard* [1975] 1 W.L.R. 1319 and *Gilham v. Tall and May* [1985] C.L.Y. 1066 (address falsely given as a candidate's home address: elections declared void); *Talbot v. Gordon and Thornley* [1989] C.L.Y. 1390 (nomination forms incorrectly stated that candidates were qualified by residence rather than as electors: election declared void).

any improper inclusion to be challenged on an election petition: *per* Sedley J. in *Ex p. Saunders*,[72] refusing a Liberal Democrat candidate leave to apply for judicial review of a decision of the acting returning officer to accept as valid the nomination papers delivered for Richard John Huggett as a "Literal Democrat" candidate for a forthcoming European election. At that election, Mr Huggett polled over 10,000 votes and the Liberal Democrat candidate, Mr Saunders, lost by 800 votes to the Conservative. An election court subsequently rejected an election petition challenging the result, in *Saunders v. Chichester*.[73] The court held that there was no requirement that the optional description on the ballot paper be true, fair or not confusing, provided that with the other particulars it was sufficient to identify the candidate. The returning officer had no power to investigate the validity of the description.

The formalities of nomination are complete when the candidate has submitted a consent to nomination in writing, attested by one witness, stating that he is qualified as required by law and giving particulars of his qualification.[74]

Under section 96 of the Representation of the People Act 1983,[75] a candidate is entitled for the purpose of holding public meetings in furtherance of his candidature to the free use, at reasonable times between the notice of election and the day preceding the day of election, of any room which it is the practice to be let for public meetings and which is maintained wholly or mainly at public expense, and any suitable school room.[76]

Election agent[77]

Except in the case of parish or community council elections the candidate **11–13** is required to appoint an election agent; he may appoint himself and will be taken to have appointed himself if in fact he makes no appointment. The agent's office must be in the local government area, or in the constituency or one of the constituencies in which the area is comprised, or in a borough or district which adjoins it. The agent is to be generally concerned with the candidate's affairs, but certain specific duties are put on him by statute, particularly in the matter of expenses, the appointment of messengers, clerks and polling agents and the hiring of rooms. The following extract from the Final Report of the Committee on Electoral Reform on the requirement as to the appointment of election agents indicates an agent's functions[78]:

"The object of the requirement is that there shall be an experienced person

---

[72] *The Times*, May 30, 1994.
[73] *The Times*, December 2, 1994.
[74] r. 6, Appendix.
[75] As substituted by the Representation of the People Act 1985, Sched. 4, para. 38, and amended by the Education Reform Act 1988, Sched. 12, Part I, para. 31.
[76] The right is a private law right enforceable in an action for a declaration or injunction: *Ettridge v. Morrell* (1987) 85 L.G.R. 100, C.A.
[77] Representation of the People Act 1983, ss.67, 69–71, as amended by the Representation of the People Act 1985, Sched. 4, paras. 20, 22, 23.
[78] Cmd. 7286 (1947–48).

responsible to the candidate and to the public for the proper management of the candidature and in particular for the control of expenditure. The employment of an agent is of great benefit to the candidate, and a competent agent can do much to promote due observance of electoral law."

The responsibility of a candidate for the acts of his agent is considerably greater than the responsibility normally flowing from the principal/agent relationship, where in general a principal is responsible only for the acts of his agent which come within the scope of the authority he has given. So far as responsibility is concerned, the relationship is more one of master and servant, the master being responsible for the acts of his servant within the course of his employment. Lush J. said in the *Harwich* case[79]:

"The relation between a candidate and a person whom he constitutes his agent is much more intimate than that which subsists between an ordinary principal and an agent.... [T]he candidate is responsible for all the misdeeds of his agent committed within the scope of his authority, although they were done against his express directions, and even in wilful defiance of them. There is never any difficulty or doubt as regards this proposition."

Voting[80]

11–14 Electors record their votes in person at the polling stations to which they are allotted by the returning officer, as published in the notice of poll. Exceptions are made in the case of persons falling within one of the following groups:

(a) An elector may vote by post if he is shown in the absent voters list as entitled to vote by post.

(b) An elector may vote by proxy if he is shown in the absent voters list as entitled to vote by proxy, unless, before a ballot paper has been issued for him so to vote, he applies at the polling station allotted to him for a ballot paper for the purpose of voting in person.

(c) An elector may vote in person at any polling station in the electoral area if

   (i) he is not entitled to an absent vote; and

   (ii) he cannot reasonably be expected to go in person to the polling station allotted to him, by reason of the particular circumstances of his employment, either as a constable or by the returning officer, on the date of the poll, for a purpose connected with the election.

An elector may be entitled to an absent vote (1) for an indefinite period or (2) for a particular election. He will be eligible for an absent vote for an indefinite period:

(a) if he is or will be registered as a service voter; or

---

[79] *Harwich* (1880) 3 O'M & H. 61 at p. 69.

[80] Representation of the People Act 1983, s.46; Representation of the People Act 1985, ss.5–9, Sched. 2, s.6 as amended by the Representation of the People Act 1990, s.1. Representation of the People Regulations 1986 (S.I. 1986 No. 1081), as amended by S.I. 1991 No. 1198, S.I. 1992 No. 722 and S.I. 1995 No. 1948, Part IV (absent voters), Part V (postal ballot papers).

(b) if he is no longer resident at his qualifying address or at any other address in the same area,[81]
(c) if he cannot reasonably be expected to go in person to the polling station allotted or likely to be allotted to him, or to vote unaided there, by reason of blindness or other physical incapacity; or
(d) if he cannot reasonably be expected to go in person to that polling station by reason of the general nature of his occupation, service or employment or that of his spouse; or
(e) if he cannot go in person from his qualifying address to that polling station without making a journey by air or sea.

Applications must be made to the registration officer, and must meet the prescribed requirements. The officer must keep a record of successful applications.

An elector will be eligible for an absent vote at a particular election if his circumstances on the date of the poll will or are likely to be such that he cannot reasonably be expected to vote in person at the polling station allotted or likely to be allotted to him. Again, applications must be made to the registration officer and must meet the prescribed requirements.[82] These provisions do not apply to a person eligible for an absent vote for an indefinite period, but such a person entitled to vote by post may apply, in respect of a particular election, to the registration officer (a) for his ballot paper to be sent to a different address in the United Kingdom, or (b) to vote by proxy. The officer must grant such an application if it meets the prescribed requirements.

The registration officer must, in respect of each election, keep an "absent voters list" of all persons entitled to vote by proxy or by post.

A person entitled to vote *as* proxy may do so in person at the polling station allotted to the elector unless he is included in the special list of such persons entitled to vote as proxy by post.

In a contested election the counting of votes is the responsibility of the **11–15** returning officer.[83] This is done under conditions of secrecy in the presence of the candidates, their spouses, election agents and counting agents, and the official counting staff, and such other persons as may be approved by the returning officer after consultation with the agents. All such persons must make a formal declaration of secrecy. The decision of the returning officer on any question relating to the validity of a ballot paper or the voting or other mark thereon is final, but is subject to review on an election petition. If there is equality of votes he casts lots. When the result of the poll has been

---

[81] This ground was added by the Representation of the People Act 1990, s.1. Two addresses are in the same area if they are in the same parliamentary constituency in Greater London or a metropolitan county, in the same electoral division (and, if either address is in a parish, the same parish) in a non-metropolitan county in England, or in the same electoral division of a county in Wales and in the same community: *ibid.*
[82] Requirements that such applications be attested were abolished by S.I. 1990 No. 520, reg. 21, except where the claim relates to the applicant's health on polling day when the relevant circumstances could not have been foreseen earlier.
[83] Local Election (Principal Areas) Rules 1986 (S.I. 1986 No. 2214), rr. 38 *et seq.*

ascertained he must declare the result forthwith and as soon as possible publish it, with the number of votes given to each candidate, and the numbers of rejected ballot papers in the different categories. He then formally reports the result to the proper officer of the authority, to whom he hands over the election documents for custody. In an uncontested election, the returning officer is required, as soon as practicable after the latest time for the delivery of notices of withdrawals of candidature, to declare elected the person or persons remaining validly nominated and to notify the proper officer of the council and to give public notice of their names.

Election expenses[84]

11–16   The total sum which a candidate may incur by way of election expenses is limited. Election expenses are expenses incurred before, during or after an election on account of or in respect of the conduct or management of the election. The maximum is £205 plus 4p for every entry in the register.[85] Where there are two joint candidates the maximum of each is reduced by one-fourth; where there are more than two, by one-third. Candidates are joint candidates for this purpose where they employ the same election agent or employ the same clerks or messengers, or hire the same committee rooms, or publish a joint election address.

11–17   A candidate or election agent who knowingly contravenes the rules is guilty of an illegal practice. All expenses (apart from the personal expenses of the candidate and certain petty expenses) must be paid by or through the election agent. No expenses may be incurred in holding public meetings or organising public displays, or issuing advertisements, circulars or publications, or otherwise presenting to the electors the candidate or his views, or the extent or nature of his backing or disparaging another candidate, with a view to promoting or procuring the election of a candidate,[86] except by the candidate, his election agent and persons authorised in writing by the election agent. A party political broadcast is not an expense within the terms of section 63 of the Representation of the People Act 1949 (now section 75 of the 1983 Act).[87]

All payments made by an election agent (except where they are less than £20, or £10 in parish council elections) must be vouched for by a bill, stating the particulars, and by a receipt, and all election expenses are to be paid within 28 days of the declaration of the result of the election. Within 35 days after the declaration of the election result, the election agent must deliver to the returning officer a return as to election expenses, together with a declaration as to the election expenses that to the best of his knowledge and

---

[84] Representation of the People Act 1983, ss.72–90, and Sched. 4, as amended by the Representation of the People Act 1985, s.14 and Sched. 4, paras. 24–33, 89. Section 76A, inserted by the 1985 Act, s.14(4), empowers the Secretary of State to vary the specified maxima by statutory instrument.

[85] Representation of the People (Variation of Limits of Candidates' Election Expenses) Order 1994 (S.I. 1994 No. 747), reg. 6.

[86] It is sufficient to establish an intention to prevent the election of a candidate: *D.P.P. v. Luft* [1977] A.C. 962 (literature advising the electorate not to vote for National Front candidates).

[87] *Grieve v. Douglas-Home* 1965 S.L.T. 186.

belief the return is true and correct. At the same time, or within seven days afterwards, the candidate must deliver to the returning officer a declaration in similar terms. If a candidate or agent makes a false declaration he is guilty of a corrupt practice; a failure to send in the return or declaration within the prescribed time is an illegal practice but relief against the consequences of this failure may, in certain circumstances, be granted.

F. Questioning an Election[88]

Election petition[89]

An election may be challenged by means of an election petition presented **11–18** in the prescribed form to the Queen's Bench Division of the High Court either by four or more persons who voted or were entitled to vote at the election, or by a candidate. A person whose election is questioned and a returning officer of whose conduct the petition complains may be made a respondent. The petition may be founded on one or more of the following grounds:

(a) that the candidate was disqualified at the time of the election;
(b) that the candidate was not duly elected;
(c) that the election was avoided by corrupt or illegal practices;
(d) that corrupt or illegal practices have so extensively prevailed that they may be reasonably supposed to have affected the result;
(e) that the candidate or his election agent personally engaged as a canvasser or agent someone whom he knew or had reasonable grounds for supposing to be subject to incapacity by reason of his having been guilty of a corrupt or illegal practice or having been convicted more than once of bribery and corruption of members or officers of public bodies under the Public Bodies Corrupt Practices Act 1889.

A copy of the petition is forwarded by the court to the local authority for **11–19** publication in the area.

It is for the court to decide on the evidence as a whole whether there has been a substantial compliance with the law as to elections or whether an act or omission affected the result.

> *Re Kensington North Parliamentary Election.*[90] A parliamentary election petition was brought by Sir Oswald Mosley for a scrutiny of the votes recorded as having been cast in the election for the North Division of the Parliamentary Borough of Kensington, and for a determination that the Member in fact elected was not duly elected, and that his election and return were void on the ground that in the holding of the election divers illegal practices and breaches of the statutory rules governing the conduct of the election were committed by the

---

[88] Representation of the People Act 1983, ss.127–163, as amended by the Representation of the People Act 1985, Sched. 4, paras. 48–51 and Sched. 5; Election Petition Rules 1960 (S.I. 1960 No. 543 as amended by S.I.s 1979 No. 543 and 1985 No. 1278).
[89] See *Levers v. Morris* [1972] 1 Q.B. 221 for an example of this proceeding.
[90] [1960] 1 W.L.R. 762.

returning officer and/or his servants or agents. *Held*, dismissing the petition, that, although certain breaches of the rules had been proved, there was no evidence that there had been a substantial breach, and that such breaches as there had been had not affected the result of the election. It was further held that the burden of proof in an election petition is not on the respondent to the petition; it is for the election court to decide on the evidence as a whole whether there has been a substantial compliance with the law as to elections or whether an act or omission affected the result.

> *Thompson v. Dann; In re a local government election for Eel Brook Electoral Division of Hammersmith and Fulham London Borough Council.*[91] The Divisional Court refused to declare a vote void on the ground of personation. All that was established was that a voter (who had appointed a proxy) had not voted in person and that a ballot paper attributed to her had been found among the votes. To establish personation it had to be shown that another person had personated the particular person who had not voted. Here, it was much more likely that there had been a mistake by the polling clerk in marking the register than that an unknown person had deliberately impersonated the voter in question.

No local government election is to be declared invalid by reason of any act or omission of the returning officer or any other person in breach of his official duty or otherwise of the local elections rules if it appears that the election was so conducted as to be substantially in accordance with the law and that the act or omission did not affect its result.[92]

> *Gunn v. Sharpe.*[93] There was a failure to stamp ballot papers in a local election with the official mark. This disfranchised over half the voters at one polling station and resulted in two candidates being elected who otherwise would not have been. *Held*, the election was void as it had not been conducted substantially in accordance with the rules.
>
> *Morgan v. Simpson.*[94] Forty-four unstamped papers out of 24,000 resulted in a candidate having a majority of 11 votes, whereas had they been stamped and therefore counted, his opponent would have been elected with a majority of seven. *Held*, the election was void. Although it had been conducted substantially in accordance with the law, the result had in fact been affected by breaches of the rules.
>
> *Ruffle v. Rogers.*[95] The mere fact that a voter wrote the name of his chosen candidate on his ballot did not of itself invalidate the paper. The voter could not, on the facts, be clearly identified and he had made his intention clear. However, the failure to stamp four ballot papers had affected the result, as it would otherwise have been a tie: accordingly, the election was declared void.

Inspection of ballot papers can be obtained by order of a county court or an election court.[96]

---

[91] *The Times*, November 3, 1994.
[92] Representation of the People Act 1983, s.48.
[93] [1974] Q.B. 808.
[94] [1975] Q.B. 151; *cf. James v. Davies* (1977) 76 L.G.R. 189 (election not void by reason of inconsistent election notices).
[95] [1982] Q.B. 1220.
[96] Local Elections (Principal Areas) Rules 1986 (S.I. 1986 No. 2214), r. 47.

Presentation of petition

A petition founded on a corrupt practice must be presented within 21 days **11–20** from election day. This time is extended in certain circumstances. Where the petition alleges a corrupt practice relating to a payment or reward made or promised since the election, the time is 28 days after payment or promise. Where illegal practices are alleged, the latest time for presentation is 14 days after the receipt by the clerk of the return and declaration of election expenses; but where the illegal practice is the payment of money or other act done since the election, then the latest time for presentation is 28 days from the date of the payment or such act.

When the petition is presented, or within three days thereafter, the petitioner must give security for all costs which may become payable by him to any witness summoned on his behalf or to any respondent. The security is for an amount not exceeding £2,500 as the High Court directs, and must be by way of a surety[97] (or sureties) or deposit of money or a combination of both.

The election court

The election court consists of a commissioner sitting without jury. The **11–21** commissioner is a barrister of at least 15 years' standing and is appointed by the judges on the rota for the trial of parliamentary election petitions. Provision is made for the stating of a special case for the determination of the High Court. At the conclusion of the trial the election court certifies to the High Court its decision as to whether the person whose election was complained of was duly elected or whether some other person was elected, or whether the election was void. This determination is final as to the matters at issue in the petition. Where an election has been declared void and no other person has been declared elected, a new election will be held in the same way as when a casual vacancy occurs. Where illegal or corrupt practices have been alleged a further report is required of the election court stating:

(a) whether any corrupt or illegal practice is proved to have been committed by or with the consent of the candidate and the nature of the corrupt or illegal practice;
(b) whether any of the candidates has been guilty by his agents of any corrupt or illegal practice;
(c) the names of all persons guilty of a corrupt or illegal practice; and
(d) whether any corrupt practices have, or whether there is reason to believe that any corrupt practices have, extensively prevailed in the electoral area.

The election of a candidate is void if he is reported under (a) or (b) or if it is **11–22** shown that corrupt or illegal practices committed to procure his election

---

[97] This must be a third party and not the petitioner himself: *Barrett v. Tuckman, The Times,* November 5, 1984.

have so extensively prevailed that they may be reasonably supposed to have affected the result. Other consequences may flow from this report. First, the report must be laid before the Director of Public Prosecutions (who is always to be present or represented at the trial of an election petition if the election court so requests, and who otherwise has a discretion to attend), and he may prosecute offenders before the election court, or some other competent court. Where information is given to the Director that a person has been guilty of an offence under the Representation of the People Act 1983, he must make such inquiries and institute such prosecutions as the circumstances of the case appear to him to require.[98] Secondly, certain incapacities as to voting and holding office attach to persons who are reported guilty of corrupt or illegal practices. These matters are noted in earlier paragraphs.

All costs of and incidental to the presentation of an election petition and consequent proceedings are defrayed by the parties to the petition in the proportion which the election court or High Court determines.[99] The court may also direct that any costs incurred by vexatious conduct, unfounded allegations or unfounded objections shall be defrayed by the parties by whom they were caused, whether or not they were on the whole successful.

G. Election Offences

11–23 It is customary to divide election offences into two groups, those which stem from the common law and those from statute. The greater number of common law offences have now been defined in statute and for practical purposes it is the statutory offences which are important. Bribery at an election, for example, is an offence at common law; it is also an offence under the Representation of the People Act 1983, and whilst it is still open to proceed by way of the common law in the case of bribery at an election a prosecutor would normally choose the statutory procedure.

Statutory offences may be considered in three groups, corrupt practices, illegal practices, and other election offences. The distinction between a corrupt practice and an illegal practice lies more in the consequence which flows from the offence rather than in the offence itself. There is, however, this further point: speaking generally a corrupt practice involves a guilty intention; an illegal practice is something prohibited by the legislature whether it is done honestly or dishonestly. The statute law relating to corrupt and illegal practices is now contained in the Representation of the People Act 1983 and the following are corrupt practices: personation, incurring expense without authority of the candidate or agent; false declaration in relation to election expenses; bribery; treating; undue influence.[1]

For example, section 115(2)(b) of the Representation of the People Act 1983 provides that a person is guilty of undue influence if, by a fraudulent

---

[98] Representation of the People Act 1983, s.181, as amended by the Representation of the People Act 1985, Sched. 4, para. 63, Sched. 5, and the Prosecution of Offences Act 1985, Sched. 2.

[99] See *R. v. Cripps, ex p. Muldoon* [1984] Q.B. 686.

[1] Representation of the People Act 1983, ss.60, 75, 82, 113, 114, 115.

device or contrivance, he, *inter alia*, impedes or prevents the free exercise of the franchise by an elector or proxy. In *R. v. Rowe, ex p. Mainwaring*[2] the Court of Appeal held that a leaflet issued by Liberal Democrat election candidates in Tower Hamlets to look like a Labour leaflet was fraudulent, but had not been shown to have impeded or prevented the free exercise of the franchise by any elector. The leaflet was fraudulent, in that it lied about its own genesis, and notwithstanding that it comprised true statements made by Labour spokesmen in the past. The question of whether an elector was impeded was to be determined by reference to the time when the vote was cast on polling day and there was insufficient evidence of this given that the matter had to be proved beyond reasonable doubt.

Illegal practices and other election offences may be grouped under five **11–24** headings.[3] It will be noted that some offences are illegal practices only if committed by a candidate or agent.

(a) *Illegal payments:* Payments for the conveyance of electors to the poll, and to voters for exhibiting bills and notices, payments to induce withdrawal of a candidate, the provision of money for illegal payments; exceeding maximum expenses; failure to make a return and declaration as to expenses.

(b) *Illegal hiring and employment:* The hiring of conveyances for voters, and certain premises for committee rooms (licensed premises); the employment of paid canvassers. These offences are illegal practices if committed by a candidate or agent.

(c) *Restrictions on broadcasting during elections:* It is unlawful during the period commencing five weeks before polling day for an item about the electoral area to be broadcast or televised if any candidate who takes part does not consent; and, unless all candidates consent, any person taking part in the item broadcast for the purpose of promoting or procuring his election, is guilty of an illegal practice, unless the broadcast is without his consent. The use of a wireless or television station abroad for election purposes is an illegal practice.

(d) *Improper conduct of election campaign:* The publication of false statements of fact relating to the personal conduct or character of the candidate (unless the person concerned had reasonable grounds for supposing and did in fact believe that his statements were true); the publication of a false statement as to the withdrawal of a candidate; acting (or inciting others to act) in a disorderly manner at an election meeting for the purpose of preventing the transaction of business; inducing or procuring illegal practices. Under this heading may be included the failure to show the printer's name and address on election literature. This is an illegal practice if committed by a candidate or agent.

---

[2] [1992] 1 W.L.R. 1059.
[3] *ibid.* ss.61–66, 73, 75, 76, 78, 82–87, 92–94, 97, 99–102, 106–112, 168, 169, 175, 189, as amended by the Representation of the People Act 1985, Scheds. 3, 4, 5.

(e) *Voting offences:* It is an illegal practice to vote or to induce another to vote contrary to law.

11–25   A person guilty of a corrupt practice is liable to imprisonment or fine or both,[4] and other consequences and incapacities flow from a finding of guilt. He may be prosecuted before an election court which is hearing an election petition, or on indictment or summarily. A person guilty of an illegal practice, payment, employment or hiring is liable to a fine not exceeding level 5 on the standard scale.[5]

Provision is made in certain circumstances for the granting of relief from the consequences of wrongful acts. Where an illegal practice, payment, employment or hiring has been committed and the act or omission arises from inadvertence or accidental miscalculation or from some other reasonable cause of like nature, an application for relief may be made to the High Court or election court (or in certain cases to the county court).[6] The Director of Public Prosecutions or his assistant or representative may appear and make representations. An applicant must show that there has been no want of good faith, and notice of the application must be published locally. The effect of relief is to except the particular act or omission from being an illegal practice—the taint of illegality is removed so that no proceedings can be instituted in respect of that act or omission, either against the applicant or any other person.

11–26   Relief may also be granted by the High Court, an election court or a county court where a candidate or an agent fails to deliver the return and declaration as to election expenses, where the failure arises through the illness of the applicant or the absence, death, illness or misconduct of the election agent or by reason of inadvertence, provided that there is no want of good faith.[7] A candidate may also in certain circumstances avoid the consequences which would otherwise fall to him through the wrongful acts of his agent. Where such a candidate is reported by the election court to have been guilty *by his agents* of treating, undue influence or any illegal practice, and the election court further reports that the candidate has proved:

(a) that no corrupt or illegal practice was committed at the election by the candidate or his election agent and the offences mentioned in the report were committed contrary to the orders and without the sanction or connivance of the candidate or his election agent; and

(b) that the candidate and his election agent took all reasonable means for preventing the commission of corrupt and illegal practices at the election; and

(c) that the offences mentioned in the report were of a trivial, unimportant and limited character; and

---

[4] Representation of the People Act 1983, s.168(1)–(4), as substituted by the Representation of the People Act 1985, Sched. 3, para. 8.
[5] *ibid.* s.169, 175.
[6] *ibid.* s.167. See *Re Berry* [1978] Crim.L.R. 357.
[7] *ibid.* s.86.

(d) that in all other respects the election was free from any corrupt or illegal practice on the part of the candidate and of his agents.

then the election is not avoided and the candidate suffers no incapacity.[8]

It was at one time suggested that an election address was the subject of **11–27** qualified privilege, being a communication from one elector to other electors on a matter of common interest which did not come within section 10 of the Defamation Act 1952: but this view has now been clarified and overruled. In ordinary circumstances, therefore, an election address is not privileged.[9]

A person who commits the offence of personation at an election is liable to imprisonment for a term not exceeding two years.[10]

H. Elections to Fill a Casual Vacancy[11]

The procedure for the filling of a casual vacancy is substantially the same as **11–28** that for an ordinary election. A casual vacancy may arise through the failure of an elected person to make a declaration of acceptance of office, or through the death or resignation of a member, or through the failure of a member to attend any meeting of the authority or of its committees or subcommittees for a period of six consecutive months (unless the failure was due to some reason approved by the authority), or because a member ceases to be qualified, or becomes disqualified. Where a casual vacancy arises because a member ceases to be qualified or becomes disqualified or because of his failure to attend meetings, the local authority is required forthwith to declare the office vacant, unless the High Court has already made a declaration to this effect. In other cases, a vacancy may be declared by the local authority or the High Court or by notice in writing given to the proper officer by two local government electors for the area.[12] An election to fill a casual vacancy must be held within 42 days after the High Court or the council has declared the office to be vacant or within 42 days after written notice of the vacancy has been given to the authority by two electors for the area. Where a casual vacancy occurs within six months before the ordinary day of retirement from the office in which the vacancy arises, it is filled at the next ordinary election. If there is an election to fill several casual vacancies, the successful candidate with the fewer votes takes the shorter period; where the election is combined with an ordinary election of councillors and not contested, somewhat complex rules apply. A casual vacancy among parish councillors or community councillors is filled by election or by the parish or community council in accordance with the relevant election rules. Where

---

[8] Representation of the People Act 1983, s.158.
[9] *Plummer v. Charman* [1962] 1 W.L.R. 1469.
[10] Representation of the People Act 1983, s.168(1), as substituted by the Representation of the People Act 1985, Sched. 3, para. 8.
[11] Local Government Act 1972, ss.86, 87, 89, 90, 91, as amended by the Local Government Act 1985, Sched. 14, paras. 8–11, the Education Reform Act 1988, Sched. 13, Part I, and the Local Government (Wales) Act 1994, Sched. 15, para. 24.
[12] Local Government Act 1972, s.89.

there are so many vacancies among parish or community councillors that the council may be unable to act, the district council or, in Wales, the principal council may by order make temporary appointments until other councillors are elected to take up office.[13]

---

[13] *ibid.* s.91, as amended by the Local Government (Wales) Act 1994, Sched. 15, para. 24.

CHAPTER 12

LOCAL AUTHORITY FINANCE

THE topic of local government finance can be divided into a number of issues **12–01** and headings relating to the financial transactions and administration of local government. All finance is deemed to be either revenue or capital.

The revenue income of local authorities is at present obtained largely from the three sources of grants from central government, the non-domestic rate, and the council tax. Each of these sources is examined in detail in a separate chapter, the first, funded by the national exchequer, in chapter 14 and the other two, based on taxation with different degrees of central control and local discretion, in chapters 15 and 16. The raising of other revenue by the more minor means of fees and charges is considered in this chapter.

The ability of local government to conduct its business is determined not only by the level of its revenue income, but also by the balance between these different sources and the discretion left to the authority. Nationally, this balance varies both between authorities and also over time, determined by political and economic factors. Thus central grants have in the past amounted to up to 65 per cent of total revenue funding for local government. Within that overall figure for central grant the balance between non-specific support grant and grants for particular purposes can also affect the discretion of the authority.[1] At other times, the majority of revenue funding came from locally raised taxes under the rating system.[2]

The rating system was subject to a number of criticisms and a number of different systems, including local income tax, were examined.[3] The Local Government Finance Act 1988 introduced a radically different system for locally raised taxation. Rates were retained, in an amended centrally controlled form, for non-domestic property. The level of this tax is set centrally and the income collected by local authorities but then pooled and redistributed to authorities according to a centrally set formula.[4] Rates on domestic property, however, were abolished in favour of a tax on individuals, the community charge, which was not related to income. This, however, was to prove what Auld J. described as "a singular and short-lived concept",[5]

---

[1] See § 14–01.
[2] For a brief explanation of the old rating system, see § 15–01.
[3] See for example the Committee of Inquiry into Local Government Finance (Layfield), 1976, Cmnd. 6453.
[4] See § 15–21.
[5] *Cherwell District Council v. Hodges* [1991] R.V.R. 163.

and it remained only until the end of the financial year 1992–93.[6] Thereafter, it was replaced by a new system of domestic property charge known as the council tax. The council tax may best be described as a mixture of the previous two systems in that it is a tax on domestic property which retains some personal element, but less than the community charge.[7]

Under the old rating system, but continued with both the community charge and council tax, there has also been introduced systems of revenue or expenditure capping which also may in practice affect the discretion of a local authority.[8]

The law relating to capital finance is considered in this chapter. Again the discretion of local government is in practice affected by the extent to which it remains free to raise capital and engage in capital expenditure. This has varied over time, influenced by economic and political factors. At present, the system may be characterised as one of strong central control, and it is being used to encourage the use of private finance.[9]

The law must also make provision for the administration of financial transactions, including mechanisms for accountability. Some of those relating to the internal operation of the local authority are dealt with in this chapter. Those relating to internal and external control through the audit system, which have become more extensive and important in recent years, are examined in Chapter 13.

While the following chapters in this section of the book examine particular topics in more detail, this chapter deals with the general framework for local authority finance, and other matters, under the following headings: (a) basic framework for expenses and receipts; (b) charges; (c) capital expenditure and finance: (d) financial reserves: (e) investments.

A. Framework for Expenses and Receipts

Funds and accounts

12–02   The basis of the administration of financial transactions is the requirement to maintain certain funds for certain transactions. This not only facilitates audit, but can be used to facilitate control of expenditure. While some of the law relating to basic funds is different for England and Wales, there are a number of specific funds, and other provisions relating to the basic funds, which are common to both countries, discussed below.

While authorities in Wales were previously subject to substantially the

---

[6] While the community charge remains relevant in regard to some collection and enforcement matters, the section relating directly to the community charge has been removed from this edition. Readers requiring information on the community charge should refer to the previous edition, while much of the material on collection and enforcement of the council tax in chapter 16 is relevant to the community charge.

[7] For further explanation, see § 16–01 to § 16–04.

[8] See § 16–13.

[9] See § 12–36 and § 12–37.

same requirements as England, the Local Government (Wales) Act 1994 introduced a new framework for the new principal councils from April 1, 1996. These councils must establish and maintain a fund, known as the council fund, into which all sums received, and from which all payments, must be paid, with the exception of transactions relating to trust funds.[10] The council may not delegate their functions in relation to the council fund.[11] Provision is made for general and special accounts within this fund, and for the Secretary of State to make regulations relating to separate funds within the council fund.[12] The Secretary of State may also make regulations in relation to precepts of local and major precepting authorities.[13]

For England, under Part VI of the Local Government Finance Act 1988,[14] district councils, London borough councils, and the Councils of the City of London and the Isles of Scilly, as billing authorities for the council tax, are required to maintain a collection fund and a general fund.[15]

From 1993–94, receipts in respect of council tax, community charge and non-domestic rates are to be paid into the collection fund, together with any other sums specified in regulations by the Secretary of State.[16] From that fund the billing authority must make payments of precepts to major precepting authorities and payments to the Secretary of State in respect of non-domestic rates.[17] (Major precepting authorities, as defined in section 39 of the 1992 Act, do not include parish councils and the like, which are defined as local precepting authorities.) Finally, the billing authority must transfer, from its collection fund to its general fund, the amount which it has calculated is to be raised by council tax to meet its own net expenditure (including allowances for contingencies and financial reserves) adjusted in respect of its share of the estimated surplus or deficiency on the collection fund at the end of the previous year.[18]

The general funds were originally established on April 1, 1990, by transfer of the balances on the general rate funds formerly maintained by the authorities under section 148(1) of the Local Government Act 1972. Except for sums attributable to the collection fund or a trust fund, all receipts and payments must be made into or out of the general fund.[19] General funds now contain the following items which before 1993–94 were included in collection funds but are not so included under section 90 as amended:[20] revenue support grant and redistributed non-domestic rates payable to English authorities: precepts of local precepting authorities; interest receiv-

---

[10] Local Government (Wales) Act 1994, s.38(1)–(4).
[11] ibid., s.38(5).
[12] ibid., s.38(7)–(8).
[13] ibid., s.38(9)–(10). See the Local Authorities (Precepts) (Wales) Regulations 1995 (S.I. 1995 No. 2562).
[14] As amended by the Local Government Finance Act 1992, and the Local Government (Wales) Act 1994, Sched. 12.
[15] Local Government Finance Act 1988, ss.89–94.
[16] ibid., s.90(1).
[17] ibid., s.90(2).
[18] ibid., s.99.
[19] ibid., s.91.
[20] ibid.

able or payable in respect of collection fund monies. Regulations may require that any other fund established by an authority, other than its collection fund or a trust fund, should be maintained as a separate fund but falling within its general fund.[21] Further regulation-making powers in respect of funds are conferred by sections 89, 94, 98 and 99.

County councils are required to keep a county fund and joint authorities established by the Local Government Act 1985 a general fund. All its receipts are carried to the fund and all its liabilities discharged therefrom.[22]

Section 148(5) of the 1972 Act[23] provides that principal councils shall keep accounts of receipts carried to, and payments made out of, the county fund, in the case of a county, the collection fund and the general fund, in the case of a district or London borough council, and that separate accounts shall be kept for general expenses and each class of special expenses.

12–03 The Local Authorities (Funds) (England) Regulations 1992[24] make detailed provision for the discharge by a billing authority of its liabilities to pay amounts in respect of precepts from its collection and general funds and to make transfers between those funds to meet its estimated expenses. They also make provision for the annual division between a billing authority and its major precepting authorities of any estimated surplus or deficit in the billing authority's collection fund,[25] and provision as to the holding investment and use of sums paid into a billing authority's collection fund.[26] The Local Authorities (Precepts) (Wales) Regulations 1995[27] make provision for payment of precepts for Welsh authorities.

The Collection Fund (General) (England) Specification and Directions 1992 and 1994, and the Collection Fund (Community Charges) (England) Directions 1992, and made under sections 90(1)(e), (2)(e) and (3), 98(4) to (6) and 140(4) of the 1988 Act, specify sums to be paid into billing authorities' collection funds and direct transfers between collection funds and general funds.

12–04 The Local Government Finance Act 1987, sections 1 and 2, require local authorities to maintain revenue accounts in respect of their rate funds and county funds and define income and expenditure to be included in and excluded from those accounts. These provisions were made in the context of the previous rate support grant system. They have not been repealed or amended by the 1988 Act.

Section 41 of the Local Government and Housing Act 1989 requires all expenditure incurred by a local authority, in England and Wales, other than expenditure excluded by section 42, to be charged to a revenue account, either an account which the authority is required to keep by statute or in order to comply with proper practices, or an account which the authority

---

[21] *ibid.*, s.92.
[22] Local Government Act 1972, s.148; Local Government Act 1985, s.72.
[23] As amended by S.I. 1991 No. 1730.
[24] S.I. 1992 No. 2428, as amended.
[25] *ibid.*, regs. 10–12.
[26] *ibid.*, reg. 13.
[27] S.I. 1995 No. 2562.

decides to keep in accordance with proper practices. Proper practices are broadly, accounting practices required by enactment or generally regarded (by reference to a published code or otherwise) as proper accounting practices for local authorities.[28] Expenditure is normally to be charged in the year in which it is incurred, that is, when the authority becomes liable to make a payment, but it may be charged to an earlier or later year if that accords with proper practices.[29] Expenditure for this purpose also includes, under section 41(3), amounts set aside as provision for contingent liabilities and, with some exceptions, as provision for credit liabilities.[30]

Expenditure excluded by section 42 from the *requirement* to charge to revenue account (but which may be so charged if consistent with proper practices) is mainly expenditure for capital purposes which is (i) capitalised by virtue of a credit approval,[31] or (ii) met out of capital receipts, or (iii) met out of grant or contribution from some other person. Also excluded from the requirement are (iv) the repayment of the principal of borrowed money, (v) the discharge of liabilities under credit arrangements, and (vi) the placing of surplus funds in approved investments[32]; *cf.* the requirement under section 41(3), noted above, to charge to revenue account provision for credit liabilities.

There are a number of other more minor provisions relating to the establishment and maintenance of particular funds. In regard to those relating to superannuation, and trust and other funds, see paragraphs 12–38 to 12–41 below.

The local government finance report and setting of council tax
For each financial year from 1993–94 onwards, the Secretary of State is **12–05** obliged to lay before Parliament a local government finance report. That report must contain two elements. First, details of the total amount of revenue support grant and the proposed basis of distribution based on the Standard Spending Assessment (S.S.A.).[33] Secondly, the total amount and proposed distribution of the pooled non-domestic rate.[34] As soon as reasonably practicable after the approval by the House of Commons, the Secretary of State is to calculate the amounts payable to each receiving authority in accordance with the basis of distribution in the amended report. The sums provided under these two sources provide the majority of the income of the authority.

The third source is the council tax. Section 30 of the Local Government Finance Act 1992 provides that a billing authority[35] must set its council tax on

---

[28] Local Government and Housing Act 1989, s.66(4), and see § 13–02.
[29] *ibid.*, ss.41(1), 66(2)(a). On the annual basis of local authority finance see *Westminster City Council v. Greater London Council* [1986] A.C. 668.
[30] See § 12–34.
[31] See § 12–29.
[32] See § 12–40.
[33] See § 14–07.
[34] See § 15–24.
[35] Billing authority means, in relation to England, a district council or London borough council, the Common Council or the Council of the Isles of Scilly, and in relation to Wales, a county council or county borough council.

or before March 11 in the preceding financial year, but that the tax will not be invalid if set after that date. Precepting authorities are required to issue their precepts before March 1; again failure to do so does not involve invalidity.[36] The setting of the council tax involves a series of processes and calculations, resulting in a separate amount of tax for properties in each of the eight bands (A to H) in which properties have been valued under Chapter II of the 1992 Act.[37]

Levying bodies

12–06   A levying body, under section 74 of the Local Government Finance Act 1988, is a statutory body (other than a precepting authority, combined police or fire authority, magistrates' committee or probation committee) with pre-existing power to raise its expenses from a local authority. The existing powers of such bodies were repealed by section 117 of the Act, but section 74 enabled the Secretary of State to make regulations conferring powers to issue levies to the councils concerned, which may be either billing or precepting authorities.

The Secretary of State is also empowered by sections 75 and 118 of the 1988 Act to make regulations abolishing or modifying the rating powers of any existing authority and conferring on them the power to make a special levy on a prescribed billing authority.

In England, levies on a billing authority are not, like precepts, charged to the collection fund. They are charged to the general fund and become a component of the authority's own budgeting.

Limitation of council tax and precepts

12–07   Chapter V of the Local Government Finance Act 1992 prescribes a scheme of limitation of charges under which the Secretary of State may designate a billing or precepting authority for limitation of council tax or precept on the ground that its budget requirement for the year is excessive or that it represents an excessive increase over that for the previous financial year.[38] For the operation of this system see paragraph 16–17.

Judicial review

12–08   Sections 138 of the Local Government Finance Act 1988 and 66 of the Local Government Finance Act 1992 provide that the following matters, *inter alia*, shall not be questioned except by application for judicial review: the setting of council tax, the issue of precepts and calculations relating thereto; the issue of a levy or special levy under section 74 or 75 of the 1988 Act.

The following cases on judicial review in respect of rates and precepts may still have relevance. A rate or precept could be quashed on judicial review if it was made in part for financing expenditure which the authority could not

---

[36] Local Government Finance Act 1992, ss.40(5), 50(2).
[37] See § 16–12.
[38] Local Government Finance Act 1992, s.54.

lawfully incur: *Bromley London Borough Council v. Greater London Council.*[39]

> *R. v. Liverpool City Council, ex p. Ferguson.*[40] The council fixed a rate which was inadequate to meet the projected level of net revenue expenditure. When it appeared that its money would run out, the council resolved to issue notice to all its teachers that they would be dismissed with effect from December 31, 1985. The applicant sought a declaration that the decision and the notices were *ultra vires. Held*, allowing the application, (1) that the rate was illegal, being contrary to the provisions of the General Rate Act 1967; (2) that the decision to dismiss the teachers was *ultra vires* because it was the direct consequence of the fixing of an illegal rate and because it was not taken for education reasons in furtherance of the council's duties as local education authority.

While there is now a statutory date for setting council tax and precepts,[41] **12–09** before the Local Government Act 1986, there was no express provision stating by what date an authority should make a rate. However, in *R. v. London Borough of Hackney, ex p. Fleming,*[42] Woolf J. held that in accordance with general principles the discretion as to when to fix a rate must be exercised reasonably, and that failure to make a rate within a reasonable time—weeks rather than months—after the beginning of the financial year would, in the absence of a reasonable explanation, be *prima facie* unreasonable and therefore in breach of duty. See also *Smith v. Skinner* and *Lloyd v. McMahon.*[43]

In *R. v. Secretary of State for the Environment, ex p. Hammersmith and Fulham London Borough Council,*[44] the House of Lords dismissed appeals by the local authority against the refusal of lower courts to quash caps imposed by the Secretary of State under earlier legislation. The authorities submitted that the caps should be set aside as irrational, but the House held that in such a case, depending on political judgment approved by the House of Commons, the courts could not interfere unless the Secretary of State had acted in bad faith, or from an improper motive, or his decisions were so absurd that he must have taken leave of his senses—none of which applied in the cases under appeal.

Expenses of parish and community councils

The expenses of parish and community bodies are generally paid by the **12–10** bodies themselves or, in the case of meetings, by the corresponding council, and an appropriate precept is made on the council of the principal area in which the community is situated for the sums required.[45] However, the expenses of a community meeting where there is no community council are paid by the district council.[46] This exception derives from the fact that the community meeting does not necessarily have continuity of existence and no

[39] [1983] 1 A.C. 768.
[40] *The Times*, November 20, 1985.
[41] Local Government Finance Act 1992, ss.40(5), 50(2).
[42] (1985) 85 L.G.R. 626.
[43] (1986) 26 R.V.R. 45 (D.C.), [1987] A.C. 625 (C.A. and H.L.), and see § 13–35.
[44] [1991] 1 A.C. 521.
[45] Local Government Act 1972, s.150(2), (7).
[46] *ibid.*, s.150(3).

one is charged by law to keep its accounts.[47] It may also be noted that expenses relating to the election of parish and community councils are met by the district council and chargeable on the parish or community.[48]

Cheques and orders for payment by parish and community councils are required to be signed by two council members.[49]

Financial administration

12–11   Every local authority is required to make arrangements for the proper administration of its financial affairs and to secure that one of its officers has responsibility for the administration of those affairs.[50] This also applies to authorities set up by the Local Government Act 1985[51]; and to police and combined fire authorities.[52] This chief finance officer must be qualified through membership of a professional accountancy body.[53] The House of Lords has held that the duties of this officer may be validly performed by a member of his staff acting on his authority.[54]

12–12   Under earlier law, payment out of the county fund or borough fund could only be made by the treasurer and his duties in that respect were the subject of case law which may still be applicable under the present legislation. Although, as described below, there are now other reporting and accountability mechanisms, it is submitted that the new provisions were not intended to repeal the common law responsibilities.

> *Att.-Gen. v. De Winton*.[55] The facts in this case are not important. But of the borough treasurer, Farwell J. said: "[he] is not a mere servant of the council: he owes a duty and stands in a fiduciary relation to the burgesses as a body; he is the treasurer of the borough; all payments to and out of the borough fund must be paid to and by him; ... although he holds office during the pleasure of the council only, this does not enable him to plead the orders of the council as an excuse for an unlawful act. In my opinion the observations of Erle J. in *R. v. Saunders*[56] with relation to a county treasurer, apply with equal force to a treasurer under the Municipal Corporations Act: 'If an order be made on a county to pay expenses wholly disconnected with county matters, such an order is without jurisdiction, and one which the county treasurer would be bound to disobey.' "[57]

12–13   Section 114 of the Local Government Finance Act 1988 places more detailed responsibilities upon the chief finance officer.[58] He must make a report if it appears to him that the authority has made or is about to make a

---

[47] *ibid.*, s.27(1); *cf.* ss.9(1), 150(6) re parish meetings.
[48] Representation of the People Act 1983, s.36(3).
[49] Local Government Act 1972, s.150(5).
[50] *ibid.*, s.151.
[51] Local Government Act 1985, s.73.
[52] Local Government Finance Act 1988, s.112, as amended.
[53] Local Government Finance Act 1988, s.113. An exception was made for those already in post.
[54] *Provident Mutual Life Assurance Association v. Derby City Council* (1981) 79 L.G.R. 89.
[55] [1906] 2 Ch. 106.
[56] (1855) 24 L.J.M.C. 45 at p. 48.
[57] See also § 13–38.
[58] The officer appointed under section 151 of the 1972 Act.

decision to incur unlawful expenditure, or has taken or is about to take unlawful action likely to cause a loss or deficiency, or is about to enter an unlawful item of account, or will incur expenditure in excess of its resources.[59] This function must be undertaken by the chief finance officer personally.[60] Copies of the report are to be sent to each member of the authority and to the auditor.[61] The authority must consider the report at a meeting within 21 days, and is prohibited from pursuing the course under report until that meeting has been held.[62]

Local authorities are also required to appoint a monitoring officer, who may not be the chief finance officer.[63] The duties of the two officers overlap: the monitoring officer is required to report to the authority on any proposal, decision or omission by the authority or its committees which has given or may give rise to a contravention of law or statutory code of practice or to such maladministration or injustice as is mentioned in Part III of the Local Government Act 1974. Provisions as to the consequences of such a report are similar to those relating to the chief finance officer's report described above, except that a copy of the monitoring officer's report need not be sent to the auditor.

Before issuing their respective reports, the chief finance officer and the monitoring officer must consult with each other and with the head of paid service appointed under section 4 of the 1989 Act.[64]

Revenues from undertakings

Statutes which authorise the operation of trading undertakings generally **12–14** deal with the application of surplus moneys. Any such provision is not overridden by the general provisions of sections 148 to 150 of the Local Government Act 1972.[65]

Expenditure and the ultra vires rule

No expenditure may be incurred unless there is specific statutory **12–15** authority for the particular purpose.[66] There is an exception to this rule—under section 137 of the Local Government Act 1972, as amended, a local authority may incur expenditure which in its opinion is in the interests of its area or any part of it or all or some of its inhabitants and will bring direct benefit thereto.[67] The benefit must be commensurate with the expenditure incurred. Expenditure cannot be incurred for a purpose for which it is authorised by any other statutory provision. An authority may also, under this provision, contribute to charitable funds and the like.[68] The

---

[59] Local Government Act 1988, s.114(2), (3).
[60] *ibid.*, s.114(5).
[61] *ibid.*, s.114(4).
[62] *ibid.*, s.115.
[63] The Local Government and Housing Act 1989, s.5.
[64] *ibid.*, s.5(3); Local Government Finance Act 1988, s.114(3A).
[65] Local Government Act 1972, s.152.
[66] See §§ 1–19 to 1–30.
[67] An amended version was printed in Schedule 2 to the Local Government and Housing Act 1989, which added to previous amendments and substantially re-cast the power.
[68] s.137(1), (3).

limit of expenditure under section 137 in any financial year, subject to some disregards, is the sum produced by multiplying the relevant population of the area[69] by such sum as is in operation for that class of authority, as specified either in the Act or in an order of the Secretary of State.[70] Such sums, however, must be within the overall expenditure limits of the council, which in recent years has reduced the importance of this power.

12–16 In *Manchester City Council v. Greater Manchester County Council*,[71] the House of Lords upheld the validity of payments under this section by the county council (which had no educational functions) to a trust set up to provide assisted places in independent schools. In *Lobenstein v. Hackney London Borough Council*,[72] Pain J., upholding a grant under section 137 towards expenses in connection with the Moscow Olympics, indicated that the word "interests" should not be given too restricted a meaning, and that review by the court of the council's opinion was governed by *Wednesbury*[73] principles. In *R. v. District Auditor for Leicester, ex p. Leicester City Council*[74] the Court of Appeal held that apportioned expenditure on staffing, accommodation and other overhead costs relating to projects authorised under the powers of section 137 must be charged to the account of expenditure under the section and be counted against the expenditure limit.

12–17 As noted in Chapter 1, an authority has power to do anything which is calculated to facilitate, or is conducive or incidental to, the discharge of any of its functions.[75] Anything authorised by means of s.111 cannot be undertaken by means of s.137 and should not be allocated to the s.137 financial limit.

There are, additionally, certain fairly widely expressed powers.[76] An authority may spend money on gifts of real or personal property donated for the benefit of the inhabitants of the area. The gift may be related, or unrelated, to a statutory purpose. In the latter case expenditure relating to such gifts counts against the section 137 limit referred to above.[77]

---

[69] As determined by the Local Authorities (Discretionary Expenditure) (Relevant Population) Regulations 1993 (S.I. 1993 No. 40).
[70] s.137(4)–(4B) and the Local Authorities (Discretionary Expenditure Limits) Order 1993 (S.I. 1993 No. 41) provide that the appropriate sums are £1.90 for county and non-metropolitan district councils, £3.55 for Greater London authorities and for metropolitan districts which are constituent councils in a scheme of grants to voluntary organisations under section 48 of the Local Government Act 1985, £3.80 for other metropolitan districts and £3.50 for parish and community councils. The Local Authorities (Discretionary Expenditure Limits) (England) Order 1995 (S.I. 1995 No. 651) provides that the appropriate sum for a new unitary authority, under a structure change order, is £3.80. The problem of "double-counting" in regard to expenditure under s.137 by a county, county borough or district council to a parish council, which would otherwise fall to be also included in the s.137 of the parish is resolved by the Local Authorities (Expenditure Powers) Order 1995 (S.I. 1995 No. 3304).
[71] (1980) 78 L.G.R. 560; *cf. R. v. District Auditor No. 3 Audit District of West Yorkshire Metropolitan County Council, ex p. West Yorkshire Metropolitan County Council* (1985) 26 R.V.R. 24: trust financed under s.137 for various purposes held invalid.
[72] (1980), unreported.
[73] See § 10–25.
[74] (1985) 25 R.V.R. 191.
[75] See §§ 1–25 *et seq.*
[76] Local Government Act 1972, ss.138, 139.
[77] *ibid.*, s.139.

A principal council may spend money or grant loans in connection with emergencies and disasters affecting a part or the whole of its area and in contingency planning in respect thereof.[78]

B. Charges

Although many local authorities considered that an implied power to charge **12–18** was to be found in s.111 of the Local Government Act 1972, this view was rejected by the House of Lords in *R. v. Richmond Upon Thames London Borough Council, ex p. McCarthy and Stone*.[79] There it was held that a power to charge had to be authorised by statute either expressly or by necessary implication. In applying this test, no distinction is to be drawn between statutory discretions and duties.[80]

A general power in relation to charges is, however, provided by statute. Section 150 of the Local Government and Housing Act 1989 empowers the Secretary of State to make regulations authorising principal councils (and other authorities defined in section 152) to make charges for services rendered, documents issued or other things done, for which there is no existing power to charge. The regulations may provide that the amount of a charge is at the authority's discretion, or at its discretion subject to a maximum.

Section 151 enables the Secretary of State, by regulation, to repeal or amend statutory provisions which empower (but not those which oblige) the same classes of authority to make a charge. Such regulations may, as under section 150, confer a discretion or impose a maximum but may not require a charge to be made.

Neither section 150 nor section 151 can apply to excepted functions as defined in section 152, including education in schools, libraries (for which special provision is made in section 154), fire-fighting, elections, registration of electors, and most police functions. Nor may charges be made for temporary traffic signs.[81]

C. Capital Expenditure and Finance

Part IV of the Local Government and Housing Act 1989 inaugurated a **12–19** completely new regime for capital finance of local authorities. It replaced both the borrowing powers of Schedule 13 to the Local Government Act 1972 and the system of "prescribed expenditure", laid down in Part VIII of the Local Government, Planning and Land Act 1980 by a single structure covering the control of capital expenditure and its financing, whether by borrowing or otherwise.

---

[78] *ibid.*, s.138, as amended.
[79] [1991] 4 All E.R. 897. See § 1–28.
[80] For a recent case illustrating the principles of charging see *R. v. Brighton Borough Council, ex p. McCue*, unreported, July 21, 1994, CO/931/92.
[81] Local Government and Housing Act 1989, s.153.

The system, though technical and complicated, can be understood simply as, in relation to matters brought into the system by the definition of capital expenditure, central control through limitations on borrowing (and credit arrangements which have the same effect as borrowing), by means of an annual credit approval. In determining the credit approval, the Minister may take into account capital receipts. Subject to the controls over borrowing, the authority may spend more than its credit approval limit if, subject to other demands, it is financed from the annual revenue budget.

12–20   Section 39, as amended, applies the system to all principal councils, the Common Council of the City of London, the Council of the Isles of Scilly, joint authorities and waste disposal authorities established by the Local Government Act 1985, National Parks and Broads authorities, police authorities under the Police Act 1964, and fire authorities. It may also be applied to other bodies by regulations, and this power has been used, *inter alia*, to apply the provisions to levying bodies, local authority controlled or influenced companies, and passenger transport executives.[82]

12–21   Reference may also be made to Department of the Environment Circular 11/90 which summarises the provisions of Part IV of the 1989 Act and of the regulations made under it, describes the main principles underlying the new system; and covers sundry matters of detail. Welsh Office Circular 18/90 covers the same ground.

Expenditure for capital purposes

12–22   This is defined by section 40 to cover most expenditure on tangible assets, including plant and vehicles. Expenditure on maintenance, repair or improvement of assets, however, will only be expenditure for capital purposes to the extent that the works amount to "enhancement" of the asset, that is, that they are intended to lengthen substantially the life of the asset or increase substantially its open market value or the extent to which it can be used for the authority's functions.

The definition also includes the acquisition of investments other than "approved" investments[83] and the making of grants, advances or other financial assistance towards expenditure by other persons on tangible assets or investments. The definitions may be amended by regulations, and the Secretary of State may direct that particular expenditure by a local authority shall be treated as capital.[84]

Charging to revenue account

12–23   Capital expenditure may be financed by borrowing, capital receipts, grants, the private sector,[85] or from revenue account.

---

[82] There are various specific orders and also an order of general application: the Local Authorities (Companies) Order 1995 (S.I. 1995 No. 849).

[83] See § 12–42.

[84] The detailed definitions have been extended, and some excluded, by the Local Authorities (Capital Finance) Regulations 1990 (S.I. 1990 No. 432, as amended).

[85] See § 12–36.

The starting point of the new system is that, in order to limit the amount of credit which an authority may have outstanding, and to link this to the controls on revenue finance, all expenditure, including capital expenditure, must be charged to a revenue account in the year in which it is incurred, unless it is proper accounting practice to allocate to an earlier or later year.[86] Crucially, however, there are a number of exceptions provided by statute and by regulation where it need not, but may, be so charged.[87] Thus excluded from the requirement to charge to revenue account are discharge of liabilities under a "credit arrangement",[88] discharge of any borrowing liability, capital expenditure funded within a basic "credit approval",[89] expenditure on approved investments, expenditure which is the application of "reserved" or "usable portion" of capital receipts,[90] expenditure which is to be reimbursed or met by another person, excluding an institution of the E.U., such as central grants or private contribution, payments out of an authority's superannuation fund, and payments out of a charitable trust.

Borrowing

Section 43 of the 1989 Act confers on local authorities a general power to **12–24** borrow, subject to the provisions of the Act. Except with the approval of the Secretary of State, borrowing is limited to three methods: (i) by overdraft or short-term loans from recognised banks; (ii) from the Public Works Loan Board; and (iii) by loan instrument, that is, a document which acknowledges that money has been lent or that a payment or repayment is due in respect of the provision of funds to the authority and specifies when payments or repayments are to be made. Without the consent of the Treasury, authorities may not borrow outside the United Kingdom or otherwise than in sterling. These provisions replace the former provisions under which loans could be raised by mortgages, stock, bonds, etc.

Section 44 requires each local authority to keep the amount of its outstanding borrowing plus the cost of any credit arrangements within its aggregate credit limit.[91] The authority must also set limits before the beginning of each financial year for (i) its maximum outstanding borrowing; (ii) its total short-term borrowings (repayable without notice or within one year); (iii) its borrowings at variable interest rates. Section 45 provides that these decisions cannot be delegated.

Section 46 of the 1989 Act requires local authorities to maintain a register **12–25** of loans, including all loans made by way of loan instrument and previous loans (other than short-term and P.W.L.B. loans) still outstanding. The register must record the dates and amounts of repayments, or the method by

---

[86] Local Government and Housing Act 1989, s.41.
[87] *ibid.*, s.42, and the Local Authorities (Capital Finance) Regulations 1990 (S.I. 1990 No. 432, as amended).
[88] See § 12–27 below.
[89] See § 12–29 below.
[90] See § 12–30 below.
[91] See §§ 12–31 to 12–33.

which repayments are to be calculated, and except for bearer loans, the name and address of the person to whom repayments are due. The Local Authorities (Borrowing) Regulations 1990[92] make detailed administrative provisions relating to loan instruments and registers of loans.

Section 47 repeats former provisions that all money borrowed shall be charged indifferently on all the revenues of the authority and that all securities shall rank equally. It also provides that lenders may apply to the court for appointment of a receiver when a sum of more than £5,000 due in respect of borrowing remains unpaid for two months after demand in writing.

12–26   In *Hazell v. Hammersmith and Fulham London Borough Council*[93] the House of Lords held that interest rate swaps and similar transactions were not capable of being within the powers of local authorities. The Divisional Court, on the application of the auditor under section 19 of the Local Government Finance Act 1982, had held all such transactions unlawful, but the Court of Appeal had held that while authorities were not empowered to carry on a trade of such transactions with a view to profit, a swap clearly linked to a particular debt could be lawful under section 111 of the Local Government Act 1972 as "calculated to facilitate or conducive or incidental to" the function of borrowing by way of interest rate risk management. The House of Lords, however, held that Schedule 13 to the 1972 Act, in providing a code which closely defined the powers relating to borrowing, thereby precluded swap activities being treated as incidental to borrowing, and that swap transactions did not facilitate the original function of borrowing—they were a distinct speculative activity aimed at reducing the burden of interest on money already borrowed. The House therefore reinstated the original orders of the Divisional Court declaring all the relevant items of account contrary to law.

Credit arrangements

12–27   Sections 48 to 52 of the 1989 Act deal with the definition and control of credit arrangements. The intention is to place these arrangements, which are regarded as having the same effect as borrowing, within the same system of control as borrowing itself.

A credit arrangement is defined as any lease by which the authority become lessee of property or goods or any other transaction, other than borrowing, under which a local authority estimate that the consideration still to be given by it at the end of any financial year will be greater than the consideration still to be received by it at the start of the same year. This means that a transaction where a local authority estimate that it will receive benefits more than one financial year in advance of paying for them will be a credit arrangement. The Secretary of State may prescribe by regulation that other types of transaction shall be treated as credit arrangements.

12–28   A local authority may not enter into a credit arrangement unless the following conditions are met[94]:

(a) It must be for capital purposes as defined by section 40.

---

[92] S.I. 1990 No. 767, as amended.
[93] [1992] 2 A.C. 1. See § 1–27.
[94] Local Government and Housing Act 1989, s.50.

(b) The authority must have "credit cover" for its cost. Its cost is defined by formula under section 49, calculating the estimated value of the total payments or other consideration to be given by the authority under the arrangement, discounted to the year the arrangement is entered into at a rate prescribed for that year by regulation. (This is to eliminate the element reflecting the cost of the credit itself, *i.e.* the equivalent of interest.) Credit cover may be obtained by using a "credit approval" or by setting aside sums from revenue or from "usable capital receipts"[95] as provision to meet capital liabilities.

(c) The cost of the arrangement together with the cost of other credit arrangements and with the amount of the authority's outstanding borrowing must in total be within the authority's aggregate credit limit.[96]

Section 51 of the 1989 Act makes detailed provision in respect of variation of credit arrangements. Part IV of the Local Authorities (Capital Finance) Regulations 1990,[97] makes further provision with respect to credit arrangements.

Credit approvals

Before the beginning of each financial year the Secretary of State must **12–29** issue each local authority with a basic credit approval, though the amount of this may be nil.[98] It will normally cover all classes of capital expenditure, though particular descriptions of expenditure may be excluded. Regulations may require basic approvals to specify "amortisation periods" during which amounts determined by the regulations must be set aside from revenue account to meet credit liabilities.

Supplementary credit approvals may be issued by any Minister and may either cover all classes of expenditure or only a particular project or programme.[99]

In determining the amount of any credit approval, the issuing Minister may take into account the authority's usable capital receipts and any expected grants or contributions towards capital expenditure, but not the ability of the authority to finance capital from revenue.[1]

Credit approvals may be used either as authority to enter into credit arrangements or as authority to capitalise expenditure in accounts,[2] thus increasing the aggregate credit limit and hence the borrowing powers.[3] Section 57 of the 1989 Act and Part V of the Local Authorities (Capital Finance) Regulations 1990[4] make detailed provision as to the effect of certain capital grants on credit approvals.

[95] See §§ 12–29, 12–30.
[96] See § 12–31.
[97] S.I. 1990 No. 432, as amended.
[98] Local Government and Housing Act 1989, s.53.
[99] *ibid.*, s.54.
[1] *ibid.*, s.55.
[2] *ibid.*, s.56.
[3] See §§ 12–31, 12–24.
[4] S.I. 1990 No. 432, as amended.

Capital receipts

12–30 Section 58 of the 1989 Act defines capital receipts as (i) those sums received by a local authority in respect of the disposal of any interest in an asset where expenditure on the acquisition of the asset would be expenditure for capital purposes; (ii) the disposal of any investment other than an "approved" investment[5]; and (iii) the repayment of capital grants and advances. Receipts of a superannuation fund are excluded. In the case of the disposal of a leasehold interest the capital receipt will generally be any premium paid on a grant or assignment and any consideration received in respect of a surrender, but there is provision for certain rents to be included in capital receipts. The Secretary of State may add sums to, or exclude sums from, the definition by regulation.[6]

Local authorities are required to set aside a "reserved" part of most capital receipts as provision to meet credit liabilities.[7] While, under the original provision, the reserved part was to be 75 per cent of receipts from the sale of houses held under Part II of the Housing Act 1985 and 50 per cent of other receipts, the Secretary of State may by regulation alter these percentages to any figure from nil to 100 per cent, and differentiate by both type of receipt and authority.[8] The balance of these receipts—the "usable" part—may be applied by a local authority to meet expenditure incurred for capital purposes or as provision to meet credit liabilities.[9]

Where a local authority receives a consideration not wholly in money for a capital disposal, it will be required to set aside as provision for credit liabilities a sum equal to the reserved part it would have had to set aside if the consideration had been wholly in money.[10]

Aggregate credit limit

12–31 An authority's aggregate credit limit determines whether the authority may enter into a credit arrangement[11] and sets the limit of its borrowing powers, since it may not borrow an amount which would cause the amount outstanding of borrowed money plus the aggregate cost of credit arrangements to exceed the aggregate credit limit.[12]

Section 62 of the 1989 Act defines the aggregate credit limit of an authority at any time as the sum of four components: (i) a temporary revenue borrowing limit; (ii) a temporary capital borrowing limit; (iii) a "credit ceiling"; (iv) "approved" investments and cash, less usable capital receipts. An authority's limit may be increased for a specified period by direction of the Secretary of State.

The temporary revenue borrowing limit is designed, broadly, to cover revenue expenses paid in advance of receipt of the corresponding revenues.

---

[5] See § 12–40.
[6] Local Authorities (Capital Finance) Regulations (S.I. 1990 No. 432, as amended).
[7] Local Government and Housing Act 1989, s.59.
[8] Local Authorities (Capital Finance) Regulations (S.I. 1990 No. 432, as amended).
[9] Local Government and Housing Act 1989, s.60.
[10] *ibid.*, s.61.
[11] *ibid.*, s.50(4). See also § 12–27.
[12] *ibid.*, s.44(1).

The temporary capital borrowing limit is the total expenditure for capital purposes in the previous 18 months which is due to be reimbursed by some other person, not including money due from an institution of the European Community.

The "credit ceiling" is closely defined.[13] It can be regarded as roughly **12–32** equivalent to the total outstanding advances from the loans fund under previous legislation, adjusted to take account of credit arrangements and the setting aside of capital receipts to meet credit liabilities. Broadly, the initial credit ceiling on April 1, 1990, comprised the outstanding advances from the authority's loans fund plus the cost of its transitional credit arrangements, if any,[14] less the capital receipts held immediately before that date which were set aside as provision for credit liabilities. Thereafter the credit ceiling increases by the amount of any credit approval used.[15] Thus, when an authority authorises capitalisation of expenditure by the use of a credit approval, it will be able to borrow to finance the expenditure.

The credit ceiling will generally decrease whenever sums are set aside as **12–33** provisions for credit liabilities.[16] The sums set aside will be available to repay external debt, defray liabilities under credit arrangements, or substitute for new external borrowing. But for as long as they are held in approved investments and cash, the effect on the aggregate limit of the reduction in the credit ceiling will be offset by the fourth component of the aggregate credit limit. Local authorities will thus not have to repay external debt immediately.

Part VII of the Local Authorities (Capital Finance) Regulations 1990[17] makes further detailed provision in respect of the credit ceiling.

The fourth component of the aggregate credit limit is the amount of approved investments and cash held by the authority less its usable capital receipts. Where an authority has more usable receipts than it has approved investments and cash, the fourth component will be negative.[18] This will only occur where an authority has temporarily used the cash from usable capital receipts in substitution for external borrowing, and in such cases it will be appropriate for its aggregate credit limit to be reduced.

Sums set aside to meet credit liabilities

Section 63 and Schedule 3, Part IV, provide that, without prejudice to **12–34** other provisions requiring sums to be set aside to meet credit liabilities, authorities shall set aside the following sums:

(a) from revenue, an amount determined by the authority, being not less than the minimum revenue provision prescribed by Schedule 3, Part IV;

[13] *ibid.*, Sched. 3, Part III.
[14] *ibid.*, s.52, and see § 12–28.
[15] *ibid.*, Sched. 3, paras. 9–11.
[16] *ibid.*, para. 12.
[17] S.I. 1990 No. 432, as amended.
[18] Local Government and Housing Act 1989, s.62(6).

(b) any sums received by way of commutation of annual payment of government grant; and

(c) any sum received from a European Community institution as grant on capital expenditure.

The minimum revenue provision in any year under Schedule 3 will be the sum of an amount in respect of principal and an amount in respect of notional interest on credit arrangements. The amount in respect of principal, except as otherwise provided by regulations, will be a percentage, prescribed by regulations, of the credit ceiling of the authority at the end of the previous financial year. The amount in respect of notional interest will generally be calculated by multiplying the cost of each credit arrangement by the discount rate applying when the credit arrangement was entered into or last varied.[19]

12–35 Section 64 provides that sums set aside to meet credit liabilities may be used only for the following purposes:

(i) to repay principal of money borrowed;

(ii) to meet liabilities in respect of credit arrangements; and

(iii) to defray expenditure in respect of which a credit approval has been used as authority not to charge it to revenue.

Where the authority's credit ceiling is a negative amount, regulations may permit amounts set aside to meet credit liabilities to be applied in specific ways or to be transferred to another body.[20]

Private Finance Initiative and Challenge Funding

12–36 Under a general programme known as the Private Finance Initiative (P.F.I.), new legislative measures have been introduced to give local authorities a greater incentive to enter joint ventures with the private sector in the lead; to dispose of assets to the private sector; to target local authorities' spending to encourage new public/private partnerships and unlock private investment; and to encourage more flexible procurement and rationalisation of local authority non-housing property. While much of this involves changes to the regulation of local authority companies,[21] a major element has been the use of the capital finance system. This programme has been introduced through various stages. In 1995, packages of new measures included: fewer financial controls over local authority participation in companies led by the private sector; provisions to facilitate the transfer of public assets to local authority companies and the movement of such companies into the private sector; time-limited incentives to dispose of assets to the private sector, namely airports, bus companies, retail property, crematoria, and car parks; and widening the scope for leasing of non-housing property by making revenue treatment available for leases up to 10 years rather than the existing three year period. This was achieved partly by

---

[19] *ibid.*, Sched. 3, paras. 15, 19.

[20] The Local Authorities (Capital Finance) Regulations 1990 (S.I. 1990 No. 432, as amended), Part VIIIA, specify the purposes for which such amounts may be applied and the bodies to which they may be transferred.

[21] See §§ 4–88, *et seq.*

increasing to 75 per cent or 90 per cent, the usable portion of the receipts from the disposal of assets,[22] and partly by freeing authorities from the capital finance impact from a company's operation if it left the public sector permanently. The capital finance elements of this were included in the Local Authorities (Capital Finance) (Amendment) Regulations 1995,[23] and Local Authorities (Capital Finance and Approved Investments) (Amendment No. 2) Regulations 1995,[24] which amended the Local Authorities (Capital Finance) Regulations 1990.[25]

Further stages have involved altering the usable proportion of receipts from the sale of county farms, educational assets, and shares in education companies; reductions in the capital cost when authorities enter "design, build, finance and operate" contracts for replacement and upgrading by the private sector of facilities such as schools, leisure centres, and theatres; and giving greater scope for the financing of replacements of assets sold, by deducting the cost of replacement before calculating set aside parts.[26] The capital finance elements of this were included in the Local Authorities (Capital Finance and Approved Investments) (Amendment) Regulations 1996,[27] which also amend the main 1990 Regulations.

Another method of capital funding involving the private sector has been **12–37** introduced following a consultation paper in 1996.[28] "Challenge funding", whereby authorities compete for funding, has been used previously for specific spending schemes such as transport and regeneration schemes. The purpose of the consultation paper was to consider whether the challenge concept should determine the distribution of Government support for local authorities' mainstream capital spending, through the introduction of challenge for the award of credit approvals. Those proposals which involved a high degree of private involvement would be favoured. Following the consultation exercise, it has been decided to test this by a three year pilot project commencing in April 1997. It allocates £600 million of the capital allocation which would have been available under the normal credit approval process, and awards will take the form of supplementary credit approvals. If the pilot is converted to the normal process for capital allocation, this will mark a fundamental shift in the system of capital funding.

D. FINANCIAL RESERVES

The Local Government Act 1972, as originally enacted, provided that local **12–38** authorities could establish loans funds, capital funds and renewal and repairs

---

[22] See § 12–30.
[23] S.I. 1995 No. 1526.
[24] S.I. 1995 No. 1982.
[25] S.I. 1990 No. 432.
[26] See § 12–30.
[27] S.I. 1996 No. 568.
[28] Department of the Environment, January 1996.

funds. Insurance funds and other funds were also maintained by authorities under local legislation. The Local Government (Miscellaneous Provisions) Act 1976 replaced the provisions relating to capital funds and renewal and repairs funds by a general power to establish such funds as the authority considered appropriate for meeting expenditure on its functions. Further amendments were made by the Local Government Finance Act 1988 and the Local Government and Housing Act 1989, but the matter is now governed by sections 32(2) and 43(2) of the Local Government Finance Act 1992, which required billing and major precepting authorities to budget for financial reserves which the authority estimates (i) as appropriate to raise for meeting estimated future expenditure and (ii) as sufficient to meet revenue account deficits for earlier financial years.

12–39   Under section 91 of the Local Government Finance Act 1988 all receipts and payments of a "relevant authority", except those relating to a trust fund or the collection fund, must be paid into or out of the general fund. "Relevant authorities" are the councils of districts, a county to which the functions of the district have been transferred by a structure order, London boroughs and the Isles of Scilly. Section 92 enables the Secretary of State to make regulations providing for separate funds to be held within the general fund, but no such regulations have been made. Receipts and payments of county councils and of joint authorities under the Local Government Act 1985 must be carried to and from the county fund and general fund respectively.[29] Section 41 of the Local Government and Housing Act 1989 enables all local authorities under Part IV of that Act to charge expenditure to any revenue account which the authority decides to keep in accordance with proper practices. This indicates that separate revenue accounts may be kept within the general fund or county fund, which would apparently enable separate revenue accounts to be kept for such reserves as the authority decides to maintain in accordance with section 32 or 43 of the Local Government Finance Act 1992.

E. Investments

Superannuation funds

12–40   The history of the current provisions is that the Local Government Superannuation (Amendment) (No. 2) Regulations 1983[30] substituted a new regulation governing use and investment of superannuation fund moneys for earlier regulations under which investment had been governed by the Trustee Investments Act 1961 with some modifications.[31] The 1983 Regulations were revoked by the Local Government Superannuation Regulations 1986,[32] their substance being reproduced, with minor amendments, in regulation P3 of the 1986 Regulations. In turn, after further amendment,

---

[29] Local Government Act 1972, s.148; Local Government Act 1985, s.72.
[30] S.I. 1983 No. 1270.
[31] The changes made by the 1983 Regulations were explained in Department of the Environment Circular 24/83.
[32] S.I. 1986 No. 24.

these have been repealed and consolidated by the Local Government Pension Scheme Regulations 1995.[33]

Under the 1995 Regulations, administering authorities are required to invest superannuation fund moneys not for the time being required for the payment of benefits. Investment, for this purpose, includes (a) financial futures and traded options, as defined; (b) use by the administering authority for any purpose for which it has a statutory borrowing power; (c) a contract constituting the carrying on an insurance business as defined; (d) a stocklending arrangement as defined; and (e) entering as a limited partner into a partnership as defined.[34] Interest on such use must be calculated on a daily basis at a rate no lower than the lowest rate at which the same amount could be borrowed at seven days' notice.[35] Limitations are imposed, however, to restrict the proportion of the fund's investments which may be placed in seven categories.[36] These are: (a) securities not listed on a reputable stock exchange (maximum 10 per cent of total value of investments); (b) single holdings, as defined (10 per cent—not more than 25 per cent in unit trusts managed by one body); (c) deposits with a single bank, institution or person other than the National Savings Bank (10 per cent); (d) loans to persons or bodies (including local authorities), other than the Government or bankers and the like (as defined), *plus* use by the authority itself under borrowing powers (10 per cent in aggregate); (e) contracts constituting insurance business (25 per cent); (f) stocklending arrangements (25 per cent); and (g) contributions to a particular partnership (as defined) (2 per cent) or to partnership in general (5 per cent).

An administering authority must have regard to the need for diversification and the suitability of investments, and to proper advice obtained at reasonable intervals.[37] Functions may be delegated to officers or to outside investment managers, subject to the requirements of regulation as to appointment and reports of managers, review of their decisions, and competence of officers.[38]

Other funds

The investment of funds held on charitable or other trusts is subject to the **12–41** provisions of the Trustee Investments Act 1961. These provisions also apply to an Art Fund established under the Public Libraries and Museums Act 1964,[39] and may be specifically applied to other funds established under local Act or otherwise. The 1961 Act enables trustees to invest a part of their funds in equities, subject to certain safeguards. If a trustee wishes to use this power he must divide the trust fund into two parts equal at the time of

---

[33] S.I. 1995 No. 1019.
[34] *ibid.*, reg. L5.
[35] *ibid.*, reg. L7.
[36] *ibid.*, reg. P3(4), (5).
[37] *ibid.*, reg. L5(3).
[38] *ibid.*, regs. L4, L8, L9, L10 and L11.
[39] Trustee Investments Act 1961, s.15 and Sched. 2, para. 4.

division. One part must be invested in what the Act calls the narrower-range investments (these are, broadly speaking, government and public authority securities and company debentures) and the other part may be invested in the wider-range investments (equities, etc.), or partly in the wider and partly in the narrower range.[40] Provisions relating to advice, similar to those relating to superannuation funds (above) apply to wider-range investments and to certain narrower-range investments listed in Part II of Schedule 1.[41]

The Local Authorities (Funds) (England) Regulations 1992[42] restrict investment by charging authorities of sums paid into a collection fund which are not immediately required for the purpose of making payments or transfers from the fund in accordance with the regulations.[43] Investment may be made only in deposits with banks, building societies or, if repayable at not more than seven days' notice, with a body specified in paragraph 12 or 13 of Schedule 2 to the Banking Act 1987.

12–42 The scope of investment of other funds is not now specifically restricted by statute. However, the Local Government and Housing Act 1989 introduced distinctions between the statutory treatment of "approved investments"[44] and that of other investments. The Local Authorities (Capital Finance) (Approved Investments) Regulations 1990[45] contain a list of approved investments.

Approved investments are effectively treated by Part IV as equivalent to cash. Expenditure on approved investments is not expenditure for capital purposes under section 40.[46] Nor is it required to be charged to revenue account.[47] The disposal of an approved investment is not a capital receipt.[48] Together with cash, and subject to the deduction of usable capital receipts, approved investments, other than those of superannuation and trust funds, are a component of the aggregate credit limit.[49]

12–43 On the other hand non-approved investments, except for those of superannuation funds and charitable trust funds, are treated for Part IV purposes in broadly the same way as tangible capital assets. Expenditure on such investments is expenditure for capital purposes.[50] It is required to be charged to revenue account under section 41 unless it is met out of usable capital receipts or covered by use of a credit approval.[51] In the latter case it would increase the credit ceiling and hence the minimum sums to be set aside from revenue to meet credit liabilities.[52] The proceeds of disposal of such

---

[40] *ibid.*, s.2.
[41] *ibid.*, s.6.
[42] S.I. 1992 No. 2428.
[43] *ibid.*, reg. 13, Sched. 3.
[44] Defined by s.66(1)(a) of the 1989 Act to mean investments approved for the purposes of Part IV of the Act by regulations made by the Secretary of State.
[45] S.I. 1990 No. 426, as amended.
[46] Local Government and Housing Act 1989, s.40(4), and see § 12–22.
[47] *ibid.*, s.42(2)(d), and see § 12–04.
[48] *ibid.*, s.58(1)(d), and see § 12–30.
[49] *ibid.*, s.62(1)(d), and see § 12–31.
[50] *ibid.*, s.40(4)(b).
[51] *ibid.*, s.42(2).
[52] *ibid.*, Sched. 3, paras. 11, 15, and see §§ 12–32, 12–34.

investments are capital receipts under section 58(1)(b) and are therefore subject to the requirement to set aside a reserved part to meet credit liabilities.[53] Finally, non-approved investments are not a component of the aggregate credit limit under section 62(1)(d).

---

[53] *ibid.*, s.59 and see § 12–30.

CHAPTER 13

AUDIT

THE administration of financial transactions must be subject to some form of **13–01** check and accountability. In addition to political accountability through elected members and central government, and judicial review through the courts, there is accountability and control through the audit system. Internal audit controls are governed mostly by the non-statutory "proper practices" developed by the professions. External audit controls are subject to a much greater body of law and, while always important, have become more extensive in recent years and are seen as an essential element in the Citizen's Charter initiative.[1]

The audit of local authority accounts for periods commencing on or after April 1, 1983, is governed by Part III of the Local Government Finance Act 1982, which also extends to other bodies specified in the Act and to accounts of officers.[2]

A. INTERNAL AUDIT

The Local Government and Housing Act 1989 requires authorities to follow **13–02** proper practices in regard to revenue accounts and accounting for capital expenditure.[3] Proper practices are defined as being those accounting practices: (a) which the authority are required to follow by any enactment; and (b) regarded, by reference to a generally published code or otherwise, as proper accounting practices for local authorities.[4] Where there is any inconsistency between these two elements the former prevails.

Section 23 of the Local Government Finance Act 1982 authorises the Secretary of State to make regulations on matters including the keeping of accounts and the form and preparation of accounts. Under these regulations a number of duties are placed on the authority, but many of these in turn depend on the concept of proper accounting practices. The responsible financial officer is, subject to detailed requirements in the regulations, required to determine the accounting system, records, and the form of accounts and to ensure that the system and records are maintained in accordance with proper practices.[5] The authority is required to maintain an

---

[1] See *The Citizen's Charter*, 1991, Cm. 1599. See also Part I of the Local Government Act 1992.
[2] Local Government Finance Act 1982, as amended, ss.12, 25, 31.
[3] See § 12–23.
[4] Local Government and Housing Act 1989, s.66(4).
[5] Accounts and Audit Regulations 1996 (S.I. 1996 No. 590), reg. 4(1). In regard to records and control systems see reg. 4(3) and (4) respectively.

adequate and effective system of internal audit of their records and control systems.[6] The authority is also required to prepare statements of accounts for each period in accordance with proper practices and the detailed provisions of the regulation.[7] Further provision is made in regard to the signing, approval and publication of the accounts,[8] and to statements of costs in regard to specified activities relating to the costs of work falling within defined activities for the purpose of Part I of the Local Government Act 1988.[9]

There is no single source of proper practice, but reference should be made to the Code of Practice on Local Authority Accounting in Great Britain 1995: A Statement of Recommended Practice,[10] and other more detailed publications from the Chartered Institute of Public Finance and Accountancy.

B. External Audit

The Audit Commission

13–03   The Local Government Finance Act 1982 established the Audit Commission for Local Authorities in England and Wales to take responsibility for audit arrangements. The Commission is appointed by the Secretary of State, after consultation with local authority associations and professional accountancy bodies.[11] The Secretary of State may give the Commission directions on the discharge of its functions.[12] The Commission must appoint a chief officer, known as the Controller of Audit, and such other officers as it considers necessary. The first Controller was appointed by the Secretary of State and subsequent appointments to the office require his approval.[13]

Section 20 of the National Health Service and Community Care Act 1990 extended the functions of the Commission to the National Health Service and altered its title to become the Audit Commission for Local Authorities

---

[6] *ibid.*, reg. 5.

[7] *ibid.*, reg. 6, from April 1, 1997 in regard to the records and control systems operated from April 1996. Until then the existing provision, the Accounts and Audit Regulations 1983 (S.I. 1983 No. 1761) reg. 7, remains in force in relation to the records and control systems operated under the 1983 regulations.

[8] *ibid.*, regs. 8 and 9, from April 1, 1997. Until then the existing provisions, the Accounts and Audit Regulations 1983 (S.I. 1983 No. 1761) regs. 13 and 15, remain in force in relation to the records and control systems operated under the 1983 regulations.

[9] *ibid.*, reg. 10 and Schedule, from April 1, 1997. Until then the existing provisions, the Accounts and Audit Regulations 1983 (S.I. 1983 No. 1761) reg. 15A and Schedule, inserted by the Accounts and Audit (Amendment) Regulations (S.I. 1994 No. 3018), remain in force. On Part I of the 1988 Act, see §§ 7–38, *et seq.*

[10] Developed by a C.I.P.F.A./L.A.S.A.A.C. Joint Committee in accordance with the Accounting Standards Board's code of practice for the development of Statements of Recommended Accounting Practice (S.O.R.P.s).

[11] Local Government and Housing Act 1989, s.11. Detailed provisions as to the Commission appear in Sched. 3, as amended.

[12] *ibid.*, Sched. 3, para. 3(1).

[13] *ibid.*, Sched. 3, para. 7.

and the National Health Service in England and Wales. The functions of the Commission and its auditors in respect of the National Health Service are outside the scope of this book.

Appointments of auditors

The auditor for each local government body covered by Part III of the **13–04** Local Government Finance Act 1982 is appointed by the Commission after consultation with the body.[14] The auditor may be an officer of the Commission or a private accountant or firm of accountants.[15] He must be a member of one of the accountancy bodies specified in section 13(6) or have such other qualification as may be approved by the Secretary of State.[16] The Commission may arrange for joint audits, in which the auditors may act jointly or separately for different parts of the accounts or in discharge of different functions.[17] The Commission may also approve arrangements for persons assisting an auditor to carry out such of the auditor's statutory functions as may be specified.[18]

These arrangements differ substantially from the former provisions for the appointment of auditors in Part VIII of the Local Government Act 1972. Bodies subject to audit under that Act were empowered to choose whether their accounts should be audited by a district auditor, appointed by the Secretary of State with the consent of the Minister for the Civil Service, or an "approved auditor," that is, a private accountant appointed by the body and approved by the Secretary of State. The 1982 Act does not use the title "district auditor", but the Commission has retained the title for its own officers appointed as auditors under section 13 of the Act.

Code of audit practice

Section 14 of the Local Government Finance Act 1972 provides for a code **13–05** of audit practice to be prepared, kept under review and published by the Commission and to be approved by each House of Parliament at intervals of not more than five years.[19] The Commission may make alterations in the intervals between parliamentary approval and these must be laid before Parliament.[20] Local authority associations and accountancy bodies must be consulted before the preparation and alteration of the code.[21] The code must embody what appears to the Commission to be the best professional practice with respect to the standards, procedures and techniques to be adopted by auditors.[22] The auditor is under a duty to comply with the code.[23]

There had not previously been statutory provision for a code of local

---

[14] *ibid.*, ss.12(1), 13(3).
[15] *ibid.*, s.13(1).
[16] *ibid.*, s.13(5).
[17] *ibid.*, s.13(2).
[18] *ibid.*, s.13(8), (9).
[19] *ibid.*, as amended by the National Health Service and Community Care Act 1990, s.14(1), (3), (5).
[20] *ibid.*, s.14(4), (5).
[21] *ibid.*, s.14(6).
[22] *ibid.*, s.14(2).
[23] *ibid.*, s.15(2).

government audit practice, but a non-statutory code had been in force, with the knowledge of Parliament, since 1973.[24]

The current Code of Audit Practice for England and Wales, prepared by the Commission and approved by Parliament in accordance with section 14 of the 1982 Act, came into force on July 21, 1995.[25] The main provisions of the Code are in five parts. The first part sets out the purpose and scope of audit. The second outlines the powers and duties of the auditor, and refers to requirements placed on the auditor in accordance with the considerations of independence, integrity, objectivity and professional care, together with the duties in regard to detailed conduct of the audit. These are the detailed duties with respect to economy, efficiency and effectiveness; financial standing, financial systems; fraud, irregularities and corruption; legality; and performance indicators. The third part sets out the audit approach including general principles; planning, controlling and recording, and evidence; and in respect of the detailed duties. The fourth part deals with outputs from the audit process, namely reporting arrangements; audit certificate and opinion; reports in the public interest; reports on economy efficiency and effectiveness; reports on the regularity audit and management letters. The fifth part describes the exercise of special powers with regard to the audits of local government bodies and health service bodies respectively. It is made clear in the introduction to the Code that it represents the Commission's view of best practice but that its application must depend on the specific circumstances and on what is reasonable and appropriate in these circumstances.

Economy and impact studies

13–06   Apart from the duties of the Audit Commission in relation to audits and auditors, the Local Government Finance Act 1982 imposes directly on the Commission itself certain duties in relation to bodies audited under the Act. Section 26 requires the Commission, after consultation with relevant associations, to undertake or promote comparative and other across-the-board studies concerning economy, efficiency, effectiveness and financial or other management of bodies subject to audit. It may also undertake or promote other studies relating to services of bodies under audit. Section 27 provides for the Commission to undertake or promote studies on the impact on the operation of any statutory provision and also the impact of any directions by a Minister relating to economy, efficiency and effectiveness in section 26. Before undertaking section 27 studies, the Commission must consult the relevant Minister, local authority associations and the Comptroller and Auditor General. The Commission is to report on studies under sections 26 and 27, and the Comptroller and Auditor General may inquire into matters arising from reports under section 27 and report thereon to the House of Commons.[26]

The Commission may also assist the Secretary of State, at his request, in

---

[24] DoE Circular 79/73, Annex II.
[25] This replaced and revised the Code which came into effect on July 28, 1990, which had been amended by the Commission on October 1, 1992.
[26] Local Government Finance Act 1988, ss.26(3) and 27(2)–(4).

any study designed to improve economy, efficiency, effectiveness and quality of performance by local authorities in the discharge of social service functions.[27] A local authority included in such a study is required to supply such information or make available such documents, and any officer or member of such an authority is also required to supply such information, as the Commission require.[28] Any information supplied under these provisions may be disclosed for the purposes of any functions of the Secretary of State connected with the discharge of social services functions by local authorities.[29] Any report is to be published jointly and the Commission is prohibited from providing assistance in such a study unless the Secretary of State agrees to pay the full cost of the assistance.[30]

The Commission consider that the national studies promote good management practice in specific services or in overall management arrangements, and are governed by guidance issued annually by the Commission.[31] Such studies are linked to the audit of individual authorities in that the Commission consider that the auditor, when identifying potential review areas and carrying out the audit work, should consider the use of comparative performance indicators where possible.[32]

Performance standards

The Local Government Act 1992 requires the Audit Commission to give **13–07** such directions as it thinks fit for requiring relevant bodies to publish information facilitating comparisons between such bodies of standards of performance in respect of cost, economy, efficiency, and effectiveness.[33] Relevant bodies are bodies subject to audit under Part III of the 1982 Act, excluding health service bodies, passenger transport executives, parishes and communities and other specified minor authorities.[34] The Secretary of State may by order apply the requirement to parish and community councils and charter trustees.[35]

Bodies so directed to publish information for a financial year must make necessary arrangements for collecting and recording accurate and complete information, must publish it by one of the permitted methods within nine months of the end of the year, and must keep a document containing the information available for inspection by interested persons.[36] The permitted methods are either a newspaper printed for sale and circulating in the area or a newspaper or other periodical distributed free of charge by another

---

[27] *ibid.*, s.28AA(1), inserted by the Audit (Miscellaneous Provisions) Act 1996, s.1.
[28] *ibid.*, s.28AA(4)–(5).
[29] *ibid.*, s.28AA(6).
[30] *ibid.*, s.28AA(8)–(9).
[31] Code of Audit Practice, 1995, para. 40.
[32] *ibid.*
[33] Local Government Act 1992, s.1(1).
[34] *ibid.*, ss.1(7), (8), 28(2).
[35] *ibid.*, s.4.
[36] *ibid.*, s.1(2), as amended by the Audit (Miscellaneous Provisions) Act 1996, s.5.

person, other than a local authority company.[37] In regard to the latter, all reasonable steps are taken by the authority to secure that it is distributed to each dwelling in the area and, if the authority consider that the information is of concern to business persons, to business premises in the area.[38] Interested persons are local government electors for the area. They are entitled to inspect and make copies without charge, and to be supplied with copies on reasonable terms.[39]

Sections 2 and 3 of the 1992 Act contain supplementary provisions in respect of directions under section 1. In particular, directions imposing new requirements are to be preceded by consultations with such associations of bodies and other persons as the Commission thinks fit[40]; directions are to be published by the Commission as appropriate to bring them to public attention[41]; auditors are required to satisfy themselves that bodies have taken action required by section 1[42]; and the Commission are required to undertake studies to determine what directions it should make and what comparative information it should itself publish about standards of performance achieved.[43]

The Commission publish annually guidance which auditors must take into account in carrying out the audit work during which they must satisfy themselves that the necessary arrangements are in place.[44]

Miscellaneous duties and powers of the Commission

13–08   Section 29 of the 1982 Act, as amended, provides that the Commission, if so required by the body concerned, shall make arrangements for certifying claims on government departments and public authorities, contractual payments due from government departments, and other statutory calculations and returns. The body must be charged a fee to cover the full cost. Detailed arrangements for certification of grant claims are set out in Department of the Environment Circular 10/84. For certain claims, it is a condition of grant that claims are certified by an auditor appointed by the Commission. For the remainder, authorities will be free to engage other professional accountants to certify their claims.

Section 29(2) enables the Commission to promote or undertake value-for-money studies into transactions of a body if the body, after consulting employees' associations, so requests. Section 29(3) enables the Commission, with the consent of the Secretary of State, to audit by agreement the accounts of bodies connected with local government which are not subject to

---

[37] *ibid.*, s.1A, as inserted by the Audit (Miscellaneous Provisions) Act 1996, s.5. A local authority company is any company under the control of the authority as defined by s.68(1) of the Local Government and Housing Act 1989. See § 4–89.
[38] *ibid.*
[39] *ibid.*, s.1(4), (5).
[40] *ibid.*, s.2(3).
[41] *ibid.*, s.2(5).
[42] *ibid.*, s.3(1).
[43] *ibid.*, s.3(3).
[44] Code of Audit Practice, 1995, para. 54.

audit under Part III. Any other relevant statutory provisions (*e.g.* the Companies Acts) will apply; otherwise the terms of the audit are for agreement. Services under section 29(2) and (3) must be charged at full cost.[45]

If so required by the Local Government Commission, the Audit Commission shall provide it, at full cost, with a written opinion as to the likely impact of any proposed structural changes under Part II of the Local Government Act 1992 on economy, efficiency and effectiveness. Bodies under audit may be required by the Audit Commission to provide it with information for this purpose.[46] **13–09**

Additional powers to bring audit matters to the attention of the public are given to the Commission by section 7 of the Local Government Act 1992, which empowers it to publish information on the following matters (except in respect of health service bodies)[47]: **13–10**

(a) contravention by a body of its obligations under section 1(2) of the Act as to information on standards of performance[48];
(b) audit reports and action taken thereon[49];
(c) contravention by a body of accounts regulations.

Publication may relate to matters occurring before the Act but is restricted in respect of decisions made while the public were excluded from a meeting.[50] Prior notice of publication to the body concerned is required.[51]

General duties of auditors
Section 15(1) of the 1982 Act requires the auditor to satisfy himself: **13–11**

(a) that the accounts are prepared in accordance with regulations made under section 23 of the Act and otherwise comply with statutory provisions;
(b) that proper practices have been observed in the compilation of the accounts[52];
(c) that the body has made proper arrangements for securing economy, efficiency and effectiveness in its use of resources; and
(d) that where the body are required to publish performance information under section 1 of the Local Government Act 1992 they have made

---

[45] Local Government Finance Act 1982, s.29(4), (5).
[46] Local Government Act 1992, s.16.
[47] Local Government Act 1992, s.7(1)–(3)(a).
[48] § 13–07.
[49] See § 13–14 to § 13–18.
[50] Local Government Act 1992, s.7(4), (3)(b).
[51] *ibid.*, s.7(5).
[52] "Proper practices" are defined by s.66(4) of the Local Government and Housing Act 1989 to mean accounting practices which the authority are required to follow by statute or which, whether by reference to any generally recognised published code or otherwise, are regarded as proper accounting practices to be followed by local authorities and are not in conflict with statute. See § 13–02.

required arrangements for collecting, recording and publishing the information.

Paragraph (c) of section 15(1) was a new provision; but the 1973 Code of Practice had recognised that it was the auditor's function (as earlier exercised by district auditors) to look into questions of "value for money", which comprises the concepts of economy, efficiency and effectiveness. These terms are defined and operationalised in current Code of Practice, in the foreword and paragraphs 16–18 and 37–44. Paragraph (d) was inserted by section 3(1) of the Local Government Act 1992.

13–12   The traditional view taken by the courts of the responsibility of the district auditor was restated by Lord Denning M.R. in *Asher v. Secretary of State for the Environment*[53] in the following terms:

> "The district auditor holds a position of much responsibility. In some respects he is like a company auditor, He is a watchdog to see that the accounts are properly kept and that no one is making off with the funds. He is not bound to be of a suspicious turn of mind: see *In re Kingston Cotton Mill Co. (No. 2)* [1996] 2 Ch. 279; but, if anything suspicious does turn up, it is his duty to take care to follow it up: see *In re Thomas Gerrard & Son Ltd* [1968] Ch. 455. In other respects, however, the duties of a district auditor go far beyond those of a company auditor. He must see whether, on the financial side, the councillors and their officers have discharged their duties according to law. He must listen to any elector who makes objection to the accounts. He must make his own investigation also. If he finds that the councillors or the officers, or any of them, have expended money improperly, or unreasonably, or allowed it to be so expended, it is his duty to surcharge them: see *Roberts v. Hopwood* [1925] A.C. 578 and *Pooley v. District Auditor No. 8 Audit District* (1964) 63 L.G.R. 60 and in the Court of Appeal (1965) 63 L.G.R. 236."

13–13   In *West Wiltshire District Council v. Garland; Cond and others, third parties*,[54] it was held, by Morritt J., that an auditor under the Local Government Finance Act 1982 did not owe a duty of care to officers of an audited authority and that no action lay against him for breach of such a duty; but that he did owe a statutory duty to the Council, a breach of which gave rise to a right of action by the Council against the auditor. In the light of his finding on the statutory duty, Morritt J. did not consider it necessary to deal with the question of whether the auditor owed a common law duty which would give rise to an action in negligence. In the Court of Appeal,[55] the decision was upheld in regard to the statutory duty owed to the Council and to there being no liability to any officer. However, the Court refused to strike out the action in negligence on the ground that: "there may be co-existent remedies for negligence in breach of a statutory duty and in tort. Certainly it is not so clear and obvious that the two causes of action cannot co-exist as to justify striking out on that ground alone the claims sounding in tort as disclosing no cause of action".

---

[53] [1974] Ch. 208 at p. 219. The word "surcharge" no longer appears in the audit provisions. For corresponding current powers of the auditor, see §§ 13–32 to 13–37.
[54] [1993] 3 W.L.R. 626.
[55] [1995] 2 W.L.R. 439.

The auditor's reports

Section 15(3) of the 1982 Act provides that the auditor is to consider **13–14** whether in the public interest he should make a report on any matter coming to his notice in the course of the audit in order that it may be considered by the body concerned or brought to the attention of the public. He is also to consider whether the public interest requires an immediate report rather than a report at the conclusion of the audit. A report (other than an immediate report) is to be sent to the body under audit not later than 14 days after the conclusion of the audit; all reports must be considered by the body under audit as soon as practicable after receipt. Copies of reports go to the Commission.[56] The body to whom an immediate report is made must supply a copy forthwith to every member of the body and must forthwith advertise in the local press, identifying the subject-matter of the report and stating that any member of the public may inspect and obtain copies of the report for a reasonable sum at specified times and places.[57] Failure to comply with the additional publicity for immediate reports involves liability to a fine of up to level 3 of the standard scale. Allowing for further notification, the auditor may also notify or supply a copy of any immediate report he has made to any person he thinks fit.[58] The agenda for the meeting of the authority to which the report is submitted must be accompanied by the report, which must not be excluded from the documents to be made available to the press and public under the Public Bodies (Admission to Meetings) Act 1960 and Part VA of the Local Government Act 1972.[59] Local government electors may inspect and copy, or pay for copies of, auditors' reports and statements of accounts, and obstruction or refusal entails liability to a penalty of up to level 3 of the standard scale.[60] Availability of the report for inspection must be advertised, and contravention of this requirement is an offence.[61]

The Code of Audit Practice contains sundry comments and examples **13–15** concerning audit reports. Paragraph 76 points out that auditors should not be deflected from making a report because its subject matter is critical or unwelcome, since the auditor must remain independent and impartial and such reports are an important means of informing the public. However, it states that it is not the function of the auditor to express his opinion as to the wisdom of particular decisions taken by authorities in the lawful exercise of their discretion, and that reports relating to such decisions should only refer to facts which have not previously been brought to the notice of the authority or which ought to be brought to the attention of the public. Paragraph 43 states that it is not the auditor's function to question policy, but makes it clear that it is his responsibility to consider the effects of policy and to

[56] Local Government Finance Act 1982, s.18(3), (4).
[57] *ibid.*, s.18A, inserted by the Local Government Finance (Publicity for Auditors' Reports) Act 1991.
[58] *ibid.*, s.18A(5).
[59] *ibid.*, s.18(5), as amended.
[60] *ibid.*, s.24(1), (3).
[61] Accounts and Audit Regulations 1983 (S.I. 1983 No. 1761), regs. 14(2), and (17). From April 1, 1997 these will be superseded by the Accounts and Audit Regulations 1996 (S.I. 1996 No. 590) regs. 16(2) and 19. See § 13–53.

examine the arrangements by which policy decisions are reached, and gives examples of aspects of policy decisions into which he should inquire, such as the methods for identification, consideration and evaluation of policy options; whether policy aims conflict; whether policy aims are communicated clearly; and whether the costs of alternative levels of service are considered. Comparison with paragraph 76 appears to indicate that the bar on "questioning" policy relates rather to the limitation that the auditor should not express his own opinion on the wisdom of council decisions in the lawful exercise of discretion.

13–16   Decisions of the courts are also relevant to the question of the auditor's function in respect of policy decisions. In *Anns v. Merton London Borough Council*,[62] Lord Wilberforce indicated that policy was to be equated with discretion, and it is well established that it is the auditor's function, under section 19 of the 1982 Act and its predecessors, to consider whether discretion has been exercised lawfully.[63] If discretion has been exercised lawfully, the Irish case of *R. (Drury) v. Dublin Corporation*,[64] referring to audit legislation not significantly different, indicates that the auditor nevertheless has power to report on (and hence to inquire into) matters within the discretion of the authority (*i.e.* policy matters) in order that the public might be informed and the authority give further consideration to those matters, the ultimate discretion of the authority being unimpaired. To the same effect is a dictum in *R. v. Roberts*.[65]

13–17   The Code of Audit Practice also advocates another non-statutory type of report, designated a "management letter". This is described as: "addressed to members which will give a summary of the audit activities and details of the significant matters which have arisen from all aspects of the audit".[66] Letters may be issued in full or summary form provided sufficient supporting information exists and that they summarise all issues of substance or significance.[67] While there should normally be one only each year for each audited body, auditors should consider whether to issue an interim management letter in exceptional circumstances.[68] A management letter should be discussed in draft form with the officers and, the auditor having ensured that the final letter is issued to all members, should seek a meeting with members to answer questions. The Code states that it is for the auditor to decide when to report by way of a public interest report and gives examples of circumstances pointing to the use of a public interest report, such as, *inter alia*, delayed preparation of the accounts; excessive or inadequate balances or prospective deficits; absence or weakness in securing economy, efficiency, and effectiveness; lack of action on previous reports of the auditor; misconduct, fraud; and objections received at audit.[69]

---

[62] [1978] A.C. 728, 754.
[63] See § 13–22.
[64] (1907) 41 I.L.T.R. 97, 100, 105.
[65] [1908] 1 K.B. 407, 434.
[66] Code of Audit Practice, 1995, para. 55(f).
[67] *ibid.*, para. 84.
[68] *ibid.*, para. 85.
[69] *ibid.*, para. 74.

Duty to consider auditor's report or recommendation

Section 5 of the Local Government Act 1992 places a duty on bodies to **13–18** which it applies to give consideration in accordance with sections 5 and 6 to auditors' reports under section 15(3) of the 1982 Act and to any other written recommendation by an auditor who states therein that, in the auditor's opinion, it should receive such consideration. Thus section 5 may apply to a management letter if the auditor so chooses. Section 5 does not apply to health service bodies, to passenger transport executives or to specified types of minor authority, but applies to all other bodies audited under the 1982 Act, including parish and community authorities.[70]

The requirements of sections 5 and 6 as to the consideration to be given under the sections are as follows:

(1) Consideration must be at a meeting of the body itself, with no delegation permitted, held within four months of the issue of the report or recommendation, unless the auditor is satisfied that it is reasonable to allow more time.[71]

(2) Seven clear days' notice of the meeting must be given in a local newspaper, with particulars of its purpose and of the subject-matter of the report or recommendation.[72]

(3) The body is under a duty to decide at the meeting (i) whether the report requires the body to take any action or whether the recommendation is to be accepted, and (ii) what, if any, action to take in response to the report or recommendation.[73]

(4) The body must notify the auditor, as soon as practicable after the meeting, of the decisions made under section 5(2)(b).[74]

(5) The body must ensure that a notice containing a summary of those decisions is promptly published in a local newspaper.[75] The notice is not required to summarise decisions made while the public were excluded from the meeting under statutory authority, but must indicate documents open to inspection under such authority.[76]

Paragraphs 89 to 91 of the Code of Audit Practice reflect the provisions of sections 5 and 6 of the Local Government Act 1992. It is stated that, while section 5 will apply automatically to a public interest report, in regard to management letters to which the auditor wishes the provisions to apply, this must be specified in writing and that recommendations under section 5 made in management letters should normally be in a section headed "Recommendations Requiring a Public Response" near the beginning of the letter.[77] The Code states that it is for the auditor to decide whether to attach such a requirement to any recommendation in a management letter, but

[70] Local Government Act 1992, ss.5(6), 28(2).
[71] *ibid.*, s.5(2)(a), (3), (4).
[72] *ibid.*, s.6(1).
[73] *ibid.*, s.5(2)(b).
[74] *ibid.*, s.6(2)(a).
[75] *ibid.*, s.6(2)(b).
[76] *ibid.*, s.6(3).
[77] Code of Audit Practice, 1995, paras. 89 and 91.

takes the view that this should be considered where authorities have responded inadequately to recommendations by auditors, or disagreed with such recommendations and the auditor sees advantage in wider public debate.

The auditor's certificate and opinion on the accounts

13–19   Section 18(1) of the Local Government Finance Act 1982 requires the auditor, at the conclusion of the audit, to enter on the statement of accounts prepared pursuant to regulations: (a) a certificate that he has completed the audit in accordance with the Act, and (b) his opinion on the statement of accounts. For authorities not required to prepare a statement of accounts (parish councils and the like) the certificate and opinion are to be entered on the accounts themselves. Where the auditor makes a report under section 15(3) at the close of the audit he may include his certificate and opinion in that report.[78]

The Code of Audit Practice requires the auditor to refer expressly in his opinion (a) to whether the audit has been completed in accordance with the Code; (b) the respective responsibilities with regard to the statements of accounts of the audited body, its officers and auditors making it clear that the auditor's responsibility is not for the statements but the opinion on those statements; (c) the basis of that opinion; and (d) the opinion, stating whether the statement of accounts presents fairly the financial position of the authority.[79] Where the auditor is unable to give an affirmative opinion on these matters, he is to qualify his opinion by referring to all material matters about which he has reservations.[80] The Code sets out detailed requirements concerning auditors' opinions on statements of accounts.[81]

Access to documents, etc.

13–20   An auditor has a right of access at all reasonable times to all documents relating to an audited body which appear to him to be necessary for the purposes of his statutory functions.[82] The auditor may also require any person holding or accountable for such a document, and any member or officer of the body, to give information or explanation which he thinks necessary for the purposes of his functions, and to attend before him for that purpose or to produce the document. The audited body must give the auditor all facilities and information which he may reasonably require. The Audit Commission has similar powers to those of the auditor to require information and documents.[83] Particular powers are granted in regard to the provision of information and documents for joint studies into social services functions.[84]

---

[78] Local Government Finance Act 1982, s.18(2).
[79] Code of Audit Practice, 1995, para. 58.
[80] *ibid.*, para. 15.
[81] *ibid.*, Part 4.
[82] Local Government Finance Act 1982, s.16.
[83] *ibid.*, ss.28(1) (a general power), 13(4), 28(2) (specific powers relating to the appointment of auditors and the maintenance of audit standards).
[84] *ibid.*, s.28AA, as inserted by the Audit (Miscellaneous Provisions) Act 1996, s.1. See § 13–06.

A person who without reasonable excuse fails to comply with an auditor's requirement in this regard, or that of the Commission,[85] is liable on summary conviction to a fine of up to level 3 on the standard scale under the Criminal Justice Act 1982 and to an additional fine of £20 for each day on which the offence continues after conviction.[86] The defence of "reasonable excuse" does not extend to ignorance or mistake as to the law, even if this is in doubt at the time of the offence.[87]

It is well established by the case law under earlier similar provisions that the auditor's powers are not restricted to officers or documents of the authority; they apply, for example, to contractors and their documents.[88]

Information obtained by or on behalf of the Commission or an auditor **13–21** under Part III of the 1982 Act may not be disclosed except with consent of the body or person concerned, or for the purposes of the functions of Commission or auditor, or for the purpose of criminal proceedings. Contravention is punishable on summary conviction or indictment.[89] In *Bookbinder v. Tebbit (No. 2)*,[90] the court set aside subpoenas served by the plaintiff in a libel action to obtain evidence from audit staff who had enquired into expenditure relevant to the subject-matter of the alleged libel. It was held that audit evidence would involve breach of the above provisions, since although the local authority had consented to disclosure of the information, the individual officers who had supplied it to the audit staff had not consented. It was also held that public interest immunity applied, under established case law, where disclosure of information obtained in statutory investigations was likely to inhibit the obtaining of information in such investigations, and that this was such a case.

Unlawful items of account

Where it appears to the auditor that an item of account is contrary to law **13–22** he may apply to the court for a declaration to that effect.[91] The phrase "contrary to law" has been the subject of much litigation under earlier law which gave the district auditor power to surcharge illegal expenditure on the members or officers responsible for incurring it. This clearly includes an item that is *ultra vires* in the narrow sense.

> In *North Tyneside Metropolitan Borough Council v. Allsop*[92] the Court of Appeal upheld the Divisional Court in granting an application by the district auditor for a declaration that payments under an enhanced severance scheme for voluntary redundancy were contrary to law. The court rejected the council's

---

[85] *ibid.*, under s.28(1).

[86] *ibid.*, ss.16(4), 28(3). See also the Criminal Justice Act 1993, s.65, under which the court, before fixing the amount of a fine to reflect the seriousness of the case, must inquire into the financial circumstances of the offender, and take account thereof, up to the maximum fine.

[87] *R. v. Reid (Philip)* [1973] 3 All E.R. 1020.

[88] *Re Hurle-Hobbs* [1994] 2 All E.R. 261; and *R. v. Hurle-Hobbs, ex p. Simmons* [1945] K.B. 165.

[89] Local Government Finance Act 1982, s.30. By s.30(1A), this is subject to an exception in regard to joint studies into social services functions under s.28AA, as inserted by the Audit (Miscellaneous Provisions) Act 1996. See § 13–06.

[90] [1992] 1 W.L.R. 213.

[91] Local Government Finance Act 1982, s.19(1).

[92] (1992) 90 L.G.R. 462.

claim that redundancy payments in excess of those under specific statutes were authorised by the general provisions of section 111 of the Local Government Act 1972.[93]

In the above case, the Court rejected the argument that the council had discretion to pay enhanced sums. However, discretionary powers may also be exercised in a manner which is contrary to law and expenditure under discretionary powers has been held to be contrary to law if it is unreasonable in its extent or excessive and incurred by abuse of discretion.

> *Roberts v. Hopwood.*[94] Under the Metropolis Management Act 1855 the Poplar Council had authority to employ such servants as might be necessary and to pay such servants such wages as the council thought fit. The council resolved to pay a minimum wage of £4 per week to its employees, a figure higher than that paid to persons doing similar work in the district. In an affidavit the council stated that "a public authority should be a model employer and that a minimum rate of £4 is the least wage which ought to be paid to an adult." The district auditor disallowed what he considered to be excess wages and surcharged the members of the council. The House of Lords upheld the disallowance. The headnote to the report, which has been much quoted, records it to have been held "(l) that the discretion conferred upon the council must be exercised reasonably, and that the fixing by the council of an arbitrary sum for wages without regard to existing labour conditions was not an exercise of that discretion; (n) that an expenditure upon a lawful object might be so excessive as to be unlawful, and that to the extent by which the amount exceeded legality the auditor was bound to disallow it and surcharge the excess upon the persons responsible," and that the disallowance and surcharge were therefore rightly made.

13–23 The *ratio decidendi* of *Roberts v. Hopwood* has been the subject of comment and interpretation in subsequent cases, however, and in *Pickwell v. Camden London Borough Council* (below) Ormrod L.J. said that the headnote of *Roberts v. Hopwood* did not accurately reflect the *ratio decidendi* of the case.

> In *Associated Provincial Picture Houses Ltd v. Wednesbury Corporation*[95] Lord Greene M.R. said, "When the case [*Roberts v. Hopwood*] is examined, the word 'unreasonable' is found to be used rather in the sense I mentioned a short while ago, namely, that in fixing £4, they had fixed it by reference to a matter which they ought not to have taken into account and to the exclusion of those elements which they ought to have taken into consideration in fixing a sum which could fairly be called a wage. That is no authority whatsoever to support the proposition that the court has power, a sort of overriding power, to decide what is reasonable and what is unreasonable."
>
> *Giddens v. Harlow District Auditor.*[96] The appellant had objected at the audit, alleging that a loss had been incurred by negligence or misconduct because of the council's failure to charge reasonable rents. She also objected to the expenditure of some £5,000 on the purchase of a wood as a nature reserve, claiming that the wood would benefit only a privileged minority of ratepayers. The district auditor considered the evidence and, applying the principles in *Associated Provincial Picture Houses Ltd v. Wednesbury Corporation*, above,

---

[93] For further details, see § 1–29.
[94] [1925] A.C. 578.
[95] [1948] 1 K.B. 223 at p. 232; and see § 10–25.
[96] (1972) 70 L.G.R. 485.

decided that none of the conditions required to establish unreasonable and unlawful exercise of discretion was satisfied. He accordingly dismissed the objection. The applicant appealed against the auditor's decision. *Held*, dismissing the appeal, that whether or not the authority's conduct was politically motivated, the auditor had applied the correct principles in deciding that it had acted lawfully, and nothing justified the contention that he had erred in law in reaching his decision. Ashworth J. said at p. 487, "It is perhaps worth just citing the three reasons on which, as he says rightly, he could and should interfere: (a) the council have taken into account matters which it ought not to have taken into account; or (b) it had refused or neglected to take into account matters which it ought to take into account; or (c) it had come to a conclusion so unreasonable that no reasonable authority could ever have come to it."

Pickwell v. Camden London Borough Council.[97] The council made a local **13–24** settlement with its manual workers who, in common with other local government workers, were striking for higher pay and reduced working hours. The local settlement was substantially higher than the national settlement reached shortly afterwards. The district auditor applied to the court, under s.161 of the Local Government Act 1972, for a declaration that the payments under the Camden settlement were in part contrary to law. He relied on *Roberts v. Hopwood* and also on the *Wednesbury* case, on the basis that the respondents must have taken irrelevant matters into account or failed to take account of matters which they ought to have considered, or alternatively that the decision was one which no reasonable authority could have reached. Ormrod L.J. said that the headnote to *Roberts v. Hopwood* did not accurately reflect the *ratio decidendi*. The true reason for that decision, he said, was that the local authority had purported to exercise their powers to pay wages in order to make gifts to their staff rather than pay wages; the payments were accordingly *ultra vires* and contrary to law. As to the *Wednesbury* case, Ormrod L.J. said that a failure to take into account relevant matters, or the taking into account of irrelevant matters (and also excessive expenditure) were in effect only evidence that the authority may have acted *ultra vires* and therefore contrary to law. That did not, however, amount to illegality in itself. Attention was to be paid to the quality of the decision rather than to the method by which it was reached. For the district auditor to succeed, he must establish that the council had acted outside its powers, either by showing that the decision was not a real exercise of the power to pay wages but was made for an ulterior purpose, or by satisfying the court that no reasonable authority could have made such a decision. The first of these alternatives had not been put forward. The second would require clear and compelling evidence, leading almost to a finding that the council had acted in bad faith; the evidence before the court was quite insufficient to permit the court to make any such finding of fact. The application therefore failed. The judgment of Forbes J. was based more closely on *Wednesbury* principles. He said that there was no direct evidence of breach of those principles and that it could not be inferred from the amount of the payments that the council ignored relevant material, were guided by improper motives or acted in such a way that no reasonable council could act.

It is arguable that the judgment of Forbes J. was based "on a narrow ground confined to the necessities of the decision", that the wider propositions of Ormrod L.J. went beyond those necessities, and that the reasoning of Forbes J. should therefore be taken as the true *ratio decidendi*.[98] However, the words of Ormrod L.J. must carry great weight and may be

---

[97] [1983] 1 Q.B. 962.
[98] *Gold v. Essex County Council* [1942] 2 K.B. 293 at p. 298.

taken as precluding audit action on alleged excessive expenditure unless there is evidence to show an ulterior purpose or that no reasonable authority could have made such a decision.

13–25   In the next case the authority had a discretion to recover certain sums but chose not to do so. In the circumstances of this case it was held by the High Court that the district auditor was right in making a surcharge against members of the authority for having acted "contrary to law".

> *Taylor v. Munrow*.[99] The facts of this case are somewhat involved but, stated shortly, the authority was obliged to pay to the landlords of requisitioned property the full standard rent under the Rent Acts, the difference between that and the actual rent paid by the occupier being borne by the general rate fund unless the authority should "otherwise determine", by revising the rent. The authority failed to make a determination, paying the whole of the difference, arguing, *inter alia*, that a means test would be involved and was undesirable. The auditor surcharged the councillors with the sums falling to the general rate fund and in addition he found the members of the council to have been guilty of negligence. The court on appeal upheld the district auditor in his view that the discretion given to the council under the Requisitioned Houses and Housing (Amendment) Act 1955 was a discretion which the council was bound to exercise and was bound to exercise reasonably, for the council had always a duty to preserve a balance between a duty owed to the general body of ratepayers and a duty owed to particular tenants.

Roberts v. Hopwood (read in the light of the *Giddens* and *Camden* decisions, above) is an authority for the view that excessive expenditure may be held contrary to law if it is shown to have stemmed from an abuse of discretion. *Taylor v. Munrow* may be taken as an authority for the view that an improper failure to exercise a discretion at all may be equally regarded as contrary to law.

13–26   If unlawful exercise of discretion produces expenditure which is objectively reasonable, it cannot be held contrary to law. In *Re Walker's Decision*,[1] the district auditor disallowed payments of children's allowances to employees on the grounds that an employee's living expenses (and therefore family size) were irrelevant considerations in fixing remuneration. The court held that the amounts paid were not contrary to law because they were not in themselves unreasonable. Goddard L.J. said "If the result is a reasonable sum, that is enough to justify the payment", and referred with approval to a dictum of Lord Sumner in *Roberts v. Hopwood*,[2] in which he said that even in case of bad faith, if "the councillors' evil minds had missed their mark and the expenditure itself was right, then the expenditure would not be contrary to law".

13–27   The meaning of the phrase "contrary to law" was considered in *Beecham v. Metropolitan District Auditor*[3] in a somewhat different context from *Roberts v. Hopwood*, *Giddens* and *Camden*. The appellant objected at

---

[99] [1960] 1 All E.R. 455.
[1] [1944] 1 K.B. 644.
[2] *op. cit.*, at p. 604.
[3] (1977) 75 L.G.R. 79.

district audit to expenditure on demolition of property on the grounds that planning permission for the demolition was required and had not been obtained. He argued that the demolition was contrary to law and that accordingly the expenditure incurred was contrary to law. The district auditor disallowed the objection. The objector appealed, and failed, Boreham J. said, at p. 83:

> "... the council in the present case has power to demolish their houses and to expend money in so doing. They were therefore in that regard acting *intra vires*. Secondly, the failure to obtain planning permission or consent, assuming that such permission was required, does not in my view render *ultra vires* what was otherwise *intra vires*. It follows, therefore, that the item to which the appellant was objecting was not contrary to law ... Of course, if planning permission was required in this case, and if the council's failure to obtain it were in the future to lead to loss, then it would be incumbent no doubt upon the district auditor to consider whether such loss ought to be surcharged upon the person responsible ..."

The auditor may not make application to the court in respect of an item of **13–28** account sanctioned by the Secretary of State.[4] This appears as a dispensing power in the hands of the Secretary of State, for an auditor cannot in effect look at an account where payment has been approved in this way notwithstanding the fact that it is *ultra vires* or otherwise illegal; but the sanction does not legalise a payment, and an elector who objects to any account may exercise the other (though more expensive) remedies available.[5]

The policy originally adopted by the Local Government Board in issuing sanctions still appears substantially to be followed by the Secretary of State. The Board said in its Annual Report for 1887–88:

> "The power of sanction is intended to be used in those cases where the expenditure is incurred bona fide but in ignorance of the strict letter of the law, or inadvertently without the observance of requisite formalities, or under such circumstances as make it fair and equitable that the expenditure should not be disallowed by the auditor ... We do not regard the Act as intended to supply the want of legislative or other authority for particular expenditure or classes of expenditure, and as justifying us in giving prospective sanction to recurring expenses."

Where the court makes the declaration asked for it may order repayment **13–29** by the person concerned and may order the rectification of accounts. Where the person concerned is a member and the expenditure exceeds £2,000 he may be disqualified from membership for a specified period. The court in making an order must have regard to the person's ability to pay and is precluded from making one if satisfied that he acted reasonably or in the belief that the expenditure was authorised by law.[6]

A person answerable under these provisions is one responsible for

---

[4] Local Government Finance Act 1982, s.19(1). See also *R. v. Grain, ex p. Wandsworth Guardians* [1927] 2 K.B 205, and *Att.-Gen. v. East Barnet Urban District Council* (1911) 9 L.G.R. 913.
[5] See Chap. 10.
[6] Local Government Finance Act 1982, s.19(2), (3).

incurring or authorising expenditure declared unlawful. He is responsible if he voted in favour and he may be responsible if he abstained from voting, or even if he does not attend the meeting.[7]

Both the High Court and the county courts have jurisdiction for these purposes, but applications must be commenced in the High Court. The High Court may order transfer of the proceedings to a county court having regard to specified criteria.[8] As to appeals by an objector dissatisfied by an auditor's decision not to apply for a declaration under section 19(1), and the power of the court in respect of expenses relating to applications and appeals, see paragraph 13–50 below.

13–30   In two cases where district auditors, in reports under section 15(3) of the 1982 Act, have expressed doubts as to the legality of items of account, the local authorities have taken the initiative to resolve the matter by applying for judicial review and asking for declarations.[9] In each case the court expressed some reservations about dealing with the matter by judicial review rather than on application by the district auditor under section 19 of the 1982 Act, but agreed to do so since both parties agreed that the matter should be determined quickly. Subsequent to these cases the auditor was given express power under section 25D of the 1982 Act to seek judicial review.[10] The question of the ability of the local authority to seek judicial review arose again in:

> *R. v. Arthur Young (a firm), ex p. Thamesdown Borough Council.*[11] The council had proposed to enter into a "factoring" agreement similar to one subsequently held unlawful, on the application of the auditor under section 25D of the 1982 Act, in *R. v. Wirral Metropolitan Borough Council, ex p. Milstead.*[12] The auditor appointed by the Audit Commission, in a report under section 15(3), urged the Thamesdown council to refrain from proceeding with the agreement pending the decision of the court in the *Wirral* case. The council then applied for judicial review, asking for an order of *certiorari* to quash what was alleged to be a decision of the auditor and for a declaration that their proposed agreement would be lawful. Leave to apply for judicial review was granted *ex parte*, but the auditor applied for it to be set aside, arguing that he had made no decision capable of being subject to *certiorari* and that section 31(2) of the Supreme Court Act 1981 did not permit of a declaration being made on judicial review where no prerogative order was available.
>
> Pill J. said that the claim for *certiorari* was in his judgment hopeless, but the question of entitlement to argue for a declaration was more difficult. He found considerable force in the auditor's submissions, but, bearing in mind that the court should not defeat the purpose of the leave procedure by going into the matter in depth, he would, in the exercise of his discretion, refuse the

---

[7] See generally *Roberts v. Hopwood* [1925] A.C. 578; *R. v. Browne* [1907] 2 I.R. 505; *R. v. Hendon Rural District Council, ex p. Chorley* [1933] 2 K.B. 696 at p. 703; *Att.-Gen. v. Tottenham Local Board* (1872) 27 L.T. (N.S.) 440 and *Rothnie v. Dearne Urban District Council* (1951) 50 L.G.R. 123.

[8] Local Government Finance Act 1982, s.19(6), as substituted by the High Court and County Courts Jurisdiction Order 191 (S.I. 1991 No. 724, arts. 2(8), 6, 7(6), Sched., Pt. I).

[9] *R. v. District Auditor, ex p. West Yorkshire Metropolitan County Council* (1985) 26 R.V.R. 24; and *R. v. District Auditor, ex p. Leicester City Council* (1985) 25 R.V.R. 191.

[10] Inserted by the Local Government Act 1988, s.30.

[11] [1989] C.O.D. 392.

[12] (1989) 87 L.G.R. 611.

application to set aside the leave granted, so that the matter would be left to be determined at the substantive hearing. By the time that the matter came before the court for a full hearing, however, judgment had been given in the *Wirral* case. It was then conceded by the Thamesdown council that the decision defeated their substantive case on the factoring agreement. The procedural question whether they were entitled to seek judicial review on the basis of the auditor's report was not therefore considered by the court.

The Code of Audit Practice states that, in order to ensure the legality of **13–31** items of account, auditors should, *inter alia*: review the minutes of the audited body's principal committees; hold discussions with officers; have regard to the authority's implementation of significant new legislation or statutory requirements; review the local applicability of relevant national issues; and take account of advice issued by the Audit Commission.[13] In deciding whether to take action under section 19 of the 1982 Act to have the item of account declared unlawful, the auditor must: exercise the discretion personally; ensure that all persons who may be directly affected have a fair and adequate opportunity to reply to any allegations and charges; take account of all relevant factors including the significance of the point of law and the sum in question; and consider seeking legal advice.[14]

Misconduct and failure to account

Where a person has failed to bring into account a sum which ought to have **13–32** been included, or where there is loss or deficiency due to wilful misconduct, the auditor may certify a sum due from the person responsible, which, subject to rights of appeal, is then recoverable either by the auditor or the body. The auditor's expenses in enforcing recovery are recoverable from the body unless the court otherwise directs. If that person is a member and the amount exceeds £2,000 he will, subject to appeal, be disqualified for a period of five years. Provisions as to the jurisdiction of courts and transfer of proceedings, as described at paragraph 13–29, apply also to appeals under this head.[15]

Liability under earlier law was for loss or deficiency due to "negligence or **13–33** misconduct".[16] In *Asher v. Lacey*,[17] the failure of the councillors of the Clay Cross Urban District Council to increase council house rents as required by the Housing Finance Act 1972 was held to be negligence or misconduct. Members were surcharged for the resulting "loss or deficiency". There had been a breach of duty.

Graham v. Teesdale.[18] A sum was certified due from the former chairman of a

---

[13] Code of Audit Practice, 1995, para. 52.
[14] *ibid.*, paras. 96–97.
[15] Local Government Finance Act 1982, s.20, as amended by the High Court and County Courts Jurisdiction Order 1991 (S.I. 1991 No. 724, arts. 2(8), (6), 7(5), Sched., Pt. I).
[16] The word "misconduct" was considered in this context in *R. v. Roberts* [1908] 1 K.B. 407; *Roberts v. Hopwood* [1925] A.C. 578; and *R. v. Browne* [1907] 2 I.R. 505.
[17] [1973] 1 W.L.R. 1412.
[18] (1981) 81 L.G.R. 117.

parish council in respect of payments made to him in purported reimbursement of out-of-pocket expenses and to others for his benefit (car repairs and insurance) during a period when he had taken on the responsibility of the council's financial and general administration. No detailed accounts or vouchers were produced for the alleged out-of-pocket expenses; the appellant alleged that such accounts and vouchers had been passed to another member of the council, who did not admit their receipt. The majority of the payments were not authorised by the council; as to the remainder the district auditor found that the council's approval had been obtained by misrepresentation. The appeal was on the grounds, *inter alia*, (1) that the district auditor had misdirected himself in law as to the meaning of "wilful misconduct" and (2) that he had failed to observe the requirements of natural justice in that (a) he failed to permit the appellant to question witnesses; (b) he heard evidence adverse to the appellant in his absence. *Held*: (i) that "wilful misconduct" in section 161(4) of the 1972 Act meant "deliberately doing something which is wrong knowing it to be wrong or with reckless indifference whether it is wrong or not"; (ii) that the requirements of fairness by a district auditor were (a) that any material adverse to a person must be put to him and he must be allowed to deal with it by adducing evidence and otherwise; (b) that if there is a hearing (though no hearing is statutorily required) he must be allowed to question witnesses who give evidence at the hearing, through his legal representative, if any, or otherwise through the district auditor; (iii) that the district auditor had correctly directed himself under (i) and had met the requirements of fairness under (ii); (iv) that the appeal should be dismissed.

13–34   In defining misconduct the judgment refers only to "doing something" and does not specifically cover wrongful omission to act, as do other cases cited in the judgment.[19] However, the judgment later refers to "acts or omissions" which the district auditor had found to constitute misconduct, and does not distinguish between acts and omissions in upholding the auditor's decision. It is not therefore in conflict with the clear authority of such cases as *Forder* and *Horabin* that wilful misconduct includes wrongful omission to act where the omission is known to be wrongful or there is reckless indifference whether it is wrongful or not.

13–35   *Smith v. Skinner, Gladden v. McMahon*.[20] The district auditors certified sums due from members of Lambeth London Borough Council and Liverpool City Council in respect of losses due to their wilful misconduct in delaying the making of rates for the year 1985–86. On appeal to the Divisional Court it was *held*: (1) that the councillors' decisions in delaying the making of the rates were for an improper and extraneous reason, namely to put pressure on the Secretary of State by the threat that chaos would ensue if he did not make more funds available, and were therefore unlawful; (2) that in wilfully disregarding advice to that effect from their officers and the district auditor the councillors showed that they were at least reckless as to whether they were acting wrongly or not and were therefore guilty of wilful misconduct as correctly defined in *Graham v. Teesdale* (above); (3) that since the auditors had not, at the time, been able to quantify the loss arising from late payment of rate income generally, it was appropriate for them to assess loss on two specific items only—instalments of rate rebate subsidy and Crown contributions in lieu of rates forgone; (4) that the auditors had not acted unfairly in inviting representations from the councillors in writing rather than orally.

[19] *e.g. Forder v. G.W.R. Co.* [1905] 2 K.B. 532; and *Horabin v. B.O.A.C.* [1952] 2 All E.R. 1016.
[20] (1986) 26 R.V.R. 45 (D.C.).

An appeal by the Liverpool councillors to the Court of Appeal[21] was rejected. (The Lambeth councillors did not appeal.) The Court of Appeal upheld the reasoning of the Divisional Court under heads (1) to (3), above. Under head (4) some differences appeared in the judgments. Lawton L.J. held: (a) that the auditor was not required to hold an oral hearing in all cases but had a constitutional duty to act fairly; (b) that on the facts he was justified in inviting written representations in the first instance, since oral hearings at the outset might have taken an inordinate time; but (c) that he ought subsequently, in fairness, to have given the councillors an opportunity of an oral hearing to enable them to establish, if they could, their good faith and credibility; (d) that any unfairness there may have been was cured by the appeal to the Divisional Court, since that appeal was a rehearing at which the councillors had every opportunity of giving any evidence they wished. The other members of the court agreed with Lawton L.J. under heads (a), (b) and (d), but under head (c) Dillon L.J. found it unnecessary to reach a final conclusion and Woolf L.J. held that justice did not require the offer of an oral hearing.

The House of Lords dismissed an appeal by the councillors from the decision of the Court of Appeal.[22] The Lords rejected the view of Lawton L.J. in the Court of Appeal that the auditor ought in fairness to have offered an oral hearing. It was held that in all the circumstances the auditor had not acted unfairly and the procedure that he had followed of inviting written representations had not involved any prejudice to the councillors. They also expressed the view *obiter*, that a court hearing an appeal under section 20(3) of the 1982 Act against an auditor's certificate could cure a procedural defect by the auditor by inquiring into the merits of the case and arriving at its own decision.[23]

Fleming v. Lees.[24] An objector submitted at audit that members of Hackney **13–36** L.B.C. had caused loss by wilful misconduct (1) in failing to levy a rate for 1985–86 until May 22, 1985; and (2) in incurring costs by resisting judicial review proceedings instituted by himself, which had resulted in the issue of an order of mandamus commanding the council to make a rate by May 31, 1985. The auditor rejected the first submission but found a *prima facie* case in respect of the second and gave the councillors concerned an opportunity to answer that case. A sum was then paid in on behalf of the councillors to meet the costs of the judicial review proceedings. The objector submitted that the auditor should nevertheless certify that sum due from the councillors because it was due at the date to which the accounts were made up. The auditor rejected this submission. The objector appealed against the auditor's decisions.

Held, dismissing the appeal, (1) that the councillors were not in breach of duty in not making a rate until May 22, 1985; the judgment in the review proceedings did not suggest that there was such a breach and the making of an order of mandamus does not necessarily imply an extant breach of duty; (2) that the proper construction of section 20(1) of the 1982 Act, which uses the words "is due", requires the auditor to focus on whether there is a loss at the date of certification or refusal to certify.

As with section 19, in deciding whether to take action under section 20 of **13–37** the 1982 Act to recover amounts caused by wilful misconduct, the auditor must: exercise the discretion personally; ensure that all persons who may be directly affected have a fair and adequate opportunity to reply to any allegations and charges; and consider seeking legal advice.[25]

[21] *Sub nom. Lloyd v. McMahon* [1987] A.C. 625.
[22] Also reported at [1987] A.C. 625.
[23] See Lord Bridge [1987] A.C. 625, at pp. 708–709.
[24] [1991] C.O.D. 50.
[25] Code of Audit Practice, 1995, para. 97.

Responsibilities of officers

13–38   In cases of illegality or misconduct where the primary responsibility is that of the members of the council or other body some responsibility may also be borne by officers. In *R. v. Saunders*[26] it was held that a county treasurer who was ordered to make an illegal payment should disobey the order. In *Att.-Gen. v. De Winton*[27] it was similarly held that a borough treasurer stood in a fiduciary relationship to the burgesses and could not plead the orders of the council for an unlawful act.[28] In *Re Hurle-Hobbs, ex p. Riley*,[29] the court upheld a surcharge on the Town Clerk of Finsbury on the ground that loss had been caused by his misconduct in withholding information from the council on the instructions of the leader of the majority group (who was also surcharged). The court rejected the clerk's defence that he acted under threat of dismissal.

13–39   While the offices of county and borough treasurer and town clerk are no longer statutory, the officer responsible for administration of a body's affairs under section 151 of the Local Government Act 1972 has duties which effectively include those of treasurers under earlier legislation, and the chief executive officer and chief legal adviser of a body (under whatever title or titles) is or are as much "an important part of the machinery of local government" as the town clerk who was so described in *Riley's* case. It would therefore appear that these officers would be under a duty, first to advise the council against any unlawful action or misconduct to the detriment of ratepayers, and in the last resort to refuse to implement instructions which are manifestly illegal, such as for the making of illegal payments. Similar considerations would presumably apply to other chief officers and are consistent with the general rule of law, applicable to all officers, that an order of a superior or other duress is not recognised as an excuse for an act which is known to be unlawful.[30] In *Riley's* case Viscount Caldecote C.J. said that "the integrity of the administration of public affairs is such that publicity may be safely relied on to secure protection for anyone in the position in which the Town Clerk was said to have been placed". It would seem that surer protection is now provided by statute, on the assumption that dismissal for refusal to obey unlawful instructions would be held to be unfair within the meaning of the Employment Rights Act 1996 and would therefore result, on complaint to an industrial tribunal, in an order of reinstatement or compensation under that Act.[31]

---

[26] (1854) 3 E. & B. 763.

[27] [1906] 2 Ch. 106.

[28] See § 12–13.

[29] (1944) unreported. A full report of the judgments appears in Hurle-Hobbs, *The Law Relating to District Audit* (1955), now out of print, and a summarised note, with extracts of judgments, in R. Jones, *Local Government Audit Law* (2nd ed.), App. D.4.

[30] Clerk and Lindsell, *Torts*, 17th ed., para. 3–64.

[31] Employment Rights Act 1996, ss.98, 111–132; *cf. Morrish v. Henlys (Folkestone) Ltd* [1973] I.C.R. 482. See also § 12–13 as to the duties of report placed on the chief finance officer and on the monitoring officer by the Local Government Finance Act 1988 and the Local Government and Housing Act 1989.

Prohibition Orders and the power to apply for judicial review

Section 25A of the 1982 Act empowers a local government auditor to issue **13–40** a prohibition order requiring a body or officer under audit to desist from making or implementing decisions, or taking action, which the auditor has reason to believe would result in unlawful expenditure or other unlawful items of account, or would be unlawful and likely to cause a loss or deficiency.[32] A prohibition order does not have effect unless the auditor, within seven days of serving the order, serves a statement of reasons on the body and on any officer to whom an order has been addressed. The auditor may revoke, but may not vary, a prohibition order. The auditor may not issue a prohibition order in respect of any matter on which the chief finance officer has made a report to the council in exercise of his powers under the Local Government Finance Act 1988, section 114,[33] during the period between the issue of that report and the council's consideration of it.[34]

The body (but not an officer) may appeal to the High Court against a prohibition order. Subject thereto, any action in contravention of an order will be unlawful. The court may order payment by the body of expenses incurred by the auditor on an appeal and the auditor may recover other expenses relating to the issue of an order. The court's right to award costs of an appeal against the auditor is unaffected; otherwise no action will lie against the auditor for loss or damage caused by an order made in good faith.[35]

Section 25D of the 1982 Act empowers an auditor to make application for judicial review of any decision of a body under audit, or of any failure by the body to act, which in either case it is reasonable to believe would have an effect on the accounts of the body.[36] Again the court may order the payment by the body of the auditor's expenses relating to the application. An application by a district auditor for judicial review under this section was upheld in *R. v. Wirral Metropolitan Borough Council, Ex p. Milstead.*[37]

The Code of Audit Practice advises that auditors, when considering **13–41** whether to exercise these powers, should take into account all relevant considerations, including the significance of the points of law, and the size of the sum, loss or deficiency in question.[38] In deciding whether to apply for judicial review the auditor should additionally consider the extent of the effect which the decision or failure in question would be likely to have on the statements of the accounts of the relevant body.[39] It is also stated that, while there is no right for local electors in regard to these powers, the auditor should always consider them in relation to matters raised by others, and also

---

[32] Inserted by s.30 and Sched. 4 of the Local Government Act 1988.
[33] See § 12–13.
[34] Local Government Finance Act 1982, s.25AA of the 1982 Act, inserted by the Local Government Finance Act 1988, s.137, Sched. 12, para. 3(3).
[35] *ibid.*, ss.25B, 25C(2). See § 13–51 as to expenses.
[36] Inserted by s.30 and Sched. 4 of the Local Government Act 1988.
[37] (1989) 29 R.V.R. 66, on which see § 13–30.
[38] Code of Audit Practice, 1995, para. 107.
[39] *ibid.*

in regard to any report by a chief finance officer or monitoring officer.[40] The Code also advises that, while there is no duty to consult with the authority before exercising the powers, and that in some circumstances it would not be appropriate to do so, the auditor should give the authority or officer concerned an opportunity to respond to the matters giving cause for concern, so far as is consistent with the prompt exercise of the powers in the public interest.[41]

Public rights

13–42   Section 17(1) of the Local Government Finance Act 1982 provides that all persons interested may inspect the accounts to be audited and all books, deeds, contracts, bills, vouchers and receipts relating thereto, and they may make copies of them.[42] The right is "to all persons interested", a term which is wider than "ratepayer", or "local government elector".[43] An interested person would appear entitled to depute an agent to make an inspection on his behalf.

> *R. v. Bedwellty Urban District Council.*[44] A ratepayer, the secretary of the local ratepayers' association, appointed an accountant who was not a ratepayer, to inspect with him the books of account and to report to the association thereon. The accountant was refused permission to see the books of account on the ground that he was not a "person interested". *Held*, that a person interested was entitled to inspect by an agent. Charles J. said (at p. 341): "the whole purpose of the section would be defeated if only the ratepayer were allowed to inspect, without a skilled person at his elbow to act as his agent for the inspection".

13–43   A local government elector for any area to which the accounts under audit relate, or his representative, may question the auditor about the accounts, and may attend before the auditor and make objections—(a) as to matters on which the auditor could take action under section 19 or 20 of the 1982 Act; or (b) as to any other matter on which he could make a report under section 15(3).[45] The objector must give written notice of a proposed objection, stating its grounds, the facts relied on, and particulars of the action which it is proposed that the auditor should take.[46]

Accounts and other documents must be made available for inspection under section 17(1) for 15 full working days before the date appointed by the auditor for the exercise of rights under section 17(2) and (3). At least 14 days' public notice must be given of the rights available under section 17, by

---

[40] *ibid.*, para. 108.

[41] *ibid.*, para. 109.

[42] As to the meaning of "voucher", see *R. v. Monmouthshire County Council* (1935) 33 L.G.R. 279.

[43] *Marginson v. Tildsley* (1903) 1 L.G.R. 333. Presumably also "council tax payer".

[44] [1934] 1 K.B. 333.

[45] Local Government Finance Act 1982, s.17(2)–(5).

[46] Accounts and Audit Regulations 1996 (S.I. 1996 No. 590), reg. 15, from April 1, 1997, in regard to the accounts kept from April 1996 under these regulations. Until then the existing provision, the Accounts and Audit Regulations 1983 (S.I. 1983 No. 1761), reg. 12, remains in force in regard to accounts kept under the 1983 regulations.

advertisement in local newspapers.[47] Once made available for inspection, the accounts can be altered only with the consent of the auditor.[48] Contravention of the inspection or notice requirements is an offence.[49]

Section 11 of the Local Government and Housing Act 1989 provides, in **13–44** respect of accounts from 1990–91 onwards, that nothing in section 17 shall entitle any person to inspect personal information about a member of staff held in respect of his employment or to require such information to be disclosed in answer to a question. The courts may regard the audit procedure as more appropriate than judicial review as a mechanism for challenge.

In *R. v. Westminster City Council, ex p. Hilditch*[50] an elector who had made an objection at audit alleging illegality of council decisions and who subsequently, before the objection was determined, applied for judicial review of the same decisions was refused leave since the audit procedure was more apt to decide the disputed factual issues raised and there were no exceptional circumstances justifying judicial review over the same ground.

The Audit Commission considers that auditors must at all times be **13–45** mindful of their responsibilities to the public, consider any information received from the public whether under statutory rights or at any other time, and that the auditor may remind electors of the right to make an objection where they think it appropriate.[51] Where representations are made, or information given or otherwise obtained, the auditor is to decide whether the matter is such as to merit prompt investigation and action, whether by way of section 19 (unlawful item of account), 20 (recovery of amount), 25A (prohibition order), or 25D (judicial review).

Audit proceedings

The conduct of audit proceedings in regard to questions, objections, and **13–46** the consideration of formal proceedings is subject to the requirements of the Code of Audit Practice and to principles laid down in case law.

The Code advises that the auditor should not admit questions on general matters such as the authority's policies, finances, and procedures which are beyond the scope of the actual accounts for the year under audit, should not without the consent of the authority disclose information not available for public inspection, or disclose personal information about the remuneration or other benefits of staff of the authority.[52]

Like any other tribunal with investigatory functions, the auditor should **13–47** (a) consider all relevant evidence which a party wishes to submit; (b) inform

---

[47] *ibid.*, regs. 11, 12, and 14, from April 1, 1997. Until then the existing provisions, the Accounts and Audit Regulations 1983 (S.I. 1983 No. 1761), regs. 8, 11, and 14, remain in force in regard to accounts kept under the 1983 regulations.

[48] *ibid.*, reg. 13, from April 1, 1997. Until then the existing provision, the Accounts and Audit Regulations 1983 (S.I. 1983 No. 1761), reg. 10, remains in force in regard to accounts kept under the 1983 regulations.

[49] *ibid.*, reg. 19, from April 1, 1997. Until then the existing provision, the Accounts and Audit Regulations 1983 (S.I. 1983 No. 1761), reg. 17, remains in force in regard to accounts kept under the 1983 regulations. See § 13–53.

[50] [1990] C.O.D. 434.

[51] Code of Audit Practice, 1995, paras. 93–94.

[52] *ibid.*, para. 98.

every party of the objection and all the evidence to be taken into account, whether derived from another party or from his own investigations, consistent with fairness and the good conduct of the enquiry[53]; (c) allow witnesses giving oral evidence to be questioned; and (d) allow comment on the evidence and argument on the whole case including, if the auditor considers it is required in fairness, provisional views on the matters investigated.[54] It also appears that he is not bound by the legal rules of evidence, but may take into account any material which as a matter of reason has some probative value.[55] The auditor is not statutorily required to hold an oral hearing but the Code suggests that consideration should be given to whether justice or fairness would best be served by giving those affected the opportunity of an oral hearing and, if so, whether it should be in public.[56] Where one is held, the auditor should give notice of the hearing to any person who may be adversely affected and should afford opportunity for questioning of witnesses either by legal representatives or, if a party is not represented, through the auditor himself.[57]

13–48   *R. v. District Auditor, No. 10 Audit District, ex p. Judge.*[58] Leave had initially been granted to the applicant to seek judicial review of the auditor's decision to dismiss his objections made under section 17 of the Local Government Finance Act 1982. The applicant's principal complaint was that he had not been given an oral hearing. The auditor applied for the leave initially granted to be set aside. He cited an *obiter dictum* of Woolf L.J.[59] to the effect that section 17(3) of the 1982 Act did not confer a right to oral hearings of objections, and submitted that even if there were such a right the objector should have raised it by appeal under section 19(4) of the 1982 Act and not by judicial review. He also pointed out that the objector had failed, in his initial application for leave, to disclose material matters, including his choice not to pursue his statutory right of appeal.

Rose J. set aside the leave previously granted, holding that questions of procedural fairness under sections 19 and 20 of the 1982 Act, such as the right to an oral hearing, should be dealt with by the statutory right of appeal rather than by judicial review, and that in all the circumstances of the case it was appropriate to take the exceptional step of exercising the inherent jurisdiction of the court to set aside leave previously granted.

The Court of Appeal refused leave to appeal against this decision, upholding the judge's reasoning.

13–49   While the Code advises that it is for the auditor to decide whether an oral hearing should be in public,[60] it is the general practice for the public and press to be admitted to the formal oral hearings of objections (though not to any preliminary meetings which may be necessary to state or clarify the terms of the objection, since allegations might be made at such meetings

---

[53] *ibid.*, para. 102.

[54] *ibid.*

[55] *R. v. Deputy Industrial Injuries Commissioner, ex p. Moore* [1965] 1 Q.B. 456, at pp. 488 and 490.

[56] Code of Audit Practice, 1995, para. 103.

[57] *ibid.* See also *Graham v. Teesdale* (1981) 81 L.G.R. 117, 131; and *Smith v. Skinner* and *Lloyd v. McMahon*, § 13–35.

[58] *The Times*, December 26, 1988, CO/1267/88, *sub nom. R. v. District Auditor Chelmsford.*

[59] *Lloyd v. McMahon* [1987] A.C. 625, 662.

[60] Code of Audit Practice, 1995, para. 103.

without those attacked having notice and the opportunity to answer[61]). In *R. v. Farmer, ex p. Hargrave*,[62] however, the auditor had decided for special reasons to hear an objection in private. On application by the objector to compel a public hearing it was held that there was no requirement of law that hearings of objections should be held in public, since the tenor of the statutory provisions was against anyone other than the objector being allowed to attend. The issue decided by the case was that the auditor was not required to admit the public; the general practice of holding oral hearings in public, in the absence of special reasons to the contrary, was not expressly disapproved and has continued.

Appeals

A person who has made an objection at audit and is aggrieved by the **13–50** auditor's decision, and a person from whom the auditor has certified a sum due, may require the auditor, not later than six weeks after the decision has been notified, to state in writing the reasons for his decision, and may appeal against the decision.[63]

On an appeal under these provisions, and on an application to the court by an auditor, the court may order payment by the audited body of expenses incurred by the auditor or other parties.[64]

Questions of fairness in audit proceedings should be raised by way of the statutory appeal procedure, not by judicial review.[65]

Fees for audit

Section 21 of the Local Government Finance Act 1982 provides for the **13–51** Audit Commission, after consultation with local authority associations and accountancy bodies, to fix scales of fees payable to the Commission which may be varied according to the work involved in a particular audit. The fee must be the same whether the auditor is an officer of the Commission or not. The Secretary of State is given a reserve power to set fee scales, after consultation, in place of those prescribed by the Commission.[66]

Extraordinary audit

The Audit Commission may direct an auditor to hold an extraordinary **13–52** audit of accounts of any body subject to audit if it appears to them desirable, either on application by a local government elector or otherwise, and the Secretary of State may require the Commission to do so.[67] Three days' notice must be given to the body. All the normal audit provisions apply, except the public rights of inspection of accounts and questioning the auditor. The cost

---

[61] *cf. Hearts of Oak Assurance Co. v. Att.-Gen.* [1932] A.C. 392.
[62] (1980) 79 L.G.R. 676.
[63] Local Government Finance Act 1982, ss.19(4), (6), 20(2), (3), (9) above. As to the courts having jurisdiction, and the commencement and transfer of proceedings, see § 13–29.
[64] *ibid.*, ss.19(5), 20(7). Such an order is not limited to taxed costs: *Wilkinson v. Doncaster Metropolitan Borough Council*, unreported, December 21, 1983, CO/203/83.
[65] *Supra*, § 13–48.
[66] Local Government Finance Act 1982, ss.21(7), 35(3).
[67] *ibid.*, s.22.

is met by the Commission in the first instance, but may be recharged to the body. A possible use for the extraordinary audit procedure would be to enable an objection to be heard in advance of the date appointed under normal procedure for the exercise of public rights of inspection and challenge under section 17. Public notice must be given of the right to make objection at an extraordinary audit.[68]

Accounts—regulations

13–53   Most of the provisions of the Accounts and Audit Regulations 1996[69] have been incorporated into the explanation above. It should be noted that while regulations 3, 4, and 5 of the 1996 Regulations, which establish the records and control systems, came into force on April 1, 1996, the other provisions do not come into force until April 1, 1997. The existing provisions under the 1983 Regulations are therefore also given in footnotes since these apply to the records kept in regard to records kept under the 1983 Regulations until April 1996.

By section 23(3) of the 1982 Act a person who without reasonable excuse contravenes a regulation made under the section, the contravention of which is declared by the regulations to be an offence, is liable on summary conviction to a fine at level 3 of the standard scale.[70] Regulation 19 of the 1996 Regulations declares as offences contravention of certain regulations.[71]

Separate regulations, the Accounts and Audit (Passenger Transport Executives and the London Transport Executive) Regulations 1983[72] were made in respect of the authorities named in the title. For the most part they follow the main regulations.

Local Government Act 1985—joint authorities and residuary bodies

13–54   All the audit provisions of Part III of the Local Government Finance Act 1982 are applied to the joint authorities established by the Local Government Act 1985.[73]

For the residuary bodies set up by the 1985 Act, section 79 of that Act applies the 1982 Act audit provisions with the exception of sections 15(1)(a) (auditor's duty as to compliance with statutory provisions), 17 (public inspection of accounts and right of challenge), 19 (unlawful items of account), 20 (failure to account and wilful misconduct), 22 (extraordinary

---

[68] Accounts and Audit Regulations 1996, (S.I. 1996 No. 590), reg. 18, from April 1, 1997. Until then the existing provision, the Accounts and Audit Regulations 1983 (S.I. 1983 No. 1761), reg. 16, remains in force. Contravention of this regulation is an offence: see § 13–53.

[69] S.I. 1996 No. 590.

[70] See § 7–31, above.

[71] From April 1, 1997. Until then the Accounts and Audit Regulations 1983 (S.I. 1983 No. 1761), reg. 17, remains in force.

[72] S.I. 1983 No. 1849.

[73] s.72(3); also to the authorities established by the Waste Regulation and Disposal (Authorities) Order 1985, (S.I. 1985 No. 1884 art. 9(2)), and to the South Yorkshire Pensions Authority, (S.I. 1987 No. 2110, Sched. 1, para. 6). The London Government Reorganisation (Pensions etc.) Order 1989 (S.I. 1989 No. 1815) applies the provisions of section 79 of the 1985 Act to the London Pensions Fund Authority, with the exception that section 22(2) of the Local Government Finance Act 1982 (power of Secretary of State to direct extraordinary audit) is also applied to the Authority (Sched. 1, para. 7(3), (4) of the 1989 Order).

audit), 23 (regulations) and 24 (right to inspect statement of accounts and auditor's report). However, section 79 of the 1985 Act itself confers similar rights on local government electors in respect of inspection and copies of accounts and documents and of statements of accounts and auditors' reports. No sanctions are provided against obstruction of these rights. Electors may also question the auditor and draw his attention to any matter on which he could make a report. At the conclusion of an audit copies of the statement of accounts and auditor's report must be sent to the Secretary of State and laid by him before Parliament.

CHAPTER 14

THE GRANT SYSTEM

EXCHEQUER grants in aid of local authority services fall into two groups, **14–01** specific grants towards expenditure on particular services and revenue support grant in general aid of local authorities' finances. The balance between these two sources may vary widely for each authority but is important in regard to the overall impact on local authority finance and discretion as discussed in Chapter 12.[1]

A. SPECIFIC GRANTS

There are numerous specific grants which can be made under the legislation **14–02** relating to the different functions. These differ in terms of a number of crucial factors such as significance, level of control by central government, whether fully reimbursed or a percentage only, whether transitional or permanent, and the conditions to be satisfied before payment. A table of specific grants appears in Appendix F, showing some of the main statutory provisions under which such grants are made.

Special grants

A general power to make specific grants lies in section 88B of the Local Government Finance Act 1988[2] which confers on the Secretary of State a general power to make special grants to billing authorities, major precepting authorities, and metropolitan county passenger transport authorities.[3] It was envisaged initially that the power would be used to pay grants towards the cost of implementing the community charge, but it has subsequently been seen as the basis for paying other grants, *e.g.* to authorities taking over the responsibilities of the Inner London Education Authority and other matters such as reorganisation.[4] Before making a grant under this section the Secretary of State must obtain the consent of the Treasury and must lay before the House of Commons for approval a special grant report, and as

---

[1] See § 12–01. In 1993–94, specific grants amounted to 43.2 per cent, and general grants to 56.8 per cent, of the total.
[2] Inserted by the Local Government Finance Act 1992, Sched. 10.
[3] Billing authorities mean, in relation to England, a district council, London borough council, the Common Council of the City of London and the Council of the Isles of Scilly, and in relation to Wales, a county or county borough council. Major precepting authorities are county councils not having the functions of district councils in England, police authorities, the Receiver of the Metropolitan Police District, the London and metropolitan county fire and civil defence authorities.
[4] Vol. 511, H.L.Deb., cols. 1442–1443, October 25, 1989.

soon as is reasonably practicable after the report is laid the Secretary of State must send a copy of any relevant authority to whom a special grant is proposed to be paid. Such reports must specify the amounts of grants, the authorities to which they are to be paid, the purpose of the grants, and must contain an explanation thereof. They may also specify conditions to be imposed on the payment of grant.

Commutation of payment

Section 147 of the Local Government and Housing Act 1989 enables the Secretary of State to commute payments of grants which would otherwise be paid annually or periodically into a single payment or a reduced number of payments. The money may be paid, in whole or part, directly to the Public Works Loan Commissioners in redemption of debt due from the authority.

B. REVENUE SUPPORT GRANT

14–03 Revenue support grant was introduced, with effect from April 1, 1990, by Part V of the Local Government Finance Act 1988, as amended by the Local Government and Housing Act 1989. Revenue support grant replaced the former rate support grant, which had been subject to widespread criticism. In a consultation paper issued in 1987 the Department of the Environment accepted that the block grant, which formed the major part of the rate support grant, was so complicated that it was understood by only a few specialists in central and local government, and that it was unstable, because each authority's entitlement could change substantially from year to year for a variety of reasons.

The consultation paper went on to propose a new and simpler system of revenue support grant under which grant entitlement would be fixed at the beginning of each year and would not vary with expenditure, as it did under the block grant system. The actual cost or benefit of higher or lower expenditure would thus, under the new system, fall directly on the community charge payer. It was also proposed that the method of distributing grant should be more stable from year to year, and that in England grant would not be split, as formerly, between different tiers of authority; instead it would be paid into the collection funds of charging authorities together with the revenue from the community charges of that time and the authority's share of the non-domestic rating pool distributed by the Secretary of State. (In Wales grant was to continue to be paid direct to both tiers of authority.)

14–04 These proposals were enacted by the 1988 Act. The central element of revenue support grant continues to be a system of equalisation based upon a needs assessment for each authority, like the grant-related expenditure assessment under the rate support grant system. The objective, as expressed by the consultation paper of that time when the community charge was envisaged, was that "if each authority in an area spends at the level of its needs assessment, local residents will pay a common community charge unless they are entitled to rebates. The common charge will be the same for all authorities' areas". A further proposal in the consultation paper was that the system of needs assessment should be simpler than under the previous system, with fewer separate indicators of need. The paper did not spell out any detail in this respect. Neither does the Act, which provides only a framework for the new grant system. The detail is filled in by a series of reports which the Secretary of State is required by the Act to lay before the House of Commons for approval.

Local government finance report

From 1990–91 there operated a system of reports dealing revenue support **14–05** grants and distribution reports under sections 78 and 80 of the 1988 Act respectively. These were then replaced for each financial year from 1993–94 onwards, by local government finance reports under section 78A of the Local Government Finance Act 1988,[5] which requires the Secretary of State to lay such a report before the House of Commons for approval, and as soon as is reasonably practicable after the report is laid the Secretary of State must send a copy to each receiving authority.[6] Separate reports are in practice made for England and Wales. These reports also contain the distributable amount and basis of the distribution of the pooled non-domestic rates.[7] The reports must specify two elements in regard to revenue support grant.

First, the determination made under section 78(3) as to the total amount **14–06** of the grant for the year, the amount to be distributed among "receiving authorities", and the individual amounts to be paid to "specified bodies". "Specified bodies" are bodies providing services to local authorities and specified in regulations made by the Secretary of State (*e.g.* Local Government Training Board, Local Government International Bureau and also the Commission for Local Administration).[8] "Receiving authorities" are the billing authorities and major precepting authorities.[9] Before making the determinations under section 78(3) the Secretary of State must consult such representatives of local government as appear to him to be appropriate, and obtain the consent of the Treasury.

The second element is the basis on which he proposes to distribute among receiving authorities the aggregate revenue support grant available to them under the sections 78(3) determination. Before making the report the Secretary of State is required to notify, to such representatives of local government as appear to him to be appropriate, the general nature of the basis of distribution. However, he is not required to consult those

---

[5] Inserted by the Local Government Finance Act 1992, Sched. 10.
[6] For the finance reports for 1996–97, see the Local Government Finance Report (England) 1996/7, H.C. 164, and the Local Government Finance Report (Wales) 1996/97, H.C. 141.
[7] See § 15–24.
[8] Revenue Support Grant (Specified Bodies) Regulations 1992 (S.I. 1992 No. 89), as amended by the Revenue Support Grant (Specified Bodies) Regulations of 1993 and 1995 (S.I. 1993 No. 139 and S.I. 1995 No. 3184). The Commission for Local Administration is to be treated as a specified body for this purpose by virtue of the Local Government Act 1974, Sched. 4, para. 6, as substituted by s.24 of the Local Government and Housing Act 1989.
[9] See n.3.

representatives and in this respect the provision differs from that relating to the section 78(3) determination, and also from corresponding provisions in earlier legislation. A further departure from earlier legislation is the omission of any provision that the principles by which grant will be distributed must be principles applicable to all authorities.

14–07   The detailed application of the system is therefore left to be specified in the local government finance report. This has remained largely the same since the introduction of the new reports in 1993–94. The foundation of the system is the Standard Spending Assessment (S.S.A.), to be calculated annually by the Secretary of State for each charging authority and for each precepting authority (with the exception of parish councils and the like, the assessment of whose spending is included in the S.S.A. of the district). The S.S.A. for each authority is intended to represent the amount of net revenue expenditure (to be borne by council tax, share of non-domestic rates pool, and revenue support grant) which it would be appropriate for the authority to incur in the year to provide a standard level of service consistent with the Secretary of State's view of the appropriate overall level of local government expenditure.

14–08   The S.S.A. for each authority is based on an assessment of the cost of each of the main services for which it is responsible, using information for each authority about factors which lead to differences in the costs of providing services to a common standard, such as the number of pupils to be educated and the miles of road to be maintained. The system is similar to, but simpler than, that used in the calculation of grant-related expenditure assessments under the previous rate support grant system.

For England, in place of the 63 separate assessments in the previous system there are now 13 components: 11 covering the five major services (education, with five sub-divisions, social services, with three sub-divisions, police, fire and civil defence, and highway maintenance), another covering all other services, and one reflecting the financing costs of capital expenditure. In general, the method involves fixing a unit cost of providing each service and multiplying this by the number of clients for that service; adjustments are then made for factors leading to variation of costs between authorities. For example, the basic calculation for primary education is to multiply a unit cost by the number of pupils aged 5 to 10 years for whose education the authority is financially responsible. Cost adjustments are incorporated in the formula to reflet the increased costs associated with the additional educational needs of some pupils (*e.g.* children of single parents), the provision of free school meals and milk, the sparsity of population in an area and differences between areas in the costs of providing education. The sum of all the relevant S.S.A. elements produces a final S.S.A. However, subject to any legal duties imposed by functional legislation, the authority retains discretion both between and within services so virement is possible.[10]

For Wales, a different system operates and the S.S.A. is constructed from a number of needs indicators, currently 47, together with some additions for

---

[10] For further detail, see the Local Government Finance Report (England) 1996/97, H.C. 164.

special factors.[11] However no part of the revenue grant in Wales is earmarked for particular services so authorities have discretion over the allocation of this resource.

For both England and Wales, revenue support grant is distributed on the **14–09** basis that if each billing authority, each major precepting authority, and each principal council were to spend at the level of its S.S.A. then, subject to certain qualifications, all billing authorities could set broadly the same council tax, known as the Council Tax for Standard Spending (C.T.S.S.) for dwellings listed in the same valuation band. The qualifications relate to items which are not taken into account for the purposes of distributing grant but may affect council tax in some areas.[12]

Where services are provided by more than authority in an area in England (for example, non-metropolitan district councils and county councils) the C.T.S.S. is divided between the authorities on the basis of national shares of S.S.A. for the services which each provides. Annex B to each of the local government finance reports state the amount of C.T.S.S. for valuation band D dwellings, known as the "*standard tax element*", for all classes of authority.

The grant entitlement for each of receiving authority is then calculated by **14–10** deducting from its own S.S.A. the sum of:

(i) its share of the non-domestic rating pool, broadly in proportion to population as estimated by the Registrar General;
(ii) its notional council tax income. This is obtained by multiplying its "*standard tax element*" by its "*council tax base for revenue support grant purposes*". This tax base is stated by, or calculated in accordance with, Annex C to each local government finance report. It is the total obtained by multiplying the number of dwellings in each valuation band by a factor which produces an equivalent number of Band D dwellings, having regard to the proportions of tax payable for dwellings in that band, under section 5 of the Local Government Finance Act 1992.

Calculation and payment of grant

Once the local government finance report for a financial year has been **14–11** approved by the House of Commons, there is a right for specified bodies to be paid the grant and for receiving authorities to be paid the sum distributed in accordance with sections 82 and 83 of the 1988 Act.[13] Under section 82(1), the Secretary of State is, as soon as reasonably practicable, to calculate the amounts payable to each receiving authority in accordance with the basis of distribution in the report. For this purpose, among other purposes under the Act, he is empowered to require authorities to supply him with information;

---

[11] For further detail, see the Local Government Finance Report (Wales) 1996/97, H.C. 141.
[12] For the qualifications see section 3 in each of the Local Government Finance Report (England) 1996/7, H.C. 164, and the Local Government Finance Report (Wales) 1996/97, H.C. 141.
[13] Local Government Finance Act 1988, s.79.

and if information is not supplied by a date specified he is entitled to take into account any other information available to him, to make such assumptions as he thinks fit about an authority, and to leave out of account information received after dates notified to the authority.[14] It is open to him to make one revised calculation of the sums payable to each receiving authority, however, to enable him to correct errors or to adjust the first calculation in the light of further information.[15] This further calculation can be made at any time before the end of the financial year following that to which the report relates. As soon as is reasonably practicable after making an original or revised calculation the Secretary of State must inform each receiving authority of the sum he calculates falls to be paid.[16] The sums may be paid by instalments of such amounts and at such times as the Secretary of State determines with the consent of the Treasury and, while the sums under an original calculation for receiving authorities must be paid within the financial year, those for specified bodies may be within or after that financial year.[17] Under corresponding earlier legislation it was held, in *R. v. Secretary of State for the Environment, ex p. Brent London Borough Council,*[18] that such determinations were not immutable, and that the Secretary of State was therefore entitled to defer payments until he had made a decision on the exercise of certain transitional powers. Where revised calculations are made under section 82(2), adjustments are not to be effected until after the end of the financial year concerned.[19]

Amending reports

14–12   While a revised calculation under section 82(2) is still to be made on the basis of distribution set out in the local government finance report, the Secretary of State also has the power, under section 84A, to make an amending report to change the basis of distribution. This may be made at any time before the end of that financial year or the following financial year. As with the original report, before making the amended report the Secretary of State is required to notify to, but not consult, such representatives of local government as appear to him to be appropriate, the general nature of the amendments he proposes. The proposed amendments require the approval of the House of Commons, and as soon as is reasonably practicable after the report is laid the Secretary of State must send a copy to each receiving authority.[20] Once the proposal is approved by the House of Commons, no further amending reports may be made in relation to the same local government finance report.[21] However, if the House of Commons does not

---

[14] *ibid.*, ss.84(4), (5), 139A.
[15] *ibid.*, s.82(2).
[16] *ibid.*, s.82(6) and (7).
[17] *ibid.*, ss.79(6) and 83(2). See also the Local Government Finance (Payments) (English Authorities) Regulations 1992 (S.I. 1992 No. 2996) and the Local Government Finance (Payments) (Welsh Authorities) Regulations 1993 (S.I. 1993 No. 613).
[18] [1983] 3 All E.R. 321.
[19] Local Government Finance Act 1988, s.83(4), (5).
[20] *ibid.*, s.84A(5).
[21] *ibid.*, s.84A(6).

approve a proposed amendment the Secretary of State may make further proposals until one is accepted.

Under section 84B, the Secretary of State is, as soon as reasonably practicable after the approval by the House of Commons, to calculate the amounts payable to each receiving authority in accordance with the basis of distribution in the amended report. Again, it is open to him to make one revised calculation of the sums payable to each receiving authority, but this must be made before either the end of the financial year following the financial year to which the amended report relates, or three months after the approval of the amending report, whichever is later.[22] The provisions regarding information which apply to the original and revised calculations, under section 82, apply also in relation to calculations made under section 84B.[23] Where a calculation or revised calculation has been made under an amended report under section 84B, adjustments are not to be effected until after the end of the financial year concerned.[24]

Additional grant

An amending report may change only the basis of distribution and **14–13** subsequent calculations, and cannot increase the total sum available for distribution. However, the Secretary of State has the power, under section 85 of the 1988 Act, to lay before the House of Commons for approval a report relating to additional grant. This power may be invoked if, before the year ends, he forms the view that fresh circumstances affecting the finances of local government have arisen since the approval of the local government finance report for that financial year.[25] In that event, he may make determination, with the consent of the Treasury, which contains both the global total of additional grant for that year and also the basis of its distribution among receiving authorities.[26] This determination must be specified in a report laid before the House and as soon as is reasonably practicable after the report is laid the Secretary of State must send a copy to each receiving authority. This provision therefore adds further flexibility to make an additional amount of revenue support grant available, with or without a change in the basis of distribution. If the House of Commons approves the report then the sums specified in the report fall due to be paid on the basis in the determination.[27] Additional grant is to be paid at such time, or in such instalments and at such times, as determined by the Secretary of State and may be paid in or after the financial year to which the grant relates.[28]

[22] *ibid.*, s.84B(3).
[23] *ibid.*, s.84B(4).
[24] *ibid.*, s.84C.
[25] *ibid.*, s.85(1).
[26] *ibid.*, s.85(4).
[27] *ibid.*, s.86(2).
[28] *ibid.*, s.86(3).

Judicial review

14–14   In general, the withholding or underpayment of grant may be questioned by judicial review, but interest on grant unlawfully withheld or underpaid cannot be awarded in such proceedings.[29] Challenges to the amount of S.S.A. or revenue support grant are also challengeable in law but only in exceptional circumstances.

> In *R. v. Secretary of State for the Environment, ex p. Nottinghamshire County Council*[30] the House of Lords considered the jurisdiction of the courts to intervene by judicial review in a case where a decision by the Secretary of State was subject by statute to the approval of the House of Commons in the same way as distribution and other reports in respect of revenue support grants are so subject under the Local Government Finance Act 1988. The council had applied for judicial review of such a decision in respect of the former rate support grant on the ground, inter alia, that the decision was so disproportionately disadvantageous to some authorities that it was unlawful as a perversely unreasonable exercise of discretion. It was held, dismissing the application, that it was not constitutionally appropriate, save in very exceptional circumstances, for the courts to intervene on grounds of *Wednesbury* unreasonableness[31] to quash a decision framed by the Secretary of State and approved by the House of Commons; examination of the detail of the decision or its consequences would be justified only if a prima facie case were to be shown that the Secretary of State had acted in bad faith, or for an improper motive, or that the consequences of the decision were so absurd that be must have taken leave of his senses.[32]
>
> In *R. v. Secretary of State for the Environment, ex p. Avon County Council*,[33] the Divisional Court dismissed an application for judicial review of the Distribution Report for 1990–91 on grounds of unfairness in that if neighbouring authorities spent at the level of their S.S.A.s the community charges in one would be £10 higher than in the other. It was held, following the *Nottinghamshire* case, above, that the court had no power to override a minister's decision under statutory powers unless it was perverse; that House of Commons approval, in the absence of deception by a minister, presented an almost inseparable argument against perversity; that the unfairness resulted from a conflict of lawful administrative decisions which it was for negotiation or Parliament to resolve.
>
> In *R. v. Secretary of State for the Environment, ex p. Hackney London Borough Council*[34] in a case challenging the withholding of grant, the Court of Appeal rejected a claim that it is necessarily unreasonable or perverse for the Secretary of State to set limits within which the authority cannot discharge its statutory duties.

---

[29] *R. v. Secretary of State for Transport, ex parte Sheriff and Sons, The Independent*, January 12, 1988.
[30] [1986] A.C. 240.
[31] See § 10–25.
[32] See also *R. v. Secretary of State for the Environment, ex p. Hammersmith & Fulham London Borough Council* [1991] 1 A.C. 521.
[33] (1990) 89 L.G.R. 498.
[34] (1985) 84 L.G.R. 32.

CHAPTER 15

NON-DOMESTIC RATES

RATING in England and Wales grew out of the system imposed by the Poor **15–01** Relief Act 1601, commonly referred to as the Statute of Elizabeth. Section 1 of that Act required the overseers of the poor to raise sums from inhabitants and occupiers of land in the parish to provide materials to enable the poor to be set to work and to maintain the lame, impotent, halt and blind. Liability fell on residents and on occupiers of property within the parish, and in an early case[1] it was held that assessments should be made according to the visible estate, both real and personal, of those living within the parish. Statutory recognition was given in the Parochial Assessments Act 1836 to the principle of ability to pay as disclosed by the estimated annual letting value of occupied property, and the liability of residents, as opposed to occupiers of property, was removed by the Poor Rate Exemption Act 1840. The Act of 1836 had been repealed, but the principle which it established remained substantially valid under later legislation, until a new system was introduced by the Local Government Finance Act 1988. Section 1 of the 1836 Act provided that no rate for the relief of the poor should be allowed unless it was made on an estimate of the net annual value of the property rated, *i.e.*, on an estimate of the rent at which the property might reasonably be expected to be let from year to year, free of all tenant's rates and taxes and deducting therefrom the probable annual average cost of repairs, insurance and other expenses necessary to maintain the property in a state fit to command such rent. It was at that time thought that the wording of the section was such that only real property could be the subject of rating, but a decision to the contrary[2] led to the passing of the Poor Rate Exemption Act 1840, which removed all doubt on this point.

The Local Government Finance Act 1988 introduced a radically different system. Rates were retained, in an amended centrally controlled form, for non-domestic property. Rates on domestic property, however, were abolished in favour of a tax on individuals, the community charge, which was not related to income.

Thereafter, it was replaced by a new system. The Local Government Finance Act 1992 introduced the new system for a domestic property charge known as the council tax. Rates were retained, in the centrally controlled form, for non-domestic property, although the 1992 Act also made some amendments to this tax.

---

[1] *Sir Anthony Earby's* Case (1633) 2 Bulst. 354.
[2] *R. v. Lumsdaine* (1839) A. & E. 157.

While it may be thought that most of the law relating the non-domestic rating system is no longer part of local government law, since it is under direct central control, it is retained in this edition because the revenue raised it is still an important part of local government funding, local authorities operate as collection agents, and there remains political pressure to return control over the level of non-domestic rates to local government.

Non-domestic rates are considered under the following headings: (a) the basis of rateability, (b) the measure of liability and setting the rate, (c) exemptions, special cases and personal reliefs, (d) valuation for rating, (e) the collection and recovery of rates, (f) pooling and distribution of rates.

A. THE BASIS OF RATING

15–02 Non-domestic rates can be levied on three categories of person. Occupation is the general basis of rateability, so the rate is levied on the occupier of any hereditament shown in the local non-domestic rating list as subject to a non-domestic rate.[3] However, it may also be levied on owners, where the hereditament is unoccupied,[4] or on persons named in a central rating list in regard to undertakings which operate in more than one area, such as transport or energy.[5]

The concept of the hereditament is defined by the 1988 Act as that which existed under the General Rate Act 1967, together with certain land used for advertising.[6] Every *relevant non-domestic hereditament* must be entered in a local rating list, unless exempt or entered in the central rating list. "Relevant hereditament" is defined as property within the following broad descriptions—lands; coal mines; other mines; sporting rights; advertising.[7]

> *Westminster City Council v. Woodbury (Valuation Officer).*[8] It was held that a vessel permanently moored alongside the Victoria Embankment of the River Thames, no longer having an engine, connected up to mains services, and used as a restaurant was not a rateable hereditament in itself as a "restaurant and premises", under the General Rate Act 1967. The Court of Appeal confirmed that, while chattels are not in principle rateable, they may be if they are occupied with the land.[9] For the vessel to be rateable, it therefore had to be occupied with some rateable land. It was argued that it occupied the river bed and the embankment. However, the river bed did not form such rateable land, being exempt under section 178(1) of the Port of London Act 1968. No firm finding was expressed on whether the vessel was a chattel occupying the embankment, because under the 1967 Act which governed this case, as opposed to the new provisions in section 42(1) of the 1998 Act, if a hereditament was partly exempt then the whole was exempt. The court, *obiter*, expressed some doubt over whether it would be possible to have lateral occupation of the

---

[3] Local Government Finance Act 1988, s.43.

[4] *ibid.*, s.45.

[5] *ibid.*, ss.52–54.

[6] *ibid.*, s.64. Thus the existing case-law is preserved, see *Gilbert v. Hickinbottom (S.) & Sons Ltd* [1956] 2 Q.B. 40.

[7] *ibid.*, s.64(4).

[8] [1992] R.A. 1.

[9] For an example of this, see *Storehire (U.K.) v. Wojcik (Valuation Officer)* [1991] R.A. 39, where it was held that shipping containers used for storage could be rateable.

embankment but, while not having to decide the matter, appeared more willing to accept that the suggestion that the mooring, as enhanced by the vessel, was rateable.[10] This is an important difference in valuation terms, since the starting point for the valuation would be the licence fee, not the value of the restaurant.

"Non-domestic" is defined largely negatively as a hereditament which consists entirely of property which is not domestic, or is a composite hereditament.[11] Thus the definition of "domestic" becomes important, and is defined as property used wholly for the purposes of living accommodation; a yard, garden or outhouse belonging to such accommodation; a private garage used wholly or mainly for the accommodation of a private motor vehicle; and private storage premises used wholly or mainly for the storage of articles of domestic use.[12] A mooring is included if used for a boat which is the sole or main residence of an individual, and caravans are included if used as the sole or main residence of an individual.[13] A hereditament is composite if part only of it consists of domestic property.[14] Property is not domestic if it is time-share.[15]

The concept of occupation is to be determined by reference to the rules **15–03** which would have been applied for the purposes of the General Rate Act 1967, before its repeal by the 1988 Act.[16] However, there is no statutory definition of occupation, its meaning in rating having developed through a mass of complicated case law from which certain fairly clear principles have emerged. Occupation to be rateable involves first possession, a *de facto* possession which embraces some form of use or enjoyment; secondly, there must be at least some element of permanence; thirdly, the occupation must be beneficial. The first two points are referred to in *R. v. St Pancras Assessment Committee*[17]; the third in *Jones v. Mersey Docks and Harbour Board*[18] A definition mentioned in *John Laing and Son Limited v. Assessment Committee for Kingswood Assessment Area*[19] identifies a fourth ingredient—the occupation must be exclusive as well as actual.

R. v. St Pancras Assessment Committee.[20] The facts in this case are not of as

---

[10] See, *e.g.*, *Peak v. Stacey* [1965] R.A. 363. Under the Local Government Finance Act 1988, s.64(3A), as enacted by the Local Government Finance Act 1992, s.104 and Sched. 5, the Secretary of State may make regulations to treat groups of moorings as one hereditament in the occupation of the owner rather than as a number of separately occupied hereditaments.
[11] Local Government Finance Act 1988, s.64(8).
[12] *ibid.*, s.66, as amended.
[13] *ibid.*, s.66(3), (4), (4A) as substituted by the Rating (Caravans and Boats) Act 1996, which clarified the previous position. The changes are deemed to have to retrospective effect to April 1, 1990 so sums payable may accordingly be recovered: s.1(4) of the 1996 Act.
[14] *ibid.*, s.64(9).
[15] *ibid.*, s.66(2E).
[16] *ibid.*, s.65(2).
[17] (1877) 2 Q.B.D. 581. See also *Kingston upon Thames London Borough Council v. Marlow* [1996] R.A. 87 where the respondent was held not liable for unoccupied property rates as he was not the person entitled to possession because, in response to forfeiture proceedings, he had vacated the premises, handed over the keys and told the landlord that he was relinquishing the tenancy.
[18] (1865) 11 H.L.C. 443.
[19] [1949] 1 K.B. 344.
[20] *supra*, n.17.

much importance as the speech of Lush J. which is continually referred to in rating law. He said[21]: "It is not easy to give an accurate and exhaustive definition of the word 'occupier'. Occupation includes possession as its primary element, but it also includes something more. Legal possession does not of itself constitute an occupation. The owner of a vacant house is in possession, and may maintain trespass against anyone who invades it, but as long as he leaves it vacant he is not rateable for it as an occupier. If, however, he furnishes it, and keeps it ready for habitation whenever he pleases to go to it, he is an occupier, though he may not reside in it one day in a year. On the other hand, a person who, without having any title, takes actual possession of a house or piece of land, whether by leave of the owner or against his will, is the occupier of it. Another element, however, besides actual possession of the land, is necessary to constitute the kind of occupation which the Act contemplates, and that is permanence. An itinerant showman who erects a temporary structure for his performances, may be in exclusive actual possession, and may, with strict grammatical propriety, be said to occupy the ground on which his structure is placed, but it is clear that he is not such an occupier as the statute intends ... A transient, temporary holding of land is not enough to make the holding rateable. It must be an occupation which has in it the character of permanence; a holding as a settler not as a wayfarer."

Jones v. Mersey Docks and Harbour Board.[22] The Board claimed that it was not rateable for the docks for it was required by statute to apply moneys received in defraying conservancy and pilotage expenditure and other expenditure prescribed by statute. No member of the Board derived a benefit from the execution of the trusts. *Held*, the Board was liable. In the course of his judgment Lord Cranworth discussed the term "beneficial occupation". He said[23]: "If by beneficial occupation is meant any occupation of something valuable, something in its own nature beneficial to someone, I think it is fair to consider that word as impliedly included in the statute. It was not meant to impose the duty of contributing to the relief of the poor or anyone merely because he might be the occupier of a barren rock, neither yielding, nor capable of yielding, any profit from its occupation. But I can discover nothing either in the words or in the spirit of the Act exempting from liability the occupier of valuable property, merely because the profits of the occupation are not to be enjoyed by him or by anyone on whose behoof he is occupying, but are to be devoted to the benefit of the public."

John Laing and Son Ltd v. Assessment Committee for Kingswood Assessment Area.[24] The plaintiffs erected contractors' offices, canteens and other structures on land belonging to the Air Ministry. The site was handed over to the plaintiffs but under the terms of the contract the work was subject to the Ministry's officers. It was argued for the plaintiffs that occupation to be rateable must be something more than occupation by subordinates for the purposes of the predominant occupier. *Held*, the control exercised under the contract had relation only to the performance of the contract and was not such as to interfere with the exclusive occupation of the hereditament by the contractors for the purposes of their business. Jenkins J. said[25]: "It seems to me that their

---

[21] *ibid.*, at p. 588.
[22] *supra*, n. 18.
[23] *ibid.*, at 507.
[24] *supra*, n. 20. *cf: Forces Help Society and Lord Roberts Workshops v. Canterbury City Council* (1978) 77 L.G.R. 541, where it was held that, in the case of property occupied by a licensee, the question of who was in rateable occupation must be determined having regard to the degree of control exercised by the owner and the purpose for which the licensee was allowed to occupy the property.
[25] *ibid.*, at p. 357.

possession was nonetheless exclusive because they were subject to the general controlling authority of the superintending officers." Tucker L.J., in the course of his judgment, referred to the general principles of law relating to rateable occupation. He said[26]: "First, there must be actual occupation; secondly, that it must be exclusive for the particular purposes of the possessor; thirdly, that the possession must be of some value or benefit to the possessor; and fourthly, the possession must not be for too transient a period."[27]

Unoccupied property

On the principles settled by these cases the owner of an unoccupied **15–04** property would not be rateable, since there is possession but no use or enjoyment,[28] but under the 1988 Act liability for such premises falls on the owner.[29] For unoccupied new buildings, a completion notice may be served by the authority, and this notice establishes the date from which liability to council tax in regard to that dwelling begins.[30] It was held in *Bayliss v. Chatters*[31] that the owner of empty bungalows advertised as being available for letting was in beneficial occupation. In this case four bungalows formed part of a group of six, which were let when tenants could be found. During the winter the furniture was taken out of the four bungalows and stored in a fifth. The Divisional Court held that there was evidence on which the justices were entitled to find that the owner was in beneficial occupation of all the bungalows. By contrast, in *Wirral Borough Council v. Lane*[32] the Divisional Court decided that, where an owner did not sleep in his house but had some furniture there, kept the property heated and used the telephone for private and business calls, the magistrates' conclusion that he was not in rateable occupation would not be set aside. The magistrates might well have come to the opposite conclusion but the question for the Divisional Court was not whether they had reached a wrong decision but whether it was one which they could not reasonably have reached. In *R. v. Melladew*[33] it was held that an empty warehouse would be beneficially occupied if it were ready to receive goods and advertised as such, for a warehouse is full, half-full or empty from time to time according to the fluctuations of trade, and warehousemen must contemplate the use for considerable periods of parts of the premises as spare room. This case was distinguished in *Associated*

---

[26] *ibid.*, at p. 350.

[27] Applying the principles of occupation, it has been held in *Brook (Valuation Officer) v. Greggs plc* [1991] R.A. 61 that market stallholders are in exclusive occupation of their stalls.

[28] *R. v. St. Pancras Assessment Committee* (1877) 2 Q.B.D. 581. Lord Russell of Killowen stated this as a broad rule in *Westminster City Council v. Southern Ry.* [1936] A.C. 511, where he said, at p. 529: "The owner of an empty house has the legal possession, but he is not in rateable occupation."

[29] Local Government Finance Act 1988, s.45.

[30] Local Government Finance Act 1988, s.46A and Sched. 4A, as enacted by the Local Government and Housing Act 1989, s.139 and Sched. 5. Where a completion notice is served on a building which is not yet complete, the notice specifies a "completion day", which is to be not more than three months after service of the notice. This date may be altered on appeal to the valuation tribunal. Even if the dwelling is not completed by that date, the "relevant date", it is nevertheless deemed to have been completed for the purpose of liability.

[31] [1940] 1 All E.R. 620.

[32] (1979) 251 E.G. 61, D.C.

[33] [1907] 1 K.B. 192.

Cinema Properties Ltd v. Hampstead Borough Council.[34] Here a company acquired a lease of premises intending to use them as offices if their existing accommodation became unusable through enemy action. They left the premises vacant, did not use them in any way, and did not install any furniture or other goods. It was held that there was no rateable occupation, du Parcq L.J. stating[35]:

> "It is significant that no case could be cited in which occupation has been held to be established without proof of some overt act amounting to evidence of user. In *R. v. Melladew* the owner had advertised the premises as a warehouse. In most cases user has been proved by showing that the house had been furnished, or equipped for some business purpose ... in our judgment, a mere intention to occupy premises on the happening of a future uncertain event, cannot, without more, be regarded as evidence of occupation."

The *Hampstead* case was followed in *Bexley Congregational Church Treasurer v. London Borough of Bexley*.[36] A manse had been vacant for 11 months and during that time was held available for the next minister. The Divisional Court held that it was "occupied", relying on *Gage v. Wren*[37] and *R. v. Melladew*, but the Court of Appeal reversed this decision, holding that a mere intention to occupy the premises did not constitute occupation. In *British Telecommunications v. Kennet District Council*[38] the House of Lords held that a telephone exchange was in rateable occupation during the installation of telephone equipment. Lord Keith said that the question at issue was "whether that hereditament was during the relevant period serving the business purpose of the respondents, in the sense that they were enjoying the accommodation which it afforded". The nature of occupation was also considered in *Re Briant Colour Printing Co. Ltd*[39] where it was held that an owner of a factory who is totally excluded from the premises by a "work-in" by former employees is not to be regarded as being in rateable occupation during the period of such exclusion to be regarded as being in rateable occupation during the period of such exclusion. In *Barnet London Borough Council v. London Transport Property*[40] it was held that the parking of buses at their depot overnight as a normal incident of their everyday use was held not to be storage for the purposes of the Non-Domestic Rating (Unoccupied Property) Regulations 1989.[41]

[34] [1944] 1 K.B. 412.
[35] *ibid.*, at p. 416.
[36] [1972] 2 Q.B. 222.
[37] (1902) 87 L.T. 271.
[38] [1983] R.A. 43.
[39] [1977] 1 W.L.R. 942.
[40] [1995] R.A. 235.
[41] S.I. 1989 No. 2261.

B. THE MEASURE OF LIABILITY AND SETTING THE RATE

The amount which falls to be paid in respect of any non-domestic **15–05** hereditament depends primarily on its rateable value. The value is ascertained on the basis of the principle set out in the 1988 Act as[42]:

> "the rent at which it is estimated the hereditament might reasonably be expected to let from year to year if the tenant undertook to pay all usual tenant's rates and taxes and to bear the cost of the repairs and insurance and the other expenses (if any) necessary to maintain the hereditament in a state to command that rent."

The annual value taken for rating purposes is the estimated rental value on year-to-year lettings. Lord Herschell L.C. said in *London County Council v. Erith Parish (Churchwardens, etc.)*[43]:

> "Whether the premises are in the occupation of the owner or not, the question to be answered is: Supposing they were vacant and to let, what rent might reasonably be expected to be obtained for them?"

Scott L.J. said in *Robinson Bros. (Brewers) Ltd v. Houghton and Chester-le-Street Assessment Committee*[44]:

> "The rent to be ascertained is the figure at which the hypothetical landlord and tenant would, in the opinion of the valuer or the tribunal, come to terms as a result of bargaining for that hereditament, in the light of competition or its absence in both demand and supply, as a result of 'the higgling of the market'. I call this the true rent because it corresponds to real value."

In *Garton v. Hunter (Valuation Officer)*[45] it was held that in arriving at the rent which a hypothetical tenant would pay for the particular hereditament, its actual rent and those of truly comparable hereditaments might be useful but were not necessarily decisive. In a proper case, other relevant evidence, such as evidence on the profits or contractor's basis, should also be admitted. Such a case would be a caravan site or premises in respect of which there were only rarely true comparables. All relevant evidence was admissible. The merits of it would go only to weight, and not to admissibility.

The Secretary of State has power to substitute, by regulation, other assumptions in respect of hereditaments of a prescribed description.[46] This continues the previous practice of dealing with matters where rental values would be difficult to assess. An unsuccessful challenge has been made to such an order, on the basis of wide principles of law.

R. v. Secretary of State for the Environment and Secretary of State for Wales, ex p. British Telecommunications plc.[47] The Telecommunications Industry

---

[42] Local Government Finance Act 1988, s.56 and Sched. 6, para. 2(1), which is very similar to the formulation of the General Rate Act 1967, s.19, which itself consolidated much of the rating legislation.
[43] [1893] A.C. 562 at p. 588.
[44] [1937] 2 K.B. 445 at p. 470.
[45] [1969] 2 Q.B. 37.
[46] Local Government Finance Act 1988, s.56 and Sched. 6, para. 2(8).
[47] [1991] R.A. 307.

(Rateable Values) Order 1989[48] was challenged by judicial review on the basis that:

(i) the wide discretion of the Secretary of State was limited in that it was necessary to seek to produce a valuation system which had the same nature and characteristics as the normal system, namely "the rent at which it is estimated the hereditament might reasonably be expected to let from year to year";

(ii) that the Secretaries of State had given a legitimate expectation that such a system would be set;

(iii) it was the land which had to be valued and not the land and the equipment;

(iv) the Secretaries of State had misapplied the "contractor's test" of valuation; and

(v) the Secretaries of State had taken into account the irrelevant consideration of attempting to achieve fairness, rather than correctness, between the applicant and another communications company and other ratepayers in general.

All grounds were rejected by the High Court on the basis that:

(i) although the claim was not defeated by the Parliamentary approval of the Order,[49] the formulation did not frustrate the policy behind the Act which was to give the Secretary of State a free hand in departing from the normal principles where they were difficult to apply;

(ii) there was neither legitimate expectation established on the facts, nor any unfairness which was required for the doctrine to operate;

(iii) under Schedule 6, it was possible to value the equipment and the land;

(iv) the "contractor's test" was correctly applied since it was based not simply on capital cost but included an overall allowance for depreciation etc.;

(v) matters of fairness were relevant considerations, and the weight to be given to them was a decision for the Secretary of State with which the court would be slow to interfere.

Setting the rate

15–06   Under the previous system, the local authority set the amount of the rate to be applied to the rateable value of the property. Under the 1988 Act, this has been replaced by a multiplier set by the Secretary of State and applied nationally.[50] The original figure having been set for the financial year 1990–91, the increase in the multiplier each year is tied to the increase in the retail prices index, unless a smaller figure is specified. The setting of the multiplier can be challenged only by judicial review.[51] All receipts are pooled centrally and the Secretary of State redistributes these to local authorities,[52] the distribution and basis for it having to be set out in an annual local government finance report to be approved by the House of Commons.[53] This procedure is discussed further at paragraph 15–21.

The amount to which a ratepayer is liable is calculated on a daily basis,

---

[48] S.I. 1989 No. 2478.

[49] See *Nottinghamshire County Council v. Secretary of State for the Environment* [1986] A.C. 240 and *R. v. Secretary of State for the Environment, ex p. Hammersmith & Fulham London Borough Council* [1991] 1 A.C. 521.

[50] Local Government Finance Act 1988, Sched. 7.

[51] *ibid.*, s.138.

[52] *ibid.*, s.60 and Sched. 8.

[53] *ibid.*, as amended by the Local Government Finance Act 1992, s.104 and Sched. 10.

according to a specified formula which differs according to whether the hereditament is occupied or unoccupied. For occupied hereditaments, the liability is determined by the formula $A \times B/C$, where A is the rateable value, B the multiplier for the financial year, and C the number of days in the financial year.[54] Where the ratepayer is a charity, or trustees for a charity,[55] the amount is reduced to 20 per cent of that amount. For unoccupied hereditaments, the calculation is by the same method, but reduced by 50 per cent, including that for charities.[56]

In order to mitigate the effect of this new system on those hereditaments which because of the new system would have been subject to large increases in the amount of liability, transitional arrangements have been made to stage the increases over the period 1990–95.[57] In addition, power has been given to the Secretary of State to make rules for the period beyond 1995, for the further five-year periods which will follow revaluations.[58] These provisions have been amended as to the operation of the increases by the Non-Domestic Rating Acts of 1993 and 1994, the latter of which also amends the power of the Secretary of State to make regulations for 1995 onwards and places further duties on the Secretary of State to make good any shortfall from the estimated amounts available.[59]

Although the non-domestic ratepayer now has no direct interest in the level of council tax, the billing authorities and certain precepting authorities, are required by section 65 of the Local Government Finance Act 1992 to consult representatives of the non-domestic ratepayers in regard to their expenditure for each financial year.[60]

C. EXEMPTIONS, SPECIAL CASES AND PERSONAL RELIEFS

Certain classes of hereditament are exempt from rating, and in certain cases **15–07** the measure of liability is calculated on a different basis. Under the 1988 Act,[61] there are several cases where relief, in whole or part, may be claimed by bodies or individuals, and the present law largely reflects that which existed under the General Rate Act 1967.

---

[54] *ibid.*, s.43.
[55] See § 15–10.
[56] Local Government Finance Act 1988, s.45.
[57] *ibid.*, s.57, as amended by the Local Government and Housing Act 1989, further amended by the Non-Domestic Rating Act 1992. The primary purpose of the 1992 Act is to ensure that at a time of recession businesses should not have their costs worsened by a real increase in the non-domestic rate.
[58] *ibid.*, s.58.
[59] See also the Non-Domestic Rating (Chargeable Amounts) Regulations 1994 (S.I. 1994 No. 3279, as amended).
[60] See also the Non-Domestic Ratepayers (Consultation) Regulations 1992 (S.I. 1992 No. 3171).
[61] Local Government Finance Act 1988, s.51 and Sched. 5.

Crown property

It is a general principle of law that the Crown is not bound by statute unless expressly named.[62] The Crown was not mentioned in the Statute of Elizabeth and therefore Crown properties were not rateable. Premises occupied by the departments of state and the fighting services such as government offices, army barracks, prisons and hospitals under the control of area health authorities clearly come within this category. The Crown exemption is extended to properties occupied for the purposes of the Crown in the carrying out of functions of the Central Government, even though the occupants are not strictly the servants of the Crown, so that exemption had been afforded to police stations.[63] However, under the 1988 Act, all hereditaments provided and maintained for purposes connected with the administration of justice, police purposes and other Crown purposes by a specified authority are excluded from this exemption.[64] Where the hereditament falls within these classes, it must be entered in the rating list.[65]

The exemption of Crown property has not significantly affected the income of rating authorities. It has been the practice for the Treasury to make a contribution in lieu of rates in respect of Crown properties, on the basis of a valuation made by the Treasury Valuer by reference to the principles applicable to the valuation of other hereditaments. The position is now governed by section 59 of the 1988 Act, which provides that where any hereditament would be subject to a non-domestic rate but for the rules of Crown exemption, and a contribution in aid is made, it should be paid to the Secretary of State.[66]

Places of public worship

15–08 The 1988 Act follows section 39 of the General Rate Act 1967 in exempting from rating places of public religious worship, extending to church and chapel halls and similar buildings used in connection with any such place of public worship and "so used for the purposes of the organisation responsible for the conduct of public religious worship in that

---

[62] Although subject to much criticism and rejected by the Inner House of the Court of Session, this rule has been reaffirmed by the House of Lords in *Lord Advocate v. Dumbarton District Council* [1990] 2 A.C. 580.

[63] See, *e.g.* Lord Blackburn in *Coomber v. Berkshire JJ.* (1882) 2 App.Cas. 61, where he said, at p. 67, "I do not think it can be disputed that the administration of justice, both criminal and civil, and the preservation of order and prevention of crime by means of what is now called police, are among the most important functions of government, nor that by the constitution of this country these functions do, of common right, belong to the Crown."

[64] Local Government Finance Act 1988, s.64(5). By s.64(7), the authorities are specified as a county council; a district council; a London borough council; the Common Council; a metropolitan county police authority; and the Northumbria Police Authority. By ss.64(7A)–(7C), added by the Local Government and Housing Act 1989, s.139 and Sched. 5, the Secretary of State may prescribe additional classes of hereditaments.

[65] *ibid.*, s.64(6).

[66] As amended by the Local Government and Housing Act 1989, s.139 and Sched. 5. In the unamended 1988 Act, the sum was to be paid to the charging authority in whose area the hereditament is situated, unless it fell within the classes to be prescribed by regulation.

place".[67] However, it also extends that exemption to any buildings used for carrying out administrative and other activities relating to the organisation of public religious worship.[68]

Agricultural land and buildings

Schedule 5 of the 1988 Act follows the General Rate Act 1967, as amended, in giving total exemption from rates to agricultural land, agricultural buildings, and fish farms.[69] Agricultural land includes any land "used as arable, meadow or pasture ground only". This is the most important part of the definition. Certain other lands are included in the term, such as nursery grounds, market gardens and land exceeding 0.10 hectare used for poultry farming. Land used for sport or recreation or a racecourse, and land occupied together with a house as a park, is specifically excluded. Agricultural buildings consist of buildings (other than dwelling-houses) occupied with agricultural land or forming part of a market garden, and in either case used solely in connection with agricultural operations on the land. The words "only" and "solely" in the definition are of particular significance, the following being examples of the restrictive effect of these words. **15–09**

> *Meriden and Solihull Rating Authority v. Tyacke.*[70] A farmer sold turf from one of his fields primarily to rid the land of parasites which injured his young cattle. Adult cattle grazed in the field whilst the turf was being removed. *Held*, during the removal of the turf the land was being used for pasture, but not for pasture only. The land did not therefore come within the derating provisions.

> *W. & J. B. Eastwood v. Herrod (Valuation Officer).*[71] An enterprise used 1,150 acres of farm land and a large number of buildings for the production, slaughtering and packing of broiler chickens. The farmland produced only four per cent of the necessary food and the hens never went on the land. *Held*, the buildings were rateable. Lord Reid was of the opinion that it would "be a travesty of language to say that these buildings are used solely in connection with agricultural operations on this land."[72]

> *Hambleton District Council v. Buxted Poultry Ltd.*[73] The company owned two hereditaments in the same village for the purposes of its poultry business, carried on in 67 farms situated up to 120 miles distant. The first hereditament was a mill used to provide feed. Between six and eight per cent of the feed was supplied to farms other than those of the company. The second was a processing factory used for the slaughter and processing of poultry from the company's farms. The House of Lords agreed with the Court of Appeal that, while two

---

[67] Local Government Finance Act 1988, s.51 and Sched. 5, para. 11. The buildings must belong to the Church of England, Church of Wales, or be certified as a place of public worship under the Places of Worship Registration Act 1855.

[68] *ibid.*, The Act has not reproduced the previous provisions which required rates to be paid if a church hall was let for other than church purposes and generated surplus income once expenditure on the premises had been deducted.

[69] Local Government Finance Act 1988, s.51 and Sched. 5, paras. 1 and 9.

[70] [1950] All E.R. 939.

[71] [1971] A.C. 160.

[72] *ibid.*, p. 169.

[73] [1993] 1 All E.R. 117.

areas of land or buildings could be said to be "occupied together with" each other for the purposes of farming, nevertheless distance was relevant factor to bear in establishing this relationship, and so the Lands Tribunal had been wrong to conclude that the geographical test was not a relevant consideration. Their Lordships stressed that the buildings had to be in the same occupation and the activities jointly managed or controlled, effectively forming a single agricultural unit. While not conclusive, the geographical test can indicate whether these criteria do apply. In addition, since the six to eight per cent of production of feed which went to other farms was continuous, rather than a temporary change in output, the Court of Appeal concluded that it could not be said that the use was "solely" in connection with the agricultural use of the 67 farms.

Charitable and other organisations

15–10   Charitable organisations and certain other bodies which exist for public benefit are eligible for rating relief in two ways. First, under sections 43 and 45 of the 1988 Act, charities pay only one-fifth of the non-domestic rate that would otherwise be payable on occupied or unoccupied property. To qualify for this relief, the ratepayer must be a charity or trustees for a charity, and the hereditament must be wholly or mainly used, or if unoccupied will next be used, for charitable purposes (whether of that or other charities).

Secondly, the authority may reduce the amount of rates otherwise payable in regard to three classes of organisation.[74] The first is where the ratepayer is a charity or trustees for a charity, and the hereditament is wholly or mainly used for charitable purposes (whether of that or other charities). In that event, relief may be given beyond the existing 80 per cent. The second class covers hereditaments, not being excepted, where all or part is occupied for the purposes of one or more institutions or organisations, none of which is conducted for profit and each of whose main objects are charitable or are otherwise philanthropic, religious or concerned with education, social welfare, science, literature or the fine arts. The third class covers hereditaments, not being excepted, wholly or mainly used for purposes of recreation, and all or part is occupied for the purposes of a club, society or other organisation not established or conducted for profit.

A charity is defined as an institution or other organisation established for charitable purposes only, or any persons administering a trust established for charitable purposes only.[75] While registration under the Charities Act 1960 is conclusive for rating purposes, an organisation whose application for registration has been refused by the Charity Commissioners can have its status decided differently for rating purposes.[76]

The phrase "wholly or mainly used for charitable purposes" has been considered judicially.

> *Glasgow City Corporation v. Johnstone.*[77] A house and church were parts of a single building, and the only access to the house was through the church premises. Under the terms of his contract of service the church officer was required to live in the house. The House of Lords held that his employers

[74] Local Government Finance Act 1988, s.47.
[75] *ibid.*, s.67(10).
[76] *Over Seventies Housing Association v. Westminster City Council* [1974] R.A. 247.
[77] [1965] A.C. 609.

"occupied" the house for the purposes of a Scottish provision similar to the English Act. Lord Reid said[78]: "If the use which the charity makes of premises is directly to facilitate the carrying out of its main charitable purposes that is, in my view, sufficient to satisfy the requirements that the premises are used for charitable purposes."

Shops occupied by charitable organisations qualify for rating relief under section 64(11) of the 1988 Act, continuing the relief authorised by the Rating (Charity Shops) Act 1976 in respect of shops used wholly or mainly for the sale of goods donated to a charity.[79]

Disabled persons

The Rating (Disabled Persons) Act 1978 replaced earlier provisions for **15–11** rating relief for disabled persons which had caused some difficulty and provided for rebates in respect of two categories of property. The 1988 Act substituted a system of full exemption for property used wholly for any of the specified purposes, these being the provision of facilities for training, or keeping suitably occupied, persons who are disabled or who are or have been suffering from illness; the provision of welfare services for disabled persons; the provision of facilities under section 15 of the Disabled Persons (Employment) Act 1944; the provision of a workshop or other facilities under section 3(1) of the Disabled Persons (Employment) Act 1958.[80]

Unoccupied property

Although unoccupied premises are subject to rates,[81] there are exceptions **15–12** provided for by regulation.[82] These are hereditaments unoccupied for less than three months; where the owner is prohibited by law from occupying the premises; where the hereditament is kept vacant due to action by the Crown, or a local or other public authority; listed buildings, ancient monuments; industrial, storage, mineral and electricity generation hereditaments; small hereditaments where the rateable value is less than £1,500; where the owner is in possession only by virtue of being the personal representative of a deceased person; where there is a bankruptcy order in respect of the owner's estate; where the owner is in possession only by virtue of being a trustee under a deed of arrangement; where the owner is a company subject to a winding-up order, or which is being wound-up voluntarily; and where the owner is in possession only by virtue of being a liquidator.

---

[78] *ibid.*, p. 735.
[79] That Act reversed the ruling of the House of Lords in *Oxfam v. Birmingham City Council* [1976] A.C. 126.
[80] Local Government Finance Act 1988, s.51 and Sched. 5, para. 16.
[81] *ibid.*, s.45.
[82] Non-Domestic Rating (Unoccupied Property) Regulations 1989 (S.I. 1989 No. 2261, as amended). In *Barnet London Borough Council v. London Transport Property* [1995] R.A. 235 it was held that the parking of buses at their depot overnight as a normal incident of their everyday use was held not to be storage for the purposes of 1989 regulations.

Other exemptions and special cases

15–13   There are a number of other classes of occupation which are exempt from rating—some are mentioned briefly here without reference to limiting or other factors: property occupied by diplomats,[83] public parks, certain property of Trinity House, sewers, property of drainage authorities, air-raid protection works, swinging moorings, road crossings over watercourses, and property in enterprise zones.[84] The Secretary of State has power to include further classes by regulation, but only if the exemption was enjoyed in practice immediately before the passing of the 1988 Act, and was conferred by local Act or order.[85]

Personal reliefs

15–14   A rating authority has, under section 49 of the 1988 Act, a general power to reduce or remit the payment of any rate if satisfied that the ratepayer would sustain hardship if the authority did not do so, and it is reasonable to do so having regard to the interests of the council taxpayers. Unlike previous legislation, there is now a right to recover any sums overpaid.[86]

D. RATING VALUATION

15–15   Non-domestic rating is based upon the rating list,[87] whether local or central, which may not contain property which is wholly domestic or wholly exempt.[88] The Commissioners of Inland Revenue are required to appoint a valuation officer for each authority and also the central valuation officer, to compile the local and central rating lists respectively.[89] The first lists were required to be compiled on April 1, 1990, and to be compiled on the same date every fifth year afterwards.[90] The list comes into force on the day it is compiled, and it is required to be maintained for as long as is necessary "so that the expiry of the five-year period for which it is in force does not detract from the duty to maintain it."[91]

Before a list is formally compiled, the valuation officer is under a duty to take such steps as are reasonably practicable to ensure that the list is

---

[83] This stemmed from the Diplomatic Privileges Act 1708: see now International Organisations (Immunities and Privileges) Act 1950; Diplomatic Immunities (Commonwealth Countries and Republic of Ireland) Act 1952; Diplomatic Privileges Act 1964.

[84] Local Government Finance Act 1988, s.51 and Sched. 5, paras. 12–15 and 17–19.

[85] *ibid.*, Sched. 5, para. 20.

[86] *ibid.*, Sched. 9, reg. 2A, as enacted by the Local Government and Housing Act 1989, s.139 and Sched. 5. See also § 15–20.

[87] The rating lists replaced the valuation lists which operated under the General Rate Act 1967. The Local Government Act 1948 relieved rating authorities of their valuation functions and abolished those bodies having statutory duties in relation to the valuation lists—the assessment committees, county valuation committees and the central valuation committee. Part III of the Act transferred this work to the valuation officers of the Commissioners of Inland Revenue.

[88] See § 15–03.

[89] Local Government Finance Act 1988, s.61.

[90] The statutory requirement for quinquennial revisions of the valuation lists, under the General Rate Act 1967, was abolished by s.28 of the Local Government, Planning and Land Act 1980.

[91] Local Government Finance Act 1988, ss.41(7) and 52(7).

compiled accurately.[92] To facilitate this, powers are given to requisition information and enter premises.[93] Not later than December 31 of the year preceding that in which a list is to be compiled, the valuation officer must send a copy of the local list he proposes to compile to the authority, and the central list to the Secretary of State, and the recipient must deposit it at the relevant principal office as soon as reasonably practicable and, in the case of local lists, the authority must take such steps as it thinks most suitable for giving notice.[94] In addition, once the list is formally compiled, the valuation officer must send a copy of the list to the authority or the Secretary of State as appropriate, and the recipient must deposit it at the relevant principal office as soon as reasonably practicable.[95] Inspection of the list or relevant documents is provided for by regulation.[96]

The local list must show, for each day in the financial year, each hereditament which is non-domestic and situated within the authority's area, not being or required to be included in the central rating list, and it must distinguish between property which is entirely non-domestic and that which is composite.[97] In addition, it is required to show the rateable value and whether any part of the hereditament is exempt from local non-domestic rating. The Secretary of State has power to prescribe further requirements by regulation.[98] The central list is required to show the name of the designated person, and each hereditament which is occupied or (if unoccupied) owned by that person, if it falls within a prescribed class.[99] The classes and designated persons are determined by regulation, the Central Lists Regulations 1989 designating a number of bodies and prescribed hereditaments—canal, electricity supply, gas, railway, telecommunications, water supply, and long-distance pipelines.[1] The validity of the rating lists may be challenged by means of judicial review,[2] and by defence to proceedings for payment of rates.[3]

---

[92] *ibid.*, ss.41(4) and 52(4).
[93] *ibid.*, Sched. 9, paras. 5–7. It is an offence to fail to supply such information without reasonable excuse, or to supply false information knowingly or recklessly.
[94] *ibid.*, ss.41(5)–(6), and 52(5)–(6).
[95] *ibid.*, ss.41(6A) and (6B), 52(6A) and (6B), as amended by the Local Government and Housing Act 1989, s.139 and Sched. 5.
[96] *ibid.*, Sched. 9, para. 8.
[97] *ibid.*, s.42.
[98] See the Non-Domestic Rating (Miscellaneous Provisions) Regulations 1989 (S.I. 1989 No. 1060), under which he has required the list to show for each hereditament, a description, the address, the reference number ascribed by the valuation officer, and whether an alteration was the result of a direction of the valuation or community charge tribunal or Lands Tribunal.
[99] Local Government Finance Act 1988, s.53.
[1] S.I. 1994 No. 3121.
[2] *R. v. Paddington Valuation Officer, ex p. Peachey Property Corporation* [1966] 1 Q.B. 380. An example of challenge to the central list by means of judicial review has been provided by *R. v. Secretary of State for the Environment and Secretary of State for Wales, ex p. British Telecommunications plc* [1991] R.A. 307, see § 15–05.
[3] *Wandsworth London Borough Council v. Winder* [1985] A.C. 461. The High Court, in *Hackney London Borough Council v. Mott and Fairman* [1994] R.A. 381 decided that the magistrates' court has no jurisdiction to determine the validity of an entry in the non-domestic rating list. Thus the fact that the valuation officer had not informed the ratepayer within the prescribed period of the alteration to the list was no defence against making the liability order.

Alteration of lists

15–16   The local rating lists may be altered on his own initiative by the valuation officer,[4] or as a result of a proposal by a relevant authority, the ratepayer, or those with a legal or equitable interest in the hereditament.[5] Once the alteration is made, the valuation officer must notify the authority within six weeks and the authority must then alter the copy deposited with it, and also within six weeks he must notify the taxpayer of the effect of the alteration, unless the alteration is to reflect a clerical error or other prescribed matters.[6] In general, the alteration takes effect from the day on which the circumstances giving rise to the alteration occurred.[7]

Proposals to alter the list may be made in a number of circumstances, although these are more restricted than under the General Rate Act 1967 and time limits have been introduced.[8] A proposal may be made by relevant authorities or interested persons, at any time before a new list is compiled, if they are of the opinion that a hereditament is wrongly included or excluded, and they may also make a proposal if of the opinion that the rateable value is wrong, because of either a material change of circumstances or a decision of a valuation tribunal, the Lands Tribunal or a court, provided that it is made within six months of the change or decision. In addition, an interested person may make a proposal if aggrieved by the value shown in the list, by any statement made in or omitted from the list, or by an alteration to the list, provided that the proposal is made within six months of the compilation or alteration. A person who becomes a ratepayer after the list is in force may make a proposal if he is of the opinion that the rateable value shown is wrong, or that any statement in the list relating to the hereditament is wrongly included or excluded, provided that the proposal is made before the expiry of six months of becoming the ratepayer and no similar proposal arising from the same facts has been determined by the valuation tribunal or the Lands Tribunal.[9]

Among other requirements, a proposal must be made in writing, identify both the property and the person making the proposal, and include a statement of the reasons for believing the list to be incorrect and the manner in which the list is proposed to be altered.[10] Acknowledgment must be given within four weeks of receipt, unless the valuation officer serves an invalidity

---

[4] Although no specific power has been given in the legislation, it would appear that it is authorised impliedly by the duty, under s.41 of the 1988 Act, to maintain the list.
[5] Local Government Finance Act 1988, s.55 and the Non-Domestic Rating (Alteration of Lists and Appeals) Regulations 1993 (S.I. 1993 No. 291), reg. 2. Under the General Rate Act 1967, the right to make proposals was conferred on "persons aggrieved" which allowed third parties to be "aggrieved" by the under-assessment of another hereditament, see *Arsenal Football Club v. Smith (Valuation Officer)* [1979] A.C. 1.
[6] *ibid.*, reg. 18.
[7] *ibid.*, regs. 13, 15, 16 and 44.
[8] *ibid.*, reg. 4.
[9] *ibid.*, Such proposals are excluded where it is to alter the same list in relation to the same dwelling on the same facts as has been determined by a valuation tribunal or the High Court, or the new taxpayer has become so only by a transaction between companies of which one or both are a subsidiary of the other or another company, or by the formation of a new partnership containing a partner from the previous partnership.
[10] *ibid.*, reg. 5.

notice.[11] If the valuation officer considers the proposal to be invalid, he must notify the person making the proposal of his reasons, within four weeks, by means of an invalidity notice.[12] Within four weeks of that notification, the proposer may either make a further proposal (unless the invalidity notice was itself in response to a further proposal) or appeal to the valuation tribunal, which is initiated by serving notice of disagreement on the valuation officer. If he treats the proposal as valid, the valuation officer must, within six weeks, serve a copy of the proposal on the ratepayer (if not the proposer) and, in certain circumstances, the authority.[13] The valuation officer may then accept the proposal and alter the list accordingly[14]; the proposal may be withdrawn[15]; an alteration may be made on terms other than those stated in the proposal, provided all the relevant persons agree[16]; and a financial adjustment may be required, including the payment of interest.[17] Or where there is no agreement and the proposal is not withdrawn, the valuation officer must refer the matter as an appeal to the valuation tribunal within six months of the date of the proposal being served on him.[18] Similar provisions exist in relation to amendment of the central rating list by the central valuation officer, and proposals by the designated officer.[19] Appeals may also be made in relation to completion notices and certification.[20]

Appeals

The valuation tribunals are governed by section 136 and Schedule 11 of **15–17** the 1988 Act, as amended by section 15 of the Local Government Finance Act 1992. The jurisdiction, members and staff of the former local valuation courts were transferred to the new valuation and community charge tribunals under the 1988 Act, which were then renamed by the 1992 Act.[21] The tribunal for each area is to maintain a permanent office and appoint a clerk.[22] Further members may be appointed by the appropriate councils,[23] and a person is not disqualified simply by being a member of a billing authority. However, such members may not exceed one third of the number of members of the tribunal.[24] A member of an authority may not take part in

---

[11] *ibid.*, reg. 6.
[12] *ibid.*, reg. 7.
[13] *ibid.*, reg. 8.
[14] *ibid.*, reg. 9.
[15] *ibid.*, reg. 10.
[16] *ibid.*, reg. 11.
[17] Local Government Finance Act 1988, s.55(7), as amended by the Local Government Finance Act 1992, s.104 and Sched. 10.
[18] Non-Domestic Rating (Alteration of Lists and Appeals) Regulations 1993 (S.I. 1993 No. 291), reg. 12.
[19] *ibid.*, regs. 19–28.
[20] *ibid.*, regs. 29–30.
[21] Valuation and Community Charge Tribunals (Transfer of Jurisdiction) Regulations 1989 (S.I. 1989 No. 440).
[22] Valuation and Community Charge Tribunals Regulations 1989 (S.I. 1989 No. 439, as amended).
[23] *ibid.*, Sched. 1.
[24] *ibid.*, reg. 5(2) as substituted by the Valuation and Community Charge Tribunals (Amendment) (England) Regulations 1995, reg. 4.

an appeal against a decision of that authority or its registration officer.[25] In *Williams v. Bristol District Valuation Officer and Avon Valuation Tribunal,*[26] an objection that there was a breach of natural justice because the Tribunal was chaired by a member of Avon County Council which benefited from council tax valuations was rejected.

15–18   An appeal may be withdrawn,[27] proceed to full hearing, or be dealt with by written representations provided that all parties agree in writing.[28] It is also possible for the parties to agree to have the matter referred to arbitration, the arbitrator having the same power to make an order as the tribunal.[29] Under the written representations procedure, the clerk must serve a notice of the procedure on each party, and within four weeks of this notice each party may serve on the clerk a notice containing either the reasons for the disagreement leading to the appeal or a statement that no further representations will be made.[30] Following the supply of these statements to the other parties, there is a period of four weeks during which the parties may serve a further notice stating either the reply to the other party or that no further representations will be made, and the clerk must also send a copy of any such statement to the other parties.[31] After the expiry of that four week period, the clerk must submit any information and notices to the tribunal, which has the power to require the parties to supply further particulars, which are to be served on the other parties, or to order a full hearing.[32]

     In the event of a full hearing, the clerk must give the parties four weeks notice of the date, time and place of the hearing and advertise this by a notice at the offices of the tribunal or some other conspicuous place within the authority's area.[33] Any party may appear in person or be represented,[34] before a tribunal which, while normally consisting of three members including the chairman, may be composed of any two members with the consent of all parties, and the hearing shall take place in public unless the tribunal accepts the application of a party that the interests of that party would be affected prejudicially.[35] The tribunal may dismiss the appeal if only the valuation officer or listing officer appears or, for a completion notice appeal, if the appellant does not appear, and if any party fails to appear the tribunal may determine the appeal in their absence. The tribunal is given the power to administer an oath; to hear the parties in such order as it determines, although in most situations the valuation officer or relevant

---

[25] Non-Domestic Rating (Alteration of Lists and Appeals) Regulations 1993 (S.I. 1993 No. 291), reg. 38.

[26] [1995] R.A. 189.

[27] Non-Domestic Rating (Alteration of Lists and Appeals) Regulations 1993 (S.I. 1993 No. 291), reg. 34.

[28] *ibid.*, reg. 34.

[29] *ibid.*, reg. 48. Section 31 of the Arbitration Act 1950 applies.

[30] *ibid.*, reg. 35(2).

[31] *ibid.*, reg. 35(3) and (4).

[32] *ibid.*, reg. 40(5)–(7).

[33] *ibid.*, reg. 37.

[34] *ibid.*, reg. 39.

[35] *ibid.*, reg. 40.

authority must begin the hearing; to adjourn for such time, to such place, and on such terms as the tribunal determines, provided notice is given to every party; and to inspect any hereditament which is the subject of the appeal.[36] Otherwise, the procedure is for the tribunal to determine as being most suitable to the clarification of the issues and the just handling of the proceedings, while seeking to avoid formality and not being subject to the strict rules of evidence. Information is admissible provided that not less than two weeks notice of the details of the information and the dwelling or person has been given to every other party, and any person who has given 24 hours notice is allowed to inspect it and make a copy of, or extract from, a document or, if not a document, a print-out, photographic image or other reproduction which has been obtained from the storage medium.[37] The contents of a list or a completion notice may be proved by a copy certified to be a true copy by the valuation officer or the proper officer of the billing authority respectively.[38]

The decision of the tribunal may be by majority, but in the event of a tribunal of two failing to agree the matter must be remitted for decision by a tribunal consisting of different members.[39] The decision on a hearing may be reserved or given orally and, in either event and for written representations, it must be communicated or confirmed in writing to the parties as soon as reasonably practicable together with a statement of the reasons for the decision.[40] In consequence of that decision, the tribunal may order a list to be altered.[41]

The decision of the tribunal can, on written application by a party within four weeks of the notice being given, be reviewed or set aside by itself, and it is provided that as far as possible this is to be done by the same members who took the original decision. The decision may be reviewed or set aside on the grounds that the decision was wrongly made as a result of a clerical error; a party did not appear and can show reasonable cause why he did not do so; that the decision is affected by a decision of, or appeal from, the High Court or Lands Tribunal in relation an appeal in respect of the hereditament concerned.[42]

The clerk is responsible for recording the decision, sending a copy to the parties, and retaining a copy for a period of six years. In addition, any person may inspect the record of any decision of the tribunal, it being an offence for the keeper of the record to obstruct such inspection without reasonable excuse.[43]

An appeal may be made by any party to the appeal, within four weeks of the original decision or order or review decision or order, to the Lands

---

[36] *ibid.*
[37] *ibid.*, reg. 41.
[38] *ibid.*, reg. 42.
[39] *ibid.*, reg. 43(1).
[40] *ibid.*, reg. 43(2)–(5).
[41] *ibid.*, reg. 44. Any such order may also require any matter ancillary to its subject-matter to be attended to.
[42] *ibid.*, reg. 45.
[43] *ibid.*, reg. 46.

Tribunal, which may confirm, vary, set aside, revoke or remit the decision, and make any order the tribunal could have made.[44] Where the authority had not had an opportunity to comment on the basis of valuation adopted by the Lands Tribunal it was held by the Court of Appeal in *Aquila and Carberry v. London Borough of Havering* that this constituted a breach of natural justice.[45]

E. THE RECOVERY OF RATES

15–19 The authority must serve a demand notice on each ratepayer, for each financial year, as soon as practicable after April 1, of the relevant year.[46] Thus the demand notice is really an estimate of the liability for the whole financial year, and the sum demanded will have to be altered, and a fresh demand notice issued, if the relevant circumstances of the ratepayer change during that year.[47] Unless the ratepayer has agreed a different method of payment with the authority, the normal method of payment is by equal monthly instalments.[48] Where the notice is issued on or after January 1 of the relevant financial year, the full amount is due on the expiry of a period of not less than 14 days.[49] If the ratepayer continues to fail to pay an instalment after seven days of a reminder notice being served, then the balance of the complete estimated liability for the financial year becomes payable within a further seven days.[50]

15–20 To recover unpaid sums, the authority may raise an action for civil debt "in court of competent jurisdiction",[51] or enforce by means of distress but, if the former proceedings have been instituted, it may not obtain a liability order for the latter method.

If enforcing by distress, it must first obtain a liability order from the magistrates' court, the application having to be made within six years from the day on which the sum became due.[52] Unless a stipendiary magistrate is

---

[44] *ibid.*, reg. 47.

[45] (1993) 66 P. & C.R. 39.

[46] Non-Domestic Rating (Collection and Enforcement) Regulations 1989 (S.I. 1989 No. 1058, as amended), regs. 4 and 5. Reg. 5, permits the demand notice to be served before April 1, provided the non-domestic multiplier has been set, but in either event not before the billing authority has set amounts of council tax for the relevant financial year. See also the Community Tax and Non-Domestic Rating (Demand Notices) (England) Regulations 1993 (S.I. 1993 No. 191, as amended) and the Non-Domestic Rating (Demand Notices) (Wales) Regulations 1993 (S.I. 1993 No. 252, as amended).

[47] *ibid.*, Sched. I, Part II. In *Ford v. Burnley Borough Council* [1995] R.A. 205, it was decided that the Non-Domestic Rating (Collection and Enforcement) (Miscellaneous Provisions) Regulations were not intended to create a situation where a liability to pay rates is imposed for the whole of the hereditament on an occupier of part of a hereditament.

[48] *ibid.*, reg. 7.

[49] *ibid.*, Sched. I, para. 2.

[50] *ibid.*, reg. 8.

[51] *ibid.*, reg. 20. This reverses the effect of *Liverpool Corporation v. Hope* [1938] 1 K.B. 751 which had held that unpaid rates cannot be recovered in this way.

[52] *ibid.*, reg. 12. In *Royal Borough of Kingston upon Thames v. Kholi*, unreported, April 30, 1993 CO/30/92, decided that no estoppel may operate to frustrate the duty of the authority to obtain a liability order, even though the authority had made a clear representation that the respondent was not liable for non-domestic rates because of the terms of his lease.

authorised by another enactment, the application should be heard by at least two justices.[53] If the magistrates are satisfied that the sum had become payable and has not been paid, they must make the order. It is not open to the ratepayer to argue at this stage any matter that could have been raised in relation to the alteration of the list.[54] The amount of the order is the aggregate of the sums due together with the reasonable costs of the authority in obtaining the order, these costs also being due in the event of the ratepayer paying after the order was applied for, but before it is made.[55]

Once obtained, the authority can enforce the order through distress. However, a local authority has no power of distress to recover rates over goods of a company which are subject to a floating charge after that charge has crystallised.[56] Appeal lies to the magistrates' court on the ground that the levy was irregular.[57] However, it was held in *R. v. Basildon JJ., ex p. Holding & Barnes plc* that the magistrates were under no duty no hear a complaint where they decided that the facts and legal complexities meant that the alternative remedy of civil proceedings in the County or High Court should be utilised.[58]

> In *Steel Linings Ltd and Harvey v. Bibby & Co.*,[59] further guidance on the process of distress was given by the Court of Appeal. In that case, the ratepayer company owed £7,358 and the bailiffs attended, seized and removed industrial equipment including three vehicles, a forklift truck, three large boxes of tools, and a valuable lathe which the ratepayer company alleged amounted to a total value of £46,340. The process caused great hostility between the parties, involved at least six bailiffs, and took 12 hours resulting in a more than usually large bill for charges from the bailiffs of £5,910. County court proceedings were issued by the company claiming excessive levy of distress and damage to their property, and a director of the company claimed personal injury. The County Court issued an injunction restraining the sale or disposal of the assets and making the goods available for collection by the company. In the Court of Appeal, the bailiffs argued that the county court judge had no power to grant such an injunction since the statutory scheme of distress was such that the magistrates' court alone had the jurisdiction to receive appeals in connection with distress for rates and alone had the power to require bailiffs to return distrained goods. This was rejected by the Court of Appeal which found, among other points, that the county court had jurisdiction to issue the injunction since an excessive distress for rates was a wrongful act because the regulations only empowered the authority to levy "the appropriate amount by distress and sale" and the wrongful act constituted the tort of wrongful interference with goods under the provisions of the Torts (Interference with Goods) Act 1977. In addition, the regulations provided for the recovery of damages "by proceedings in trespass or otherwise" and there was no reason why the court's injunctive powers should not be invoked since the complaint process specified would in

---

[53] *ibid.*, reg. 21.
[54] *ibid.*, reg. 23. In *Tower Hamlets London Borough Council v. Fallows and Fallows* [1990] R.A. 255, the Court of Appeal held that the burden of proving that the rates had not been paid fell on the authority.
[55] *ibid.*, reg. 12, as amended.
[56] *Re ELS Ltd* [1994] 2 All E.R. 833.
[57] Non-Domestic Rating (Collection and Enforcement) Regulations 1989 (S.I. 1989 No. 1058, as amended), regs. 15 and 15.
[58] [1994] R.A. 157.
[59] [1993] R.A. 27.

the present case have proved an ineffective means of redress because the distraining authority was free to sell immediately it seized the goods.[60] It was considered that damages were not an adequate remedy because the goods seized were the tools of the company's trade urgently needed to fulfil customers' contracts. While this case seems to give great support to the debtor, the Court added the warning that

"... we would sound this note of warning to future debtors tempted to build upon this present decision. Only very exceptionally will it be appropriate to invoke the interlocutory jurisdiction of the county court to secure the return of distrained goods. Defaulting ratepayers (or other debtors) will need to present a powerful *prima facie* case for saying that the distraint has indeed been in some respect unlawful. Where, as here, the allegation advanced is one of excessive distraint, debtors should expect a generally sceptical reaction to their own estimation of their goods' worth. In short, the civil courts will not allow themselves to become a ready means of escaping the proper processes and consequences of statutory distraint."

If the value of the goods obtained is insufficient,[61] the authority may apply to the magistrates' court for the issue of a warrant to commit the debtor to prison, and the court must be satisfied, as a result of its inquiries in the debtor's presence, that the failure to pay the liability order was due to wilful refusal or culpable neglect before a warrant is issued.[62] The order in the warrant shall state a period not exceeding three months, and the period may be reduced by the proportion of the amount, including reasonable costs, paid after the proceedings. The amount due may also be deemed a debt for the purpose of bankruptcy proceedings against an individual or a company.[63] For relevant judicial interpretations of similar recovery provisions in regard to the council tax and community charge, see paras. 16–37 to 16–39.

Similar provisions exist in relation to the collection and enforcement of the rates due under the central list, although in regard to this any sum which has not been paid cannot be recovered by distress, only by an action for civil debt "in a court of competent jurisdiction".[64]

Overpayment of rates is corrected by either repayment if the ratepayer so requires, or by repayment or credit against any future liability to pay non-domestic rates at the discretion of the authority or the Secretary of State as appropriate.[65]

---

[60] Non-Domestic Rating (Collection and Enforcement) (Local Lists) Regulations 1989 (S.I. 1989 No. 1058, as amended), regs. 14(7) and 15.

[61] *ibid.*, reg. 14, as amended, provides that goods which satisfy the basic domestic needs of the debtors family cannot be seised.

[62] *ibid.*, reg. 16.

[63] *ibid.*, reg. 18.

[64] Non-Domestic Rating (Collection and Enforcement) (Central Lists) Regulations 1989 (S.I. 1989 No. 2260, as amended).

[65] Local Government Finance Act 1988, Sched. 9, reg. 2A, as enacted by the Local Government and Housing Act 1989, s.139 and Sched. 5 and the Non-Domestic Rating (Collection and Enforcement) Regulations 1989 (S.I. 1989 No. 1058, as amended), reg. 9; Non-Domestic Rating (Collection and Enforcement) (Central Lists) Regulations 1989 (S.I. 1989 No. 2260 as amended by S.I. 1992 No. 1513) reg. 9. Where rates are paid under a mistake of fact or of law, they are recoverable at common law: *Tower Hamlets London Borough Council v. Chetnick Developments* [1988] 1 All E.R. 961; *Woolwich Building Society v. Inland Revenue Commissioners (No. 2)* [1992] 3 All E.R. 737.

F. Pooling and Distribution of Rates

While billing authorities are responsible for the collection of rates, their **15–21** income from this source is only such sums as are permitted by the Secretary of State. All receipts are pooled centrally and the Secretary of State redistributes these to all billing and major precepting authorities.[66] The total amounts of redistributed non-domestic rates, the distribution, and the basis for it have to be set out in an annual local government finance report to be approved by the House of Commons.[67] This process is established by Schedule 8 of the 1988 Act.[68]

The account

Under Part I of Schedule 8, the Secretary of State is required to keep an **15–22** account for each financial year to which is to be credited the income received from non-domestic rating in the central list,[69] the amounts paid on crown property in lieu of rates,[70] and the non-domestic rating contributions paid by billing authorities. From this account is to be debited any payments to authorities. Any deficit or surplus is to be carried forward to the following year.

Contributions

Under Part II, the rules for calculating contributions from billing **15–23** authorities for any financial year are to be determined by the Secretary of State in regulations to be made before January 1 in the preceding financial year.[71] In determining the rules, which are to produce an amount broadly the same as the amount which would be obtained by the authority if it "acted diligently" in collection, the Secretary of State may take account of such deductions as he thinks fit in regard to costs of collection, the various reliefs which may be granted by the authority,[72] and other matters he thinks fit. These regulations may also include adjustments relating to the previous financial year. The billing authority is then under duty, by such time before the financial year as the Secretary of State directs, to calculate and notify to

---

[66] Billing authorities are, by s.1 of the Local Government Finance Act 1992, as amended, in relation to England, a district council or London borough council, the Common Council or the Council of the Isles of Scilly and, in relation to Wales, a county council or county borough council. Major precepting authorities are, by s.39 of the 1992 Act, a county council [in England]; a police authority established under section 3 of the Police Act 1964; a metropolitan county fire and civil defence authority; the London Fire and Civil Defence Authority; and the Receiver for the Metropolitan Police District.

[67] For the finance reports for 1996–97, see the Local Government Finance Report (England) 1996/7, H.C. 164, and the Local Government Finance Report (Wales) 1996/97, H.C. 141.

[68] Local Government Finance Act 1988, s.60 and Sched. 8 as amended by the Local Government Finance Act 1992, s.104 and Sched. 10.

[69] See § 14–15.

[70] See § 14–07.

[71] Local Government Finance Act 1988, Sched. 8 (as amended), para. 4.

[72] In regard to the reliefs, see §§ 15–07 to 15–14.

the Secretary of State their non-domestic rating contribution, known as the "provisional amount," and failure to do so, or the Secretary of State's belief that the authority has not followed the rules in operation, enables the Secretary of State to make his own calculation of the provisional amount, which he must then notify to the authority.[73] The provisional amount is then payable by the authority in such instalments and at such times as the Secretary of State directs, with the consent of the Treasury. After the end of the financial year, the billing authority must again calculate the contribution. All calculations of the amount are to be made on the basis of information available to the decision-maker at the time, but the rules for calculating contributions may prescribe that the information be read subject to assumptions and that certain information may be disregarded if it is not practicable to take it into account or if it was received after a prescribed date.[74] The final calculation must be notified to the Secretary of State by such time as the Secretary of State directs, and certified by the Audit Commission which must send the certification to the Secretary of State.[75] If the amount notified by the authority is greater than the provisional amount, the billing authority must pay the difference at such time as the Secretary of State directs. If the notified amount is less, the Secretary of State shall either pay the difference to the authority, with the consent of the Treasury, or, having informed the authority that he does not believe the calculation has been in accordance with the regulations, recalculate the amount. Provision is also made for such adjustments where the certified amount differs from the notified amount. All sums payable are recoverable in a court of competent jurisdiction.[76]

Distribution

15–24   Under Part III of Schedule 8, the distribution of the amounts from the fund may be made to any billing or major precepting authority. The Secretary of State must include in the annual local government finance report the total amount of the sum available for distribution to these receiving authorities. The Secretary of State must also, following consultation with such representatives of local government as appear to him to be appropriate, include in the annual report the basis of the proposed distribution.[77] Separate reports are in practice made for England and Wales, and these reports also contain the amount and distribution of revenue support grant.[78] The basis of distribution of non-domestic rate depends on resident population.[79]

[73] Local Government Finance Act 1988, Sched. 8 (as amended), para. 5.
[74] *ibid.*, para. 6.
[75] *ibid.*, para. 5. Failure to comply with the time-limit may result in payments of redistributed non-domestic rates to the authority being suspended.
[76] *ibid.*, para. 7.
[77] *ibid.*, para. 9 and 10.
[78] See § 14–05.
[79] Further details of the basis of distribution can be found in section 6 of each of the annual local government finance reports. For the finance reports for 1996–97, see the Local Government Finance Report (England) 1996/97, H.C. 164, and the Local Government Finance Report (Wales) 1996/97, H.C. 141.

Calculation and payment of redistributed rates

Once the local government finance report for a financial year has been **15–25** approved by the House of Commons, the Secretary of State is, as soon as reasonably practicable, to calculate the amounts payable to each receiving authority in accordance with the basis of distribution in the report.[80] For this purpose, among other purposes under the Act, he is empowered to require authorities to supply him with information; and if information is not supplied by a date specified he is entitled to take into account any other information available to him, to make such assumptions as he thinks fit about an authority, and to leave out of account information received after dates notified to the authority. It is open to him to make one revised calculation of the sums payable to each receiving authority, however, to enable him to correct errors or to adjust the first calculation in the light of further information. This further calculation can be made at any time before the end of the financial year following that to which the report relates. As soon as is reasonably practicable after making an original or revised calculation the Secretary of State must inform each receiving authority of the sum he calculates falls to be paid. The sums may be paid by instalments of such amounts and at such times as the Secretary of State determines with the consent of the Treasury and, while the sums under an original calculation for receiving authorities must be paid within the financial year, but where revised calculations are made adjustments are not to be effected until after the end of the financial year concerned.[81]

Amending reports

While a revised calculation is still to be made on the basis of distribution **15–26** set out in the local government finance report, the Secretary of State also has the power to make an amending report to change the basis of distribution.[82] This may be made at any time before the end of that financial year or the following financial year. As with the original report, before making the amended report the Secretary of State is required to notify to, but not consult, such representatives of local government as appear to him to be appropriate, the general nature of the amendments he proposes. The proposed amendments require the approval of the House of Commons, and as soon as is reasonably practicable after the report is laid the Secretary of State must send a copy to each receiving authority. Once the proposal is approved by the House of Commons, no further amending reports may be made in relation to the same local government finance report. However, if the House of Commons does not approve a proposed amendment the Secretary of State may make further proposals until one is accepted.

The Secretary of State is, as soon as reasonably practicable after the approval by the House of Commons, to calculate the amounts payable to each receiving authority in accordance with the basis of distribution in the

---

[80] Local Government Finance Act 1988, Sched. 8 (as amended), para. 11.
[81] *ibid.*, para. 12.
[82] *ibid.*, para. 13.

amended report.[83] Again, it is open to him to make one revised calculation of the sums payable to each receiving authority, but this must be made before either the end of the financial year following the financial year to which the amended report relates, or three months after the approval of the amending report, whichever is later. The provisions regarding information which apply to the original and revised calculation apply also in relation to calculations under amended reports. Where a calculation or revised calculation has been made under an amended report, adjustments are not to be effected until after the end of the financial year concerned.[84]

[83] *ibid.*, para. 14.
[84] *ibid.*, para. 15.

CHAPTER 16

COUNCIL TAX

UNDER the Local Government Finance Act 1988, rates on domestic property **16–01** were abolished in favour of a tax on individuals, the community charge, which was not related to income. This, however, was to prove what Auld J. described as "a singular and short-lived concept",[1] and it remained only until the end of the financial year 1992–93.[2]

Thereafter, it was replaced by a new system. As the first stage in the possible change in the system of finance, section 3 of the Local Government Finance and Valuation Act 1991 authorised a valuation of all domestic property for the purpose of compiling and maintaining a list, differentiated according to bands of values. The Local Government Finance Act 1992 introduced the new system for a domestic property charge known as the council tax from the financial year 1993–94.[3]

The council tax may best be described as a mixture of the previous two systems in relation to domestic property. Although based primarily on the capital value of the property, it is not simply a property tax like the domestic rating system; nor is it simply a charge on the individual like the community charge. Instead it can be seen as a property based tax, with 50 per cent elements for each of the property itself and the residency of individuals. For the property element, an extensive, if crude, valuation exercise placed all residential property into one of eight valuation bands, based on capital value, and the contribution in relation to that property is calculated according to that broad band, rather than an exact value as under the domestic rating system. For the personal element, it is assumed that two eligible adults are resident and liability is calculated accordingly, with dwellings in the highest band liable to pay three times that to be paid by those in the lowest band.[4] There is no increase in the tax to be paid if there are more than two eligible adults residing in the property, but where there is only one eligible adult resident a discount of 25 per cent will operate.[5] In this way the tax retains a limited personal element, although there is a single bill

---

[1] *Cherwell District Council v. Hodges* [1991] R.V.R. 163.
[2] While the community charge remains relevant in regard to some collection and enforcement matters the section relating directly to the community charge has been removed from this edition. Readers requiring this should refer to the previous edition, while much of the material on collection and enforcement of the council tax is relevant to the community charge.
[3] Local Government Finance Act 1992, s.1.
[4] *ibid.*, s.5.
[5] *ibid.*, s.11.

per property with liability to pay falling not on all eligible adults but on a specified person.[6] There are also further exemptions and discounts.

As with the community charge, the level of the tax is set by the local authority, subject to "capping", after taking account of income from rates and grants.[7]

The council tax is considered under the following headings: (a) the tax, (b) the lists, (c) setting the tax, (d) liability, (e) appeals, (f) collection and enforcement.

A. THE TAX

16–02 Section 1 of the Local Government Finance Act 1992 establishes the basic duty for a billing authority to levy and collect the council tax in respect of dwellings within its area. A "billing authority" is defined as a metropolitan or non-metropolitan district council, London borough council, the Common Council, or Council of the Isles of Scilly and in Wales as a county or county borough.[8] A number of factors specified by this Act affect the liability to pay the council tax and, for each of these, section 2 specifies that the situation which exists at the end of the day is deemed to have existed throughout the day. The factors are, whether the property is a dwelling subject to the tax; what valuation band is shown as applicable to the dwelling; the person liable to pay the tax in respect of the dwelling; and any discount applicable to the dwelling.

16–03 Council tax is not payable in regard to all dwellings, but only "chargeable dwellings", defined in two stages. First, a "dwelling" is defined, essentially negatively, as any property which would have been included within the relevant definition of rateable hereditament under the old rating system, under the General Rate 1967, but which has neither been incorporated into the new non-domestic rating system, nor exempted from such under the 1988 Act.[9] For the properties which would otherwise be exempt because of Crown exemption, these shall be included in the definition of "dwelling".[10] More positively, the definition includes composite hereditaments together

---

[6] *ibid.*, s.6.

[7] *ibid.*, Part I, Ch. V.

[8] *ibid.*, s.1(2), as amended. By subs. (3), the Secretary of State is permitted to make regulations to deal with the situation where the dwelling is situated in more than one authority's area, by treating it as situated in only one of the areas. For the regulations, see the Council Tax (Situation and Valuation of Dwellings) Regulations 1992 (S.I. 1992 No. 550, as amended).

[9] *ibid.*, s.3, and see The Council Tax (Chargeable Dwellings) Order 1992 (S.I. 1992 No. 549) and the Council Tax (Situation and Valuation of Dwellings) Order 1992 (S.I. 1992 No. 558, as amended).

[10] See also s.19 which extends to the council tax system the approach, under s.64(5) of the 1988 Act, whereby all hereditaments provided and maintained for purposes connected with the administration of justice, police purposes and other Crown purposes by a specified authority were excluded from exemption by virtue of Crown status, see § 15–07. Thus, for dwellings which fall within the classes specified in s.19, or in regulations made by the Secretary of State, Crown exemption is removed from dwellings and the person who would otherwise be liable to pay the council tax for a chargeable dwelling shall be so liable.

with any hereditament which is used wholly for the purposes of living accommodation, but excluded from the definition are types of premises which are considered as a dwelling only if they form part of a larger property which is itself a dwelling.[11] Thus yards, gardens, outhouses, garages of up to 25 square metres used primarily in relation to a private car, or private storage premises for domestic goods are excluded in themselves, but they will be incorporated as part of a dwelling if associated with another property which is already within the definition of a dwelling. It has been held that each of the 340 beach huts on a stretch of sand is a "dwelling" within and so subject to council tax.[12] Wide powers are given to the Secretary of State to make regulations to amend the definition, and to deal with subdivision and incorporation of property by prescribing that certain single dwellings be classed as two or more dwellings, or that two or more dwellings be classed as a single dwelling.[13] A completion notice may be served in respect of new buildings which comprise the whole or part of dwelling, and this notice establishes the date from which liability to council tax in regard to that dwelling begins.[14] Secondly, "chargeable dwellings" is defined, also essentially negatively, as those which are not exempt by virtue of being within any class of dwelling specified by means of order made by the Secretary of State.[15]

All residential property is placed into one of eight bands in the billing **16–04** authority's valuation list. The bands are different for England and Wales, and the proportion to be paid by each band is as follows[16]:

---

[11] On the status of a maisonette above a shop, see *Williams v. Bristol District Valuation Officer and Avon Valuation Tribunal* [1995] R.A. 189.

[12] *Lewis v. Christchurch Borough Council*, unreported, March 18, 1996, CO/4064/95.

[13] Council Tax (Chargeable Dwellings) Order 1992, (S.I. 1992 No. 549). On the issue of whether an annex to a house, particularly a "granny-flat", was a self-contained dwelling, see *Rodd v. Richards* [1995] R.A. 299. The court excluded the factors of actual use, the intention or ability to sell separately, and the possible mismatch between the terms of the planning permission and liability for council tax. It was indicated that the most important factor was the precise physical layout.

[14] Local Government Finance Act 1992, s.17. Where a completion notice is served on a building which is not yet complete, the notice specifies a "completion day," which is to be not more than three months after service of the notice. This date may be altered on appeal to the valuation tribunal, see § 16–17. Even if the dwelling is not completed by that date, the "relevant date", it is nevertheless deemed to have been completed for the purpose of liability to council tax.

[15] *ibid.*, s.4, and the Council Tax (Exempt Dwellings) Order 1992 (S.I. 1992 No. 558, as amended). While confirming the width of the discretion of the Secretary of State it is made clear that some of the relevant factors may be the physical characteristics of the dwelling; that the dwelling may be unoccupied; that it is occupied for prescribed purposes; and that it is occupied or owned by persons of prescribed descriptions. Various classes have been prescribed including—dwellings to which works are being carried out; which have been unoccupied for less than six months; which are the homes of people living elsewhere or detained in specified circumstances (and not of others); where someone has died; where occupation is prohibited; which are kept for ministers of religion; which are the homes of people resident elsewhere to take care of others; which are the homes of people resident elsewhere for the purpose of their studies; which are in the possession of a mortgagee; and which is a hall of residence wholly occupied by students, or part of armed forces accommodation, unoccupied dwellings in relation to which a trustee in bankruptcy would otherwise be liable.

[16] *ibid.*, s.5.

Band	England	Wales	Proportion
A	up to £40,000	up to £30,000	6
B	£ 40,000–£ 52,000	£ 30,000–£ 39,000	7
C	£ 52,000–£ 68,000	£ 39,000–£ 51,000	8
D	£ 68,000–£ 88,000	£ 51,000–£ 66,000	9
E	£ 88,000–£120,000	£ 66,000–£ 90,000	11
F	£120,000–£160,000	£ 90,000–£120,000	13
G	£160,000–£320,000	£120,000–£240,000	15
H	exceeding £320,000	exceeding £240,000	18

Thus the properties in the highest band will be liable to pay only three times the tax payable by those in the lowest band. The Secretary of State may change the banding values and proportions by order, but only with an affirmative resolution of the House of Commons.[17]

B. The Lists

16–05 The Commissioners of Inland Revenue must appoint, for each billing authority, listing officers who shall be Crown servants paid out of central funds, rather than by the authority.[18] They must also carry out such valuations and disclose such information as they consider necessary or expedient to assist listing officers in compiling the valuation list, and for this purpose they may appoint persons not in the service to assist in the process.[19] The Commissioners may disclose to such persons any survey obtained for rating purposes, or any information obtained under the authority of section 27 of the 1992 Act,[20] but the use or disclosure of such information by the appointed person for any purpose other than valuation is an offence.[21]

16–06 The relevant date for valuation purposes is April 1, 1991, and the valuation is carried out according to assumptions and principles prescribed in regulations.[22] The basic principle is that the value is that which the dwelling might reasonably have been expected to realise if it had been sold in the open market by a willing vendor. The assumptions on which that is based are that the sale was with vacant possession; that the interest was freehold or a lease of 99 years at a nominal rent; that it was sold free of any rent charge or other incumbrance; that it was in a state of reasonable repair, and that where there are common parts that they were in a similar state, but that the costs of maintenance of the common parts could be taken into account; that fixtures are not included in the dwelling; that it would be permanently restricted to use as a dwelling; and that it had no development value other than value

[17] *ibid.*, s.5(5).

[18] *ibid.*, s.20.

[19] *ibid.*, s.21(1) and (3). In practice much of the work of the initial valuation exercise was undertaken by estate agents because of the short time-scale involved.

[20] See § 16–33 below.

[21] Local Government Finance Act 1992, s.21(4)–(6).

[22] *ibid.*, s.21(2) and Council Tax (Situation and Valuation of Dwellings) Regulations 1992 (S.I. 1992 No. 550).

attributable to permitted development.[23] Where, under section 24, it is alleged that there has been a material reduction in the value it is to be assumed that the physical state of the locality of the dwelling is the same as on the date from which the alteration of the list would have effect; and the size, layout and character of the dwelling the same as on the date from which the alteration would take place.[24]

The officer conducting the valuation may enter a dwelling in order to **16–07** survey and value it provided, first, that adequate notice in writing must be given, this being defined as three clear days' notice, excluding Saturday or Sunday, Christmas Day or Good Friday, and any other bank holiday and, secondly, that the officer must produce written authority if requested.[25] It is an offence to delay or obstruct deliberately the exercise of the power of entry.[26] A listing officer or the Commissioners of Inland Revenue may require information about properties to be made available from a number of sources.[27] A notice requiring information may be served on a charging or billing authority, a community charges registration officer, or any other person in an official capacity.[28] The information must relate to property,[29] and the listing officer or Commissioners of Inland Revenue must reasonably believe that the information will assist in carrying out their functions. The notice must also specify the information sought, and the manner, form and timing of the reply. Information may also be obtained by means of a notice served on an owner or occupier of any dwelling.[30] The information required must be specified in the notice, and the listing officer or Commissioners of Inland Revenue must state in the notice that they believe that the information will assist in carrying out their functions. Where a notice is served which conforms to these requirements, then it is the duty of those on whom the notice is served to supply the information in such manner and form as is specified in the notice. For information from official sources, the notice specifies the time within which a reply must be made, but for information from an owner or occupier the reply must be within 21 days from the date of service of the notice.[31] It is an offence for an owner or occupier to fail to comply with these duties, or to knowingly or recklessly make a false statement in reply.[32] A further duty is placed upon the charging or billing authority to provide information to the listing officer where the information has been obtained in the exercise of their functions and where the authority is of the opinion that the information would assist the listing

---

[23] Council Tax (Situation and Valuation of Dwellings) Regulations 1992 (S.I. 1992 No. 550, as amended), reg. 6.
[24] *ibid.*
[25] Local Government Finance Act 1992, s.26.
[26] *ibid.*, s.26(4).
[27] *ibid.*, s.27.
[28] *ibid.*, s.27(1).
[29] It is likely that this will be interpreted to include information about persons in that property.
[30] Local Government Finance Act 1992, s.27(2).
[31] *ibid.*, s.27(3).
[32] *ibid.*, s.27(4)–(5).

officer in carrying out his functions.[33] The listing officer or the Commissioners of Inland Revenue may take into account not merely information obtained under the provisions of this Act, but also any other information available, whatever its source.[34]

16–08   Each listing officer for a billing authority must compile and maintain a valuation list, which is technically to be "compiled" on April 1, 1993, and come into force on that day.[35] The listing officer must ensure that the list is as accurate as reasonably possible prior to its being "compiled". In order to allow the billing authority to make comments, at two stages in the process leading up to the formal compilation of the valuation list, the listing officer must send to the billing authority a copy of the proposed list.[36] Following receipt of the second proposed valuation list, publicity must be given to the list by the billing authority. Although the precise form of the publicity is left to the discretion of the authority, a copy of the list must be deposited at the principal office of the authority for public scrutiny. As soon as is "reasonably practicable" after April 1, 1993, when the list is formally "compiled", the listing officer must send a copy to the billing authority. The billing authority is required to notify the person concerned in relation to each dwelling of the valuation band shown in the proposed list, or whether the dwelling is considered to be an exempt dwelling.[37] When the final copy of the valuation list is received, the billing authority is required to deposit it at its principal office and, at this stage, there is no need for further publicity.

16–09   Each dwelling in the billing authority's area must be shown in the valuation list for each day for which it is force, together with the valuation band applicable and such other information as is prescribed.[38] Exclusion from the valuation list does not affect the status of the dwelling as a "chargeable dwelling", but the amount of tax payable could not be calculated in accordance with section 10 of the 1992 Act, so no tax could be demanded in relation to a dwelling not shown in the valuation list for that day. Any dwelling which would otherwise be exempt from liability to be shown in the list, by virtue of Crown exemption, shall be included in the list,

---

[33] *ibid.*, s.27(6).

[34] *ibid.*, s.27(7). This, presumably, should be interpreted to mean available lawfully and not, for example, supplied in breach of the Data Protection Act 1984. It should also be noted that this formulation is wider than the equivalent power in relation to Scotland, under s.90 of the 1992 Act, which restricts the relevant officer to any other information available under other enactments relating to valuation, community charges or electoral registration.

[35] *ibid.*, s.22.

[36] The first was set at not later than September 1, 1992, and the second to be within the period November 15 to December 1, 1992.

[37] Council Tax (Administration and Enforcement) Regulations 1992 (S.I. 1992 No. 613, as amended), reg. 7.

[38] Local Government Finance Act 1992, s.23. See also the Council Tax (Contents of Valuation Lists) Regulations 1992 (S.I. 1992 No. 553) which require that the lists show a reference number for each dwelling, and indicate if the property is a composite hereditament. In addition, where the list has been altered, it must show the period for, or the date from, which the alteration is to take effect, and whether the alteration was made in compliance with an order of the valuation tribunal or the High Court.

together with the applicable band and any other information required by regulation.[39]

The Secretary of State is given a general power to make regulations **16–10** concerning the alteration of valuation lists by listing officers, and before a listing officer is able to alter a valuation list, any conditions and procedures in the regulations must be fulfilled.[40] In any alteration the same assumptions and principles of valuation as the original valuation exercise shall apply.[41] Before an alteration can be made to the valuation band shown as applicable to a particular dwelling, one of three factors must have changed from the time of the original compilation of the valuation list.[42]

The first concerns the extent of domestic use and the value of the dwelling, which in turn divides into four components. Where the value has increased, the valuation band can be altered only where there has also been a "relevant transaction" in regard to all or some of the dwelling, that is a sale of the property or the grant, or transfer on sale, of a lease of seven years or longer. Where the value has decreased, that fact alone will not be sufficient. The reduction must have been due, in whole or in part, to demolition of part of the dwelling, some physical change in the locality of the property, or adaptation to meet the needs of the disabled. The third and fourth components relate to a "composite hereditament", that is a property only part of which is domestic with the rest non-domestic and thus subject to the non-domestic rating system. If a dwelling has become, or ceased to be, a composite hereditament then, as the third component, the valuation band may be altered. The fourth component would allow the valuation band to be altered where, in relation to an existing composite hereditament, there is a change in the proportion of the domestic use.

The second factor is the opinion of the listing officer as to the value of the dwelling. Two different situations are provided for, both concerning errors. The first deals with a situation where the wrong valuation has been made, and the listing officer is of the opinion that a different valuation band should have been determined by him for the dwelling. The second deals with the situation where a mistake occurs over the actual entry, and the valuation band shown in the list is not that actually determined by him at that time as applicable to the dwelling. The third factor is the order of a valuation tribunal or the High Court requiring the alteration to the valuation list to be made.

The valuation list may be altered on his own initiative by the valuation officer, or as a result of a proposal by a billing authority or an interested

---

[39] This does not, however, mean that council tax will be required to be paid. Only those dwellings which would have had Crown exemption but for s.19 of the 1992 Act will be required to pay council tax. The custom whereby the Crown may nevertheless make a contribution in aid may continue, although there is no provision in this Act similar to s.59 of the 1988 Act recognising this practice.
[40] Local Government Finance Act 1992, s.24 and the Council Tax (Alteration of Lists and Appeals) Regulations 1993 (S.I. 1993 No. 290, as amended).
[41] *ibid.*, s.24(3) and reg. 36.
[42] *ibid.*, s.24(4) and reg. 4.

person.[43] Once the alteration is made, the listing officer must notify the billing authority within six weeks and the authority must then alter the copy deposited with it, and also within six weeks he must notify the taxpayer of the effect of the alteration, unless the alteration is to reflect a clerical error or other prescribed matters.[44] Provision is made for when the alteration is to take effect.[45]

16–11   Proposals to alter the list by billing authorities or interested persons may be made in a number of circumstances.[46] First, if it is considered that the list is inaccurate because it shows a dwelling which ought not to be shown; it fails to show a dwelling which ought to be shown; the listing officer has determined as applicable a valuation band other than that which should have been determined as applicable; there has been a material increase and relevant transaction, or material reduction or change in regard to a composite hereditament; or account has not been taken of a decision of a valuation tribunal or the High Court, provided that a proposal on the last ground is made within six months of the decision.[47] In addition, no proposal (other than a further proposal) may be made in regard to the valuation band applicable to a dwelling after November 30, 1993.[48] This last restriction will not apply where a person becomes a taxpayer in regard to the dwelling for the first time after the list is in force, provided that the proposal is made within six months of becoming a taxpayer.[49] Secondly, where a listing officer has altered the list, a proposal may be made to restore the list to its original state or to make a further alteration, provided that the alteration made by the listing officer does not consist of a reference number, alteration of address, correction of clerical error, entry of a completion day, or is to take account either of a change to the area of the billing authority or of a decision of a valuation tribunal or the High Court.[50]

Among other requirements, a proposal must be made in writing to the listing officer, identify both the property and the person making the proposal, and include a statement of the reasons for believing the list to be incorrect and the manner in which the list is proposed to be altered.[51]

---

[43] Council Tax (Alteration of Lists and Appeals) Regulations 1993 (S.I. 1993 No. 290, as amended), reg. 5. "Interested person" is defined by reg. 2 as the owner, person prescribed as owner, person liable to pay council tax if the dwelling were not an exempt building, or a taxpayer in respect of the dwelling. Under the General Rate Act 1967, the right to make proposals was conferred on "persons aggrieved" which allowed third parties to be "aggrieved" by the under-assessment of another hereditament, see *Arsenal Football Club v. Smith (Valuation Officer)* [1979] A.C. 1.

[44] *ibid.*, reg. 15.

[45] *ibid.*, reg. 14. See also *Simmonds v. Dowty and others*, unreported, February 26, 1996, CO/1696/95.

[46] *ibid.*, reg. 5.

[47] *ibid.*, reg. 5(1) and (2).

[48] *ibid.*, reg. 5(3).

[49] *ibid.*, reg. 5(4). Reg. 5(5) excludes such proposals where it is to alter the same list in relation to the same dwelling on the same facts as has been determined by a valuation tribunal or the High Court, or the new taxpayers has become so only by a transaction between companies of which one or both are a subsidiary of the other or another company, or by the formation of a new partnership containing a partner from the previous partnership.

[50] *ibid.*, reg. 5(6) and (7).

[51] *ibid.*, reg. 6.

Acknowledgement must be given within 28 days of receipt, unless the listing officer serves an invalidity notice.[52] If the listing officer considers the proposal to be invalid, he must notify the person making the proposal of his reasons, within four weeks, by means of an invalidity notice.[53] Within four weeks of that notification, the proposer may either make a further proposal (unless the invalidity notice was itself in response to a further proposal) or appeal to the valuation tribunal, which is initiated by serving notice of disagreement on the listing officer. If he treats the proposal as valid, the listing officer must, within six weeks, serve a copy of the proposal on, if not the proposer, the taxpayer and, in certain circumstances, the authority.[54] The listing officer may then accept the proposal and alter the list accordingly[55]; the proposal may be withdrawn[56]; an alteration may be made on terms other than those stated in the proposal, provided all the relevant persons agree[57]; or where there is no agreement and the proposal is not withdrawn, the listing officer must refer the matter as an appeal to the valuation tribunal within six months of the date of the proposal being served on him.[58] In regard to appeals, see below § 16–17 and § 16–18.

Where the Secretary of State, under section 5(4) of the 1992 Act, alters the valuation bands, listing officers will be required to compile and maintain new valuation lists in accordance with the general provisions in relation to the lists, subject to certain modifications.[59]

Where the listing officer is maintaining a valuation list which is in force, or **16–12** has been at any time in the previous five years, then any person may require the officer to give access to such information as will enable him to establish the state of the list, either currently or at any time since it came into force.[60] This is subject to the limitation that the duty to maintain the information on a list falls five years after the list ceases to be in force. Information about the present and historic state of the list must be made available at a reasonable time and place, free of charge although relevant photocopies may be charged for. Obstruction of rights of access, or failure to comply with the requirements of allowing copies or transcripts to be made, is an offence. Similar provisions exist in relation to information concerning proposals and appeals.[61]

---

[52] *ibid.*, reg. 7.
[53] *ibid.*, reg. 8.
[54] *ibid.*, reg. 9.
[55] *ibid.*, reg. 10.
[56] *ibid.*, reg. 11.
[57] *ibid.*, reg. 12.
[58] *ibid.*, reg. 13.
[59] *ibid.*, s.25. The modifications are the date on which the list was compiled; the date by reference to which the valuations are to be treated as having been carried out; and the dates by which the listing officer must supply the billing authority with an advance copy of the new list.

[60] *ibid.*, s.28.
[61] *ibid.*, s.29.

C. Setting the Tax

16-13 The billing authorities are the London borough and metropolitan and non-metropolitan district councils, together with the Common Council of the City of London and the Council of the Isles of Scilly and, in Wales, the county and county borough councils.[62] Other local authorities may issue precepts to the appropriate billing authority,[63] depending on whether they are major[64] or minor[65] precepting authorities.

A duty is placed on the billing authority to set, for each financial year, an amount of council tax for the different categories of dwellings, according to the band in which the dwelling falls.[66] The amount is to be calculated by taking the aggregate of two sums. First, the amount which has been calculated for each category of dwelling by the billing authority as necessary for its own purposes, including any precept from a minor precepting authority. Secondly, the amount which has been calculated for each category of dwelling by the major precepting authority as necessary for its own purposes, and which has been issued to the billing authority.[67]

A major precepting authority must, and a minor precepting authority may, issue a precept to the billing authority before March 1, in the preceding financial year, although this duty is directory only and a precept issued later than that will not be invalid solely for that reason.[68] The precept of the major precepting authority may not be issued until either the prescribed period for notification of the tax base has expired, or the billing authority has actually notified the precepting authority of its calculations in relation to that tax base.[69] The Secretary of State may make regulations to allow the billing authority to anticipate, when determining its own budget requirement, the issue of a precept from a minor precepting authority.[70] The precept issued by the major precepting authority must state, first, the amount of council tax

[62] Local Government Finance Act 1992, s.1(2).
[63] *ibid.*, s.39, which defines the appropriate billing authority as one where the whole or part of its area falls within the area of the precepting authority, but it is the appropriate billing authority only for that part of the area.
[64] *ibid.*, s.39(1) which specifies the county councils, police authorities, metropolitan county fire and civil defence authorities, the London Fire and Civil Defence Authority, and the Receiver for the Metropolitan Police District.
[65] *ibid.*, s.39(2), which specifies the parish or community councils; chairman of the parish meeting; charter trustees; and the sub-treasurer of the Inner Temple and under-treasurer of the Middle Temple.
[66] *ibid.*, s.30.
[67] *ibid.*, s.30(2). If the result of the process of aggregation under subs. (2) is to produce a negative sum, then the amount set for each category of dwelling is to be nil, s.30(3). Even if there are no dwellings in a particular band, the billing authority must set an amount of council tax which would have applied to that band, s.30(5).
[68] *ibid.*, s.40 and s.41 respectively.
[69] *ibid.*, s.40(6). Any purported precept which has been issued without the necessary calculations having been undertaken, or which has been issued before the tax base has been notified or the period for notification has expired will have no legal effect: s.40(8).
[70] *ibid.*, s.41(3) and the Billing Authorities (Anticipation of Precepts) (Amendment) Regulations 1992 (S.I. 1992 No. 3239). The anticipated amounts may include any increase or decrease in the retail prices index: reg. 2(2) as amended by the Billing Authorities (Anticipation of Precepts) (Amendment) Regulations 1995 (S.I. 1995 No. 235).

which the precepting authority calculates is applicable to each category of dwellings in the area of the billing authority for that financial year and, second, the amount which the precepting authority calculates is the amount payable by the billing authority in respect of the precept for that financial year.[71] The precept of a minor precepting authority must state the authority's budget requirement for the year and it is that amount which is payable by the billing authority in respect of the precept for that financial year.[72] The amounts of council tax set by the billing authority must be set before March 11, in the preceding financial year, although failure to do so does not affect validity of an amount set after that date, but may not be set before the earlier of March 1, in the preceding financial year, or the date of issue to the billing authority of the precept from the major precepting authority.[73] A setting of an amount of council tax payable by either a billing or major precepting authority will be void and of no legal effect if it fails to meet these requirements or those relating to the relevant calculations.[74]

Each authority must therefore calculate its budget requirement for the **16–14** financial year. This is calculated by subtracting the estimated income from the estimated expenditure, as defined for each authority, but not including income from non-domestic rates, revenue support grant, additional grant or special grant.[75] For the billing authority, this will include the precept issued by a minor precepting authority and, for both the billing and major precepting authority, this will include the amount of any levy or special levy issued to it by a "levying body", as defined by section 74(1) of the Local Government Finance Act 1988.[76] The billing and major precepting authority must then calculate the basic amount of council tax (A) according to the formula $(R-P)/T$, where R is the total budget requirement; P is the aggregate of the sums payable in respect of redistributed non-domestic rates and revenue support grant, additional grant, and special grant; and T is the council tax base for the year.[77] Special provision is made for additional calculations in regard to items which relate to part only of the area, and in regard to special items.[78] Thereafter, the amount for different valuation

---

[71] *ibid.*, s.40(2). It is to be assumed that there are one or more dwellings in each of the valuation bands for each relevant part of the area, whether or not this is the case in fact. Thus a sum for each of the valuation bands must be shown in relation to each part of the area for which a different basic amount of council tax is payable: s.40(4).

[72] *ibid.*, s.41(2).

[73] *ibid.*, s.30(6) and (7). That precept must be the final one possible, other than by way of the process of substitution.

[74] *ibid.*, s.30(9) and s.40(8) respectively.

[75] *ibid.*, s.32 for the billing authority, s.43 for the major precepting authority, and s.52 for the minor precepting authority, as amended by the Local Authorities (Alteration of Requisite Calculations and Funds) Regulations 1995 (S.I. 1995 No. 234).

[76] An anticipated levy or special levy may not be included, no matter how likely it is to be issued, except in accordance with any regulations made under s.41 of the 1992 Act, and s.74 and s.75 of the 1988 Act.

[77] Local Government Finance Act 1992, s.33 and s.44 respectively, as amended by the Local Authorities (Alteration of Requisite Calculations and Funds) Regulations 1995 (S.I. 1995 No. 234). See also the Local Authorities (Calculation of Council Tax Base) Regulations 1992 (S.I. 1992 No. 612, as amended).

[78] *ibid.*, ss.34 and 35 and ss.45 and 46 respectively.

bands is calculated according to the formula A × N/D, where A is the basic amount calculated in accordance with the above formula; N is the number which is applicable to the proportion to be applied to dwellings listed in that valuation band[79]; and D is the number which in that proportion is applicable to dwellings listed in valuation band D.[80] The setting of the precept, tax or the calculation of the authority's budget requirement has to be undertaken by the authority itself and cannot be delegated to an officer, or a committee except in the case of the amount of council tax, which may be delegated to a committee of members of the authority appointed for that purpose with a fixed number and terms of office.[81]

16–15   It is possible for an authority, having already made calculations as to its budget requirement and council tax, to make a substitute calculation.[82] The authority must comply with the provisions of the original calculation, with the exception of the time-limits. A purported substitute calculation will have no legal effect in two situations. First, if either the budget requirement or the basic amount of council tax is greater than that in the previous calculation. Secondly, if the billing or major precepting authority fails to comply with the requirement to use the same amounts for the items specified in the calculation of the basic amount of tax, except that the element P may be increased if it is a result of an increase in the amount of additional grant which was not taken into account in the original calculation. A higher budget requirement or amount of council tax may be set, and other amounts taken into the calculation, when the previous calculation has been quashed for a failure to comply with the provisions of the Act. Where a precepting authority has made a substitute calculation, after a precept has already been issued, then it is under a duty to issue a substitute precept as soon as reasonably practicable thereafter.[83] Where payments have already been made to the billing authority on the basis of the original amount set, then those sums shall be treated as having been paid in relation to the new amount set and where payments have already been made to the precepting authority on the basis of the original precept, and the sums paid are greater than would have been paid in relation to the substituted precept, the billing authority has the right to require a repayment but, if the billing authority does not make such a request, then it is within the discretion of the precepting authority as to whether to repay the overpayment or to credit the sum against liability of the billing authority in regard to a precept for a future financial year.[84]

16–16   A billing authority is required to publish, in at least one newspaper circulating in the area, a notice of the amounts of council tax set, whether originally or by way of substitution.[85] Regulations may prescribe the supply

[79] *ibid.*, s.5(1), which gives the proportions as 6: 7: 8: 9: 11: 13: 15: 18.
[80] *ibid.*, s.36.
[81] *ibid.*, s.67.
[82] *ibid.*, s.37 for the billing authority; s.49 for the major precepting authority; s.51 for the local precepting authority.
[83] *ibid.*, s.42(1).
[84] *ibid.*, s.42(3) and (4).
[85] *ibid.*, s.38(2), but failure to comply does not make the setting of the amounts invalid.

of information between the billing and precepting authority.[86] The setting of the amount of a tax, or the calculation of the authority's budget requirement, can be challenged only by way of judicial review, thus excluding collateral challenge.[87]

The Secretary of State may designate an authority for "capping" of the **16–17** council tax or precept, if in his opinion its budget requirement is excessive or if there is an excessive increase over the previous year.[88] The authorities liable to this limitation are all billing authorities and all major precepting authorities with the exception of the Receiver for the Metropolitan Police District.[89] However, this broad power is modified by the requirement to apply to each authority the same principles as apply to others in the same class, or in relation to those which have or have not been designated previously, whether under the 1992 or 1988 Acts.[90] This leaves a great deal of discretion to the Secretary of State and it is possible for the principles to apply in a manner which may appear somewhat arbitrary, given that the underlying philosophy or criteria need not be made clear.[91] In *R. v. Secretary of State for the Environment, ex p. Hammersmith and Fulham London Borough Council*,[92] it was held that a decision under an equivalent provision was a matter of political opinion and did not require any prior assessment of the excessiveness of each authority's budget by reference to what a sensible authority would set in the particular circumstances of the area, and that the principles adopted, while the same for each authority, did not need to be applicable to each authority. In addition, that case held that the principles of natural justice were not to be applied to supplement the statutory procedural requirements in regard to this process, and that, since the powers were matters of political judgment subject to approval by the House of Commons, such decisions could be challenged only on the extreme grounds of bad faith, improper motive or manifest absurdity.[93]

Under section 55, there is special provision made for the first year of operation of the power, where the budget requirement is to be compared with the "relevant notional amount," which will also apply in future years where there has been a change in boundaries or functions. In order to allow the Secretary of State to decide whether to exercise these powers, the authorities are placed under a duty to notify him in writing of their budget

---

[86] *ibid.*, s.38(1) and s.52.

[87] *ibid.*, s.66.

[88] *ibid.*, s.54.

[89] *ibid.*, s.53.

[90] *ibid.*, s.54(2) and (3). There is, however, separate administration for England and Wales which allows different principles to apply, s.63.

[91] The classes specified are metropolitan districts; non-metropolitan districts; inner London boroughs; outer London boroughs; county councils, metropolitan county and the Northumbria police authorities; metropolitan county fire and civil defence authorities. In regard to the previous system of "rate-capping", the courts held that the test was satisfied by a mathematical formula and the Secretary of State need not disclose the underlying reasoning: *R. v. Secretary of State for the Environment, ex p. Hackney London Borough Council, The Times*, May 11, 1985.

[92] [1991] 1 A.C. 521.

[93] Applying *R. v. Secretary of State for the Environment, ex p. Nottinghamshire County Council* [1986] A.C. 240.

requirements and precepts from local precepting authorities, and the Secretary of State may serve a notice requiring the authority to supply such information as is specified, and he may also take into account any other information available to him, whatever its source.[94]

Where the Secretary of State decides to designate an authority, he must notify it in writing, specifying the principles employed, and the amount which he calculates should be the maximum for the budget requirement.[95] Unlike the position in regard to the principles employed in the decision to designate, the Secretary of State need not apply the same principles to each authority within a class in fixing the maximum amount after designation. If the authority does not respond within 28 days, the Secretary of State must make an order, for approval by the House of Commons, implementing the maximum amount.[96] If the authority accepts in writing within 28 days, the maximum figure becomes binding without parliamentary approval.[97] Equally the authority may make a substitute calculation for a different amount, but in this event, the amount of the substitute may not exceed the maximum amount prescribed in the designation, and the authority must use the same amounts for the items specified in the original calculation of the basic amount of tax, except that the element P may be increased if it is a result of an increase in the amount of additional grant which was not taken into account in the original calculation.[98]

If, however, the authority wishes to challenge the maximum amount, this must be done in writing within 28 days of the notice, specifying both the reasons for the challenge and a different figure.[99] Acting on whatever information or assumptions he thinks appropriate, the Secretary of State may then fix an amount which is the same as, or greater or smaller than the original maximum amount proposed by him, but it may not exceed the amount previously calculated by the authority unless the Secretary of State is of the opinion that the calculation was invalid.[1]

If the designated authority fail to comply with an agreed or imposed maximum within 21 days of the final notice, the sanction is that the authority will have no power to transfer funds from its collection fund to its general fund. It will thus have no access to its income. This prohibition continues until the authority complies with its duty to make a substitute calculation under section 60.[2]

---

[94] Local Government Finance Act 1992, s.64. If the authority fails to comply with these requirements the Secretary of State may decide to exercise his powers on the basis of such assumptions and estimates as he sees fit.

[95] *ibid.*, s.56.

[96] *ibid.*, s.59.

[97] *ibid.*, s.58.

[98] *ibid.*, ss.60 and 61.

[99] *ibid.*, s.56(4).

[1] *ibid.*, s.57. Any such order is subject to the affirmative resolution procedure of the House of Commons.

[2] *ibid.*, s.62.

D. LIABILITY

Liability depends on whether the dwelling is a "chargeable dwelling",[3] and **16–18**
the status of the person. Liability is daily charge, and it is a general principle
that for all relevant matters the state of affairs subsisting at the end of the day
is deemed to have existed throughout the day.[4]

Those persons liable are defined as the person who falls within the first of
the categories to apply, taking each in sequence, the categories being based
on two elements, residency and legal interest.[5] The top category in the
hierarchy is the person who is both a resident of the building and has a
freehold interest in whole or part of it. The hierarchy then progresses
through a variety of categories of where there is residency and differing legal
interest, namely leasehold, tenancy, contractual licence, and then no legal
interest. Finally, where there is no residency, then ownership establishes
liability. Where two or more persons fall within the same category for any
day then, unless severely mentally impaired, they will be jointly and
severally liable.[6]

"Resident", as the first of the qualifying classes, is defined as an individual **16–19**
who is both 18 years of age and occupies the dwelling as the sole or main
residence.[7] Since it is a daily tax, so an individual becomes liable from the day
on which the age of 18 is attained. As with the 1988 Act and the community
charge, this Act does not define the term "sole or main residence", and its
interpretation in this context will be influenced by the interpretation
adopted in other areas of law. The general approach of the courts has been
that the phrase should be considered in its ordinary meaning and as a matter
of fact and degree.[8] Thus, while it is accepted that a person can have more
than one residence,[9] a number of factors will be taken into account into
determining which is the main residence. However, in regard to the
community charge, although both the subjective opinion of the individual
and objective factors, such as where most of the personal belongings are
kept, are relevant, much weight was attached to the time spent at each
dwelling, since the charge was considered to be a charge for the services
provided.

> *Bradford City Metropolitan Council v. Anderton.*[10] In determining that a **16–20**
> merchant seaman had his residence in a house where he spent only 90 days of
> the year, Hutchinson J. held that apart from time, other factors in determining

---

[3] § 16–03 above.
[4] Local Government Finance Act 1992, s.2.
[5] *ibid.*, s.6(1) and (2) and the Council Tax (Liability for Owners) Regulations 1992 (S.I. 1992 No. 551, as amended).
[6] *ibid.*, s.6(3) and (4).
[7] *ibid.*, s.6(5).
[8] *Shah v. Barnet London Borough Council* [1983] 2 A.C. 309; *Hipperson v. Newbury District Electoral Officer* [1985] Q.B. 1060. In *Bradford City Metropolitan Council v. Anderton* (1991) 89 L.G.R. 681 it was held that the house where a merchant seaman spent only 90 days per year, and the rest of the year on a ship, was his sole residence. The argument that it was not his main residence was rejected on the basis that a merchant ship could not constitute a residence.
[9] *Fox v. Stirk* [1970] 2 Q.B. 463.
[10] (1991) 89 L.G.R. 681.

residence were the subjective view of what the individual regarded as his home, that it was where his wife lived, and that he had a legal interest in the house.

Stevenson v. Rodgers.[11] The Inner House of the Court of Session indicated that time was not simply one factor among others but the most important of the criteria. Thus where a person worked and slept during the week in Liverpool, but his wife and children lived in Edinburgh where he spent most weekends, the number of nights spent in each place was not evenly balanced. Only where the numbers were more evenly balanced should the other factors be considered as providing a contrary indication of residence. Differing views were expressed by the three judges as to the relevance of a legal interest in the house, where the person was registered with a G.P., where the person appeared on the electoral register, and where the rest of the family were living.

In *Ward v. Kingston upon Hull City Council*,[12] Mr Ward worked in Saudi Arabia but throughout the period of his employment and residence in Saudi Arabia his wife continued to live at their house in Hull. He returned home to be with his wife for periods of leave, totalling between six and nine weeks a year. His contract of employment was specifically for employment in Saudi Arabia, and he was provided with bachelor accommodation there. His right to remain in Saudi Arabia depended upon his job there, but his contract also contained a provision that it would be possible for him to be accompanied by his wife and family if permission could be obtained from the Saudi Arabian authorities and subject to his place on a waiting list for married accommodation at the base. There was evidence that the appellant and his wife had plans that she should join him out in Saudi Arabia at some time. He was entered on the register as subject to a personal community charge in respect of the house. Before the Valuation and Community Charge Tribunal he contended that his sole or main residence was in Saudi Arabia, not Hull. Confirming his registration, the tribunal took into consideration that Mr Ward had security of tenure on the house in Hull, but that there was no security of tenure on Mr Ward's accommodation in Saudi Arabia. The High Court dismissed his appeal on the basis that reliance on the comparison of security of tenure was relevant to the decision that it had to make, and it could not possibly be said to be unreasonable. Following the *Bradford* case, Auld J. considered that there was

"the obvious distinction between that case and this in that there the judge was concerned with the occupation by the applicant of a ship, when he was working as a seaman at sea, and of his matrimonial home when he was ashore. Here the case concerns two houses on dry land, but, apart from that distinction, there are a number of common factors. The most important of those are: that Mr Ward has security of tenure in his home in Hull, which he clearly does not have in his tied accommodation in Saudi Arabia, that the only home that he owns is the one in Hull; that he lives in the accommodation in Saudi Arabia, when he does, only because he works there; and that as in the *Bradford Metropolitan City Council* case, he spends longer away from his matrimonial home than he does in it."

Both the *Bradford* and *Ward* cases were followed in *R. v. West Somerset District Council, ex p. Fernandez*,[13] where the High Court ordered an entry

---

[11] 1992 S.L.T. 558.
[12] [1993] R.A. 71.
[13] Unreported, April 21, 1993, CO/1908/91.

which showed liability to a personal community charge to be altered to show liability to a standard community charge. In that case, the individual resided in New York, but also owned a property in Somerset in which she stayed for about one week each year. The Valuation and Community Charge Tribunal had held that this was her sole residence "in the United Kingdom". However, the court considered that there was no reason why those words should be added to a perfectly plain section of the Act. Following the *Bradford* and *Ward* cases, it was concluded that the individual's residence was in New York.

The *Bradford* case was also followed in dealing with the two residence family situation. In *Codner v. Wiltshire Valuation and Community Charge Tribunal*,[14] Laws J. refused to displace a finding of the tribunal that a barrister, whose wife and children lived in Wiltshire and whom he joined at weekends, has his primary residence in Wiltshire rather than a flat in London where he stayed for 70 per cent of his time in order to carry on his practice.

"Owner" is defined as the person with a "material interest"[15] in the whole **16–21** or any part of the dwelling, and which is not subject to an inferior material interest.[16]

In order to facilitate collection of the charges, joint and several liability is **16–22** provided for in two ways. First, where two or more persons fall into the same category for establishing liability they are jointly and severally liable.[17] Secondly, those married or living together as man and wife on any day are jointly and severally liable, provided that neither is under the age of 18.[18] Provision is made in regard to the death of a person liable.[19]

Special provision is made for caravans and boats.[20] Where a person resides **16–23** in the caravan or boat, as their sole or main residence, and is not the owner, then it is that person rather than the owner who is liable to pay the council tax, but where there is no person resident, or the owner is resident, then it is the owner who is liable to pay the council tax. Where two or more persons are thereby liable, either as joint owners or by having the caravan or boat as their sole or main residence, then they are jointly and severally liable.[21]

---

[14] [1994] R.V.R. 169. A similar finding was reached in *Cox v. London (South West) Valuation and Community Charge Tribunal and Poole Borough Council Community Charge Registration Officer* [1994] R.V.R. 171.

[15] Local Government Finance Act 1992, s.6(6) defines this as an interest which is freehold or leasehold granted for six months or more.

[16] *ibid.*, s.6(5).

[17] *ibid.*, s.6(3).

[18] *ibid.*, s.9.

[19] *ibid.*, s.18.

[20] *ibid.*, s.7.

[21] For the purposes of this section, a "caravan" is defined in accordance with Part I of the Caravan Sites and Development Act 1960. See also, for the purpose of the application of s.1 of the 1992 Act where the dwelling falls within more than one area, the definition of the "superficial extent" of a caravan or houseboat in the Council Tax (Situation and Valuation of Dwellings) Regulations 1992 (S.I. 1992 No. 550). Given the different nature of caravans and boats as opposed to other dwellings, the definition of owner in the 1992 Act has been modified to meet two special cases. Thus the "owner" is any person entitled to possession where there is a hire-purchase or conditional sale agreement or the person entitled to it apart from a bill of sale or mortgage.

The Secretary of State may, by reference to such factors as he sees fit, prescribe classes of chargeable dwellings, including pitches for caravans and moorings for boats, for which the billing authority will retain discretion to make the owner rather than the resident liable to pay the council tax.[22] The aim is to ensure that the owner pays the council tax, in situations like hostels, where the residents may be short term and difficult to trace. In this way the system is similar to, and replaces the collective community charge. The regulations have prescribed that the classes are nursing homes and other similar homes; houses of religious communities; houses in multiple occupation; residences of staff who live in houses occasionally occupied by an employer; and residences of ministers of religion. The Secretary of State may also prescribe classes of chargeable dwellings, including pitches for caravans and moorings for boats, for which the billing authority will retain discretion to make the owner rather than the resident liable to pay the council tax.[23] Where any class of chargeable dwelling has been so prescribed in regulation under this subsection and the authority decides to exercise the discretion, then the normal provisions for caravans or boats, are displaced and substituted by the provisions of section 8. Where the billing authority does decide to exercise that discretion in relation to a particular class, then it must be applied to the owners of all dwellings within that class there being no discretion to apply it within the class. Where two or more persons are liable by virtue of being owners of such dwellings then they are jointly and severally liable. The regulations may also make provision for determining who is to be considered as the owner of any dwelling in that class.

16–24 The liability for a particular dwelling is calculated on a daily basis according to the formula A/D, where A is the sum set by the billing authority for dwellings in that valuation band in that area, and D is the number of days in the financial year.[24] The amount set for the valuation band may be for the whole or part of the area, thus accommodating the setting of different amounts of council tax because of different precepts, or special expenses for different parts of the area. From this starting point, the amount may be reduced either by discounts or in accordance with regulations made by the Secretary of State.

16–25 Discounts are provided in two situations.[25] First, where there is only one resident who is not to be disregarded for the purposes of the tax. Secondly, where the property is unoccupied or where all the adults are to be disregarded. In the former case the discount is the "appropriate percentage", set at 25 per cent, and in the latter twice the "appropriate percentage",

[22] Local Government Finance Act 1992, s.8 and the Council Tax (Liability for Owners) Regulations 1992 (S.I. 1992 No. 551, as amended).
[23] ibid., s.8(2).
[24] ibid., s.10.
[25] ibid., s.11 and Sched. 1. See also the Council Tax (Discounts Disregards) Order 1992 (S.I. 1992 No. 548, as amended) and Council Tax (Additional Provisions for Discounts Disregards) Regulations 1992 (S.I. 1992 No. 552, as amended).

thus 50 per cent.[26] Discretion is given to Welsh authorities to vary the latter in regard to dwellings which are not the sole or main residence of any person, provided that the dwelling falls within a class prescribed by the Secretary of State for any financial year.[27] The determination must either reduce the discount from 50 per cent to 25 per cent or give no discount, and any such determination must be made by the authority,[28] and the determination must be publicised in a newspaper circulating locally. The classes of those to be disregarded, or "invisible", for the purposes of liability for the tax are[29]—persons in detention; the severely mentally impaired; persons in respect of whom child benefit is payable; students; hospital patients; patients in homes; care-workers; residents of hostels or similar accommodation for the homeless or itinerant; members of international headquarters and defence organisations; members of religious communities; and school leavers.

Provision is also made to allow the Secretary of State to make regulations for reduced amounts in regard to the liability of council taxpayers where the conditions specified in the regulations are met and for the purposes of transitional relief.[30] These regulations may apply irrespective of entitlement to any discounts. The Secretary of State may prescribe, by reference to such factors as he thinks fit, the conditions which permit the reduction and the amount of the reduction of council tax to which a taxpayer is liable. Among such factors are whether an application for reduction has been made; the community charge before the council tax was introduced; the circumstances of the taxpayer concerned; amounts relating to the authority concerned, provided that the amount is specified in a report which will be laid before the House of Commons; whether the dwelling is the sole or main residence of a disabled person; the circumstances of that person; and the physical characteristics or other matters, relating to that dwelling. The regulations may contain provisions for reviewing a decision of the billing authority in relation to the regulations, thus permitting some type of appeal system, but the Secretary of State may provide that such appeals should not be made to the valuation tribunal.[31] The Secretary of State may also amend any "social security instrument", either directly or indirectly in order to provide for a system of council tax benefit.[32]

[26] ibid., s.11(3). The Secretary of State may alter the "appropriate percentage" by means of order but, as required by s.11(4), such an order must be approved by the affirmative resolution procedure of the House of Commons.
[27] ibid., s.12 and Council Tax (Prescribed Class of Dwellings) (Wales) Regulations 1992 (S.I. 1992 No. 3023).
[28] ibid., s.67. In addition, the determination may not be questioned in any proceedings other than by an application for judicial review: s.66.
[29] ibid., Sched. 1, as amended.
[30] ibid., s.13.
[31] ibid. See also the Council Tax Benefit (General) Regulations 1992 (S.I. 1992 No. 1814, as amended), reg. 11, which provide for review by a review board appointed by the billing authority.
[32] ibid., s.13(9), and see the Social Security Contributions and Benefits Act 1992; the Social Security Administration Act 1992 and the Council Tax Benefit (General) Regulations 1992 (S.I. 1992 No. 1814, as amended).

E. APPEALS

16–26 Appeals may be made in relation to the council tax in a number of ways.[33] First, an appeal in regard to the alteration or proposed alteration of the valuation list.[34] Secondly, an appeal in relation to the imposition of a penalty for failure to comply with the provisions relating to the supply of information to the billing or levying authority.[35] Thirdly, an appeal against a completion notice.[36] Fourthly, an appeal under section 16 of the 1992 Act.

Section 16 of the 1992 Act establishes the right of appeal to a valuation tribunal[37] in three circumstances. First, if the person is not satisfied with the designation of a dwelling as a chargeable dwelling. Secondly, if the person is not satisfied with the decision of the billing authority that he is liable to pay council tax in respect of a chargeable dwelling. Thirdly, if the person is not satisfied with the decision of the billing authority as to any calculation or estimate of the amount of council tax to which he is liable. However, appeals on these matters may be prohibited if the grounds of appeal fall within categories prescribed by regulation.[38] In regard to these appeals, in order to try to resolve as many matters as possible without the need for an appeal, before the appeal can be made, the person aggrieved must, under section 16(4), serve a written notice on the billing authority stating the matter and grounds by which the person is aggrieved. One of three further conditions must also be met. Thus, having notified the authority, the person must remain dissatisfied after a written explanation from the authority as to why the grievance is not well founded; or remain dissatisfied after a written explanation of the steps which the authority proposes to take to meet the grievance; or have received no written notification of either result within two months commencing with the date of service of the written statement of the grievance.[39] To facilitate the speedy resolution of the matter, and to simplify the appeal procedure, the authority is also charged with the duty of considering the matters raised by such a notice and supplying reasons for their decision and any steps taken to deal with the grievance contained in the notice.[40]

16–27 The appeal to the valuation tribunal is initiated by serving on the clerk to the tribunal a notice of appeal containing the grounds of appeal,[41] or in regard to the valuation list by the listing officer referring the matter to the

---

[33] Valuation and Community Charge Tribunals Regulations 1989 (S.I. 1989 No. 439, as amended), reg. 34, and the Council Tax (Alteration of Lists and Appeals) Regulations 1993 (S.I. 1993 No. 290).

[34] Council Tax (Alteration of Lists and Appeals) Regulations 1993 (S.I. 1993 No. 290), regs. 8 and 13.

[35] Local Government Finance Act 1992, Sched. 3, para. 3(1).

[36] *ibid.*, s.17 and Sched. 4, para. 4.

[37] The valuation and community charge tribunal, as renamed by s.15 of the 1992 Act. For the composition and constitution of the tribunal see § 15–17.

[38] Valuation and Community Charge Tribunals Regulations 1989 (S.I. 1989 No. 439, as amended), reg. 35.

[39] Local Government Finance Act, s.16(7).

[40] *ibid.*, s.16(8).

[41] Valuation and Community Charge Tribunals Regulations 1989 (S.I. 1989 No. 439, as amended), reg. 37.

tribunal.[42] An appeal in regard to the imposition of a penalty is to be dealt with by the tribunal whose area of jurisdiction includes the area of the billing authority concerned, but for all other appeals by the tribunal whose area includes the dwelling to which the appeal relates.[43]

Different time-limits within which the appeal may be made operate in regard to different types of appeal.[44] For appeals in regard to the valuation list, the listing officer must refer the matter within four weeks in regard to an invalidity notice and within six months of the service of the proposal in other appeals. Where, in an appeal under section 16, the person remains dissatisfied after either a written explanation from the authority as to why the grievance is not well founded, or after a written explanation of the steps which the authority proposes to take to meet the grievance, the appeal must be pursued before the valuation tribunal within two months of the date of service of the billing authority's notification. Where, in an appeal under section 16, the authority does not notify the person of their decision within two months of his notice under section 16(4), the appeal must be pursued within four months of the date of service of the notice under section 16(4). An appeal in regard to the imposition of a penalty must be pursued within two months of the later of either April 1, 1993, or the date of service of the notice of the imposition of the penalty. An appeal in regard to a completion notice must be pursued within two months of later of either April 1, 1993, or the date of service of the notice.

An appeal may be withdrawn,[45] proceed to full hearing, or be dealt with by **16–28** written representations. It is also possible for the parties to agree to have the matter referred to arbitration, the arbitrator having the same power to make an order as the tribunal.[46] For written representations to be the method, all parties must agree in writing.[47] Then the clerk must serve a notice of the procedure on each party, and within four weeks of this notice each party may serve on the clerk a notice containing either the reasons for the disagreement leading to the appeal or a statement that no further representations will be made.[48] Following the supply of these statements to the other parties, there is a period of four weeks during which the parties may serve a further notice stating either the reply to the other party or that no further representations will be made, and the clerk must also send a copy of any such statement to the other parties.[49] After the expiry of that four week period, the clerk must

[42] Council Tax (Alteration of Lists and Appeals) Regulations 1992 (S.I. 1993 No. 290), regs. 8 and 13.
[43] Valuation and Community Charge Tribunals Regulations 1989 (S.I. 1989 No. 439, as amended), reg. 35. Where an appeal involves more than one billing authority the appellant may elect the appropriate tribunal Council Tax (Alteration of Lists and Appeals) Regulations 1993 (S.I. 1993 No. 290), reg. 3.
[44] *ibid.*, reg. 36 (although for each, the president of the tribunal may waive the limit if he is satisfied that the failure to appeal was beyond the control of the person aggrieved, reg. 36(5) and regs. 8 and 13 respectively).
[45] *ibid.*, regs. 39 and 19 respectively.
[46] *ibid.*, regs. 52 and 33 respectively. Section 31 of the Arbitration Act 1950 applies.
[47] *ibid.*, regs. 40(1) and 20(1) respectively.
[48] *ibid.*, regs. 40(2) and 20(2) respectively.
[49] *ibid.*, regs. 40(3)–(4) and 20(3)–(4) respectively.

submit any information and notices to the tribunal, which has the power to require the parties to supply further particulars, which are to be served on the other parties, or to order a full hearing.[50]

16–29 In the event of a full hearing, the clerk must give the parties four weeks notice of the date, time and place of the hearing and advertise this by a conspicuous notice at the offices of the tribunal, outside the office of the billing authority, or some other place within the authority's area.[51] Any party may appear in person or be represented.[52] The tribunal, while normally consisting of three members including the chairman, may be composed of any two members with the consent of all parties, and the hearing shall take place in public unless the tribunal accepts the application of a party that the interests of that party would be prejudicially affected.[53] If the appellant or, for an appeal relating to valuation list, if every party other than the listing officer fails to appear the tribunal may dismiss the appeal, and if any party fails to appear the tribunal may determine the appeal in their absence.[54] The tribunal is given the power to administer an oath; to hear and examine parties and witnesses in such order as the tribunal decides, except in regard to an appeal concerning the valuation list where the listing officer must begin the hearing; to adjourn for such time, to such place, and on such terms as the tribunal determines, provided notice is given to every party; and to inspect any dwelling which is the subject of the appeal.[55] Otherwise, the procedure is for the tribunal to determine as being most suitable to the clarification of the issues and the just handling of the proceedings, while seeking to avoid formality and not being subject to the strict rules of evidence.[56] Information is admissible provided that not less than two weeks notice of the details of the information and the dwelling or person has been given to every other party, and any person who has given 24 hours notice is allowed to inspect it and make a copy of, or extract from, a document or, if not a document, a print-out, photographic image or other reproduction which has been obtained from the storage medium.[57] The contents of a list or a completion notice may be proved by a copy certified to be a true copy by the listing officer or proper officer of the billing authority respectively.[58]

16–30 The decision of the tribunal may be by majority, but in the event of a tribunal of two failing to agree the matter must be remitted for decision by a tribunal consisting of different members.[59] The decision on a hearing may be reserved or given orally and, in either event and for written representations,

---

[50] *ibid.*, regs. 40(5)–(7) and 20(5)–(7) respectively.
[51] *ibid.*, regs. 41 and 22 respectively, and in regard to appeals concerning the valuation list, the chairman may, at the request of a party or at his own discretion, order a pre-hearing review, giving not less than four weeks notice: reg. 23.
[52] *ibid.*, regs. 43 and 24 respectively.
[53] *ibid.*, regs. 44(1)–(3) and 25(1)–(3) respectively.
[54] *ibid.*, regs. 44(4) and 25(4)–(5).
[55] *ibid.*, regs. 44(5)–(8) and 25(6)–(10) respectively.
[56] *ibid.*, regs. 44(9) and 25(12) respectively.
[57] *ibid.*, regs. 45 and 26 respectively.
[58] *ibid.*, regs. 46 and 27 respectively.
[59] *ibid.*, regs. 47(1) and 28(1) respectively.

it must be communicated or confirmed in writing to the parties as soon as reasonably practicable together with a statement of the reasons for the decision.[60] In consequence of that decision, the tribunal may order an estimate to be quashed or altered; a penalty to be quashed; the decision of a billing authority to be reversed; a calculation (other than an estimate) of an amount to be quashed and the amount to be recalculated; or a list to be altered.[61]

The decision of the tribunal can, on written application by a party within **16–31** four weeks of the notice being given, be reviewed or set aside by itself, and it is provided that as far as possible this is to be done by the same members who took the original decision. The decision may be reviewed or set aside on the grounds that the decision was wrongly made as a result of a clerical error; a party did not appear and can show reasonable cause why he did not do so; that the decision is affected by a decision of, or appeal from, the High Court or Lands Tribunal in relation an appeal in respect of the dwelling or person concerned; and, in the case of a completion notice, that new evidence, which could not have been ascertained by reasonably diligent inquiry or could not be foreseen, has become available since the decision.[62]

The clerk is responsible for recording the decision, sending a copy to the parties, and retaining a copy for a period of six years. In addition, any person may inspect the record of any decision of the tribunal, it being an offence for the keeper of the record to obstruct such inspection without reasonable excuse.[63]

An appeal may be made by any party to the appeal, within four weeks of the original decision or order or review decision or order, to the High Court on a question of law, and the High Court may confirm, vary, set aside, revoke or remit the decision, and make any order the tribunal could have made.[64]

F. COLLECTION AND ENFORCEMENT

No payment in respect of council tax charge is necessary until a demand **16–32** notice has been served on the person chargeable but, once served, the notice places an obligation on the person to pay in a specified manner, failing which the authority may, after the service of a further notice, seek a liability order in the magistrates' court.[65] The demand notice is to be served as soon as practicable after the setting of the amount of council tax for the relevant year for the category of dwellings within which the chargeable dwelling falls, and

---

[60] *ibid.*, regs. 47(2)–(5) and 28(2)–(4) respectively.
[61] *ibid.*, regs. 48 and reg. 29 respectively. Any such order may also require any matter ancillary to its subject-matter to be attended to.
[62] *ibid.*, regs. 49 and 30 respectively.
[63] *ibid.*, regs. 50 and 31 respectively.
[64] *ibid.*, regs. 51 and 32 respectively. It is likely that the period cannot be extended by applying the principles applicable to dismissal of an action for want of prosecution, since the Court of Appeal considered that this should not apply to an appeal from a statutory tribunal in a public law context: *Regalbourne v. East Lindsey District Council* [1994] R.A. 1.
[65] Local Government Finance Act 1992, s.14, Scheds. 2 and 4, and the Council Tax (Administration and Enforcement) Regulations 1992 (S.I. 1992 No. 613, as amended).

at least 14 days before the first instalment of payment is due.[66] Thus the demand notice is really an estimate of the liability for the whole financial year, and the sum demanded will have to be altered, and a fresh demand notice issued, if the assumptions or relevant circumstances of the taxpayer change during that year.[67] Unless the taxpayer has agreed a different method of payment with the authority, the normal method of payment is by equal monthly instalments.[68] Where the notice postdates the liability, the full amount is due on the expiry of a period of not less than 14 days.[69] If the taxpayer continues to fail to pay an instalment seven days after a reminder notice has been served, then the balance of the complete estimated liability for the financial year becomes payable within a further seven days and, if after paying in accordance with the reminder notice, the liable person fails to pay any subsequent payment, the balance of the complete estimated liability for the financial year becomes payable immediately.[70] There is also provision for discounts to be offered to taxpayers where there are lump sum or non-cash payments.[71] Penalties imposed under Schedule 3 for failure to comply with the provisions relating to the supply of information to the billing or levying authority may be collected either as if it were part of the liability for council tax or by the service of a separate notice requiring payment not less than 14 days after the issue of the notice.[72]

16–33 To recover unpaid sums, the authority must first serve a final notice, in addition to the reminder notice, stating every amount in regard to which the authority will make an application for a liability order.[73] If the amount outstanding remains wholly or partly unpaid after seven days from the issue of that notice, the billing authority may apply for a liability order from the magistrates' court, the application having to be made within six years from the day on which the sum became due.[74] Unless a stipendiary magistrate is authorised by another enactment, the application should be heard by at least two justices.[75] A statement, contained in a document of record compiled by the authority, is admissible as evidence of any fact stated in it of which direct

[66] Council Tax (Administration and Enforcement) Regulations 1992 (S.I. 1992 No. 613 as amended), reg. 19.
[67] ibid., reg. 20.
[68] ibid., reg. 21 and Sched. 1. The number of instalments is to be the number of complete months left in the financial year, up to a maximum of 10.
[69] ibid., reg. 21(7).
[70] ibid., reg. 23.
[71] ibid., regs. 25 and 26.
[72] ibid., reg. 29.
[73] ibid., reg. 33.
[74] ibid., reg. 34.
[75] ibid., reg. 53(2). A summons must be served on the person against whom proceedings are brought: regs. 34(2) and 35(2). *R. v. Leicester JJ. and Leicester City Council, ex p. Barrow and Barrow* [1991] 3 All E.R. 935 determined that, at the equivalent hearing in regard to the community charge, the unrepresented chargepayer has the right to be accompanied by a friend, assistant or adviser (known as a "McKenzie friend", *McKenzie v. McKenzie* [1970] 3 All E.R. 1034), provided that the assistant is not disruptive or disorderly. See also *R. v. Highbury Corner Magistrates' Court, ex p. Watkins* [1993] R.A. 300. In *R. v. Burnley JJ., ex p. Ashworth* [1992] R.V.R. 27 the High Court rejected an argument that the justices were under a duty to investigate the evidence more fully where the chargepayer was unrepresented.

oral evidence would be admissible, and a certificate made in respect of such a document of record produced by a computer and purported to be signed by a person occupying a responsible position in relation to the operation of the computer, shall be admissible as evidence of anything which is stated in it to the best of his information and belief.[76] If the magistrates are satisfied that the sum has become payable by the defendant and has not been paid then they must make the order for the aggregate of the sums due together with the reasonable costs of the applicant in obtaining the order, these costs also being due in the event of the taxpayer paying after the order was applied for, but before it is made.[77] A liability order may deal with one or more persons and one or more amount.[78]

Once the liability order is obtained, the person against whom an order is **16–34** made is under a further duty to supply the following information within 14 days of it being requested, in writing, by the authority:

   (a) the name and address of the debtor's employer;
   (b) the earnings or expected earnings of the debtor;
   (c) deductions or expected deductions from earnings and other attach-
       ment of earnings orders;
   (d) the debtor's work or identity number in employment;
   (e) other sources of income of the debtor;
   (f) whether anyone else is jointly or severally liable for the debt.[79]

Failure to comply without reasonable excuse, or to provide false information knowingly or recklessly, is an offence.[80]

The authority can enforce the order through either an attachment of earnings order, attachment of allowances orders in the case of elected members, distress, a winding-up petition or charging order. While only one method may be resorted to at any one time, it is possible for the authority to alternate if one proves unsuccessful, or resort to each method more than once.[81]

The authority may make an attachment of earnings order by serving a **16–35** copy in the specified form on the employer.[82] The employer is under a duty to comply with the order and make deductions in accordance with the attachment of earnings order and the regulations.[83] The employer must notify the employee of the total deductions to date each time a deduction is made and inform the authority if the debtor is not in his employment, within 14 days of the service of the order or the end of the employment, and any

---

[76] *ibid.*, reg. 53(4)–(6).
[77] *ibid.*, reg. 34(6)–(8).
[78] *ibid.*, reg. 35(1).
[79] *ibid.*, reg. 36. The regulations make special provision in relation to those jointly or severally liable for the debt: reg. 54, as amended.
[80] *ibid.*, reg. 56.
[81] *ibid.*, as amended.
[82] *ibid.*, reg. 37 and Sched. 3. Special provision is made for persons employed under the Crown: reg. 43.
[83] *ibid.*, regs. 37(3) and 38.

new employer who employs a person and knows that such an order is in force must also notify the authority within 14 days of the person becoming an employee.[84] Failure to notify the employee without reasonable excuse, or to provide false information knowingly or recklessly, is an offence.[85] The debtor is under a duty to inform the authority of any change of employment, within 14 days of that change, together with other relevant information as to the name and address of the debtor's new employer; the earnings or expected earnings of the debtor; deductions or expected deductions from earnings; and the debtor's work or identity number in employment.[86] Failure to comply without reasonable excuse, or to provide false information knowingly or recklessly, is an offence.[87] Provision is made for priority between attachment of earnings orders,[88] and for attachment of allowances orders in the case of elected members.[89]

16–36   The liability order may also be enforced by distress,[90] against which appeal to the magistrates' court lies on the ground that the levy was irregular.[91] A distress shall not be deemed unlawful because of any defect or want of form in the liability order and the person making the distress will not be deemed a trespasser on that account, but a person sustaining special damage by reason of a subsequent irregularity may recover special damages by proceedings in trespass.[92] Where the court finds the levy to be irregular, it may order the goods to be returned if in the possession of the authority or, if not, order compensation equal to the amount which would be awarded by way of special damage in an action in trespass.[93] If the value of the goods obtained is insufficient,[94] irrespective of the reason for the failure of the attempt to levy, the authority may apply to the magistrates' court for the issue of a warrant to commit the debtor to prison, and the court must be satisfied, as a result of its inquiries in the debtor's presence, that the failure to pay the liability order was due to wilful refusal or culpable neglect before the warrant had been issued.[95] The warrant may be for commitment for up to three months, or it may be postponed on such conditions as the court thinks fit, and part payment reduces the term proportionately. Where an application for a warrant has been made, and the after having determined whether the failure

[84] *ibid.*, reg. 39.
[85] *ibid.*, reg. 56.
[86] *ibid.*, reg. 40.
[87] *ibid.*, regs. 36 and 56.
[88] *ibid.*, reg. 42.
[89] *ibid.*, reg. 44.
[90] *ibid.*, reg. 45. The sum to be recovered includes the administrative cost of the distress, and this must be paid if the sum is settled before the sale of the goods, but not if the sum is settled before the goods are seized.
[91] *ibid.*, reg. 46. It has been held that a bailiff, who was unable to gain lawful entry, did not levy effective distraint on a debtor's goods by posting a written notice of distraint through the letterbox: *Evans v. South Ribble Borough Council* [1992] 1 Q.B. 757.
[92] *ibid.*, reg. 45(7).
[93] *ibid.*, reg. 46(3).
[94] *ibid.*, as amended, provides that goods which satisfy the basic domestic needs of the debtor's family cannot be seized.
[95] *ibid.*, reg. 47.

was due to wilful refusal or culpable neglect and having decided not to issue a warrant or fix a term of imprisonment, the court may remit all or part of the sum owing, that is the total of the council tax liability together with the administrative costs of the distress.[96]

The courts have developed similar principles concerning imprisonment in regard to the recovery of community charge, council tax and rates. While there appeared to be inconsistency in "the stream of decisions by judges at first instance"[97] regarding the community charge, the position now appears to be clarified. **16–37**

The confusion had arisen because in *R. v. Faversham and Sittingbourne JJ., ex p. Ursell*[98] it had been suggested that the sole consideration was the recovery of unpaid sums, to the exclusion of a punitive element.[99] Similarly in *R. v. Alfreton Magistrates, ex p. Gratton*,[1] MacPherson J. considered that a number of decisions show that "community charge liability should only be visited with prison (if I may use that shorthand expression) if there is no other way in which the money can be extracted". However, it is clear that, while the primary purpose may be recovery of the debt, the punitive element is not irrelevant.

The starting point for analysis is the case of *Re Smith (a Bankrupt)*, a case concerning equivalent powers under the General Rate Act 1967,[2] where Lord Jauncey said:

> "Two matters emerge ... namely: (1) that the issue of a warrant cannot be viewed in isolation but must be considered as part of the whole procedure for recovery of unpaid rates by way of distress and, (2) that although there may be a punitive element present in the power to issue a warrant of commitment, the predominant purpose is to coerce the defaulting ratepayer into making payment."[3]

In *R. v. Felixstowe, Ipswich and Woodbridge Magistrates' Court and Ipswich Borough Council, ex p. Herridge*,[4] Stuart-Smith L.J. concluded that "the predominant purpose is not the same as the sole purpose and I would with respect disagree with Schiemann J. who in the case of *R. v. Faversham and Sittingbourne JJ., ex p. Ursell*[4a] said that it was the sole purpose". He considered that where a suspended committal order was made, if the court could not commit the debtor where there has been a breach of conditions then a suspended order would be totally emasculated. Thus, he could not accept that such orders would frustrate the purposes of the legislation. Provided that the magistrates took into consideration the predominant

---

[96] *ibid.*, reg. 48(2).
[97] *per* Brooke J. in *R. v. Leicester Justices, ex p. Deary*, unreported, June 7, 1994, CO/3154/93.
[98] [1992] R.A. 99.
[99] *R. v. Northampton Magistrates' Court, ex p. Newell* [1992] R.A. 283. See also *R. v. Poole Magistrates, ex p. Benham* [1991] R.V.R. 217.
[1] *The Times*, December 7, 1993, CO/484/93.
[2] Sections 102 and 103 of the General Rate Act 1967.
[3] [1990] R.A. 1, at p. 7.
[4] [1993] R.A. 83.
[4a] [1992] R.A. 99 at p. 106.

purpose of obtaining payment, they were entitled to find that the debtor would not pay. Such a finding would be displaced by the court only on *Wednesbury* grounds.[5] This last point is illustrated clearly by the statement of Potts J. that while he would have been disposed to order smaller weekly payments, he was unable to say that the magistrates acted perversely.

This approach was confirmed by the Court of Appeal in *R. v. Cannock JJ., ex p. Ireland*,[6] in which Henry L.J. considered that all the authorities were consistent. Thus, subject to the principle that imprisonment is possible, the previous cases remain valid.

16–38 *R. v. Faversham and Sittingbourne Justices, ex p. Ursell*[7] and *R. v. Northampton Magistrates' Court, ex p. Newell*[8] decided that, when a term of imprisonment had been fixed for wilful refusal to pay the community charge but had been postponed on condition of future payments, there should be a further hearing, notice of which should be given to the defaulter. Since the circumstances of the defaulter may have changed, an opportunity to examine this has to be provided. However, if that person does not appear in court the justices are not thereby inhibited from committing to prison. In terms of the circumstances to be taken into account in deciding whether to commit to prison, the primary factor is whether the person has the means to pay. This was confirmed in *R. v. Poole Magistrates, ex p. Benham*,[9] where the decision of the magistrates to commit to prison someone who had no assets or income during the relevant period was quashed. The High Court was of the opinion that it was incumbent upon the magistrates to consider the alternatives to immediate commitment to prison. The committal proceedings are more than a simple means inquiry. Thus, although the issue of the liability to pay cannot be reopened at this stage, all other matters have to be proved and are susceptible to cross-examination.[10] In *Benham*, the magistrates had considered that the debtor was guilty of culpable neglect in that he had the potential to earn money but was not in employment, but Potts J. took the view that this course was not open to the justices in the absence of clear evidence that gainful employment had been available but refused by the debtor. Where such evidence did exist, he was of the opinion that in "certain circumstances a failure on the part of the debtor to work and put himself in funds to pay the community charge might constitute culpable neglect".

In *R. v. Felixstowe, Ipswich and Woodbridge Magistrates' Court and Ipswich Borough Council, ex p. Herridge*,[11] an order of 30 days' imprisonment was imposed, but the warrant postponed indefinitely on condition that the applicant paid £10.00 per week until his debt was discharged. He then became voluntarily unemployed and offered to pay £2.00 per week, but the

---

[5] *Associated Provincial Picture Houses v. Wednesbury Corporation* [1948] 1 K.B. 223. This follows the approach adopted by Tucker J. in *R. v. Thanet District Council, ex p. Haddow* [1992] R.A. 245.
[6] Unreported, November 21, 1995.
[7] [1992] R.A. 99.
[8] [1992] R.A. 283.
[9] [1991] R.V.R. 217.
[10] *R. v. Highbury Corner Magistrates' Court, ex p. Watkins* [1993] R.A. 300. See also *R. v. Wolverhampton Stipendiary Magistrate, ex p. Mould* [1992] R.A. 309.
[11] [1993] R.A. 83.

authority applied for the issue of the warrant. This was granted for 25 days imprisonment, taking account of the sums paid since the original hearing. The applicant argued that the magistrates failed to consider whether there was any alternative remedy available to the charging authority which it would have been reasonable and practicable for them to pursue and which would have resulted in the eventual collection of the outstanding relevant sum, rather than in the effective extinguishment of the remaining debt by a commitment to prison. On the first point, Stuart-Smith L.J., citing *R. v. Birmingham Magistrates' Court, ex p. Mansell*,[12] found that "it is quite clear that it is not necessary for the magistrates in every case to inquire whether there is an alternative procedure whereby the enforcement of the debt may be obtained".

In *R. v. Alfreton Magistrates, ex p. Gratton*,[13] the magistrates, who according to MacPherson J. "were quite obviously upset by the conduct of the applicant", who may well have been "somewhat supercilious and silly about the proceedings", erred by deciding not to consider payment because the applicant was already paying £10 of his £30 income support on unpaid fines. MacPherson J. found that the "cases show that this is something which ought always to be considered, even if in certain circumstances it may ultimately be rejected". He also added that

> "Prison is not to be used as a big stick or primarily as punishment but as a means of extracting the liability. For example, a prison sentence can be postponed pending payment of so much off the arrears. The object of the exercise is to collect the money from those who chose wilfully not to pay it and thus piled the liability onto their fellow community charge payers, rather than simply to throw them in prison and not extract the money. If the full sentence is served, the liability is of course extinguished."

Some other principles must be followed. In *R. v. Highbury Corner* **16–39** *Magistrates' Court, ex p. Uchendu*,[14] Laws J. found that in considering imprisonment, the court must observe the principle of proportionality in the sense that the term of imprisonment should increase with the seriousness of the case, and he expressed the opinion that failure to pay through culpable neglect was less serious than failure through wilful refusal. In determining which is the cause, the justices are required to hold an inquiry. In *R. v. Hendon Magistrates' Court, ex p. Swansea*,[15] Owen J. found that: "the word 'inquiry' connotes more than merely allowing a debtor to speak if he wishes to speak. It must involve asking such questions as will enable a decision properly to be made as to whether the further non-payment has been due to wilful refusal or culpable neglect."

Once the justices have so decided, they must state which has been found and their reasons for so doing. In *R. v. Northavon Magistrates, ex p. Clark*,[16] Latham J. quashed a committal where this was not done, stating

[12] [1988] R.V.R. 112.
[13] *The Times*, December 7, 1993, CO/484/93.
[14] [1994] R.A. 51.
[15] Unreported, March 16, 1994, CO/2941/92.
[16] Unreported, March 21, 1994, CO/1841/92.

"it seems to me that it does behove Magistrates when there is a challenge of this sort, to indicate on what basis they have come to the conclusion, which is the precondition of their imposing imprisonment on a person such as the applicant, that the applicant has been guilty of wilful refusal or culpable neglect. If they do not do so, then it seems to me that the court is entitled to infer that they have not applied their minds properly to the relevant considerations."

Applying their minds properly to the considerations involves applying a burden of proof "of a high standard, not simply the ordinary civil standard of balance of probability".[17]

There is no application of the common law privilege against self-incrimination as to means in these proceedings.[18]

16–40 Matters can be brought to court through either a case stated or by means of judicial review. Such challenges should be made by means of the former procedure to avoid the possibility of the court having wholly inadequate material on which to decide the question.[19] However, there has also been confusion over whether it was possible to obtain bail under the former procedure. As a result of a number of cases,[20] it was thought that because it was essentially a civil matter, an application for bail could not be made until the stated case had been made and lodged with the High Court. In these circumstances, an application for judicial review, while in principle undesirable, was thought to be in practice necessary. However, in *R. v. Wolverhampton Justices, ex p. Bastable* Buxton J. has held that any such fear was ill-founded since section 113 of the Magistrates Courts' Act provided that, when an application had been made to magistrates to state a case, they had jurisdiction to grant bail.[21]

16–41 The amount due may also be deemed a debt for the purpose of bankruptcy proceedings against an individual or a company.[22] The authority may also seek a charging order if at least £1,000 of the liability order remains outstanding.[23] In exercising the discretion whether to make such an order, the magistrates' court must pay particular attention to the personal circumstances of the debtor and whether any other person would be unduly prejudiced, and the order may be made subject to such conditions as the court thinks fit in regard to the time when the charge is to become enforceable or as to other matters.[24] Where the liability of the company is not

---

[17] Carnwath J. in *R. v. Kingston-Upon-Hull JJ., ex p. Broom*, unreported, November 15, 1995, following Sedley J. in *R. v. South Tyneside JJ., ex p. Martin, The Independent*, September 20, 1995. This decision of Sedley J. was also followed by Laws J. in *R. v. Mid-Hertfordshire Justices, ex p. Cox*, October 19, 1995, CO/3584/94.

[18] *R. v. Highbury Corner Magistrates' Court, ex p. Watkins* [1993] R.A. 300. It was considered that this privilege applied only to criminal proceedings and the proceedings under reg. 41 were civil proceedings for the recovery of tax.

[19] See *e.g. R. v. Ealing JJ., ex p. Cloves* [1991] R.V.R. 169; *R. v. Oldbury JJ. and Sandwell M.B.C., ex p. Smith* [1995] R.V.R. 7; and *R. v. Wolverhampton JJ., ex p. Bastable* [1995] R.V.R. 215.

[20] See *e.g. R. v. Poole Magistrates, ex p. Benham* [1991] R.V.R. 217.

[21] [1995] R.V.R. 215.

[22] Council Tax (Administration and Enforcement) Regulations 1992 (S.I. 1992 No. 613), reg. 49. See also *Preston Borough Council v. Riley and Riley* [1995] R.A. 227.

[23] *ibid.*, reg. 50.

[24] *ibid.*, reg. 51.

provable as a debt in liquidation, being neither a liability to which the company was liable at the time of liquidation nor one to which it became subject after that date by virtue of an obligation incurred before that date, the debt cannot be recovered as a liquidation expense.[25]

Overpayment of council tax is corrected by either repayment if the taxpayer so requires, or by repayment or credit against any future liability to pay council tax at the discretion of the authority.[26]

---

[25] *In re Kentish Homes* (1993) 91 L.G.R. 592.

[26] *ibid.*, regs. 24, 21 and 31. Where charges are paid under a mistake of fact or of law, they are recoverable at common law: *Tower Hamlets London Borough Council v. Chetnick Developments* [1988] 1 All E.R. 961; and *Woolwich Building Society v. Inland Revenue Commissioners (No. 2)* [1992] 3 All E.R. 737.

APPENDIX A

ALLOCATION OF PRINCIPAL FUNCTIONS

A. METROPOLITAN AREAS

All principal local government functions are exercised by metropolitan **A–01** district councils except the following:

Fire
Civil Defence (a) ⎱ Metropolitan fire and civil defence authorities
Passenger Transport Metropolitan passenger transport authorities

Waste disposal Greater Manchester and Merseyside Waste Disposal Authorities (b)

Notes

(a) Principal responsibilities lie on metropolitan district councils but the authority may carry out its functions by agreement and provide assistance.

(b) Waste disposal functions in Wigan are exercised by the district council and not the Greater Manchester Waste Disposal Authority.

B. NON-METROPOLITAN AREAS IN ENGLAND[1]

All principal local authorities are exercised by unitary authorities within **A–02** their areas. Otherwise, the position is as follows:

Non-metropolitan County Councils	*Non-metropolitan District Councils*
Education	
Youth Employment	
Personal Social Services	
Libraries	
Museums and art galleries (a)	Museums and art galleries (a)
Housing—	Housing—
Certain reserve powers	Provision
	Management
	Slum clearance
Civil defence (c)	House and area improvement
Planning—	Planning—
Structure plans	Local plans
Development control (d)	Development control (d)
	Advertisement control
Derelict land (a)	Derelict land (a)
Country parks (a)	Country parks (a)

455

Non-metropolitan County Councils	Non-metropolitan District Councils
Conservation areas (a)	Conservation areas (a)
Building preservation notices (a)	Building preservation notices (a)
	Listed building control
Tree preservation (a)	Tree preservation (a)
Acquisition and disposal of land for planning purposes, development or redevelopment (a)	Acquisition and disposal of land for planning purposes, development or redevelopment (a)
Footpaths and bridleways—	Footpaths and bridleways—
Surveys	
Creation, diversion and extinguishment orders (a)	Creation, diversion and extinguishment orders (a)
Maintenance (e)	
Protection (a)	Protection (a)
Signposting	
Transportation—	Transportation—
Highways (e)	
Traffic	
All parking (a)	Off-street parking (a)
Public transport (a) (g)	Public transport (a) (g)
	Public transport undertakings (h)
Road safety	
Highway lighting	
Footway lighting (a)	Footway lighting (a)
Environmental health—	Environmental health—
Animal diseases	Food safety and hygiene
	Communicable disease
	Slaughterhouses
	Offices, shops and railway premises (j)
	Factories
	Home safety
	Water and sewerage (k)
Refuse disposal	Refuse collection
Consumer protection (e.g. weights and measures, trade descriptions, explosives, food)	Clean air
	Building regulations
	Coast protection
	Cemeteries and crematoria
	Markets and fairs
Fire (l)	By-laws
Swimming baths (a)	Swimming baths (a)
Physical training and recreation (a)	Physical training and recreation (a)
Parks and open spaces (a)	Parks and open spaces (a)
Smallholdings	Allotments
	Local licensing
	Airports (a)
Local lotteries (a)	Local lotteries (a)

[1] This table was originally based on the table in DoE Circular 121/72.

Notes

(a) Concurrent powers exercisable by county and district councils.

456

(c) Non-metropolitan district councils may supply information and provide assistance.
(d) Primarily a district council function except in the case of "county matters".
(e) District councils may claim maintenance powers for footpaths, bridleways, and urban roads which are neither trunk roads nor classified roads.
(g) Co-ordination.
(h) Non-metropolitan district councils under local Act powers. Most bus undertakings have been transferred to public transport companies.
(j) Fire precautions under the Fire Precautions Act 1971 are a county council responsibility.
(k) Through agency.
(l) Subject to amalgamation schemes.

Local authorities have power under section 101 of the Local Government Act 1972 to arrange for the discharge of their functions by any other authority.

Powers may be vested in joint boards under various Acts and the provisions of the Local Government Act 1972 may be applied to such boards under section 241 of the Act.

Local authorities may acquire power to undertake other functions by means of local Acts.

C. WALES A–03

All principal local government functions are exercised by the unitary county and county borough councils.

APPENDIX B

PRINCIPAL POWERS AND DUTIES OF PARISH AND COMMUNITY COUNCILS

Function	Powers and Duties	Statutory Provisions	**B–01**
Allotments	Power to provide allotments. Duty to provide allotment gardens if demand unsatisfied	Small Holdings and Allotments Act 1908, ss.23–33	
Baths and washhouses	Power to provide public baths, washhouses and bathing places	Public Health Act 1936, ss.221, 222, 223 and 227	
Burial grounds, cemeteries and crematoria	Power to provide	Local Government Act 1972, ss.214 and 215. Parish Councils and Burial Authorities (Miscellaneous Provisions) Act 1970, s.1	
Bus shelters	Power to provide and maintain shelters	Local Government (Miscellaneous Provisions) Act 1953, s.4	
By-laws	Power to make by-laws in regard to— Pleasure grounds, etc.	Public Health Act 1875, s.164, Public Health Acts Amendment Act 1890, s.45. Local Government Act 1894, s.8	
	Cycle parks	Road Traffic Regulation Act 1984, s.57	
	Baths and washhouses	Public Health Act 1936, s 223; Local Government Act 1972, s.270 and Sched. 14, para. 18	
	Open spaces	Open Spaces Act 1906, s.15	
	Mortuaries and post-mortem rooms	Public Health Act 1936, s.198	
Clocks	Power to provide public clocks	Parish Councils Act 1957, s.2	
Closed churchyards	Powers as to maintenance	Local Government Act 1972, s.215	
Commons and common pastures	Powers in relation to inclosure and as to regulation and management	Inclosure Act 1845. Local Government Act 1894, s.8(4). Smallholdings and Allotments Act 1908, s.34	

459

Function	Powers and Duties	Statutory Provisions
Conference facilities	Power to provide and encourage the use of facilities	Local Government Act 1972, s.144
Community centres	Power to provide and equip buildings for use of clubs having athletic, social or educational objects	Local Government (Miscellaneous Provisions) Act 1976, s.19
Drainage	Power to deal with ponds and ditches	Public Health Act 1936, s.260
Education	Right to appoint school governor	Education (No. 2) Act 1986, s.7
Entertainment and the arts	Provision of entertainment and the support of the arts	Local Government Act 1972, ss.144 and 145
Gifts	Power to accept	Local Government Act 1972, s.139
Highways	Power to repair and maintain footpaths and bridle-ways	Highways Act 1980, ss.30, 43 and 50
	Power to light roads and public places	Parish Councils Act 1957, s.3. Highways Act 1980, s.301
	Provision of litter bins	Litter Act 1983, ss.5, 6
	Power to provide parking places for bicycles, motor-cycles and other vehicles	Road Traffic Regulation Act 1984, ss.57–60
	Power to acquire rights of way	Highways Act 1980, ss.30, 72
	Power to provide roadside seats and shelters, and omnibus shelters	Parish Councils Act 1957, s.1. Local Government (Miscellaneous Provisions) Act 1953, s.4
	Consent of parish council required for stopping up or diversion of highway	Highways Act 1980, ss.47, 116
	Power to complain to district council as to maintenance of highways or protection of rights of way and roadside wastes	Highways Act 1980, s.130
	Power to provide traffic signs and other notices	Road Traffic Regulation Act 1984, s.72
	Power as to roadside verges	Highways Act 1980, s.96
	Right to be notified of order requiring operator to provide tunnel or bridge for footpath or bridleway over railway	Transport and Works Act 1992, s.48

Function	Powers and Duties	Statutory Provisions
Investments	Power to participate in schemes of collective investment	Trustee Investments Act 1961, s.11
Land	Acquisition	Local Government Act 1972, ss.124–127
	Rights of way over land (other than highways)	Local Government Act 1894, s.8(1)(g)
Litter	Provision of receptacles	Litter Act 1983, ss.5, 6
Lotteries	Power to promote	Lotteries and Amusements Act 1976, s.7
Mortuaries and post-mortem rooms	Power to provide mortuaries and post-mortem rooms	Public Health Act 1936, s.198
National Park	Duty of Secretary of State to appoint parish members of National Park authorities	Environment Act 1995, Sched. 7
Nuisances	Power to deal with offensive ditches	Public Health Act 1936, s.260
Open spaces	Power to acquire land	Public Health Act 1875, s.164. Open Spaces Act 1906, ss.9 and 10
Parish property and documents	Management and custody	Local Government Act 1972, s.227
Postal and telecommunications facilities	Power to pay the Post Office, British Telecommunications or any other public telecommunications operator any loss sustained in providing additional post or telegraph office or telecommunications facilities	Post Office Act 1953, s.51. British Telecommunications Act 1981, Sched. 4, para. 12. Telecommunications Act 1984, s.97
Public buildings and village halls	Power to provide buildings for offices and for public meetings and assemblies	Local Government Act 1972, s.133. Local Government (Miscellaneous Provisions) Act 1976, s.19
Public conveniences	Power to provide	Public Health Act 1936, s.87
Recreation	Power to acquire land for recreation grounds, public walks and open spaces and to manage and control them.	Local Government Act 1894, s.6. Public Health Acts Amendment Act 1890, s.44. Open Spaces Act 1906, ss.9 and 10
	Power to provide gymnasiums, playing fields, holiday camps	Local Government (Miscellaneous Provisions) Act 1976, s.19
	Provision of boating pools	Public Health Act 1961, s.54

B–02

461

Function	Powers and Duties	Statutory Provisions
Town and country planning	Rights to be notified of planning applications	Town and Country Planning Act 1990, s.252, Sched. 1, para. 8, Sched. 14, para. 1
Tourism	Power to encourage	Local Government Act 1972, s.144
Village greens	Power to provide	Public Health Act 1875, s.164. Local Government Act 1972, Sched. 14, para. 27
War memorials	Power to maintain, repair, protect and adapt war memorials	War Memorials (Local Authorities' Powers) Act 1923 s.1, as amended by Local Government Act 1948, s.133
Water supply	Power to utilise well, spring or stream and to provide facilities for obtaining water therefrom	Public Health Act 1936, ss.125, 260

Appendix C

TABLE OF THE MORE COMMONLY USED SPECIFIC STATUTORY POWERS AUTHORISING THE PURCHASE OF LAND COMPULSORILY

Functions	*Basic Statutory Provisions*	*Purposes*	**C–01**
Aerodromes	Civil Aviation Act 1982, ss.30, 41, 42. Airports Act 1986, s.59	Provision of aerodromes and airports. Purposes of civil aviation	
Allotments	Small Holdings and Allotments Act 1908, ss.25(1), 39, as amended	Provision of allotments	
Caravan sites	Caravan Sites and Control of Development Act 1960, s.24	Purchase of sites	
Cemeteries	Local Government Act 1972, s.214(2), Sched. 26	For cemetery purposes	
Civil defence and emergency services	Civil Defence Act 1948, s.4	For the purposes of the Act	**C–02**
Coast protection	Coast Protection Act 1949, ss.14, 27	Carrying out of coast protection work	
Diseases of animals	Animal Health Act 1981, s.55	Provision of wharves or other places; provision of burial grounds for carcasses	
Education	Education Act 1944, s.90 (1), as amended	Land required for the purposes of any school or college or otherwise for the purposes of the Education Acts	
Fire services	Fire Services Act 1947, s.3(5)	For the purposes of the Act	**C–03**
Highways	Highways Act 1980, ss.238 to 255	For construction and improvement of highways and other specified highway purposes. Mitigating adverse effect of highway works or use	
	Road Traffic Regulation Act 1984, s.40	Provision of parking places	
	Road Traffic Regulation Act 1984, s.97	For discharge of functions relating to traffic wardens	

Functions	Basic Statutory Provisions	Purposes
Housing	Housing Act 1985, s.300(3)	Purchase for temporary accommodation of houses unfit for human habitation
	Housing Act 1985, ss.9(3), 17(3)–(4)	Purposes of Part II of the Act (provision of housing accommodation)
	Housing Act 1985, s.290(3)–(4)	Land comprised in, or surrounded by or adjoining a clearance area
	Housing Act 1985, s.255(1)	Land adjoining or within a general improvement area
	Housing Act 1985, s.243(2)	Housing accommodation in housing action area
Markets	Food Act 1984, s.110	To establish a market (but not to acquire an existing market)
Parks and recreation facilities and open spaces	Local Government (Miscellaneous Provisions) Act 1976, s.19	Various recreational facilities, both indoor and outdoor
	National Parks and Access to the Countryside Act 1949, ss.12(4), 13(8), 21, 53, 54 and 103(1), as amended by the Local Government, Planning and Land Act 1980, s.1(7); Sched. 7, para. 1(1)	Provision of accommodation, camping sites, parking places, etc., in National Parks improvement of waterways for open-air recreation, provision of ferries for long-distance routes and nature reserves
	Caravan Sites and Control of Development Act 1960, s.24	Provision of caravan sites
	National Parks and Access to the Countryside Act 1949, ss.76, 77 and 103(1)	To secure public access for open-air recreation
	National Parks and Access to the Countryside Act 1949, s.89, as amended	To enable trees to be planted to preserve or enhance the natural beauty of the land; or to deal with derelict land
	Countryside Act 1968, ss.7, 9 and 10	For functions as to country parks and other related purposes
C–04 Planning	Town and Country Planning Act 1990, ss.226 to 228, 231	Development, redevelopment, improvement and other planning purposes, land necessary for the public service and land for exchange

Functions	Basic Statutory Provisions	Purposes
	Planning (Listed Buildings and Conservation Areas) Act 1990, ss.47–51	Listed buildings in need of repair
Police	Metropolitan Police Act 1886, ss.2 and 4(11), as amended	For offices, police stations, houses and buildings required for the purposes of the Metropolitan Police
Slaughterhouses	Slaughterhouses Act 1974, ss.15, 18, as amended by the Local Government Act 1974, s.35 and Sched. 6	Provision of public slaughterhouses and cold-air stores

TABLE OF PRINCIPAL LICENSING AND REGISTRATION FUNCTIONS

A. FUNCTIONS EXERCISED BY DISTRICT COUNCILS

Nature of Licence	*Statutory Provisions and Statutory Instruments* **D–01**
Acupuncture, tattooing, ear-piercing and electrolysis	Local Government (Miscellaneous Provisions) Act 1982, ss.13–17
Betting tracks	Betting, Gaming and Lotteries Act 1963, s.6 and Sched. 3
Bingo and other group games	Lotteries and Amusements Act 1976, s.16 and Sched. 3
Camping sites	Public Health Act 1936, s.269
Caravan sites	Caravan Sites and Control of Development Act 1960
Cinemas and cinema clubs	Cinemas Act 1985, s.1
Common lodging houses	Housing Act 1985, ss.401–416
Dogs	Local Government Act 1988, s.37 (power to establish a dog registration scheme by regulations)
Dog breeding	Breeding of Dogs Act 1973, s.1, as amended by the Local Government, Planning and Land Act 1980, s.1(6), Sched. 6, para. 15, Sched. 34, Pt. VI and the Protection of Animals (Amendment) Act 1988, s.3
Filling materials: Registration of premises Licence in respect of premises where rag flock is manufactured or stored	Rag Flock and Other Filling Materials Act 1951, s.2, as amended by the Local Government, Planning and Land Act 1980, s.1(6), Sched. 6, para. 6
Food: Food premises	Food Safety Act 1990, s.19 (power to make regulations for registration and licensing of food premises)
Game: To kill game Gamekeeper to kill game Gamedealer Sell game to licensed dealer	Game Act, 1831, ss.5, 6, 17, 18, 21–23 Game Licences Act 1860 Customs and Inland Revenue Act 1883 Local Government Act 1894, ss.21(3), 27 Local Government Act 1972, s.213(1)
Gaming machines not on licensed premises	Gaming Act 1968, s.34 and Sched. 9, as amended

Nature of Licence	*Statutory Provisions and Statutory Instruments*
Hackney carriage and hackney carriage drivers	Public Health Act 1875, s.171 Town Police Clauses Act 1847, ss.37, 38, 40–68, as amended by the Local Government Act 1972, s.180 and Sched. 14, paras. 24, 25 and the Local Government, Planning and Land Act 1980, s.1(6) and Sched. 6, para. 1 Local Government (Miscellaneous Provisions) Act 1976, Part II Transport Act 1985, ss.10–17
House to house collections	House to House Collections Act 1939, s.2, as amended by the Local Government Act 1972, Sched. 29, para. 23 (to be repealed by the Charities Act 1992 from a day to be appointed: see the 1992 Act, ss.66–74)
Kennels: Boarding establishments for cats or dogs	Animal Boarding Establishments Act 1963, s.1, as amended by the Local Government Act 1974, Sched. 6, para. 17, Sched. 8, and the Protection of Animals (Amendment) Act 1988, s.3
Knackers yards	Slaughterhouses Act 1974, s.1
Lotteries: Societies promoting	Lotteries and Amusements Act 1976, s.5, Sched. 1 as amended by the National Lottery Etc. Act 1993, ss.48, 49, 64, Scheds. 7, 10
Moveable Dwellings	Public Health Act 1936, s.269
Parking: off-street	Road Traffic Regulations Act 1984, s.44. Control of Off-Street Parking (England and Wales) Order 1978 (S.I. 1978 No. 1535); Control of Off-Street Parking (England and Wales (Metropolitan Districts) Orders 1986 (S.I. 1986 No. 225)
Pet animal shops	Pet Animals Act 1951, s.1, as amended by the Local Government Act 1974, Sched. 6, para. 8
Pleasure boats Boatmen	Public Health Acts (Amendment) Act 1907, s.94, as amended by the Local Government Act 1974, Sched. 6, para. 1, the Local Government (Miscellaneous Provisions) Act 1976, s.18, and the Local Government, Planning and Land Act 1980, s.186
Pool promoters' registration	Betting, Gaming and Lotteries Act 1963, s.4 and Sched. 2
Private hire vehicles, operators and drivers	Local Government (Miscellaneous Provisions) Act 1976, Part II Transport Act 1985, ss.10–17

Nature of Licence	*Statutory Provisions and Statutory Instruments*
Private music, dancing and similar entertainment	Private Places of Entertainment (Licensing) Act 1967, as amended
Public Entertainments	Local Government (Miscellaneous Provisions) Act 1982, s.1, Sched. 1
Refreshment houses which are open between 10 p.m. and 5 a.m.	Late Night Refreshment Houses Act 1969, s.2, as amended by the Local Government Act 1972, s.204(9) and the Local Government Act 1974, Sched. 6, para. 24 and the London Authorities Act 1990, s.20
Riding establishments	Riding Establishments Act 1964, s.1, as amended by the Riding Establishments Act 1970, the Local Government Act 1974, Sched. 6, para. 18 and the Protection of Animals (Amendment) Act 1988, s.3
Scrap metal dealers	Scrap Metal Dealers Act 1964, s.1
Sex Shops and Sex Cinemas	Local Government (Miscellaneous Provisions) Act 1982, s.2, Sched. 3
Slaughterhouses	Slaughterhouses Act 1974, ss.1–10
Street collections	Police, Factories, etc., (Miscellaneous Provisions) Act 1916, s.5, as amended by Local Government Act 1972, s.251 and Sched. 29 (to be repealed by the Charities Act 1992, Sched. 7, and replaced by Part II (ss.65–74) from a day to be appointed)
Street trading	Local Government (Miscellaneous Provisions) Act 1982, s.3 and Sched. 4
Sunday Trading (register of permitted Sunday opening hours for larger shops)	Sunday Trading Act 1994
Theatres	Theatres Act 1968, ss.12–14, 18 and Sched. 1, as amended by the Local Government Act 1972, s.204(6) and the Local Government, Planning and Land Act 1980, s.1(6), Sched. 6, para. 11, Sched. 34, Pt. VI
Wild animals	Dangerous Wild Animals Act 1976
Zoos	Zoo Licensing Act 1981

B. Functions Exercised by Non-Metropolitan County Councils and Fire Authorities

Sale of explosives including fireworks	Explosives Act 1875, ss.15, 67, as amended by the Local Government Acts 1972, Sched. 29, para. 19 and 1985, Sched. 11, para. 3

D–02

469

Nature of Licence	*Statutory Provisions and Statutory Instruments*
Petroleum and carbide	Petroleum (Consolidation) Act 1928, ss.1–4, as amended by the Local Government Act 1972, Sched. 29, para. 32, S.I. 1974 No. 1942 and the Local Government Act 1985, Sched. 11, para. 4
	Petroleum (Transfer of Licences) Act 1936, s.1

C. FUNCTIONS EXERCISED BY NON-METROPOLITAN COUNTY AND METROPOLITAN DISTRICT COUNCILS

D–03

Agencies for supply of nurses	Nurses Agencies Act 1957, s.2, as amended by the Local Government Act 1972, Sched. 29, para. 30 and the Nurses, Midwives and Health Visitors Act 1979, Sched. 7, para. 9
	Nurses Agencies Regulations 1961 (S.I. 1961 No. 1214) as amended
Employment of children in street trading	Children and Young Persons Act 1933, s.20, as amended by the Children and Young Persons Act 1963, s.35, and the Employment Act 1989, s.10 and Sched. 3, and the Sunday Trading Act 1994, Sched. 4, para. 24
Homes—residential homes for old persons, disabled, mentally disordered	Registered Homes Act 1984
	Residential Care Homes Regulations 1984 (S.I. 1984 No. 1345), as amended
Homes—residential homes for children	Children Act 1989, Part VIII (ss.63–65, Scheds. 6, 7)
Nurseries and child-minders	Children Act 1989, Part X (ss.71–79 and Sched 9)
Performing animals	Performing Animals (Registration) Act 1925, as amended by the Local Government Act 1974, Sched. 6, para. 2, Sched. 8, and the Local Government Act 1985, Sched. 8, para. 17
Poisons—sale	Poisons Act 1972, s.5, as amended by the Local Government, Planning and Land Act 1980, Sched. 6, para. 13, s.11, as amended by the Local Government Act 1985, Sched. 8, para. 16
	Poisons List Order 1982 (S.I. 1982 No. 217), as amended
	Poisons Rules 1982 (S.I. 1982 No. 218), as amended

Nature of Licence	*Statutory Provisions and Statutory Instruments*
War charities and charities for disabled persons—registration	War Charities Act 1940, ss.2, 10, as amended by the Local Government Act 1972, s.210(8) National Assistance Act 1948, s 41, as amended by the Local Government Act 1972, Sched. 23, para. 2(a) and the Registered Homes Act 1984, Sched. 1, para. 1
Waste management	Environmental Protection Act 1990, ss.35–44, 74

D. Functions Exercised by County and District Councils

Charities-index of local charities	Charities Act 1993, s.76

E. Functions Exercised by the Police

Accommodation addresses	Official Secrets Act 1920, s.5
Aliens	Immigration Act 1971, s.4(3) The Immigration (Registration with Police) Regulations 1972 (S.I. 1972 No. 1758), as amended
Firearms	Firearms Act 1968, Part III
Shotguns	Firearms Act 1982
Firearms dealer	Firearms (Amendment) Act 1988
Pedlars	Pedlars Act 1871, s.5

D–04

LIST OF PRINCIPAL BY-LAW MAKING POWERS

The list is reproduced overleaf.   **E–01**

Function	Purpose of Subject-Matter of By-Law	Statutory Provisions	Confirming Authority
	Good rule and government	Local Government Act 1972, s.235	Secretary of State for the Home Department
Aerodromes	Regulations for the use and operation of airports including the control of noise, vibration and pollution	Airports Act 1986, s.63	Secretary of State for Trade and Industry
Allotments	Rules as to letting, and generally	Small Holdings and Allotments Act 1908, s.28 as amended by the Local Government, Planning and Land Act 1980, s.1(5); Sched. 34, Pt. V	Not applicable
Ancient monuments	As to access, preservation and protection	Ancient Monuments and Archaeological Areas Act 1979, s.19	Secretary of State for the Environment
Animals	For the purposes of the Animal Health Act 1981 (power of the Minister to make orders and local authority to make regulations)	Animal Health Act 1981, s.2	Not applicable
Burials and cremation	Management, charges and use of mortuaries and post-mortem rooms	Public Health Act 1936, s.198(1)	Secretary of State for the Environment
Cemeteries	Management thereof	Local Government Act 1972, s.214(3). Sched. 26, para. 11	do.
Charities	For the regulation of street collections	Police, Factories (Miscellaneous Provisions) Act 1916, s.5 (to be repealed by the Charities Act 1993, Sched. 7)	Secretary of State for the Home Department
Children and young persons	Street trading by children and young persons	Children and Young Persons Act 1933, s.20, as amended by the Employment Act 1989, s.10 and Sched. 3	Secretary of State for the Home Department
Food	As to slaughterhouses and knackers' yards	Slaughterhouses Act 1974 s.12 as amended by the Local Government, Planning and Land Act 1980, s.194; Sched. 34, Pt. I; and the Food Safety Act 1990, Sched. 3, para. 18(c)	Minister of Agriculture, Fisheries and Food

	Description	Enabling Act	Authority
	Securing sanitary and cleanly conditions and practices in connection with handling, wrapping and delivery of food and in connection with sale or exposure for sale of food in the open air	Food Act 1984, s.15; Food Safety Act 1990, Sched. 4, para. 7 (existing by-laws continue in effect notwithstanding repeal of s.15 by Sched. 5)	Secretary of State for Health
	As to public slaughterhouses	Slaughterhouses Act 1974, s.16 as amended by the Local Government, Planning and Land Act 1980, s.194; Sched. 34, Pt. I and the Food Safety Act 1990, Sched. 3, para. 18(d)	Minister of Agriculture, Fisheries and Food
Highways	Restricting the use of a road for the purpose of providing playground facilities for children	Road Traffic Regulation Act 1984, s.31	Secretary of State for the Environment
	Regulation as to ferries	Ferries (Acquisition by Local Authorities) Act 1919, s.2	Secretary of State for Transport
	Priority and queues in relation to persons waiting to enter public vehicles	Public Health Act 1925, s.75	Secretary of State for the Home Department
	Prevention of danger from wireless apparatus liable to fall in any street or public place	Public Health Act 1925, s.26	do.
	Regulation of hackney carriages	Public Health Act 1875, s.171, Town Police Clauses Act 1847, s.68	do.
	Regulation of the use of cabmen's shelters	Public Health Acts Amendment Act 1890, s.40(2)	do.
	Parking places for bicycles and motor cycles	Road Traffic Regulation Act 1984, s.57	Secretary of State for the Environment
	Regulation of public conveniences for road users	Highways Act 1980, s.114(3)	do.
	Regulation as to persons using walkways	Highways Act 1980, s.35(6)	do.

475

Function	Purpose of Subject-Matter of By-Law	Statutory Provisions	Confirming Authority
Housing	Management, use and regulation of houses provided by local authorities, and as to local authority lodging houses	Housing Act 1985, s.23	do.
Inland waters and waterways	Regulation of use	Transport Act 1968, s.113, as amended by the Water Act 1989, Sched. 25, para. 38(3) Water Resources Act 1991, ss.210–212 and Scheds. 25, 26	do.
Land drainage	Efficient working of drainage systems, drainage works against flooding	Land Drainage Act 1991, s.66 and Sched. 5	Minister of Agriculture, Fisheries and Food
Libraries and museums	Regulation of use of libraries, museums, art galleries	Public Libraries and Museums Act 1964, s.19	Secretary of State for Education and Employment
Parks, recreational facilities and open spaces	Preservation of order and prevention of damage in National Parks and areas of outstanding natural beauty	National Parks and Access to the Countryside Act 1949, s.90	Secretary of State for the Home Department
	The prevention of danger, obstruction and annoyance to persons using a seashore	Public Health Acts Amendment Act 1907, s.82	do.
	Regulation of pleasure fairs and roller skating rinks	Public Health Act 1961, s.75 (extended by the Local Government (Miscellaneous Provisions) Act 1976, s.22)	do.
	Regulation of pleasure boats	Local Government, Planning and Land Act 1980, s.185, as amended by the Water Act 1989, Sched. 25, para. 61(5)	Secretary of State for the Home Department
	Regulation of seaside pleasure boats	Public Health Act 1961, s.76 (extended by the Local Government (Miscellaneous Provisions) Act 1976, s.17)	do.

Regulation of pleasure boats in parks and pleasure grounds	Public Health Acts Amendment Act 1890, s.44(2)	do.
Regulation of public walks, and pleasure grounds	Public Health Act 1875, s.164	do.
Regulation of ancient monuments	Ancient Monuments and Archaeological Areas Act 1979, s.19	Secretary of State for the Environment
Preservation of order, etc., in country parks	Countryside Act 1978, s.41	Secretary of State for the Home Department
Prevention of nuisance and preservation of order on commons	Commons Act 1899, ss.1 and 10	do.
Regulation of esplanades and promenades, including, *inter alia*, prescribing the nature of traffic for which they may be used, and regulating hawking and selling	Public Health Acts Amendment Act 1907, s.83	do.
Use of facilities in or near National Parks	Countryside Act 1968, s.12(5)	Secretary of State for the Environment
Regulation of lakes in National Parks	Countryside Act 1968, s.13	do.
Regulation of public conveniences for users of roads	Highways Act 1980, ss.113(7), 114(3)	do.
Regulation of open spaces and burial grounds, including preservation of order and prevention of nuisances	Open Spaces Act 1906, s.15	Secretary of State for the Home Department
Regulation of sailing, boating, bathing, fishing and works and services in country parks	Countryside Act 1968, s.8(5)	Secretary of State for the Environment
Public health — As to hop-pickers and other persons doing similar work	Public Health Act 1936, s.270	Secretary of State for the Environment
Regulation of fish frying and offensive trades	Public Health Act 1936, s.108	do.
As to common lodging houses	Housing Act 1985, s.406	do.

Function	Purpose of Subject-Matter of By-Law	Statutory Provisions	Confirming Authority
	As to public sanitary conveniences	Public Health Act 1936, s.87(3)	do.
	Regulation of acupuncture, tattooing, ear-piercing and electrolysis	Local Government (Miscellaneous Provisions) Act 1982, ss.14–16	Secretary of State for Health
	Regulation of hairdressers and barbers	Public Health Act 1961, s.77	Secretary of State for the Environment
	Regulation of public bathing including the areas and hours permitted	Public Health Act 1936, s.231 (extended by the Local Government (Miscellaneous Provisions) Act 1976, s.17)	Secretary of State for the Home Department
	Regulation of swimming baths and bathing pools not under the management of local authority *inter alia* as to purity of water and prevention of accidents	Public Health Act 1936, s.233	Secretary of State for the Environment
	Prevention of nuisance from snow, filth, etc., and from animals	Public Health Act 1936, s.81	do.
	Regulating the removal through streets of offensive matter or liquid	Public Health Act 1936, s.82	do.
	Regulation of the use of cabmen's shelters	Public Health Acts Amendment Act 1890, s.40(2)	do.
	Regulating tents, vans, etc., used for human habitation	Public Health Act 1936, s.268. Public Health (Control of Disease) Act 1984, s.56	Secretary of State for Health
Weights and measures	Sale of solid fuel	Weights and Measures Act 1985, Sched. 5, para. 9	Secretary of State for Trade and Industry
Miscellaneous	Regulation of municipal baths and washhouses and bathing places	Public Health Act 1936, s.223	Secretary of State for the Environment
	Prevention of danger from whirligigs and swings driven by steam power, and from the use of firearms in shooting ranges and galleries	Public Health Acts Amendment Act 1890, s.38 (repealed by the Public Health Act 1961, s.75(7) (without prejudice to by-laws already in force))	Secretary of State for the Home Department

Regulating the use or markets maintained by a local authority	Food Act 1984, s.60	do.
Relating to the provision of heat, hot air, hot water or steam	Local Government (Miscellaneous Provisions) Act 1976, s.12	do.

479

TABLE OF SPECIFIC GRANTS*

Function	Grant provisions
Administration of Justice	
Expenses of Magistrates' Court Committees.	Justice of the Peace Act 1979, s.59.
Probation—revenue expenditure.	Probation Service Act 1993, ss.20–22.
Probation and bail hostels.	Probation Service Act 1993, s.20.
Children	
Provision of secure accommodation.	Children Act 1989, s.82(2).
Guardians *ad litem.*	Children Act 1989, s.41(12).
Civil defence	
General functions.	Civil Defence Act 1948, s.3.
Coast protection	Coast Protection Act 1949, s.21.
Consumer advice	Competition Act 1980, s.20.
Council Tax	
Transitional relief.	Local Government Finance Act 1988, s.88A.
Council tax benefit scheme	Social Security Administration Act 1992, ss.135–137, 140.
Education	
Student grants — mandatory awards.	Education Reform Act 1988, s.209.
Training of teachers and others working in specified fields.	Education (No. 2) Act 1986, s.50, as amended.
Education expenditure on Dept. of Employment schemes — technical and vocational education initiative, work related further education, careers service strengthening.	Employment and Training Act 1973, s.2(2)(d), as substituted by Employment Act 1988, s.25.
Welsh language training.	Education Act 1980, s.21.
Education support grants.	Education (Grants and Awards) Act 1984, s.1; Education (Amendment) Act 1986.

* This table is not intended to be comprehensive, but to point to some of the main provisions.

Function	*Grant provisions*
Education of travellers and displaced persons.	Education Reform Act 1988, s.210.
Liabilities to former employees in higher or further education.	Education Reform Act 1988, s.133, as amended.
Farms attached to agricultural colleges.	As under Smallholdings, below.

Emergencies and disasters

Expenditure to safeguard life and property, etc.	Local Government and Housing Act 1989, s.155.

European Community grants

School milk and milk products.	E.C. Regulations — Intervention Board for Agricultural Produce. (IBAP).
Butter subsidy.	E.C. Regulations — Intervention Board for Agricultural Produce. (IBAP).
Regional development projects.	E.C. Regulations — European Regional Development Fund. (ERDF).
Projects for improvements of conditions for marketing and processing agricultural and fish products.	E.C. Regulations — European Agriculture Guidance and Guarantee Fund. (FEOGA).
Projects for improving employment opportunities.	E.C. Regulations — European Social Fund. (ESF).

Gypsies

Provision of caravan sites.	Local Government, Planning and Land Act 1980, s.70, as amended.

Harbours

Harbour-related improvements and repairs which assist fishing industry.	Fisheries Act 1955, s.2.

Highways and transport

Advances for highway purposes.	Highways Act 1980, s.272.
Transport supplementary grant.	Local Government Finance Act 1988, s.87.
Improved facilities for road transport in development or intermediate areas.	Industrial Development Act 1982, s.13.
Bus fuel duty.	Finance Act 1965, s.92, as amended.
Rural bus grant.	Transport Act 1985, s.109.
Rehousing indemnity claims.	Land Compensation Act 1973, s.42.
Public transport infrastructure projects.	Transport Act 1968, s.56.
Pensions costs, former Road Construction Units staff.	Highways Act 1980, s.9.

Function	*Grant provisions*
Historic buildings	Historic Buildings etc., Act 1953, ss.5B, 6; National Heritage Act 1983, Sched. 4, para. 7.
Housing	
Housing Revenue Account subsidy.	Local Government and Housing Act 1989, s.79.
Improvement and renovation grants.	Local Government and Housing Act 1989, s.132.
Group repair schemes.	Local Government and Housing Act 1989, ss.127–130.
Environmental improvements in renewal areas.	Local Government and Housing Act 1989, s.96.
Home improvement agencies.	Local Government and Housing Act 1989, s.169.
Slum clearance.	Local Government and Housing Act 1989, s.165.
Improvements for sale.	Housing Act 1985, s.429.
Reinstatement and repurchase of defective dwellings sold to private owners.	Housing Act 1985, s.569.
Agricultural housing.	Housing Act 1985, Sched. 15, Pt. II.
Housing benefit scheme.	Social Security Administration Act 1992, ss.135, 140.
Mortgage interest relief scheme (MIRAS).	Income and Corporation Taxes Act 1988, ss.369–379.
Commutation of grants paid on loan charges basis, 1992–5.	Local Government and Housing Act 1989, s.157.
Temporary accommodation to replace short-term leases.	Local Government Grants (Social Needs) Act 1969, s.1.
Planning, development and industry	
Research and education.	Town and Country Planning Act 1990, s.304.
Conservation areas, preservation or enhancement.	Planning (Listed Buildings and Conservation Areas) Act 1990, s.72.
Environmental improvements in Wales.	Welsh Development Agency Act 1975, s.15.
Acquiring and carrying out works of reclamation or improvement of derelict land.	Derelict Land Act 1982, ss.1, 2; Welsh Development Agency Act 1975, s.16.
Remedial operations on unstable tips.	Mines and Quarries (Tips) Act 1969, s.25.
National Parks.	Local Government Act 1974, s.7, as amended.
Regeneration of urban areas.	Housing and Planning Act 1986, s.27, as amended.

483

Function	*Grant provisions*
Police	
General.	Police Act 1964, s.31.
Public health and drainage	
Smoke control.	Clean Air Act 1993, Sched. 2, para. 4.
Port health services — medical examinations.	Immigration Act 1971, s.31.
Land drainage improvements or new works carried out under ss.30, 31, 91(6), 98, 99 and 100 of the Land Drainage Act 1976.	Land Drainage Act 1976, s.91.
Rent officers service	Rent Act 1977, s.63.
Social needs	
Expenditure incurred through existence of special social need in any urban area (or rural area in Wales).	Local Government Grants (Social Needs) Act 1969, s.1.
Commutation of grants paid on loan charges basis.	Local Government and Housing Act 1989, s.157.
AIDS and HIV.	Local Government Grants (Social Needs) Act 1969, s.1.
Ethnic minority population.	Local Government Act 1966, s.11.
Smallholdings	
Works or facilities of a capital nature for agricultural improvement and farm diversification.	Agriculture Act 1970, s.29.
Modernisation of farms, and mountain and hill farming in less favoured areas, in accordance with EEC directives (Development grants).	European Communities Act 1972, s.2(2).
Improving agricultural efficiency (Farm and Conservation grants).	European Communities Act 1972, s.2(2).
Farm diversification — non-capital feasibility and marketing grants.	Farm Land and Rural Development Act 1988, s.1.
Welfare services	
Employment of blind, partially sighted and other disabled persons in sheltered workshops and placement schemes.	Disabled Persons (Employment Act) 1944, s.15(5)(c).
Employment of blind persons—home workers.	Disabled Persons (Employment Act) 1944, s.15(5)(c).

Function	Grant provisions
Resettlement units.	Supplementary Benefits Act 1976, s.30, Sched. 5, as amended.
Employment rehabilitation of disabled persons—capital grants.	Employment and Training Act 1973, s.2(2)(d), as substituted by Employment Act 1988, s.25.
Development of services of mentally handicapped (Wales only).	National Health Service Act 1977, s.28B.
Elderly initiative scheme (Wales only).	National Health Service Act 1977. s.28A.
Community care joint finance.	National Health Service Act 1977, s.28B.
Training Support Grant.	Health Services and Public Health Act 1968, s.63, as amended (England); National Health Service Act 1977, s.28B(1)(a) (Wales).
Social services re mental illness.	Local Authority Social Services Act 1970, s.7E(a).
Payments to voluntary organisations re alcohol/drugs dependence.	Local Authority Social Services Act 1970, s.7E(b).
Central Funding for flexible community care (Wales only).	National Health Service Act 1977, s.28B.
Development programme (community care for elderly people) (Wales only).	National Health Service Act 1977, s.28B.
Development programme (assessment and care management) (Wales only).	National Health Service Act 1977, s.28B.
Community Care—Special transitional grant.	Local Government Finance Act 1988, s.88B.

485

INDEX